BIOLOGY
OF THE
REPTILIA

BIOLOGY OF THE REPTILIA

Edited by

CARL GANS

*The University of Michigan
Ann Arbor, Michigan, U.S.A.*

VOLUME 9

NEUROLOGY A

Coeditors for this volume

R. GLENN NORTHCUTT

*The University of Michigan
Ann Arbor, Michigan, U.S.A.*

and

PHILIP ULINSKI

*University of Chicago
Chicago, Illinois, U.S.A.*

1979

ACADEMIC PRESS

LONDON   NEW YORK   SAN FRANCISCO

A Subsidiary of Harcourt Brace Jovanovich, Publishers

ACADEMIC PRESS INC. (LONDON) LTD.
24/28 Oval Road
London NW1

United States Edition published by
ACADEMIC PRESS INC.
111 Fifth Avenue
New York, New York 10003

British Library Cataloguing in Publication Data
Biology of the Reptilia
  Vol. 9: Neurology A
  1. Reptiles
  I. Gans, Carl   II. Northcutt, R. Glenn
  III. Ulinski, Philip
  598.1   QL641   68–9113

  ISBN 0–12–274609–0

Text set in 11/12 pt. Monotype Ehrhardt, printed by letterpress,
and bound in Great Britain at The Pitman Press, Bath

Contributors to Volume 9

MONIKA VON DÜRING, *Postfach 2148, Universitätstrasse 150, 4630 Bochum, Federal Republic of Germany.*

JAMES A. HOPSON, *Department of Anatomy, The University of Chicago, 1025 East 57th Street, Chicago, Illinois 60637, U.S.A.*

MALCOLM R. MILLER, *Department of Anatomy, School of Medicine, University of California, San Francisco, California 94143, U.S.A.*

ROLAND PLATEL, *Faculté des Sciences de Paris, Laboratoire d'Anatomie Comparée, 2 Place Jussieu, Université Paris 7, 75-Paris V, France.*

W. B. QUAY, *Department of Anatomy, University of Texas Medical Branch, Galveston, Texas 77550, U.S.A.*

DAVID G. SENN, *Zoologisches Institut, Universität Basel, Markgräflerstrasse 35, CH-4057 Basel, Switzerland.*

D. STARCK, *Zentrum der Morphologie, Theodor Stern Kai 7, Frankfurt am Main, Federal Republic of Germany.*

Preface

The present introduction to the reptilian nervous system marks a milestone. It begins the last major section into which the Biology of the Reptilia has been divided, and offers the first treatment on topics that logically tie together reptilian morphology with their physiology and behavior. The shapes and some pathways of reptilian nervous systems were described almost 200 years ago, during the earliest days of comparative anatomy. However, our knowledge has, until recently, been most scanty; even thirty years ago, the spectacular diversity exhibited by the nervous systems of Recent reptiles was barely conceived.

Since then, we have seen the development of many new approaches, each in turn speeding up analysis of regions and their connections. Classical Golgi techniques (cf. Ebbesson *et al.*, 1975; Valverde, 1970; Ramón-Moliner, 1970) have achieved a new importance, because they complement the analysis of the individual cells with the electron microscope. These Golgi techniques allow one to visualize individual neurons in their entirety and to work out the geometry of the dendrites and axons within a region of interest. However, Golgi techniques stain only a fraction of the neurons present; only a few of the functional contacts among neurons become apparent. In contrast, electron microscopy permits one to visualize synaptic contacts, but the magnifications are generally so high that a global perspective is lacking (Heimer, 1970). Recently described procedures now allow one to combine the advantages of Golgi and electron microscopy (Fairén and Peters, 1977).

Other advances have been made in tracing the connections of disjunct parts of reptilian brains. Prior to the 1950's this was almost impossible because the existing techniques did not permit the study of those unmyelinated fiber systems that constitute the bulk of reptilian pathways. Shortly thereafter a series of silver compounds were introduced, which selectively stain degenerating axons, even those that are unmyelinated (cf. Ebbesson, 1970). When a particular structure is lesioned, the trajectory of severed axons may now be traced. Complications due to inadvertent damage to axons passing the lesion site may be circumvented by utilizing newer autoradiographic tracing techniques (Cowan and Cuénod, 1975). Tritiated amino acids are injected into a brain structure where they are taken up by neurons near the injection site. The labelled amino acids are incorporated into proteins which are then transported actively through the axons to the synaptic terminations of the labelled neurons; they may there be visualized by standard autoradiographic techniques. Horseradish peroxidase (HRP) is also transported actively by axons, both toward and away from the cell body (LaVail, 1975). A particular advantage of its use has been that HRP may completely fill neurons, giving a Golgi-like preparation. Finally, specific techniques have been developed for the visualization of biogenic amines (Parent, volume 10), and these techniques have led to the analysis of several previously unsuspected neuronal systems.

In parallel with these primarily anatomical techniques, physiological approaches have started to provide more quantitative and functional data. Detailed examination of the physiological properties of neurons at each successive structure in a neuronal pathway permits analysis of the flow of information (Belekhova, volume 10). Recently, students of the nervous system have begun to combine anatomical and physiological techniques and to approach a more complete concept of neuronal function. For example, marker substances can be injected into a particular neuron after its physiology has been studied (Kater and Nicholson, 1973). The physiology of a particular neuron may then be correlated directly with its structure. Regions and nuclei in the reptilian brain may now be associated with particular physiological and behavioral responses.

It seems redundant to recite the significant new discoveries about reptilian neurobiology achieved with such techniques, and better to let the authors present their own conclusions. For each topic, we have asked that the treatment not only emphasize recent discoveries, but that it should also summarize the general area. Beyond that, the authors have been asked to note the ways in which the reptilian system resembles and those in which it differs from those characterizing the other classes of vertebrates. This first volume begins with two treatments of the skeletal system surrounding the brain, treating these from an embryological and an historical viewpoint, and emphasizing the interaction between the form of the central nervous system, its afferents and efferents, and the capsules, fenestrae and foramina that contrain these. This is followed by a discussion of brain-weight relationships that utilizes the comparative method to derive generalizations about the patterns seen in major reptilian groupings. A review of major trends in the embryology of the several regions of the central nervous system is followed by an overview of the enormous amount of work published on the parietal-pineal complex; while there are as yet no definite answers, it is becoming clear that this system may have a very major controlling influence on the rhythms in ectothermal metabolism. Finally, there is an account of the structure of the major sensory endings of the integument and some deeper regions.

We have again been fortunate in being able to interest major authorities in contributing these several chapters on topics to which they have made significant contributions. We appreciate their willingness to have us match the style and extent of their chapters to those of others. Beyond this, we are grateful to many colleagues for discussions and advice regarding the subject matter to be covered in the present volume. It is a particular pleasure again to acknowledge the assistance of Drs Werner H. Stingelin and Rudolf Nieuwenhuys who arranged for the funding and the organization of the very successful planning conference on questions of Reptilian Neurobiology held on the Island of Texel, The Netherlands, during December, 1971 (cf. Gans and Northcutt, 1972, *Brain, Behav. Evol.*). Drs H. R. Barghusen, A. d'A. Bellairs, M. R. Braford, Jr., G. Burnstock, A. B. Butler, C. B. G. Campbell, W. L. R. Cruce, R. M. Eakin, E. G. Gaffney, S. J. Gould, G. Craig Gundy, M. Halpern, H. J. Jerison, B. Jones, L. Landmann, A. H. M. Lohman, P. F. A. Maderson, Malcolm R. Miller, R. Nieuwenhuys, E. C. Olson, T. S. Parsons, E. H. Peterson, C. L. Prosser, W. B. Quay, L. B. Radinsky, O. Rieppel, D. G. Senn, and M. von Düring reviewed individual manuscripts and Drs G. Zug and H. Wermuth critically read the entire set of manuscripts and checked the proofs for current usage and accuracy of the Latin names employed. I thank my coeditors for their efforts in handling editorial chores, and Mary Sue Northcutt for aid with the complex problems of Dr Senn's manuscripts. The index was compiled by P. Ulinski. The Division of Biological Sciences of The University of Michigan and the Department of Anatomy, The University of Chicago contributed part of the considerable bills for postage.

May, 1978   Carl Gans

References

Cowan, W. M. and Cuénod, M. (1975). "The Use of Axonal Transport for Studies of Neuronal Connectivity." Elsevier, New York.

Ebbesson, S. O. E. (1970). The selective silver-impregnation of degenerating axons and their synaptic endings in nonmammalian species. *In* "Contemporary Research Methods in Neuroanatomy." (W. J. H. Nauta and S. O. E. Ebbesson, eds.). Springer Verlag, New York, pp. 132–161.

Ebbesson, S. O. E., Schroeder, D. M., and Butler, A. B. (1975). The Golgi method and the revival of comparative neurology. *In* "Golgi Centennial Symposium." (M. Santini, ed.). Raven Press, New York, pp. 153–160.

Fairén, A. and Peters, A. (1977). A new procedure for examining Golgi impregnated neurons by light and electron microscopy. *J. Neurocytol.* **6,** 311–337.

Heimer, L. (1970). Bridging the gap between light and electron microscopy in the experimental tracing of fiber connections. *In* "Contemporary Research Methods in Neuroanatomy." (W. J. H. Nauta and S. O. E. Ebbesson, eds.). Springer Verlag, New York, pp. 162–172.

Kater, S. B. and Nicholson, C. (1973). "Intracellular Staining in Neurobiology." Springer Verlag, New York.

La Vail, J. H. (1975). Retrograde cell degeneration and retrograde transport techniques. *In* "The Use of Axonal Transport for Studies of Neuronal Connectivity." (W. M. Cowan and M. Cuénod, eds.). Elsevier, New York, pp. 217–248.

Ramón-Moliner, E. (1970). The Golgi-Cox technique. *In* "Contemporary Research Methods in Neuroanatomy." (W. J. H. Nauta and S. O. E. Ebbesson, eds.). Springer Verlag, New York, pp. 32–55.

Valverde, F. (1970). The Golgi method. A tool for comparative structural analyses. *In* "Contemporary Research Methods in Neuroanatomy." (W. J. H. Nauta and S. O. E. Ebbesson, eds.). Springer Verlag, New York, pp. 12–31.

Contents

CHAPTER 1

Cranio-Cerebral Relations in Recent Reptiles

D. STARCK

Zentrum der Morphologie, Frankfurt am Main,
Federal Republic of Germany

I. Introduction

The skull of living reptiles is the result of a protracted historical development. The complex syncranium results from the fusion in ontogeny of three elements that arose at different times in phylogeny: the neural endocranium and sensory capsules, the splanchnocranium, and the dermal exoskeleton. Variation among the skulls of diverse reptiles is determined by various factors; among these the position of the brain and relative development of the sense organs, as well as the disposition of the head muscles and the mechanics of feeding, are particularly important. Some of these factors influence the orbitotemporal region of the braincase which exhibits the greatest variation among reptiles.

The present chapter describes the ossification of the lateral wall of the braincase. It notes the variation in the resulting basal and orbitotemporal regions and the result of this ossification on the distribution of the cranial nerves that pass through these regions. The meninges are closely related to the central nervous system, the cranial nerves and to the walls of the endocranium. Thus the relationships and development of the meninges are also considered. Finally, the position and shape of the brain are discussed with reference to the morphology of the head. The relative position and size of the sense organs are seen to exert the primary effects on brain shape, exceeding those of feeding-related demands of the skull.

II. The Structure of the Lateral Wall of the Braincase

A. General

1. *Organization*

The cranium contains several major regions. From rostral to caudal, they are termed the ethmoid, orbitotemporal, otic and occipital. The ventral

1

aspect of the cranial base forms a unit, the central stem. Each region is defined in terms of its place relative to the central braincase and the independently developing paired, sensory capsules. The orbitotemporal region differs markedly among reptiles, while the reptilian occipital and otic regions show relatively few differences.

In the embryo, the cranium starts to form as a chondrocranium, which consists of a cartilaginous precursor for the braincase that surrounds the developing sensory centers. It should be regarded as a changing and adaptable structure, rather than a functionless stage. The chondrocranium also provides the base on which the adult skull is ultimately constructed (Gaupp, 1900;

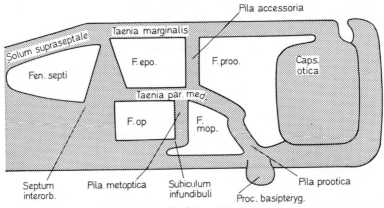

FIG. 1. Schematic view of the lateral wall of the orbitotemporal region in a lizard. Typical structures of the cartilaginous skull. Caps. otica, Capsula otica; F. epo., fenestra epioptica; F. mop., fenestra metoptica; F. op., fenestra optica; F. proo., fenestra prootica; Fen. septi., fenestra septi; Proc. basipteryg., processus basipterygoideus; Septum interorb., septum interorbitale; Taenia par. med., taenia parietalis media.

Versluys, 1936; de Beer, 1937; Romer, 1956; Jollie, 1960; Guibé, 1970). Consequently, it shows variable retention in diverse adult forms.

2. *Braincase*

The base of the braincase is composed of three independent elements, the parachordals, the acrochordal plate and the trabeculae (Rieppel, 1976a). The parachordals, which cover the cranial part of the chorda dorsalis, contribute to the basal plate (posterior base) of the braincase and reach rostrally to the hypophyseal region. The trabeculae form the cranial base anterior to the hypophysis. Posterior to the site of the hypophysis and the fenestra basicranialis anterior, the crista sellaris, which develops from the acrochordal plate, closes the rostral portion of the basal plate (the Crocodilia may lack such a crista). Anterior to the exit of the fifth cranial nerve (V) the walls of the braincase chondrify as independent sphenolateral plates (Fig. 1). These plates cover the exits of the oculomotor and trochlear nerves (III, IV) and lie between the cerebrum and eye to form the anterolateral portions of the braincase (Sphenolateralplatte, Versluys, 1936; Orbital cartilage, de Beer, 1937; Alisphenoidalknorpel, Sewertzoff, 1895; Ostosphenoidalplate, Howes and Swinnerton, 1901; and Arcus Mesencephalicus, Shaner, 1925). While this plate has been referred to as alisphenoidal cartilage, the term is inappropriate, because the alisphenoid of mammals is in part a visceral element that does not form the wall of the primary braincase, but is homologous to the epipterygoid (Gaupp, 1902), which is secondarily included in the neurocranial wall of theromorphs (Barry, 1965).

3. *Sensory Capsules*

The skeleton of the olfactory capsule is composed of the ethmosphenoidal plate, which is formed by a fusion of the trabeculae and the sphenolateral plate. Posteriorly, the trabeculae fuse to the anterolateral edges of the crista sellaris. Rostrally, the trabeculae fuse with each other and form the base of the interorbital septum. This septum splits dorsally and forms two plates, the planum and solum supraseptale, which lie below the olfactory bulbs. The planum supraseptale covers the olfactory canal, which is closed dorsally by dermal bones. The interorbital septum is of paired origin, but usually fuses early during ontogeny; in some *Emys*, the two cartilaginous lamellae remain separated by a small gap (Kunkel, 1911, 1912).

The skeletal elements of the orbital capsule need not here be dealt with as they do not fuse to the braincase (Underwood, 1970). The interorbital septum continues rostrally into the septum nasi. The paraseptal cartilages appear to develop autonomously on the ventral surface of the nasal capsule.

The otic capsule chondrifies independently and very early. A gap, the foramen prooticum, remains between the otic capsule and sphenolateral cartilage. It is traversed by the fifth nerve. The trigeminal ganglion lies extracranial to the foramen prooticum. Of the branches of the fifth nerve, the V_1 passes medial and the $V_{2,3}$ lateral to the epipterygoid.

The occipital pillars extend dorsally and cover the foramen magnum posterior to the otic capsules. The dorsal closure may be produced by a tectum posterius, formed by the occipital pillars, or by a tectum synoticum, developing from the otic capsules. Turtles possess only a synotic tectum. The occipital pillar has three to four foramina hypoglossi, suggesting that the occipital region includes three occipito-vertebral neural arches between the most anterior foramen of the twelfth nerve and foramen magnum. The fissura metotica is a gap between the otic capsule and the occipital pillar, and the ninth and tenth nerves and the internal jugular vein traverse it. The recessus scalae tympani results from a subdivision of the fissura metotica at a later stage.

4

4. *Variation*

In Recent reptiles, the otic and occipital regions are rather uniform. However, the several orders and families show numerous differences in the structure of the orbitotemporal region. Ancestral vertebrates presumably had an almost complete cartilaginous lateral wall in the orbitotemporal region. In lizards, the side wall is broken up into a fine meshwork, that may be reduced in various genera (*Calotes*, *Chamaeleo*, Figs 2B, C). Bars remain between the windows (fenestrae), defining what may be considered as primary nerve exits. The reduction of the lateral wall is almost complete

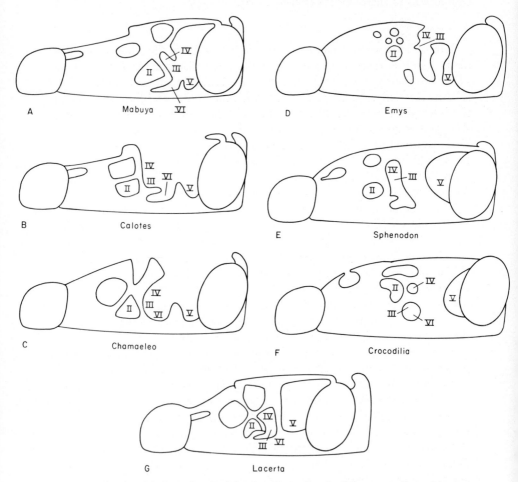

Fig. 2. Structure of the lateral wall of the chondrocranium in different reptiles, with nerve exits (II–VI). A. *Mabuya*. B. *Calotes*. C. *Chamaeleo*. D. *Emys*. E. *Sphenodon*. F. Crocodilia. G. *Lacerta*.

in very kinetic forms, such as snakes. A further modification leads to a secondary completion of the lateral walls by the formation of new cartilages. This clearly occurs in several marine turtles, e.g. *Dermochelys*, Fig. 3, and is due to the hypertrophy of cartilage in marine vertebrates.

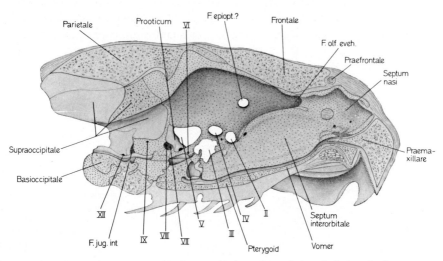

FIG. 3. *Dermochelys coriacea*. Median sagittal section of the skull (cartilaginous and osseous) of an adult demonstrating the retention of cartilage in marine turtles (after Nick, 1912). F. epiopt., Fenestra epioptica; F. jug. int., foramen jugulare internale; F. olf. eveh., foramen olfactorium evehens.

B. THE CHONDROCRANIUM OF *Lacerta*

Gaupp (1900) described the taeniae as rudimentary horizontal bars of the lateral wall, and pilae as vertical connections between the taeniae and the base. Because taeniae, pilae, and fenestrae are fully developed in *Lacerta*, a description of its chondrocranium may serve as a basis for understanding the simpler chondrocranium of other forms.

The anterior and posterior parts of the orbitotemporal region are formed in distinct ways. Anteriorly, the chondrocranium consists merely of the very narrow interorbital septum. In the temporal region, the chondrocranium is widened and formed of cartilaginous bars. These spatial relations correlate with the narrow anterior base, the intermediate interorbital septum, and the wide posterior basal plate. The internal carotid artery enters the braincase through the posterolateral corner of the hypophyseal fenestra. Sometimes there is a separate carotid foramen. The basitrabecular processes arise from the caudal ends of the trabeculae, near their attachment to the crista sellaris (Fig. 5). They are not involved in the formation of the ventrolateral borders of the primary cranial cavity. The ganglion of the fifth nerve lies between the epipterygoid and the wall of the primary braincase (Fig. 5). Near the dorsal edge of the lateral wall, the taenia marginalis (Fig. 5) connects the otic capsule with the planum supraseptale. Parallel to this, but more ventral to the posterolateral corner of the solum supraseptale, lies the taenia parietalis media, which posteriorly reaches the middle of the lateral wall. Here it is connected to a vertical pillar, the pila prootica (antotica), slightly anterior to the otic capsule. The base of the pillar is pierced by the foramen for the abducens nerve (Fig. 5).

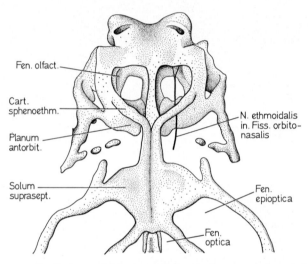

FIG. 4. *Lacerta agilis*. Embryo of 31 mm total length. Reconstruction of the nasal and interorbital region of the chondrocranium in dorsal view (after Gaupp, 1900). Cart. sphenoethm., Cartilago sphenoethmoidalis; Fen. epioptica, fenestra epioptica; Fen. olfact., fenestra olfactoria; Fen. optica, fenestra optica; Planum antorbit., planum antorbitale; Solum suprasept., solum supraseptale.

Another space is defined by the posterior rim of the interorbital septum, the lateral basal edge, and the pila antotica. It is roofed by the taenia parietalis media. The pila metoptica divides it into a rostral portion, the foramen opticum (exit of the second nerve), and a more posterior fenestra metoptica (exit of the third and fourth nerves). The lower end of the pila metoptica fuses with the subiculum infundibuli, a chondral plate resting dorsal to the trabeculae (Fig. 4). The fenestra epioptica is defined by the taenia marginalis, the taenia parietalis media, and the posterior rim of the solum supraseptale; it is bordered posteriorly by a pila accessoria.

No nerves pass through the fenestra epioptica. The large fenestra prootica (Figs 1, 2) is defined by the taenia marginalis, pila accessoria, taenia parietalis media, pila prootica, lateral rim of the basal plate and the otic capsule; its lower portion contains both the exit and ganglion of the trigeminal nerve. The interorbital septum may include a window (fenestra septi) closed by connective tissue.

The fenestra olfactoria provides for passage of the olfactory nerve. Posterolaterally it is bordered by the sphenoethmoidal cartilage. More

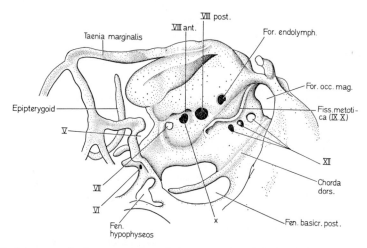

FIG. 5. *Lacerta agilis*. Reconstruction of the otic and occipital region of the chondrocranium of an embryo of 31 mm total length in oblique dorsal view (after Gaupp, 1900). For. endolymph. (Foramen endolymphaticum); For. occ. mag. (Foramen occipitale magnum); Fiss. metotica (Fissura metotica); Chorda dors. (Chorda dorsalis); Fen. basicr. post. (Fenestra basicranialis posterior); Fen. hypophyseos (Fenestra hypophyseos); Ant. (anterior); post. (posterior). × not chondrified part of the otic capsule.

ventral lies the fissura orbitonasalis, through which passes the ethmoid nerve (V) from the orbit to the nasal cavity.

C. VARIATIONS

The basic pattern thus described is modified in the various groups (Fig. 2). The fenestrae are relatively small in the Crocodilia and *Sphenodon*. In crocodilians, the pila prootica is broadened and the foramen prooticum narrowed. The Gekkonidae lack the pila prootica and pila accessoria, but show three large windows posterior to the fenestra optica (Kamal, 1964). *Calotes* has only rudiments in the region of the otic capsule.

In Crocodilia, turtles and *Sphenodon*, the opening for the fourth nerve may be separated from the fenestra metoptica. The abducens generally passes through its own foramen, that penetrates the base of the pila antotica (e.g. *Lacerta*). Embryos of *Emys* (Kunkel, 1912), lack the taenia marginalis, but these occur in those of *Chrysemys* (Shaner, 1925). The reduction of the taenia marginalis of turtles, which have a rather solid chondrocranium, may be related at least in part to the early development of massive membrane bones dorsal to the orbitotemporal region. Reductions in the lateral orbito-temporal wall occur not only in the Anguidae, Chamaeleonidae, and Cordy-lidae, but also in groups showing extreme burrowing adaptations (*Acontias*, Anniellidae).

The snakes examined thus far lack even traces of the lateral wall of the chondrocranium. In snakes, the trabeculae do not fuse posterior to the nasal septum (platytrabecular skull), and the vertical pillars regress.

III. Ossification of the Lateral Wall of the Braincase

A. Posterior Braincase

The uniform development of the posterior walls of the reptilian braincase also extends to its mode of ossification. The occipital region always contains the typical basioccipital, supraoccipital, and two exoccipitals. The basi-sphenoid lies anterior to the basioccipital and may extend far rostral to reach between the trabeculae and the intertrabeculae; thus the basisphenoid may contribute to the rostrum. The basisphenoid originates from the crista sellaris. A channel (Vidian canal or parabasal canal) between the basi-sphenoid and parasphenoid is traversed by the palatine ramus of the seventh nerve, as well as the internal carotid artery. The otic capsule always includes an opisthotic and a prootic. The epioticum, described by Parker (1885) in crocodilians, represents only an overlap of the supraoccipital onto the otic capsules (Versluys, 1936).

B. Orbitotemporal Region

The ossifications of the orbitotemporal region are highly variable. The following main types may be recognized:

1. In lizards and *Sphenodon*, the side wall of the braincase in the orbito-temporal region remains cartilaginous or membranous.

2. In the digging and burrowing Amphisbaenia, the skull is of extra-ordinary solidity and shows massive ossifications in the orbitotemporal region. The large parietal extends far ventrally and is particularly important, as it stiffens this region and connects to the orbitosphenoid. The ossifications of the orbitotemporal region are solidly attached to the otic and occipital regions. There is no true interorbital septum.

3. Snakes have almost no primary orbitotemporal wall. Only a small laterosphenoid is found in the posterior part of this zone. A secondary

cranial wall has formed, in this case by dermal bones of the orbitotemporal region. It encompasses the nerves III, IV, and VI. This space resembles a cavum epiptericum in its formation and contents, but differs from it in the composition of its external wall. It undoubtedly arose independently in snakes. The foramen orbitale magnum (Gaupp, 1902), which lies between the parietal and frontal, allows the passage of the optic nerve, as well as the exit of the nerves III, IV and VI from the skull.

4. The processus descendens of the parietal of turtles also extends far ventrally. However, it articulates with the pterygoid rather than the basisphenoid, with which it connects in snakes. The epipterygoid, too, is enclosed by the descending process of the parietal. Thus the primarily extracranial cavum epiptericum becomes enclosed within the secondary bony side-wall of the orbitotemporal region. Many Testudines retain cartilaginous relicts of the primary lateral wall of the skull (they are lost in *Chelonia*). The nerves of the eye muscles and VI traverse the cavum epiptericum lateral to the dura mater, though they lie medial to the parietal bone (Shiino, 1912). *Dermochelys* has secondarily returned to a state resembling the presumed ancestral condition (Nick, 1912); the primary lateral wall of the skull is entirely cartilaginous throughout the orbitotemporal region. The descending process of the parietal is thus reduced. The cartilaginous neurocranial wall persists in the adult. In turtles, the processus descendens of the parietal generally assumes the functional role of the epipterygoid in other reptiles.

5. In the Crocodilia, the orbital wall of the braincase is completely closed by an ossified chondral bone in the broadened pila antotica. Even though this ossified element was formerly referred to as an alisphenoid, it belongs to the lateral wall of the primary skull. Therefore, it is not homologous to the alisphenoid of mammals. It should, more properly, be referred to as the pleurosphenoid (Versluys, 1936; Rieppel, 1976b). The mammalian alisphenoid represents a visceral element, secondarily incorporated in the cranial wall and homologous to the epipterygoid. The more rostrally positioned orbitosphenoid, which ossifies in the pila metoptica, is homologous in crocodiles and mammals.

IV. Relationships of Cranial Nerves to the Skull

A. OLFACTORY NERVE (I)

The rostral forebrain of the Crocodilia, Squamata, and Rhynchocephalia is different from that of Testudines. In the former groups, the olfactory bulbs lie anterior to the eyes. Long, fine fibers, the so-called "Zwischenstück" (Haller v. Hallerstein, 1934a) or olfactory peduncle (Goldby and Gamble,

1957), connect the bulbs to the bulk of the forebrain. They lie in the cavum supraseptale and contain a ventricle. In the amphisbaenid, *Leposternon microcephalum*, the olfactory peduncle is very short. In contrast, turtles have short or sessile olfactory bulbs (Fig. 19). The interorbital inset is short and close to the bulb. An annular ridge separates it from the hemisphere. A long olfactory nerve traverses the interorbital space of turtles from the forebrain to the nasal cavity, whereas other reptiles have a long interorbital inset and short olfactory nerve (Figs 15–18).

The fenestra olfactoria is a wide opening in the posterodorsal wall of the capsule. The posterior rim of the fenestra is formed by the sphenoethmoidal cartilage (Gaupp, 1900). Both fenestrae olfactoriae meet at the dorsal margin of the nasal septum. The olfactory bulbs lie immediately dorsal to the fenestrae. Numerous olfactory nerve fibers pass into the nasal fossa through the fenestrae.

The ethmoidal ramus of the ophthalmic nerve (V_1) emerges from the orbit to reach the fenestra olfactoria directly ventral to the sphenoethmoidal cartilage, across the orbitonasal fissure. There it reaches the lateral aspect of the olfactory bulb, and they jointly enter the nasal capsule (Fig. 4).

The posterior aperture of the fenestra olfactoria (foramen olfactorium evehens) and the opening of the nasal capsule (foramen olfactorium advehens) lie on different levels. The foramen olfactorium evehens is defined by the posterodorsal edge of the nasal capsule, the dorsal rim of the nasal septum, and the sphenoethmoidal cartilage. The latter reaches from the posterodorsal edge of the nasal capsule to the solum supraseptale. The fissura orbitonasalis lies ventral to the capsule, bordered ventrally by the planum antorbitale. The foramen olfactorium advehens, representing the olfactory passage into the nasal cavity, is limited by the roof of the nasal capsule, the planum and septum antorbitale (= lamina orbitonasalis, de Beer, 1937). The space extending from foramen olfactorium evehens to the foramen olfactorium advehens, the cavum orbitonasale (= recessus supracribrosus of mammals), is therefore a space that is primarily extracranial. By contrast, the lamina cribrosa of mammals lies adjacent to the foramen olfactorium advehens (fenestra cribrosa) so that the recessus supracribrosus is part of the osseous skull.

B. Optic Nerve (II)

The optic nerve emerges from the primary wall of the cranial cavity via the optic foramen. The foramen is defined by the pila metoptica, the taenia parietalis and the posterior rim of the septum interorbitale. Both of the optic foramina are closely adjacent in the median plane. The hypochiasmatic cartilage lies immediately ventral to the optic chiasm.

C. Nerves to Extrinsic Eye Muscles (III, IV, VI)

Generally, the oculomotor and trochlear nerves cross the primary lateral wall (foramen metopticum) together. The abducens nerve penetrates the base of the pila antotica. In early embryos of *Sphenodon* the outlet of the abducens nerve is separated from the fenestra metoptica by a cartilaginous bar. However, the two apertures fuse later. An autonomous, protruding aperture for the abducens nerve is mentioned for Crocodilia (Parker, 1885; Shiino, 1914) and turtles (*Chelonia, Dermochelys*, Nick 1912). During ossification, this aperture becomes included in the basisphenoid. Where the originally extracranial space is secondarily incorporated into the cranial cavity, the abducens nerve passes in the extradural space between the retractor bulbi muscle before emerging via the foramen orbitale.

D. Trigeminal Nerve (V)

The trigeminal nerve has two components of different origins. The ophthalmic nerve (superficialis and profundus, V_1) is the sensory nerve of the rostral part of the head. It probably cannot be homologized with any other nerve. On the contrary, the maxillo-mandibular nerve ($V_{2,3}$) corresponds to the mandibular arch and is a true branchial nerve. The mandibular nerve is a posttrematic branch. The maxillary nerve arises from the maxillary segment of the mandibular arch. The exceptional position of nerve V_1, in contrast to nerves $V_{2,3}$, is consistent with its ontogeny, morphology and topographic relations (Haller v. Hallerstein, 1934b; Poglayen-Neuwall, 1953a,b, 1954; Soliman, 1964).

Sensory ganglia are associated with both components. The ophthalmic and maxillo-mandibular ganglia fuse in amphibians and mammals to form a complex trigeminal or semilunar ganglion. However, in most reptiles, especially the Squamata, the two ganglia remain separated. In species which retain an extracranial cavum epaptericum limited laterally by the epipterygoid, the ganglia of the trigeminal nerve lie mesial to the epipterygoid. The profundus division passes anteriorly mesial to the epipterygoid, while the maxillary and mandibular branches pass laterally of the epipterygoid (Watkinson, 1906; Willard, 1915). The ophthalmic ganglion is, furthermore, located rostral and dorsal to the maxillo-mandibular ganglion. In snakes and turtles, which have a processus descendens parietalis, the trigeminal ganglion lies medial to this (Poglayen-Neuwall, 1953a; Soliman, 1964).

The trigeminal root leaves the cranial cavity and penetrates the primary cranial wall near the foramen prooticum. The frontal and dorsal parts of the enlarged fenestra prootica are closed by connective tissue. The trigeminal nerve exits the posteroventral part of the fenestra. In lizards and *Sphenodon*, this exit is included in the anterior edge of the prootic bone. The resulting incisura (= Incl. otosphenoida, Siebenrock, 1893, 1897) may be transformed into a foramen by being completely covered by the prootic (Dinosauria, Crocodilia) or by the ossification of the pila prootica as a pleurosphenoid (see Section IIIB, *Crocodylus*). A bony-edged foramen prooticum is present in the Amphisbaenia. If the descensus of the parietal and frontal bone causes the formation of a secondary side wall to the skull (Testudines), the foramen prooticum leads from the cranial cavity into the cavum epiptericum. In snakes, $V_{2,3}$ leave the cranial cavity jointly via a single opening of the prootic (Scolecophidia; Haas, 1930, 1964) or by means of separated apertures, as in most snakes (Haas, 1930).

In turtles, the secondary side wall, formed from the parietal, reaches the epipterygoid. Cavum cranii and cavum epiptericum remain separated by a membranous wall, in which residues of the chondrocranium may be retained. Only in *Dermochelys* is a cartilaginous wall of the cavum cranii reformed (see Section IIIB; Fig. 3, Nick, 1912). The ophthalmic and maxillo-mandibular ganglia are fused in turtles. The nerve V_1 typically reaches the orbit via the foramen orbitale magnum (Fissura orbitalis auct.). Nerves $V_{2,3}$ leave the skull via a foramen prooticum. The definitive aperture is rostrally limited by the processus descendens parietalis and, therefore, lies more lateral than the exit of the primary side wall. This aperture is often called "foramen sphenoidale" although it has no relation to parts of the sphenoid complex. Wegner (1959) called it foramen interpilare. The designation is also impractical, as the real pila of the chondrocranium does not contribute to this limit. The term foramen otico-parietale emphasizes the demarcation opposite the exit of the primary side wall and is, hence, used.

E. FACIAL AND STATOACOUSTIC NERVES (VII, and VIII)

The facial nerve is associated with the hyoid arch. Its pretrematic and pharyngeal branches form the palatine nerve. The posttrematic branch forms the hyoid nerve, supplying the hyoid arch and its musculature. The viscerosensory, internal mandibular branch passes from the hyoid nerve to the floor of the mouth as the chorda tympani. The facial root courses from caudal to cranial and forms an anteriorly concave arch, the genu. The geniculate ganglion lies near the genu.

The facial root penetrates the wall of the primary skull, so that the geniculate ganglion is always located outside of the cranial cavity. The facial foramen usually lies between the basal plate and bony labyrinth, directly posterior to the foramen prooticum (N. $V_{2,3}$), but separated from it by the prefacial commissure. In sauropsids, the cochlear portion of the membranous labyrinth develops in stages. Thus mesenchyme originating from the basal plate is induced by the membranous labyrinth early in ontogeny and contributes to the bony labyrinth as the pars sacculocochlearis. Consequently, the facial foramen lies at the edge of the pars sacculocochlearis and pars utriculoampullaris of the bony labyrinth. The external aperture of the facial canal is then located in the wall of the lateral ear capsule, near the prootic foramen. The original conditions are illustrated in Gaupp's (1900) model of *Lacerta* (Fig. 5). The internal auditory meatus is formed by ossification of the medial wall of the otic capsule. Foramina for the seventh and eighth nerves lie at its base (Fig. 5). The foramen for the seventh nerve usually lies rostral, while the anterior and posterior acoustic foramina lie more posteriorly and contain the vestibular ganglion.

The acoustic foramina lie in the prootic. The anterior foramen (Fig. 5) is located somewhat dorsal and caudal to the foramen for the facial nerve, and is shielded by the utricular prominence. The eighth nerve is commonly divided into acoustic and vestibular branches. However, this terminology is not correct, because both of these branches have different functional components. Therefore, the terms anterior (vestibular) and posterior (acoustic) branches are preferable. Fibers are positioned in the nerves according to the topographic arrangement of their peripheral receptors. Consequently, the two branches may contain fibers from different sensory organs. The anterior branch usually includes nerves for the utriculus and the lateral and anterior ampullae. Fibers from the lagena, papilla neglecta, papilla basilaris and posterior ampulla run in the posterior branch. Fibers from the sacculus may join either the anterior or the posterior branch, may be distributed in both branches, or may form a branch of their own.

F. Glossopharyngeal and Vagoaccessory Nerves (IX and X)

The metotic fissure is the gap persisting between the otic capsule and the occipital pillar of the chondrocranium (Figs 5, 6). It transmits the glossopharyngeal and vagoaccessory nerves and the internal jugular vein. The perilymphatic duct passes from the bony labyrinth via the internal orifice (= foramen jugulare internum) of the metotic fissure to the cranial cavity. The subdivision of the metotic fissure leads to the formation of the anterior recessus scalae tympani and the posterior jugular foramen (Gaupp, 1900; Fig. 6). The glossopharyngeal nerve always emerges through the anterior portion of the metotic fissure. The jugular foramen contains the vagus nerve and the posterior cerebral vein.

The postotic region is modified in adult reptiles. In lizards (Gaupp, 1900), the edge of the fissura metotica ossifies. The connective tissue of the fissure simultaneously ossifies into periosteal bone, so that the recessus scalae tympani, anteriorly, and jugular foramen, posteriorly, are separated by a bony bar (Fig. 7). The channel for the tenth nerve may also join the anterior part of the hypoglossal foramen (*Gerrhosaurus, Varanus, Lophura*; Versluys, 1936). Consequently, only two foramina are present on the outside of the skull, the anterior one for nerves X and $XII_{1,2}$ and the posterior one for nerve XII_3. In *Sphenodon*, nerves IX and X pass jointly through a narrow

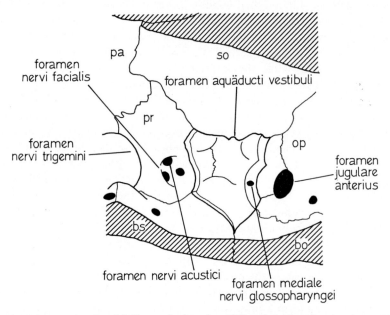

F<small>IG</small>. 6. *Chelydra serpentina*. Median sagittal section of the otic region showing the position of foramina for the nerves V to X bo (basioccipital); bs (basisphenoid); op (opisthotic); pa (parietal); pr (prootic); so (supraoccipital) (from Gaffney, 1945).

channel. In lizards, the perilymphatic sac in the recessus scalae tympani shifts to the lateral aperture. This lateral aperture is separated from the tympanic cavity by a secondary tympanic membrane; it functionally corresponds to the fenestra rotunda of mammals. However, the two are not homologous because they are positioned and bordered differently (de Beer, 1937; Frick, 1952).

The condition in crocodilians is similar to that in lizards. The recessus scalae tympani has a bony base, the processus subcapsularis, which may represent cranial ribs (de Beer, 1937). The fenestra pseudorotunda is delimited by a bony labyrinth and the processus subcapsularis. No cyst-like diverticulum of the perilymphatic space penetrates the recessus scalae tympani.

In turtles, the rostralmost component of the fissura metotica is separated from the residue of the cleft by a cartilaginous projection of the basal plate. This segment contains the channel for the glossopharyngeal nerve, which leaves the cranial cavity via the internal glossopharyngeal foramen, reaches the pars saccularis of the bony labyrinth (Fig. 7), and enters the lateral part of the recessus scalae tympani via an aperture in the posterior wall of the otic capsule. Nerve X and the vena cerebri posterior enter the posterior

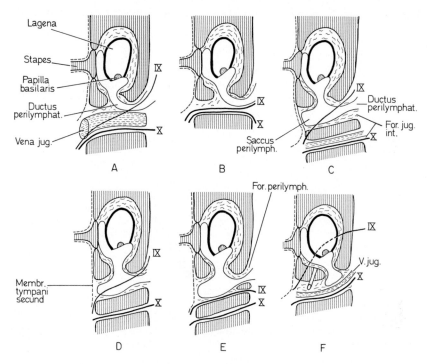

Fig. 7. Schematic representation of the topographical relations in the region of the fissura metotica and recessus scalae tympani in Recent reptiles (from Versluys, 1936). A. *Sphenodon*, embryo. B. *Sphenodon*, adult. C. *Lacerta*, embryo. D. Sauria, adult. E. *Gekko*. F. Testudines.

segment (Fig. 7), which is defined by the exoccipital, quadrate, bony labyrinth and pterygoid. A special aperture for the vagus, the posterior jugular foramen (Fig. 8), may furthermore be separated from the fenestra postotica (Figs 7, 8).

The condition in snakes is insufficiently known. As in turtles, nerve IX passes the pars saccularis of the bony labyrinth and then to the recessus scalae tympani. From there it usually enters the jugular foramina (Baird, 1960).

G. Hypoglossal Nerve (XII)

The zone between head and trunk has anterior spinal nerves that become incorporated into the occipital region of the skull (Van der Horst, 1934). Sauropsida generally have three such nerve roots (nerves a, b, c, Fürbringer, 1897) that leave the cranium via their own foramina in the exoccipital. Externally, the three roots join into a hypoglossal nerve and innervate the lingual musculature, occasionally sending a dorsal branch to components of

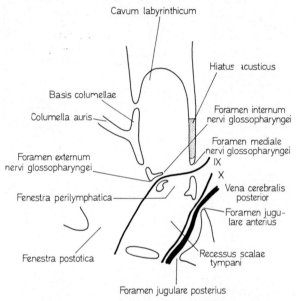

FIG. 8. *Chelydra serpentina*. Horizontal section through the cavum labyrinthi and cavum acustico-jugulare. Cartilage is shown stippled. (Modified from Baird, 1960, by Gaffney, 1972.)

the autochthonous spinal muscles. Sauropsida lack the dorsal roots and the spinal ganglia associated with the hypoglossal in some mammals. Consequently, the first complete spinal nerve is the fourth nerve of the body wall. Reptiles occasionally have only two hypoglossal roots, which results from a reduction of a or an amalgamation of a and b.

Because of the origin of the XII roots in the rhombencephalon, the hypoglossal foramina lie somewhat ventral to the foramen for nerve X. There are usually three separate hypoglossal foramina in the chondrocrania of *Emys*, *Crocodylus*, *Sphenodon*, *Lacerta*, and *Natrix*, but there are often only two in adult skulls. The most rostral foramen may reach the vagal channel while still in the cranial wall, so that the external aperture provides for the exit of both nerves. In amphisbaenians, the apertures for the ninth, tenth and eleventh nerves may be secondarily united. In *Varanus komodoensis*, a relatively large foramen for the tenth nerve includes a hypoglossal channel.

V. The Meninges

A. GENERAL

The meninges of reptiles have scarcely been investigated (Zander, 1899; Sterzi, 1900, 1901, 1913; van Gelderen, 1926; Haller v. Hallerstein, 1934a).

The meningeal membranes arise from the mesenchyme, filling the space between the epidermis and central nervous system. It is usually assumed that this mesenchyme is of mesodermal origin, but vital staining and transplantation experiments suggest that the neural crest participates in the formation of perineural mesenchyme in urodeles (du Shane, 1935; Hörstadius, 1950).

The skeletal elements divide this mesenchyme into external (cutis, subcutis) and internal (perineural mesenchyme) strata as they develop. The external stratum is positioned close to the skeleton (interior periosteum, endorhachis, endocranium) and is mechanically important as a bracing system. The internal stratum forms the meninges, which further differentiate into the tela chorioidea Vertebrates first show a uniform perineural mesenchyme, the meninx primitiva. Details of these events are still controversial, but there have been two major theories. Sterzi (1900) suggested that only the internal stratum of the perineural mesenchyme forms the meninx primitivia. The peripheral position of the skeleto-neural intermediate stratum (Haller v. Hallerstein, 1934b) is endosteum; it belongs to the skeleton functionally and lacks any relation to the meninges. Sterzi (1900) also speculated that the external stratum (pachymeninx, dura) differentiates from the interior one. In amphibians and reptiles (Sterzi, 1900, 1913), the dura arises from the remaining central part of the perineural mesenchyme, after the primary secretion of the endosteum, and it alone should be designated as meninx primitiva. Consequently, the intermediate stratum would be located between the endosteum and the meninx. However, such a primary separation of the strata is difficult to prove, particularly because close morphological relations between the different mesenchymal positions remain evident, at least locally. Most recent students (van Gelderen, 1926; Haller v. Hallerstein, 1934a; Schaltenbrand, 1955) accept a second theory (Fig. 9), which was first defined by Gegenbaur (1898) and which is also of interest in the context of human embryology (Hochstetter, 1939). In this view, the entire primary perineural mesenchyme, including the skeleto-neural intermediate stratum of Haller v. Hallerstein (1934a), should be interpreted as meninx primitiva. The interior cover, lying immediately upon the central

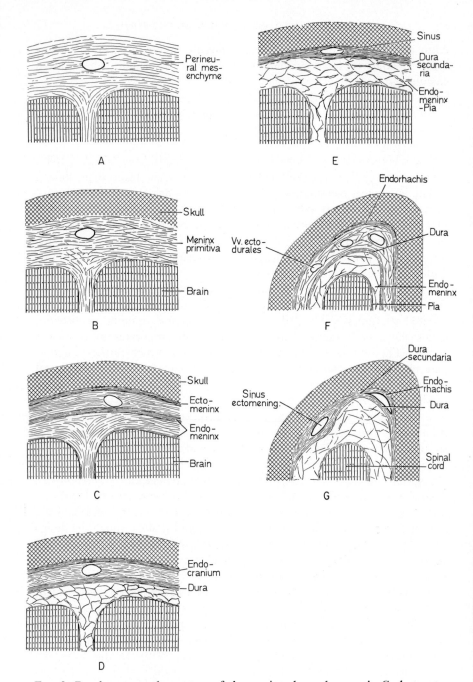

FIG. 9. Development and structure of the meningeal membranes. A. Cyclostomata, embryonic. B. Cyclostomata, adult. C, D, E. Sauria, different stages. F. Crocodilia. G. Testudines. Figs 9F G, from the cervicospinal region (modified from van Gelderen, 1926).

nervous system, becomes endomeninx and the external stratum, located adjacent to the skeleton, becomes ectomeninx. A slack, vascular inter-meningeal stratum lies between them and, in fishes, may be rich in adipose and mesenchymal tissues. The intermeningeal stratum fills the space between the cranial cavity and the brain. The ectomeninx splits into endosteum (endorhachis and endocranium) and dura. The intermeningeal tissue becomes reduced as cerebral size increases. Within the skull, endosteum and dura again fuse and form the "dura secundaria". This phase occurs in birds and mammals, and occasionally in reptiles. In turtles, the ectomeninx does not split within the spinal canal, as the vertebral column is securely incorporated into the shell. Turtles also lack intermeningeal tissue. However, dura and endorhachis are separated by intermeningeal tissue in regions where the cervical spinal column is mobile (Zander, 1899).

B. Variation in Meninges

1. General

The meninges do not show radical differences among the orders of Recent reptiles. The conditions in Rhynchocephalia, Sauria, Amphisbaenia, and Serpentes are nearly identical, so they can be discussed together. Different conditions are seen in Testudines and Crocodilia. It should be noted that Recent reptiles show no differences in the formation of cerebral and spinal meninges until the stage of meninx primitiva. In the following stages, separated limiting strata (pia–dura–endosteum) arise via the endoectomenix stage in the cranium and, in the Crocodilia, in the spinal canal as well. Dura and endosteum always fuse into dura secundaria within the reptilian skull. Consequently, the peridural veins have changed to sinuses (without their own mesenchymal wall). In the spinal canal the ectomeninx remains homo-geneous for Rhynchocephalia, Squamata, and in the carapacial zone of turtles. It only shows local splitting where veins pass. The ectomeninx is more extensively split in the cervical zone of turtles. It seems obvious to consider the condition seen in the Rhynchocephalia and Squamata as primitive and to refer the condition seen in turtles to a similar original state. The regional differentiation in turtles might reflect the stiffening of the carapacial region. In Crocodilia, the dura and endosteum of the spinal canal remain separated from the beginning by a large, veined ectomeningeal intermediate stratum. Archosaurian specializations obviously diverged early from those of the other groups.

2. Lepidosaurs

Relatively few species of lepidosaurs have thus far been investigated. Van Gelderen (1926) studied *Lacerta agilis*, *Chalcides*, and *Sphenodon punctatus*, and I studied *Lacerta agilis*, *L. sicula*, *Chalcides sphenopsiformis*, *Acantho-dactylus erythrurus*, *Anolis carolinensis*, *Tarentola mauritanica*, *Calotes versi-color*, *Chamaeleo dilepis*, and *Sphenodon punctatus*. Early embryonic stages of all reptiles show a slack, homogeneous and avascular mesenchyme between the epidermis and central nervous system. Perineural venous plexuses quickly develop in the mesenchyme. As the skeletal rudiments appear, the mesenchyme is divided into cutaneous and perineural strata. The latter stratum is the meninx primitiva (Fig. 9), including the rudiments of the endocranium and meninges and comprising the venae meningeae primitivae.

In the cranial region, the meninx primitiva differentiates into two homo-geneous strata, that is to say into the internal, slack endomeninx and the tighter, external ectomeninx. The hypophysis cerebri, ectomeningeal veins and saccus endolymphaticus lie in the ectomeninx. The pia mater is a tiny, membranous, limiting stratum formed within the endomeninx. The rest of the endomeninx becomes slender and forms the intermeningeal (= endo-meningeal) intermediate stratum (Fig. 13). Simultaneously the ectomeninx starts to define a limiting stratum (= dura mater) along the interstitial tissue and to form the basis for an endocranium (endorhachis) along the skeletal rudiments. The venae ectomeningeales (= peridural veins) lie in the ecto-meningeal stratum, intermediate between the ectomeningeal limiting strata. The parietal eye also lies peridurally. The dura is always more sharply demarcated towards the intermeningeal tissue than towards the peridural. In those regions of the skull having little space between dura and endo-cranium, both strata amalgamate secondarily to form a uniform dura secon-daria (Fig. 9). By the time adult size is reached, only the hypophysis cerebri, saccus endolymphaticus, parietal eye and peridural veins remain between the two separated sheets of the ectomeninx. The peridural mesenchyme becomes completely reduced around the veins, and these are then considered sinuses.

Reptiles lack dural wrinkles and septa (van Gelderen, 1926). However, some larger adults (*Sphenodon*, Gisi, 1907; Dendy, 1910; *Varanus*, Säve-Söderbergh, 1946; pers. obs.) have numerous, more compact connective tissue funiculi (Fig. 10), that connect the pia with the dura via the inter-meningeal cavity. Especially when the cranial cavity is only partly occupied by the brain, these funiculi may be ribbon-like and doubtless furnish support to the central nervous system. Funicular connections are especially well-developed near the pedicle of the parietal eye in *Sphenodon* (Fig. 10). The funiculus there encloses the pineal nerve as well as the associated artery and shows widened, transverse wings. The dura forms an external capsule of peridural tissue around the parietal eye. The capsule is relatively wide-meshed and contains numerous arterial branches, as well as a thin limiting stratum about the parietal eye (the internal capsule). Supporting ribbons

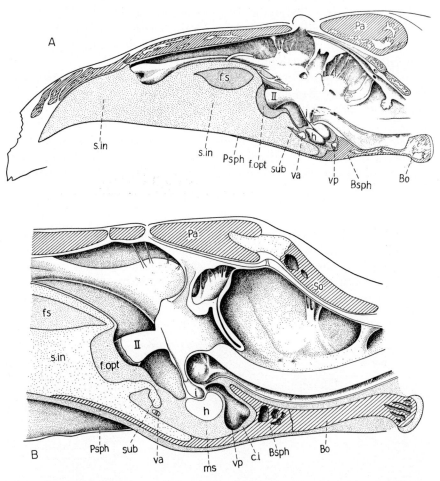

FIG. 10. Median section through the head. A. *Sphenodon punctatus*. Brain and pituitary, *in situ*. B. *Varanus salvator*. Bo, Basioccipital; Bsph, basisphenoid; c. i, Art. carotis interna and its foramen in the basisphenoid; f. opt., fenestra optica; fs, fenestra septi; h, hypophysis; i, infundibulum; ms, median membraneous septum; Pa, parietal; Psph, parasphenoid; s. in, septum internasalis; So, supraoccipital; sub, subiculum infundibuli; va, vena anastomotica; vp, vena pituitaria; II, optic nerve.

also run from rostrolateral to mediocaudal along the rhombencephalon of *Sphenodon* (Gisi, 1907). They support the central nervous system during horizontal head motions. Contrary to the opinion of Sterzi (1900), reptiles generally possess only two cerebral meninges and always lack an arachnoidea.

It should be mentioned that the so-called dura apophysis (falx, tentorium cerebelli) does not result from wrinkles of the ectomeninx (Hochstetter,

1939). The primary falx cerebri is composed of the tissues of the meninx primitiva and is in direct connection with the tissues of the tela choroidea. The falx and tentorium differentiate *in situ*. Their presence is closely correlated with the growth of cerebrum and cerebellum.

In Rhynchocephalia and Squamata, the meninges of the spinal canal develop differently than do the cranial ones. Only near venous trunks is the ectomeninx widened locally, but dura and endorhachis are never separated completely. Consequently, the membranes resemble those present inside the adult cranium, but differ in origin. The homogeneous dura secundaria is always formed by additional intergrowth of two previously separated strata within the cranium. In the spinal canal, the divison of the ectomeninx is delayed.

3. *Testudines*

Conditions similar to those present in the Squamata occur in the skulls of Testudines. *Chelydra, Chrysemys* (van Gelderen, 1926), *Chelydra, Eretmochelys, Chelonia* (pers. obs.), *Testudo graeca* (Zander, 1899) and *Emys* (Bojanus, 1819) have been studied. A large specimen of *Chelonia mydas* (Fig. 11) shows especially robust suspensory ligaments passing from the

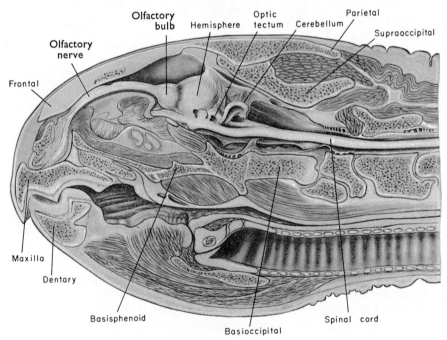

FIG. 11. *Chelonia mydas,* old male. Median section through the head. Topographic relations of brain and meningeal membranes.

tectum and cerebellum to the dura, beginning with the leptomeninx in the caudal pole of the telencephalon. There are never more than two cerebral meninges; the claim of Zander (1899) for an arachnoidea could not be confirmed.

The spinal meninges of turtles differ from those of the Squamata; the difference is greatest for those within the shell (Zander, 1899; van Geldern, 1926). In the carapacial region, the ectomeninx is very thin and homogeneous; it only widens and splits into dura and endorhachis where veins

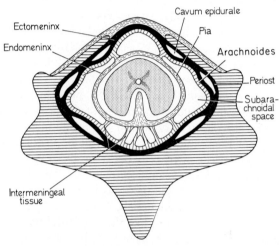

FIG. 12. Transverse section through the vertebral column in the cervical region of turtles. Spinal meningeal membranes (modified from Zander, 1899).

are surrounded by two meningeal sheets; they thus resemble a sinus (Fig. 12), as no ectomenigeal interstitial tissue is formed.

4. *Crocodilia*

The cerebral meninges of the Crocodilia are similar to the above description, but their spinal meninges are quite different. Pia, dura and endocranium are typically differentiated within the skull. The intermeningeal interstitial tissue is largely slack. The tissue between dura and endocranium remains relatively compact and stretched. Dura and endocranium are embryologically separate in the ectomeninx, but they later amalgamate to form a homogeneous dura secundaria. Only the hypophysis cerebri remains peridural, but all veins assume the characteristic of true sinuses. Crocodilia lack parietal organs. Along the spinal canal, the limiting strata of the ectomeninx remain separated as dura and endorhachis; the situation in the cervical and postcervical zones are identical. This condition remains constant through ontogeny, and the two strata never amalgamate. The venae peridurales are also preserved. In ontogeny, the spinal meninges remain at a stage passed by the cerebral meninges.

C. Histology of the Meninges

We lack specific studies of the histology of reptilian meninges. These very sensitive membranes often deform in serial sections, particularly because reptiles lack specialized tissue structures, such as those in the peridural spaces of fishes. The slack tissue of the intermediate strata is typical mesenchyme (Fig. 13); its intercellular spaces may vary (*Chalcides*), so that the sections may be similar to those of a mammalian cavum leptomeningicum.

The meninges of many reptiles, especially of Sauria, are rich in melanocytes. The number and kind of pigment cells differ considerably with region, and they tend to be especially common in rhombencephalic and spinal zones. In *Sphenodon* (Gisi, 1907) the pigment density is greatest above the rhomboid fossa and in the region of the pineal. The dorsolateral zone, particularly the olfactory canal and the region of the cavum bulbi, is only sparsely pigmented. The area between the occipital region and spinal column lacks pigment. Pigment cells occur in all strata, as well as in the derivatives of the endomeninx and ectomeninx. They also penetrate the connective tissue sheaths of the peripheral nerves and the endosteum (perineural pigment cells) (Weidenreich, 1912; Starck, 1965). Hypotheses regarding the functional significance of the meningeal pigments are unconvincing. Thus far only a very few have been investigated, and it has been impossible to correlate the kinds of pigments with their distribution among species with different habitats. Important differences in the distribution of pigments seem to occur among animals showing similar environments. If it be assumed that many pigments could afford protection from ultraviolet rays, it would be expected that fossorial species would show a reduction of the pigmentation. This does not hold, as many of these (particularly scincomorphs) are especially rich in meningeal pigment. The conditions are consequently quite similar to those of the peritoneal (visceral) pigmentation (Bellairs, 1969). Pigment cells are derivatives of the neural crest, and embryologic studies are needed to determine the extent to which the number of pigment cells relates to the extent of the neural crest and to the relative size of the mass of ectomesenchyme.

VI. Brain Position in Relation to Head Morphology

A. General

Reptiles differ from mammals in that the shapes of their skulls and the total contours of their heads are hardly influenced by the shapes of their

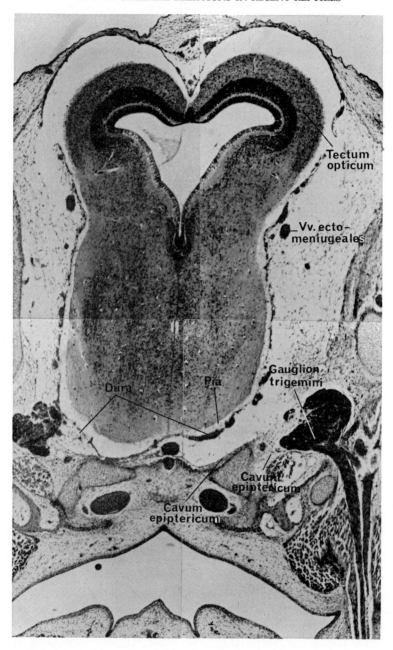

FIG. 13. *Chelydra serpentina*, older embryo. Arrangement of the meningeal membranes in the midbrain region.

brains. On the other hand, the visceral apparatus and the development of the sense organs are most important determinants of reptilian head shape. Especially critical are the size and the position of the eyes, as well as the otic and olfactory capsules. Contrary to the situation for birds and mammals,

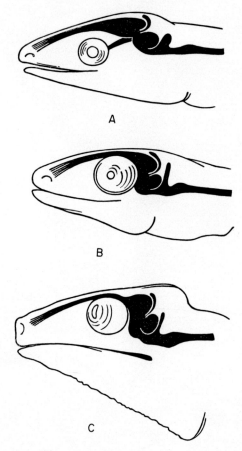

FIG. 14. Relation of the brain position and size of the eye. A. *Lacerta*. B. *Agama caucasica*. C. *Chamaeleo*. (Modified from Starck, 1955.)

these topographic relations have hardly been considered in reptiles. In his essay on *Sphenodon*, Gisi (1907) makes valuable comparative statements about cranio–cerebral topography. Starck (1955) illustrates some extreme examples among the Sauria (Fig. 14). Some relations concerning crocodilians, are discussed by Iordansky (1973). Dullemeijer (1956) discusses *Vipera berus* and Gans (1960) Amphisbaenia.

B. BRAIN–BODY RELATIONS

The statements of Gisi about *Sphenodon* (1907) and my own investigations of many other reptiles deal with a spectrum of topographic relations among and within the individual orders. Volumetric proportions are certainly a very important determinant of topographic relations (cf. Platel, Chapter 3, this volume). The size of the brain depends on the absolute body size and on the level of neural complexity. Furthermore, the relative volumes of the individual cerebral segments are independent of each other, but reflect the specializations of the sense organs. In reptiles, the mechanical loading during ingestion and food preparation is more critical to the construction of the skull than is cerebral size. Consequently, reptiles frequently show a considerable discrepancy between the size of the endocranial cavity and the total size of the skull; the brain only partly fills the cranial cavity. Among Recent species, this applies especially to large marine turtles, to *Sphenodon*, and to many lizards (Figs 10, 11). However, in snakes and amphisbaenians, the space between the brain and the cranial wall is very narrow. Many Testudines and Crocodilia show an intermediate position. It must be remembered that these relations not only show group specific differences, but also ontogenetic and possibly sexual ones.

C. POSITION OF BRAIN

Most Recent reptiles (many Testudines, Crocodilia, and Sauria) typically show an extended cerebral position in which the longitudinal axis of the brain either runs nearly parallel to the basal axis of the neurocranium or forms an angle of less than 25°. This is equivalent to the orthocranial basal type (Hofer, 1952). The space for the brain may be compressed when the eyes are larger. The forebrain is then apt to be inclined, producing an airencephalic skull (Fig. 14). These relations are manifested early in ontogeny, as the eyes quickly reach considerable size. The angle between the cerebral and cranial axes may attain values of 60° or more (*Chamaeleo*). *Sphenodon*, all Gekkonidae, and *Lacerta* possess an extended brain. Many agamids (Fig. 14) and *Anolis* are intermediate in this characteristic. Chamaeleons have the largest eyes and show extreme values.

D. INFLUENCE OF EYES

The size of the eyes also influences their relative position in the horizontal direction. The eyes lie near the center of the head in *Sphenodon*, *Lacerta*, and *Anolis*. As the total construction of the snout appears to reflect feeding functions, the eyes cannot enlarge in a rostral direction. Consequently, the occipital segments of the head are more likely to be compressed. The eyes are thus located in the posterior half of the head, and the relative snout length (distance from snout tip to anterior edge of the eyeball) will be relatively large (many Agamidae, *Chamaeleo*, Gisi, 1907). Crocodilians show special conditions because of the secondary prolongation of the snout

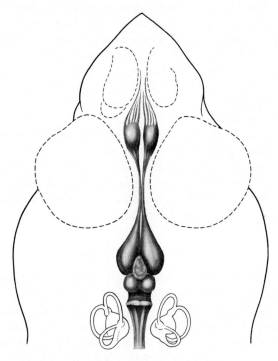

FIG. 15. *Sphenodon punctatus.* Topographic relations and shape of the brain, eyeball, auditory organ and head. (Modified from Gisi, 1907.)

(Iordansky, 1973). If the brain is compressed in the occipital direction, the medulla oblongata becomes more convex ventrally (*Chamaeleo*; Fig. 14).

The width of the interorbital region, and thus the shape of the orbital skull, reflect the size of the eye. In *Chamaeleo* and *Anolis*, the medialmost portion of the sclera reaches very close to the median plane. This distance is only slightly larger in *Sphenodon* (Fig. 15), *Gekko* and *Lacerta*. The level of the interorbital distance of the bulbs least reflects the plane of the oral fissure (Gisi, 1907). It is relatively low in *Gekko*, very high in *Agama stellio* and *Amphibolurus*, and intermediate in *Sphenodon* and *Chamaeleo*.

E. Influence of Nasal Capsules

The olfactory organ has little influence on the cerebral shape, because it lies near the front of the head and lacks direct topographic relation to the brain. The olfactory tracts and nerves lie in the cavum supraseptale at the dorsal edge of the interorbital septum, their position and shape reflecting the size of the eyes. The differentiation and magnitude of these structures of course depends on the importance of the olfactory system to the species. Consequently, they differ considerably. A direct correlation exists between the size of the olfactory organ and the bulb. In Lepidosauria, the bulb

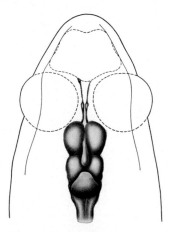

Fig. 16. *Chamaeleo* species. Topographic relations and shape of the brain, eyeball, auditory organ and head. (Modified from Gisi, 1907.)

generally lies far anteriorly, and the tract passes through the total length of the cavum supraseptale (*Sphenodon*, *Lacerta*, *Agama*). The bulb only possesses a short pedicle. The bulb of *Chamaeleo* (Figs 16, 17) lies far posterior to the cavum; consequently, it has occasionally been overlooked (Stannius, 1856). The bulb of *Sphenodon* is relatively small, and the tract very thin.

F. Feeding Adaptations

Feeding adaptations vary remarkably in the Serpentes (Fig. 17). In response to the swallowing of large prey objects, the cerebral capsule has solidified as protection for brain and sense organs. In contrast, the palato-maxillary apparatus is mobile and its connections to the cerebral capsule mainly ligamentous and muscular. The formation of a secondary lateral wall of the skull, consisting of dermal bones (see Section IIIB), results in a homogeneous,

tubular neural skull intercalated between the eyes. Thus the interorbital
septum disappears, except for some macrophthalmic types (*Dispholidus*).
While the eyes of snakes are often small and unimportant in the formation
of the head (cf. Fig. 17A with Fig. 17B), the differences within the order are
nevertheless considerable. The relative size of the eyes of *Zaocys* compared
to those of *Xenopeltis* is about 20:1 (Gisi, 1907). But even in macrophthalmic
species the interocular distance (= distance between the most medial point

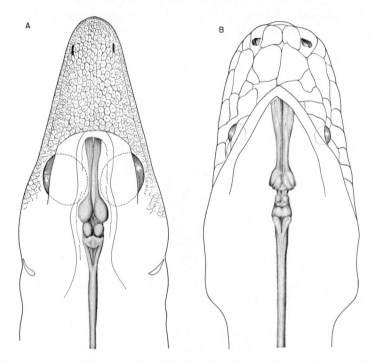

Fig. 17. A. *Varanus salvator*. B. *Python reticulatus*. Topographic relations and shape of
the brain, eyeball, auditory organ and head.

of each eyeball) always remains considerably larger than in lizards (1·5–
2·5% of the width in Sauria; *Macropisthodon*, 12%; *Xenopeltis*, 28%; Gisi,
1907. *Python reticulatus*, 60%; pers. obs.). In some species (Boiga), the
olfactory bulbs are nearly sessile, and almost join the rostral pole of the
hemisphere. When the interorbital gap is large, the olfactory bulbs and
nerves diverge rostrally. In snakes, the relative snout length (distance from
the snout tip to the eye/head leangth) is generally somewhat less than in
Sauria.

G. LABYRINTHIC ORGANS

The labyrinthic organs extend the width of the medulla oblongata and, thus, influence cerebral shape. The influence is unimportant in turtles, *Sphenodon* and Amphisbaenia (Fig. 15). In *Lacerta*, the utriculus is enlarged; the entire labyrinth stretches far dorsally. The external shape of the rhomben-cephalon reflects this; its height is greater than its width. In *Chamaeleo* (Fig. 16), the labyrinth is especially voluminous and shifted far dorsally. The medulla is more sharply confined. In some turtles, the Gekkonidae and snakes, the saccus endolymphaticus is positioned dorsally and filled with

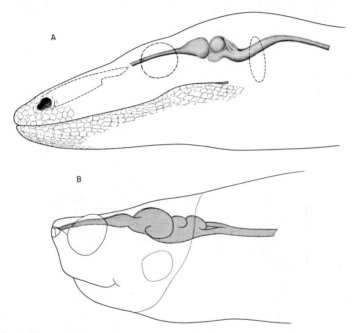

FIG. 18. A. *Varanus salvator.* B. *Pseudemys* sp. Topographic relations and shape of the brain, eyeball, auditory organ and head.

calcium crystals. The sacculus is also rather voluminous. The cyst-like diverticulum of the saccus endolymphaticus extends dorsal and posterior to the tectum.

H. BRAIN INTERACTIONS

Furthermore, it must be noted that there is a mutual interaction between the shapes of the tectum and adjacent cerebral parts. If the tectum is large (as in all macrophthalmic species), it will project to the surface between the

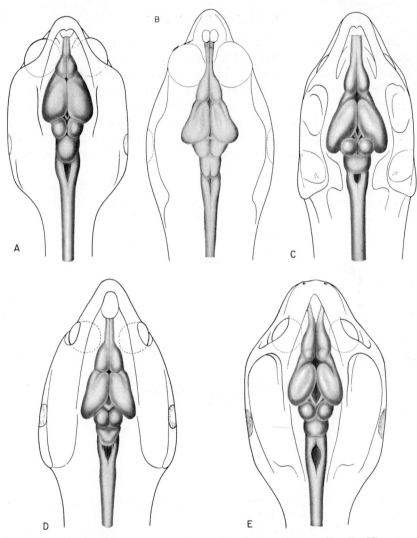

Fig. 19. A. *Kachuga tecta*. B. *Pseudemys* species. C. *Terrapene carolina*. D. *Kinosternon leucostomum*. E. *Testudo hermanni*. Topographic relations and shape of the brain, eyeball, auditory organ and head.

telencephalon and the cerebellum and will lie dorsally (*Sphenodon*, Sauria). In contrast, if the tectum is small, its dorsal side will lie ventral to the dorsal side of the forebrain. This may result in a partial overlap of the forebrain over the tectum (*Pseudemys* and *Kinosternon*), even though reptiles do not show midbrain overlap to the extent seen in mammals (Starck, 1963).

I. Systematic Considerations

The situation in turtles differs from that in other reptiles in several ways (Fig. 18). First, all turtles, regardless of their interorbital width, have sessile bulbs. The olfactory tract is generally reduced so that the bulb sits directly on the telencephalon. The olfactory nerves pass through the interorbital region. Gisi's (1907) statement that *Chelonia mydas* has an olfactory pedicle has not been checked for a large individual (Fig. 11). The wall of the olfactory canal, the planum supraseptale, is double in early stages. The planum

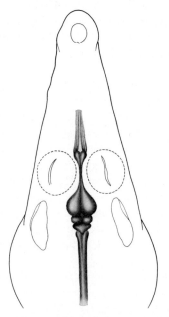

Fig. 20. *Crocodylus porosus*. Topographic relations and shape of the brain, eyeball, auditory organ and head. (Modified from Bellairs, 1969.)

generally is quite wide, but the interorbital width may vary considerably. It is small in *Emys* and *Pseudemys* (Fig. 19), but very large in *Chelonia*. The olfactory bulbs usually contact the posterior edge of the eye and their pointed ends intercalate between the eyeballs, so that only the olfactory nerves are located between the eyes (Figs 18, 19) of *Pseudemys*, and *Kinosternon*. However, in *Testudo* and *Kachuga*, the entire olfactory bulb lies between the eyes, and the olfactory nerve only begins anterior to the eyeballs. In the species investigated, the olfactory nerves are parallel and closely adjacent. Considerable divergence is found in *Testudo* (Fig. 19E). In turtles, the eyes are situated far anteriorly. The small size of the eyeballs makes the skull orthocraneous. The Crocodilia differ from other Recent reptiles by their widened telencephalon, with the indication of an impressio orbitalis (Fig. 20). The interorbital gap is narrow (*Crocodylus*) and is passed by the narrow, long, extended tractus olfactorii. The olfactory bulbs are large and lie immediately anterior to the eyes.

VII. Summary

A. The braincase is formed embryonically by three elements: the parachordals, the trabeculae, and the sphenolateral plates. The parachordals form the basal plates as far rostrally as the hypophyseal region, while the trabeculae form the cranial base rostral to the hypophysis. The lateral wall (sphenolateral plates) of the braincase chondrifies rostral to the trigeminal nerve.

B. The optic capsule housing the inner ear chondrifies independently of the braincase, and the olfactory capsule is composed of the ethmosphenoid plate, formed by fusion of the trabeculae and part of the sphenolateral plate.

C. The occipital region of the braincase is characterized by three to four hypoglossal foramina, suggesting that in primitive reptiles this region contained at least four postotic head segments.

D. The optic and occipital regions of Recent reptiles show little variation, while their orbitotemporal regions vary markedly. Ancestral vertebrates apparently possessed an almost complete cartilaginous lateral wall of their braincase, while the skulls of lizards and some snakes are characterized by extreme reduction of the lateral wall. Other snakes show extensive secondary chondrification in this region.

E. Ossification of the occipital braincase always results in a basioccipital, a supraoccipital and exoccipitals. However, ossification of the orbitotemporal region is highly variable. In lizards and *Sphenodon*, the wall remains cartilaginous or membranous. In amphisbaenians, the wall ossifies. Snakes lack a primary orbitotemporal wall, and most turtles have cartilaginous relicts of the primary lateral wall. Finally, crocodilians are characterized by an ossified chondral bone (incorrectly described as an alisphenoid), formed by the primary lateral wall.

F. Variation in the development of the orbitotemporal region and the position of the brain with respect to the lateral wall of the braincase result in different peripheral courses for the cranial nerves and blood vessels in the different reptilian orders.

G. The meninges arise from mesenchyme with possible involvement of neural crest in the formation of perineural mesenchyme. Dermal skeletal development divides the mesenchyme into external and internal strata. The external stratum forms the endosteum, while the internal stratum forms the meninges and the chorioid plexuses. Cranially the internal stratum (meninx primitiva) differentiates into an internal endomeninx and an external ectomeninx. The cranial meninges of reptiles show little variation. The spinal meninges of reptiles do not differentiate as completely as do the cranial meninges.

H. In reptiles the shape of the skull is only slightly influenced by the size of the brain. However, the jaw apparatus and sense organs, particularly the eyes, are important determinants of head shape.

Acknowledgements

I wish to thank many colleagues for their generosity in supplying me with specimens. I mention especially Dr K. Klemmer, Natur Museum Senckenberg, and Dr H. Wermuth, Staatliches Museum für Naturkunde, Stuttgart-Ludwigsburg. I thank most heartily Dr C. Gans for many comments and for supervising the linguistic and stylistic preparation of my contribution, and Mr H. Schneeberger for preparing the drawings.

References

Baird, I. L. (1960). A survey of the periotic labyrhynth in some representative Recent reptiles. *Kansas Univ. Sci. Bull.* **41**, 891–981.

Barry, T. H. (1965). On the epipterygoid–alisphenoid transition in Therapsida. *Ann. S. Afr. Mus.* **48**, 399–426.

Bellairs, A. d'A. (1969). "The Life of Reptiles." Weidenfeld and Nicholson, London, 2 vols.

Bojanus, L. H. (1819). "Anatome Testudinis Europaeae." Vilno (also reprint 1970 *Facsim. Repr. Herpetology* (26) Soc. Stud. Amph. Rept.).

de Beer, G. R. (1937). "The Development of the Vertebrate Skull." Oxford University Press, London.

Dendy, A. (1910). On the structure, development and morphological interpretation of the pineal organs and adjacent parts of the brain in the Tuatara (*Sphenodon punctatus*). *Phil. Trans. R. Soc. Ser. B* **201**, 227–331.

Dullemeijer, P. (1956). The functional anatomy of the head of the common viper, *Vipera berus* (L). *Archs néerl. Zool.* **11**, 387–497.

du Shane, G. P. (1935). An experimental study of the origin of pigment cells in Amphibia. *J. exp. Zool.* **72**, 1–32.

Frick, H. (1952). Zur Morphogenese der Fenestra rotunda. *Verh. Anat. Ges., 50. Vers, Marburg/L.* (Ergänzungsheft *Anat. Anz.* 99) 194–203.

Fürbringer, M. (1897). Über die spino-occipitalen Nerven der Selachier und Holocephalen und ihre vergleichende Morphologie. Gegebaurs-Festschrift. W. Engelmann, Leipzig, **3**, 351–788.

Gaffney, E. S. (1972). An illustrated glossary of turtle skull nomenclature. *Am. Mus. Novit.* (2486), 1–33.

36   D. STARCK

Gans, C. (1960). Studies on amphisbaenids (Amphisbaenia, Reptilia) I. A taxonomic revision of the Trogonophinae and a functional interpretation of the amphisbaenid adaptive pattern. *Bull. Am. Mus. nat. Hist.* 119(3), 133–204.

Gaupp, E. (1900). Das Chondrocranium von *Lacerta agilis*. *Anat. Hefte* 15, 433–595.

Gaupp, E. (1902). Über die Ala Temporalis des Säugerschädels und die Regio orbitalis einiger anderer Wirbeltierschädel. *Anat. Hefte* (59) 19, 159–230.

Gegenbaur, C. (1898). "Vergleichende Anatomie der Wirbeltiere." Engelmann, Leipzig.

Gisi, J. (1907). Das Gehirn von *Hatteria punctata*. *Zool. Jb.* (*Anat.*) 25, 1–166.

Goldby, F. and Gamble, H. J. (1957). The reptilian cerebral hemispheres. *Biol. Rev.* 31, 383–420.

Guibé, J. (1970). Le squelette cephalique. *In* "Traité de Zoologie". (P. P. Grassé, ed.). Masson et Cie, Paris, 14(2), 78–143.

Haas, G. (1930). Über das Kopfskelet und die Kaumuskulatur der Typhlopiden und Glauconiiden. *Zool. Jb.* (*Anat.*). 52, 1–94.

Haas, G. (1964). Anatomical observations on the head of *Liotyphlops albirostris* (Typhlopidae, Ophidia). *Acta Zool.* 45, 1–62.

Haller v. Hallerstein, Graf V. (1934a). Hüllen des Zentralnervensystems. *In* "Handbuch der vergleichenden Anatomie der Wirbeltiere". (L. Bolk, E. Göppert, E. Kallius and W. Lubosch, eds). Urban und Schwarzenberg, Berlin and Wien, 2(1), 309–318.

Haller v. Hallerstein, Graf V. (1934b). Kranialnerven. *In* "Handbuch der vergleichenden Anatomie der Wirbeltiere". (L. Bolk, E. Göppert, E. Kallius and W. Lubosch, eds). Urban und Schwarzenberg, Berlin and Wien, 2(1), 541–684, 835–840.

Hochstetter, F. (1939). Über die Entwicklung und Differenzierung der Hüllen des menschlichen Gehirns. *Morph. Jb.* 83, 359–494.

Hörstadius, S. (1950). "The Neural Crest." Oxford University Press, London.

Hofer, H. (1952). Der Gestaltswandel des Schädels der Säugetiere und Vögel mit besonderer Berücksichtigung der Knickungstypen und der Schädelbasis. *Verh. anat. Ges. 50. Vers. Marburg/L.* (Ergänzungsheft *Anat. Anz.* 99) 102–121.

Howes, G. B. and Swinnerton, H. H. (1901). On the development of the skeleton of the tuatara, *Sphenodon punctatus. Trans. zool. Soc. Lond.* 16(1), 1486.

Iordansky, N. N. (1973). The skull of the Crocodilia. *In* "Biology of the Reptilia". (C. Gans and T. S. Parsons, eds). Academic Press, London, 4(2), 201–262.

Jollie, M. T. (1960). The head skelcton of the lizard. *Acta Zool.* 41, 1–64.

Kamal, A. M. (1964). Notes on the chondrocranium of the gecko *Tropiocolotes steudneri. Bull. zool. Soc. Egypt* 5(19), 73–83.

Kunkel, B. W. (1911). Zur Entwicklungsgeschichte und vergleichenden Morphologie des Schildkrötenschädels. *Anat. Anz.* 39, 354–364.

Kunkel, B. W. (1912). The development of the skull of *Emys lutaria. J. Morph.* 23(4), 693–781.

Nick, L. (1912). Das Kopfskelet von *Dermochelys coriacea* L. *Zool. Jb.* (*Anat.*) 33, 1–238.

Parker, W. K. (1885). On the structure and development of the skull in the Crocodilia. *Trans. zool. Soc. Lond.* 11, 263–310.

Poglayen-Neuwall, Ingemar (1954). Die Kiefermuskulatur der Eidechsen und ihre Innervation. *Z. wiss. Zool.* 158, 79–132.

Poglayen-Neuwall, Ivo (1953a). Untersuchungen der Kiefermuskulatur und deren Innervation bei Schildkröten. *Acta Zool.* 34, 241–292.

Poglayen-Neuwall, Ivo (1953b). Untersuchungen der Kiefermuskulatur und deren Innervation an Krokodilen. *Anat. Anz.* 99, 257–276.

Rieppel, O. (1976a). Die orbitotemporale Region im Schädel von *Chelydra serpentina* Linnaeus (Chelonia) und *Lacerta sicula* Rafinesque (Lacertilia). *Acta Anat.* 96, 309–320.

Rieppel, O. (1976b). The homology of the laterosphenoid bone in snakes. *Herpetologica* 32, 426–429.

Romer, A. S. (1956). "Osteology of the Reptiles." Univ. of Chicago Press, Chicago.

Säve-Söderbergh, G. (1946). On the fossa hypophyseos and the attachment of the retractor bulbi group in *Sphenodon*, *Varanus*, and *Lacerta*. *Ark. Zool.* 38(11), 1–24.

Schaltenbrand, G. (1955). Plexus und Meningen. *In* "Handbuch der mikroskopischen Anatomie des Menschen". (W. H. W. v. Möllendorff, ed.). Springer Verlag, Berlin, 4(2), 1–139.

Sewertzoff, A. N. (1895). Die Entwicklung der Occipitalregion der niederen Vertebraten. *Bull. Soc. imp. Naturalistes Moscou* 1895.

Shaner, R. F. (1925). The development of the skull of the turtle with remarks on fossil reptile skulls. *Anat. Rec.* 32, 343–367.

Shiino, K. (1912). Beitrag zur Kenntnis der Gehirnnerven der Schildkröten. *Anat. Hefte* 47, 1–34.

Shiino, K. (1914). Studien zur Kenntnis des Wirbeltierkopfes. I. Das Chondrocranium von *Crocodilus* mit Berücksichtigung der Gehirnnerven und der Kopfgefässe. *Anat. Hefte* 50, 253–382.

Siebenrock, G. (1893). Zur Osteologie des *Hatteria*-Kopfes. *Sbr. k. Akad. Wiss. Wien, math.-naturw. Kl.* 102(1), 1–19.

Siebenrock, F. (1896). Das Kopfskelet der Schildkröten. *Sbr. k. Akad. Wiss. Wien, math. naturw. Kl.* 106(1), 1–84.

Soliman, M. A. (1964). Die Kopfnerven der Schildkröten. *Z. wiss. Zool.* 169, 216–312.

Stannius, H. (1856). Die Amphibien. *In* "Die Wirbelthiere." Vol. 2. *In* "Handbuch der Zootomie" (v. Siebold and H. Stannius, eds). Veit und Co., Berlin, 2, 1–270.

Starck, D. (1955). Die endokraniale Morphologie der Ratiten, besonders der Apterygidae und Dinornithidae. *Morph. Jb.* 96, 14–72.

Starck, D. (1963). "Freiliegendes Tectum mesencephali" ein Kennzeichen des primitiven Säugetiergehirns? *Zool. Anz.* 171, 350–359.

Starck, D. (1965). Herkunft und Entwicklung der Pigmentzellen. *In* "Handbuch der Haut- und Geschlechtskrankheiten". (O. Gans, ed.). Springer Verlag, Berlin, 1(2), 139–175.

Sterzi, G. (1900/1901). Ricerche intorno all' anatomia comparata ed all' ontogenesi delle meningi. *Atti. Inst. ven. Sci.* 60; *also* (1902). *Arch. ital. Biol.* 37, 257–269.

Sterzi, G. (1913). Intorno alle meningi midollari ed al legamento denticolato degli ofidi. *Anat. Anz.* 43, 220–227.

Underwood, G. (1970). The eye. *In* "Biology of the Reptilia". (C. Gans and T. S. Parsons, eds). Academic Press, New York and London, 2(1), 1–97.

van Gelderen, C. (1926). Die Morphologie der Sinus durae matris. Die vergleichende Ontogenie der Hirnhäute mit besonderer Berücksichtigung der Lage der neurokraniellen Venen. *Z. Anat. EntwGesch.* 78, 339–489.

van der Horst, C. I. (1934). Spinalnerven. *In* "Handbuch der vergleichenden Anatomie der Wirbeltiere". (L. Bolk, E. Göppert, E. Kallius and W. Lubosch, eds). Urban und Schwarzenberg, Berlin and Wien, 2(1), 505–540.

Versluys, J. (1936). Kranium und Visceralskelett der Sauropsiden. 1. Reptilien. *In* "Handbuch der vergleichenden Anatomie der Wirbeltiere". (L. Bolk, E. Göppert, E. Kallius and W. Lubosch, eds). Urban und Schwarzenberg, Berlin and Vienna, 4, 699–808.

Watkinson, G. B. (1906). The cranial nerves of *Varanus bivittatus*. *Morph. Jb.* 35, 450–472.

Wegner, R. N. (1959). Der Schädelbau der Lederschildkröte *Dermochelys coriacea* Linné (1766). *Abh. dt. Akad. Wiss. Berlin, Kl. Chemie, Geol., Biol.* 1959(4), 1–80.

Weidenreich, F. (1912). Die Lokalisation des Pigmentes und ihre Bedeutung in Ontogenie und Phylogenie der Wirbeltiere. *Z. Morph. Anthrop.*, *Suppl.* **2,** 59–140.

Willard, W. A. (1915). The cranial nerves of *Anolis carolinensis. Bull. Mus. comp. Zool. Harv.* **59,** 17–116.

Zander, R. (1899). Beiträge zur Morphologie der Dura mater und zur Knochenentwicklung. *Festschrift C. V. Kupffer*, Fischer Verlag, Jena, 63–78.

CHAPTER 2

Paleoneurology

JAMES A. HOPSON

Department of Anatomy,
University of Chicago
Chicago, Illinois, U.S.A.

I. Introduction

The tissues of the nervous system normally decay rapidly after the death of an organism; hence the study of paleoneurology of necessity deals with the nervous system only indirectly. The evidence bearing on the morphology of the nervous system in extinct vertebrates is derived entirely from the study of those fossilized hard parts which lay in close proximity to elements of the nervous system and upon which these elements had left indications of their former existence. The size and shape of the endocranial cavity of the skull provide information on the size and external morphology of the brain, and the size and location of cranial foramina yield information on cranial nerves. The neural canal within the vertebrae may provide clues about local enlargements of the spinal cord but otherwise yields little significant information.

The brains of living reptiles, unlike those of mammals and birds, usually do not fill the cranial cavity. Therefore, a cast of the reptilian braincase cavity usually provides only a general impression of the superficial topography of the brain. Nevertheless, such a cast may yield a great deal of useful information about the brain, for, as pointed out by Romer (1956, p. 21): "The internal contours of the braincase are, in general, molded by the brain." The extent to which the brain fills the braincase varies among living reptiles, and this appears to have been the case for extinct groups as well. Non-neural elements such as venous sinuses also occupy part of the intracranial space, and these too show different degrees of development in different reptiles. When the influences of non-neural tissues on the topography of the cranial cavity are taken into account, it is sometimes possible to gain a great deal of information from a cast of this cavity.

The literature on the paleoneurology of reptiles is large (see Edinger,

1975, for a recent summary), but much of it consists of secondary references or oft-repeated comments on the brains of dinosaurs in non-technical publications. Original descriptions of endocranial casts of fossil reptiles are in fact relatively few, and of these, the majority pertain to dinosaurs and other archosaurian groups. We know very little about the brains, as interpreted from casts of their cranial cavities, of most groups of extinct reptiles.

Very few endocranial casts, or endocasts, of fossil reptiles were described before Yale paleontologist O. C. Marsh, in the 1870s and 1880s, made paleoneurology a recognized area of research with his important studies of the endocasts of early Cenozoic mammals and Mesozoic birds and giant reptiles. Marsh (1876, 1885) espoused the view that the mammals of the early Cenozoic and the birds and reptiles of the Mesozoic all had much smaller brains than do their modern descendants. From this he arrived at general "laws of brain growth", principally (1) that there was a gradual increase in brain size during the evolutionary histories of these vertebrate groups and (2) that this increase was confined mainly to the cerebral hemispheres. Marsh described and illustrated endocranial and endosacral casts of a number of dinosaurs.

Many endocasts of fossil reptiles have been described since the last two decades of the nineteenth century, usually, however, incidental to the description of the skull or other aspects of cranial osteology. The literature on paleoneurology prior to 1929 was reviewed by T. Edinger (1929) in her monograph *Die fossilen Gehirne*. She provided a general discussion of paleoneurology, including the relation of endocasts to the brain and the influence of the meninges and other non-nervous structures on the endocast. Certain of the topics with which she dealt are treated in the present volume by Starck (see Chapter 1); others are treated later in this chapter. A second part of Edinger's monograph consists of a systematic review of the endocasts of extinct vertebrates, with some 27 pages (pp. 115–142) devoted to reptiles. A supplement to this mongraph was published by Edinger in 1937. Recently, an annotated bibliography of paleoneurology, which Dr Edinger was compiling at the time of her death in 1967, was published (Edinger, 1975). This work covers the literature from 1804 to 1966; it should be consulted for a complete listing of references to the paleoneurology of reptiles prior to 1967.

The present review is organized much the same as Edinger's 1929 monograph. Section II reviews the nature of the evidence which an endocast is capable of providing about the brain and cranial nerves. An important part of this section is a detailed comparison in the recent species *Caiman crocodilus* of the endocast with the brain and the non-neural contents of the cranial cavity. Some information is also provided on the ontogenetic changes which occur both in the endocast and in the brain of *Caiman*. Unless the relation of endocast to brain is understood in living reptiles, it is difficult to derive much reliable information from the endocasts of extinct reptiles. Section III reviews available information on relative brain size in fossil reptiles; the pioneering methods of Dr H. J. Jerison are reviewed, and the problems involved in determining brain and body weights in fossil reptiles are discussed. Section IV is a systematic review of current knowledge of the endocranial casts of fossil reptiles.

The following abbreviations are used for designating museum specimens: A.M.N.H., American Museum of Natural History, New York; B.M. (N.H.), British Museum (Natural History), London; F.M.N.H., Field Museum of Natural History, Chicago; Geol. Surv. Mus., Geological Survey Museum, London; K.U., University of Kansas Museum of Natural History, Lawrence; M.I.W.G., Museum of Isle of Wight Geology; N.M.C., National Museum of Canada, Ottawa; R.O.M., Royal Ontario Museum, Toronto; S.A.M., South African Museum, Cape Town; S.M., Senckenberg Museum, Frankfurt; U.C.M.P., University of California Museum of Paleontology, Berkeley; U.M., University of Michigan Museum of Paleontology, Ann Arbor; U.S.N.M., United States National Museum of Natural History, Washington; U.U.V.P., University of Utah (Vertebrate Paleontology Collection), Salt Lake City.

II. The Nature of the Evidence Which the Endocast Provides about the Brain

A. What Are Endocasts?

1. Natural Endocasts

A natural endocast—or *Steinkern*—is one in which the rock matrix filling the cranial cavity is exposed by removal of the surrounding skull bones so as to leave a stone cast of the endocranial cavity. Such a cast resembles, to a greater or lesser extent, the brain which in life lay within the cranial cavity. Natural endocasts from which the surrounding bone has been eroded away in the field are discovered only infrequently; an example of such a specimen is the endocast of the mammal-like reptile *Thrinaxodon liorhinus* (described originally as *Nythosaurus larvatus*, Fig. 29c). More commonly, natural endocasts are prepared in the laboratory by removing bone by artificial means in order to expose the matrix filling of the cranial cavity. In specimens in which the endocast is partially exposed by natural means, additional removal of bone will yield a more complete replica of the contents of the cranial cavity. This was done in the pterosaur *Parapsicephalus purdoni* (Newton, 1888) (Fig. 12) from which the frontal bone was removed to expose the cerebral hemisphere and olfactory bulb.

2. *Artificial Endocasts*

Naturally exposed endocasts are extremely rare in nature, and it is often impractical to expose the natural endocranial filling of a fossil skull, either because the matrix filling is too soft and friable to yield a good surface or, as is the case in most reptiles, because the cranial bones are very thick relative to the size of the deep-lying cranial cavity. In such cases it is usually easier to clear the matrix from the cranial cavity and use the cavity as the mold for an artificial cast of some appropriate casting material. Edinger (1929) describes older methods of casting using such materials as gelatin, glue, and gutta percha. At the present time, the most convenient and satisfactory casting material is latex (Radinsky, 1968). In all cases, the artificially produced endocast may be used as the basis for a mold and plaster casts produced. Most endocasts of fossil reptiles have been prepared in this way, often by sectioning a skull sagittally or by opening up the braincase along natural fractures. Incomplete braincases or isolated roofing bones have also been used as molds from which partial endocasts have been made (see Figs 13, 18, 19A, B).

A second method for artificially producing a replica of the cranial cavity is by means of serially grinding a fossil skull and reconstructing the outline of the cavity graphically or in wax. This method was used by Olson (1944) and Boonstra (1968) to construct endocasts for a series of mammal-like reptiles (see Figs 27, 28).

B. FACTORS WHICH INFLUENCE THE SHAPE OF THE ENDOCAST

Endocasts of reptiles normally reflect features of the cranial cavity as well as those of the brain and cranial nerves. Several of these features are considered by Starck in this volume. For example, the endocast reflects the shape of the dural envelope which surrounds the brain and this may be very thick in places (see Starck, Figs 9, 10). Intradural venous sinuses may occupy a substantial amount of space within the cranial cavity. The discrepancy between the size of the brain and the size of the cavity it occupies will be discussed below. Blood vessels within the braincase sometimes leave grooves and foramina in the cranial walls, and these are reflected as ridges and processes on the endocast. The endolymphatic sac also opens into the cranial cavity, and its foramen is sometimes preserved as a small protuberance on the endocast.

Other features of the endocast are the result of postmortem changes in the skull. In the braincases of many living reptiles, such as *Sphenodon*, lizards, and turtles, large portions of the orbitotemporal region are formed from cartilage or membrane. This was also true in many extinct groups. Furthermore, the anterodorsal portion of the supraoccipital bone, underlying the parietals, frequently remains cartilaginous in many reptiles (see Zangerl, 1960). After death, all unossified portions of the skeleton decay along with the soft tissues, and the space which they occupied may become filled with sediment. Thus the endocast will usually include extracranial spaces which in life were separated from the cranial cavity by a partition now lost, or which in life were occupied by a mass of unossified skeletal tissue. Such postmortem changes may invite misinterpretation about the true limits of the cranial cavity. Immature individuals, in which the skull contains more cartilage, naturally pose the greatest problems.

The braincase of crocodilians, snakes, and amphisbaenians is almost completely ossified. In these living forms, and in their extinct relatives, one would expect the endocast to reflect the shape of the cranial cavity with relatively great accuracy. This is fortunate because, although endocasts of fossil snakes and amphisbaenians are virtually unknown, the endocasts of crocodilians and other archosaurs (thecodonts, dinosaurs, and pterosaurs) are relatively common. The endocasts of fossil archosaurs do indeed resemble those of living crocodiles in their degree of faithfulness to the shape of the endocranial cavity.

C. Relation of Brain to Endocast in Living Reptiles

1. *Introduction*

Dendy (1911) points out that the brain of *Sphenodon* fills only about one-half of the cranial cavity. Edinger (1929) figures endocasts and brains of *Alligator* and *Chelonia* and notes that the endocast of the turtle provides little information about the shape of the brain whereas that of the crocodilian reflects the relative proportions of the different parts of the brain quite well. Ostrom (1961) cites Papez (1929), who commented on the great disparity in size between the brain and the cranial cavity in turtles. Papez also notes that the brain of squamates more nearly fills the cranial cavity, a condition which Ostrom verified by dissection of several species of large lizards and of *Sphenodon*. Ostrom adds that his dissections of *Alligator* crania establish that "the dura mater occupies a major portion of the endocranial cavity here also".

2. *Iguana*

Jerison (1973) notes that the volume of the brain of a small specimen of *Iguana iguana* is only one-half that of casts made from the cranial cavity of the same individual. He draws attention to the fact that in living reptiles such as *Iguana*, in which the braincase is partly cartilaginous, a distinction must be made between a cast of the cranial cavity with cartilages intact and one made after the cartilages have been removed. The former "chondrosteoendocast" is "moderately brainlike in appearance" and, in Jerison's example, has a volume (0·96 ml) almost twice that of the brain (0·51 ml). The latter "osteoendocast" is a cast only of the bony portion of the cranial cavity and lacks all detail of the sides and floor of the braincase in front of the pituitary fossa. Its volume (0·83 ml), however, still greatly exceeds that of the brain.

Details of the brain of *Iguana* are difficult to determine from an endocast. The close apposition of the optic tectum to the cerebrum renders the tectum indistinguishable on the endocast, even in the smallest individuals. Jerison (1973, Fig. 2.1) points out that a more posterior bulge on the cast (caused by venous sinuses?) could be misindentified as the impression of the optic tectum.

3. *Caiman*

In order better to interpret the morphology of fossil endocasts, I have compared a series of endocasts made from the skulls of recent *Caiman crocodilus* with (i) preserved brains and (ii) a dissected head in which the arteries and veins had been injected with colored latex. Endocasts of a very small (skull length = 30·9 mm) and a medium-sized (skull length = 247 mm) caiman are illustrated in Figs 1 and 2, along with figures of the brain and other intracranial structures of *Caiman* and *Crocodylus*. The morphology of the larger endocast is described in terms of the soft tissues within the cranial cavity which have influenced its morphology.Ontogenetic changes in morphology both of the endocast and of the endocranial soft tissues are discussed subsequently.

The braincase of *Caiman* is, as in all other living crocodilians, completely ossified except for the floor of the canal for the olfactory peduncles, which remains cartilaginous. The endocast reflects the major regions of the brain with a greater or lesser degree of fidelity. The principal gross features of the forebrain are accurately represented, but those of the mid- and hindbrain are indicated only vaguely. The dural envelope surrounding the forebrain is relatively thin and the bony walls of the braincase lie close to the cerebral hemispheres. The dural covering of the mid- and hindbrain is generally much thicker and, in addition, the posterior portion of the midbrain and the entire hindbrain are overlain by the large longitudinal venous sinus and its principal branches. This results in the preservation on the endocast of only the grossest aspects of these regions of the brain, and also leads to possible misinterpretation of details of their morphology.

The endocast clearly reflects the anteroposterior limits of the main parts of the forebrain. The position of the olfactory bulbs is indicated by an expansion of the cavity in which they lie between the ventrally directed pillars of the prefrontals. Posteriorly, the trough on the undersurface of

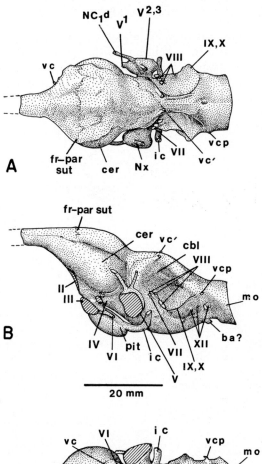

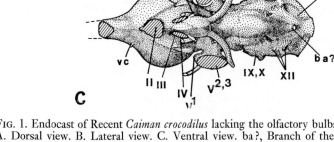

Fig. 1. Endocast of Recent *Caiman crocodilus* lacking the olfactory bulbs and peduncles. A. Dorsal view. B. Lateral view. C. Ventral view. ba?, Branch of the basilar artery?; cbl, cerebellum; cer, cerebrum; fr-par sut, frontal-parietal suture; ic, internal carotid artery; mo, medulla oblongata; NC_1d, motor branch of the trigeminal nerve to the levator bulbi muscle; Nx, unidentified branch of trigeminal nerve; pit, pituitary fossa; vc, minor vascular canals; vc′, branch of longitudinal sinus; vcp, diverticulum of longitudinal sinus; II, optic foramen; III, oculomotor foramen; IV, trochlear foramen; V^1, canal for ophthalmic branch of the trigeminal nerve; $V^{2,3}$, foramen for maxillary and mandibular branches of the trigeminal nerve; VI, canal for the abducens nerve; VII, facial foramen; VIII, foramina for the auditory nerve; IX, X, foramen for the glossopharyngeal and vagus nerves; XII, foramina for the hypoglossal nerve.

the frontal gradually narrows for about half its length, then gradually widens and merges with the cerebrum. In the specimen illustrated (Fig. 1), the cerebral cast is about as long as it is wide; in smaller individuals the cerebral cast is proportionally wider (cf. Fig. 2A) and in larger individuals

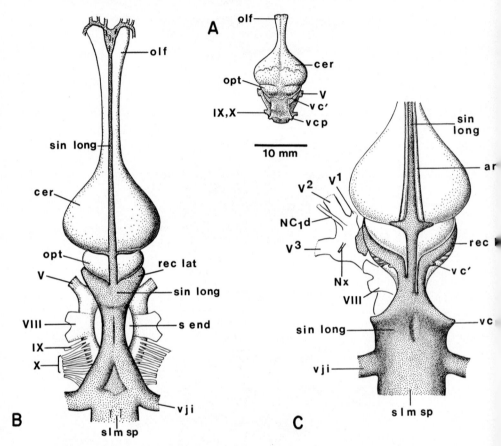

FIG. 2. A. Endocast of juvenile *Caiman crocodilus* (skull length = 30·9 mm) in postero-dorsal view to show impressions of cerebral hemispheres and optic lobes. B. Dorsal view of the brain and longitudinal venous sinus of *Crocodylus niloticus* (after Hochstetter, 1906). C. Dorsal view of the brain and longitudinal venous sinus of *Caiman crocodilus*. B and C not to scale. art, "Arteria cerebri posterior"; cer, cerebrum; olf, olfactory bulb; opt, optic lobe; rec lat, recessus lateralis of longitudinal sinus; s end, endolymphatic sac; sin long, longitudinal venous sinus; s l m sp, sinus longitudinalis medullae spinalis; vc′, branch of the longitudinal sinus; vcp, diverticulum of the longitudinal sinus; v j i, internal jugular vein posterior to the skull; NC_1d, motor branch of the trigeminal nerve to the levator bulbi muscle; Nx, unidentified branch of the trigeminal nerve; V, trigeminal nerve; V^1, ophthalmic branch of the trigeminal nerve; V^2, maxillary branch of the trigeminal nerve; V^3, mandibular branch of the trigeminal nerve; VIII, auditory nerve; IX, glossopharyngeal nerve; X, vagus nerve.

it is narrower. These changes in endocast proportions reflect changes in forebrain shape during ontogeny. The shape of the endocast closely reflects the shape of the cerebral hemispheres except in the regions of the dorsal and ventral midlines. Dorsally, the cast bears a slight longitudinal median ridge whereas on the brain the paired hemispheres are separated by a deep median cleft. The dura is continuous across this median depression, and it contains the anterior continuation of the longitudinal venous sinus and a pair of arteries which run forward to the nasal cavity (Fig. 2). The slight midline elevation of the endocast may be a reflection of these vascular elements. On the dorsolateral surface of the endocast is a longitudinal ridge representing the suture between the frontal and laterosphenoid bones into which the latex had penetrated. The transverse fronto-parietal suture is also evident on the dorsal surface of the endocast. The endocast does not reflect the ventral cleft between the paired hemispheres, nor does it reflect the distinct separation between the ventral borders of the hemispheres and the infundi-bulum; in all cases, the dural covering rounds off sharp boundaries and smooths over depressions.

The pineal of the caiman is a small finger-like projection extending upward from between the optic lobes and the caudal border of the cerebral hemispheres. It is overlain in the living animal by the longitudinal venous sinus and is not represented on the surface of the endocast. The cast of the pituitary fossa lies below the posterior part of the cerebrum and appears as an elongate oval, narrowest proximally, in both lateral and ventral views. It is triangular in transverse section, with a flat posterodorsal surface and flat ventrolateral walls which meet in a blunt midventral ridge. The dimen-sions of the cast are much greater than those of the neural tissue contained in the fossa. The infundibulum occupies the proximal half of the fossa and the pituitary body a small part of the distal half. The remainder of the distal portion is occupied by the internal carotid artery and venous sinuses.

The position of the optic tectum is indicated on the endocast by the posterior constriction of the sides of the cerebral cast and by the drop in height of the cast behind the cerebral region. Lateral swellings above the cast of the trigeminal ganglion appear to indicate the transverse dimensions of the optic tectum but, as will be indicated below, these swellings reflect lateral branches of the dorsal venous sinus. The optic tecta are, in fact, completely prevented from leaving evidence of their size and shape by the relatively great thickness of the dura surrounding them and by the presence of the prominent vascular elements interposed between them and the cranial wall.

The cerebellum of the caiman is about equal in height to the optic tectum but is transversely narrower. The endocast is constricted in its upper half behind the level of the optic tecta, but the precise position, size, and shape of the cerebellum are totally obscured by the presence in life of the thick, broad, dorsal venous sinus. The endocast behind the level of the optic tectum provides more evidence about the morphology of the longitudinal venous sinus and its branches than it does about the cerebellum (see below).

The longitudinal venous sinus obscures the dimensions and morphology of the medulla oblongata both dorsally and laterally. At the level of the foramen magnum, both the height and the width of the endocast better reflect the dimensions of the intracranial venous sinus than those of the medulla. The cross-sectional area of the medulla is much smaller than suggested by the endocast. However, the undersurface of the medulla is reflected more accurately on the endocast. In lateral view, the ventral profile of the medulla has a sigmoid curvature which is clearly reflected on the endocast.

The cranial foramina which transmit the cranial nerves are usually indicated on the endocast as short processes. The olfactory bulbs and peduncles are discussed above. The optic nerves in crocodilians leave the braincase via a single large median foramen below the anterior half of the cerebrum. In the caiman, the size of the foramen closely reflects the cross-sectional area of the nerves. Behind and below the optic foramen is a second, large median foramen which represents the metoptic fenestra of the chondrocranium. It is incompletely subdivided below by the basisphenoid rostrum and it appears on the endocast as two anterolaterally directed foramina on the sides of the cast of the pituitary fossa. The foramen transmits the oculomotor (III) nerve and the ophthalmic branch of the internal carotid artery (Müller, 1967, Fig. 22). The oculomotor nerve, though the largest of the three cranial nerves innervating the intrinsic ocular muscles, is nevertheless much smaller in cross-section than the foramen. A short distance above the oculomotor foramen is a small foramen for the small trochlear (IV) nerve. At the posterolateral extremity of the short process which marks the oculomotor foramen is a short, slender, caudally directed process which marks the anterior opening of the narrow canal through the basisphenoid which transmits the small abducens (VI) nerve. The posterior opening of the canal lies on the floor of the cranial cavity below the trigeminal foramen; it is marked on the endocast by a very small anteroventrally directed process on the underside of the medullary region.

The very prominent trigeminal (V) nerve leaves the cranial cavity via the large trigeminal foramen. Lateral to the trigeminal foramen is a very large semicircular hollow, partially walled dorsolaterally but otherwise open laterally, formed by the prootic and laterosphenoid bones. The Gasserian ganglion fills the hollow and gives off large maxillary (V^2) and mandibular (V^3) rami through the lateral opening; these, of course, are not seen as separate trunks on the endocast. The ophthalmic (V^1) branch of the trigeminal nerve passes forward in a short slit-like canal between the braincase wall and a more lateral downgrowth of the laterosphenoid. The cast of this canal is seen on the right side of the figured endocast (Figs 1A, C). From the roof of the hollow for the trigeminal ganglion two narrow canals pass upward into the side wall of the braincase. The slightly wider anterior canal opens on to the lateral surface of the laterosphenoid below the supratemporal fenestra. It transmits a small motor nerve from the dorsal surface of the trigeminal ganglion to the levator bulbi muscle, a remnant of the dorsal constrictor of the mandibular arch (Schumacher, 1973, p. 130). It is labeled NC_1D in Fig. 1A, following Schumacher (1973). The small posterior canal passes posterodorsally and somewhat medially into the anterior part of the tympanic cavity. It transmits a second small nerve from the trigeminal ganglion which, after passing through the prootic bone, continues upward to the roof of the middle ear cavity. According to Killian (1890) this small branch of the trigeminal nerve anastomoses with the glossopharyngeal and vagus nerves.

A short distance behind the cast of the trigeminal nerve are three very small processes lying closely together, one above the other, and behind these, a larger, anteroposteriorly elongate process. The most anteroventral of these four processes represents the cast of the proximal portion of the foramen for the small facial (VII) nerve. The two processes immediately overlying it represent two rami of the vestibular branch of the statoacoustic (VIII) nerve and the larger process behind them represents the cochlear branch of this nerve. The branches of the auditory nerve pass laterally through the prootic into the cavity of the inner ear. The large common trunk of the statoacoustic and facial nerves, which lies below the bulbous otic capsule within the cranial cavity, is surrounded by the dura and, thus, does not leave an impression on the endocast.

Behind the cast of the cochlear branch of the eighth nerve, on the posteroventral margin of the large depression in the endocast which reflects the bulbous otic "bulla", is an elongate process which filled the slit-like common foramen for the glossopharyngeal (IX) and vagus (X) nerves.

The hypoglossal (XII) nerve lies posterior to the lower half of the glossopharyngeal-vagus foramen on the ventrolateral surface of the medulla. It may have two or three roots in *Caiman*. The available endocasts have either two or three hypoglossal roots; in the figured endocast (Fig. 1) there are three, a large posterior root and two smaller anterior roots. Other specimens show only one small root anterior to the large one.

Aspects of the intracranial circulation are markedly reflected on the caiman endocast. The arterial system is indicated principally by the internal carotid artery. It passes through a canal in the basicranium which is reflected on the endocast as a prominent curved process. The carotid canal leaves the middle ear cavity a short distance behind the trigeminal root and curves downward, inward, and forward within the basisphenoid to open into the posterodorsal part of the pituitary fossa. The ophthalmic branch of the internal carotid artery, as noted above, leaves the fossa via the same foramen through which the oculomotor nerve emerges from the cranial cavity (Müller, 1967). The only other probable arterial element reflected on the endocast is a small midline canal which passes posteroventrally into the floor of the braincase a short distance in front of the foramen magnum; this canal was probably passed by a minor branch of the basilar artery.

The venous system of the head has a greater influence on the form of the reptilian endocast than does the arterial system. Consequently, the intra-cranial venous circulation in *Caiman* is here described in some detail. The major features of the crocodilian intracranial venous system are described and figured by Hochstetter (1906).

The principal element of the intracranial venous circulation in *Caiman* is the longitudinal sinus. In a juvenile (skull length: 67 mm) the sinus is very well developed above the hindbrain; it decreases in prominence anteriorly so that above the forebrain it is reduced to a slender vein about one-tenth the diameter it has at the level of the foramen magnum (Fig. 2c). The posterior part of the sinus, at the level of the hypoglossal nerve, is much wider than the medulla. The sinus narrows markedly between the bulbous otic capsules, but expands again anterior to them, where it sub-divides into paired lateral branches and a single median branch. In *Croco-dylus niloticus* (Hochstetter, 1906, Fig. 33; Fig. 2B), each lateral branch ("recessus lateralis" of Hochstetter) merges with the median sinus at the same anteroposterior level. In *Caiman* the branching is asymmetrical; the lateral recess of the right side joins the common median trunk well behind the level at which the recess of the left side joins the median trunk. The variation of branching of the sinus is not reflected on endocasts, as such details are hidden by the thick dural covering of the sinus. The width of the anterior continuation of the longitudinal sinus above the optic lobes is perhaps one-fifth its more posterior diameter. At the level of the transverse sulcus between optic lobes and cerebral hemispheres the sinus gives off a pair of lateral branches ("vena cerebri posterior" of Hochstetter). It then continues forward as a small vein above the forebrain and into the nasal cavity. A low midline elevation of the cerebral portion of the endocast may reflect the course of the anterior extension of the sinus (and an associated pair of arteries). Otherwise, the longitudinal sinus and its branches anterior to the lateral recesses are not definitely reflected on the endocast.

The large lateral recess of the longitudinal sinus passes downward and slightly forward on the side of the brain to the dorsal surface of the root of the trigeminal nerve. The recess overlies the posterior border of the optic tectum and the anterior border of the cerebellum including the auricles (floccular lobes). It gives off several small branches on the lateral surface of the brain into a thick pocket of the dura which lies in a broad depression in the anterolateral wall of the otic "bulla". These branches break up into small vessels which penetrate the bone of the otic capsule. On the endocast these vessels are indicated by numerous tiny processes on the swelling which represents the dura-filled pocket on the otic capsule. This swelling on the endocast, which lies directly above the trigeminal ganglion, might easily be mistaken for the cast of the optic tectum on a fossil endocast. The optic tectum however, lies further anteriorly and, with the exception of pterosaurs and the dinosaur *Stenonychosaurus*, seems never to be reflected on the endocast of reptiles (cf. Jerison, 1973, Fig. 2.1).

A small branch from each lateral recess passes dorsally into the supra-occipital bone just behind the suture of the latter with the parietal. Further posteriorly, just behind the constriction of the longitudinal sinus between the otic capsules, the sinus sends a short, bluntly rounded extension laterally into a pit in the exoccipital bone. One or more tiny vessels enter the distal wall of the pit. On the endocast, this extension of the longitudinal sinus appears as a small process on the side of the medullary region above the two posterior roots of the hypoglossal nerve. Additional small branches of the major intracranial veins penetrate the surrounding bones of the cranial cavity but only those described above appear to be identifiable on fossil endocasts.

Additional but unidentified vascular elements (either venous or arterial) may be seen on the *Caiman* skull and endocast. On the lateral surface of the forebrain, anterodorsal to the optic foramen, is a slender process which undoubtedly marks the foramen of a small blood vessel, probably a vein. This vessel was not found on the dissection. It may occur on both sides or only on one side (Fig. 1); it is totally absent in other endocasts. A process in this approximate locations is frequently present on fossil endocasts.

Another small vessel which could not be located on the dissected head is indicated by a slender but distinct ridge on the ventrolateral surface of the cerebral hemisphere, just dorsal to the trochlear foramen (Fig. 1). The ridge on the endocast (representing a groove on the inner surface of the braincase) ends abruptly at the point at which the vessel passed anteriorly through a small canal in the laterosphenoid. A faint depression on the endocast, which passes anteromedially to contact the lateral border of the optic foramen, represents a groove on the external surface of the latero-sphenoid bone; it marks the anterior continuation of the vessel which passed through the small canal.

In *Caiman*, as one would expect, the discrepancy between the volume of the brain and the volume of the endocranial cavity (and therefore of the endocast) increases during ontogeny. However, an analysis of three brains from animals with skull lengths ranging from 30 to 100 mm compared with six endocasts from animals with skull lengths of 30 to 200 mm indicates that the increasing discrepancy is localized in certain regions of the braincase. The transverse diameters of the cast of the cerebrum, midbrain, and medulla between the otic capsules maintain a rather constant relationship to the diameters of these regions of the brain. On the other hand, the rate of increase in both transverse and dorsoventral diameters of the cast of the medulla (at the level of the posterior root of the hypoglossal nerve) is much greater than the rate at which these dimensions increase on the brain. This disproportionate increase in the height and breadth of the medullary region is probably attributable to the increase in volume of the longitudinal venous sinus during ontogeny. Unfortunately, the size range of the sample is inadequate to provide evidence on the effect of the venous sinuses on the relative volumes of the brain to endocast in full-grown individuals.

The dimensions of the smallest *Caiman* endocasts are almost the same as the dimensions of the smallest brains. The endocast illustrated in Fig. 2A is extremely brain-like, showing the paired cerebral hemispheres and optic tectum. On slightly larger endocasts, however, the distinctly paired nature of these areas becomes obscured.

The endocasts of juvenile caimans suggest that, at least in fossil archosaurs, one might expect the endocasts of small individuals to provide a good reproduction of the brain, especially of the forebrain. This is borne out in some, but not all, cases (see Figs 12, 13, 18).

D. Evidence on the Relation of Brain to Endocast in Fossil Reptiles

Dendy (1911) observes that the brain of *Sphenodon* fills about one-half of the endocranial cavity and concludes that the shape of the latter provides no reliable indication of the former. He further notes that this is probably true of many fossil reptiles, so that the greatest caution should be exercised in drawing conclusions from the study of casts of the cranial cavity. Osborn (1912, p. 21), taking heed of Dendy's admonition, refers to the endocast of *Tyrannosaurus* as a cast of the dura mater envelope of the brain. Following Dendy's observation that the cubic capacity of this envelope in *Sphenodon* appears to be double that of the brain, he uses the same proportion in estimating the volume of the brain of *Tyrannosaurus* from its endocast. Subsequent workers on the endocasts of fossil reptiles have accepted as fact that, in most cases, there is a great deal of space within the braincase which is not filled by the brain.

In his studies of relative brain size, Jerison (1969, 1973) assumes that the brains of fossil reptiles were about half the size of their endocasts. He notes that the assumption is not completely satisfactory and that it would be desirable to have a more accurate set of data on brain: endocast relations from living species. He suggests that it is more likely that the fraction of the cranial cavity occupied by the brain is a negative function of body size, as suggested by Aronson (1963) for fish. Gould (1975) has picked on this point as a possible weakness in Jerison's methodology, because were it the case that the brain filled a decreasing fraction of the cranial cavity in increasingly large reptiles, then Jerison's conclusion that dinosaurs had relative brain sizes within the expected reptilian range for their body sizes would probably be false. Dinosaurs would, in fact, have had smaller brains than predicted on the basis of the brain to body size allometry seen in living reptiles.

It would indeed be desirable to have data from living reptiles on the rate of change of brain volume and of braincase volume with change of body size. As noted above, endocast volume in *Caiman* does increase allometrically in relation to brain volume over a narrow size range of juvenile individuals. The increase is concentrated primarily in the posterior half of the endocast, i.e. in the part that reflects the longitudinal venous sinus to the greatest extent. The forebrain, and midbrain regions and the more ventral part of the medullary region do not show such an allometric dimensional relationship of brain to endocast, at least over the small size range for which data exist. These limited data suggest that the *total* volume of the endocast may increase allometrically relative to brain volume in fossil reptiles, so that the use of a constant fraction of endocast volume (such as Jerison's use of 50%) to estimate brain volume may be incorrect. However, in the absence of data on the ratio of brain to endocast volume in large living crocodilians, it is not possible to determine what the allometric relationship of these features might have been in large extinct forms.

An examination of the endocasts of fossil reptiles suggests that if an allometric relationship does exist between brain and endocast volume, it differs among different groups. For example, in some archosaurs the endocast is wholly or partially brain-like in appearance, suggesting that the walls of the cranial cavity lay very close to the surface of the brain. The most spectacular example is that of the pterosaurs (Fig. 12), in which the entire endocast is extraordinarily brain-like. In several medium-sized (estimated body weight about 45 kg) carnivorous dinosaurs the cast of the forebrain shows the modeling of the brain surface in great detail, although the preserved parts of the midbrain and cerebellar regions are less clearly shown (Fig. 13). Floccular lobes of the cerebellum are impressed on the braincase in a number of extinct forms, such as pterosaurs, most therapsids, and carnivorous dinosaurs; this occurs in very large as well as in small animals. Likewise, the cast of the forebrain region varies in its degree of resemblance to the actual brain in different groups and the degree of resemblance among medium-sized to large animals is poorly correlated with absolute size. For example, in hadrosaurian ornithischians (estimated body weight: 3–4 metric tons; Colbert, 1962), endocasts reflect the shape of the cerebral hemispheres as faithfully as do those of living crocodilians of less than 1/40th their body weight and far better than that of the ceratopsian *Protoceratops* of 1/20th their body weight (see Figs 1, 17, 22). It is likely that the forebrains of hadrosaurs nearly filled their portions of the braincase.

The variability in the degree to which all or parts of the brain filled the cranial cavity in both living and fossil reptiles suggests that we ought not anticipate a regular relationship of brain to endocast volume across a broad taxonomic spectrum of extinct reptiles.

E. EVIDENCE ON THE MORPHOLOGY OF THE BRAIN IN FOSSIL REPTILES

1. *Overall Shape*

Although the endocast usually does not represent the surface contours of the brain in much detail, it may nevertheless reflect the flexure of the brain, its overall shape, and the relative sizes of its parts. Frequently, the flexure can be related to the orientation and size of the braincase in the skull and to the orientation of the skull on the neck. If the semicircular canals are represented on the endocast, the horizontal canal (which is usually held horizontally in living tetrapods; DeBeer, 1947; Delattre and Fenart, 1958) can be used to give the probable life orientation of the cranial cavity and therefore of the skull. Knowledge of the orientation of the head relative to the neck may permit an interpretation of the functional significance of cranial proportions; this, in turn, can provide insight into the functional significance of overall brain shape.

Head orientation and the shape of the brain appear to be correlated in sauropod dinosaurs, on the one hand, and cynodont therapsids on the other. The endocast of the sauropod *Diplodocus* (Fig. 16) is short and compact and shows distinct flexures. The temporal region of the *Diplodocus* skull is extremely short, the facial region is turned sharply downward on the cranium, and the posterodorsally placed orbit is very large. All of these factors have combined to crowd the braincase far back in the skull; hence the brain is shaped to fill the available space most economically. In cynodont therapsids, to illustrate the opposite extreme, the skull is straight, the temporal region is long, and the orbit is proportionately small; in consequence the brain is elongate and nearly unflexed (Fig. 29). Within a single group of closely related genera, the effect of skull shape on the shape of the endocast is clearly demonstrated by comparing the endocasts of the long- and short-headed dicynodont therapsids (Fig. 28).

The influence of skull size on the shape of the cranial cavity (and, consequently, of the brain) is best shown by comparing the endocasts of closely related animals with skulls of similar shape but of very different size. Because brain size increases at a slower rate than skull size in increasingly larger animals, the endocasts of smaller species are more compact and usually show a greater degree of flexure than do those of larger species. Examples are provided by the pachycephalosaurian (Fig. 19), ankylosaurian, and ceratopsian (Figs 22, 23) ornithischians and by the carnosaurian saurischians.

It is useful to have some measure of the degree of flexure of the endocast between forebrain and midbrain (cephalic flexure) and between the metencephalon and myelencephalon (pontine flexure). Where a distinct pontine flexure is discernible, I have adopted the convention of orienting the medulla oblongata horizontally; the amount of flexure is then determined by the acute angle between the horizontal axis of the medullary region and the oblique axis of the midbrain region. Likewise, the acute angle between the usually horizontal axis of the forebrain region and the inclined axis of the midbrain region is a measure of the magnitude of the cephalic flexure. In some groups, such as the hadrosaurian ornithischians (Fig. 17), the medullary region continues the oblique axis of the midbrain region; in such cases, the forebrain axis is considered to be horizontal and only a cephalic flexure can be determined.

2. *Regions of the Brain and Cranial Nerves*

a. *General.* In this section is summarized the general nature of the evidence derived from endocasts relating to the major regions of the brain and to the cranial nerves in fossil reptiles.

b. *Telencephalon.* (i) Olfactory bulbs and peduncles. The olfactory bulbs and peduncles frequently leave paired impressions on the undersurface of the cranial roof, so their approximate lengths and widths can be determined (see Figs 13, 19, 29). In most reptiles, the floor of the olfactory portion of the brain is not ossified and the ventral margins of the tracts are not preserved. In many archosaurs, with an ossified laterosphenoid (orbitosphenoid) and presphenoid, part or all of the olfactory peduncles and bulbs may be enclosed in bone. Information on the relative sizes of the olfactory region of the brain in most archosaur groups and advanced therapsids is provided by the endocast.

(ii) Cerebral hemispheres. The cerebrum usually occupies the widest portion of the endocast. It is clearly demarcated from the midbrain region in relatively few specimens; more frequently, the endocast narrows gradually in a posterior direction and the posterior borders of the hemispheres are not clearly demarcated from the midbrain and cerebellar regions. The dura

covering the cerebrum is relatively thin in living crocodilians, and the endocast provides a relatively good reproduction of this region of the brain. In
small saurischian and ornithischian dinosaurs and in pterosaurs, as already
noted, the cerebral hemispheres closely fit the braincase in life, and their
shapes and limits can be determined with relatively great accuracy. Even in
some large dinosaurs, e.g. hadrosaurs, the cast of the cerebral cavity is much
broader than the adjacent parts of the brain and its limits are more clearly
defined than is usual in large reptiles.

In many archosaur endocasts, the side of the forebrain cast bears a pointed
projection which many authors have identified as marking the foramen of a
minor vascular element. Janensch (1936) identifies this foramen on the
braincases of several dinosaurs as the foramen epioptica, which in embryonic
reptiles transmits the anterior cerebral vein. In the adult it probably transmitted a small vein.

c. *Diencephalon*. The diencephalon is not seen on the endocast except for
its outgrowths, the infundibulum and pituitary ventrally, and, where a
parietal foramen is present, the parietal (parapineal) organ dorsally. The cast
of the optic foramina, but not usually the optic chiasma, is visible anteroventrally, below the cerebrum.

The pituitary fossa in living reptiles is only partially filled by the pituitary.
It also contains arteries, venous sinuses, and, sometimes, the attachment
areas of certain of the extrinsic eye muscles (Säve-Söderbergh, 1946).
Therefore, one cannot exactly estimate the size of the gland from the size
of its fossa. The size of the fossa, and presumably of the gland itself, appears
to have an allometric relation more closely related to total body size than to
brain size (Edinger, 1942). Its size therefore increases more rapidly with
increase in body size than does the cranial cavity, and it is extraordinarily
large in the giant sauropods (Janensch, 1938). No precise quantitative data
in support of this conclusion are available, but the cast of the pituitary fossa
is often large in fossil reptiles, especially so in dinosaurs.

Paired processes extending posteroventrally and laterally from the lower
part of the pituitary cast are the canals of the internal carotid arteries. A
pair of smaller canals passes anteroventrally from the floor of the medulla
through the dorsum sellae to open just lateral to the pituitary fossa. These
canals transmitted the abducens (VI) nerves. The cast of the anterior
opening of the abducens canal usually joins the cast of the pituitary fossa
because the latter also includes some space which lies lateral to the fossa
proper, including the walls of the fenestra metoptica through which nerve
VI enters the orbit. This fenestra (which may be subdivided in different
groups) often forms a large lateral opening in the side of the pituitary cast;
in living crocodilians it transmits the ophthalmic branch of the internal
carotid artery and the VIth cranial nerve from the braincase.

The presence of a parietal (parapineal) eye is indicated in many extinct reptiles by the presence of a parietal foramen lying between the parietal bones on the skull roof. A parietal foramen, often of very large size, is present in primitive reptiles as it was in their anthracosaurian labyrinthodont predecessors. The foramen is retained in the marine orders, in primitive lepidosaurs, including sphenodontids and many lizards, and in all but the most advanced mammal-like groups. It is absent in turtles, some lepidosaurs (rhynchosaurs, many lizards, and almost all amphisbaenians and snakes), and all but three of the earliest genera (*Proterosuchus, Erythrosuchus, Mesorhinosuchus*) of archosaurs. The foramen is very large in the so-called "diadectomorph" cotylosaurs (diadectids, procolophonids, and pareiasaurs), and dinocephalian therapsids. It is discussed by Edinger (1955).

A parietal foramen has been attributed to several sauropods (*Diplodocus, Dicraeosaurus, Barosaurus*) by Janensch (1936), but the large, variably present, opening between the parietals of these forms has more often been interpreted as a fontanelle or unossified zone rather than a true foramen (Marsh, 1896; Pompeckj, 1920; Edinger, 1975). Its functional significance is not known.

d. *Mesencephalon.* The mesencephalon is usually not indicated on the endocast because the optic tectum is overlain by dura which is often thicker than that over the cerebrum and by the longitudinal venous sinus and its lateral branches which further obscure their outline. Optic tectum impressions are clearly evident in pterosaurs and are also visible in the medium-sized carnivorous dinosaur *Stenonychosaurus* (Russell, 1969). They have been identified on the endocast of *Tyrannosaurus* by Osborn (1912), but the swellings so identified are more likely to represent parts of the cerebral hemispheres (see Fig. 15).

The foramen for cranial nerves III and IV (foramen metoptica) frequently occurs on the endocast behind and below the optic foramen. Crocodilians and other archosaurs have a separate foramen for the trochlear nerve dorsal to that for the oculomotor nerve.

e. *Metencephalon.* The cerebellar region is sometimes expanded over the midbrain region. It is sometimes elevated slightly above the midbrain region as an elongate ridge or a more-or-less blunt, backwardly directed protuberance (as in *Stegosaurus*, Fig. 20, or *Corsochelys*, Fig. 6). This protuberance on the endocast has been described as an indication of a large cerebellum (or even as an enlarged cerebrum or optic tectum), but it represents the cartilaginous, anterodorsal portion of the supraoccipital which underlies the parietals and often fails to ossify in living reptiles (Oelrich, 1956; Zangerl, 1960). The cerebellum normally is not closely molded by the braincase, being overlain by the longitudinal venous sinus, so only a vague indication of its form and position are seen on the endocast. The variability in height and contours of this region are probably a consequence of the relative development of the venous sinus. Two major exceptions to this generalization exist: the cerebellum, including the very large floccular lobes, is well shown on the endocast of pterosaurs, and the floccular lobes, though not the medial portion of the cerebellum, are well represented on the endo-casts of therapsids (Watson, 1913; Olson, 1944). A floccular fossa has also been identified on the endocasts of carnivorous dinosaurs.

The foramina of the trigeminal and facial nerves are normally well shown on the endocast. The space in the cavum epiptericum occupied by the trigeminal ganglion is usually represented by a large bulbous process on the ventrolateral surface of the endocast. In some archosaurs, in which the ophthalmic branch of cranial nerve V passes anteriorly within a separate channel in the laterosphenoid, the course of this nerve is represented on the endocast as a distinct, anteriorly directed process separate from the common root for the second and third branches of nerve V (Figs 14, 23). The seventh cranial nerve is usually seen as a process of small diameter behind the large trigeminal root and in front of the cavity which housed the inner ear (which, on the endocast, is usually not completely represented).

The small abducens nerve pierces the dorsum sellae below and medial to the trigeminal nerve and passes downward, forward, and somewhat lateral, to exit from the dorsum sellae lateral to the pituitary fossa.

One or two branches of the acoustic nerve are infrequently represented on the endocast; these pass posteriorly from the base of the canal for the facial nerve into the inner ear cavity (Langston, 1960, Fig. 163).

Most endocasts show an oblique ridge on the lateral surface of the cere-bellar region which passes up and back from just above the trigeminal foramen. It has been sometimes interpreted as representing the endo-lymphatic duct, but this lies more posteriorly and is a less prominent feature. In crocodilians, this position is occupied by a prominent venous element, the lateral recess of the longitudinal sinus. This vein develops ontogenetically from the vena cerebralis media, which primitively drains into the lateral head vein. Janensch (1936) interprets the ridge in dinosaurs as representing a groove in the endocranial cavity for the vena cerebralis media. A similar groove in the cranial cavity of cynodonts is also interpreted as housing this vein (Hopson, 1964).

The small foramen of the endolymphatic duct on the inner surface of the optic capsule is rarely evident on fossil endocasts.

f. *Myelencephalon.* The cast of the posterior part of the medulla oblongata often widens toward the foramen magnum. The medulla may be long, as in hadrosaurs, or short, as in sauropods. The canal for cranial nerves IX and X and the posterior cerebral vein (internal jugular vein) is represented by a large process extending outward and posteroventrally, either from behind the cast of the inner ear cavity or from its posterolateral corner. This canal, often called the jugular foramen, represents the metotic fissure of the chondrocranium. It may be variously subdivided so that the nerves and vessels leaving the skull may have separate foramina. The glossopharyngeal nerve may exit in some reptiles (e.g. mosasaurs, Camp, 1942; hadrosaurs, Langston, 1960) via a separate small foramen below the fenestra ovalis. The internal jugular vein usually leaves the skull with the vagus nerve, but in some reptiles (such as crocodilians) it is lost and its function is taken over by drainage via the foramen magnum.

The hypoglossal nerve may have one, two, or three separate roots represented on the endocast ventromedial and somewhat posterior to the vagus canal.

On the endocast of many archosaurs is a round protuberance behind the inner ear cavity and above the hypoglossal foramina. Janensch (1936) described in several dinosaur braincases a blind depression in the wall of the cranial cavity, which he interpreted as the remnant of a canal which transmitted in the juvenile or the embryo a branch of the posterior cerebral vein. This, he believed, was later replaced by a more posterior branch which exited through the foramen magnum (as in adult crocodilians and some lizards). In *Caiman*, a similar protuberance on the endocast (Fig. 1) represents a diverticulum of the longitudinal venous sinus from which small veinlets enter the surrounding bone. I interpret the process on the endocast of fossil archosaurs as representing such a diverticulum of the longitudinal sinus.

III. Relative Brain Size in Extinct Reptiles

A. Methods for Studying Relative Brain Size

Jerison (1969, 1970, 1973) has presented analyses of the relationship between brain size and body size in several orders of extinct reptiles. His study concerns only three groups—dinosaurs, pterosaurs, and therapsids— but, for a variety of reasons, these are the extinct reptiles of greatest interest to students of evolution. I here present a brief description of Jerison's methods and conclusions and then discuss the problems and areas of uncertainty in studies of relative brain size in fossil reptiles.

Jerison (1969, 1973) plots brain and body weights of 198 living vertebrates (data from Crile and Quiring, 1940) on log–log coordinates and shows that the points for mammals and birds and those for fishes and reptiles form two non-overlapping clusters with the former lying above the latter. To demonstrate the outer limits of these natural groupings, Jerison enclosed the arrays of points for "higher vertebrates" (mammals and birds) and for "lower vertebrates" (fishes and reptiles) in minimum convex polygons of the sort shown by Platel (this volume). Both polygons have approximately the same slope, which Jerison indicates by placing visually fitted lines having slopes of 0·67 through the approximate centroid of each array of data. The y intercepts of these lines are 0·07 for higher vertebrates and 0·007 for lower vertebrates; these values, Jerison suggests, are indicative of a tenfold increase in relative brain size in the shift from lower to higher vertebrates.

On the basis of these data, Jerison determines that a best-fitting line for brain:body data takes the form

$$E = kP^{2/3}$$

where E is the brain weight and P the body weight (in grams) and k is a proportionality constant equal to the y intercept of the equation in logarithmic form. For "lower vertebrates", as noted above, $k = 0·007$. Thus, if body weight is known, the equation

$$E_e = 0·007P^{2/3}$$

may be used to determine the "expected" brain weight of an average fish or reptile of that body weight. The expected brain size may then be compared with the actual brain size, which in a fossil form would be determined from the endocast. The ratio of actual to expected brain size for an animal of a given body size is the "encephalization quotient" for that animal, and is determined by the equation

$$EQ_i = E_i/E_e$$

Brain and body size data for fossil vertebrates are plotted by Jerison in relation to the minimum convex polygons determined for living vertebrates. All points for fossil reptiles fall within or as extensions of the main trend of the polygon for living reptiles (Fig. 3).

The main conclusions of Jerison's analysis of fossil reptiles is that dinosaurs, pterosaurs, and therapsids are all typically reptilian with respect to relative brain size. Therefore, they are all similar to other "lower vertebrates" in level of neural adaptation and are thus distinct from the far more encephalized birds and mammals. Although great differences in relative brain size appear to exist among fossil reptiles (approximately five- to sixfold differences in dinosaurs), Jerison points out that "the brain's size has been determined by approximately the same rule in the bony fish, amphibians, and reptiles throughout their radiation in time and in space" (Jerison, 1973, p. 154). His analysis suggests that: (1) mammal-like reptiles, though approaching mammals in many morphological and presumably physiological features, were still at the reptilian level of brain evolution; (2) the brains of pterosaurs, though they show specializations paralleling those of

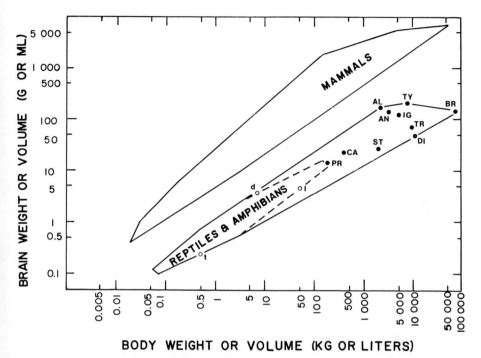

FIG. 3. Brain to body size relations in fossil reptiles superimposed on minimum convex polygons for living species (modified from Jerison, 1973). Dinosaurs: AL, *Allosaurus*; AN, *Anatosaurus*; BR, *Brachiosaurus*; CA, *Camptosaurus*; DI, *Diplodocus*; IG, *Iguanodon*; PR, *Protoceratops*; ST, *Stegosaurus*; TR, *Triceratops*; TY, *Tyrannosaurus*. Therapsids: d, *Diademodon*; l, *Lystrosaurus*; t, *Thrinaxodon*.

birds, were still reptilian in size; and (3) dinosaur brains, which have been commonly presumed to be of relatively smaller size than those of living reptiles (Marsh, 1885; and many later references), were in fact within the expected size range for lower vertebrates when the allometry of brain size to body size is taken into account.

Jerison has concluded that brain size in fossil reptiles was within the expected range for reptiles (though see Gould's, 1975, caveat concerning dinosaur brain sizes). However, he states repeatedly: "The kind of brain: body analysis that I prefer . . . tends to emphasize regularities and obscure differences" (p. 154). Therefore, if one wishes to perform comparative studies among related groups of reptiles, methods which bring out the significant intergroup differences must be sought and levels of resolution finer than those which concerned Jerison are required.

The methods used by Jerison in determining endocast volume are straightforward and are easily repeated with a small amount of variance in results. The volume of an endocast may be determined by the water displacement method or, if only illustrations are available, by the method of "graphic double integration" developed by Jerison (1969, 1973). In this method the brain is modelled as an elliptical cylinder. The length of the brain from tip of the forebrain (the olfactory bulbs and peduncles are excluded) to the exit of cranial nerve XII is the length of the cylinder; the average width of the brain cast is the major axis and the average height is the minor axis of the elliptical cross-section of the cylinder. Jerison (1969, 1973) states that the difference between the volume so obtained and that determined by water displacement never exceeded 5 per cent.

B. PROBLEMS IN DETERMINING RELATIVE BRAIN SIZE IN FOSSIL REPTILES

1. *General*

It is clear that a number of areas of uncertainty exist in the determination of relative brain size in fossil reptiles. The two most obvious problems are: (1) the estimation of brain size from a cast of the cranial cavity which may have had a capacity perhaps twice that of the brain which it housed in life; and (ii) the estimation of body size (weight or volume) in an animal represented only by its skeleton (which may often be very incomplete). In addition, the endocast and body size are often determined from different individuals, which introduces another source of possible error in estimating relative brain size.

2. *Determination of Brain Size*

The problem of determining how much of the endocast was filled by the brain is discussed in Section IID. Indeed, the extent to which the brain fills the cranial cavity is highly variable among living reptiles and appears to have been highly variable among fossil reptiles as well. Another problem, that of deformation, can ordinarily be recognized in the asymmetry of the endocast. A badly crushed or deformed specimen should not be used for determining volume, though moderate distortion can be corrected for.

The use of illustrations to determine endocast volume introduces a common source of error; published scales may be inaccurate. If possible, the scale of the figure should be checked against published measurements of the endocast or of the braincase. For example, Gilmore (1920, Plate 36) figured the endocast of the medium-sized carnivorous dinosaur *Ceratosaurus* at natural size, but stated in the figure caption that it was reproduced at one-half size. Swinton (1958) later combined this figure with those of a series of other dinosaur endocasts all presumed to be illustrated to the same scale. He commented on the large size of the *Ceratosaurus* endocast relative to that of *Tyrannosaurus*; in fact, as figured by Swinton, the endocast of the medium-sized *Ceratosaurus* is absolutely larger than that of the very large-bodied *Tyrannosaurus*.

3. *Determination of Body Weight*

Two principal methods are used by Jerison to determine body weight of extinct vertebrates. One method is applied to fossil mammals only. Jerison plots measurements of body length against body weight for living mammals (data from Walker, 1964) on a log–log scale. From the calculated regression axis of these data, a formula is derived which allows body weights of fossil forms to be estimated from body lengths. This method might be applied profitably to reptiles. However, because the size range of fossil forms exceeds the maximum size range of living species by almost two orders of magnitude, and because body form varies so widely in both living and fossil groups, it remains to be seen how useful such an approach would be. It has the advantage, as will be pointed out, of being less subjective than the second, and more widely used, method of determining body weights in fossils.

Paleontologists have determined body volumes and weights in fossil vertebrates by the use of scale models; this was done by Romer and Price (1940) for pelycosaurs, by Colbert (1962) for dinosaurs, and by Bakker (1975a,b; pers. commun.) for a variety of extinct reptiles, amphibians, and mammals. This method is discussed at length by Colbert (1962). In all such cases, the accuracy of the determination is only as good as the accuracy of the model. Furthermore, the greater the difference in scale between model and animal, the greater the potential error. As Colbert (1962, p. 6) notes, "Slight inaccuracies in small models will loom large when the volumes of such models are expanded to natural size." This is shown dramatically by comparing two restorations and the resulting weight determinations of the giant sauropod dinosaur *Brachiosaurus*, of which only a single complete skeleton exists. Colbert (1962), using a model of extreme bulkiness, with very thick legs and neck, arrives at a weight (assuming a density of 0·9) of 78·26 metric tons. Bakker (1975b), using a more gracile model, arrives at a weight of 40·0 metric tons. This twofold difference in weight estimates of the same specimen reflects a basic difference in how the restorers view dinosaurs as biological entities. The older view of dinosaurs is one of clumsy, sluggish, and dull-witted ectotherms; the more recent one is of agile, active, and alert endotherms. This example demonstrates that, when it comes to fleshing out the bare bones, there is room for a large degree of subjectivity. This suggests cautious use of body-weight estimates of large fossil vertebrates when these are based on extrapolations from small scale models.

A variation of the scale model method of determining body volumes is the use of illustrations of skeletons or life restorations to known scale. This method is applied by Jerison (1973) to determine body volumes of two late Paleozoic labyrinthodont amphibians. Jerison estimates body volume as equal to a cylinder of three-fifths the body length, with body length and diameter determined from published restorations and measurements. He also estimates body sizes in three species of mammal-like reptiles from published skeletal reconstructions, but gives no details of the procedure.

4. Determination of Brain Size: Body Size Relationships

When the possible sources of error in determining brain size and body size are taken into account, other sources of error may be introduced by the necessity of combining E and P values derived from different individuals.

Frequently, specimens suitable for having their cranial cavity cleared of matrix for endocast preparation are much too fragmentary to provide adequate information on total body size. Therefore, endocast size must often be determined from one individual of a taxon and body size estimated from another. This problem often cannot be avoided, but a few of the more obvious sources of error can be anticipated and consequently minimized.

Sexual dimorphism is one possible source of error that cannot be adequately dealt with in most species of fossil reptiles. It has been recognized in only a few species to date (Kurzanov, 1972, for *Protoceratops*; Dodson, 1975, and Hopson, 1975, for crested hadrosaurs); most fossil specimens cannot now be sexed. Ontogenetic changes are less of a problem as juvenile specimens can often be recognized on the basis of incomplete ossification of the ends of limb bones or of the paroccipital processes and cranial base in the skull. Also, cranial sutures may show a lack of fusion or a loose interdigitation. The endocast of *Diplodocus* figured by Osborn (1912) and used by Jerison (1969, 1973) as the basis for a brain size determination is from a young individual (Holland, 1906). How much smaller this individual (represented by a partial skull) was in life than the specimen on which the body weight was determined (a complete skeleton) is not known. However, in the case of this sauropod, even if the body weight estimate should be reduced by one-half, the resulting brain:body size ratio would still be low relative to that of most non-sauropod dinosaurs (Fig. 3).

Another source of possible error lies in determining the relative brain size for a genus by using the endocast of one species of a genus and the body weight of another species. Fossil forms are so commonly dealt with on the generic rather than the specific level that it is sometimes forgotten that natural populations derived from species, not genera. In determining body weights of dinosaurs, Colbert (1962) gives figures for genera, not for species. Jerison (1969, 1973) also determines brain:body size relationships for genera. For the Early Cretaceous ornithopod *Iguanodon*, Jerison uses Colbert's body volume figure, which was determined for the large species *I. bernissartensis*, but he bases his brain volume (from Andrews, 1897) on the smaller species *I. mantelli*. Maximum body length in the former species is 8 m whereas it is 6 m in the latter species. Body volume in *I. mantelli* is 0.75^3, or about 42% that of *I. bernissartensis*. This gives *I. mantelli* an expected brain volume (E_e) of 115 ml, which is slightly lower than that determined on the basis of the endocast ($E_i = 125$ ml). According to Jerison (1973, p. 145), *Iguanodon* would have had an EQ of 0.63; after using a more appropriate body size estimate the EQ is determined to be 1.09. Although still falling within the reptilian range, *Iguanodon* is seen to have been a relatively encephalized reptile.

IV. Systematic Survey of Brain Morphology in Fossil Reptiles

A. INTRODUCTION: CLASSIFICATION OF REPTILES

The major subdivisions of the Reptilia as listed by Romer (1966) are accepted in this survey. For discussions of reptilian classification, see Romer (1956, 1966, 1967, 1968). The problems relating to the origin and early radiation of reptiles are discussed by Carroll (1969a, b, c, 1970a, b) and Panchen (1972). Many papers deal with the problems of the classification of specific subgroups, but these are too numerous to consider here.

Below are listed all of the subclasses and orders, and, in some cases, suborders, with comments on the evidence pertaining to the brain for each. Romer (1966) recognizes six subclasses and 17 orders of reptiles. Of these, information about the brain is available for five subclasses and 12 orders.

Subclass Anapsida
  Primitive reptiles with the temporal region of the skull not fenestrated; includes the ancestral group (cotylosaurs), several early radiations (mesosaurs, millerosaurs), and turtles.
  Order Cotylosauria: Pennsylvanian to Late Triassic in age; includes the ancestors of later reptiles and specialized, mostly herbivorous, types of questionable relationship to other reptiles, i.e. procolophonids,

pareiasaurs, and possibly the diadectids which are placed in the
Amphibia by Romer.

Suborder Diadectomorpha: includes the highly specialized herbivorous Diadectidae and perhaps the procolophonids and pareiasaurs.
An endocast is known only for *Diadectes*.

Order Mesosauria: small aquatic reptiles of the Early Permian. No endocasts known.

Order Testudines (= Chelonia or Testudinata): turtles; Middle Triassic
to Recent. Endocasts known for two Cretaceous genera.

Subclass Lepidosauria

Lizard-like reptiles which primitively possess both upper and lateral
temporal fenestrae (diapsid condition) or have lost one or both temporal
bars during their subsequent history.

Order Eosuchia: the ancestral lepidosaurs of the Late Permian. No
endocasts known.

Order Squamata: Triassic to Recent lizards, snakes, and amphisbaenians.
Endocasts known for Cretaceous marine lizards (mosasaurs) and an
Oligocene amphisbaenian; none for snakes.

Order Rhynchocephalia; *Sphenodon* and its fossil relatives, Triassic to
Recent. No endocasts known.

Subclass Archosauria

Diapsid reptiles in which the skull primitively possesses an antorbital
fenestra and the implantation of the teeth is thecodont. Endocasts known
for all orders.

Order Thecodontia; primitive archosaurs of the Triassic; includes the
ancestry of the remaining orders.

Suborder Aetosauria: quadrupedal, armored thecodonts. Endocast known
for *Desmatosuchus*.

Suborder Phytosauria; Long-snouted crocodile-like theocodonts. Endocasts are known from several specimens all of which may fall within the
genus *Rutiodon*.

Order Crocodilia: crocodilians; Late Triassic to Recent. Endocasts
known for several genera.

Order Pterosauria: flying reptiles of the Late Triassic to Late Cretaceous.
Endocasts are known for several genera.

Order Saurischia: dinosaurs of the Middle Triassic to Late Cretaceous in
which the pelvis is of the triradiate type with a forwardly directed pubis.

Suborder Theropoda: carnivorous dinosaurs. Endocasts known for
members of the major families.

Suborder Sauropodomorpha: herbivorous saurischians; includes the
Triassic prosauropods and the Jurassic and Cretaceous sauropods

(brontosaurs). Endocasts known for the prosauropod *Plateosaurus* and several sauropods.

Order Ornithischia: dinosaurs in which the pelvis is bird-like with the pubis rotated backwards to parallel the ischium. All ornithischians were herbivorous.

> Suborder Ornithopoda: the central group of ornithischians, all bipedal, including small primitive Triassic forms and large highly-specialized Cretaceous forms such as *Iguanodon* and the hadrosaurs. Endocasts are known for *Iguanodon* and several genera of hadrosaurs.

> Suborder Pachycephalosauria: bipedal forms with a greatly thickened skull roof. Endocasts are known for three genera.

> Suborder Stegosauria: quadrupedal forms with small heads and a double row of enlarged dermal plates extending along the back and tail. Endocasts known for *Stegosaurus* and *Kentrosaurus*.

> Suborder Ankylosauria: heavily armored quadrupedal forms. Endocasts known for *Struthiosaurus* and *Euoplocephalus* ("*Ankylosaurus*").

> Suborder Ceratopsia: horned dinosaurs. Endocasts known for several genera.

Subclass Euryapsida (= Synaptosauria)

Primarily marine reptiles of the Mesozoic with an upper temporal fenestra (euryapsid condition) in which the limbs become modified for swimming but the body does not become fish-like in form.

Order Areoscelida: small terrestrial forms of the Permian and Triassic possessing an upper temporal fenestra which cannot be readily allocated to other subclasses but which show no special affinities to the following orders. No endocasts known.

Order Sauropterygia: marine fish-eating forms with necks moderately to greatly elongated.

> Suborder Nothosauria: relatively small, slender-bodied Triassic sauropterygians in which aquatic specializations are moderately developed. Endocasts known for *Nothosaurus*.

> Suborder Plesiosauria; Highly specialized Jurassic and Cretaceous aquatic forms in which the neck may be greatly elongated and the limbs form long flippers. One poor endocast is known.

Order Placodontia; marine mollusc-eating forms of the Triassic with short sturdy jaws and enlarged crushing teeth. Endocasts are known for *Placodus*.

Subclass Ichthyopterygia

Fish-shaped Mesozoic marine forms with an upper temporal fenestra.

Order Ichthyosauria: No endocasts of ichthyosaurs are known and the braincase is so poorly ossified that it provides no useful evidence about the morphology of the brain.

Subclass Synapsida

Mammal-like reptiles possessing a lateral temporal fenestra (synapsid condition).

Order Pelycosauria: primitive synapsids of the Pennsylvanian to Middle Permian. An endocast known only for *Dimetrodon*.

Order Therapsida: moderately to very advanced mammal-like reptiles of the Middle Permian to Middle Jurassic from which mammals arose in the Late Triassic.

Suborder Phthinosuchia: the most primitive therapsids. No endocasts known.

Suborder Anomodontia: moderately advanced, primarily herbivorous therapsids including the infraorder Dinocephalia (large forms with greatly thickened skull roofs) and the infraorder Dicynodontia (small to large forms with turtle-like beaks). Endocasts of several dinocephalians and dicynodonts are known.

Suborder Theriodontia: primarily carnivorous therapsids including the moderately advanced infraorders Gorgonopsia and Therocephalia and the advanced infraorder Cynodontia. Evidence of the brain is known for all three groups, but good endocasts are known only for the cynodonts.

B. Subclass Anapsida

1. *Order Cotylosauria*

Endocasts of the primitive anapsid reptiles of the Pennsylvanian and Permian are unknown, except for that of the enigmatic Early Permian form, *Diadectes*. The systematic position of *Diadectes*, is uncertain; it can be only distantly related to the captorhinomorphs which form the central stock leading to the great majority of later reptiles and, in fact, may technically be considered an amphibian (Romer, 1966). Whatever its systematic position, it has achieved a reptilian grade of organization in its skeleton and is described here because it provides the only evidence of the brain of the basal reptilian stock. In addition, the brain of a pareiasaur is also discussed, based upon the morphology of its cranial cavity.

Cope (1886) describes and figures an endocast of *Diadectes* derived mainly from a specimen in which the basicranium was lost prior to fossilization and, according to Watson (1916), a good deal of the prootic was subsequently removed. Edinger (1975, p. 34) notes that this endocast is a composite containing portions derived from two additional skulls. Furthermore, it is evident that most of the cranial foramina and the pituitary fossa were not cleared of matrix before casting, so that the specimen provides a very limited amount of information on these features. The inadequacies of the endocast led Cope to draw several erroneous conclusions about the

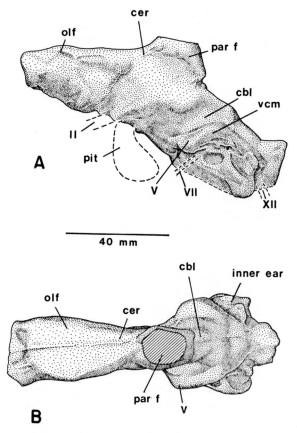

FIG. 4. Endocast of *Diadectes* sp., A.M.N.H. 4441. A. Lateral view. B. Dorsal view. Restored portions are indicated by broken lines. cbl, Cerebellar region; cer, cerebral region; olf, olfactory bulb?; par f, parietal foramen; pit, pituitary fossa; vcm, ridge marking the course of the middle cerebral vein; II, optic nerve; V, trigeminal foramen; VII, facial nerve; XII, hypoglossal nerve.

morphology of the brain and von Huene (1913) later introduced additional misinterpretations. The following description takes into account information on braincase structure provided by Watson (1916), Gregory (1946), and Olson (1966).

The endocast of *Diadectes* (Fig. 4) shows moderate cephalic and pontine flexures. The portion of the periotic bone which forms the medial wall of the inner ear is extremely thin in *Diadectes* (Olson, 1966); it was lost in the present specimen so that the endocast includes a partial cast of the vestibule and the bases of the semicircular canals. Certain of the canal bases were misinterpreted by von Huene (1913) as the roots of cranial nerves. Watson (1916) provides an accurate description of the inner ear cavity.

The forebrain is enclosed within an ossified sphenethmoid but it is not well shown in the endocast and the olfactory tracts cannot be demarcated from the cerebrum. The anterior end of the cast appears to include the olfactory bulbs which, therefore, constitute the widest part of the telencephalon. Behind the presumed olfactory bulbs, the cast tapers gradually back to the level of a very large parietal foramen. At this level, the cerebral cast is 13·5 mm wide and 27·0 mm high. The extraordinary narrowness of the cerebral and midbrain regions may be an artifact of preservation, but a equally narrow fore- and midbrain is seen in the primitive sauropterygian *Nothosaurus* (see Fig. 24).

The position of the optic foramina and pituitary fossa are probably indicated by two rounded projections on the undersurface of the cast. In figures of sagittally sectioned braincases (Watson, 1916, Fig. 6; Olson, 1966, Fig. 101A), the sella turcica extends posteriorly as a large cavity below a broad, horizontally oriented dorsum sellae. The pituitary is restored on the basis of these data.

The tube within the parietal bones for the parietal eye is of very large size. At the base of the tube, on either side, is an elongate horizontal projection suggesting a canal or unossified zone in the dorsolateral wall of the cranial cavity. Posteroventral to the tube is a flat horizontal process extending backwards into the cranial roof above the cerebellar region; this may represent an unossified zone in the braincase.

Behind the parietal tube, the dorsal surface of the endocast slopes gently posteroventrally to meet the more horizontally oriented medulla. Two slight swellings break the smooth descent. The anterior swelling, identified as "optic lobe" by Cope (1886, Figs 1 and 2), probably overlies the cerebellum, whereas the posterior one, called "cerebellum" by Cope, cannot be identified as a significant brain feature. No midbrain features can be identified on the cast.

The position of the trigeminal foramen is indicated by an obliquely elongate projection below the cerebellar swelling. The projection represents an unossified area between the sphenethmoid and the prootic (prootic fenestra). A similar opening occurs in the braincase of pareiasaurs (Watson, 1914) and *Nothosaurus* (see below). Only the lower part of the opening represents the exit of the trigeminal nerve from the braincase; the upper part would have been covered by membrane in life. The small facial nerve exit is seen on the braincase and is indicated in Fig. 4A. In dorsal view, the cerebellar region expands greatly from the extraordinarily narrow fore- and midbrain region so that it appears nearly circular. Between the casts of the inner ear cavities the medulla narrows, as is usual in reptiles, then expands slightly behind them. The posterior portion of the medulla is transversely narrow; its depth is uncertain.

The jugular canal, which presumably passed cranial nerves IX and X, is indicated on a wax model of the inner ear figured by Olson (1966). A single foramen for the hypoglossal nerve is described by Watson (1916).

In summary, Cope's endocast indicates that the brain of *Diadectes* was of a generalized reptilian type, specialized in the very large size of the parietal organ (much greater than in contemporary captorhinomorphs), and perhaps primitive in the extraordinary narrowness of the fore- and midbrain.

Although endocasts of pareiasaurs are not known, the internal structure of their braincase can be compared with the endocast of *Diadectes*. The endocranial cavity is described by Watson (1914) and Boonstra (1934) as being long, wide and low. It shows even less flexure than does that of *Diadectes*. The space for the olfactory tracts is shallow compared with that for the cerebrum. The large parietal foramen lies relatively further forward than does that of *Diadectes*. Anterodorsal to the pituitary fossa (which is lacking its lower portion), are two foramina. The larger and more ventral is identified by Watson as being for cranial nerves II and III; the smaller and more dorsal for nerve IV. The trigeminal nerve passed out in the lower part of a large, vertically elongate opening (prootic fenestra) as in *Diadectes*. As figured by Watson, the medulla is extremely long and low. The position of the cerebellum is not clearly indicated, but it may have lain at the level of the posterodorsal end of the large prootic fenestra.

2. Order Testudines (= Chelonia or Testudinata)

a. *General.* In the brain of turtles, the olfactory bulbs lie in close proximity to the cerebral hemispheres so that they lack distinct olfactory peduncles. Distal to the bulbs are long olfactory nerves which pass forward between the orbits to the nasal cavity. Turtles usually have a secondary side wall of the orbitotemporal region formed by a descending process of the parietal. The primary wall of this region is cartilaginous or membranous; however, the descending process of the parietal may reflect impressions of the sides of the cranial cavity anterior to the basisphenoid–prootic region (see Fig. 7).

Although turtles are quite abundant as fossils, shells form the major part of the record and skulls are relatively uncommon (though not rare). To date, only four endocasts of fossil turtles have been described. Zangerl (1960) describes the endocast of a Cretaceous cheloniid sea turtle. Gaffney and Zangerl (1968) and Gaffney (1977) describe three endocasts of a Creta-ceous pelomedusid pleurodire. Edinger (1934) had earlier provided a

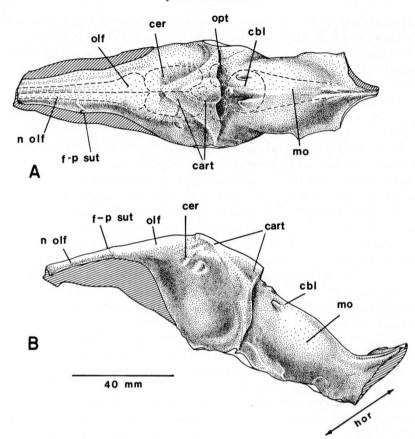

Fig. 5. Endocast of a Recent *Chelonia mydas*, F.M.N.H. 22066 (redrawn from Zangerl 1960). A. Dorsal view with the outline of the brain of another individual indicated by broken lines. B. Lateral view. The horizontal axis of the endocast is indicated by the double-headed arrow marked "hor". cart, Filling of the space for the cartilaginous portion of the supraoccipital; cbl, cerebellum; cer, cerebrum; f-p sut, frontal-parietal suture; mo, medulla oblongata; n olf, olfactory nerve; olf, olfactory bulb; opt, optic lobe.

redescription of the natural cast of the inside of the skull (including the temporal fossae and dorsal surface of the endocranial cavity) of a large marine turtle (possibly *Protosphargis*; Edinger, 1975, p. 50), which had been interpreted in its entirety as the "brain" of a plesiosaur by Fritsch (1905). Only the narrow central area of the specimen represents the cast of the cranial cavity and this provides no information useful to the present study.

b. *Suborder Cryptodira.* Zangerl (1960), for his study of the endocast of the Late Cretaceous cheloniid *Corsochelys haliniches* from Alabama, prepared casts from skulls of the Recent *Chelonia* and *Caretta*. His figure of the cast of *Chelonia* with the outline of the brain superimposed on the dorsal view is redrawn in Fig. 5. The endocast of *Caretta* differs little from that of *Chelonia*. The brain is much smaller than the cranial cavity so that the major parts of the brain are indicated only vaguely. The cast shows the position of the flexures of the brain which, in these turtles, occur at the forward end of the medulla oblongata and at the posterior end of the olfactory region. The

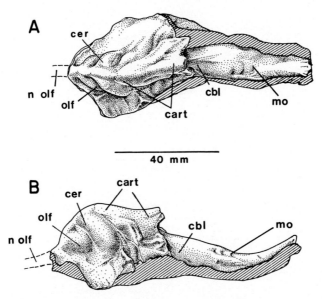

FIG. 6. Endocast of *Corsochelys haliniches*, F.M.N.H. PR 249, (redrawn from Zangerl, 1960). Restored portion indicated by broken lines. cart, Filling of the space for the cartilaginous portion of the supraoccipital; cbl, cerebellar region; cer, cerebrum; mo, medulla oblongata; n olf, olfactory nerve; olf, olfactory bulb.

middle region of the brain is oriented at a high angle to the horizontal. The other notable feature of this cast is the large triangular area above the posterior part of the cerebrum; this represents the cartilaginous anterior end of the supraoccipital, which is lost during maceration of the skull.

The endocast of the fossil turtle *Corsochelys* (Fig. 6) resembles that of *Chelonia*, but it shows an interesting difference from this and other large turtles in that the cast clearly reflects the cerebral hemispheres and olfactory bulbs. These are typically turtle-like as to their position on the endocast and in the position of the olfactory bulbs adjacent to the cerebrum. Zangerl attributes the close apposition of the skull bones to the forebrain in *Corsochelys* to the "unusual thickness of the bones and the massiveness of the construction of the skull" in this animal (p. 291).

The endocast of *Corsochelys* lacks the more ventral parts and so provides no information about cranial nerves and the floor of the braincase.

c. *Suborder Pleurodira*. Partial endocasts of two species of the pelomedusid pleurodire *Bothremys* are described by Gaffney and Zangerl (1968) the more complete specimen (Fig. 7) is from the type skull of *B. cooki* (A.M.N.H. 2521) from the Late Cretaceous of New Jersey, the other from

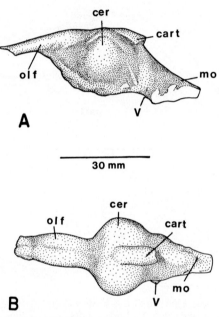

FIG. 7. Endocast from the type skull of *Bothremys cooki* (redrawn from Gaffney and Zangerl, 1968). A. Lateral view. B. Dorsal view. cart, Filling of the space for the cartilaginous portion of the supraoccipital; cer, cerebrum; mo, medulla oblongata; olf, olfactory bulb; V, trigeminal nerve.

the larger, very fragmentary skull of *B. barberi* (F.M.N.H. PR 247) from the Selma Formation (of Late Cretaceous age) of Alabama. *Bothremys* is one of the earliest pleurodires known. The endocasts were compared by Gaffney and Zangerl with an endocast of the Recent *Podocnemis madagascariensis*.

These endocasts show fair detail of the principal regions of the brain. The degree of flexure in the better-preserved *Bothremys cooki* is comparable to that in *Podocnemis* but much less than in *Chelonia*. The olfactory region of *B. cooki* is set off from the broad cerebral area by a very prominent constriction. The cast of the olfactory bulbs indicates that they were elongate oval structures. The olfactory region of *B. barberi* is relatively less expanded and is not so sharply set off from the cerebral region. The cerebral area of *B. cooki* is extraordinarily broad, with its widest part rather far forward as compared with *Podocnemis* and *B. barberi*. In the latter two specimens, the cerebral region is oval in dorsal view, with its posterior half being the broader. On the dorsal surface of the *Bothremys* casts is a squarish process, the "rider" of Gaffney and Zangerl, i.e. the remnant of the unossified anterior portion of the supraoccipital. Behind the cerebral region, the cerebellar and medullary parts narrow and drop down to the foramen magnum. In *B. cooki*, lateral swellings above the trigeminal root perhaps reflect the optic tectum. The larger *B. barberi* lacks such swellings.

Gaffney and Zangerl note that the differences in endocasts are greater between *Bothremys cooki* and *B. barberi* than between *B. cooki* and *Podocnemis*. They explain this in terms of the absolute size difference between the large skull of *B. barberi* and the small skulls of the other two turtles. The skull of *B. barberi* is twice the size of that of *B. cooki*. "But the brains were probably only slightly different in size (if recent reptiles are a correct analogy). Therefore although the brains were probably very similar, the cavities housing them were not" (Gaffney and Zangerl, 1968, pp. 229–230).

Gaffney (1977) has recently described an isolated natural endocast of *Bothremys* (not identifiable to species) which preserves the cast of the floor of the cranial cavity and includes a cast of the orbital cavities. Though the new endocast is about the same size as that of *B. barberi*, it more closely resembles that of *B. cooki* in degree of expansion of the cerebral cavity. Gaffney notes that this tends to refute the contention of Gaffney and Zangerl (1968) that the differences in the cranial cavities of the two species are due solely to differences in skull size.

C. Subclass Lepidosauria

1. Order Squamata

a. *General.* Of the three lepidosaurian orders (Eosuchia, Rhynchocephalia, and Squamata), fossil endocasts are known only for the Squamata.

Despite the fact that squamates comprise by far the majority of living reptiles, the fossil record of the group is relatively poor. Fossil snakes and amphisbaenians are rare and, except for the giant marine mosasaurs of the Late Cretaceous, fossil lizards are not common. Endocasts of lizards are known only from mosasaurs. A single, incomplete, endocast has been described from a fossil amphisbaenian. Endocasts from fossil snakes are unknown.

b. *Suborder Sauria (also Lacertilia).* Mosasaurs are large, fully marine, platynotan lizards of the Late Cretaceous, known from many well-preserved, essentially complete specimens. Camp (1942) figures an endocast of the mosasaur *Platecarpus* sp. (U.C.M.P. 34781) in lateral view with details

added from a specimen of *P. coryphaeus* (U.C.M.P. 32136). He also figures
the forebrain region of *Clidastes turtor* (U.C.M.P. 34535) in dorsal view.
Russell (1967, Fig. 16) reproduces Camp's figure of the *Platecarpus* endocast
with slight modifications. That illustration is presented here as Fig. 8. The
following account is based on the above publications, with some details
modified on the basis of information on the osteology of the braincase of
mosasaurs (Russell, 1967) and modern lizards (Oelrich, 1956).

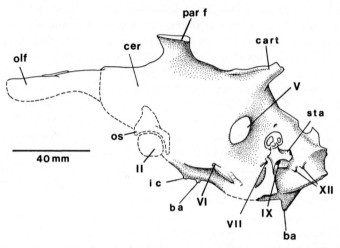

FIG. 8. Lateral view of the endocast of the mosasaur *Platecarpus* sp., U.C.M.P. 34781,
with details added from U.C.M.P. 32136 (redrawn from Russell, 1967). Restored portions
indicated by broken lines. The orbitosphenoid is restored from *Kolposaurus bennisoni*.
ba, Branches of the basilar artery; cart, filling of the space for the cartilaginous portion of
the supraoccipital; cer, cerebral region; ic, internal carotid artery; olf, olfactory bulb;
os, orbitosphenoid; par f, parietal foramen; sta, fossa lateral to inner ear for reception of
the stapes; II, optic nerve; V, trigeminal nerve; VI, abducens nerve; VII, facial nerve;
IX, glossopharyngeal nerve; XII, hypoglossal nerve.

Except for a relatively small orbitosphenoid located behind the optic
foramen, the braincase of lizards is usually unossified anterior to the basisphenoid–prootic region. Therefore, the shape of the forebrain region is
represented only on the undersurface of the cranial roofing bones. The
endocast of living lizards does not provide a good representation of the
brain (see Jerison, 1973). That of the mosasaur *Platecarpus* resembles the
endocast of a full-grown *Iguana iguana* and provides about the same amount
of information about the brain, cranial nerves and intracranial circulation.

The endocast of *Platecarpus* suggests that the brain was flexed much as
in *Iguana*. No details of the size and shape of the different regions of the
brain are indicated except for the olfactory portion. As in other lizards, the

olfactory bulbs are elongate structures which merge posteriorly into extremely slender olfactory peduncles. The cerebrum appears to have been relatively narrow, but otherwise its form is indeterminable. The position of the optic nerves in Fig. 8 is indicated by the orbitosphenoids in *Kolposaurus bennisoni* preserved in presumed life position (see Camp, 1942, Fig. 15). The parietal foramen is large in *Platecarpus*, as it is in several other genera of mosasaurs (Russell, 1967). The optic tectum and the cerebellum lie below the level of the cerebrum, but no details of their morphology are indicated on the cast. A posterodorsally directed process above the cerebellar region represents the cartilage between the parietal and supraoccipital. The pituitary fossa is shallow; paired canals for the internal carotid and basilar arteries pierce its lower surface.

Behind the cartilage process, the upper surface of the cast drops steeply down to the foramen magnum. The posteroventral surface of the cast, behind the pituitary fossa, is broadly convex. A large anteroventrally directed process on the ventral surface of the medullary region represents a large bilobate foramen which passes into the basioccipital and carried the basilar arteries forward to the pituitary fossa (Russell, 1967).

The trigeminal root lies high on the side of the cast. Anteroventral to nerve V is the abducens nerve. The facial nerve and the closely associated branches of the acoustic nerve are separated widely from the trigeminal nerve. The glossopharyngeal nerve left the cranial cavity via a foramen lying posteroventral to nerves VII and VIII. It passes into the perilymphatic fossa, as it does in *Varanus* and *Ctenosaura*. The vagus foramen is not indicated on the endocast figured by Camp and Russell, but it lay on the inner surface of the opisthotic, posterodorsal to the foramen for nerve IX, and above the anterior two of the three hypoglossal foramina (see Russell, 1967, Fig. 13). Only two of the hypoglossal roots are indicated on the *Platecarpus* endocast, lying relatively high on the sides of the medullary region. Camp and Russell both erroneously label the anterior of these roots as "X, XI". The cast of the cranial opening of the vagus nerve may be hidden on the figured endocast by the posterolaterally directed process of the inner ear cast ("sta"), which represents the deep fossa lateral to the inner ear proper (which is bounded laterally by the fenestra ovalis), into which the proximal end of the stapes fitted.

The dorsal location of the posterior cranial nerves on the *Platecarpus* endocast, as compared with their more ventral positions in *Varanus*, *Ctenosaura*, or *Iguana*, suggests that the lower part of the medullary cavity of the braincase was not occupied by the brain, but rather by a large basilar artery and perhaps other vascular elements. Camp (1942, Fig. 24B) consequently restores the medulla of *Platecarpus* as much less deep than it appears to be on the endocast.

c. *Suborder Amphisbaenia.* The braincase of amphisbaenians, like that of snakes, is completely ossified so that it should provide a complete cast of the endocranial cavity. Taylor (1951) figures and describes a natural endocast of the extinct rhineurine *Hyporhina galbreathi* from the Early Oligocene of Colorado. The specimen (K.U. 8219) as preserved is 8·5 mm long; the complete skull could hardly have been more than 10 mm in length. The present discussion is based on Taylor's work but my interpretation of the endocast differs somewhat from that of Taylor.

The endocast of *Hyporhina* has an elongate oval outline in dorsal view with the widest part toward the rear. Between the orbits, at the narrowest part of the skull, are a pair of ovoid swellings which Taylor interprets as optic tectum ("corpora bigemina"), but which must represent the olfactory bulbs. Anterior to these structures is the cast of the lateral portion of the nasal cavity, which forms a posterolateral lobe in front of the orbit. Taylor erroneously interprets these lobes as parts of the cerebral hemispheres. The remainder of the endocast broadens considerably behind the olfactory bulbs. As in other amphisbaenians, the olfactory bulbs lie close to the cerebrum and distinct peduncles are not visible. It is not possible to delimit cerebral, midbrain, and hindbrain regions on the cast. The presumed cerebral area is subdivided into three longitudinal regions by two shallow sulci. Further back, a pair of grooves mark off an anteriorly pointing V-shaped area in front of the foramen magnum. I interpret this V as marking the position of the supraoccipital bone. The specimen provides no information on the cranial nerves.

D. SUBCLASS ARCHOSAURIA

1. *Introduction*

By far the most detailed record of brain evolution among extinct reptiles exists for the subclass Archosauria because: (i) archosaur braincases are more completely ossified than those of any other group, (ii) the brains of archosaurs appear to have molded the cranial cavity to a greater extent than is usual among reptiles, and (iii) numerous well-preserved specimens exist of a size conveniently large to facilitate clearing the matrix from the endocranial cavity.

The skulls of archosaurs, except in a few primitive genera, lack a parietal foramen and, hence, a parietal eye. A small parietal foramen exists in the Early Triassic proterosuchian thecodonts *Proterosuchus* (*Chasmatosaurus*) (Cruickshank, 1972) and *Erythrosuchus* (Romer, 1956), and in the primitive phytosaur *Mesorhinosuchus* (Romer, 1956). Parietal foramina have been described in the prosauropod *Plateosaurus* and in several sauropods, but these were presumably zones of cartilage in life in which ossification did not occur.

2. *Order Thecodontia*

The order Thecodontia comprises a horizontal grade of primitive archosaurs whose members have not diverged sufficiently from the ancestral stock to merit separation at the ordinal level. The ancestors of the progressive archosaurian orders are believed to lie in the thecodont suborder Pseudosuchia. Unfortunately, the only described thecodont endocasts pertain to members of the suborders Aetosauria and Phytosauria, highly specialized groups far from the central pseudosuchian stock. Aetosaurs are quadrupedal armored forms of probable herbivorous food habits, and phytosaurs are aquatic forms convergent on the large crocodilians. The undescribed endocast of a probable pseudosuchian from the Chañares Formation (early Middle Triassic) of Argentina is to be described by Dr Juan Quiroga of the Universidad Nacional de La Plata. This specimen is the oldest archosaurian endocast yet known. It is remarkable for the extremely small transverse diameter of the cerebral region.

The best thecodont endocast described to date is that of *Desmatosuchus spurensis*, an aetosaurid from the Late Triassic of North America (Case, 1921). Less well-preserved endocasts are known for several phytosaurs. Cope (1887) describes the endocast of the phytosaur *"Belodon"* which differs markedly from endocasts of other archosaurs and was probably made from a poorly prepared braincase; it has not been used in preparing the following account. Case (1922) describes an incomplete endocast of *"Leptosuchus?"* and Camp (1930) describes the endocranial cavity and restores the brain of *"Machaeroprosopus"* *gregorii*, as well as figuring the endocranial cavity of *"M."* *zunii* (Camp, 1942, Fig. 21). The latter two genera are currently included in *Rutiodon*, and it is likely that Cope's specimen also pertains to this genus.

In overall shape, the endocasts of aetosaurs (Fig. 9) and phytosaurs are of the unspecialized archosaurian type seen in crocodilians and carnosaurian dinosaurs. The degree of flexure of the brain was about as in modern Crocodilia.

The phytosaur endocasts described by Cope and Camp show a large median process above the midbrain region which these authors interpret as having housed a very large epiphysis. A much smaller dorsal process occurs in the aetosaurid *Desmatosuchus*. Comparison with living reptiles indicates that in life this space was probably occupied, at least in part, by a cartilaginous portion of the supraoccipital. It is unlikely that such dorsal spaces in the skull were occupied by processes of the brain.

The olfactory tracts and bulbs of phytosaurs were enclosed in bone over their entire length; the bulbs are elongate and closely appressed and lie at the ends of very long, slender peduncles. In *Desmatosuchus* the floor of the telencephalon is not ossified and only the dorsal surface of the olfactory region is preserved as impressions in the undersurface of the skull roof. Well-separated, shallow ovoid swellings in front of the cerebrum appear to

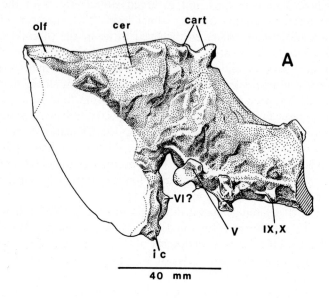

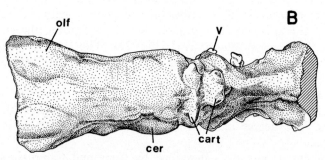

FIG. 9. Endocast of the aetosaurid thecodont *Desmatosuchus spurensis*, U.M. 7476. A. Lateral view. B. Dorsal view. cart, Filling of the space for the cartilaginous portion of the supraoccipital; cer, cerebrum; ic, internal carotid artery; olf, probable impression of the olfactory bulb; V, trigeminal nerve; VI?, probable canal for abducens nerve; IX, X, foramen for the glossopharyngeal and vagus nerves.

represent the olfactory bulbs. If so, they were joined to the cerebrum by unusually short, slightly divergent, olfactory peduncles of which no evidence is present on the endocast. Short, divergent olfactory tracts are known elsewhere among archosaurs in ankylosaurs.

The cerebral hemispheres of phytosaurs and aetosaurs are longer than wide, with proportions similar to those of a living crocodilian of similar body size. In phytosaurs they taper gradually anteriorly into the olfactory tracts, as in crocodilians. In *Desmatosuchus* they taper only slightly before widening into the olfactory region.

The optic foramina are preserved in phytosaurs but not in *Desmatosuchus*. Camp (1930) figures a small foramen lying posteroventral to the optic foramina which he considered to have transmitted cranial nerves III and IV. Camp (1942) later illustrates a slightly more anterodorsal foramen which he identifies as that for nerve III. Comparison with conditions in Crocodilia suggests that this foramen passed the IVth cranial nerve and the more posteroventral opening passed the IIIrd (Fig. 1).

The pituitary fossa of phytosaurs and aetosaurs is elongate and oriented vertically or slightly posteriorly from vertical. The internal carotid arteries entered at the base of the fossa. In phytosaurs, a pair of foramina in the lateral parts of the dorsum sellae (figured but not identified by Camp, 1930, Fig. 36) transmitted the abducens nerve. In *Desmatosuchus* similar foramina are identified by Case (1922) as representing the internal carotid arteries, but it is more likely that they are for the abducens nerves, the carotid foramina being indicated by paired projections at the distal end of the pituitary cast (Fig. 9A).

No evidence of midbrain features is seen on these endocasts.

The dorsal borders of the phytosaur and aetosaur endocasts, behind the so-called epiphyseal projection, slopes smoothly back and down to the medulla. The cerebellum was probably much as in crocodilians. The foramina for the Vth, VIth, and VIIth cranial nerves, insofar as they can be made out, are as in other reptiles.

The medulla is oriented obliquely posteroventrally and is relatively long. The inner ear is preserved in Case's "*Leptosuchus?*" and in specimens described by Camp. The foramen for nerves IX and X was large. Two pairs of hypoglossal foramina occur in phytosaurs.

3. Order Crocodilia

a. *General.* Fossil crocodiles are extremely abundant and endocasts have been described for specimens ranging in age from Early Cretaceous to Early Cenozoic. No endocast has been described for the small early crocodilians of the suborder Protosuchia known from the Late Triassic, or of the Late Jurassic to Early Cretaceous members of the highly specialized marine suborder Thalattosuchia. Natural endocasts of several genera of meso-suchians have been described from the Early Cretaceous (Wealden) of Europe, and an artificial endocast has been described from the aberrant South American *Sebecus*, which is placed in a distinct suborder Sebecosuchia. Among fossil eusuchians, natural endocasts have been described for *Tomistoma* from the Paleocene of Europe and the Eocene of China.

The endocast of the Recent *Caiman crocodilus* is figured and described in Section IIC. The endocasts of the fossil crocodilians differ from those of living crocodilians principally in proportions and degree of flexure. Edinger (1975) provides a translation of the remarks of Koken (1887), who describes the endocasts of Early Cretaceous crocodilians and reviews earlier work on the cranial cavities of Jurassic forms: "Only one conclusion can be drawn, namely that the tenacity with which crocodilians have retained one type of

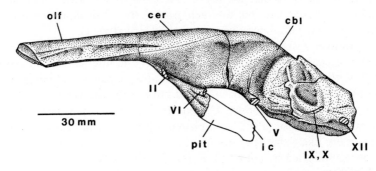

FIG. 10. Lateral view of the endocast of *Pholidosaurus meyeri* (redrawn from Koken, 1887). The pituitary fossa is restored from a specimen figured by Edinger (1938). cbl, Cerebellar region; cer, cerebrum; ic, canal for the internal carotid artery; olf, olfactory bulb; pit, pituitary fossa; II, optic nerve; V, trigeminal nerve; VI, anterior foramen for abducens nerve; IX, X, foramen for the glossopharyngeal and vagus nerves; XII, hypoglossal nerve.

skeleton build from the Liassic to now is present in almost miraculous fashion also in the structure and shape of the cranial cavity and the position of the nerve foramina: a sufficient basis for the assumption that the brain, too, has remained essentially the same" (p. 368). With regard to external morphology, Koken's observation appears to be correct.

b. *Suborder Mesosuchia.* Mesosuchian crocodilians are predominantly of Jurassic and Cretaceous age and include both amphibious fresh-water forms and highly adapted aquatic marine forms. Koken (1887) describes two natural endocasts of the long-snouted marine pholidosaurid *Pholidosaurus* ("*Macrorhynchus*"). Additional specimens of *Pholidosaurus*, and several of the amphibious goniopholid *Goniopholis pugnax*, all of Early Cretaceous age, are described by Edinger (1938). The goniopholids lie close to the ancestry of the modern suborder, the Eusuchia.

Endocasts of *Pholidosaurus meyeri* and *P. schaumburgensis*, as described by Koken and Edinger, are essentially identical. They are more elongated, shallower, and less strongly flexed than the endocasts of modern crocodilians (cf. Figs 1, 10). Their dorsoventral diameter hardly varies from the front of the cerebral region to the foramen magnum. The forebrain plus midbrain regions, which cannot be distinguished from one another on the cast, are long and shallow. The olfactory tracts in dorsal view are broad with straight sides which pass directly into the cerebral area without a constriction to indicate the boundary between the two regions. The olfactory bulbs cannot be distinguished on the figures. The cerebral area has smoothly rounded sides as in living crocodilians but it is less expanded than that of modern specimens with the same foramen magnum diameter.

The cast of the pituitary fossa is damaged in Koken's specimens but is complete in a specimen of *Pholidosaurus* described by Edinger (1938, Fig. 4); it has been restored in Fig. 10. It is a posteroventrally oriented, elongated process with slightly convex sides.

The general location of the midbrain of *Pholidosaurus* is indicated by a gradual narrowing of the cast between its widest part and the root of the trigeminal nerve. A swelling posterodorsal to the trigeminal is interpreted by Edinger as the optic tectum. Comparison with the *Caiman* endocast (Fig. 1) suggests that it represents the lateral recess of the longitudinal venous sinus. Behind nerve V the cast is flexed slightly downward; it straightens back to the horizontal at the level of the jugular foramen.

The morphology of the cerebellar and medullary regions of *Pholidosaurus* is much as in *Caiman*. The otic capsules are reflected by the deep lateral depressions which leave a narrow ridge between them. Behind the ear region, the medullary area is broad and essentially parallel-sided. The depth of this region is about half its width. The similar morphology of the endocast of *Caiman* reflects the characteristics of the longitudinal venous sinus rather than of the brain itself; this suggests that a similar pattern of endocranial circulation was present in *Pholidosaurus*.

The endocast of *Goniopholis*, as described and figured by Edinger (1938, Fig. 2), is less well preserved than that of *Pholidosaurus* but is extremely similar to the latter in most aspects of its morphology.

c. *Suborder Sebecosuchia*. Sebecosuchians were a peculiar group of South American crocodilians characterized by the possession of a deep, laterally compressed snout and a low number of laterally flattened, serrated teeth. Colbert (1946) describes an artificial endocast made from the disarticulated skull of *Sebecus icaeorhinus* from the Eocene of Patagonia. As Colbert notes, the endocast of *Sebecus* is very similar to that of *Crocodylus* (which he illustrates). (It also resembles that of *Caiman*, though it is more like specimens larger than that illustrated in Fig. 1). The olfactory bulbs and tracts are essentially identical in *Sebecus* and *Crocodylus*. The cerebrum is perhaps somewhat longer and narrower in *Sebecus* and it tapers more gradually into the olfactory peduncles. Colbert (1946, p. 250) notes: "All in all, one gets the impression that the forebrain was enlarged to a lesser degree in *Sebecus*."

The dorsal profile of the *Sebecus* endocast rises behind the cerebral region to a high, broadly rounded swelling above the cerebellar region (Fig. 11). Colbert speculates that this possibly indicates an enlarged cerebellum. If the swelling indeed represents a real feature of the cranial cavity (the supraoccipital is missing in the specimen from which the cast was

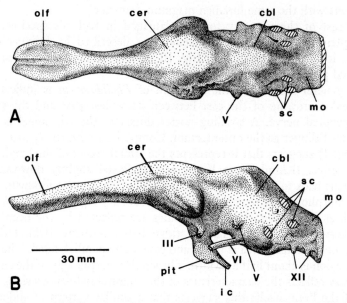

FIG. 11. Endocast of *Sebecus icaeorhinus*, A.M.N.H. 3160 (redrawn from Colbert, 1946). A. Dorsal view. B. Lateral view. cbl, Cerebellar region; cer, cerebrum; ic, internal carotid artery; mo, medulla oblongata; olf, olfactory bulb; pit, pituitary fossa; sc, positions of the semicircular canals; III, oculomotor nerve; V, trigeminal nerve; VI, abducens nerve; XII, hypoglossal nerve.

made), it is more likely to be a reflection of an enlarged longitudinal sinus than a part of the brain. Lateral swellings behind the root of the trigeminal nerve probably represent the lateral recesses of the dorsal sinus.

The most unusual aspect of the endocast of *Sebecus*, figured but not discussed by Colbert, is the very posterior location of the inner ear cavity (as represented by the position of the semicircular canals). The medulla extends further ventrally in *Sebecus* than in *Crocodylus* because, according to Colbert, the foramen magnum of *Sebecus* lies lower on the skull than it does in the living form.

The most interesting aspect of the endocast of *Sebecus* is its extremely close resemblance to that of a modern eusuchian crocodile. The Sebecosuchia split from the ancestry of the eusuchian lineage well back in the Cretaceous (Langston, 1973); therefore, it is likely that the crocodilian brain has changed little, at least in those aspects of external morphology visible on the endocast, since early in the Cretaceous.

d. *Suborder Eusuchia*. All living crocodilians are included in the Eusuchia. The earliest apparent eusuchians are of Early Cretaceous age. The only fossil eusuchian endocasts which have been described pertain to Early Cenozoic longirostrine forms which are currently placed in the genus *Tomistoma* (though this allocation is uncertain due to the common occurrence of convergently slender-snouted crocodylids in the fossil record). Lemoine (1883–84) described three incomplete natural endocasts from the Paleocene of France which he referred to *Gavialis macrorhynchus* but which Edinger (1975, p. 96) notes have more recently been placed in *Tomistoma*. Two natural endocasts from the Eocene of Kwantung Province, China, are described by Yeh (1958) as *Tomistoma petrolica*.

Lemoine's endocasts resemble those of living crocodilians in most respects, except that the cerebral hemispheres, as noted by Edinger, appear to be less expanded and the brain as a whole appears to have been almost unflexed. Yeh's specimens, insofar as their morphology can be interpreted from his figures, show no differences from modern forms. On the basis of this scanty evidence, it appears that the crocodilian brain has changed little in external morphology during the past 70 million years. The endocasts of the mesosuchians of the Early Cretaceous suggest that the basic crocodilian pattern was established even further back in the history of the group.

4. *Order Pterosauria*

The Pterosauria were Mesozoic archosaurs which paralleled the birds in becoming active flyers. The wing of pterosaurs was a skin web supported by a greatly elongated fourth finger. Some well-preserved specimens preserve a hair-like body covering, suggesting that pterosaurs, like birds and bats, were endothermic.

The earliest known pterosaur is from the Late Triassic of Italy (Zambelli, 1973). Well-preserved specimens are known from the Early Jurassic, but the best record of pterosaurs is from the Late Jurassic lithographic limestones of Germany in which specimens are preserved in superb detail. Pterosaurs survived to the end of the Cretaceous and were world-wide in distribution. Sizes range from that of a sparrow to a recently discovered gigantic form estimated to have had a wingspan of about 17 meters. The larger pterosaurs were undoubted gliders rather than active flyers.

The order Pterosauria is divided into two suborders: the Rhamphorhynchoidea, for the more primitive, usually long-tailed and shorter-faced forms, and the Pterodactyloidea, for the more derived, short-tailed and long-snouted, forms.

Natural endocasts of pterosaurs are not uncommon, but most are incomplete and show only a portion of the total cranial cavity. The base of the cranial cavity is not known in any pterosaur and the courses of the cranial nerves have not been described. Edinger (1927, 1929) reviews earlier knowledge of the brain of pterosaurs and also presents a detailed description of

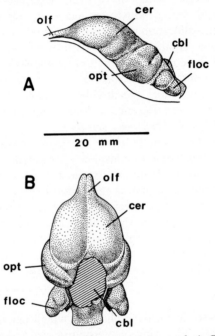

FIG. 12. Endocast of the pterosaur *Parapsicephalus purdoni*, Geol. Surv. Mus. 3166 (redrawn from Newton, 1888, with details added from the original specimen). The cerebellum is damaged. cbl. Cerebellum; cer, cerebral hemisphere; floc, flocculus; olf, olfactory bulb; opt, optic lobe.

the endocast of the Late Jurassic *Pterodactylus elegans*, with a review of the endocast in this genus (Edinger, 1941). I have restudied the Early Jurassic *Parapsicephalus* ("*Scaphognathus*") *purdoni* (Geol. Surv. Mus. 3166), which possesses perhaps the best endocast of any pterosaur.

The brain of pterosaurs, like that of birds and mammals, appears to have filled the braincase almost completely so that the endocast provides a much more accurate and detailed replica of the brain than exists in any other group of reptiles. The endocast is sufficiently similar throughout the order to allow the following description of *Parapsicephalus purdoni* to serve as a general description of the endocast of all pterosaurs (Fig. 12). Brief remarks on the variation among the different genera will follow.

Parapsicephalus purdoni is an early rhamphorhynchoid from the Early Jurassic of England. The skull contains a nearly undistorted natural endo-cast exposed on the left side in dorsal and lateral views. The skull, as preserved, measures 140 mm, but about 50 mm of the anterior end of the snout is missing (Newton, 1888). The endocast measures 25 mm in length and 17 mm in greatest width (across the optic tectum). It is relatively shallow dorsoventrally, although its true ventral margin cannot be deter-mined.

The olfactory bulbs, as in all pterosaurs, are closely-appressed, short, and taper anteriorly. The cerebral hemispheres are smooth ovoid swellings separated from one another by a deep furrow. The paired hemispheres are slightly greater in width (16·0 mm) than in length (13·4 mm). On the ventrolateral surface of the cerebrum is a shallow depression which separates the posterior third of the hemisphere from the anterior two-thirds. Edinger (1941, p. 670) compares this groove with the vallecula of birds, but as will be discussed further below, I question the validity of this interpretation.

The large optic tectum of *Parapsicephalus* forms the widest part of the endocast. It lies laterally on the cast, overlaid by the cerebellum. In the sulcus between the cerebrum and optic tectum is a narrow, elongate swelling which extends anteroventrally from the dorsal surface of the endocast down around the posterolateral portion of the cerebrum. On the posterior surface of the optic tectum is a similar swelling paralleling the course of the first. These features reflect broad grooves on the inner surface of the braincase, and probably represent the courses of vascular elements. The more anterior channel occupies the position of the "posterior cerebral" artery and vein of crocodilians (see Fig. 2). The posterior channel occupies the position of the lateral recess of the dorsal venous sinus of crocodilians (see Fig. 2) or the middle cerebral vein of other reptiles.

In the small triangular space on the cranial roof of *Parapsicephalus* between the posteromedial borders of the cerebral hemispheres and the anterior end of the cerebellum is a small median protuberance which may represent a cast of the pineal organ.

The cerebellar region and dorsal surface of the medulla oblongata are badly damaged in the *Parapsicephalus* specimen so that it is not possible to determine the exact size and shape of the cerebellum. Newton (1888, p. 510) notes that the preserved portion suggests that the cerebellum extends forward between the optic tecta. Edinger (1941) established that the cerebellum of *Pterodactylus* extended forward to contact the posterior border of the cerebrum, thus separating the optic tecta well to the side of the dorsal midline. The posterior limit of the cerebellum is determinable on the *Parapsicephalus* cast; it lay at about the level at which the proximal ends of the vertical semicircular canals meet. The cerebellum has very large posterolaterally directed floccular lobes which are partially sub-divided by a shallow groove lying nearly transverse to their long axis. The flocculi are much larger than those of similar-sized birds (Edinger, 1927).

Other genera of pterosaurs show some variation in the relative sizes of parts of the brain. The dorsal surface of the related *Rhamphorhynchus* of the Late Jurassic shows large, well-separated cerebral hemispheres and sections through the cerebellum and the flocculi (Edinger, 1927, Fig. 2). Edinger (1941) claims that with breadth:length ratios up to 1·5, *Rhampho-rhynchus* had the most bird-like forebrain among reptiles. Endocasts of the small pterodactyloid, *Pterodactylus*, are discussed by Edinger (1941). These are always preserved with their lateral surfaces oriented parallel to the bedding planes of the sediments in which they occur and, therefore, are somewhat laterally compressed. As a result, width measurements are not available. However, Edinger suggests that because *Pterodactylus* skulls are always preserved on their sides, the braincase, and therefore the brain, was slender and that the forebrain was not as wide as long. In the advanced Late Cretaceous pterodactyloid which Edinger (1927) refers to *?Pteranodon*, the cerebral hemispheres are much wider than long. She therefore considers that both suborders of pterosaurs show a trend toward progressive increase in cerebral breadth.

The *?Pteranodon* endocast has olfactory bulbs that are reduced to tiny processes. The optic tectum is not preserved on the upper half of the endocast, the only part available, and Edinger believes that it must have extended far ventrolaterally, as in birds. Therefore, reduction of the olfactory apparatus and further ventral migration of the optic lobes are additional trends in which pterosaurs parallel birds.

In the specimen of *Pterodactylus elegans*, Edinger (1941) notes that the endocast is avian in having a ventrally oriented medulla oblongata. The olfactory bulb appears to be proportionally smaller than that of *Parapsi-cephalus*. The cerebrum is subdivided on its lateral surface by a longitudinal furrow which Edinger believes corresponds to the avian vallecula. A vertical groove descending from this furrow is interpreted as "a vallecula Sylvii such as separates the frontal and temporal sections of the basal part of the forebrain in birds" (Edinger, 1941, p. 670). In a photograph of the endocast of this specimen (Edinger, 1941, Pl. 1, Fig. 2), the surface of the cerebrum appears to be damaged, and I question whether these grooves are genuine features of the endocast; I suggest that the evidence for avian-type fissures on the forebrain of pterosaurs is uncertain.

The brain of pterosaurs is extraordinarily birdlike in appearance, pre-sumably as a consequence of similar sensory and neural adaptations to the demands of active flight. The olfactory apparatus is greatly reduced from a primitive archosaurian condition; the cerebrum and cerebellum appear to be enlarged and in contact medial to the optic lobes; the optic lobes are laterally situated, and there are large flocculi.

In his analysis of relative brain size in flying reptiles, Jerison (1973) concludes that pterosaurs were reptilian, not avian, in relative size of their brains. He suggests that the brainlike appearance of the pterosaur endocast may have been a consequence of weight-reduction adaptations in the skull; i.e. the cranial bones became very thin and closely fitted to the enclosed tissues. He doubts that the avian form of the pterosaur brain is evidence that "the brain contained sufficiently expanded neural tissue to function at the advanced levels achieved by birds" (Jerison, 1973, p. 165). For the present, I accept Jerison's conservative view that the brains of pterosaurs were not expanded to an avian level, despite obviously bird-like specializations of parts of the pterosaur central nervous system.

5. Order Saurischia

a. *Suborder Theropoda.* The carnivorous dinosaurs are all included in the suborder Theropoda. Two infraorders are recognized: the Coelurosauria for the smaller, more lightly built theropods with relatively small heads and well-developed forelimbs; and the Carnosauria for the larger, more heavily built theropods with large heads and a tendency to reduce the forelimbs. A third, seemingly intermediate, group, for inclusion of the family Dromaeosauridae, has been designated the infraorder Deinonychosauria (Colbert and Russell, 1969; Ostrom, 1969). I include the dromaeosaurids in the Coelurosauria for convenience. Because coelurosaurs are the ancestors of birds (Ostrom, 1976), their endocasts have special phylogenetic significance.

Endocasts are known for members of both infraorders, but the record is far better for the Carnosauria. The Coelurosauria are represented by two incomplete endocasts of Late Cretaceous forms.

(i) Infraorder Coelurosauria. No endocast is available for primitive coelurosaurs of the Late Triassic and Jurassic. Casts of the undersurface of isolated cranial roofs of the dromaeosaurid *Stenonychosaurus* (Russell, 1969) and the ornithomimid *Dromiceiomimus* (Russell, 1972), both of Late Cretaceous age, have yielded important information on the fore- and midbrains of these small to medium-sized carnivores, but the absence of the more ventral and posterior portions of the endocasts of these animals leaves some important questions unanswered. Russell has concluded that the brains of both of these dinosaurs were extremely large and has estimated that relative brain size was comparable to that of ratite birds. This problem is discussed at greater length below.

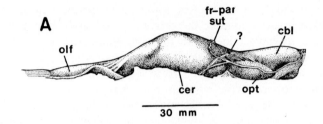

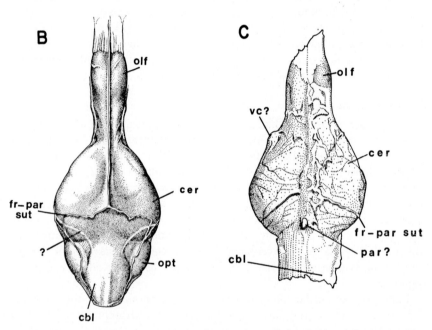

FIG. 13. Partial endocasts of coelurosaurian saurischians. A, B. *Stenonychosaurus inequalis*, A.M.N.H. 6174. A. Lateral view. B. Dorsal view. C. Dorsal view of *Dromiceiomimus brevitertius*, N.M.C. 12228. All drawn to the same scale. cbl, Cerebellar region; cer, cerebral hemisphere; fr-par sut, frontal-parietal suture; olf, olfactory bulb; opt, optic lobe; par?, cast of a hollow in the skull roof for the parietal organ?; vc?, possible vascular canal; ?, faint ridge possibly marking the course of a blood vessel.

A latex cast of the undersurface of a skull roof consisting of frontals, parietals, and portions of the laterosphenoids of the dromaeosaurid *Stenony-chosaurus* (A.M.N.H. 6174) shows the dorsal surface of the cranial cavity in remarkable detail. Russell (1969, Fig. 3) figures this cranial fragment and the dorsal surface of the endocranial cast made from it and provides a brief description of the cranial cavity. The following description is based on a new latex endocast made from an excellent plaster cast of the cranial fragment.

The endocast reproduces the dorsal surfaces of the olfactory bulbs and tracts, cerebral hemispheres, optic tectum, and cerebellar region (Fig. 13A,B). The cast of the forebrain shows a degree of surface modelling which, with the exception of the pterosaurs, may be unique among reptiles and which strongly suggests that this part of the brain lay in very close proximity to the bony walls of the cranial cavity. The outline of the olfactory bulbs is also well shown; these are elongate oval structures lying close to the midline and joined to the cerebrum by peduncles which are equal in length to the bulbs but which narrow slightly in a caudal direction. On either side of the olfactory peduncles is a dorsally convex, curved ridge which reflects a groove on the frontal bone. This ridge may represent a vascular channel, but it may equally well mark the attachment area of the cartilaginous sphenethmoid which floored the olfactory portion of the brain.

The cerebrum is roughly heart-shaped, being very narrow anteriorly where it joins the olfactory peduncles and widest about three-quarters of the way back from this point. The hemispheres are distinctly paired on the endocast. Several surface features of the cerebrum can be distinguished. Anterolaterally is a low swelling which corresponds in position to a slightly more prominent bulb on the endocast of the ostrich dinosaur *Dromiceiomimus* (Fig. 13c). This swelling does not appear to represent a foramen or the opening of a canal in *Stenonychosaurus*. Posterior to this swelling each hemisphere is a smoothly rounded oval, separated from the opposite hemisphere by a distinct sulcus which is narrow and rather deep anteriorly but which becomes wider and less distinct posteriorly. There is the slight indication of a differentiation of the hemisphere into a narrow, more convex anterior swelling which forms the highest part of the hemisphere and a more broadly rounded, posterior region which slopes down and back. A faint, smoothly curving ridge passes back and inward across the posterolateral surface of the cerebrum on to the anterior part of the cerebellar region. It may mark the course of a blood vessel, but this is uncertain. When the cast is viewed from in front, the ventrolateral surfaces of the hemispheres are seen to curve inward rather abruptly, so that although the underside of the forebrain is not preserved, the available portion indicates that its depth was less than half its width.

The preserved part of the cerebellar region of *Stenonychosaurus* is less than half the width of the cerebrum. It is an elongate oval in dorsal view, with smoothly rounded sides and a faint middorsal ridge which increases in prominence toward the rear. In lateral view, its upper profile is approximately horizontal and slightly convex. The cast of the cerebellar region does not appear accurately to reproduce the form of the underlying brain, as the cerebral cast so clearly does. It is likely that the cerebellum of *Stenony-chosaurus* was overlain by the longitudinal venous sinus as in other reptiles so that the cerebellum is reflected on the cast only in a general way.

On the sides of the cast of *Stenonychosaurus*, between the cerebrum and cerebellum, are large paired swellings which Russell (1969) interprets as impressions of the optic lobes. In the endocast of *Caiman* similar swellings lie in the position of the lateral branches of the longitudinal venous sinus. However, their position immediately adjacent to the cerebral hemispheres and their broadly rounded form support Russell's view that in *Stenonycho-saurus* they represent the optic lobes. This is one of very few cases in which the optic tectum leaves an impression on the braincase of a fossil reptile. Russell (1969) suggests that the optic lobes were shifted ventrolaterally as they are in birds due to the enlargement of the cerebral hemispheres. Possibly an anterior expansion of the cerebellum, as occurred in pterosaurs, also contributed to the lateral displacement of the optic lobes.

Information on the more ventral part of the endocast of dromaeosaurids is provided by *Dromaeosaurus* (Colbert and Russell, 1969) and *Saurornithoides* (Barsbold, 1974). The braincase of the latter indicates that the brain was strongly flexed and the forebrain dorsoventrally compressed, as was inferred for *Stenonychosaurus*. In *Dromaeosaurus*, a figure of the internal wall of the braincase indicates the presence of a floccular fossa. Colbert and Russell (1969) comment on the great breadth of the endocranial cavity, especially in the anterior medullary region. They remark that "if the posterior moiety of the brain even approximately filled this space, it must have been very broad indeed" (Colbert and Russell, 1969, p. 19).

A partial endocast of the ornithomimid *Dromiceiomimus brevitertius* was described and figured by Russell (1972). It consists of the dorsal and part of the lateral surface of the forebrain and cerebellar region (Fig. 13c). The olfactory bulbs and peduncles are short and relatively broad compared with those of *Stenonychosaurus*, and appear to be dorsoventrally very shallow. The cerebral hemispheres are similar in shape to those of *Stenonychosaurus*. Russell notes that they are slightly wider but much deeper and more broadly rounded in lateral aspect than those of *Stenonychosaurus*. He believes that the cerebrum of *Dromiceiomimus* had twice the volume of that of *Stenonycho-saurus*. A rounded projection on the anterolateral surface of the left hemi-sphere may represent a venous canal, but this is uncertain. The surface of the cerebrum is covered by very fine arborizing ridges which are indicated in Russell's figures and in Fig. 13c. These represent intracranial vascular channels such as appear on the endocasts of birds and mammals. They provide good evidence that the surface of the brain was closely appressed to the bone in this region.

A small median protuberance between the posterior ends of the cerebral hemispheres is interpreted by Russell (1972) as a parietal organ housed in a recess in the undersurface of the parietal. The cerebellar region is broader than that of *Stenonychosaurus* but otherwise it is not well preserved. Cranial fragments of the related *Struthiomimus* indicate the presence of a floccular fossa which is much larger than that of *Dromaeosaurus*, and a medullary cavity which is shorter and deeper than in the latter (Russell, 1972, p. 386).

Russell (1969, 1972) estimates relative brain weights for *Stenonychosaurus* and *Dromiceiomimus* which are comparable to those of living ratite birds and much larger than those of any other reptiles. The weight of the brain of *Stenonychosaurus* is estimated to be about 45 g on the basis of a clay model patterned after the endocranial cast of the frontoparietal region and the general shape of the brain in archosaurs. Estimating the body weight to be similar to that of a ratite bird of equal femoral circumference, he obtains a weight of 45 300 g. These figures yield a brain:body weight ratio of about 0·001, or about seven times that of a living crocodilian of similar body weight (0·000 138) and "comparable to, if not larger than those of living ratites" (Russell, 1969, p. 599). A comparable brain:body weight ratio is noted for *Dromiceiomimus* (Russell, 1972).

I have independently estimated the size of the brain of *Stenonychosaurus*, and obtain a weight of 37 g, which, though lower than that obtained by Russell (1969), nevertheless still falls within the range of living ratite birds (Hopson, 1977). The unusually large size of the brains of these coelurosaurs has been noted by Dodson (1974) and Bakker (1974) in support of the hypothesis that dinosaurs were endothermic. I argue elsewhere (Hopson, 1977) that coelurosaurs, at least, were probably endothermic.

(ii) Infraorder Carnosauria. Endocasts are known for three families of carnosaurs. Megalosaurid endocasts are known for the Late Jurassic *Ceratosaurus* of North America (Marsh, 1884b, 1896; Gilmore, 1920) and the Cretaceous *Orthogoniosaurus* (*Indosaurus*) of India (von Huene and Matley, 1933). The Allosauridae is represented by three endocasts of the Late Jurassic *Allosaurus* (*Antrodemus*) of North America: an artificial endocast (A.M.N.H. 5753), figured by Osborn (1912, Fig. 9), a natural endocast (U.U.V.P. 294) in the University of Utah Vertebrate Paleontology Collection (Madsen, 1976, Fig. 9F), and an unnumbered and undescribed artificial endocast in the latter collection. Fig. 14 is based on the latter two specimens. The Late Cretaceous Tyrannosauridae is represented by an excellent endocast of the North American *Tyrannosaurus*, well figured by Osborn (1912) and redrawn here in Fig. 15. The endocast of the Mongolian tyrannosaur *Tarbosaurus* (Maleev, 1965) is very similar.

The endocasts of carnosaurs show a basic similarity from one genus to another, the principal differences probably relating to differences in size.

When the figured specimens are reoriented to probable life position (i.e. with the long axis of the medulla aligned horizontally), it is seen that all possess a pontine flexure of about 40°. The endocast of *Ceratosaurus* is the smallest, most anteroposteriorly compact of the three North American genera; that of *Tyrannosaurus* is the largest and most elongated.

The endocast of *Ceratosaurus* is best figured by Gilmore (1920) in wash drawings prepared under Marsh's direction. These drawings are probably natural size although stated to be "one-half nat. size" in the figure legend. The skull from which the endocast was made is badly crushed transversely (Gilmore, 1920), so that the symmetrical endocast has probably been restored to an indeterminate degree. The cast shows relatively little detail, and few of the nerve roots are indicated. The olfactory bulbs form a large oval expansion joined to the cerebral region by short, relatively deep, and transversely narrow peduncles. The cerebral region is broad and deep, with smoothly rounded sides. The optic nerve and a very large process, identified by Marsh as the oculomotor nerve, lie below the anterior half of the cerebrum. Edinger (1929) comments on the remarkably large size of this process but other dinosaurs have a large opening (fenestra metoptica) for nerve III. The cast of the pituitary fossa is moderately large, with a constricted infundibular region and a rounded distal expansion.

The midbrain region of *Ceratosaurus* endocast probably lies just behind the widest portion of the cast and just in front of a distinct near-vertical ridge which probably represents the groove for the middle cerebral vein. The cerebellum is presumed to have lain beneath a blunt dorsal projection on the obliquely sloping, transversely narrow region behind the vertical ridge. The position of the inner ear is indicated just behind the trigeminal root, but no details are shown. The medullary region is short and has an unusually small transverse diameter (probably the result of lateral compression. Its dorsoventral dimension is low as in all carnosaurs.

The three known endocasts of *Allosaurus* show little variation among them. In the absence of an ossified presphenoid, the cast lacks both a floor to the olfactory region and an anterior wall to the pituitary fossa (Fig. 14). The shape of the olfactory bulbs is reflected by depressions on the undersurface of the frontal bones. They are elongate ovals which join the cerebral region by means of short, broad peduncles. The cerebral region widens gradually posteriorly to a maximum width above the pituitary fossa. The cast of the cerebral region rises well above the level of the olfactory bulbs and terminates dorsally in a rugose area below the parietal bone. The rugose extension presumably represents the cast of the unossified anterior portion of the supraoccipital. On the ventrolateral surface of the endocast, anterodorsal to the optic foramina, is a slender, elongate process (vc? in Fig. 14) which probably represents a vascular canal.

The optic foramina of the *Allosaurus* endocast are large and paired. Directly lateral to the optic foramina are large foramina metoptica for passage of the oculomotor and, presumably, the trochlear nerves. A separate foramen for the trochlear nerve is not seen on any of the *Allosaurus* endocasts. The pituitary fossa lies between and slightly posterior to them. The posterior wall of the pituitary fossa is preserved only in the artificial endocast

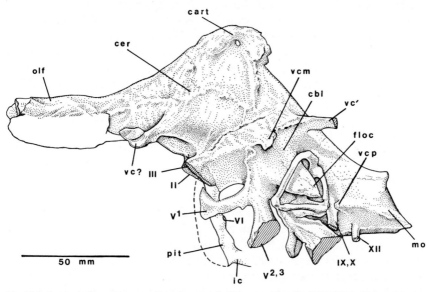

FIG. 14. Lateral view of a natural endocast of *Allosaurus fragilis* (U.U.V.P. 294), with the pituitary fossa restored from another specimen. cart, Filling of the space for the cartilaginous portion of the supraoccipital; cbl, cerebellar region; cer, cerebrum; floc, flocculus; ic, internal carotid artery; mo, medulla oblongata; olf, olfactory bulb; pit, pituitary fossa; vc?, probable venous channel; vc', branch of the longitudinal sinus; vcm, middle cerebral vein; vcp, diverticulum of the longitudinal sinus; II, optic nerve; III, fenestra metoptica for the oculomotor and probably the trochlear nerves; V¹, ophthalmic branch of the trigeminal nerve; V²,³, maxillary and mandibular branches of the trigeminal nerve; VI, abducens nerve; IX, X, foramen for the glossopharyngeal and vagus nerves; XII, hypoglossal nerve.

in the collections of the University of Utah. The wall extends a short distance below the level of the floor of the medulla. A large canal, presumably for the internal carotid artery, passes posteroventrally from its base. Halfway down its posterior face, the canal for the abducens nerve enters the fossa.

Behind the dorsal cartilage-filling, the endocast of *Allosaurus* slopes steeply posteroventrally to the foramen magnum. Two processes on the side of the cast, one above the trigeminal root and the second posterodorsal to the first, are probably fillings of canals for branches of the longitudinal venous sinus. The more anterior of these may have transmitted the middle cerebral vein. Comparable canal fillings in *Tyrannosaurus* lie much more dorsally on the cast (see below). The cast of the trigeminal root also lies low on the side of the medulla compared with that of *Tyrannosaurus*. The trigeminal cast possesses a prominent ophthalmic branch passing antero-laterally and a maxillary and mandibular branch of larger diameter passing ventrolaterally. A small facial root lies posteroventral to nerve V, but is hidden from view in Fig. 14 by the cast of the inner ear cavity.

The medulla of *Allosaurus* is short compared with that of *Tyrannosaurus*. A prominent, posteroventrally directed projection lies posterior and dorsal to the trigeminal root in all three *Allosaurus* endocasts. In the natural endocast, the process passes between the anterior vertical semicircular canal and the crus commune (Fig. 14), demonstrating that it is the filling of a floccular recess. The inner ear cast includes an elongate ventrally directed cochlea. Behind the inner ear cavity is a large ventrolaterally directed process representing the canal for nerves IX and X. There are two hypoglossal roots, a larger one posteromedial to the vagus root and a smaller one (not seen in Fig. 14) directly medial to the vagus. Directly posterior to the latter is a short anterolaterally directed process which probably repre-sents a branch of the longitudinal venous sinus.

The endocast of *Tyrannosaurus* (Fig. 15), figured by Osborn (1912), appears rather tubular in dorsal view, and lacks any notable expansions. The casts of the olfactory bulbs are large and join the cerebral region by means of relatively short, broad tracts lying close to the midline. The lower half of the olfactory portion of the cast is restored in the figures because the floor of this region was not ossified. The cerebrum is narrow, being only slightly wider than the medullary region. Dorsal to the optic nerve roots, the side of the cast forms a distinct, smoothly rounded bulge which Osborn identified as the optic tectum, but which more likely represents the postero-lateral part of the cerebrum. The dorsal surface of the cerebral region is traversed by curved ridges which probably represent the frontoparietal suture. Dorsolateral ridges and a blunt process indicate the position of the suture between the frontal and laterosphenoid; the process may represent a venous foramen.

The confluent optic foramina of *Tyrannosaurus* are separated from the pituitary fossa by a thin bar of the laterosphenoid. Anterodorsal to the optic roots is an unidentified small process (? in Fig, 15) which is comparable in position to the larger, more anterodorsal process in *Allosaurus* (vc? in Fig. 14). The process may represent a venous canal. The root of the oculomotor nerve lies a short distance behind the pituitary fossa and the trochlear root directly above the oculomotor root.

The dorsal surface of the *Tyrannosaurus* endocast, behind the cerebral and midbrain regions, rises well above the level of the forebrain to form a

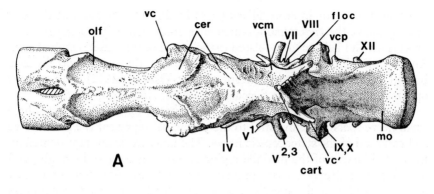

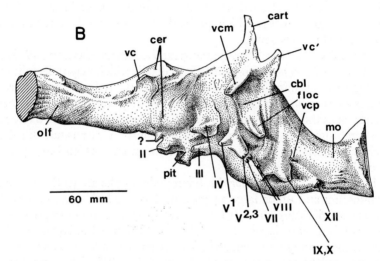

FIG. 15. Endocast of *Tyrannosaurus rex*, A.M.N.H. 5029 (redrawn from Osborn, 1912). A. Dorsal view. B. Lateral view. cart, Filling of the space for the cartilaginous portion of the supraoccipital; cbl, cerebellar region; cer, cerebrum; floc, probable flocculus; mo, medulla oblongata; olf, olfactory bulb; pit, proximal portion of the pituitary fossa; vc, minor vascular canal; vc', branch of the longitudinal sinus; vcm, middle cerebral vein; vcp, diverticulum of longitudinal sinus; II, optic nerve; III, oculomotor nerve; IV, trochlear nerve; V^1, ophthalmic branch of the trigeminal nerve; $V^{2,3}$, maxillary and mandibular branches of the trigeminal nerve; VII, facial nerve; VIII, auditory nerve; IX, X, foramen for the glossopharyngeal and vagus nerves; XII, hypoglossal nerve; ?, unidentified process.

narrow ridge capped by a slender, dorsally directed median process, presumably filling an unossified zone in the cranial roof. Ventrolateral to this process are paired projections directed posterodorsolaterally, which I interpret as the fillings of canals for branches of the longitudinal venous sinus such as occur in crocodilians (see Fig. 2c). On the sides of the cast directly above the trigeminal foramen is an anteroventrally sloping ridge or process which I believe to be related to the course of the middle cerebral vein. Another prominent process on the side of the cast, this one a short distance behind the trigeminal, was interpreted by Osborn (1912) as a venous opening, but it is clearly the floccular recess (cf. *Allosaurus*, Fig. 14).

The trigeminal nerve is preserved with a separate opthalmic ramus. Three small nerve roots posteroventral to the trigeminal represent the facial nerve and two rami of the statoacoustic nerve. The inner ear is not represented on the cast. The cast of the medulla region is relatively long and straight, and is wider than deep. A large process represents the foramen for cranial nerves IX and X, and some distance posterolateral to it is a smaller process representing the last root of the hypoglossal nerve, the more anterior roots of which are not indicated on Osborn's figure. Posterodorsal to the vagus root is a short process which probably represents a diverticulum of the longitudinal venous sinus.

The endocast of the Asian tyrannosaur *Tarbosaurus* (Maleev, 1965) differs from that of *Tyrannosaurus* primarily in details which may reflect differences in degree of cleaning of the endocranial cavity. It lacks the posterodorsal processes seen in *Tyrannosaurus*. The swelling above the optic nerve is identified as the optic tectum but, as in *Tyrannosaurus*, it more likely reflects the cerebrum. The ophthalmic branch of nerve V is misidentified as the facial nerve. Maleev identifies as nerve V the process which I interpret as the flocculus.

b. *Suborder Sauropodomorpha*. Sauropodomorphs are (i) the sauropods—brontosaurs and other large to gigantic long-necked, quadrupedal, herbivorous saurischians—and (ii) the more primitive prosauropods—smaller forms of the Late Triassic which included both bipedal and quadrupedal, and carnivorous and herbivorous members. A partial endocast is known for the prosauropod *Plateosaurus* (von Huene, 1907–08, 1932). Endocasts have been described for the following sauropods: *Antarctosaurus* (von Huene and Matley, 1933), *Barosaurus* (Janensch, 1935–36), *Brachiosaurus* (Janensch, 1935–36), *Camarasaurus* (Marsh, 1880, 1889; Osborn and Mook, 1921; Ostrom and McIntosh, 1966), *Cetiosaurus* (described as *Megalosaurus bucklandi* by von Huene (1906), *Dicraeosaurus* (Janensch, 1935–36), and *Diplodocus* (Holland, 1906; Marsh, 1884a, 1896; Osborn, 1912).

The endocast of *Plateosaurus* described by von Huene (1907–08, 1932) is incomplete anteriorly. It differs from that of sauropods in being less anteroposteriorly compressed.

The endocast of sauropods shows little variation among genera; the present description is based mainly on that of *Diplodocus* (Fig. 16). It is short and very deep, with prominent cerebral and pontine flexures. Most specimens have a large projection above the fore- and midbrain regions. This may represent an unossified zone in the braincase rather than a parietal foramen. In some forms, this unossified zone penetrates the cranial roof to form a fontanelle, in others it is covered dorsally. This projection of the

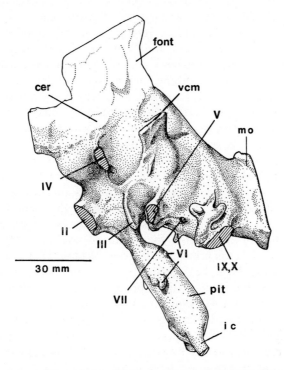

FIG. 16. Lateral view of the endocast of *Diplodocus longus*, A.M.N.H. 694. cer, Cerebrum; font, filling of an unossified zone or fontanelle in the skull roof; ic, internal carotid artery; mo, medulla oblongata; pit, pituitary fossa; vcm, middle cerebral vein; II, optic nerve; III, foramen for the oculomotor nerve; IV, foramen for the trochlear nerve and probably a vein; V, trigeminal nerve; VI, foramina for the abducens nerve; VII, facial nerve; IX, X, foramen for the glossopharyngeal and vagus nerves.

endocast may have been filled by part of the cartilaginous endocranium in life, or it may have been a space occupied perhaps by the dorsal venous sinus.

The anterior part of the olfactory tracts and the olfactory bulbs lay anterior to the ossified braincase and are never preserved on the endocast. The posterior portions of the olfactory tracts are relatively broad. The cerebral region, which forms the widest part of the endocast, is short, deep, and swollen in appearance in most specimens. It bulges forward above the optic foramen and has its greatest width at about its midlength, or even slightly forward of this point (as in *Camarasaurus grandis*). The forebrain appears to be both wider and deeper than it is long. Its posterior limit is presumed to be marked by a prominent transverse constriction.

The optic nerves lie far below the level of the olfactory peduncles. Above them, on the side of the forebrain swelling is a large process identified by Janensch (1935–36) as representing the "fenestra epioptica"; Janensch believed that it passed the anterior cerebral vein and, in some genera, the trochlear nerve. In other genera, the IVth cranial nerve may have exited with the oculomotor nerve through a more ventrally located, slit-like opening (fenestra metoptica) just behind the optic nerves.

The cast of the pituitary fossa is very long, with a short, narrow infundibular stalk and a long, broader pituitary portion oriented posteroventrally. The pituitary cast, when viewed from in front, widens gradually toward its distal end so that it appears as an elongate triangle. The internal carotid canals enter the triangle at its distolateral corners. A lateral process at its midheight is probably the exit of the abducens nerve from the pituitary region. On the rear of the cast at about this level are small protuberances marking the anterior ends of the abducens canals; above and behind them on the floor of the medulla are the posterior entrances to these canals.

The endocast is constricted at the presumed level of the midbrain; no evidence of optic lobes is present on the cast. Behind this region the lateral surface of the cast, above the trigeminal root, extends outward as a rounded bulge. On this bulge is an elongate process which is continuous anteroventrally with the low ridge which marks the course of the vena cerebralis media. The process probably represents the filling of a venous canal which opens onto the skull roof in other sauropod skulls (Janensch, 1936). The trigeminal nerve is represented by a dorsoventrally elongate process. Directly behind it is the small root of the facial nerve.

The middle region of the endocast descends steeply from the level of the forebrain and tapers gradually in to the area in which the medulla becomes horizontal. The dorsal profile of the sloping portion is nearly straight; it forms a rounded ridge which widens posteroventrally. The sides of the cast are constricted slightly between the inner ear cavities and become broader and rounder behind this region. The cerebellum probably lay beneath the steeply sloping portion of the cast, but the overlying longitudinal sinus would be expected to obscure it on the endocast.

The inner ear is beautifully preserved in *Brachiosaurus* (Janensch, 1935–36) and is partially represented in *Diplodocus* (restored from the right side in Fig. 16). In the latter, the orientation of the horizontal semicircular canal suggests that the orientation of the head was such that the face turned downward at a sharp angle. The large canal for the glossopharyngeal and vagus nerves (and internal jugular vein?) begins as a ridge high on the lateral surface of the medulla. The hypoglossal nerve is not indicated on the *Diplodocus* endocast; two pairs of canals are preserved in other specimens.

The horizontally oriented medulla does not increase in width behind the level of the vagus canal, as is usual in most dinosaurs. The medulla is very short in most sauropods, another reflection of the space constraints on the brain in these small-headed reptiles. A bluntly rounded process on the side of the medulla behind the vagus canal in *Brachiosaurus* and *Camarasaurus grandis* marks the presumed diverticulum of the longitudinal venous sinus discussed earlier.

6. Order Ornithischia

a. *General.* The Ornithischia have the best representation of endocasts of any order of fossil reptiles. Several examples of each suborder are available and comparisons among the principal groups are possible. Within the Ornithischia is a very great range of variation in endocast, and presumably brain, morphology, so that it is possible to characterize the endocast specializations of each suborder.

I follow Maryánska and Osmólska (1974) in separating the pachycephalosaurs from the suborder Ornithopoda as the suborder Pachycephalosauria.

b. *Suborder Ornithopoda.* Among the ornithopods, the majority of endocasts are from members of the Hadrosauridae, which is the latest and most specialized family of ornithopods to appear. Of earlier forms, several good endocasts are known from *Iguanodon* (Andrews, 1897; Swinton, 1958) and evidence on the endocast has been derived from the braincase of *Camptosaurus* (Marsh, 1896).

Hadrosaurs are large ornithopods (usually about 9·5 m in length but reaching 16·5 m) which underwent abundant speciation in the Late Cretaceous. They are noted for diverse and often bizarre modifications of the nasal and premaxillary bones associated with the development of conspicuous supracranial crests. The function of these cranial features has recently been interpreted as serving in intraspecific display behaviors (Dodson, 1975; Hopson, 1975). Numerous hadrosaur endocasts have been described and all are similar and characteristic of the family. The best specimen is that of *Kritosauras notabilis* described in detail by Ostrom (1961) and refigured here (Fig. 17). Endocasts have been described for: *Anatosaurus* (Lull and Wright, 1942; Ostrom, 1961), *Bactrosaurus* (Langston, 1960), *Edmontosaurus* (Lambe, 1920; Ostrom, 1961), *Lophorhothon* (Langston, 1960), *Orthomerus* ("*Limnosaurus*"; Nopcsa, 1900), "*Trachodon*" (Brown, 1914; identified as *Anatosaurus* sp. by Ostrom, 1961), and *Tsintaosaurus* (Young, 1958).

The endocast of hadrosaurs (and of the similar *Iguanodon*) is distinguished from that of non-ornithopod ornithischians by the possession of a greatly inflated, smoothly rounded cerebrum and the absence of a pontine flexure.

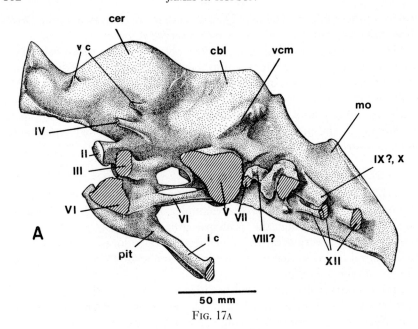

50 mm

FIG. 17A

The orientation of the cranial cavity within the skull is obliquely antero-dorsal. The foramen magnum faces posteroventrally and the spinal cord probably continued the oblique orientation of the medulla into the neck.

The olfactory tracts appear to have been relatively large but their impressions show some variation among genera. In *Kritosaurus* they widen anteriorly but they are parallel sided in *Anatosaurus* and *Edmontosaurus*. The location of the olfactory bulbs is not known in any hadrosaur, for they left no impression on the cranial roof and lay in front of the ossified braincase. Ostrom (1961) restores them at the end of long olfactory tracts by analogy with conditions in crocodilians and lizards. He suggests that as the nasal capsule of hollow-crested lambeosaurine hadrosaurs lay within the supra-cranial crest, the olfactory tracts turned upward anterior to their emergence from the cranial cavity and passed into the crestal cavity. Evidence in the skull for this course is lacking. The expansion of the olfactory stalks of *Kritosaurus* close to the front of the cerebrum suggests that the olfactory bulbs may have lain close to the brain in hadrosaurs, approximately between the anterior rim of the orbits.

The cast of the cerebral region is a large, smoothly rounded dome, which extends well above the level of the olfactory tracts and of the midbrain and cerebellar regions. Its large size is reflected on the skull roof of hadrosaurs by doming of the frontals, a feature which is especially conspicuous in juveniles. The cerebrum is about as long as it is wide, with its greatest

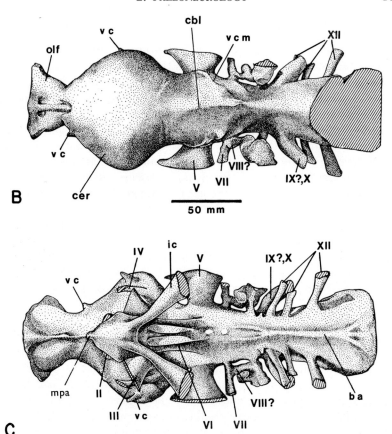

FIG. 17. Endocast of the hadrosaur *Kritosaurus notabilis*, A.M.N.H. 5350. A. Lateral view. B. Dorsal view. C. Ventral view. ba, Groove for basilar artery; cbl, cerebellar region; cer, cerebrum; ic, internal carotid artery; mo, medulla oblongata; mpa, median palatine artery; olf, probable olfactory bulb; pit, pituitary fossa; vc, minor vascular canals; vcm, middle cerebral vein; II, optic nerve; III, oculomotor nerve; IV, trochlear nerve; V, trigeminal nerve; VI, canal and foramen (metoptic fissure) of abducens nerve; VII, facial nerve; VIII? probable branch of the auditory nerve; IX?, X, foramen for the vagus nerve and possibly the glossopharyngeal nerve; XII, hypoglossal nerve.

width about two-thirds of the distance from its anterior end. The cerebral cavity has the general form of the cerebral hemispheres of living crocodilians and many lizards. I believe, therefore, that it faithfully reproduces the gross form of the cerebrum, much as does the endocast of a crocodilian many times smaller in body size. The large size and smoothly ovoid shape of the cerebral endocast strongly suggests that the size of the cerebrum of hadrosaurs was relatively greater than that of other large ornithischians and of large saurischians.

Small processes on the surface of the cerebral endocast are interpreted as vascular canals.

Large optic foramina lie below the cerebrum. A small canal above and behind the optic nerves transmitted the trochlear nerve. A larger opening posteroventral to the optic nerves probably transmitted the oculomotor nerve. The pituitary fossa is large but not greatly elongated. Below a narrow infundibular region it expands anteroposteriorly. Large internal carotid canals enter it posterolaterally and a smaller median canal, identified by Ostrom as carrying the median palatine artery, leaves it anteriorly. A large lateral opening in the wall of the fossa transmitted the abducens nerve but, in view of the large size of the opening, vascular elements and perhaps extraocular muscles also may have passed through it (see Säve-Söderbergh, 1946). Piercing the rear wall of the pituitary fossa are canals in the dorsum sellae for the VIth nerves and the ramus caudalis of the internal carotid artery (Ostrom, 1961).

The endocast is constricted at the level of the midbrain, the degree of constriction varying among genera. It is greatest in *Kritosaurus* and less in *Edmontosaurus* and *Bactrosaurus*. The optic tectum has left no impression on the braincase.

The metencephalic region is expanded slightly between the midbrain and posterior constrictions. The cerebellar region is somewhat triangular in transverse section in *Kritosaurus*, but in the much smaller *Bactrosaurus* is more broadly rounded. In lateral view, the dorsal profile of the cerebellar region of *Kritosaurus* is straight and horizontal but posteriorly it bends sharply at a 45-degree angle and drops to the upper surface of the medulla. The profile of this region varies in different specimens, probably because of differing degrees of development of the longitudinal venous sinus and of ossification in the anterior portion of the supraoccipital. In the cast of *Bactrosaurus*, for example, the posterior part of the cerebellar region forms a prominent elevation above the general level of the midbrain.

A feature of all specimens is a linear ridge extending obliquely posterodorsally on the side of the cerebellar region from just above the trigeminal foramen. Ostrom suggests that this ridge may mark the position of the endolymphatic sac, but comparison with other reptilian endocasts supports Janensch's (1936) interpretation that the ridge marks the groove in the cranial wall for the middle cerebral vein. In some specimens a small canal opening high on the lateral parietal surface is associated with the groove.

The trigeminal root is very large. The small canal for the facial nerve gives off a short branch which passes backwards to the inner ear chamber in *Kritosaurus* (Ostrom, 1961), *Bactrosaurus*, and *Lophorhothon* (Langston, 1960). Langston interprets the latter as transmitting the acoustic nerve, or at least its anterior branch.

The cast of the medulla region is oval in transverse section, being slightly higher than wide. It is straight and passes obliquely posteroventrally to the foramen magnum. The large canal immediately behind the vestibule is best interpreted as having transmitted the ninth and tenth cranial nerves, although Langston (1960) believes the ninth nerve exited by a separate foramen below the fenestra ovalis. Three pairs of canals lie ventromedial to and behind the vagus canal. A small canal medial to the latter is believed by most authors to have transmitted the jugular vein, but all three canals are probably hypoglossal foramina. The posterior-most canal is the largest.

c. *Suborder Pachycephalosauria.* Pachycephalosaurids are small to medium-sized Cretaceous ornithischians in which the skull roof is greatly thickened

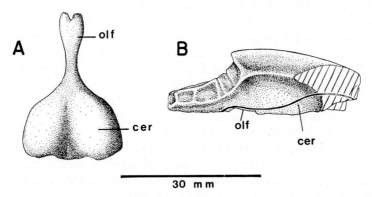

FIG. 18. *Yaverlandia bitholos*, M.I.W.G. 1530. A. Dorsal view of endocast of forebrain. B. Lateral view of cranial fragment with the profile of the endocranial cavity indicated by a heavy line. cer, Cerebral hemisphere; olf, olfactory bulb.

above the endocranial cavity. This thickened cranium probably functioned as a battering-ram, used in head-to-head combat among conspecifics (Galton, 1970, 1971). Endocasts are known for two genera from the Late Cretaceous of North America. A complete endocast of the most advanced and largest genus, *Pachycephalosaurus grangeri*, is described by Brown and Schlaikjer (1943). Several partial endocasts of the earlier and smaller form, *Stegoceras validus*, have been taken from isolated "skullcaps", the greatly thickened portions of the cranium which form the most frequently found remains of this genus. The present description of *Stegoceras* is based on two such partial endocasts, R.O.M. 803 and N.M.C. 138; the latter specimen has been figured and discussed by Maryánska and Osmólska (1974). Galton (1971) refers the moderately-thickened cranial fragment of a small Early Cretaceous ornithischian to the Pachycephalosauridae; a cast of the dorsal surface of the telencephalic region of the cranial cavity of this animal, named *Yaverlandia bitholos* by Galton, is described here.

The endocast of *Yaverlandia* (Fig. 18) is sufficiently different from that of the Late Cretaceous genera to cast doubt on the pachycephalosaurid relationships of the genus; therefore, it is described separately from the other pachycephalosaurs. Its cerebral region is short and very broad with the oval hemispheres separated by a distinct median sulcus. The widest part of the cerebrum is behind its midlength. Anteriorly, the cerebrum tapers rather abruptly to merge into the slender olfactory peduncles. The olfactory bulbs are distinct but lie close together. *Stegoceras* and *Pachycephalosaurus* (Fig. 19) differ from *Yaverlandia* in possessing much broader and more divergent olfactory bulbs and much larger olfactory peduncles. The cerebral region of *Stegoceras* is the same length as that of *Yaverlandia* but is much narrower and lacks a midline sulcus between the hemispheres.

Stegoceras was a much smaller animal than *Pachycephalosaurus*; the estimated length for the *Stegoceras* skulls for which endocasts are available is about 127 mm whereas that of the complete skull of *Pachycephalosaurus* is 642 mm. The two endocasts of *Stegoceras* are 45 mm in length and that of *Pachycephalosaurus* is 162 mm; thus the endocast of the smaller animal is about 35% the length of the skull whereas that of the larger animal is only 25%. Many of the differences in shape between the endocasts of the two genera can be attributed to the effects of allometrically varying space constraints on the brain in skulls of such disparate sizes. The endocast of *Stegoceras* gives the impression of anteroposterior compactness whereas that of *Pachycephalosaurus* appears to be greatly attentuated. Also, as expected in view of its larger size, the latter provides a poorer indication of the morphology of the brain.

The casts of the olfactory bulbs of *Stegoceras* are large ovoid masses which are in contact posteromedially and diverge from the sagittal plane at an angle of 40° in N.M.C. 138 and 45° in R.O.M. 803. They are joined to a short, broad trunk, nearly circular in cross-section, which merges smoothly into the anterior end of the cerebral region.

Viewed from above, the cerebrum plus cerebellar region of *Stegoceras* endocast N.M.C. 138 is roughly diamond-shaped, with the broadest part across the posterolateral portion of the cerebrum; that of R.O.M. 803 is more oval in outline. The surface modelling of the two specimens differs slightly, perhaps reflecting somewhat different degrees of ossification of the inner surface of the braincase. The presumed posterior limits of the hemispheres are indicated in both specimens by a slight transverse drop in the dorsal surface down to the lower level of the cerebellar region. The latter region of the cast tapers posteriorly into a small dorsomedian process in N.M.C. 138 and to two small parasagittal processes in R.O.M. 803; these are presumed to represent cartilaginous areas of the braincase. Further ventrolaterally are a pair of backwardly directed, pointed processes. These

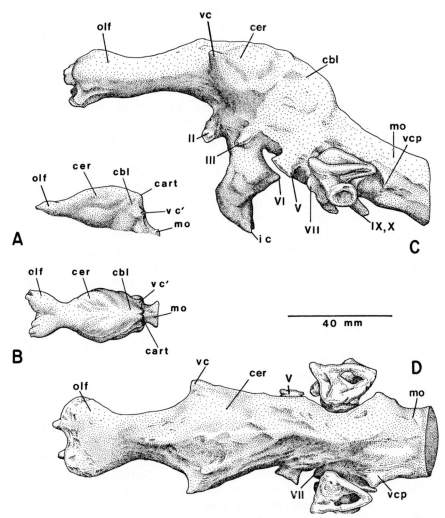

FIG. 19. Endocasts of pachycephalosaurid ornithischians. A. B. Partial endocast of *Stegoceras validus*, R.O.M. 803. A. Lateral view. B. Dorsal view. C, D. *Pachycephalosaurus grangeri*, A.M.N.H. 1696 (redrawn from Brown and Schlaikjer, 1943). C. Lateral view. D. Dorsal view. All drawn to the same scale. cart, Filling of the space for the cartilaginous portion of the supraoccipital; cbl, cerebellar region; cer, cerebrum; ic, internal carotid artery; mo, medulla oblongata; olf, olfactory bulb; vc, minor vesicular canal; vc', branch of the longitudinal sinus; vcp, diverticulum of the longitudinal sinus; II, optic nerve; III, oculomotor nerve; V, trigeminal nerve; VI, abducens nerve; VII, facial nerve; IX, X, foramen for the glossopharyngeal and vagus nerves.

probably correspond to the small projections of the longitudinal venous sinus which penetrate the supraoccipital in *Caiman* (see Fig. 2c).

We lack a reliable horizontal orientation plane for these incomplete specimens; if they are oriented as in Fig. 19, the rear of the cerebellar region drops off nearly vertically and the dorsal surface of the medullary region lies below the level of most of the cerebrum. Although the posterior-most part of the cranial cast is not preserved on either specimen, the orientation of the foramen magnum in the one complete skull of *Stegoceras* indicates that the posterior part of the medulla was oriented at an angle of about 45°. The endocast is constricted between the inner ear cavities; its breadth behind the inner ear cannot be determined in these incomplete specimens.

None of the cranial nerves (except the olfactory nerve) is indicated on the partial endocasts of *Stegoceras*.

The olfactory bulbs and tracts of *Pachycephalosaurus* are similar to those of *Stegoceras* but the tracts in the larger genus are relatively longer. The cerebral region is also longer and narrower and carries a large anterolaterally directed projection on its dorsolateral surface, similar to that in some ceratopsians (see Fig. 23). This process may well represent a vascular canal. The dorsal surface of the cerebral region curves smoothly postero-ventrally into the cerebellar region without a clear demarcation between the two. The cerebellar region is distinguished from the medulla by a slight steepening of its posterodorsal profile. The medulla is long and nearly straight, and extends posteroventrally at an angle of about 30° to the horizontal, much as in hadrosaurs.

The optic nerves leave the cranial cavity nearly at right angles to the sagittal plane, much as in ankylosaurs. Behind the optic nerve is a small root, presumed to represent the oculomotor nerve. On this interpretation, the endocast lacks evidence of a separate trochlear foramen. The cast of the pituitary fossa is a large ovoid structure with processes extending posteriorly from its proximal half, presumably representing the canals for the abducens nerves. Paired distal processes, directed posteroventrally, may represent the canals for the internal carotid arteries.

The root of the trigeminal nerve is preserved on the endocast and shows a small anterior projection presumed to represent the canal for the ophthalmic branch of the nerve. The root of the facial nerve lies just in front of and slightly below the fenestra ovalis. The canal for cranial nerves IX and X is confluent with the posteroventral portion of the inner ear cavity. The published figures do not show distinct hypoglossal foramina, but Brown and Schlaikjer (1943) note that nerve XII is situated about halfway along the length of the medulla. Possibly these authors interpret the prominent process on the lateral surface of the medullary region behind the posterior semicircular canal as the hypoglossal nerve. However, this structure more probably represents the diverticulum of the longitudinal venous sinus seen in many other archosaurs.

d. *Suborder Stegosauria*. Although the brain of the Late Jurassic American genus *Stegosaurus* has figured prominently in discussions of the brain of dinosaurs, knowledge of stegosaur endocasts is, in fact, extremely inadequate. Marsh (1880, 1881, 1896; also, Gilmore, 1914, and Ostrom and McIntosh, 1966, reproduce figures prepared by Marsh) has provided figures and brief descriptions of the endocasts of two species of *Stegosaurus*, but Edinger (1962) has pointed out that these endocasts are composites based on several specimens. The more complete reconstruction, that attributed to *S. armatus* by Marsh, contains errors which have led to a faulty understanding of the *Stegosaurus* brain (see below). The second endocast, pertaining to *S. ungulatus*, is sufficiently different from the first specimen to cast doubt on the accuracy of both specimens. Von Huene's (1914) discussion and figure of the endocranial cavity of *Stegosaurus armatus* contains misinterpretations of the positions of the pituitary fossa and various nerve foramina. A third stegosaur endocast has been described by Hennig (1925) from the East African Jurassic genus *Kentrosaurus* ("*Kentrurosaurus*"). Though incomplete anteriorly, this specimen is probably the most reliable of the three and aids in pinpointing the faults of the other two. Useful information on the internal morphology of the braincase of *Kentrosaurus* is provided by Janensch (1936).

The endocast of *Stegosaurus armatus*, as figured by Marsh, is presented in Figs 20A and C. The lateral view includes the sagittally sectioned braincase on which the endocast is primarily based. Figure 20B shows my interpretation of the endocast with information on the positions of cranial nerves taken from *Kentrosaurus*. Every author who has discussed this endocast of *Stegosaurus* has commented on the posterior position and unusual rearward curvature of the pituitary fossa. Comparison with *Kentrosaurus*, or any other reptile for that matter, indicates that the pit in the floor of the braincase (Fig. 20A) cannot be the pituitary fossa as it lies below the medulla oblongata well behind the level of both the pontine flexure and the bony structure identified here as the dorsum sellae. Instead, the pit probably represents an unossified zone within the basicranium. The braincase appears to pertain to a subadult individual in which cartilaginous areas between the bones are represented by ridges on the endocast; in such a specimen the floor of the cranial cavity may have been poorly ossified. Correct placement of the pituitary fossa anterior to the dorsum sellae and below the foramen of the oculomotor nerve results in a reptilian endocast of more conventional appearance (Fig. 20B).

The following description is based primarily on the corrected restoration of the endocast of *Stegosaurus armatus* and the reliable but less complete endocast of *Kentrosaurus*.

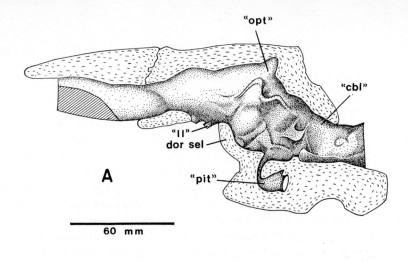

"opt"

"cbl"

"II"
dor sel

"pit"

60 mm

A

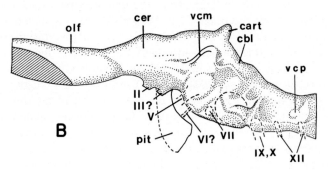

olf   cer   vcm   cart
cbl
vcp

II
III?
V

pit   VI?   VII

IX,X   XII

B

C

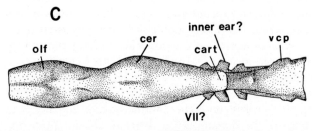

inner ear?   vcp
cer   cart
olf

VII?

FIG. 20. Endocast of *Stegosaurus armatus*, U.S.N.M. 4936 (redrawn from Marsh, in Ostrom and McIntosh, 1966). A. Lateral view of the braincase with the endocast in place. Labeled parts of the endocast are according to the interpretation of Marsh. The true dorsum sellae of the braincase is indicated. B. Lateral view of the endocast indicating the revised interpretation of parts. Note the corrected position of the pituitary fossa. Restored portions are indicated by broken lines. C. Dorsal view indicating the revised interpretation of parts. The transverse diameter of the endocast is probably too small. cart, Filling of the space for the cartilaginous portion of the supraoccipital; cbl, cerebellar region; "cbl", cerebellar region according to Marsh, probably part of the medulla oblongata; cer, cerebrum; dor sel, dorsum sellae; olf, olfactory bulb; "opt", optic lobe of Marsh; pit, pituitary fossa; "pit", pituitary fossa according to Marsh, probably an unossified zone in the basicranium; vcm, middle cerebral vein; vcp, diverticulum of the longitudinal sinus; II, optic nerve; "II", optic nerve of Marsh; III?, probable oculomotor nerve; V, restored root of the trigeminal nerve; VI?, probable position of canal for abducens nerve; VII, restored root of the facial nerve; IX, X, restored foramen of the glossopharyngeal and vagus nerves; XII, restored roots of the hypoglossal nerve.

The stegosaur endocast indicates that the brain was long and relatively low with moderate cerebral and pontine flexures (the absence of flexure in the endocast of *Stegosaurus ungulatus* is probably incorrect). The olfactory bulbs (preserved only in *S. armatus*) are extraordinarily broad with short peduncles tapering gradually backward into the narrow cerebral hemispheres. The cerebrum and cerebellar region are very narrow in *S. armatus*; comparison with the dorsal view of the *S. ungulatus* endocast suggests that the unusual narrowness is unnatural. The cerebrum is hardly wider than the medulla and does not rise above the level of the olfactory bulbs and cerebellar region. The optic nerves passed out midventrally below the cerebrum and the oculomotor nerves slightly posterolaterally to them. The anterior wall of the pituitary fossa is not preserved in *S. armatus* (it is in *Kentrosaurus*) but, as noted above, the position of the pituitary body is indicated by the positions of the dorsum sellae and the foramina for the oculomotor nerves.

The cerebellar region appears to lie at about the same vertical level as the cerebrum. This area is identified by Marsh as representing the optic tectum, but the tectum would have lain further anteriorly, approximately above the dorsum sellae as in other reptiles. On the lateral surface of the cerebellar region of the endocast is an oblique ridge which must represent the groove on the braincase for the vena cerebralis media. The curved posterior continuation of this ridge probably represents an unossified gap between the supraoccipital and the otic capsule.

The medulla oblongata is long and widens posteriorly to about the same breadth as the forebrain. The probable locations of cranial nerves V through XII are indicated in Fig. 20B. Probable nervous or sensory structures figured in dorsal view (Fig. 20C) cannot be identified with certainty; from their positions they seem to be, from front to back, the facial nerve, a portion of the inner ear cavity, and the common canal for cranial nerves IX and X. A rounded bulge on the lateral surface of the medulla probably represents the depression for a diverticulum of the longitudinal venous sinus.

e. *Suborder Ankylosauria.* The suborder Ankylosauria is an isolated group within the Ornithischia without close affinities to any other suborder. With the exception of the possible ankylosaur *Scelidosaurus* of the Early Jurassic of England, the ankylosaurs are a strictly Cretaceous group. They were covered with a carapace of dermal armor and the tail was terminated by a mass of bone believed to have served as a bludgeon. Endocasts are known from two Late Cretaceous species: the European acanthopholid *Struthiosaurus transsylvanicus*, described by Nopsca (1929), and the North American nodosaurid *Euoplocephalus* ("*Ankylosaurus*"), described by Coombs (in press). The specimen (A.M.N.H. 5337) on which Coombs' description is based is redescribed here.

The endocast of *Struthiosaurus* is illustrated in dorsal and lateral views

(Nopsca 1929, Fig. 1c and Pl. 4, Figs 5, 6) but all figures are poor and show only the grosser features of the specimen. As with the smaller pachycephalosaurs, the endocast of *Struthiosaurus* is more compact and provides a better indication of brain morphology than does that of the much larger *Euoplocephalus*. The cerebral hemispheres appear relatively broader and the cerebellar region higher and more distinct than in *Euoplocephalus*. The orientation of the specimen relative to a horizontal axis is not possible, but if it is oriented like that of *Stegoceras*, with the dorsal surfaces of the cerebral and cerebellar regions at about the same level, then the medulla is oriented posteroventrally at an angle of about 20 degrees. On the dorsal midline, above the cerebellar region, is an ovoid protuberance identified by Nopsca as the epiphysis. However, this structure, and a similar feature on the endocast of *Euoplocephalus*, are probably not part of the brain (see below). The olfactory tracts are very short and broad and the large olfactory bulbs appear to be directly joined to the front of the cerebrum.

The endocast of *Euoplocephalus* (Fig. 21) is more elongate than that of *Struthiosaurus* and the forebrain and cerebellar regions are not so distinctly differentiated from the brainstem. Using the horizontal semicircular canal as a guide, the forebrain and medulla are oriented horizontally and the cerebral and pontine flexures are approximately 30 degrees.

The cast of the olfactory tracts is broadly joined to the cerebrum, with the short peduncles diverging at nearly 45 degrees from the sagittal plane. The tracts broaden slightly distally, but the exact location of the bulbs is uncertain; in all likelihood they are represented by the anterior expansions of the tracts.

The cerebrum appears to be short and broad, though its maximum width is hardly greater than that of the anterior part of the medullary region. In lateral view the cerebral region tapers slightly anteriorly and shows a slight drop in height posteriorly.

The optic nerves diverge almost directly laterally, extending slightly forward and downward. The trochlear nerve is represented by a slender process behind and slightly above the optic nerves. The oculomotor nerve presumably passed laterally from the cranial cavity below the IVth nerve through the large fenestra metoptica. The anterior portion of the VIth nerve also left the braincase through this foramen after passing through the dorsum sellae.

The cast of the pituitary fossa is directed slightly anteriorly to the vertical. It is anteroposteriorly compressed and very wide transversely. Three processes extend outward from its lateral surface; the lowest of these represents the canal for the internal carotid, the other two probably also represent vascular canals but their identification is uncertain. The small dorsal canal lying just in front of the large fenestra metoptica may be for

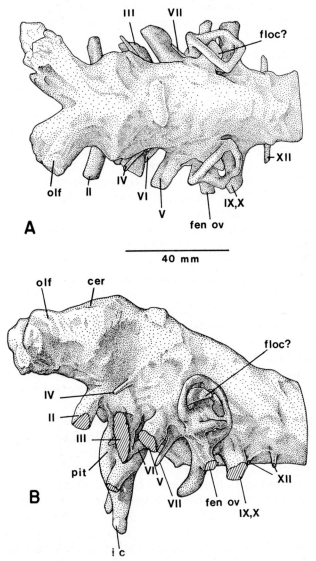

Fɪɢ. 21. Endocast of *Euoplocephalus tutus*, A.M.N.H. 5337. A. Dorsal view. B. Lateral view, cer, Cerebrum; fen ov, fenestra ovalis; floc?, possible flocculus; ic, internal carotid artery; olf, probable olfactory bulb; pit, pituitary fossa; II, optic nerve; III, foramen for the oculomotor and abducens nerves (fenestra metoptica); IV, trochlear nerve; V, trigeminal nerve; VI, canal for the abducens nerve; VII, facial nerve; IX, X, foramen for the glosso-pharyngeal and vagus nerves; XII, hypoglossal nerve.

the ophthalmic branch of the internal carotid. Coombs (in press) identifies it as the canal for the median palatine artery and the larger middle one for the palatine artery.

On the dorsal surface, above the midbrain or cerebellum, is a transversely elongated, raised area resembling the process in *Styracosaurus* which Nopcsa (1929) identified as the epiphysis. The brain in this region was undoubtedly overlain by the longitudinal venous sinus and therefore this feature probably does not represent part of the brain. Possibly, it represents a diverticulum of the sinus or, less likely, the unossified area of the supraoccipital which was filled in life by cartilage (it may lie too far forward on the skull to represent part of the supraoccipital). Behind the raised area the broadly rounded cerebellar region drops in a gently convex curve to the roof of the medulla. In dorsal view it narrows posteriorly between the inner ear cavities.

The Vth through Xth cranial nerves occupy an unusually short longitudinal segment of the endocast when compared with endocasts of other ornithischians. The root of the Vth nerve is undivided on the cast. The small VIIth nerve lies closely against it posteroventral border. On the undersurface of the cast, the VIth nerves pass anterolaterally and slightly dorsally to join the common opening with the IIIrd nerve.

The inner ear is completely represented in the endocast, including an elongate anteroventromedially curving lagena. Between the anterior vertical semicircular canal and the crus communis is an elongate, dorsoventrally flattened process which is directed posterolaterally. Its similarity to the floccular lobe of therapsids and of theropods suggests that it may represent this structure.

The portion of the cast containing the medulla oblongata is moderately elongated behind the inner ear. It is slightly higher than wide and increases in breadth only slightly toward the foramen magnum. The large canal for the glossopharyngeal and vagus nerves lies closely behind the inner ear. Ventromedial to it are two small processes and behind these a third larger process, all of which are identified here as representing roots of the hypoglossal nerve. High on the lateral surface of the medulla above the last hypoglossal root is a low, rounded process which I believe represents a diverticulum of the longitudinal venous sinus, similar to that seen in crocodilians.

f. *Suborder Ceratopsia.* Ceratopsians are among the most distinctive and familiar of dinosaurs, characterized by the presence of a large, frill-like outgrowth of the skull overlying the neck and, in all but a few genera, by one or more horns on the face. They are entirely a Late Cretaceous group and, thus, the last suborder of ornithischians to appear. Endocasts have been described for three genera: *Protoceratops* (Brown and Schlaikjer, 1940), *Anchiceratops* (Brown, 1914), and *Triceratops* (Marsh, 1890, 1891, 1896;

Hatcher *et al.*, 1907; Hay, 1909). The first of these, a small primitive form, is placed in the family Protoceratopsidae; the others, larger and advanced forms, are placed in the Ceratopsidae.

The endocast of *Protoceratops grangeri* (Fig. 22) is much the smallest of described ceratopsian endocasts and that of *Triceratops sulcatus* the largest. Correlated with the size differences, the cerebral and pontine flexures are greatest in *Protoceratops* (approximately 40 degrees from the horizontal),

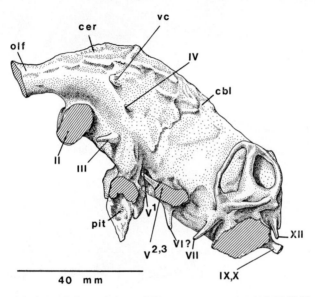

FIG. 22. Lateral view of the endocast of *Protoceratops grangeri*, A.M.N.H. 6466. cbl, Cerebellar region; cer, cerebrum; olf, olfactory peduncle (position of bulb uncertain); pit, pituitary fossa; vc, minor vascular canal; II, optic nerve; III, oculomotor nerve; IV trochlear nerve; V^1, ophthalmic branch of the trigeminal nerve; $V^{2,3}$, maxillary and mandibular branches of the trigeminal nerve; VI?, possible canal for the abducens nerve; VII, facial nerve; IX, X, foramen for the glossopharyngeal and vagus nerves; XII, hypoglossal nerve.

intermediate in *Anchiceratops* (about 30 degrees), and least in *Triceratops* (about 20 degrees). The medulla and forebrain are oriented horizontally in all three. In none of the genera does the endocast provide a good representation of the morphology of the brain. In *Protoceratops* and *Triceratops* the endocast has a swollen appearance with no clear distinction between cerebral, midbrain, and cerebellar regions. The anterior portion of the *Anchiceratops* cast (Fig. 23) is abnormally flattened dorsoventrally because it was made from a partially crushed skull; therefore the extraordinarily small size of the forebrain in this specimen is an artifact of preservation.

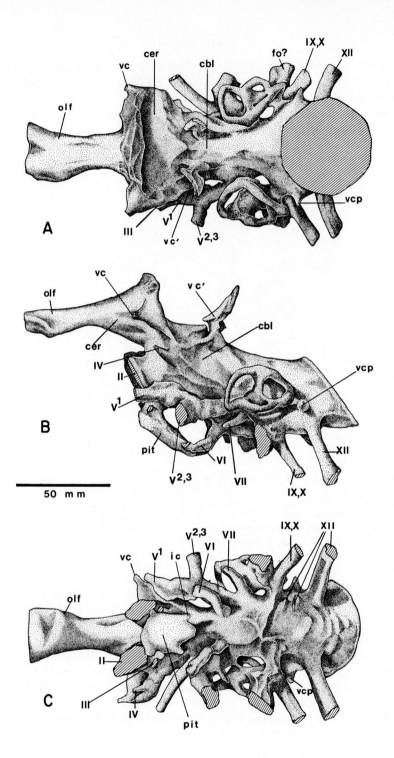

A

B

50 mm

C

The cerebral region of ceratopsians tapers anteriorly into elongate olfactory peduncles. The position of the olfactory bulbs is not clearly indicated in any specimen, but they are probably represented by the distal expansion of the tracts in *Anchiceratops* and in Marsh's figure of *Triceratops serratus* (1896, Pl. 61, Fig. 7). The cerebrum is moderately broad, but its shape and posterior limits are not clearly demarcated. It is dorsoventrally relatively shallow. The dorsal surface of this part of the *Protoceratops* endocast is rugose and the midline suture of the frontals and dorsolateral ridges marking the frontal-laterosphenoid suture are comparable to what is seen in *Caiman* (see Fig. 1). Laterally directed processes high on the sides of the cerebral region in all three genera represent vascular foramina.

The optic foramina of *Protoceratops* are confluent (Brown and Schlaikjer, 1940), as are those of crocodilians; in the two ceratopsid genera they lie far apart and are separated by a bony partition. The oculomotor nerves are represented by small processes behind the optic nerves in *Protoceratops*, and by somewhat larger processes posteroventral to the optic nerves in the two ceratopsids. The trochlear nerve lay behind the upper border of the optic nerves in all three genera.

The cast of the pituitary fossa is oriented vertically in *Protoceratops* and, as preserved, is not expanded transversely. In the other genera the pituitary cast has a short, cylindrical, anteroventrally directed infundibular portion and a transversely widened distal portion which is elongated posteroventrally. Carotid canals pass down and back from the pituitary cast and a pair of smaller processes passes anterolaterally from the region of the flexion. The latter are identified by Hay (1909) and Brown (1914) as representing the opthalmic branch of the internal carotid artery. In *Protoceratops* the cast indicates a large lateral opening into the pituitary fossa which appears to correspond to a much smaller opening in *Anchiceratops* (but not in *Triceratops*). A comparable opening in hadrosaurs is described by Ostrom (1961) as transmitting the abducens nerve from the region of the pituitary fossa.

In all three genera the endocast slopes posteroventrally from the cerebral

---

FIG. 23. Endocast of *Anchiceratops ornatus* A.M.N.H., 5259. Note that the cerebral region has been dorsoventrally crushed. A. Dorsal view. B. Lateral view. C. Ventral view. cbl, Cerebellar region; cer, cerebrum; fo?, fenestra ovalis?; ic, internal carotid artery; olf, olfactory bulb; pit, pituitary fossa; vc, minor vascular canal; vc′, branch of longitudinal sinus; vcp, diverticulum of longitudinal sinus; II, optic nerve; III, oculomotor nerve; IV, trochlear nerve; V¹, ophthalmic branch of the trigeminal nerve; V²,³, maxillary and mandibular branches of the trigeminal nerve; VI, abducens nerve; VII, facial nerve; IX, X, foramen for the glossopharyngeal and vagus nerves; XII, roots of the hypoglossal nerve.

region without providing a clear indication of the position of the optic tectum or cerebellum. In dorsal view the area posterior to the cerebral region is nearly as wide as the cerebral region but it becomes narrower as it passes down and back between the inner ears. In the two ceratopsids, the dorsolateral surface of the sloping cerebellar region bears paired postero-dorsally directed processes such as also occur in *Tyrannosaurus*. Comparison with *Caiman* (Figs 1, 2c) indicates that they represent canals for branches of the longitudinal venous sinus passing up into the skull roof. Previous identifications of these structures as processes of the cerebellum (Hay, 1909) or as the epiphysis (Case, 1921) are untenable. Brown (1914) notes that these processes in *Anchiceratops* lie in the suture between the parietal and adjacent bones and suggests that they probably transmit veins. Such processes are only weakly indicated in *Protoceratops* on what appears to be the suture of the parietal with the supraoccipital or prootic.

In all three genera, the cast of the trigeminal foramen has a distinct ophthalmic branch which passes anterodorsally within a channel covered laterally by a bar of the laterosphenoid, as in crocodilians and many other archosaurs. Medial to the trigeminal root, the posterior part of the canal for the abducens nerve passes forward and outward in the two ceratopsids. In *Protoceratops*, the processes identified by Brown and Schlaikjer (1940) as the abducens canals lie very close to the trigeminal roots and pass directly downward and slightly outward. This is an unusual direction for the proximal part of the VIth nerve canal and the structures may be misidenti-fied; however, what else they might represent is not known.

The facial nerve lies well behind the trigeminal nerve in *Protoceratops*, closer to the nerve in the ceratopsids. In *Anchiceratops*, two small canals pass posterolaterally into the inner ear cast on the right side. Figure 23 shows only the posterior one, because the anterior one is hidden by the root of nerve VII. Brown (1914) believes that these canals transmit veins but it is more likely they carry two rami of the stato-acoustic nerve.

The medulla oblongata is very short in *Protoceratops* and nearly circular in cross-section. In the ceratopsids it is somewhat longer and a transversely elongate oval in section. The canal for cranial nerves IX and X passes posteroventrally from the rear of the inner ear cast in all three genera.

The hypoglossal nerve has two roots in all specimens, a more anteromedial root and a more posterolateral one. They are small processes in *Proto-ceratops* but are very large in the ceratopsids. Dorsal to the anterior root, on the lateral surface of the medulla, is a pointed process representing a diverti-culum of the longitudinal venous sinus. This process is prominent in the two ceratopsids but is not identifiable with certainty on the abbreviated medulla of *Protoceratops*.

E. Subclass Euryapsida (Synaptosauria)

1. Order Sauropterygia

a. *Suborder Nothosauria.* Nothosaurs are amphibious marine reptiles of the Triassic, possibly ancestral to plesiosaurs, but with limbs not modified to form specialized paddles. The skulls of nothosaurs are very flat and the temporal region long. Endocasts of the genus *Nothosaurus* have been described by Koken (1890, 1893), Edinger (1921; Fig. 24) and Gorce (1960). Despite the availability of well-preserved material, a number of

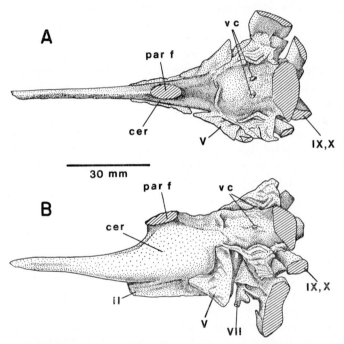

FIG. 24. Endocast of *Nothosaurus mirabilis* (redrawn from Edinger, 1921). A. Dorsal view. B. Lateral and slightly dorsal view. cer, Probable cerebral region; par f, parietal foramen; vc, venous canals from longitudinal sinus; II, optic foramen; V, foramen for the trigeminal nerve; VII, facial nerve; IX, X, foramen for the glossopharyngeal and vagus nerves.

unusual features of the nothosaur endocast cannot be fully understood on the basis of the available descriptions and figures.

Correlated with the extreme length and flatness of the temporal region, the endocast of *Nothosaurus* is straight, without noticeable flexure, and shows extremely long olfactory tracts. There is a well-ossified sphenethmoid and the brain is enclosed in bone along its entire length. The cast of the olfactory tracts is very long and thin, oval in cross-section, deeper than broad, and without division into left and right tracts. Edinger (1921) describes an oval cavity between the orbits and interprets this as having housed the olfactory bulbs.

The olfactory tracts gradually widen posteriorly to merge without a break into the region of the cerebrum. The roof of the cavity rises from the level of the olfactory tracts to the anterior border of the parietal foramen. The space below the parietal foramen, which presumably housed the cerebrum, is extraordinarily narrow in all described specimens. It increases only slightly in width back to the level at which the trigeminal nerves leave the endocast. This space included the midbrain toward its posterior end. Behind this transversely narrow region, the hindbrain area is slightly wider than the point anterior to the trigeminal nerves. The optic nerves are described by Edinger as small, anteriorly directed processes beneath the forebrain. The optic nerves must have been extremely long and compressed toward the midline for much of their length because the orbits lay far in front of the optic foramina. Koken describes paired processes, oval in section and of very large size, as the optic nerves. These processes increase in size posteriorly and extend back close to the midline below the trigeminal nerves. It is doubtful that these structures are related to the optic nerves. As discussed below, it is more likely that they represent vascular canals associated with the basicranium and the pituitary fossa.

The parietal opening is a large anteroposteriorly elongated oval in all specimens. In the German specimens described by Koken and Edinger it lies anterior to the level of the trigeminal root; in the Tunisian specimen described by Gorce it lies directly above the nerve root.

The nature of the pituitary fossa is unclear. Koken considers it to be absent. Edinger (1921) identified a roughened midventral area on the endocast as possibly representing an elongated, flattened hypophyseal fossa, but she later (Edinger, 1975, p. 48) retracted this identification. Gorce (1960, Pl. II, Fig. 2) illustrates a cross-section of a nothosaur endocast at the level of the anterior semicircular canal. This shows a midventral cavity, the "cavité hypophysaire," separated by a thin transverse lamina of bone from the floor of the cranial cavity and completely subdivided by a thin midline septum. On a more complete specimen, Gorce describes the pituitary fossa as exposed in a more anterior position on the braincase, but still subdivided by the median septum. She also notes that paired canals of rather large diameter (identified as for the internal carotids) enter this cavity ventrally and rather anteriorly.

The above evidence would suggest that the pituitary fossa of *Nothosaurus* is elongate parallel to the long axis of the skull and is at least partly subdivided by a median vertical septum. Gorce's material shows large carotid canals entering this region from a ventrolateral direction and Koken's specimen indicates that very large paired canals passed backward from the pituitary fossa in the floor of the cranial cavity beneath the medulla (these canals are also indicated in Edinger's specimen but misidentified as jugular ganglia). The latter channels may represent the course of the basilar artery (see Russell, 1967, for mosasaurs). Indeed, only a relatively small fraction of the pituitary fossa may have been filled by the pituitary (cf. that of lizards and *Sphenodon* described by Säve-Söderbergh, 1946).

The exit of the trigeminal nerve on all specimens is indicated by a large, vertically elongate process which represents the prootic fenestra between the sphenethmoid and prootic ossifications similar to the condition seen in *Diadectes* and pareiasaurs (see Section IVB1). The upper part of the opening was undoubtedly closed in life by membrane and the nerve foramen lay in its lower half.

The cranial cavity widens markedly behind the level of the trigeminal foramen, and the hindbrain has parallel sides back to the foramen magnum. The roof of the hindbrain region is flat and horizontal, providing no evidence of the position or size of the cerebellum. A transverse crest above the fifth nerve and, more posteriorly, one or two pairs of small rounded elevations on the dorsal surface of the endocast (seen in Koken's and Edinger's material) were identified by Edinger (1921) as possibly representing roots of the trochlear nerve; she later (1975, p. 48) abandoned this opinion, considering the structures to be of non-neural origin. Most likely, these features represent short diverticula of the longitudinal venous sinus into the cranial roof, similar to those seen in crocodilians.

The root of the facial nerve passes ventrolaterally and gives off antero-ventral and posteroventral branches, presumably palatine and hyomandi-bular rami bifurcating within the cranial wall. The inner ear cavity is partially represented in Edinger's specimen but is beautifully preserved, though not adequately illustrated, in the Tunisian material described by Gorce (1960). The foramen for cranial nerves IX and X is very large and lies entirely behind the inner ear cavity, very close to the posterior end of the medulla. Hypoglossal foramina are not preserved on any of the specimens.

The endocast of *Nothosaurus* is characterized by its straight long axis greatly elongate, laterally compressed olfactory tracts, and extraordinarily narrow forebrain.

b. *Suborder Plesiosauria.* The only endocast of a plesiosaur is a wax cast modelled from isolated cranial elements of the elasmosaurid *Brancasaurus* from the Early Cretaceous of Europe (skull described by Wegner, 1914). The cast was originally figured by Edinger (1928, 1929) as "*Plesiosaurus* sp.", but was later correctly identified (Edinger, 1930). Edinger does not provide a description of the specimen as it shows little useful detail. Only the hindbrain, inner ear cavity, and pituitary fossa are indicated. In Edinger's figure, the foramen magnum is indicated by the left hand end of a metal pin. When the horizontal semi-circular canal is oriented horizontally, the floor of the medulla slopes slightly downward and forward. It rises anteriorly to the region of the pituitary. The cast of the pituitary fossa is a short finger-like projection. The canal for the VIth nerve, the foramen for nerves IX and X, and two roots of the XIIth nerve are indicated on the cast.

The parietal foramen of plesiosaurs lies far forward on the cranial roof, between the postorbital bars. This contrasts with the condition in nothosaurs in which the parietal foramen usually lies well back on the cranial roof. This difference implies a difference in relative proportions of the parts of the brain. The entire brain behind the olfactory tracts in *Nothosaurus* is comparatively short. In plesiosaurs it appears that the brain was much more elongated.

2. Order Placodontia

Placodonts were marine euryapsids of Triassic age with postcranial morphology not unlike that of nothosaurs but with large, flat teeth adapted for crushing molluscs. Edinger (1925) describes a partial natural endocast and an artificial endocast of *Placodus gigas*. The olfactory region and the ventral portion of the fore- and midbrain, including the pituitary fossa, are not preserved on either specimen. Figure 25 is a composite.

The endocast of *Placodus*, unlike that of *Nothosaurus*, has pronounced cephalic and pontine flexures. Its width from forebrain to medulla is approximately uniform. An anterior braincase ossification is lacking in placodonts, and the olfactory bulbs and tracts are unknown. The dorsal region of the cerebrum leaves an elongate oval impression in the cranial roof, in the center of which lies a large oval parietal foramen. The sides and undersurface of the forebrain are not preserved. Behind the parietal foramen, the dorsal surface of the cast slopes posteroventrally. A portion of the sloping roof is not preserved but it appears to have been convexly rounded. Edinger (1925, Fig. 1B) restores a distinct swelling here into which she believes the optic tectum extended. The foramina for cranial nerves II, III, IV, and VI are not represented on the endocast. Edinger identifies a process on the dorsolateral surface of the hindbrain as the root of the trochlear nerve; actually this is a cast of the groove and foramen for the vena cerebralis media (see Janensch, 1936).

No remnant of the pituitary fossa is preserved on either endocast, and Edinger omits it from her reconstruction of the brain. Its position and size can be restored on the basis of the figured braincase (Edinger, 1925, Fig. 1A). The dorsum sellae is high and steeply sloping, and the internal carotid foramina open on to the dorsal surface of the basisphenoid (i.e. the floor of the pituitary fossa) at about the same horizontal level as the ventral surface of the medulla. These features indicate that the pituitary fossa was

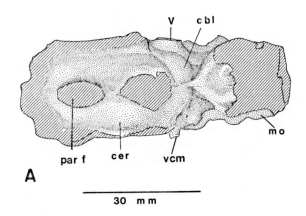

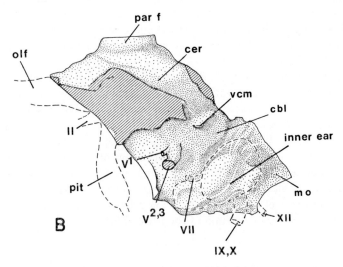

FIG. 25. Composite endocast of *Placodus gigas*, based on an artificial endocast, S.M. R359, with details added from a partial natural endocast, S.M. R4038 (modified from Edinger, 1925). A. Dorsal view. B. Lateral view. Restored parts are indicated by broken lines; damaged surfaces are indicated by diagonal lines. cbl, Cerebellar region; cer, cerebrum; mo, medulla oblongata; olf, restored olfactory peduncle; par f, parietal foramen; pit, restored pituitary fossa; vcm, middle cerebral vein; II, optic nerve; V, trigeminal nerve; V^1, ophthalmic branch of the trigeminal nerve; $V^{2,3}$, maxillary and mandibular branches of the trigeminal nerve; VII, restored facial nerve; IX, X, restored foramen of the glosso-pharyngeal and vagus nerves; XII, restored hypoglossal nerve.

large, but in the absence of bony anterior and lateral walls, its exact size cannot be determined.

The short hindbrain is oriented horizontally in the skull. A low swelling above and behind the trigeminal root is identified by Edinger as overlying the cerebellum. On the lateral surface of the swelling is a short ridge oriented obliquely down and forward toward the trigeminal root, which represents the groove on the inner surface of the prootic for the middle cerebral vein. In the natural endocast, the lower part of the ridge is drawn out to form a process presumably representing a foramen for the entrance of the vein into the cranial cavity. The large root of the trigeminal nerve is sub-divided on the natural cast into a small anteroventrally directed ophthalmic ramus and a larger, more ventrally directed, ramus for the second and third branches of the nerve. A small facial nerve root is preserved on this specimen.

The cast of the medullary region is slightly higher than wide. It is constricted dorsolaterally between the inner ear cavities. The inner ear cavity, including the semicircular canals, is represented on the natural cast but details are not clear on Edinger's figures. A large jugular canal passes ventrolaterally from behind the inner ear and a single pair of small processes on the ventrolateral surface shortly in front of the foramen magnum represents the hypoglossal foramina.

The subclass Euryapsida is represented by adequate endocasts of only two genera, so that generalizations about the euryapsid brain are impossible. The endocast of *Placodus* differs markedly from that of *Nothosaurus* and resembles endocasts of sauropod dinosaurs in its general compactness and degree of flexure. The differences in morphology can be correlated with differences in skull shape; the temporal region of *Nothosaurus* is very flat and elongated and that of *Placodus* is deep and relatively short. Although the endocast of plesiosaurs is for practical purposes unknown, it appears to differ from that of nothosaurs in being relatively longer, as indicated by the much more anterior position of the parietal foramen.

F. Subclass Synapsida

1. *General*

The Synapsida are the mammal-like reptiles, a very ancient group which split off from the ancestry of the modern reptiles and birds soon after the time of origin of the class Reptilia. The earliest synapsids are of Early Pennsylvanian age, only slightly younger than the oldest known reptiles (Carroll, 1969a). The subclass Synapsida is divided into two orders: the Pelycosauria (Early Pennsylvanian to Middle Permian) representing a primitive grade; and the Therapsida (Middle Permian to Middle Jurassic) representing an advanced, more mammal-like, grade. Advanced members of the latter order gave rise to the class Mammalia in the Late Triassic.

2. Order Pelycosauria

Pelycosaurs are, for the most part, very primitive reptiles which, except for the presence of a lateral temporal opening, show few features which would link them to the ancestry of mammals. Romer and Price (1940) recognize three suborders of pelycosaurs: the primitive carnivorous Ophiacodontia; the advanced herbivorous Edaphosauria; and the advanced carnivorous Sphenacodontia. The latter are of particular interest as they gave rise to the therapsids and, through them, the mammals.

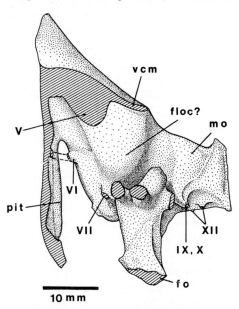

10 mm

FIG. 26. Endocast of the posterior part of the cranial cavity of *Dimetrodon incisivus*, U.M. 22201. floc?, Possible flocculus; fo, fenestra ovalis; mo, medulla oblongata; pit, pituitary fossa; vcm, notch for the middle cerebral vein; V, notch for the trigeminal nerve; VI, canal for the abducens nerve; VII, facial nerve; IX, X, foramen for glossopharyngeal and vagus nerves; XII, hypoglossal nerve.

The only described endocast of a pelycosaur is from the large, predaceous, sailbacked sphenacodontid, *Dimetrodon* (Case, 1897, 1907) of the Early Permian. The cranial cavity of *Dimetrodon* has an unossified gap between the prootic-basisphenoid region and a sphenethmoid in the interorbital region. Consequently, the endocast extends only as far forward as the pituitary fossa (Fig. 26).

The cast of the posterior part of the cranial cavity of *Dimetrodon*, taken in conjunction with the configuration of the cranial roof and the sphenethmoid, provides a generalized picture of the shape of the brain. It was probably a tubular structure lacking major expansions and was flexed about 50 degrees from the horizontally oriented medulla. The degree of flexure correlates with the extremely short postorbital length of the skull. The sphenethmoid encloses two pairs of canals that merge within the bone and open posteriorly via a single median foramen. Romer and Price (1940) believe that these canals pass two branches of the olfactory nerve and that the olfactory bulbs lie posterior to the sphenethmoid. Because primitive therapsids possess elongated olfactory tracts (see below), it is more likely that elongated olfactory peduncles occupied one pair of canals in the sphenethmoid and that the olfactory bulbs lay either in the anterior part of the sphenethmoid or entirely in front of it.

The cerebrum of *Dimetrodon* lay below the parietals in the unossified gap between sphenethmoid and prootic. Longitudinal ridges on the under-surface of the parietals probably mark the location of the sidewall of the forebrain region, indicating that the space enclosing the cerebrum was quite narrow. A well-developed parietal foramen overlay the cerebrum. The braincase slopes steeply down and back behind the parietals, and the region from Case's (1897, 1907) endocast shows this level back to the foramen magnum.

The dorsum sellae of *Dimetrodon* is a high, near-vertical transverse plate between two robust antotic pillars. The pituitary foramen lacks side and anterior walls. The cast of the posterior part of the pituitary body is a long, narrow, near-vertical process. The trigeminal nerve left the braincase via a broad semicircular notch at the level of the top of the dorsum sellae. Behind it is a slit-like notch which presumably transmitted a vein, which entered the dorsal venous sinus. The facial nerve root lies well ventral to and slightly behind the trigeminal notch on the anterior rim of the vestibular cavity. The abducens nerve passed directly forward through the dorsum sellae to exit just lateral to the infundibulum.

The inner ear cavity is widely open medially. It lies partially below the level of the floor of the cranial cavity, as is usual in synapsids. Above the inner ear cavity and posterior to the trigeminal notch, the side of the cast forms a broadly rounded swelling which Romer and Price (1940) consider to be "equivalent to the deeper one which in therapsids is interpreted as the subarcuate [floccular] fossa" (p. 71). The cerebellum presumably lay between these fossae, housing bluntly rounded floccular lobes. At the level of the posterior border of the floccular swellings, the roof of the sloping cranial cavity shows an abrupt drop downward. Behind this step, the roof gradually curves smoothly to a horizontal orientation at the level of the foramen magnum. The medullary region is roughly triangular in cross-section. Its broad floor is subdivided by a prominent longitudinal groove. The canal of the IXth and Xth cranial nerves lies low on the medulla behind the inner ear cavity. Ventromedial to it is a tiny hypoglossal root and behind this a larger one.

Evidence relating to the brain in other pelycosaurs is extremely limited. *Edaphosaurus* possesses a parietal foramen which is relatively large compared with that of sphenacodonts, but that of caseids is much larger still (Romer and Price, 1940).

3. *Order Therapsida*

The therapsids are an extremely diverse group of reptiles which include numerous highly specialized and aberrant herbivorous types as well as carnivorous types which approach the mammals in general appearance. The order is currently divided into three suborders by Romer (1966): Phthino-suchia, for poorly known, early forms which closely resemble sphenacodont pelycosaurs; Anomodontia, for specialized, mainly herbivorous types—dinocephalians and dicynodonts; and Theriodontia, specialized, mainly carnivorous types which include the ancestors of mammals. Endocasts are known only for anomodonts and theriodonts. In general, the orbitotemporal region of the therapsid braincase is not ossified, so that endocasts represent only the region behind the pituitary fossa.

a. *Suborder Anomodontia.* The Anomodontia consists of two principal groups: the infraorder Dinocephalia of Middle Permian time and the infra-order Dicynodontia of Mid-Permian to Late Triassic time. Dinocephalians were usually large, bulky creatures in which the bone of the temporal roof is enormously thickened and the skull is adapted for head-butting behavior (Barghusen, 1975). Dicynodonts were extraordinarily diverse in size and shape, but all had a turtle-like beak and in most the dentition consists of a pair of tusk-like upper canines.

(i) Infraorder Dinocephalia. Boonstra (1968) describes the braincases of a large number of South African dinocephalians, principally from serially sectioned skulls, and presents reconstructions of the cranial cavities of six genera. All conform to a single pattern, so only two are illustrated in Fig. 27.

The heads of dinocephalians were held at a high angle to the long axis of the neck so that the facial region was turned downward if the neck is oriented nearly horizontally. In this orientation, the medulla is essentially horizontal and the forebrain turns somewhat downward. The dinocephalian braincase is more completely ossified than is usual in therapsids so the endocast is unusually complete. It is elongate and tubular, with a moderate expansion below the parietal foramen, in the presumed region of the posterior part of the cerebrum, and a constriction between the inner ear cavities.

Separate short, broad olfactory tracts lie within the sphenethmoid; these widen anteriorly into expanded olfactory bulbs which lay largely in front of the ossified sphenethmoid and so are not preserved. The cerebral region

128 JAMES A. HOPSON

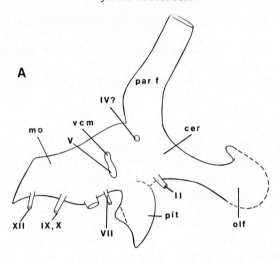

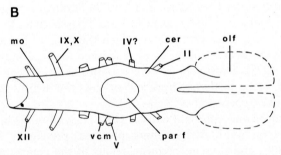

FIG. 27. Endocasts of dinocephalian therapsids. A, B. *Struthiocephalus whaitsi*, S.A.M. 12049. A. Lateral view. B. Dorsal view. C, D. *Jonkeria* sp., S.A.M. 11556. (All are redrawn from Boonstra.) cer, Cerebrum; mo, medulla oblongata; olf, olfactory bulb; par f, parietal tube and foramen; pit, pituitary fossa; vcm, foramen for the middle cerebral vein; II, optic nerve; IV?, trochlear or vascular foramen; V, trigeminal nerve; VII, facial nerve; IX, X, foramen for the glossopharyngeal and vagus nerves; XII, hypoglossal nerve.

is narrow and shallow anteriorly, but widens and deepens posteriorly. Above the cerebrum is a "truly enormous parietal canal or tube" (Boonstra, 1968, p. 207) which lies within the greatly thickened parietal bones.

The enormous parietal tube of dinocephalians has prompted a great deal of speculation as to its function. Edinger (1955) notes that the size of the parietal foramen in reptiles provides a reasonably accurate index of the

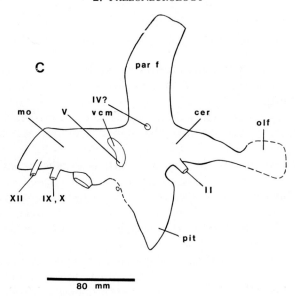

80 mm

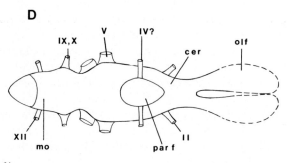

FIG. 27. (*contd.*)

size of the parietal organ, so that those extinct reptiles with a very large parietal foramen possessed a very large parietal eye. Brink (1963) and Boonstra (1968) suggest that the large parietal organ was a photoreceptor possessing a thermoregulatory function. Gundy *et al.* (1975) point out that the parietal eye of lizards plays a role in the synchronization of the normal reproductive cycle and in thermoregulation, and that lizards lacking a parietal eye tend to occur at low latitudes whereas high latitude lizards usually possess a parietal eye. In the Permian, South Africa lay at a very high southern latitude where a functional parietal eye in dinocephalians might have been an important factor in thermoregulation and regulating the reproductive cycle. The significance of the very large size of the parietal eye in dinocephalians (and certain other groups of Permian and Triassic reptiles) is still not explained.

The pituitary fossa of dinocephalians is very large; in some specimens its apparent size is increased due to incomplete ossification of the dorsum sellae (Boonstra, 1968).

The endocast turns slightly downward behind the forebrain region and narrows gradually into the more horizontal medullary region. Boonstra states that a slight bulge above the vestibule represents the flocculus.

The cranial nerves are, for the most part, as in other reptiles. A small foramen below the base of the parietal tube is designated as a trochlear foramen by Boonstra, but it appears to lie too high to have transmitted this nerve. It may be a vascular foramen. The trigeminal foramen is a vertically elongate slit which transmitted the trigeminal nerve through its lower part. The middle cerebral vein left the cranial cavity above the nerve.

(ii) Infraorder Dicynodontia. Because the dicynodont braincase is unossified between the sphenethmoid and the prootic-basisphenoid region, no complete endocasts are known. Olson (1944), Boonstra (1968) and Cluver (1971) provide reconstructions of the cranial cavity based on serial sections. An endocast of *Lystrosaurus* is figured by Edinger (1955).

The dicynodont endocast (Fig. 18) bears a superficial resemblance to that of lizards (see Fig. 8). The olfactory bulbs lay anterior to the sphenethmoid so that their size and shape are unknown. The olfactory peduncles pass back as separate slender tracts on either side of a median septum of the sphenethmoid. The anterior end of the cerebrum lay within the U-shaped posterior part of the sphenethmoid; the position of the optic nerves is sometimes indicated by a notch on the posterior edge of the bone (Cluver, 1971, Fig. 16). Above the cerebrum is a parietal tube of variable diameter and length (depending on the thickness of the parietals). The parietal foramen is large in *Lystrosaurus* and lies at the end of a relatively long tube. In other genera the foramen may be small and the tube short.

The midregion of the endocast slopes posteroventrally and the medullary region is horizontal. The unossified zone between parietals and supraoccipital is represented by a posterodorsal protuberance. The amount of flexure of the brain is directly related to the degree of shortening and deepening of the skull. *Dicynodon* (Fig. 28A) has a relatively long low skull and the endocast is flexed about 30 degrees from the horizontal; *Lystrosaurus* (Fig. 28B), with an extremely short, deep skull has a flexure of about 50 degrees.

The medullary region is short, and it is deeper than wide. A floccular fossa occurs in some dicynodonts, but it is absent or barely developed in others. The relative development of the flocculus of dicynodonts has been discussed by Olson (1944) and Cluver (1971). Olson (1944, pp. 37–38), in his study of the floccular fossa of Permian dicynodonts (and several therio-donts), considers the absence of a fossa to be primitive for therapsids, but he also believes that in the later history of therapsids, subsequent to the rapid development of a large floccular fossa, there was a secondary reduction

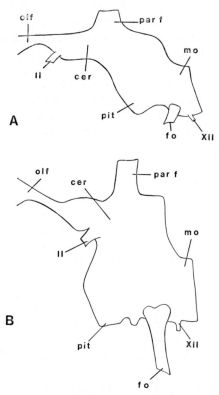

Fɪɢ. 28. Endocasts of dicynodont therapsids. A. Lateral view of *Dicynodon* sp., S.A.M. 10081 (from serial sections). B. Lateral view of *Lystrosaurus declivus*, S.A.M. K1284 (from serial sections). (Redrawn from Cluver, 1971.) Not to scale. cer, Cerebrum; fo, fenestra ovalis; mo, medulla oblongata; olf, olfactory bulb; par f, parietal foramen; pit, pituitary fossa; II, optic nerve; XII, hypoglossal nerve.

in its size. Cluver (1971, pp. 167–168) noted that a floccular fossa is present in the Early Triassic *Lystrosaurus* as a shallow depression and it is absent in several later Triassic genera. This, he believes, lends support to Olson's view that the fossa decreased in importance during dicynodont evolution.

I would point out that the depth of the floccular fossa and the size of the skull are negatively correlated in the dicynodonts; smaller skulls contain deeper fossae. Of Olson's two skulls with the deepest fossae, one ("Anomodont

B") is the smallest of his series, while the two skulls lacking fossae ("Anomo-donts A and D") are the largest. *Lystrosaurus*, with a shallow fossa, has a relatively large skull, and the later Triassic forms which lack a floccular fossa possess enormous skulls. These relationships would be expected from an allometric analysis, inasmuch as the size of the reptilian brain increases as the 2/3rds power of body size. Therefore, larger skulls contain relatively smaller brains and, consequently, more space between the brain and the cranial wall. I believe that the trend toward reduction in size of the floccular fossa in dicynodonts (though not necessarily in other therapsids) reflects nothing more than a trend toward phyletic increase in body size.

b. *Suborder Theriodontia.* Theriodonts fall into three distinct infraorders which represent increasingly mammal-like grades of evolution, the Gorgo-nopsia, the Therocephalia (including the Bauriamorpha of Romer, 1966) and the Cynodontia (including the Tritylodontia and Ictidosauria). Mammals are believed to have arisen from small insectivorous cynodonts (Hopson, 1969).

(i) Infraorder Gorgonopsia. Kemp (1969, Fig. 25B) describes the gor-gonopsian braincase in detail and attempts a reconstruction of the brain. The major landmarks in the braincase show that the brain is elongate, tubular, and nearly straight, with a long pituitary body and a well-developed parietal eye. The position and size of the olfactory bulbs cannot be deter-mined from available material; Kemp places the bulbs adjacent to the cerebrum, but it is equally likely that they lay far anteriorly, just behind the nasal capsule, with long peduncles joining them to the cerebrum. A broad depression in the orbitosphenoid below the parietal foramen probably held a moderately expanded posterolateral part of the cerebral hemispheres (and not the optic lobes as supposed by Kemp). The optic lobes probably lay behind this expanded region and above the trigeminal foramen. The hind-brain region is uniformly low along its entire length. The floccular fossa is deep in Kemp's specimens, as it is in two skulls sectioned by Olson (1944). The medullary region is long and only slightly flexed. The inner ear is widely open into the cranial cavity as is usual in therapsids.

(ii) Infraorder Therocephalia. Little evidence exists concerning the brain of therocephalians. Olson (1944) reconstructed the posterior part of the endocast for an unidentified pristerognathid. It is long and low, with a large flocculus.

(iii) Infraorder Cynodontia. The endocast of cynodonts has been well described and provides the best evidence on the brain of theriodonts. Watson (1913), Simpson (1933), and Hopson (1969) have figured and dis-cussed the superb natural endocast of the small Early Triassic galesaurid cynodont *Nythosaurus larvatus*. This species is extremely similar to *Thrinaxo-don liorhinus* and may be synonymous with it. *Thrinaxodon* is the best studied of all cynodonts and its dentition shows important similarities to that of early mammals (Hopson, 1969). Watson (1913) also describes a composite endocast of the somewhat more advanced Early Triassic *Diademodon* and Bonaparte (1966) describes an endocast of the very advanced *Exaeretodon* of the Late Triassic. Both of these genera belong to a major radiation of herbivorous cynodonts away from the line which led to mammals. A close relative and contemporary of *Diademodon* is *Trirachodon*, an endocast of which is described here. This herbivorous radiation culminated in the family Tritylodontidae; discussions of the endocranial cavity of tritylodontids are presented by Kühne (1956) for *Oligokyphus* and by Hopson (1964 and unpublished) for *Bienotherium*.

The endocasts of all cynodonts, including tritylodontids, are sufficiently stereotyped to need only a single description (Fig. 29). The endocast is long and tubular, as in other theriodonts, with the major regions not clearly demarcated. Some, but not all, cynodonts have an ossified orbitosphenoid (sphenethmoid). This element is lacking in *Thrinaxodon* and in the described specimen of *Trirachodon*, so that the floor of the braincase anterior to the pituitary fossa is unknown. The orbitosphenoid is present in advanced cynodonts such as *Exaeretodon* and tritylodontids in which it is ossified back to the prootic region, thus providing a complete floor to the brain.

Impressions of the paired olfactory bulbs, separated by a median sulcus, are visible on the underside of the frontals. These large ovoid structures appear to be joined directly to the front of the cerebrum, as they are in mammals. The bulbs are slightly broader than the cerebrum. In *Trirachodon* (Fig. 29B), the anteromedial portion of each bulb gives off what appears to be a short nerve trunk into the nasal cavity.

The cerebral region is elongated and relatively narrow. The small parietal foramen lies a short distance behind the middle of the cerebrum, the posterior border of which is perhaps indicated by a slight constriction of the sides of the cast. The midbrain probably lies in the region of the constriction, just in front of the trigeminal foramen.

The smooth area on the side of the *Trirachodon* endocast, below the posterior part of the cerebral region, is the inner surface of the expanded epipterygoid (= alisphenoid of mammals). This is not part of the cranial wall, for the cartilaginous orbitosphenoid lies medial to it. The ridge above the epipteryoid marks its contact with the parietal. The frontoparietal suture is marked on the cast of the cerebrum by a transverse ridge.

Posterior to the cerebral region the cast widens gradually and its roof rises into a large, bluntly rounded process, the cast of the cartilaginous anterior end of the supraoccipital. On each side of the posterior slope of this raised area there are, in *Trirachodon*, two low swellings which may be impressions of the lateral hemispheres of the cerebellum. The cranial cavity

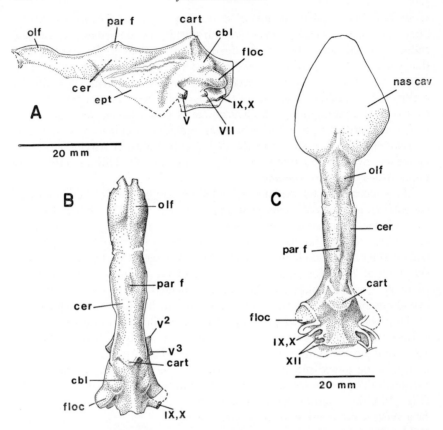

FIG. 29. Endocasts of cynodont therapsids. A, B. *Trirachodon kannemeyeri*, S.A.M. K4801. A. Lateral view. B. Dorsal view. C. Dorsal view of *Nythosaurus larvatus* (possibly identical to *Thrinaxodon liorhinus*), B.M. (N.H.) R1713. cart, Filling of the space for the cartilaginous portion of the supraoccipital; cbl, cerebellum; cer, cerebrum; ept, inner surface of the epipterygoid; floc, flocculus; nas cav, cast of the nasal cavity; olf, olfactory bulb; par f, parietal foramen; V, trigeminal nerve; V², maxillary branch of the trigeminal nerve; V³, mandibular branch of the trigeminal nerve; VII, facial nerve; IX, X, foramen for the glossopharyngeal and vagus nerves; XII, hypoglossal nerve.

is widest at this level. Very large floccular lobes extend posterolaterally and somewhat ventrally on either side of the cerebellar area.

The floor of the cranial cavity, preserved from the rear of the dorsum sellae (which is low in most cynodonts) to the foramen magnum, rises slightly and widens posteriorly. The inner ear cavity lies below the flocculus; its medial side is widely open into the cranial cavity which is the usual condition in all theriodonts except the tritylodontids. In the latter, the medial wall is ossified, leaving a depression, the internal auditory meatus, penetrated by the facial nerve anteroventrally and two branches of the stato-acoustic nerve dorsally and posteriorly. The large foramen for the IXth and Xth cranial nerves is confluent with the posterior part of the inner ear cavity. The *Nythosaurus* specimen possesses two hypoglossal roots.

The trigeminal nerve, indicated by the cast of the cavity for the trigeminal ganglion, lies low on the side of the brain. In most cynodonts there is a single trigeminal foramen. On the right side, of the *Trirachodon* endocast, as seen in dorsal view (Fig. 29B), the ganglion gives off two branches—the mandibular ramus (V^3) which passes from the skull in a posterolateral direction, and the maxillary ramus (V^2) which exits via a separate foramen in an anterolateral direction. The ophthalmic ramus (V^1) passed forward internal to the expanded epipterygoid without leaving an impression on the skull. The point of exit of the maxillary branch in cynodonts has been a source of disagreement. Simpson (1933) suggests that it left the skull anterior to the epipterygoid (= alisphenoid) as it usually does in mammals, whereas most specialists on therapsids, such as Watson (1913), believe it took the reptilian course and left via the foramen between the epipterygoid and prootic in company with V^3. In some advanced cynodonts there is a second foramen on the epipterygoid–prootic suture and Parrington (1946) has suggested that this was the exit of V^2. The braincase and endocast of *Trirachodon* show that this foramen opens medially into the hollow for the trigeminal ganglion, and thus strengthens Parrington's interpretation.

In *Exaeretodon* and *Bienotherium*, the orbitosphenoid is ossified back to the basisphenoid–prootic region to form a floor to the cerebrum. Ventro-medial optic foramina lie well forward of the pituitary fossa.

An outstanding aspect of the cynodont brain, as reflected in the endocast, is the extreme narrowness of the cerebrum, which contrasts strikingly with the expanded forebrain of their mammalian descendants. The prominent olfactory bulbs and well-developed cochlear portion of the inner ear support the view that cynodonts, like primitive living mammals, were dependent to a large degree on olfaction and audition for sensing their environment. Jerison (1973), among others, reasonably suggests that the ancestors of mammals were nocturnal creatures, as are the most primitive living mammals.

V. Conclusions

A. Comparative Studies of Relative Brain Size

The study of relative brain size in extinct reptiles has been provided with a sound methodological basis by Jerison (1969, 1973). However, in order to do comparative studies within major groups of reptiles it is necessary to refine Jerison's methods so that discriminations finer than those attempted by Jerison can be achieved. This requires better data about the relations of the volume of the brain to that of the cranial cavity (i.e. endo- cast) than are available at the present time. Such data can only be determined from the study of living species. In the case of fossil archosaurs, modern crocodilians are the only pertinent group from which to gather data on the volumetric relations of brain to endocast and to body size. Also needed are data on the size relations of different parts of the brain to the appropriate regions of the endocast. As noted earlier (Section IIC3), the crocodilian forebrain appears to fill its portion of the cranial cavity more completely than does the mid- or hindbrain; furthermore, the size discrepancy between the forebrain and the cavity it occupies remains constant or increases only at a slow rate with increasing body size. Hindbrain volume, on the other hand, lags behind as the hindbrain region of the endocast increases in volume with increase in body size. Therefore, it will be necessary to carry out detailed studies of the proportional and volumetric allometries of brain:endocast size and their relation to body size in living crocodilians before making intragroup comparisons of relative brain size in fossil archosaurs.

When these background data have been acquired, it may be possible to make comparisons within groups of dinosaurs in order to determine which dinosaurs had the relatively largest and which the smallest brains and whether relative brain size increased with the lineage through time. The data of Jerison (1973) suggest to Gould (1975) that carnivorous dinosaurs had the largest brains among the large Mesozoic reptiles, an example within the Reptilia of Jerison's generalization, based on Cenozoic mammals, that carnivores have higher EQs than do herbivores. My reanalysis of relative brain size in *Iguanodon* and several other dinosaurs suggests that the large carnivorous saurischians and the large ornithopod ornithischians had equally large brains. Most other ornithischians had EQs which were about average for reptiles and the sauropods had EQs which were very low. I offer tentative interpretations of the significance of these differences (Hopson, 1977). Gould's suggestion that carnivores in any group of vertebrates should be expected to have larger brains than their prey may explain the large brain sizes of *Allosaurus* and *Tyrannosaurus*. The large ornithopods were herbi- vores, but they may have been gregarious and may have possessed a degree of social organization (Hopson, 1975); furthermore, they lacked defensive armor or obvious weapons and may have relied more on their senses to detect predators than was necessary for other ornithischians. Sauropods appear to have had an extraordinary small ratio of brain:body size, but in this case the small brain may have been a consequence of space constraints imposed by selection for a relatively very small head.

The small carnivorous dinosaurs *Stenonychosaurus* and *Dromiceiomimus* are unique among reptiles in possessing brains which fall within the size range of living birds (Russell, 1969, 1972). Skeletal evidence indicates that these were active, agile bipeds, with grasping hands and, in the case of *Stenonychosaurus*, anterolaterally directed orbits and, therefore, a partly binocular visual field.

The fossil record of the Crocodilia is one of the longest and most continuous of any group of reptiles and crocodilian endocasts are relatively common. It is possible that one could study the change in brain size, and of the proportions of specific parts of the brain, especially the cerebrum, from the Jurassic to the present.

B. PALEONEUROLOGY AND THE STUDY OF REPTILIAN BRAIN EVOLUTION

Although endocasts provide information on the external morphology of the brain in extinct reptiles, the patterns of variation are as yet insufficiently understood to permit clear statements regarding the evolution of reptilian brains. Clearly, the gross morphology of the brain is influenced not only by neurosensory specializations but also by factors extrinsic to the nervous system such as space constraints related to size and proportions of the skull and to brain:body size allometry. Further, the reptilian brain often does not fill the cranial cavity and the endocast reflects the morphology of the brain to different degrees in animals of different size and belonging to different taxonomic groups. All of these factors obscure simple schemes matching endocast morphology to phylogenetically related factors. Nevertheless, the study of endocasts does allow some tentative conclusions about the course of brain evolution in reptiles.

The best evidence concerning brain morphology in fossil reptiles is provided by the endocasts of members of the subclass Archosauria. It is possible to distinguish the endocasts of the five orders of archosaurs and even the endocasts of the dinosaurian suborders. Thecodonts, crocodilians, and carnivorous saurischians show a generally primitive pattern of gross brain shape. These groups have a relatively elongated brain, a forebrain and medulla that are oriented approximately horizontally, and a pronounced midbrain flexure. The cerebral hemispheres of thecodonts and early crocodilians are also narrower relative to brain length than are those of living crocodilians, pterosaurs, and most dinosaurs. Modifications of the primitive archosaurian proportions are seen in sauropods and in ornithischians. In these the skull is specialized in size and shape in diverse ways. The sauropod brain is highly flexed and anteroposteriorly compressed, probably as a result of the space constraints created by the extremely small head of sauropods. In the bipedal ornithopods and pachycephalosaurs the medulla slopes obliquely down and back due to the high angle between the neck and long axis of the head. In the quadrupedal ornithischians the medulla is horizontal. Forebrain size is extremely variable within the order: pachycephalosaurs and ankylosaurs have a small forebrain and *Iguanodon* and hadrosaurs an extremely large one. The brain of pterosaurs is highly modified, probably by the neurosensory specializations associated with flight.

   The evidence for brain evolution is much poorer within the subclass Synapsida than among the archosaurs. The pelycosaur endocast is represented only by that of the large, deep-skulled *Dimetrodon*; the brain is elongated, as in archosaurs, and highly flexed. The forebrain region is not preserved on the endocast, but indications on the skull suggest that it is narrow. The brain of anomodont therapsids does not depart greatly from the condition seen in *Dimetrodon*. In theriodont therapsids, with their long, low temporal regions, the brain is elongated, little flexed, and tubular. The theriodont forebrain is much narrower than the forebrains of all but the very earliest archosaur, i.e. the presumed pseudosuchian of the Middle Triassic (see Section IVD2).

   We know little of the brain of fossil lepidosaurs but the gross morphology of the brains of *Sphenodon* and living Squamata more closely resembles that of archosaurs than that of synapsids. The same is probably true for turtles, though there are few data on the morphological variation of turtle brains.

   The brain of the marine euryapsid reptiles is very inadequately known; that of *Nothosaurus* is represented by several endocasts which are notable for the extraordinary narrowness of the forebrain region. The brain of placodonts seems to have had more typically reptilian proportions, but the endocast is, in fact, too poorly preserved to allow detailed comparison with that of other reptiles.

   Information on the brains of the earliest reptiles is of great importance for understanding patterns of brain evolution within the class Reptilia. Unfortunately, we have no information on the brains of captorhinomorph cotylosaurs, those primitive reptiles believed to include the ancestors of all living amniote vertebrates. *Diadectes* (the endocast of which is described in Section IVB1), though believed to lie on the amphibian side of the amphibian–reptilian class boundary, is considered to lie near the ancestry of the Reptilia. Its brain was moderately flexed and, more importantly, extremely narrow across the presumed cerebral region. In the latter feature it resembles the brains restored from the endocasts of labyrinthodont amphibians (Jerison, 1973).

   The evidence from endocasts available at this time suggests that the cerebral hemispheres of primitive reptiles were very narrow in transverse diameter. Their proportions were more similar to those of fossil and living amphibians than to those of living reptiles and their closest fossil relatives.

The cerebrum is relatively expanded in the modern orders of reptiles because of the large size of the dorsal ventricular ridge (DVR). The Permian history of the ancestors of the modern groups is practically unknown, but by the beginning of Triassic time (about 230 million years ago) the ancestors of the living subclasses and perhaps all of the living orders had diverged. By the end of the Triassic (about 180 million years ago) all of the living orders were in existence. One can therefore presume that the principal evolutionary developments in the central nervous system which characterize the living reptiles (and the birds) had taken place by the beginning of the Triassic. The synapsid (mammal-like) line diverged from the primitive reptilian stock by Middle Carboniferous (Early Pennsylvanian) time (about 300 million years ago), long before the origin of the living orders of reptiles. The persistently narrow cerebrum of the synapsids suggests that the DVR did not undergo an enlargement comparable to that which occurred in the ancestry of modern reptiles and birds. Even the most advanced synapsids, the cynodonts of Triassic time, did not expand the cerebral hemispheres much beyond the condition seen in *Diadectes*. Only in the Late Jurassic (about 140 million years ago) is there evidence of an expanded cerebrum in a descendant of the synapsid line, and this was in a true mammal (Jerison, 1973).

The euryapsid reptiles are of uncertain relationship to both the living groups of reptiles and the mammal-like group. The extraordinarily narrow cerebral region of *Nothosaurus* argues for a primitive unexpanded DVR in this group. Therefore, it is possible to draw the tentative conclusion from the fossil record that the great expansion of the DVR which is seen in living turtles, lepidosaurs, and archosaurs (including birds) began in the Permian *after* the separation of the Euryapsida and Synapsida from the main reptilian stock. The most important corollary of this conclusion is that the brains of modern reptiles may in many ways be as distinct from the brains of modern mammals as are the brains of modern amphibians. Living reptiles are not intermediate stages in a phylogenetic sequence linking the Amphibia to the Mammalia.

It is likely that study of additional specimens of fossil endocasts, especially of primitive reptiles (both synapsid and non-synapsid) will yield information on the primitive morphology of the reptilian brain. It is hoped that knowledge of the external form of the brain as interpreted from endocasts can contribute to further understanding of the evolution of the major aspects of internal organization as these are seen to vary among living tetrapods.

Acknowledgements

For the loan of specimens in their care I wish to acknowledge the aid of Drs A. J. Charig, M. A. Cluver, W. Coombs, E. S. Gaffney, P. M. Galton,

J. T. Gregory, the late C. W. Hibbard, J. H. Madsen, Jr., D. A. Russell, W. Wall, and R. Zangerl. Drs H. R. Barghusen, H. J. Jerison, R. G. Northcutt, and L. B. Radinsky offered advice and encouragement which I gratefully acknowledge. Thanks are also due Mrs M. Mishkin and Mrs T. Deno for typing the manuscript. I especially wish to acknowledge the contribution of Mrs C. Kryczka whose illustrations add immeasurably to the value of this review. This work has been partially supported by National Science Foundation Research Grant BMS75-01159.

References

Andrews, C. W. (1897). Note on a cast of the brain-cavity of *Iguanodon*. *Ann. Mag. nat. Hist.* 19(6), 585–591.

Aronson, L. R. (1963). The central nervous system of sharks and bony fishes with special reference to sensory and integrative mechanisms. *In* "Sharks and Survival". (P. W. Gilbert, ed.). Heath, Boston, 165–241.

Bakker, R. T. (1974). Dinosaur bioenergetics–a reply to Bennett and Dalzell, and Feduccia *Evolution, Lancaster, Pa.* 28, 497–503.

Bakker, R. T. (1975a). Experimental and fossil evidence for the evolution of tetrapod bioenergetics. *In* "Perspectives of Biophysical Ecology". (D. M. Gates and R. B. Schmerl, eds). Springer Verlag, Berlin and New York, 365–399.

Bakker, R. T. (1975b). Dinosaur renaissance. *Scient. Am.* 232(4), 58–78.

Barghusen, H. R. (1975). A review of fighting adaptations in dinocephalians (Reptilia, Therapsida). *Paleobiol.* 1, 295–311.

Barsbold, R. (1974). Saurornithoididae, a new family of small theropod dinosaurs from Central Asia and North America. *Palaeont. Polonica.* 30, 5–22.

Bonaparte, J.-F. (1966). Sobre las cavidades cerebral, nasal y otras estructuras del cráneo de *Exaeretodon* sp. (Cynodontia–Traversodontidae). *Acta geól. lilloana* 8, 5–31.

Boonstra, L. D. (1934). Pareiasaurian studies. IX. The cranial osteology. *Ann. S. Afr. Mus.* 31, 1–38.

Boonstra, L. D. (1968). The braincase, basicranial axis and median septum in the Dinocephalia. *Ann. S. Afr. Mus.* 50, 195–273.

Brink, A. S. (1963). The taxonomic position of the Synapsida. *S. Afr. J. Sci.* 59, 153–159.

Brown, B. (1914). *Anchiceratops*, a new genus of horned dinosaurs from the Edmonton Cretaceous of Alberta. With discussion of the origin of the ceratopsian crest and the brain casts of *Anchiceratops* and *Trachodon*. *Bull. Am. Mus. nat. Hist.* 33, 539–548.

Brown, B. and Schlaikjer, E. M. (1940). The structure and relationships of *Protoceratops*. *Ann N.Y. Acad. Sci.*, 40, 133–265.

Brown, B. and Schlaikjer, E. M. (1943). A study of troödont dinosaurs with the description of a new genus and four new species. *Bull. Am. Mus. nat. Hist.* 82, 115–150.

Camp, C. L. (1930). A study of the phytosaurs, with description of new material from western North America. *Mem. Univ. Calif.* 10, 1–174.

Camp, C. L. (1942). California mosasaurs. *Mem. Univ. Calif.* 13, 1–68.

Carroll, R. L. (1969a). A Middle Pennsylvanian captorhinomorph, and the interrelationships of primitive reptiles. *J. Paleont.* 43, 151–170.

Carroll, R. L. (1969b). The origin of reptiles. *In* "Biology of the Reptilia". (C. Gans,

A. d'A. Bellairs and T. S. Parsons, eds). Academic Press, London and New York, 1, (1), 1–44.

Carroll, R. L. (1969c). Problems of the origin of reptiles. *Biol. Rev.* 44, 393–432.

Carroll, R. L. (1970a). The ancestry of reptiles. *Phil. Trans. R. Soc. Ser. B* 257, 267–308.

Carroll, R. L. (1970b). Quantitative aspects of the amphibian-reptile transition. *Forma et Functio.* 3, 165–178.

Case, E. C. (1897). On the foramina perforating the cranial region of a Permian reptile and on a cast of its brain cavity. *Am. J. Sci.* 3(4), 321–326.

Case, E. C. (1907). Revision of the Pelycosauria of North America. *Carnegie Inst. Wash. Publ.* 55, 1–176.

Case, E. C. (1921). On an endocranial cast from a reptile, *Desmatosuchus spurensis*, from the Upper Triassic of western Texas. *J. comp. Neurol.* 33, 133–147.

Case, E. C. (1922). New reptiles and stegocephalians from the Upper Triassic of western Texas. *Carnegie Inst. Wash. Publ.* 321, 1–84.

Cluver, M. A. (1971). The cranial morphology of the dicynodont genus, *Lystrosaurus. Ann. S. Afr. Mus.* 56, 155–274.

Colbert, E. H. (1946). *Sebecus*, representative of a peculiar suborder of fossil Crocodilia from Patagonia. *Bull. Am. Mus. nat. Hist.* 87, 217–270.

Colbert, E. H. (1962). The weights of dinosaurs. *Am. Mus. Novit.* 2076, 1–16.

Colbert, E. H. and Russell, D. A. (1969). The small Cretaceous dinosaur *Dromaeosaurus. Am. Mus. Novit.* 2380, 1–49.

Cope, E. D. (1886). On the structure of the brain and auditory apparatus of a theromorphous reptile of the Permian epoch. *Proc. Am. Ass. Adv. Sci.* 34, 336–341.

Cope, E. D. (1887). A contribution to the history of the Vertebrata of the Triassic of North America. *Proc. Am. phil. Soc.* 24, 209–228.

Crile, G. and Quiring, D. P. (1940). A record of the body weight and certain organ and gland weights of 3690 animals. *Ohio J. Sci.* 40, 219–259.

Cruickshank, A. R. I. (1972). The proterosuchian thecodonts. *In* "Studies in Vertebrate Evolution". (K. A. Joysey and T. S. Kemp, eds). Oliver and Boyd, Edinburgh, 89–119.

De Beer, G. R. (1947). How animals hold their heads. *Proc. Linn. Soc. Lond.* 159, 125–139.

Delattre, A. and Fenart, R. (1958). La méthode vestibulaire. *Z. Morph. Anthrop.* 49, 90–114.

Dendy, A. (1911). On the structure, development and morphological interpretation of the pineal organs and adjacent parts of the brain in the tuatara (*Sphenodon punctatus*). *Phil. Trans. R. Soc. Ser. B* 201, 227–331.

Dodson, P. (1974). Dinosaurs as dinosaurs. *Evolution, Lancaster, Pa.* 28, 494–496.

Dodson, P. (1975). Taxonomic implications of relative growth in lambeosaurine hadrosaurs. *Syst. Zool.* 24, 37–54.

Edinger, T. (1921). Über *Nothosaurus*. I. Ein Steinkern der Schädelhöhle. *Senckenbergiana* 3, 121–129.

Edinger, T. (1925). Das Zentralnervensystem von *Placodus gigas. Abh. senckenb. naturforsch. Ges.* 38, 311–318.

Edinger, T. (1927). Das Gehirn der Pterosaurier. *Z. Anat. EntwGesch.* 83, 106–112.

Edinger, T. (1928). Über einige fossile Gehirne. *Paläont. Z.* 9, 379–402.

Edinger, T. (1929). Die fossilen Gehirne. *Erg. Anat. EntwGesch.* 28, 1–249.

Edinger, T. (1930). Hirnausguss des *Plesiosaurus. Paläont. Z.* 12, 135–136.

Edinger, T. (1934). Anton Fritsch's "Grosshirn von *Polyptychodon*" ist der Steinkern eines Schildkrötenschädels. *Psychiatr. en neurol. Bladen* 38, 396–404.

Edinger, T. (1937). Paläoneurologie. *Fortschr. Paläont.* 1, 235–251.

Edinger, T. (1938). Über Steinkerne von Hirn- und Ohr-Höhlen der Mesosuchier *Gonio-*

pholis und *Pholidosaurus* aus dem Bückeburger Wealden. *Acta Zool., Stockh.* 19, 467–505.

Edinger, T. (1941). The brain of *Pterodactylus*. *Am. J. Sci.* 239, 665–682.

Edinger, T. (1942). The pituitary body in giant animals, fossil and living: a survey and a suggestion. Q. *Rev. Biol.* 17, 31–45.

Edinger, T. (1955). The size of the parietal foramen and organ in reptiles. A rectification. *Bull. Mus. comp. Zool. Harv.* 114, 3–34.

Edinger, T. (1962). Anthropocentric misconceptions in paleoneurology. *Proc. Rudolf Virchow Med. Soc. New York* 19 (1960), 56–107.

Edinger, T. (1975). Paleoneurology 1804–1966. An annotated bibliography. *Erg. Anat. EntwGesch.* 49, 1–258.

Fritsch, A. (1905). Synopsis der Saurier der böhmischen Kreideformation. *Sber. K. böhm. Grs. Wiss.* 8, 1–7.

Gaffney, E. S. (1977). An endocranial cast of the side-necked turtle, *Bothremys*, with a new reconstruction of the palate. *Am. Mus. Novit.* 2639, 1–12.

Gaffney, E. S. and Zangerl, R. (1968). A revision of the chelonian genus *Bothremys* (Pleurodira: Pelomedusidae). *Fieldiana, Geol.* 16, 193–239.

Galton, P. M. (1970). Pachycephalosaurids—dinosaurian battering rams. *Discovery, New Haven* 6(1), 23–32.

Galton, P. M. (1971). A primitive dome-headed dinosaur (Ornithischia: Pachycephalosauridae) from the Lower Cretaceous of England and the function of the dome of pachycephalosaurids. *J. Paleont.* 45, 40–47.

Gilmore, C. W. (1914). Osteology of the armored Dinosauria in the United States National Museum, with special reference to the genus *Stegosaurus*. *Bull. U.S. natn. Mus.* 89, 1–143.

Gilmore, C. W. (1920). Osteology of the carnivorous Dinosauria in the United States National Museum, with special reference to the genera *Antrodemus* (*Allosaurus*) and *Ceratosaurus*. *Bull. U.S. natn. Mus.* 110, 1–159.

Gorce, F. (1960). Étude de quelques vertébrés du Muschelkalk du Djebel Rehach (Sud Tunisien). *Mém. Soc. géol. France* (n.s. 39), 88B, 1–34.

Gould, S. J. (1975). Review of "Evolution of the Brain and Intelligence". by Harry J. Jerison. *Paleobiology* 1, 125–128.

Gregory, W. K. (1946). Pareiasaurs versus placodonts as near ancestors of the turtles. *Bull. Am. Mus. nat. Hist.* 86, 275–326.

Gundy, G. C., Ralph, C. L. and Wurst, G. Z. (1975). Parietal eyes in lizards: zoogeographical correlates. *Science, N.Y.* 190, 671–673.

Hatcher, J. B., Marsh, O. C. and Lull, R. S. (1907). The Ceratopsia. *U.S. geol. Surv. Mono.* 49, 1–198.

Hay, O. P. (1909). On the skull and brain of *Triceratops*, with notes on the braincase of *Iguanodon* and *Megalosaurus*. *Proc. U.S. natn. Mus.* 36, 95–108.

Hennig, E. (1925). *Kentrurosaurus aethiopicus*: die Stegosaurier-Funde vom Tendaguru, Deutsch-Ostafrika. *Palaeontographica* Suppl. 7, 1, 101–253.

Hochstetter, F. (1906). Beiträge zur Anatomie und Entwicklungsgeschichte des Blutgefässsystemes der Krokodile. *In* "Reise in Ostafrika, 1903–1905". (A. Voeltzkow, ed.). Stuttgart, 4, 1–139.

Holland, W. J. (1906). The osteology of *Diplodocus* Marsh. *Mem. Carnegie Mus. Pittsburgh* 2, 225–278.

Hopson, J. A. (1964). The braincase of the advanced mammal-like reptile *Bienotherium*. *Postilla* 87, 1–30.

Hopson, J. A. (1969). The origin and adaptive radiation of mammal-like reptiles and nontherian mammals. *Ann. N.Y. Acad. Sci.* 167, 199–216.

Hopson, J. A. (1975). The evolution of cranial display structures in hadrosaurian dinosaurs. *Paleobiology* 1, 21–43.

Hopson, J. A. (1977). Relative brain size and behavior in archosaurian reptiles. *Ann. Rev. Ecol. Syst.* 8, 429–448.

Huene, F. von (1906). Ueber das Hinterhaupt von *Megalosaurus bucklandi* aus Stonesfield. *N. Jahrb. Min., Geol., Paläont.* 1, 1–12.

Huene, F. von (1907–08). Die Dinosaurier der europäischen Triasformation mit Berücksichtigung der aussereuropäischen Vorkommnisse. *Geol. paläont. Abh.* Suppl. 1, 1–419.

Huene, F. von (1913). The skull elements of the Permian Tetrapoda in the American Museum of Natural History, New York. *Bull. Am. Mus. nat. Hist.* 32, 315–386.

Huene, F. von (1914). Über die Zweistämmigkeit der Dinosaurier mit Beiträgen zur Kenntnis einiger Schädel. *N. Jahrb. Min., Geol., Paläont.* 37, 577–589.

Huene, F. von (1932). Die fossile Reptil-Ordnung Saurischia, ihre Entwicklung und Geschichte. *Monogr. Geol., Palaeont.* 4(1), 1–361.

Huene, F. von and Matley, C. A. (1933). The Cretaceous Saurischia and Ornithischia of the Central Provinces of India. *Mem. geol. Surv. India (Palaeont. indica)*, 21, 1–74.

Janensch, W. (1935–36). Die Schädel der Sauropoden *Brachiosaurus, Barosaurus* und *Dicraeosaurus* aus den Tendaguruschichten Deutsch-Ostafrikas. *Palaeontographica* Suppl. 7, 145–298.

Janensch, W. (1936). Über Bahnen von Hirnvenen bei Saurischiern und Ornithischiern, sowie einigen anderen fossilen und rezenten Reptilien. *Paläont. Z.* 18, 181–198.

Janensch, W. (1938). Gestalt und Grösse von *Brachiosaurus* und anderen riesenwüchsigen Sauropoden. *Biologe* 7, 130–134.

Jerison, H. J. (1969). Brain evolution and dinosaur brains. *Am. Nat.* 103, 575–588.

Jerison, H. J. (1970). Brain evolution: New light on old principles. *Science, N.Y.* 170, 1224–1225.

Jerison, H. J. (1973). "Evolution of the Brain and Intelligence." Academic Press, New York and London.

Kemp, T. S. (1969). On the functional morphology of the gorgonopsid skull. *Phil. Trans. R. Soc. Ser. B.* 256, 1–83.

Killian, G. (1890). Die Ohrmuskeln des Krokodiles, nebst vorläufigen Bemerkungen über die Homologie des Musculus stapedius und des Stapes. *Jena Z. Naturw.* 24 (n.s. 17), 632–656.

Koken, E. (1887). Die Dinosaurier, Crocodiliden und Sauropterygier des norddeutschen Wealden. *Paläont. Abh.* 3, 309–419.

Koken, E. (1890). Über die Bildung des Schädels, der Gehirnhöhle und des Gehörorgans bei der Gattung *Nothosaurus*. *Sber. Ges. naturf. Freunde Berl.* 1890, 108–111.

Koken, E. (1893). Beiträge zur Kenntnis der Gattung *Nothosaurus*. *Z. deutsch. geol. Ges.* 45, 337–377.

Kühne, W. G. (1956). "The Liassic Therapsid *Oligokyphus*." Brit. Mus. (Nat. Hist.), London.

Kurzanov, S. M. (1972). Sexual dimorphism in protoceratopsians. *Paleont. Zhur.* 1972, 104–112. (In Russian.)

Lambe, L. M. (1920). The hadrosaur *Edmontosaurus* from the Upper Cretaceous of Alberta. *Canada Dept. Mines, geol. Surv. Mem.* 120 (*Geol. Ser.* 102), 1–79.

Langston, W. (1960). The vertebrate fauna of the Selma Formation of Alabama. VI. The dinosaurs. *Fieldiana, Geol. Mem.* 3, 313–361.

Langston, W. (1973). The crocodilian skull in historical perspective. *In* "Biology of the Reptilia". (C. Gans and T. S. Parsons, eds). Academic Press, London and New York, 4(3), 263–284.

Lemoine, V. (1883–84). Note sur l'encéphale du gavial du Mont-Aime, étudié sur trois moulages naturels. *Bull. Soc. géol. Fr.* **12**(3), 158–162.

Lull, R. S. and Wright, N. E. (1942). Hadrosaurian dinosaurs of North America. *Geol. Soc. Am. spec. Pap.* **40**, 1–242.

Madsen, J. H., Jr (1976). *Allosaurus fragilis*: A revised osteology. *Bull. Utah Geol. Mineral Surv.* **109**, 1–163.

Maleev, E. A. (1965). On the brain of the carnivorous dinosaurs. *Paleont. Zhur.* **2**, 141–143. (In Russian.)

Marsh, O. C. (1876). Recent discoveries of extinct animals. *Am. J. Sci.* **12**(3), 59–61.

Marsh, O. C. (1880). Principal characters of American Jurassic dinosaurs. III. *Am. J. Sci.* **19**(3), 253–259.

Marsh, O. C. (1881). Principal characters of American Jurassic dinosaurs. IV. Spinal cord, pelvis, and limbs of *Stegosaurus*. *Am. J. Sci.* **21**(3), 167–170.

Marsh, O. C. (1884a). Principal characters of American Jurassic dinosaurs. VII. On the Diplodocidae, a new family of the Sauropoda. *Am. J. Sci.* **27**(3), 161–168.

Marsh, O. C. (1884b). Principal characters of American Jurassic dinosaurs. VIII. The order Theropoda. *Am. J. Sci.* **27**(3), 329–340.

Marsh, O. C. (1885). The gigantic mammals of the order Dinocerata. *Ann. Rep. U.S. geol. Surv.* **5**, 234–302.

Marsh, O. C. (1889). Notice of new American Dinosauria. *Am. J. Sci.* **37**(3), 331–336.

Marsh, O. C. (1890). Additional characters of the Ceratopsidae, with notice of new Cretaceous dinosaurs. *Am. J. Sci.* **39**(3), 418–426.

Marsh, O. C. (1891). The gigantic Ceratopsidae, or horned dinosaurs, of North America. *Am. J. Sci.* **41**(3), 167–178.

Marsh, O. C. (1896). The dinosaurs of North America. *Ann. Rep. U.S. geol. Surv.* **16**, 133–244.

Maryańska, T. and Osmólska, H. (1974). Pachycephalosauria, a new suborder of ornithischian dinosaurs. *Palaeontologia polonica* **30**, 45–102.

Müller, F. (1967). Zur embryonalen Kopfentwicklung von *Crocodylus cataphractus* Cuv. *Revue suisse Zool.* **74**, 189–294.

Newton, E. T. (1888). On the skull, brain, and auditory organ of a new species of pterosaurian (*Scaphognathus purdoni*), from the Upper Lias near Whitby, Yorkshire. *Phil. Trans. R. Soc. Ser. B* **179**, 503–537.

Nopcsa, F. (1900). Dinosaurierreste aus Siebenbürgen (Schädel von *Limnosaurus transsylvanicus* nov. gen. et spec.). *Denkschr. Ak. Wiss. Wien, math.-natur. Kl.* **68**. 555–591.

Nopcsa, F. (1926). Osteologia Reptilium fossilium et recentium. "Fossilium Catalogus, I. Animalia". (C. Diener, ed.). **27**, 1–391.

Nopcsa, F. (1929). Dinosaurierreste aus Siebenbürgen. V. *Geol. hung., Ser. pälaeont.* **1**(4), 1–76.

Oelrich, T. M. (1956). The anatomy of the head of *Ctenosaura pectinata* (Iguanidae). *Misc. Publ. Mus. Zool. Univ. Michigan* **94**, 1–122.

Olson, E. C. (1944). Origin of mammals based upon cranial morphology of the therapsid suborders. *Geol. Soc. Am. spec. Pap.* **55**, 1–136.

Olson, E. C. (1966). Relationships of *Diadectes*. *Fieldiana, Geol.* **14**, 199–227.

Osborn, H. F. (1912). Crania of *Tyrannosaurus* and *Allosaurus*. *Mem. Am. Mus. nat. Hist.* **1**, 1–30.

Osborn, H. F. and Mook, C. C. (1921). *Camarasaurus, Amphicoelias*, and other sauropods of Cope. *Mem. Am. Mus. nat. Hist.* **3**, 247–387.

Ostrom, J. H. (1961). Cranial morphology of the hadrosaurian dinosaurs of North America. *Bull. Am. Mus. nat. Hist.* **122**, 33–186.

Ostrom, J. H. (1969). Osteology of *Deinonychus antirrhopus*, an unusual theropod from the Lower Cretaceous of Montana. *Bull. Peabody Mus. nat. Hist.* **30**, 1–165.

Ostrom, J. H. (1976). *Archaeopteryx* and the origin of birds. *Biol. J. Linn. Soc.* **8**, 91–182.

Ostrom, J. H. and McIntosh, J. S. (1966). "Marsh's Dinosaurs. The Collections from Como Bluff." Yale Univ. Press, New Haven and London.

Panchen, A. L. (1972). The interrelationships of the earliest tetrapods. *In* "Studies in Vertebrate Evolution". (K. A. Joysey and T. S. Kemp, eds). Oliver and Boyd, Edinburgh, pp. 65–87.

Papez, J. W. (1929). "Comparative Neurology." Thomas Y. Crowell, Co., New York.

Parrington, F. R. (1946). On the cranial anatomy of cynodonts. *Proc. zool. Soc. Lond.* **116**, 181–197.

Pompeckj, J. F. (1920). Das angebliche Verkommen und Wandern des Parietalforamens. *Sber. Ges. naturf. Freunde Berl.* 109–129.

Radinsky, L. B. (1968). A new approach to mammalian cranial analysis, illustrated by examples of prosimian primates. *J. Morph.* **124**, 167–180.

Romer, A. S. (1956). "Osteology of the Reptiles." Univ. Chicago Press, Chicago.

Romer, A. S. (1966). "Vertebrate Paleontology." 3rd edn. Univ. Chicago Press, Chicago.

Romer, A. S. (1967). Early reptilian evolution re-viewed. *Evolution, Lancaster, Pa.* **21**, 821–833.

Romer, A. S. (1968). "Notes and Comments on Vertebrate Paleontology." Univ. Chicago Press, Chicago.

Romer, A. S. and Price, L. I. (1940). Review of the Pelycosauria. *Geol. Soc. Am. spec. Pap.* **28**, 1–538.

Russell, D. A. (1967). Systematics and morphology of American mosasaurs. *Bull. Peabody Mus. nat. Hist.* **23**, 1–240.

Russell, D. A. (1969). A new specimen of *Stenonychosaurus* from the Oldman Formation (Cretaceous) of Alberta. *Can. J. Earth Sci.* **6**, 595–612.

Russell, D. A. (1972). Ostrich dinosaurs from the Late Cretaceous of western Canada. *Can. J. Earth Sci.* **9**, 375–402.

Säve-Söderbergh, G. (1946). On the fossa hypophyseos and the attachment of the retractor bulbi group in *Sphenodon*, *Varanus*, and *Lacerta*. *Ark. Zool.* **38A**(11), 1–24.

Schumacher, G.-H. (1973). The head muscles and hyolaryngeal skeleton of turtles and crocodilians. *In* "Biology of the Reptilia". (C. Gans and T. S. Parsons, eds). Academic Press, New York and London, **4**(1), 101–200.

Simpson, G. G. (1933). The ear region and the foramina of the cynodont skull. *Am. J. Sci.* **226**, 285–294.

Swinton, W. E. (1958). Dinosaur brains. *New Scientist* **4**, 707–709.

Taylor, E. H. (1951). Concerning Oligocene amphisbaenid reptiles. *Univ. Kansas Sci. Bull.* **34**, 521–579.

Walker, E. (1964). "Mammals of the World". Johns Hopkins University Press, Baltimore. 3 vols.

Watson, D. M. S. (1913). Further notes on the skull, brain and organs of special sense of *Diademodon*. *Ann. Mag. nat. Hist.* **12**(8), 217–228.

Watson, D. M. S. (1914). On the skull of a pareiasaurian reptile, and on the relationship of that type. *Proc. zool. Soc. Lond.* **1914**, 155–180.

Watson, D. M. S. (1916). On the structure of the braincase in certain Lower Permian tetrapods. *Bull. Am. Mus. nat. Hist.* **35**, 611–636.

Wegner, T. (1914). *Brancasaurus brancai* Wegner, ein Elasmosauride aus Wealden Westfalens. "Branca-Festschrift." Berlin, pp. 235–305.

Yeh, K.-K. (1958). A new crocodile from Maoming, Kwantung. *Vertebr. Palasiat.* **2**, 237–242.

Young, C. C. (1958). The dinosaurian remains of Laiyang, Shantung. *Paleont. Sin.* n.s. (C) **16**, 53–138.

Zambelli, R. (1973). *Eudimorphodon ranzii* gen. nov., sp. nov., un pterosauro Triassico. *Instituto Lombardo* (*Rend. Sc.*) (B) **107**, 27–32.

Zangerl, R. (1960). The vertebrate fauna of the Selma Formation of Alabama. V. An advanced cheloniid sea turtle. *Fieldiana, Geol. Mem.* 3, 281–312.

CHAPTER 3

Brain Weight—Body Weight Relationships

ROLAND PLATEL

Laboratoire d'Anatomie comparée, Université Paris 7

I. Introduction

Quantitative study of the central nervous system employs a methodology first developed and applied to mammals. During the last 25 years this method has been extensively employed by laboratories at Kiel (W. Herre), Frankfurt am Main (H. Stephan), Paris (R. Bauchot) and Montreal (P. Pirlot). Analysis of reptilian brain structure only began during the last few years, and has thus far only been applied to a few species, mostly to lizards. There is little information on other reptiles. Such quantitative studies utilize Snell's formula (1892), a power function relating brain weight (E) to body weight (S)

$$E = kS^{\alpha}$$

where k is the intercept which is usually termed the coefficient of encephalization and α is the coefficient of allometry. Von Bonin (1937) was the first to use this equation as an allometric function and described an appropriate method for statistical analysis. Since Snell's development of this formula, a number of analyses and critiques have appeared (Anthony, 1938; Count, 1947; Sholl, 1948). More recently, White and Gould (1965), Gould (1966 and 1971), Pirlot (1969), Bauchot (1972a), Bauchot and Platel (1973), and Jerison (1973) analyzed the biological rationale and limits expressed by Snell's formula.

In practice, the study of brain–body relationships has taken two directions.

1. An examination of brain weights and body weights of a sample of all available sizes of individuals of a species allows two types of allometric analysis: the allometry of growth (comparing young and adult individuals within a species) and the allometry of size (comparing adult animals among species). The first type furnishes data on the relative growth of the brain as a whole. The second, deals with relationships

among adult animals, illustrating what Lapicque (1908) called "the inner law of the species".

2. The analysis of a group of species at the same taxonomic level (generally species comprising an order) reveals an allometric relationship that one might call allometry of filiation (Bauchot and Platel, 1973), or static allometry (Gould, 1966, 1971). Such studies among species establish indices of encephalization that may reflect grades of evolution.

In both intraspecific and interspecific studies, the study of brain–body relationships is not an end in itself. Rather, it develops a methodology as a prelude to the analysis of relative volumes of different brain areas. The present chapter will deal only with gross brain–body relationships.

If one excludes the work of Jerison (1969, 1973) on fossil forms, brain–body relationships in reptiles have been little studied. The limited data of Dubois (1913) are used only for general considerations. To date, a single study (Rose, 1957) has involved an allometric relationship, but body size was not the reference. Ebbesson and Northcutt (1976) have recently provided selected volumetric measurements on different brain areas and comparisons of these areas.

As in mammals, one can analyze the degree of encephalization of species, families, or orders within the class Reptilia, and investigate the generalized or specialized condition of different brain areas. Reptiles are a large group manifesting great diversity in locomotion, in the development of olfactory, visual and auditory functions, and in ecological adaptations. Such diversity is reflected in their central nervous system. Lizards present a wealth of interesting data and seem particularly useful for a first examination. Their phylogenetic affinities with snakes lead logically to an examination of other squamates. Analysis of turtles and crocodiles remains very limited. Comparable studies are presently being undertaken in other classes of vertebrates, enlarging a field of comparison previously limited to mammals.

II. Determination of Numerical Values

For each animal studied, measurements of the brain weight and body weight were taken according to uniform procedures. Whenever possible animals were caught in the field and sacrificed as soon after capture as possible. Captivity and controlled breeding in laboratories and zoos affect body weight in ways that are difficult to estimate. It is also desirable, in temperate climates, to avoid the weeks immediately preceding and following hibernation. The end of the reproductive period should also be avoided as body weight is necessarily altered by the weight of the large eggs.

In interspecific studies, only adults should be used. In mammals and birds, growth is limited in time, and the determination of adults is relatively easy. It is sufficient to obtain a sample of adults of each species and determine the mean body weights and brain weights. In reptiles, growth continues (theoretically) throughout life. This mode of development is also found in fishes and amphibians, and poses a problem both for definition of the adult state and for definition of an "average adult" of the species. Numerous criteria have been proposed (maturity of the gonads, body length), but none of these criteria is absolute. For instance, there are species in which sexual maturity occurs in less than a year (precocious forms) and those in which maturity may be delayed. The former condition is seen in many subtropical regions (cf. *Chalarodon madagascariensis*; Blanc, 1969), while the latter is seen in forms of cool regions (cf. the 2·5 to 4·5 year age at maturation seen in *Vipera*; Saint Girons, 1965).

When the sample size is extremely small (one to five individuals) determination of the adult type is very subjective; one computes an arithmetic mean and only employs this mean after comparison with data presented in the literature for similar cases. Once a reasonably large sample of individuals of a species is available (30 to 80 individuals) the decision regarding the definition of an adult type may be made on the basis of criteria from the allometric analysis; this is illustrated in Figs 1 and 3.

Animals were anesthetized with chloroform, then sexed and weighed to the nearest 0·1 or 0·5 g. The distance between the tip of the snout and the cloaca was measured to the nearest millimeter. After decapitation, the brains were partially exposed and fixed by immersion in Bouin's solution. The brains were removed from the cranial cavity by cutting the cranial nerves as near their origin as possible. The olfactory fibers were cut at the convexity of the olfactory bulb, and the optic tract was sectioned immediately posterior to the chiasm. The caudal limit of the brain was set at the level of the first cervical spinal nerve. The brains were weighed to the nearest 0·001 g, according to the method of Bauchot (1967). If this weight is taken during the first 30 minutes following immersion in the Bouin's solution, the weight obtained does not differ from the weight of the freshly dissected, unfixed brain. (The weight decreases 4% during the first 24 hours of fixation in Bouin's solution.)

Fifty reptilian species were measured under these conditions. This sample is still quite small, and was enlarged by using data from the literature (Dubois, 1913; Naccarati, 1922; Brummelkamp, 1940; Crile and Quiring, 1940; Count, 1947; Spector, 1956). These studies yield considerable data, some of which derive from previous work (Welcker and Brandt, 1903; Hrdlicka, 1905; Lapicque and Laugier, 1908). Frequently, the method of preparation is not indicated in these works. However, the use of the data is justified in order to enlarge the sample when specimens were not available to the author or when more recent data were unavailable. The advantages of direct measurements are several, of course, including proper fixation for further histological analysis of different brain areas.

III. Mathematical Analysis of Numerical Data

The mathematical analysis involves the application of Snell's formula, $E = kS^{\alpha}$, the logarithmic form of which is

$$\log E = \alpha \log S + \log k$$

The values for brain size and body size of each individual in a sample of individuals of the same species (intraspecific analysis) or a sample of species of the same order (interspecific analysis) permits calculation of the parameters α and k. Many mathematical methods allow the necessary regression analysis. I have utilized the method of reduced major axes (RMA) suggested by Teissier (1948, 1955). This calculation is easily performed since the exponent α corresponds to quotients of the standard deviations of the two variables. The fitness of the regression is determined by computing a product moment correlation coefficient. In each of the cases described the correlation is significant beyond the 0·01 level. A straight line with slope α and y intercept of $\log k$ is fitted to the points, graphically representing the parameters of Snell's formula. For each individual i ($\log E_i$, $\log S_i$ there corresponds a value of $\log k_i$, where k_i represents the brain weight of individual i (or species i) when the body weight is unity on the scale of measurements.

An index, independent of the unit of measurement, can be calculated by using a group's allometric function as a reference equation (Bauchot and Stephan, 1964, 1969). The allometric functions chosen can be more or less arbitrary, depending on the characteristics of the group examined. This reference allometric equation yields a value for the y intercept which is termed $\log k_o$. The index can then be defined as

$$I = \frac{k_i}{k_o} 100$$

In the case of an intraspecific study, this index is termed an *isoponderal index*; it allows comparison of brain weight in various individuals independent of body weight. In the case of interspecific studies, this index is termed an *index of encephalization*, which allows ranking of the species studied. The index of encephalization is equivalent to Jerison's (1973, 1975) encephalization quotient (EQ), and the dimensional implications of such indices are discussed by Jerison and also by Gould (1966, 1971, 1975).

IV. Results

A. INTRASPECIFIC ALLOMETRIC COEFFICIENT OF THE BRAIN–BODY RELATIONSHIP

1. *Material*

This study utilized lizards, snakes, and turtles. The species used are listed in Table I.

TABLE I

Intraspecific coefficients E: S in reptiles

Sample of species	N	α	Correlation coefficient
SAURIA			
Tarentola mauritanica	11	0·450	0·9719
Chalarodon madagascariensis	80	0·393	0·9610
Agama agama	80	0·404	0·9741
Agama inermis	46	0·441	0·8816
Chamaeleo lateralis	80	0·500	0·8127
Scincus scincus	80	0·401	0·9145
Lacerta viridis	88	0·433	0·9047
Lacerta muralis	73	0·450	0·9068
Anguis fragilis	31	0·391	0·9517
(from Platel, 1974)			
SERPENTES			
Natrix maura	6	0·438	0·9490
Natrix natrix	31	0·383	0·9496
Vipera aspis	46	0·437	0·9257
TESTUDINES			
Testudo hermanni	60	0·471	0·9511
(from Platel, 1975)			

2. *Results*

The various values of the coefficients are listed in Table I, as are the corresponding correlation coefficients. It should be noted that in each species the correlation is rather high (extreme values were 0·9741 for *Agama agama*, and 0·8127 for *Chamaeleo lateralis*). The correlation is represented graphically by the degree of scatter around the allometric line as shown, for example, in Fig. 1.

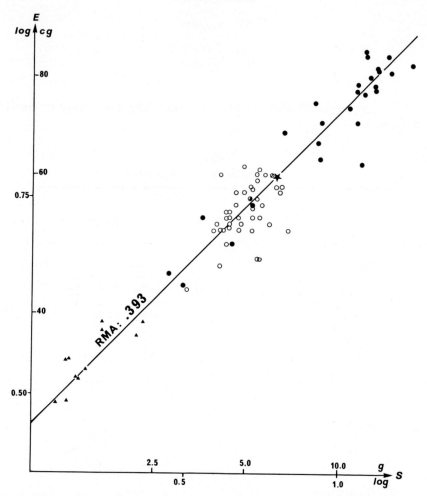

FIG. 1. *Chalarodon madagascariensis*: Brain-body weight correlation (*E*:*S*). Logarithmic scales. The allometric line is the Reduced Major Axis. This representation allows discrimination of juveniles (black triangles) from male (black dots) and female (white dots) adults. The black star marks the co-ordinates of the "average adult" of this species.

The allometric coefficients of different lizard species range from 0·391 (*Anguis fragilis*) to 0·500 (*Chamaeleo lateralis*), but eight of the nine values group between 0·391 (*Anguis fragilis*) and 0·450 (*Tarentola mauritanica, Lacerta muralis*). These values are sufficiently close to one another, despite the wide variety of species used, to justify the computation and use of an arithmetic mean. The value of this mean is 0·43, a reasonable characterization for lizards. The coefficients obtained for the three species of snakes

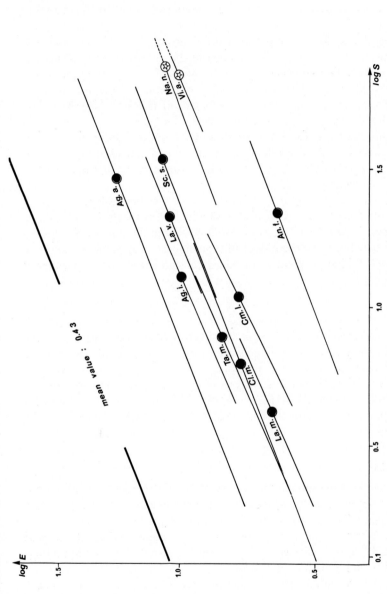

FIG. 2. Intraspecific allometric coefficients in squamates. Brain-body weight correlation (*E:S*). Logarithmic scales. Each species is represented by a dot ("average adult" of the species) and the allometric line (RMA) proper to the sample; the length of this line is limited to the extreme values for body weight. Lizards: black dots; Ta. m., *Tarentola mauritanica*; Cl. m., *Chalarodon madagascariensis*; Ag. a., *Agama agama*; Ag. i., *Agama mutabilis*; Cm. l., *Chamaeleo lateralis*; Sc. s., *Scincus scincus*; La. v., *Lacerta viridis*; La. m., *Lacerta muralis*; An. f., *Anguis fragilis*. Snakes: white stars; Na.n., *Natrix natrix*; Vi. a., *Vipera aspis*.

differ little from those for the nine species of lizards; the calculation of a mean value is again justified since the extreme values are hardly changed. Again the mean value is 0·43, which can therefore be applied to squamates in general (Fig. 2).

A comparable analysis was performed on turtles (*Testudo hermanni*) and yields a coefficient α (0·475) that is almost in the distribution of coefficients described earlier. The same is true for *Chelonia mydas* (two values published by Crile and Quiring, 1940; and one value calculated by the author: $E = 1\cdot508$ g; $S = 1625$ g). This yields a coefficient of 0·394 for the three data points with a correlation coefficient of 0·9946. The value $\alpha = 0\cdot4$ may be a characteristic measure for most reptiles. Crocodilians differ from other reptiles according to the five values published by Crile and Quiring (1940) for *Alligator mississippiensis*. Their data yield a value of 0·320 for α, with a correlation coefficient of 0·9905.

An isoponderal index for comparing brain weights independently of body weights was performed on adult individuals of both sexes in 10 species. *Vipera aspis*, *Anguis fragilis*, *Chamaeleo lateralis* and *Lacerta viridis* possess a bimodal distribution of the index, and the highest mean value is that of the males (Platel, 1975b). At present the biological significance of this peculiarity is unknown.

3. *Body Length*

The snout–cloacal length, A, can be substituted for body weight in the brain–body analysis, as there is generally a high correlation between these two size parameters (Platel and Bauchot, 1970; Bauchot *et al.*, 1972). This strong $E:A$ relationship permits analysis as shown in Fig. 3. The transformation required is discussed by Platel (1974). This substitution of length for body weight may be useful to compensate for the variance introduced by feeding and pregnancy.

4. *Discussion*

Intraspecific studies among many vertebrates also demonstrate allometric coefficients for plots of brain/body weight with ontogenetic change within a single species. This relationship has yet to be explained.

The intraspecific allometric coefficient for mammals is about 0·25 (Lapicque, 1908) or 0·23 according to recent studies by Bauchot and Guerstein (1970) and Bauchot and Diagne (1973). The calculated value for squamates and testudines (0·4) is significantly different. Other vertebrates also differ (Table II).

With the exception of the Chondrichthyes, the various coefficients cited are in the interval 0·36 to 0·48 (fresh-water and terrestrial animals) and

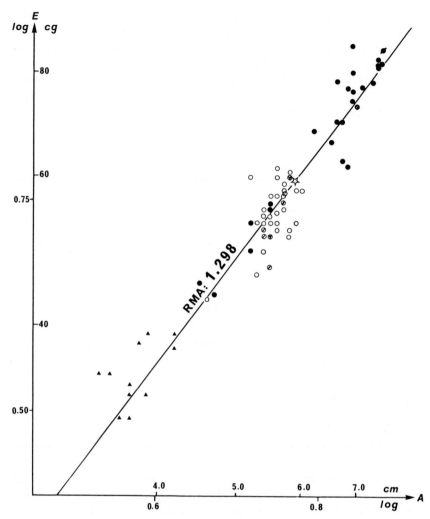

FIG. 3. *Chalarodon madagascariensis*: Brain weight—Snout-to-cloaca length correlation (*E*:*A*). Logarithmic scales. (Explanations as in Fig. 1.)

extend to 0·50 (marine teleosts) (J. M. Ridet, pers. commun.). The establishment of values for other groups of vertebrates (anurans, for example) will enable us to erect a classification based on the value of the allometric coefficient. For example, *Scyliorhinus canicula* with a high coefficient presently provides the upper limit of the range for classification. It will eventually be necessary to determine the significance of the differences observed among vertebrate classes.

It is well established that the pattern of brain growth differs between mammals and nonmammals. Intraspecific studies among mammals reveal an allometric coefficient of about 1·0 (isometry) calculated for embryos and very young animals (for example, *Rattus norvegicus*—17 days after birth; Bauchot and Guerstein, 1970). This coefficient about the unit (isometry) corresponds to an active period of mitosis of neuroblasts; cell multiplication results in a decrease of the allometric coefficient to 0·23. Except for birds,

TABLE II

Intraspecific coefficients E:S in vertebrates

Species	α	References
MAMMALIA		
Rattus norvegicus	0·24	Bauchot and Guerstein, 1970
Hemicentetes semispinosus	0·23	Bauchot and Diagne, 1973
AVES		
Gallus domesticus	0·365	Platel *et al.*, 1972
Larus argentatus—Larus fuscus	0·402	Delfini *et al.*, 1973
AMPHIBIA CAUDATA		
Salamandra salamandra	0·480	Thireau *et al.*, 1973
TELEOSTEI		
Eight species (mean value)	0·461	Ridet, 1973
CHONDRICHTHYES		
Torpedo marmorata	0·491	Bauchot *et al.*, 1976
Scyliorhinus canicula	0·566	Ridet *et al.*, 1973

there is no information regarding a first isometric phase among other vertebrates. However, it is reasonable to assume that mitosis continuing after hatching leads to allometric coefficients greater than 0·23. Birds represent an intermediate stage. They are similar to reptiles in many respects (allometric coefficients for *Gallus domesticus*, 0·365, *Larus argentatus* and *Larus fuscus*, 0·402). However, *Gallus domesticus* shows a high allometric coefficient (0·671) during the first 17 days of incubation (Platel *et al.*, 1972). Most avian species reach an essentially mammalian grade of brain–body ratios at the end of the growth period. Endothermy should not be considered a cause of the brain–body relationship found in mammals as this relationship is very different from that found in birds, which are also endothermic. The mechanisms for endothermy may differ between these two classes. Perhaps that of mammals is a consequence of their specialized method of reproduction.

B. INTERSPECIFIC ALLOMETRIC COEFFICIENT

1. General

The interspecific allometric coefficient is determined from samples of different species, each species represented by mean adult brain and body weights. This coefficient will be presented for various orders of reptiles.

2. Squamates

a. *Material.* The 48 species studied are listed in Tables III and IV. The 32 values for lizards, the one for an amphisbaenian, and the values for eight

TABLE III

Sauria. Values for E (*brain weight) and* S (*body weight), indices of encephalization*

Species	S(g)	E(g)	Origin	Index of encephalization
1 *Hemidactylus mabouia*	2·5	0·033	Reunion	115
2 *Phelsuma cepediana*	5·0	0·059	Mauritius	134
3 *Tarentola mauritanica*	7·8	0·070	Tunisia	120
4 *Gekko gecko*	54·8	0·198	—	100
5 *Chalarodon madagascariensis*	6·3	0·060	Madagascar	117
6 *Anolis auratus*	10·5	0·073	French Guiana	103
7 *Liolaemus chiliensis*	26·0	0·1035	Chile	83
8 *Hoplurus sebae*	51·0	0·267	Madagascar	141
9 *Iguana iguana*	253·5	0·606	French Guiana	117
10 *Agama inermis*	12·9	0·099	Tunisia	124
11 *Calotes versicolor*	14·6	0·097	Reunion	112
12 *Agama agama*	29·3	0·173	Ivory Coast	129
13 *Uromastyx acanthinurus*	164·0	0·335	Algeria	85
14 *Chamaeleo lateralis*	10·9	0·061	Madagascar	85
15 *Chalcides mionecton*	6·4	0·030	Morocco	58
16 *Chalcides chalcides*	18·8	0·0555	S.-E. France	55
17 *Chalcides ocellatus*	32·0	0·090	Tunisia	63
18 *Scincus scincus*	34·1	0·116	Algeria	79
19 *Eumeces schneiderii*	51·7	0·1715	Tunisia	90
20 *Psammodromus hispanicus*	2·1	0·025	SE France	97
21 *Lacerta vivipara*	3·2	0·028	SW France	84
22 *Lacerta muralis*	4·2	0·046	SW France	115
23 *Psammodromus algirus*	4·3	0·045	Portugal	112
24 *Lacerta viridis*	21·2	0·109	SW France	100
25 *Lacerta lepida*	70·8	0·224	SW France	96
26 *Cordylus cordylus*	56·5	0·175	—	86
27 *Zonosaurus quadrilineatus*	82·7	0·209	Madagascar	81
28 *Zonosaurus maximus*	386·4	0·565	Madagascar	84
29 *Ameiva* species	27·1	0·231	French Guiana	181
30 *Callopistes maculatus*	50·3	0·318	Chile	169
31 *Anguis fragilis*	22·0	0·044	France	39
32 *Varanus griseus*	254·2	0·722	Algeria	139

(from Platel, 1975)

of the 15 species of snakes were obtained by the method described earlier. Values for the other seven species of snakes were taken from the literature.

TABLE IV

Serpentes—Amphisbaenia. Values for E (brain weight) and S (body weight), indices of encephalization

Species	S(g)	E(g)	Origin	Index of encephaliza- tion
SERPENTES				
x *Boa constrictor*	1829·0	0·440	Crile and Quiring, 1940	25
y *Boa constrictor*	4460·0	0·649	French Guiana	21
z *Python molurus*	6140·0	1·123	Crile and Quiring, 1940	29
a *Thamnophis sirtalis*	54·5	0·100	Crile and Quiring, 1940	51
b *Natrix natrix*	74·1	0·115	SW France	48
c *Natrix maura*	86·0	0·095	SW France	36
d *Coronella girondica*	117·0	0·088	SW France	28
e *Elaphe longissima*	148·2	0·168	SW France	45
f *Coluber viridiflavus*	285·1	0·209	SW France	37
g *Coluber constrictor*	431·0	0·291	Crile and Quiring, 1940	40
h *Naja melanoleuca*	1770·0	0·646	Dubois, 1913	36
i *Cerastes vipera*	62·1	0·076	Algeria	35
j *Vipera berus*	64·2	0·105	Dubois, 1913	48
k *Vipera aspis*	68·7	0·1015	SW France	44
l *Agkistrodon piscivorus*	728·0	0·640	Crile and Quiring, 1940	64
AMPHISBAENIA				
Tr.w. *Trogonophis wiegmanni*	6·5	0·021	Morocco	40

(from Platel, 1975)

b. *Lizards—definition of the reference species.* The static allometric analysis of the 32 lizard species yielded the following results (Fig. 4): $\alpha = 0.669$ (correlation coefficient, 0·9470). This value is very close to that predicted by Snell (1892) and found by von Bonin (1937) for a very diverse sample of mammals (0·655). Similar values have been reported using the same procedure for other vertebrate groups (Table V). Additional groups are now being studied, and the new values will probably fall within the interval of 0·60 and 0·70.

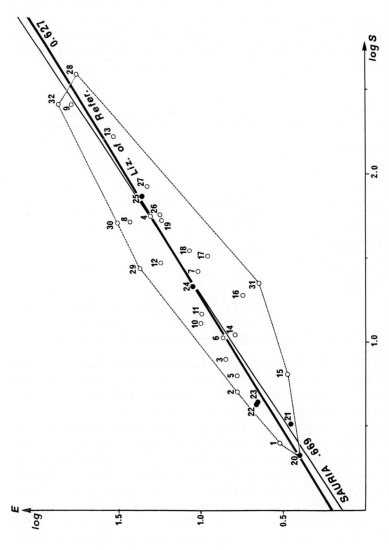

FIG. 4. Interspecific allometric coefficient in lizards. Brain–body weight correlation. Logarithmic scales. The numbers refer to Table III. The two straight lines correspond respectively to the whole sample (32 species; RMA = 0·669) and to the six reference lacertids (Platel, 1975; RMA = 0·627).

The value 0·667 reveals that the weight of the brain is proportional to the surface of the body in a large sample of species (Brandt, 1867). This indicates that for all the species in this sample there is a conservation of function at the expense of body form. This was easily verified in the present sample of lizards. Gould discusses this issue in his analysis of "static interspecific allometry" (1966, 1971). The conservation of form in a sample is translated into an allometric coefficient $\alpha = 1$, that is isometry, which shows that the brain is capable of taking on new functions (Starck, 1965; Gould, 1971).

TABLE V

Interspecific coefficients (of allometry of filiation) in various vertebrates

Taxonomic group	Author(s)	(RMA)
Basal Insectivora	Bauchot and Stephan, 1969	0·634
Insectivora	Bauchot and Stephan, 1969	0·704
Prosimians	Bauchot and Stephan, 1969	0·711
Simians	Bauchot and Stephan, 1969	0·704
Chiroptera		
Megachiroptera	Pirlot and Stephan, 1970	0·668
Microchiroptera	Pirlot and Stephan, 1970	0·609
Rodents	Compoint, 1973	0·649
Teleosts	Ridet, 1973 (46 species)	0·653
	Ridet et al., 1975 (118 species)	0·669
	Bauchot et al., 1977 228 (species)	0·663

This evolutionary phenomenon is also indicated by data on insectivores and primates (Bauchot, 1972b); it is this hypotheses that was formulated with the value 0·939 obtained for a sample of chondrichthyans (Bauchot et al., 1976). The summary considers comparable phenomena in reptiles.

The coefficient obtained for 32 lizard species is changed relatively little by additional data from other species. The choice of a stable reference for calculating indices of encephalization is heuristic. The six lacertids (20–25, Table III) are a reasonable choice for this purpose due to their homogeneity and absence of specialization. Therefore, they were chosen as the *reference saurians* (Platel, 1975a). Their characteristics are as follows: allometric coefficient, 0·627; correlation coefficient, 0·9908; y intercept (log k_0), 0·208; centroid, $\log E = 0·758$, $\log S = 0·877$. The indices of encephalization for the other lizards are calculated relative to the allometry of the reference saurians and are indicated in Table III.

Analysis of the indices of encephalization can be performed in various ways (Platel, 1975); only two will be presented here. One may then investi-

gate the difference in the values of the allometric coefficient in the two categories of lizards proposed by Senn (1970) and Northcutt (1972): type I
lizards (Northcutt, 1972; Northcutt and Butler, 1974) (Gekkonidae, Scincidae, Lacertidae, Cordylidae, Gerrhosauridae and Anguidae); and type II
lizards (Northcutt, 1972; Northcutt and Butler, 1974) (Teiidae, Varanidae,
Iguanidae, Agamidae and Chamaeleonidae).

The allometric coefficients for both types of lizards are within the interval
mentioned earlier (0·6–0·7) but the average indices of encephalization are
very different and significant at the 0·01 level. This indicates a definite
difference in the two levels of organization.

		N	*Allometric coefficient*	*Correlation coefficient*	*Mean index*
Type I	Lizards	19	0·603	0·9402	89·9
Type II	Lizards	13	0·685	0·9567	121·9

(From Platel, 1975)

The index value may be related to the mode of life, in particular, to the
mode of locomotion. Low indices (39 to 79) characterize limbless animals
(*Anguis fragilis*) or limb reduction (Scincidae). Indices from 80 to 95 occur
in slow-moving animals that spend considerable time sunning. Chamaeleons,
which are almost exclusively arboreal, also fall in this category, probably
because of their extreme slowness of movement. Indices of 96–130 appear
in terrestrial animals that are more or less fast-moving. Higher indices (i.e.
greater than 130) occur among species extremely well adapted to an arboreal
existence or virtually bipedal in locomotion. Varanids also possess high
indices but there is no obvious correlation with locomotion.

c. *Snakes.* The average allometric coefficient for a sample of 15 snakes
(Table IV) was 0·549. This differs from coefficients for other groups of
vertebrates. The graphic analysis (Fig. 5) suggests a separation of the Boidae
from other snakes, and thus a division of ophidians into Caenophidia (12
species) and Henophidia (3 species). The allometric coefficient is 0·664 for
the first group and 0·750 for the second group (Platel, 1975). The boid value
should be checked by the addition of more species, particularly smaller
species. On the other hand, the allometric coefficient for advanced snakes
(Caenophidia, Hoffstetter, 1939, 1955, 1962) agrees with the values for
other groups, particularly for lizards. In these two cases, the reference
lizards allow the calculation of indices of encephalization (Table IV and
Fig. 6). Considerable diversity occurs among the former, but the highest
index is only 64. The lowest index found thus far is that of the Boidae.

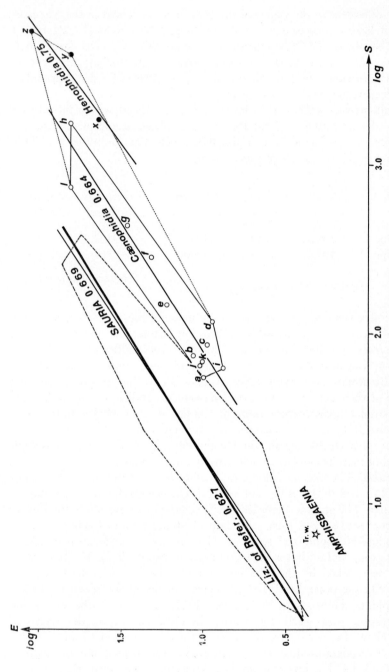

Fig. 5. Interspecific allometric coefficients in snakes. Brain-body weight correlation (E:S). Logarithmic scales. The division into Caenophidia (white dots) (RMA = 0·664) and Henophidia (black dots) (RMA = 0·750) reveals two levels of encephalization in snakes: advanced snakes and boids. The abbreviations are as given in Table IV (from Platel, 1975).

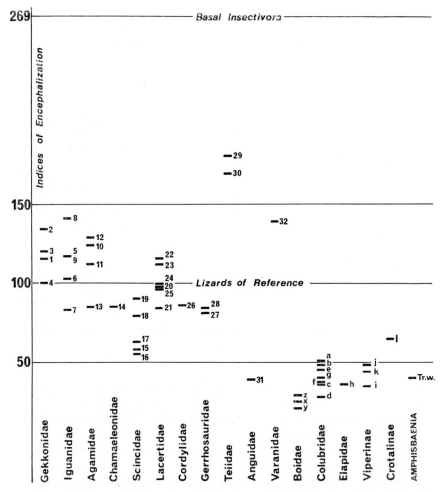

FIG. 6. Indices of encephalization in squamates. The species are regrouped in their respective families (vertical columns); the indices are calculated with reference to the six lacertids (lizards of reference), the mean value is 100. The most encephalized lizards are teiids and varanids. Snakes and limbless lizards show the lower values (modified from Platel, 1972, 1974 and 1975).

3. *Turtles*

Values for brain–body relationships in turtles are, for the most part, taken from literature (Table VI). The analysis is limited to graphic presentation (Fig. 7), as the data possess limited validity. If the data are treated in polygonal form, the polygon representing turtles falls between the lizard and snake polygons with a slope of 2/3.

TABLE VI

Testudines, Crocodilia. Values for E (*brain weight*) *and* S (*body weight*)

Species	S(g)	E(g)	Origin
TESTUDINES			
1. *Chelydra serpentina*	5 125	0·98	Crile and Quiring, 1940
2 *Macroclem temminckii*	1 848	1·01	Crile and Quiring, 1940
3 *Emys orbicularis*	250	0·25	Crile and Quiring, 1940
4 *Pseudemys scripta*	1 418	0·738	Quay, 1972
5 *Clemmys guttata*	2 163	1·36	Crile and Quiring, 1940
6 *Testudo graeca*	267·5	0·318	Platel, present paper
7 *Testudo hermanni*	693·4	0·476	Platel, present paper
8 *Chelonia mydas*	114 300	8·60	Crile and Quiring, 1940
9 *Caretta caretta*	5 443	2·70	Crisp, 1855
10 *Trionyx ferox*	3 253	2·50	Crile and Quiring, 1940
CROCODILIA			
A *Alligator mississippiensis*	205 000	14·08	Crile and Quiring, 1940
B *Crocodylus acutus*	134 000	15·60	Crile and Quiring, 1940
C *Crocodylus acutus*	110 000	11·00	Spector, 1956

4. Crocodilians

Values for brain–body relationships of crocodilians are limited to three species cited by Crile and Quiring (1940) or Spector (1956) (Table VI). The graphic representation reveals the crocodilian polygon to be an extension of the testudinian polygon (Fig. 7).

Values for the unique living representative of the remaining order of reptiles, *Sphenodon punctatus*, were unavailable.

Brain–body relationships for turtles and crocodilians remain to be determined. The available data suggest that these two groups are not more encephalized than the lizards available, as all the values fall below the average allometric line of reference lizards. This is apparent from the position of the testudinian polygon in Fig. 7.

V. Summary

A. SQUAMATES

In 1971 Gould demonstrated that the coefficients of encephalization (values of k in the formula $E = kS^\alpha$) are not independent, but in fact proportional to body size. Bauchot (1972b) provided an empirical test of

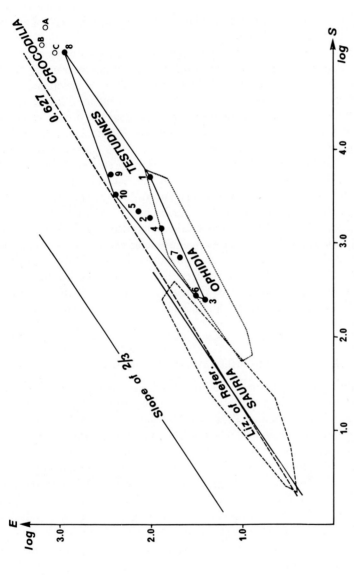

Fig. 7. Interspecific allometric coefficients in turtles and crocodiles. Brain–body weight correlation (*E*:*S*). Logarithmic scales. All dots corresponding to turtles (black dots) and to crocodiles (white dots) are beneath the allometric lines for lizards. No individual of those first two groups is more encephalized than the average lizard.

this observation, for a sample of species representing different evolutionary grades, by a study of allometry in insectivores and primates.

Among reptiles, only squamates show a high degree of uniformity. Many authors believe snakes are derived from a stock of primitive fossorial lizards, such as Feylinidae or Dibamidae (Bellairs and Underwood, 1951; Underwood, 1957; Senn and Northcutt, 1973).

The study of brain–body relationships among various squamates indicates that within this group there are three linear, parallel allometric functions with a slope of 2/3. This is evidence for three grades of encephalization which characterize, lizards, modern snakes, and Boidae. However, an increase in body size is accompanied by a reduction in the degree of encephalization or, alternately, a decrease in the size of the brain in snakes relative to lizards. The $k:S$ relationship yields the same general result with an allometric coefficient of 0·289 and a correlation coefficient of 0·6083 (Platel, 1975). The loss of limbs may explain the reduction in the indices of encephalization in snakes. A similar pattern occurs among limbless lizards (*Anguis fragilis*), scincids, and amphisbaenians. The hiatus that exists between the level of encephalization of the reference lizards and that of *Anguis fragilis* is of the same order of magnitude as the hiatus between the level of encephalization of the reference lizards and that of caenophidians. Snakes are not just lizards with reduced limbs; but a group that have evolved their own unique adaptative strategies. A study of relative volumes of different brain areas in snakes should yield evidence of these specializations (Platel, 1976).

B. STATUS OF REPTILES AMONG THE VERTEBRATES

Brain–body relationships among reptiles have been compared with those of other vertebrates: intraspecific allometric coefficients (Table II), interspecific allometric coefficients (Table V). In conclusion, it is interesting to note the polygons representing lizards, snakes and turtles, the three orders of reptiles studied, and to contrast these with basal insectivores (Bauchot and Stephan, 1964; Stephan, 1967), birds (data of Crile and Quiring, 1940), teleosts (data of Ridet *et al.*, 1975), anurans (data in the literature, and unpublished data of Bauchot and his colleagues), and chondrichthians (Bauchot *et al.*, 1976). Each systematic group is represented by a polygon the edges of which correspond to the extreme values of brain and body size on logarithmic coordinates (Figs 8 and 9). This graphic method was developed by Jerison (1973).

The mammalian level is represented by the basal insectivores which are the least encephalized of living mammals. These ten species are part of another allometric line with a slope of 0·634. The polygons of the other groups (with the exception of chondrichthyans) contain parallel principal axes with a slope of 2/3. These results were reported by Jerison (1969, 1973), Platel (1972), and Ebbesson and Northcutt (1976).

No reptile is as encephalized as the basal insectivores. There is a true hiatus between reptiles and living mammals. It is possible to ask questions about the positions achieved by fossil forms with respect to this kind of

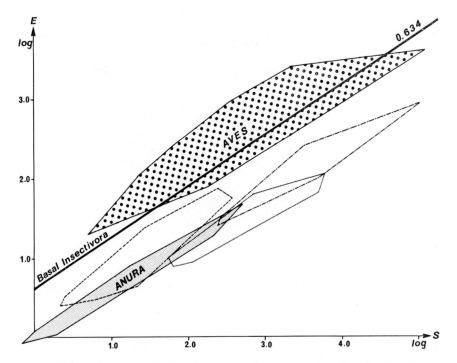

FIG. 8. Brain–body weight relationships in vertebrates. Logarithmic scales. Basal insectivora are figured by their allometric line (RMA = 0·634). Aves and Anura are represented by polygons. The polygons of the three group of reptiles studied are drawn with dotted lines. Explanation in text (modified from Platel, 1972).

analysis. One can determine, in effect, the brain weight as a fraction of the endocranial volume, and as a function of the body weight as determined from the skeleton. Jerison has shown that neither dinosaurs, pterosaurs, nor mammal-like reptiles possessed values which bridge this gap (Jerison, 1969, 1970, 1973). Only *Archeopteryx* possessed a level of encephalization intermediate between that of living reptiles and that of living birds (Jerison, 1968, 1973).

Birds fall on both sides of the allometric function of the basal insectivores;

their polygon is quite distinct from that of the reptiles. The anuran amphi-
bian polygon, on the other hand, intersects that of lizards, snakes and turtles.
Their average level of encephalization is between that of turtles and snakes
(Fig. 8).

The teleost polygon is very extended and almost coincides with the
reptilian polygon (Fig. 9). Finally, the Chondrichthyes bridge this gap.

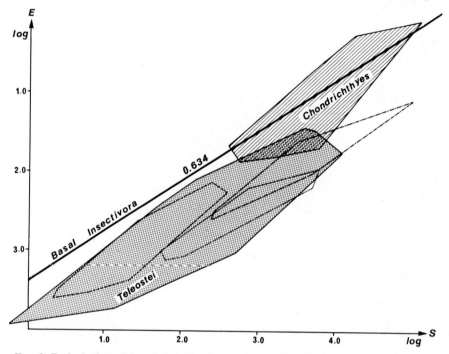

FIG. 9. Brain–body weight relationships in vertebrates. Logarithmic scales. Basal insectivores are represented by their allometric lines (RMA = 0·634). Teleosts and Chondrichthyes are represented by polygons; the polygons of the three groups of reptiles studied
here are drawn with dotted lines. Explanations in text (Bauchot *et al.*, 1976).

Their data results in a polygon, the principal axis of which is almost isometric
($\alpha = 1$). The largest specimens have a level of encephalization greater than
that of the basal insectivores. I noted earlier some of the interpretations
possible for this peculiarity (Bauchot *et al.*, 1976) which were considered
briefly by Ebbesson and Northcutt (1976).

Acknowledgements

I wish to express my gratitude to Dr H. J. Jerison, without whose help
the manuscript of this article would have been far less intelligible. Dr R. G.

3. BRAIN WEIGHT—BODY WEIGHT RELATIONSHIPS

Northcutt also provided helpful comments, and Mrs Mary Sue Northcutt brought a friendly contribution to final achievement.

References

Anthony, R. (1938). Essai de recherche d'une expression anatomique approximative du degré d'organization cérébrale autre que le poids de l'encéphale comparé au poids du corps. *Bull. Mém. Soc. Anthropol. Paris* **9**, 17–67.

Bauchot, R. (1967). Les modifications du poids encéphalique au cours de la fixation. *J. Hirnforsch.* **9**, 253–283.

Bauchot, R. (1972a). Le degré d'organisation cérébrale des Mammifères. *In* "Traité de Zoologie". (P.-P. Grassé, ed.). Masson et Cie, Paris **16**(4), 360–384.

Bauchot, R. (1972b). Encéphalisation et phylogénie. *C. r. hebd. Séanc. Acad. Sci. Paris* **275**, 441–443.

Bauchot, R., Bauchot, M.-L., Platel, R. and Ridet, J.-M. (1977). Brains of Hawaiian tropical fishes. Brain size and evolution. *Copeia* **1**, 42–46.

Bauchot, R. and Diagne, M. (1973). La croissance encéphalique chez *Hemicentetes semispinosus* (Insectivora, Tenrecidae). *Mammalia* **37**, 468–477.

Bauchot, R. and Guerstein, M.-M. (1970). Evolution de la taille et de la densité neuronique au cours de la croissance postnatale chez le rat blanc, *Rattus norvegicus* (Berkenhout). *J. Hirnforsch.* **12**, 255–265.

Bauchot, R. and Platel, R. (1973). L'encéphalisation. *La Recherche* **4**(40), 1069–1077.

Bauchot, R., Platel, R. and Petermann, R. (1972). La variabilité pondérale de quelques organes chez l'agame (Margouillat) *Agama agama* (L.) (Reptilia, Sauria, Agamidae) *Zool. Anz.* **188**, 316–338.

Bauchot, R., Platel, R. and Ridet, J.-M. (1976). Brain–body weight relationships in Selachii. *Copeia*, **3**, 305–310.

Bauchot, R. and Stephan, H. (1964). Le poids encéphalique chez les insectivores malgaches. *Acta Zool. Stockh.* **45**, 63–75.

Bauchot, R. and Stephan, H. (1969). Encéphalisation et niveau évolutif chez les Simiens. *Mammalia* **33**, 225–275.

Bellairs, A. d'A. and Underwood, G. (1951). The origin of snakes. *Biol. Rev.* **26**, 193–237.

Blanc, C. P. (1969). Études sur les Iguanidae de Madagascar. II. Observations sue l'écologie de *Chalarodon madagascariensis* Peters, 1854. *Oecologia (Berl.)* **2**, 282–318.

Bonin, G. von (1937). Brain weight and body weight in mammals. *J. gen. Psychol.* **16**, 379–389.

Brandt, A. (1867). Sur le rapport du poids du cerveau á celui du corps chez différents animaux. *Bull. Soc. Imp. Natur., Moscow* **40**, 525–543.

Brummelkamp, R. (1940). Brain weight and body size (a study of cephalization problem). *Ned. Akad. Wet.* **39**, 1–57.

Compoint, C. (1973). L'encéphalisation chez les rongeurs. *C. r. hebd. Séanc Acad. Sci., Paris* **277**, 861–863.

Count, E. W. (1947). Brain and body weight in man: their antecedents in growth and evolution. *Ann. N.Y. Acad. Sci.* **46**, 993–1122.

Crile, C. and Quiring, D. P. (1940). A record of the body weight and certain organ and gland weight of 3690 animals. *Ohio J. Sci.* **40**, 219–259.

Crisp, E. (1855). *Proc. Zool. Soc. Lond.* **23**.

Delfini, C., Platel, R. and Raffin, J.-P. (1973). Relations pondérales encéphalo-somatiques chez le poussin et l'adult de Goéland (Goéland argenté et goéland brun). *C. r. hebd. Séanc. Acad. Sci. Paris* **277**, 213–216.

Dubois, E. (1913). On the relation between the quantity of brain and the size of the body in vertebrates. *Proc. Sci. k. Akad. Wet. Amsterdam* 16, 647–669.

Ebbesson, S. O. E. and Northcutt, R. G. (1976). Neurology of anamniotic vertebrates. *In* "Evolution of Brain and Behavior in Vertebrates". (R. B. Masterton, M. E. Bitterman, and C. B. G. Campbell, eds). Lawrence Erlbaum Assoc., Hillsdale, N.J., 115–146.

Gould, S. J. (1966). Allometry and size in ontogeny and phylogeny. *Biol. Rev.* 41, 587–640.

Gould, S. J. (1971). Geometric similarity in allometric growth: a contribution to the problem of scaling in the evolution of size. *Am. Nat.* 105, 113–136.

Gould, S. J. (1975). Allometry in primates, with emphasis on scaling and the evolution of the brain. *In* "Approaches to Primate Paleobiology". (F. S. Szalay, ed.). Karger, Basel, Contrib. Primatol. 5, 244–292.

Hoffstetter, R. (1939). Contribution à l'étude des Elapidae actuels et fossiles et de l'ostéologie des Ophidiens. *Arch. Mus. Hist. nat., Lyon* 15(3), 1–78.

Hoffstetter, R. (1955). Squamates de type moderne. *In* "Traité de Paléontologie." (J. Piveteau, ed.). Masson et Cie, Paris 5, 606–662.

Hoffstetter, R. (1962). Revue des récentes acquisitions concernant l'histoire et la systématique des squamates. *Colloques int. Cent. natn. Rech. scient.* 104, 243–279.

Hrdlicka, A. (1905). Brain weight in Vertebrates. *Smithson. misc. Collns* 48, 89–112.

Jerison, H. J. (1968). Brain evolution and *Archaeopteryx. Nature, Lond.* 219, 1381–1382.

Jerison, H. J. (1969). Brain evolution and dinosaur brains. *Am. Nat.* 103, 575–588.

Jerison, H. J. (1970). Brain evolution: New light on old principles. *Science, N.Y.* 170, 1224–1225.

Jerison, H. J. (1973). "Evolution of the Brain and Intelligence." Academic Press, New York and London.

Jerison, H. J. (1975). Fossil evidence of the evolution of the human brain. *Ann. Rev. Anthropol.* 4, 27–58.

Lapicque, L. (1908). Le poids encéphalique en fonction du poids corporel entre individus d'une même espèce. *Bull. Mém. Soc. Anthropol. Paris* 8, 313–345.

Lapicque, L. and Laugier, H. (1908). Relation entre la grandeur des yeux et le poids de l'encéphale chez les vertébrés inférieurs. *C. r. Séanc. Soc. Biol.* 64, 1108–1110.

Naccarati, S. (1922). On the relation between the weight of the internal secretory glands and the body weight and brain weight. *Anat. Rec.* 24, 255–260.

Northcutt, R. G. (1972). The teiid prosencephalon and its bearing on squamate systematics. *Program and abstracts of American Society of Ichthyologists and Herpetologists* 1972, 75–76.

Northcutt, R. G. and Butler, A. B. (1974). Evolution of the reptilian visual systems: Retinal projections in a nocturnal lizard, *Gekko gecko* (Linnaeus). *J. comp. Neurol.* 157 (4), 453–466.

Pirlot, P. (1969). L'exposant phylogénétique de Snell-Dubois chez les Chiroptères. *Biométrie-Praximétrie* 10, 22–37.

Pirlot, P. and Stephan, H. (1970). Encephalization in Chiroptera. *Can. J. Zool.* 48, 433–444.

Platel, R. (1972). Les relations pondérales encéphalo-somatiques chez les reptiles sauriens. *C. r. hebd. Séanc. Acad. Sci. Paris* 274, 2181–2184.

Platel, R. (1974). Poids encéphalique et indice d'encéphalisation chez les reptiles sauriens. *Zool. Anz.* 192, 332–382.

Platel, R. (1975a). Données nouvelles sur l'encéphalisation des Squamates. *Z. zool. Syst. Evolutionsforsch.* 13, 161–184.

Platel, R. (1975b). Encéphalization et sexe chez les reptiles squamates. *Bull. Soc. zool. Fr.* **100**, 621–631.

Platel, R. (1976). Analyze volumétrique des principales subdivisions encéphaliques chez les Reptiles Sauriens. *J. Hirnforsch.* **17**, 513–537.

Platel, R. and Bauchot, R. (1970). L'encéphale de *Scincus scincus* (L.) (Reptilia, Sauria. Scincidae). Recherche d'une grandeur de référence pour des études quantitatives, *Zool. Anz.* **184**, 33–47.

Platel, R., Bauchot, R. and Delfini, C. (1972). Les relations pondérales encéphalo-somatiques chez *Gallus domesticus* L. (Galliformes, Phasianidae). Analyse au cours de l'incubation et de la période postnatale. *Z. wiss. Zool.* **185**, 88–104.

Quay, W. B. (1972). Sexual and relative growth differences in brain regions of the turtle *Pseudemys scripta* (Schoepff). *Copeia* 1972(3), 541–546.

Ridet, J. M. (1973). Les relations pondérales encéphalo-somatiques chez les poissons téléostéens. *C. r. hebd. Séanc. Acad. Sci., Paris* **276**, 1437–1440.

Ridet, J.-M., Bauchot, R., Delfini, C., Platel, R. and Thireau, M. (1973). L'encéphale de *Scyliorhinus canicula* (Linné, 1758). Recherche d'une grandeur de référence pour des études quantitatives. *Cah. Biol. Mar. Roscoff* **14**, 11–28.

Ridet, J.-M., Guézé, P., Platel, R. and Bauchot, R. (1975). L'allometrie pondérale encéphalo-somatique chez les poissons teléostéens des côtes réunionnaises. *C. r. hebd. Séanc. Acad. Sci., Paris* **280**, 109–112.

Rose, F. (1957). Allometrische Änderungen bei der Ontogenese und Phylogenese des Eidechsengehirns. *Zool. Jb. (Anat.)* **75**, 433–480.

Saint Girons, H. (1965). Les critères d'âge chez les reptiles et leurs applications à l'étude de la structure des populations sauvages. *Terre Vie* **4**, 342–358.

Senn, D. G. (1970). Die Zusammenhänge von Grosshirnstriatum, dorsalem Thalamus und Tectum opticum bei Echsen. *Verh. naturf. Ges. Basel* **80**, 209–225.

Senn, D. G. and Northcutt, R. G. (1973). The forebrain and the midbrain of some squamates and their bearing on the origin of snakes. *J. Morph.* **140**(2), 135–152.

Sholl, D. (1948). The quantitative investigation of the vertebrate brain and the applicability of allometric formulae to its study. *Proc. R. Soc.* **B135**, 243–258.

Snell, O. (1892). Die Abhängigkeit des Hirngewichtes von dem Körpergewicht und den geistigen Fähigkeiten. *Arch. Psychiat. Nervkrank* **23**, 436–446.

Spector, W. S. (1956). "Handbook of Biological Data." Saunders, Philadelphia.

Starck, D. (1965). Die Neencephalisation. *In* "Menschliche Abstammung." G. Fischer, Stuttgart, 103–144.

Stephan, H. (1967). Zur Entwicklungshöhe der Insektivoren nach Merkmalen des Gehirns und die Definition der "Basalen Insektivoren." *Zool. Anz.* **179**, 177–199.

Teissier, G. (1948). La relation d'allométrie, sa signification statistique et biologique. *Biometrics* **4**, 14–53.

Teissier, G. (1955). Sur la détermination de l'axe d'un nuage rectiligne de points. *Biometrics* **11**, 344–356.

Thireau, M., Bauchot, R., Platel, R. and Ridet, J.-M. (1973). L'encéphale de *Salamandra salamandra fastuosa* Lacépède, 1788 (Amphibia, Caudata, Salamandridae). Étude préalable à des recherches de neuroanatomie quantitative. *Bull. Mus. Hist. nat., Paris* **106**, 49–65.

Underwood, G. (1957). On lizards of the family Pygopodidae: a contribution to the morphology and phylogeny of the Squamata. *J. Morph.* **100**, 207–268.

Welcker, H. and Brandt, A. (1903). Gewichtswerthe der Körperorgane bei dem Menschen und den Thieren. *Arch. Anthropol.* **28**, 1–89.

White, J. F. and Gould, S. J. (1965). Interpretation of the coefficient in the allometric equation. *Am. Nat.* **99**, 5–18.

CHAPTER 4

Embryonic Development of the Central Nervous System

DAVID G. SENN

Zoologisches Institut, Universität Basel, Basel, Switzerland

I. Introduction

There are few developmental studies of reptilian nervous systems. Will (1892–95), C. L. Herrick (1892), von Kupffer (1906), and Nelsen (1953) provide general treatments of reptilian neurogenesis. However, most authors have emphasized the development of specific brain regions. Such studies have focused on the rhombencephalon (Landmann, 1971; Schwab and Durand, 1974), cerebellum (Larsell, 1926, 1932), mesencephalon (Senn, 1968a), diencephalon (Bergquist, 1953, 1954; Senn, 1968a, 1970b, 1971), and telencephalon (Johnston, 1916; Faul, 1926; Kuhlenbeck, 1931; Warner, 1946; Källén, 1951; Kirsche, 1972; Hetzel, 1974; Rudin, 1975). Theoretical discussions are included by His (1893), Burckhardt (1894a, b) and Senn (1968c, 1970a). The relatively new autoradiographic techniques for determining time of origin and migration patterns of cells are only beginning to be applied to reptiles (Schwab and Durand, 1974).

This chapter describes the development of the central nervous system in reptiles, with emphasis on the embryos of a lizard (*Lacerta sicula*), a turtle (*Chelydra serpentina*), and a snake (*Natrix natrix*).

II. Reptilian Embryonic Stages

Much of the following discussion is based on new observations. The staging system described by Yntema (1968) has been used for embryos of *Chelydra serpentina*; Peter's (1904) extensive developmental study on *Lacerta agilis* has been used to stage embryos of *Lacerta sicula* and *Natrix natrix*. Comparably staged series exist for *Thamnophis sirtalis* (Zehr, 1962) but not for *Sphenodon* or the crocodilians.

Embryos of *Lacerta* and *Natrix* were incubated at 30°C and 100% relative humidity, resulting in approximate hatching times of 31 and 32 days, respect-

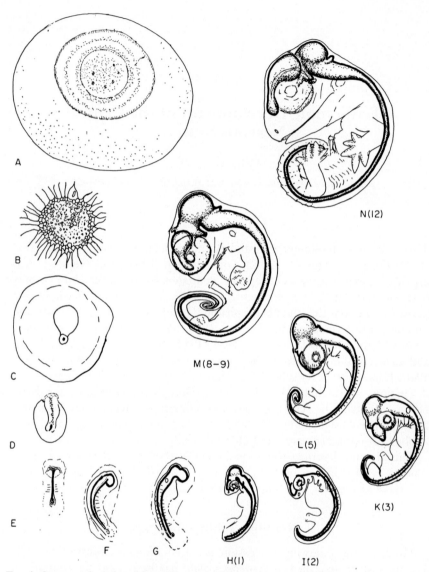

Fig. 1. Ontogenesis and position of the central nervous system in a lizard (*Lacerta sicula*). A–F. Cleavage pattern and embryonic development within the oviduct. G. Embryo at time of oviposition. H–P. Embryos between oviposition and hatching. Embryonic stages are indicated by numbers (in parentheses) of incubation days at 30°C. Q. Lateral view of adult brain *in situ* showing major structures.

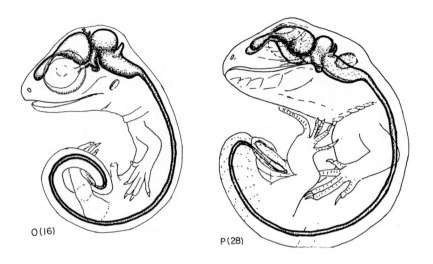

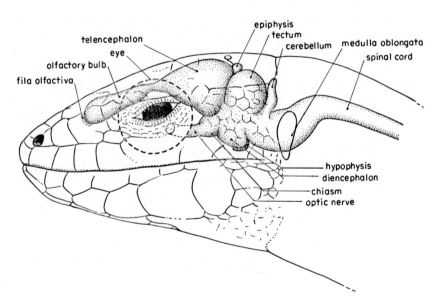

FIG. 1 *continued*.

ively. The times cited in this chapter refer to incubation days; however, it is important to note that development begins before the eggs are laid. Thus *Lacerta* embryos are at a stage of five brain vesicles (von Kupffer, 1906) on incubation day 1, and the embryos of *Natrix* are somewhat more advanced by that time.

The successful incubation of reptilian embryos requires special conditions. Freshly laid squamate eggs must not be inverted, as this kills the embryo. The eggs are best placed on cotton or peat in glass containers. A saturated Nipagine (Ciba Geigy) solution is sprayed over the substrate to prevent fungal growth. The partially covered containers are placed in a well-ventilated incubator at 30°C. A container of distilled water on the incubator floor provides a constant relative humidity of 100%.

Various embryonic stages are obtained by opening the eggs after immersion in water and fixing the embryos in AFA (90 ml of 80% ethanol, 5 ml formalin, 5 ml glacial acetic acid). Embryos are normally fixed for at least one week, then sectioned in paraffin for combined Bodian and Cresyl-violet staining (Senn, 1966).

III. Appearance and Growth of the Neural Tube

The overall pattern of reptilian neurogenesis is illustrated in Fig. 1, which shows embryos of *Lacerta sicula* at several stages. Reptilian embryos, like those of birds, develop on one side of the yolk (Fig. 1A, B, C). The neural plate extends along the midline of the embryo (Fig. 1D, E) and forms the neural tube (Nelsen, 1953). At the end of neurulation, the part of the neural tube rostral to the cervical flexure is markedly larger than the caudal part which will form the spinal cord (Fig. 1F). The rostral part of the neural tube gradually transforms into two vesicles (von Kupffer, 1906). The rostral archencephalon gives rise to the prosencephalon, while the caudal archencephalon and rostral deuterencephalon give rise to the mesencephalon. The caudal deuterencephalon becomes the rhombencephalon, which subsequently forms a dorsal metencephalon and a ventral myelencephalon (Fig. 2). Finally, the prosencephalon forms evaginated cerebral hemispheres (telencephalon) and the diencephalon.

Reptiles thus exhibit five brain vesicles, a developmental pattern common to all vertebrates (Fig. 3A). Subsequent brain development results in several flexures due to differential growth of the various vesicles (Fig. 3B). A cranial (cephalic) flexure develops around the diencephalo–tegmental boundary (Fig. 3A). The point of flexure is marked by the rostral end of the notochord; the flexion process coincides with rapid enlargement of the prosencephalon, but its cause(s) is unknown. The cranial flexure point persists in the adult (Fig. 1Q) as a depression in the rostral floor of the myelencephalon. A ventrally directed flexure (pontine flexure) occurs in the medulla, and a dorsally directed flexure (cervical flexure, Fig. 3B) occurs at the medullo-spinal junction. Both these flexures are maintained in the adult.

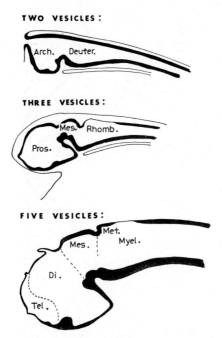

FIG. 2. Early embryonic division of the reptilian brain in sagittal view. The names of the brain vesicles (modified after von Kupffer, 1906) are formed by adding a positional unit to encephalon, e.g. arch + encephalon = archencephalon. Di., Diencephalon; Mes., mesencephalon; Met., metencephalon; Myel., myelencephalon; Tel., telencephalo

IV. Regional Development

A. GENERAL

Early formation of the wall of the neural tube is similar in the spinal cord and in each brain vesicle. Initially, the wall consists of a single layer of densely packed epithelial cells—the matrix layer (Fig. 4A). A cell-free layer—the stratum zonale (Bergquist, 1953)—forms external to the matrix layer (Figs 4A, 5A, 6A). The stratum zonale consists of the peripheral processes of matrix layer cells. Cells of the matrix layer divide and eventually migrate radially into the stratum zonale. The extent and pattern of these migrations determine the adult structure of each particular region of the nervous system. Matrix layer cells remaining near the ventricle form the ependyma.

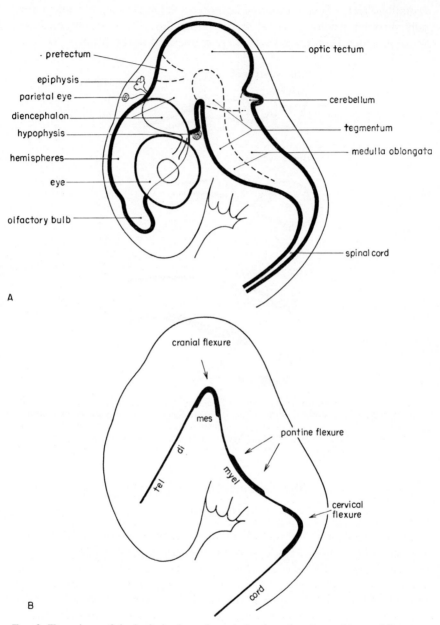

FIG. 3. Two views of the brain in the embryonic head to show its position and flexures.

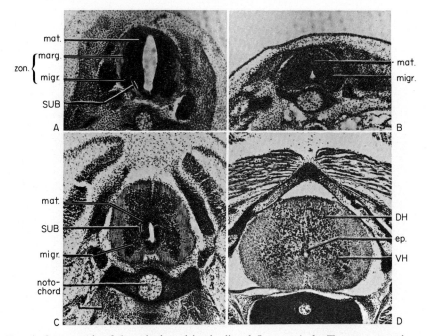

FIG. 4. Ontogenesis of the spinal cord in the lizard *Lacerta sicula*. Transverse sections; bar scale indicates 200 μm. A. Embryo at 6 incubation days. The matrix (mat.) is the early cell layer; some migrated cells (migr.) are found in the stratum zonale (zon.); a marginal zone (marg.) remains free of cells; the subcentral boundary (SUB) separates the matrix and the stratum zonale. Migrated cells form the ventral (VH) and dorsal (DH) horns. B. Stage 10. C. Stage 12. D. Stage 28. The matrix produces the ependyma (ep.) *in situ*.

A distinct subcentral boundary separates the matrix layer from the stratum zonale. Details of the development of the spinal cord and brain follow.

B. Spinal Cord

In the region of the spinal cord the neural tube consists of the roof plate, floor plate, and the alar and basal plates characteristic of all vertebrate embryos (His, 1893). The matrix layer is thick in the alar and basal plates and thin in the roof and floor plates (Figs 4A, 5A). The lumen of the tube is relatively large. The matrix layer increases in thickness during development (Figs 4C, 5B, C). Eventually, cells begin to migrate into the stratum zonale, and the matrix layer becomes thinner. Cells do not reach the periphery of the stratum zonale, but occupy the internal layer of the stratum zonale (the mantle layer), leaving a cell-free external layer (the marginal layer) which consists of longitudinally coursing fibers. The two layers are distinctly

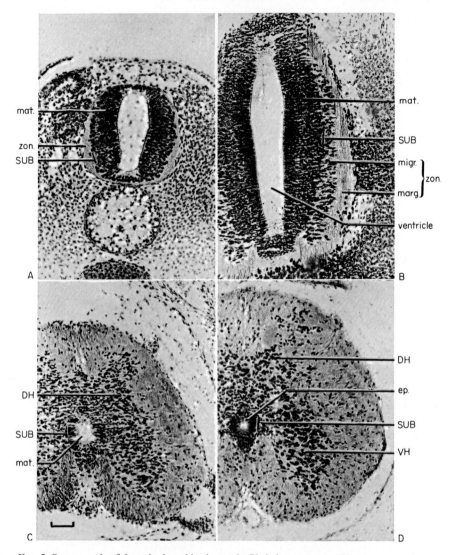

FIG. 5. Ontogenesis of the spinal cord in the turtle *Chelydra serpentina*. Transverse sections; bar scale indicates 100 μm. The stages are after Yntema (1968). A. Stage 12. B. Stage 15. C. Stage 22. D. Stage 24. Abbreviations and development as in Fig. 4.

separated by an intrazonal boundary (Senn, 1972). Cells which migrate dorsally form the dorsal horns of the cord; those which migrate ventrally (Starck, 1965) form the ventral horns (Figs 4D, 5D, 6C, 7). The matrix layer is reduced to a thin layer of ependymal cells by the end of the migration

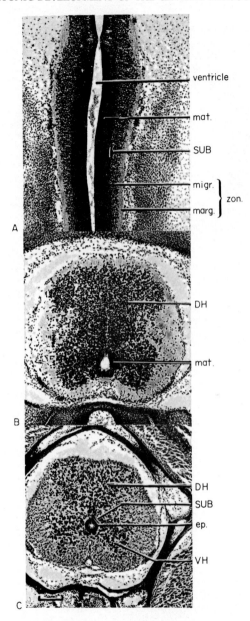

FIG. 6. Ontogenesis of the spinal cord in the snake *Natrix natrix*. Horizontal section (A) and transverse sections (B, C); bar indicates 200 μm to scale. Abbreviations and development as in Fig. 4.

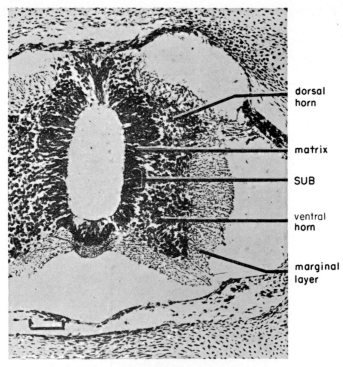

FIG. 7. Spinal cord of an embryonic *Alligator mississippiensis*. SUB, Subcentral boundary. Transverse sections; bar scale indicates 100 μm.

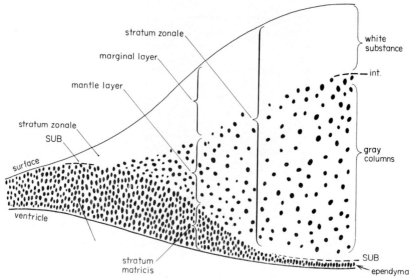

FIG. 8. Diagram of the development of the spinal cord. Differentiation is indicated from left to right. Compare with Figs 4–6. int., Intrazonal boundary; SUB, subcentral boundary.

period (Figs 4D, 5D, 6C). The migration pattern in the spinal cord is sum-marized diagrammatically in Fig. 8, which shows the undifferentiated neural tube at the left. Time is represented on the horizontal axis, and the adult condition is shown to the right of the figure.

In *Lacerta*, the course of the spinal nerve roots and dorsal sensory ganglia is more complicated than previously described (Ariëns Kappers *et al.*, 1936). The sensory neurons develop from the neural crest, and distinct dorsal and ventral populations are connected by a narrow bridge of ganglion cells (Fig. 9). The dorsal and ventral sensory populations give rise to dorsal

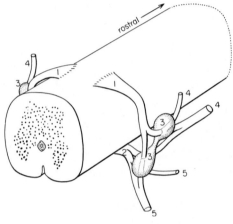

FIG. 9. Spinal nerves in the cervical area in *Lacerta sicula*. Reconstruction from dorso-caudolateral view. 1, dorsal root; 2, ventral root; 3, spinal ganglia; 4, dorsal branches; 5, ventral branches.

and ventral rootlets, respectively. These rootlets and their crest populations may correspond to epaxial and hypaxial divisions, but experimental studies are needed to confirm this.

C. RHOMBENCEPHALON

The rhombencephalon is that part of the brain which lies above the notochord. Topographically, it is recognized very early as it appears in von Kupffer's stage of three brain vesicles (Fig. 2). A number of terms—such as medulla oblongata, tegmentum and cerebellum—characterize different parts of the rhombencephalon. These terms must be defined, as they partially overlap and are used differently by different authors. The *medulla oblongata* (Fig. 10) contains the nuclei of the cranial nerves (III–XII) and fuses ventrally with the tegmentum. The *tegmentum* (Fig. 10) consists of the reticular nuclei and their derivatives which form extensive connections with the spinal cord and higher brain centers. The tegmentum includes what is usually termed the mesencephalic floor; it is massive rostrally and extends far caudally. The *cerebellum* (Fig. 10) is a cortical structure which is positioned dorsally.

The rhombencephalic wall is not of uniform thickness (Figs 2, 11, 12, 13, 14). The matrix layer is thick ventrolaterally, but thin dorsally where the

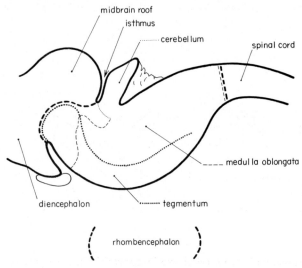

FIG. 10. Subdivisions of the rhombencephalon and adjacent areas. The definitions of medulla oblongata and tegmentum are not completely exclusive.

tela chorioidea forms. The migration pattern of the rhombencephalon is basically like that of the spinal cord, except that cells migrate further peripherally into the external zone of the stratum zonale. These cells form the various nuclear groups of the rhombencephalon. Figure 14, for example, shows the development of the vestibular nuclei in *Lacerta*.

The migration pattern of the oculomotor (Fig. 15) and trochlear (Fig. 16) nuclei differs from that of the other rhombencephalic nuclei. Oculomotor and trochlear nuclei develop from cells which remain in the matrix layer; thus the matrix layer does not become completely reduced to an ependyma. The motor neurons quickly become larger than the surrounding cells, differentiating into medium-sized, round or multipolar neurons. Axons can be recognized as soon as the neurons form cellular groupings. The axons of the oculomotor neurons grow ventrolaterally and leave the brain as the oculomotor nerve (Fig. 17). Most of these axons course ipsilaterally,

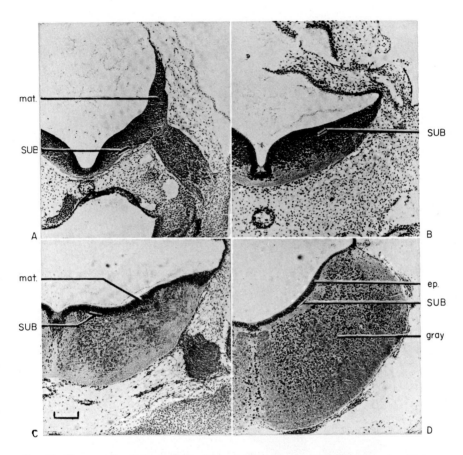

FIG. 11. Ontogenesis of the medulla oblongata in the turtle *Chelydra serpentina*. Transverse sections through the area of the Vth nerve; bar scale indicates 200 μm. A. Stage 12; the dense cellular matrix (mat.) is peripherally bounded by the subcentral boundary (SUB). B. Stage 14. C. Stages 18. D. Stages 23. In B–D, migrating cells populate the growing stratum zonale and represent the nuclei (gray). A thin portion of the matrix is left as an ependyma (ep.). Compare with Figs 4–8.

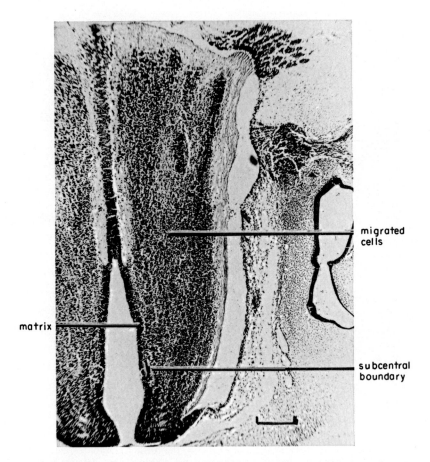

FIG. 12. Embryonic rhombencephalon of *Alligator mississippiensis*. Horizontal section; bar scale indicates 200 μm. Most cells have migrated into the stratum zonale. SUB, Subcentral boundary.

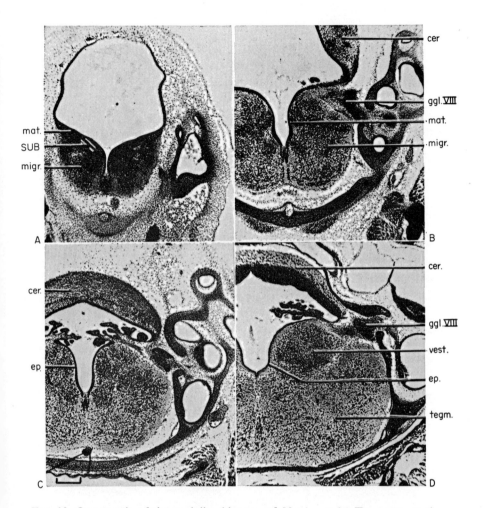

FIG. 13. Ontogenesis of the medulla oblongata of *Natrix natrix*. Transverse sections through the area of the VIIIth nerve; the bar scale indicates 200 μm. A. Stage 1. B. Stage 7. C. Stage 11. D. Stage 25. Migrated cells (migr.) leave the matrix (mat.) through the subcentral boundary (SUB). They form areas such as the vestibular region (vest.) and the tegmentum (tegm.). The ependyma (ep.) represents the remaining matrix. The cerebellum (cer.) lies dorsally, the ganglion of the VIIIth nerve (ggl. VIII) laterally.

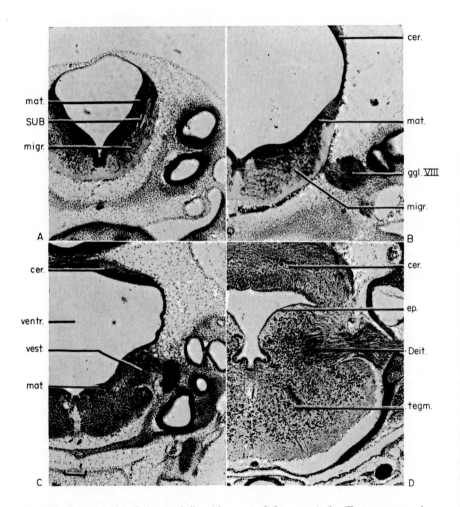

FIG. 14. Ontogenesis of the medulla oblongata of *Lacerta sicula*. Transverse sections through the area of the VIIIth nerve; the bar scale indicates 100 μm. A. Stage 6. B. Stage 7. C. Stage 10. D. Stage 20. Abbreviations and description as in Fig. 13. Deit., Deiters nucleus; ventr., ventricle.

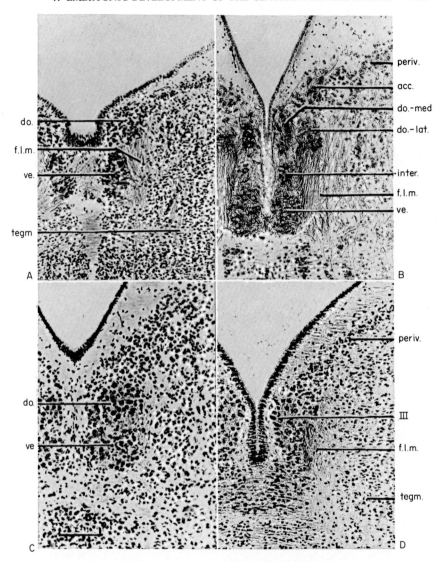

FIG. 15. Oculomotor nucleus in embryos. Transverse sections, right side; bar scale indicates 100 μm. A and B. Embryos of *Lacerta sicula* at 12 and 25 days respectively. The nuclei develop from a continuation of tectal periventricular gray (periv.). A dorsal (do.) and ventral (ve.) part are formed medially to the fasciculus longitudinalis medialis (f.l.m.). In B, a number of cell groups are distinct: acc., nucleus accessorius III; do-lat., dorso-lateral nucleus; do.-med., dorsomedial nucleus; inter., intermedial nucleus; ve, ventral nucleus. C. *Natrix natrix* (stage 21). D. *Chelydra serpentina* (stage 21). tegm., tegmentum; III, oculomotor nucleus.

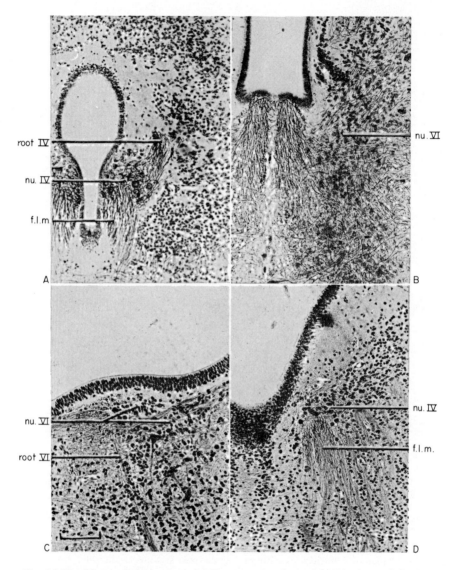

FIG. 16. Trochlear and abducens nuclei. Transverse sections, right side; bar scale indicates 100 μm. A. Nucleus IV in *Lacerta sicula* (stage 25). B. Nucleus VI in *Lacerta* (stage 25). C. Nucleus VI in *Chelydra serpentina* (stage 23). D. Nucleus IV in *Chelydra* (stage 23). f.l.m., Fasciculus longitudinalis medialis; nu. IV, trochlear nucleus; nu. VI, nucleus abducens; root VI, root of abducens; root IV, root of trochlear.

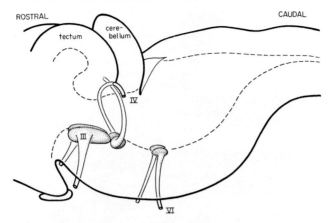

FIG. 17. Position of the eye-muscle nuclei in the rhombencephalon. Lateral view. The roots of nuclei oculomotorius (III) and abducens (VI) course in a ventral direction. The trochlear roots (IV) cross in the isthmal region. The broken line bounds the ventricle.

but a few cross in the tegmentum (Stefanelli, 1941; Senn, 1968a). The axons of trochlear neurons grow dorsally and cross in the isthmus as the trochlear decussation (Fig. 17). The oculomotor nuclei develop around the medial longitudinal fasciculus, surrounding it dorsally, medially, and ventrally (Fig. 18).

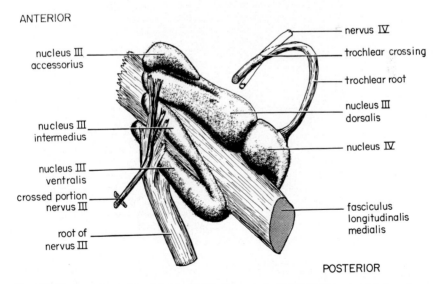

FIG. 18. Oculomotor and trochlear nuclei in *Lacerta sicula*. Mediodorsocaudal view showing arrangement of the nuclei along the fasciculus longitudinalis medialis.

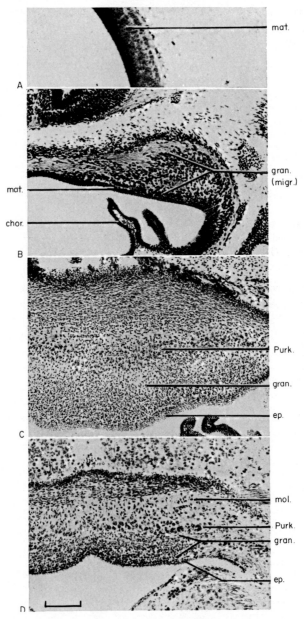

FIG. 19. Development of the cerebellum in *Lacerta sicula*. Transverse sections, right side; bar scale indicates 100 μm. A. Stage 7. B. Stage 12. C. Stage 19. D. Stage 28. The cellular matrix (mat.) gives origin to migrating cells (migr.) forming the granular layer (gran.). External cells of the granular layers differentiate the Purkinje cells (Purk.). The molecular layer (mol.) covers the layer of Purkinje cells. The thin remaining part of the matrix forms the ependyma (ep.) which continues into the chorioid plexus (chor.).

The development of the cerebellum also differs from that of the other rhombencephalic areas (Fig. 19). The cerebellum forms from paired structures situated at the dorsolateral corners of the rhombencephalon (Larsell, 1926, 1932; Weston, 1936). These two masses fuse prior to the differentiation of the cerebellar cortex (Kuhlenbeck, 1927; Senn, 1970a). The anlage of the cerebellum consists at this time of a plate (lamina metencephalica) covering the fourth ventricle (Fig. 19A). Cells leave the matrix layer of this plate and populate the stratum zonale (Fig. 19B). Most of the matrix layer cells become granule cells; however, the most centrally situated form Purkinje cells (Fig. 19c).

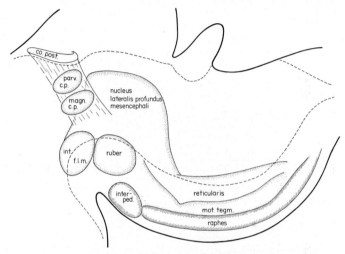

FIG. 20. Lateral view of the tegmental nuclei. Rostral is to the left. The broken line bounds the ventricle. The posterior commissure (co. post.) contains a parvocellular (parv. c.p.) and a magnocellular (magn. c.p.) nucleus among the fibers. Nucleus lateralis profundus mesencephali is in contact with the tectum; nucleus interstitialis (int. f.l.m.) produces part of the fasciculus longitudinalis medialis. Nucleus interpeduncularis (interped.) and nucleus raphes (raphes) lie in the medial part of the tegmentum. Red nucleus, nucleus motorius tegmenti (mot. tegm.) and nucleus reticularis (reticularis) are scattered more laterally.

The remaining tegmental nuclei develop by typical migrations into the stratum zonale. The largest of these nuclei is nucleus lateralis profundus mesencephali (Figs 20, 21) which migrates ventrolaterally. The cells differentiate into round or polygonal neurones of various sizes. The red nucleus and the interstitial nucleus of the medial longitudinal fasciculus (Beccari, 1923; Shanklin, 1933; Ariëns Kappers, 1947; Senn, 1968a) migrate with the nucleus profundus mesencephali (Fig. 22). The cells in this migration differentiate into medium and large polygonal neurones. Nucleus opticus tegmenti (= nucleus of the basal optic tract, basal optic

194   DAVID G. SENN

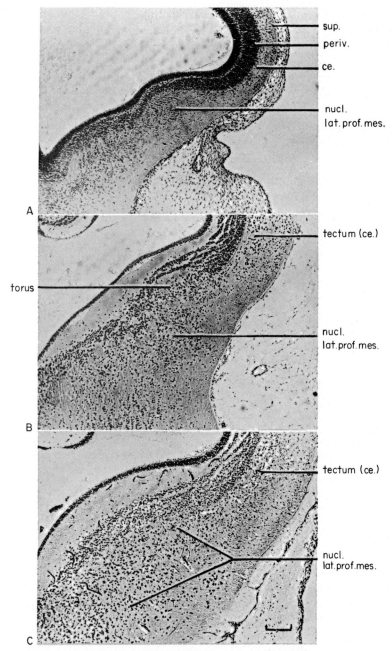

Fig. 21. Ontogenesis of nucleus lateralis profundus mesencephali in *Chelydra serpentina*.
Transverse sections, right side; the bar scale indicates 100 μm. A. Stage 18. B. Stage 23.
C. Stage 26 (hatching). Migrated cells form the nucleus lateralis profundus mesencephali
(nucl. lat. prof. mes.), which is continuous with the central layers of the optic tectum (ce.).
Superficial (sup.) and periventricular (periv.) layers are seen in the tectum.

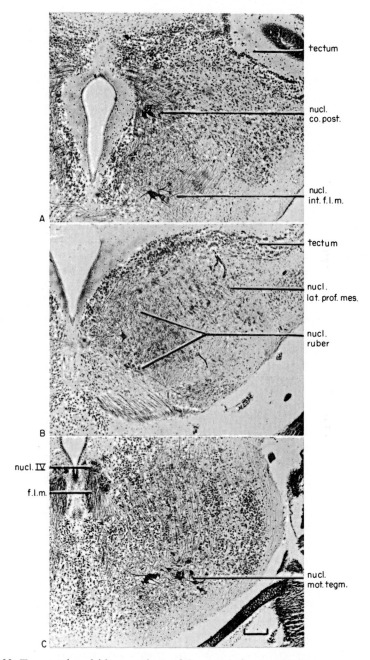

FIG. 22. Tegmental nuclei in an embryo of *Lacerta sicula*, stage 25. Transverse sections, right side; the bar scale indicates 100 μm. A. Section at a rostral level showing nucleus of the posterior commissure (nucl. co. post.) and nucleus interstitialis of the fasciculus longitudinalis medialis (nucl. int. f.l.m.). B Section ventral to the optic tectum showing red nucleus and nucleus lateralis profundus mesencephali (nucl. lat. prof. mes.). C. Section at a more caudal level showing nucleus motorius tegmenti (nucl. mot. tegm.).

nucleus or ectomammillary nucleus) develops as part of the red nucleus complex (Senn, 1968a). However, cells in the nucleus opticus tegmenti separate from the red nucleus and migrate further ventrolaterally (Fig. 23), eventually assuming a position at the tegmental surface where they receive retinal afferents. The interpeduncular and raphe nuclei originate as paired migrations in the ventrolateral tegmentum (Senn, 1968a) and subsequently approach the midline where they fuse into unpaired, midline structures.

D. MESENCEPHALON

1. *General*

The mesencephalon consists of a roof (optic tectum and tori semi-circulares) and a floor (rostral tegmentum). However, the roof and floor are remarkably different in both embryonic development and the cytoarchitecture of adult structure. The mesencephalic floor is continuous with the more caudal rhombencephalic nuclei, and no boundary exists between the mesencephalic and rhombencephalic tegmentum. The tegmentum is first recognized as a single embryonic area; later its cells migrate to form distinct nuclei. However, the mesencephalic roof develops in part from unmigrated cells, as well as from migrated cells forming cortical layers. Furthermore, the midbrain roof—unlike the tegmentum—is recognized as a distinct vesicle at an early embryonic stage. Thus, in this chapter the term mesencephalon refers only to the optic tectum and torus semicircularis.

2. *Optic tectum*

The optic tectum develops in basically the same manner in *Chelydra* and *Lacerta*, while that of *Natrix* demonstrates a pattern differing in several important respects. Development of the tectum of *Lacerta* is illustrated by sections through a series of embryos and neonates (Figs 24 to 35); the pattern is summarized in Fig. 36. Tectal development is shown in less detail for *Chelydra* (Figs 37 to 39) and *Alligator* (Fig. 40). Migration of cells into the stratum zonale begins earlier in the tectum than in the rhombencephalon (Fig. 24). The stratum zonale undergoes its greatest quantitative increase late in the first half of the incubation period. At this time the major layers of adult brains (periventricular, central, and superficial) become recognizable (Fig. 27). The periventricular layers form in the matrix zone and are separated from the central and superficial layers by a distinct subcentral boundary (Figs 25, 37). The central and superficial layers form in the internal and external parts of the stratum zonale, respectively. Further differentiation occurs within each major layer. Within the periventricular layer, fibers grow concentric with the ventricle and split the matrix zone into an internal layer of cells, which form the ependyma (zone 1 of Ramón, 1896), and an external

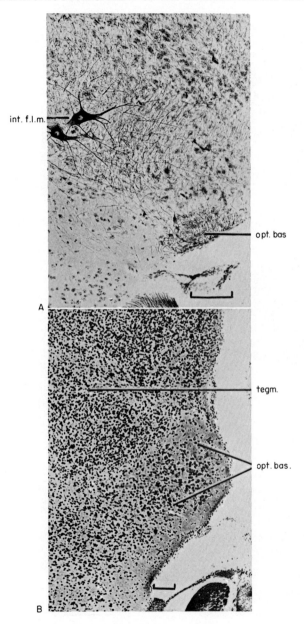

FIG. 23. Nucleus opticus basalis. Transverse sections, right side; bar scale indicates 100 μm. A. *Lacerta sicula* (stage 25). B. *Natrix natrix* (stage 28). Nucleus opticus basalis (opt. bas.) lies at the ventrolateral periphery of the tegmentum (tegm.). Int. f.l.m., nucleus interstitialis of the fasciculus longitudinalis medialis.

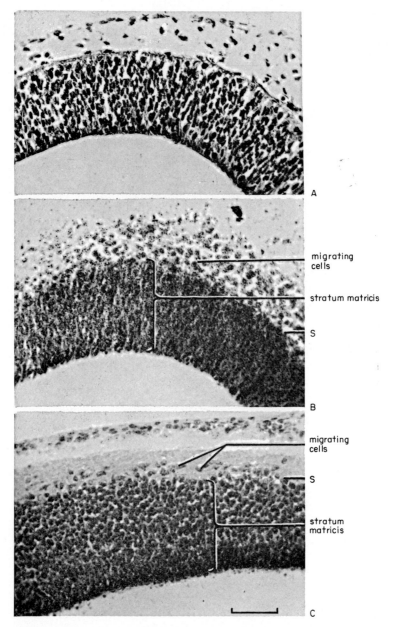

Fig. 24. Optic tectum in *Lacerta sicula*. A. Stage 2 matrix between the ventricle (below) and the surface (above). B. Stage 6 stratum zonale covering the stratum matricis is populated by the earliest migrating cells. Subcentral boundary (S) separates the two strata. C. Stage 7. Bar scale indicates 50 μm.

layer which forms layers 3 to 5 of Ramón (Figs 26, 37). The fibers constitute the stratum album profundum (Huber and Crosby, 1933) or Ramón's zone 2. Fibers in layer 4 further split the external cells, thus forming layers 3 and 5 (Figs 28, 38). Fibers situated superficial to the subcentral boundary form layer 6 (the stratum album centrale). The stratum zonale initially shows two loosely scattered layers of cells. The inner of these layers forms zone 7 (Figs 27, 38). The outer layer slowly transforms into layers 8 through 14 (Figs 29–33, 38, 39). Incoming retinal fibers are first seen at the tectal

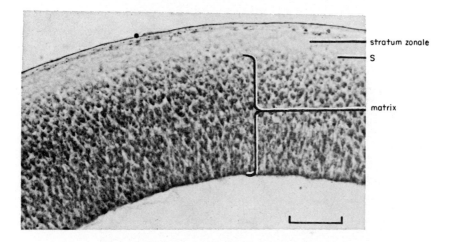

Fig. 25. Optic tectum in *Lacerta sicula*, stage 8. Bar scale indicates 50 μm. Subcentral boundary (S) separates the stratum matricis and the stratum zonale.

surface late in the first half of the incubation period (Fig. 28). They subsequently increase in number and form three layers. The first (layer 14) consists of densely packed fibers on the tectal surface. The second (layer 12) and third (layer 9) represent axon terminals.

Development of the optic tectum in *Natrix* is illustrated by sections through adult and embryonic brains in Figs 41 to 43, and is summarized in Fig. 44. The periventricular, central, and superficial layers initialiy form in the same manner as in *Chelydra*, *Alligator*, and *Lacerta*, but subsequent differentiation within the layers follows different patterns. In *Natrix* the external cell group in the stratum zonale is larger and more concentrated than the internal group (Fig. 42). The internal group forms only part of layer 7; the greater part of layer 7 splits off of the external group. Thus layer 7 is of dual origin and represents a fusion of the internal cell group

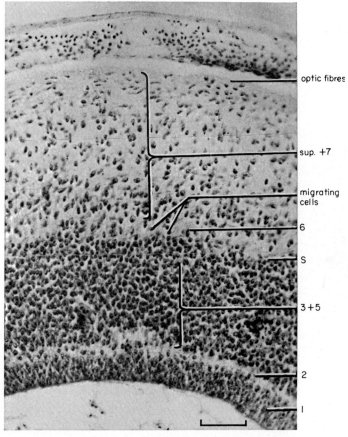

optic fibres

sup. +7

migrating
cells

6

S

3 + 5

2

1

Fig. 26. Optic tectum in *Lacerta sicula*, stage 12. Bar scale indicates 50 μm. The ependyma (zone 1) is separated from the periventricular gray (zones 3 and 5) by fibrous zone 2. Cells still migrate through fiber zone 6. The first retinal fibers are recognized at the surface of the tectum. sup. + 7, Superficial layers plus zone 7; migr., migrating cells; S, subcentral boundary.

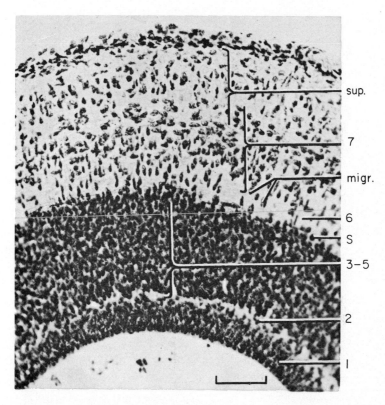

FIG. 27. Optic tectum in *Lacerta sicula*, stage 13. Bar scale indicates 50 μm. Peripheral to the subcentral boundary (S) cells begin to be arranged in a superficial and a central (zone 7) layer. sup., Superficial layers; migr., migrating cells; 1–5, zones of periventricular gray.

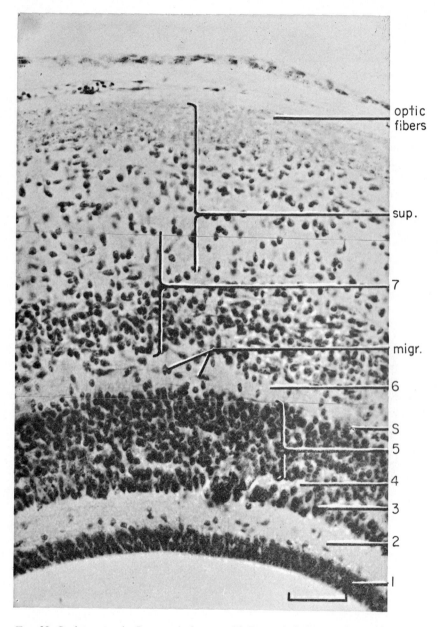

FIG. 28. Optic tectum in *Lacerta sicula*, stage 16. Bar scale indicates 50 μm. Zone 2 is a
well-developed periventricular fiber system. The periventricular gray splits into zones 3,
4 and 5. The latest migrating cells (migr.) are recognized in zone 6. sup., Superficial
layers; 7, cells of zone 7; S, subcentral boundary.

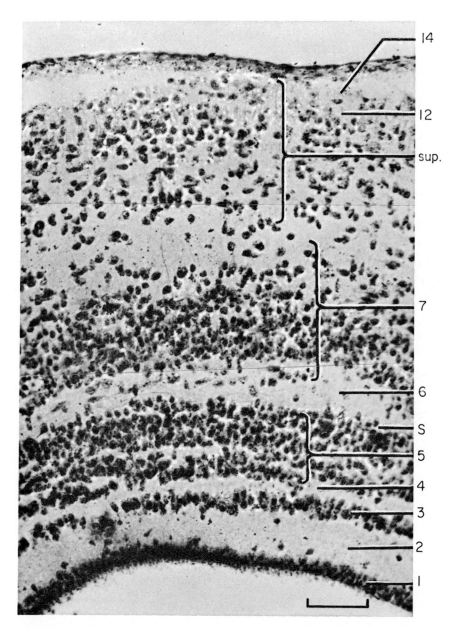

FIG. 29. Optic tectum in *Lacerta sicula*, stage 19. Zone 5 differentiates into sublaminae. The central gray (zone 7) is separated from two zones, 12 and 14, superficially. sup., Superficial layers; S, subcentral boundary; 1–5, zones of periventricular gray. Bar scale indicates 50 μm.

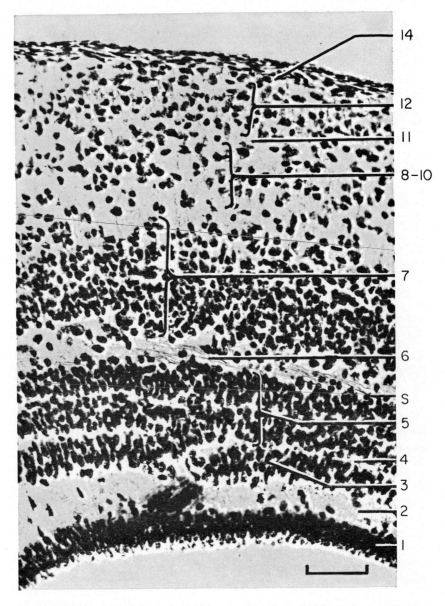

FIG. 30. Optic tectum in *Lacerta sicula* illustrating development of Ramon's zones (1–14) at stage 22. Bar scale indicates 50 μm. The superficial region is subdivided into an internal lamina representing future zones 8 and 10, and an external lamina representing future zone 12. S, Subcentral boundary.

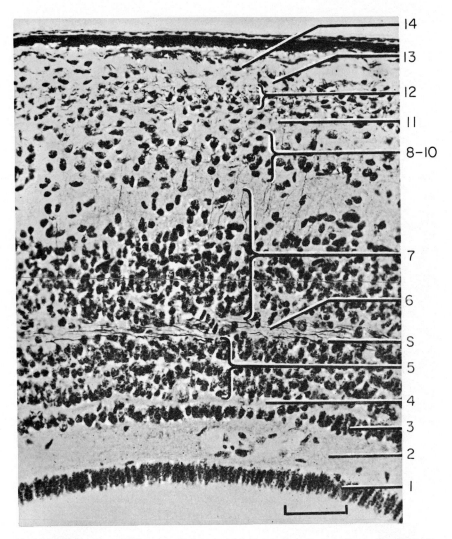

FIG. 31. Optic tectum in *Lacerta sicula*, stage 25. Bar scale indicates 50 μm. Zones 12, 13 and 14 begin to develop at the surface. S, Subcentral boundary.

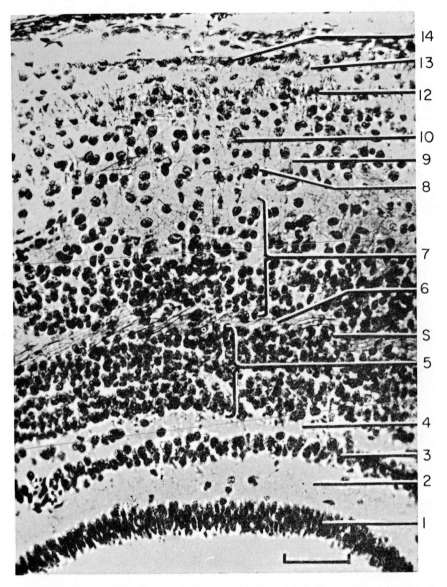

FIG. 32. Optic tectum in *Lacerta sicula*, stage 28. Bar scale indicates 50 μm. All 14 of Ramón's zones are developed. S, Subcentral boundary.

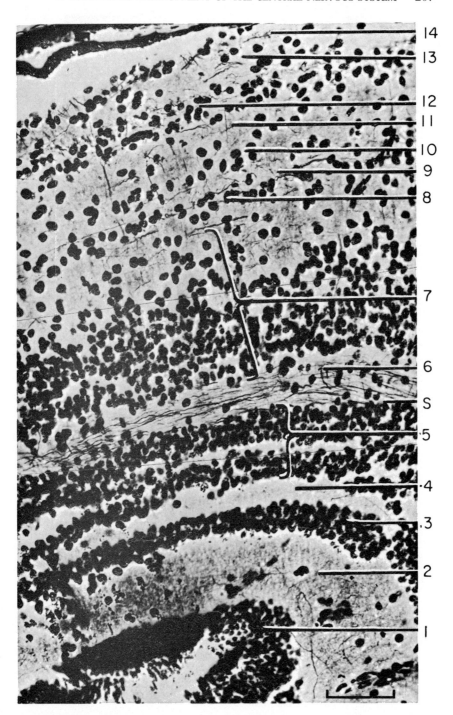

Fig. 33. Optic tectum in *Lacerta sicula* at hatching. Ramón's zones 1–14. S, Subcentral boundary. Bar scale indicates 50 μm.

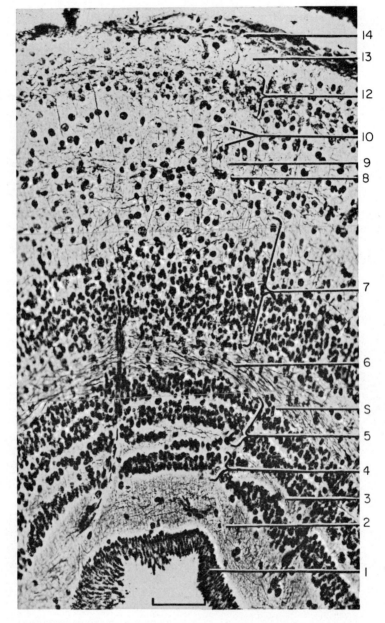

FIG. 34. Optic tectum in *Lacerta sicula* 42 days after hatching. Bar scale indicates 50 μm. Ramón's zones 1–14. S, Subcentral boundary.

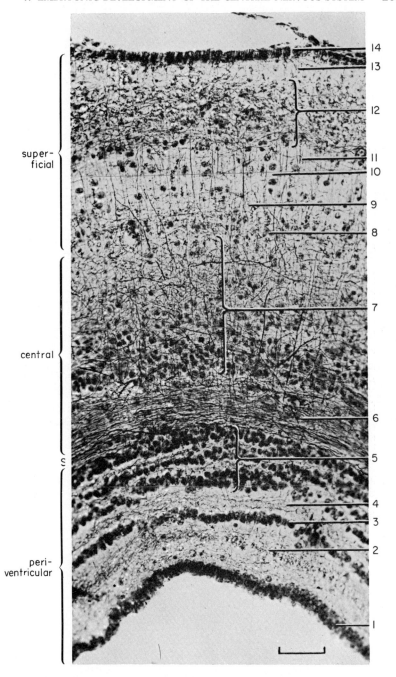

FIG. 35. Optic tectum in the adult *Lacerta sicula*. Bar scale indicates 50 μm. Periventricular zones 1–5, central zones 6 and 7, superficial zones 8–14. S, Subcentral boundary.

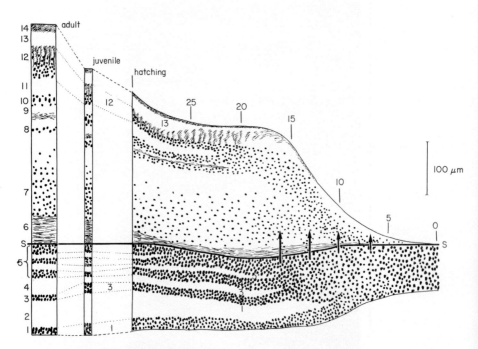

Fig. 36. Tectal differentiation in *Lacerta sicula*. The diagram shows differentiation from the right to the left. The subcentral boundary (S) separates the matrix from the stratum zonale. Arrows indicate cell migrations. Stages 0–31 (hatching) are indicated above. Juvenile and adult tecta are figured on the left. 1–14, Ramón's zones.

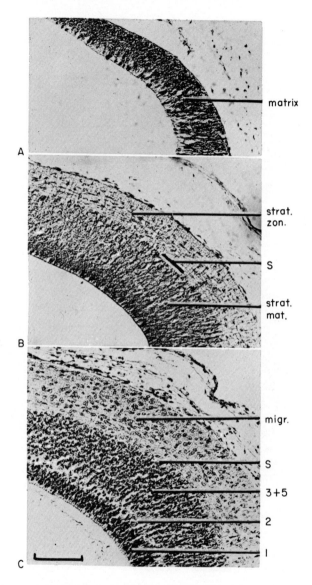

FIG. 37. Optic tectum in *Chelydra serpentina*. Bar scale indicates 100 μm. A. Cellular matrix in stage 12. B. Subcentral boundary (S) separates stratum zonale (strat. zon.) and stratum matricis (strat. mat.) in stage 17. C. Migrated cells (migr.) have settled in the stratum zonale in stage 18. Stratum matricis is split by fibrous zone 2; zones 1, 3 and 5 are distinguished.

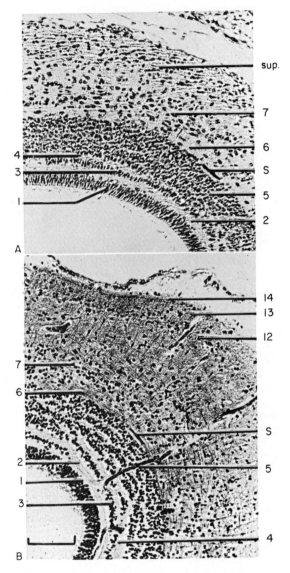

Fig. 38. Optic tectum in *Chelydra serpentina*. Bar scale indicates 100 μm. A. Stage 22. B. Stage 26 (hatching). Periventricular gray zones 1, 3 and 5 develop by a splitting of the stratum matricis. Central zones 6 and 7 appear along the subcentral boundary (S). Superficial zones (sup.) are in contact with retinal fibers (zones 12 and 14).

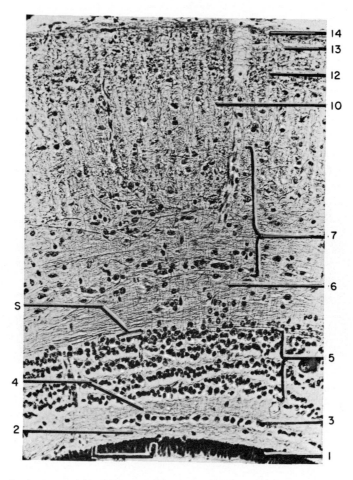

Fig. 39. Optic tectum in a subadult *Chelydra serpentina*. Bar scale indicates 100 μm. Compare Ramón's zones 1–14 with Fig. 35.

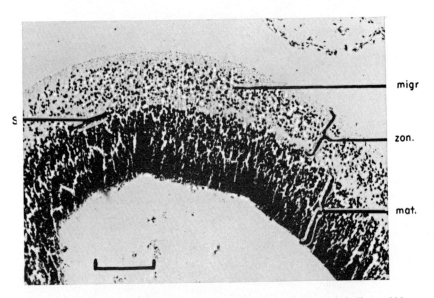

Fɪɢ. 40. Optic tectum in an embryonic *Alligator mississippiensis*. Bar scale indicates 100 μm. Migrated cells (migr.) have settled in the stratum zonale (zon.). Most cells are still found in the stratum matricis (mat.). S, Subcentral boundary.

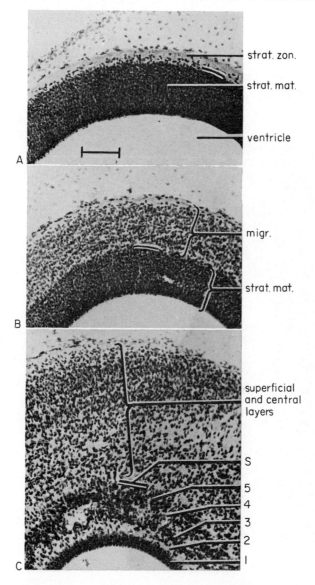

Fig. 41. Optic tectum in *Natrix natrix*. Bar scale indicates 100 μm. A. Embryo at stage 1. The dense stratum matricis is covered by a thin stratum zonale (strat. zon.). B. Stage 3. The earliest migrated cells (migr.) populate the stratum zonale. C. Stage 7. The stratum matricis (strat. mat.) subdivides into Ramón's zones 1–5 (compare with Figs 26–29). Two cellular layers (central and superficial) appear in the stratum zonale. S. Subcentral boundary.

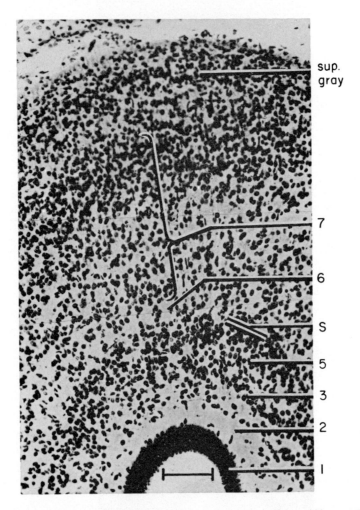

FIG. 42. Optic tectum in *Natrix natrix*, stage 15. Bar scale indicates 100 μm. Morphological penetration of periventricular zones 2–5. sup., Superficial gray; S, subcentral boundary; 1, ependyma; 6 and 7, central zones.

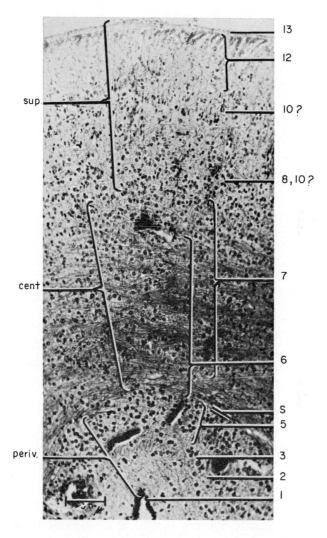

FIG. 43. Optic tectum in the adult *Natrix natrix*. Bar scale indicates 100 μm. A partial fusion of Ramón's zones 1–13 is characteristic of all snakes. sup., Superficial layers; cent., central layers; periv., periventricular layers; S, subcentral boundary; 1–13, Ramón's zones.

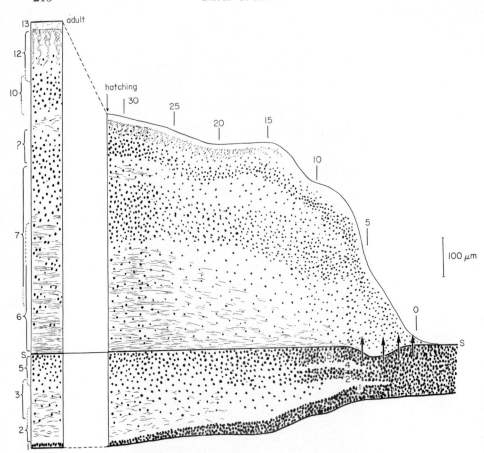

Fig. 44. Tectal development in *Natrix natrix*, stages 0–32 (hatching). Development is from the right to the left, and layers are labeled as Ramon's zones 1–13. Arrows indicate cell migrations. S, Subcentral boundary. Bar scale indicates 100 μm.

with part of the external group. The remaining external cells form the superficial gray. Consequently, zones 8, 10, and 12 are difficult to distinguish in adult snakes. The periventricular layers initially split into alternating gray and fibrous layers, but this stratification is only temporary. Zones 3 and 5 fuse and cannot be recognized in the adult, and only the ependymal zone is retained as a distinct layer. The retinal fibers form only a single layer so that a layer 14 is absent in adult snakes. The phylogenetic significance of this difference in tectal histogenesis in snakes and lizards is discussed elsewhere (Senn, 1966).

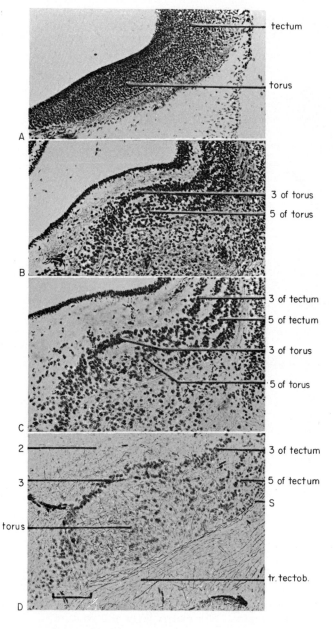

FIG. 45. Ontogenesis of the torus semicircularis in *Lacerta sicula*. Transverse sections, right side; bar scale indicates 100 μm. A. Stage 10, tectum and torus as continuous matrix. B. Stage 16, zone 3 separates in the torus and zone 5 starts to form a nucleus. C. Stage 28, zone 3 is continuous in the torus and tectum, zone 5 is nuclear in the torus and laminated in the tectum. D. Adult, zone 5 forms the main mass of the torus. Ventrally, the tractus tectobulbaris (tr. tectob.) runs along the subcentral boundary (S).

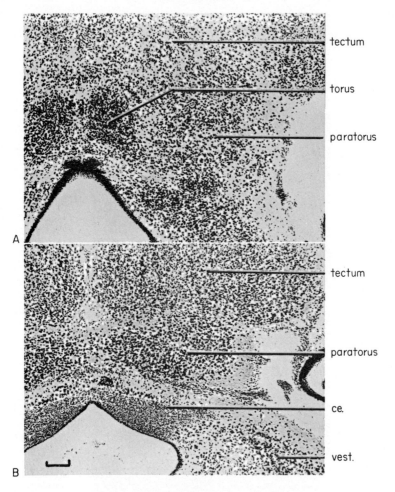

FIG. 46. Paratorus in *Natrix natrix*. Transverse section, right side; bar scale indicates 100 μm. ce, Cerebellum; vest., vestibular nucleus.

3. *Tori semicirculares*

The developmental pattern of the torus is basically the same in most groups of reptiles and results in the formation of a torus semicircularis in crocodilians, *Sphenodon*, and lizards. The toral area—like the optic tectum— shows initial differentiation of a matrix layer and stratum zonale (Fig. 45A). However, there is no significant migration of cells into the stratum zonale in the toral area; the majority of cells remain in the matrix layer. The ependymal cells form a distinct layer (Ramón's layer 1), and a split occurs between zones 3 and 5. The cells in zone 3 form a lamina covering the dorsal and medial surfaces of this nucleus (Fig. 45D). Thus the torus—unlike the optic tectum—develops entirely in a periventricular position.

The developmental pattern of the caudal midbrain roof is quite different in snakes and results in the formation of two nuclei (Fig. 46), a torus and a

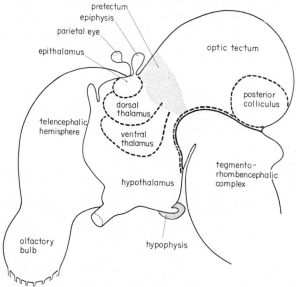

FIG. 44. Prosencephalon, tectum and rhombencephalon in diagrammatic lateral view.

paratorus (Senn, 1969). The paratorus develops by a migration of cells into the stratum zonale where a large nucleus forms. Cells remaining in the matrix layer form a small field of periventricular gray which appears to be homologous to the torus of other reptiles. The paratorus is rostrally attached to layer 7 of the optic tectum. It has direct connections with the contralateral paratorus, and connects with the contralateral tectum via axons passing rostrally through the tectal commissure into layer 6 of the contralateral tectum.

E. DIENCEPHALON

1. General

The diencephalon in embryonic reptiles can be divided into four longitudinal divisions (Fig. 47) based on differences in matrix thickness, cell migration and early fiber development. Distinct ventricular sulci characterize the reptilian diencephalon; however, these sulci do not coincide with the longitudinal cellular divisions (Nieuwenhuys and Bodenheimer, 1966; Senn, 1970a; Northcutt, 1977), as Herrick (1948) believed. The four longitudinal divisions are: epithalamus, dorsal thalamus, ventral thalamus, and hypothalamus. The pretectum is a caudal continuation of the dorsal thalamus.

2. *Epithalamus*

The development of the epithalamus is similar in all reptiles. In early embryos (Fig. 48A) the epithalamus consists of a dense matrix layer continuous ventrally with the dorsal thalamus (Bergquist, 1953). The matrix layer of the dorsal thalamus later expands (Fig. 49A) forming a dorsal diencephalic sulcus between the two structures. In the epithalamus, cells migrate into the stratum zonale more slowly than in other diencephalic structures. The lateral and medial habenular nuclei separate approximately midway through the incubation period (Figs 48B, 49A), and fibers of the stria medullaris come to occupy the intercellular space.

In the epithalamus, a number of unpaired structures vary in character among different species. In *Lacerta sicula*, a small round vesicle extends from the caudal diencephalic roof in early embryos (Fig. 50A). This anlage of the epiphysis grows dorsally, and fibers of the pineal nerve (Ariëns Kappers, 1967) extend into the stalk, connecting the epiphysis with an area near the subcommissural organ. Rostral to the epiphysis, a second vesicle forms on the habenular commissure (Fig. 50A), then shifts dorsally, reaching the skin to form the lens and retina constituting the parietal eye (Fig. 50B). A parietal nerve connects the parietal eye to the brain (Ariëns Kappers, 1967). The largest diencephalic organ is the dorsal sac (Burckhardt, 1894b). It begins as a thin epithelial sac which subsequently arches dorsally and extends between the velum transversum and the habenular commissure. The paraphysis develops rostral to the velum transversum, which is a ventrally directed fold of the tela chorioidea of the diencephalic roof.

The development of the epithalamus is considered in more detail in Chapter 5.

3. *Pretectum and Dorsal Thalamus*

The pretectum is a transitional area between the optic tectum and dorsal thalamus. It contains several nuclei, including the prominent nucleus lentiformis mesencephali. The pretectum develops by means of a large migration of cells into the stratum zonale (Fig. 51A); small ventral and large dorsal components can be distinguished soon after this migration begins (Fig. 51B). The ventral component forms the ventromedial area, which consists of densely packed cells differentiating in a periventricular position (Senn, 1968a). The dorsal component forms the remaining pretectal nuclei. Nucleus lentiformis thalami (Beccari, 1943) develops in two parts. An internal pars plicata differentiates in the matrix layer (Fig. 51B), then splits

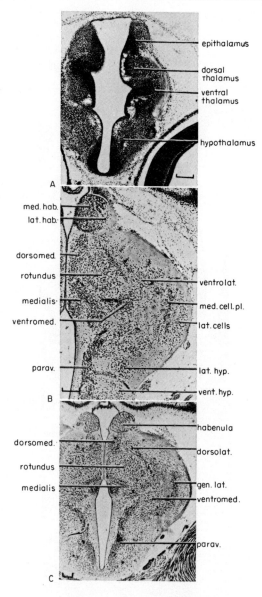

FIG. 48. Embryonic thalamus in *Lacerta sicula*. Transverse sections; bar scales indicate 100 μm. A. Stage 10. B. Stage 19. C. Stage 25. The epithalamus consists of a medial (med. hab.) and a lateral habenula (lat. hab.). The dorsal thalamus includes the nuclei dorsomedialis (dorsomed.), rotundus, medialis and dorsolateralis anterior (dorsolat.). The ventral thalamus is composed of the nuclei ventromedialis (ventromed.), ventro-lateralis (ventrolat.), geniculate lateralis (gen. lat.) including the medial cellular plate (med. cell. pl.) and lateral cells (lat. cells) within the lateral neuropil. The hypothalamus contains nucleus paraventricularis (parav.), nucleus lateralis hypothalami (lat. hyp.) and nucleus ventralis hypothalami (vent. hyp.).

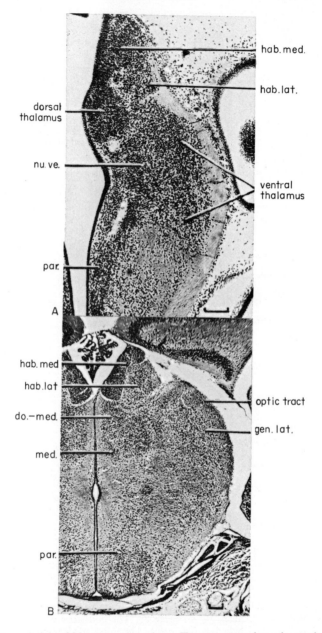

FIG. 49. Diencephalon of *Natrix natrix* embryo. Transverse sections; bar scales indicate 100 μm. A. Stage 7. B. Stage 28. The epithalamus is composed of a medial (hab. med.) and a lateral (hab. lat.) habenular nucleus. Nucleus dorsomedialis (do.-med.) and nucleus medialis (med.) are seen in the dorsal thalamus. Nucleus ventralis (nu. ve.) and the huge nucleus geniculatus lateralis (gen. lat.) form the ventral thalamus. Nucleus paraventricularis (par.) is the main cell mass of the hypothalamus.

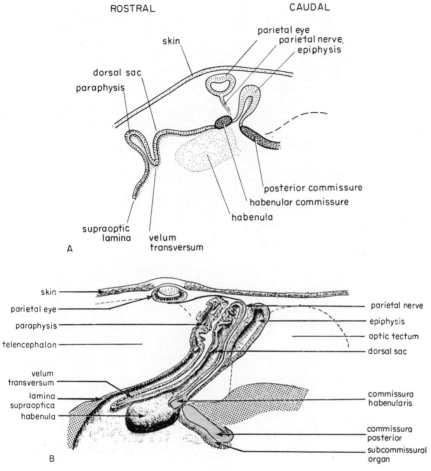

FIG. 50. The diencephalic roof of *Lacerta sicula* in sagittal view. A. Early embryo (stage 7). B. Differentiated (stage 28).

into several laminae (Fig. 52c) in *Chelydra*, *Lacerta* and, especially, in *Anniella pulchra* (Senn, 1968b). The pars plicata remains undifferentiated in *Natrix* (Fig. 53). The pars extensa is formed by a lateral migration of cells (Armstrong, 1950, 1951) into the stratum zonale (Figs 51B, 52B, C, 53). The pretectal geniculate nucleus develops as the lateral edge of this migration (Figs 52B, C, 53) and consists of an inner cell plate formed by migrated cells, and an outer fiber layer representing the superficial layer of the pretectum. Nucleus lentiformis mesencephali (Shanklin, 1930; Armstrong, 1950) and the posterodorsal nuclei (Armstrong, 1950, 1951) appear to develop relatively late in the superficial gray of the pretectum.

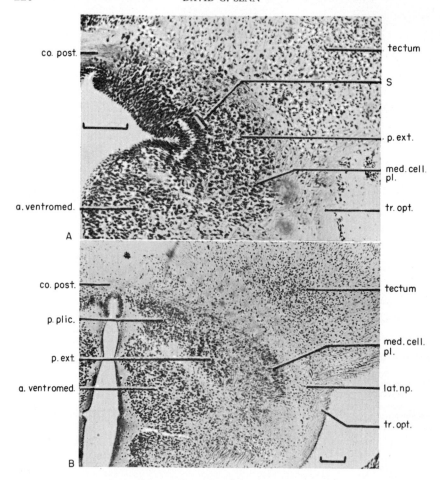

FIG. 51. Pretectum in *Lacerta sicula*. Transverse sections, right side; bar scale indicates 100 µm. Area ventromedialis (a. ventromed.) lies ventral to nucleus lentiformis thalami, which is composed of pars plicata (p. pliic.) and pars extensa (p. ext.). The medial cellular plate (med. cell. pl.) and lateral neuropil (lat. np.) form the pretectal geniculate nucleus. It is in contact with the optic tract (tr. opt.). co. post., Commissura posterior; S, subcentral boundary.

Development of the dorsal thalamus is characterized by a massive expansion of the matrix layer This expansion continues for some time in *Alligator mississippiensis*, *Chelydra serpentina*, and *Lacerta sicula*, but is short-lived in *Natrix natrix*. Cells situated near the ventricle are not involved in this expansion and remain densely packed. Laterally situated cells gradually decrease in density, and each population forms specific thalamic

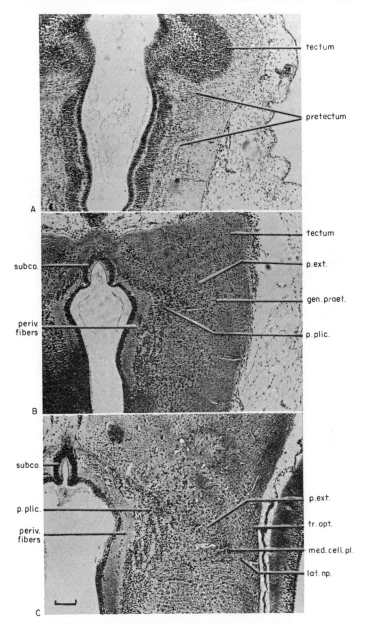

FIG. 52. Pretectum in *Chelydra serpentina*. Transverse sections, right side; bar scale indicates 100 μm. A. Stage 18, pretectum and tectum are continuous. B. Stage 22. C. Stage 26 (hatching). gen. praet., Nucleus geniculatus praetectalis, which is composed of med, cell. pl., medial cellular plate, and lat. np., lateral neuropil; p. ext., pars extensa and p. plic., pars plicata of nucleus lentiformis thalami; periv. fibers, periventricular fibers; subco., subcommissural organ; tr. opt., tractus opticus.

228   DAVID G. SENN

nuclei. The dense internal layer separates from the ependyma and forms a lamina of cells parallel to the ventricle. The dorsomedial nucleus forms rostrally in this layer (Figs 48B, 48C, 49B), and the medial nucleus forms caudally. These nuclei remain connected in the adult forms of some species. In species where nucleus rotundus is well developed, the dorsomedial and medial nuclei are separated by the medial expansion of nucleus rotundus. In *Chelydra*, the medial nucleus continues to grow after hatching and fuses with the dorsomedial nucleus at the midline in juveniles; similar processes result in nucleus reuniens (Edinger, 1899) or intermedius (Huber and Crosby,

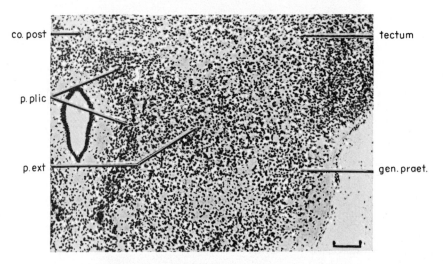

FIG. 53. Embryonic pretectum in *Natrix natrix*, stage 15. Transverse section, right side; bar scale indicates 100 μm. co. post., Commissura posterior; gen. praet., nucleus geniculatus praetectalis; p. ext., pars extensa; p. plic., pars plicata.

1926) in crocodilians. The medial nuclei remain paired in *Lacerta*. The loosely packed lateral area is dominated by nucleus rotundus, which differentiates midway during incubation (Figs 48B, C, 54, 55C). Nucleus dorsolateralis anterior develops dorsorostral to nucleus rotundus (Fig. 55B).

4. *Ventral Thalamus*

The ventral thalamus (Figs 49A, 55B) curves around the medial diencephalic sulcus (Kuhlenbeck, 1931). The majority of ventral thalamic cells remain in the matrix layer, increase in number during ontogeny, and become loosely packed. The triangular area (Huber and Crosby, 1926) forms rostrally from these cells, and the nucleus ovalis separates from the triangular area late in development. Nucleus ventralis (de Lange, 1913) forms caudally (Fig. 55B) and differentiates into nuclei ventromedialis and ventro-lateralis, separated by the dorsal peduncle of the lateral forebrain bundle. Early in development an important contingent of cells migrates from the matrix layer into the stratum zonale (Figs 48B, 54, 55B, C) to form the ventral lateral geniculate nucleus. Thus nucleus consists of two cellular laminae situated internal to the optic tract, and its size varies greatly among species.

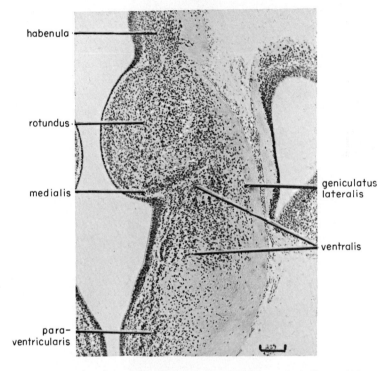

FIG. 54. Thalamus in *Chelydra serpentina*, stage 20. Bar scale indicates 100 μm.

The medial cell plate begins to differentiate into elongated cells, oriented perpendicular to the optic tract, soon after its separation; the lateral neuro-pile layer contains only scattered neurones.

5. *Hypothalamus*

   The reptilian hypothalamus consists primarily of periventricular cells which form the preoptic nucleus rostrally and the paraventricular nucleus caudally. The periventricular cells are continuous with cells in the ventral telencephalon (Kuhlenbeck, 1931; Källén, 1951; Senn, 1968a, 1970a; Kirsche, 1972; Hetzel, 1974), and the preoptic and paraventricular nuclei

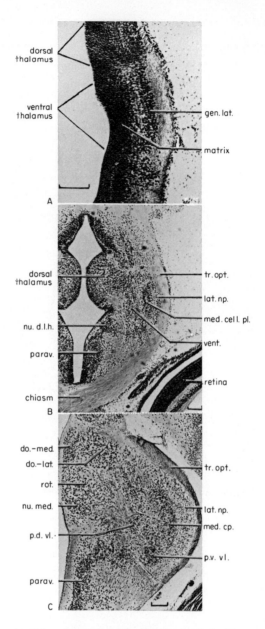

FIG. 55. Ontogenesis of the ventral thalamus in *Lacerta sicula*. Transverse sections. Bar scale indicates 100 μm. A. Stage 8, nucleus geniculatus lateralis (gen. lat.) migrates laterally. B. Stage 13, the geniculate body is composed of a medial cellular plate (med. cell. pl.) and a lateral neuropil (lat. np.). Nucleus ventralis (vent.) originates from the matrix. C. Stage 25, the lateral part of nucleus ventralis is composed of a pars dorsalis (p.d. vl.) and a pars ventralis (p.v. vl.). The dorsal thalamus includes nucleus dorsolateralis anterior (do.-lat.), nucleus dorsomedialis (do.-med.), nucleus medialis (nu. med.) and nucleus rotundus (rot.). Nucleus paraventricularis (parav.) is the main part of the hypothalamus. The optic tract (tr. opt.) covers the surface of the diencephalon. nu. dl. h., Dorsolateral hypothalamic nucleus.

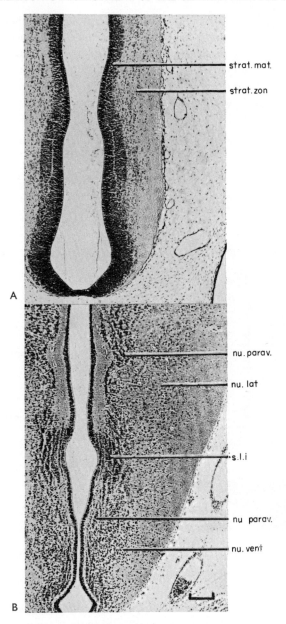

FIG. 56. Embryonic hypothalamus in *Chelydra serpentina*. Transverse sections; bar scale indicates 100 μm. A. Stage 16. B. Stage 23. nu. lat., nucleus lateralis; nu. parav., nucleus paraventricularis; nu. vent. nucleus ventralis; s.l.i., sulcus lateralis infundibuli; strat. mat. stratum matricis; strat. zon., stratum zonale.

develop from the matrix layer. Several layers may form parallel to the ventricle (Fig. 56B), and some of these layers may subsequently undergo secondary fusion. They remain continuous with the ventromedial nucleus until nearly adult stages (Fig. 48c). The periventricular cells are bounded by

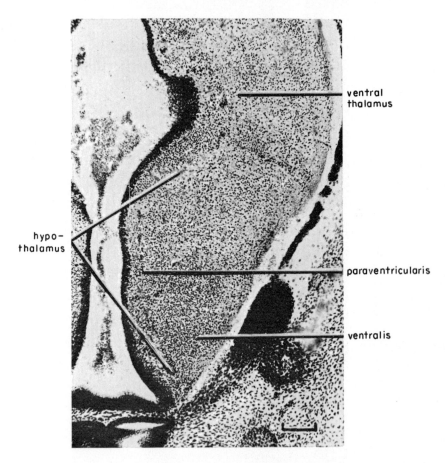

FIG. 57. Embryonic hypothalamus in *Natrix natrix*. Transverse section; bar scale indicates 100 μm.

fiber systems, primarily the medial forebrain bundles; however, some cells migrate laterally and form nuclei in the lateral hypothalamus. These nuclei include a ventral hypothalamic nucleus (Fig. 57) caudally (Senn, 1968a), a lateral hypothalamic nucleus (Huber and Crosby, 1926), mammillary nuclei (Senn, 1968b), and supraoptic nuclei rostrally.

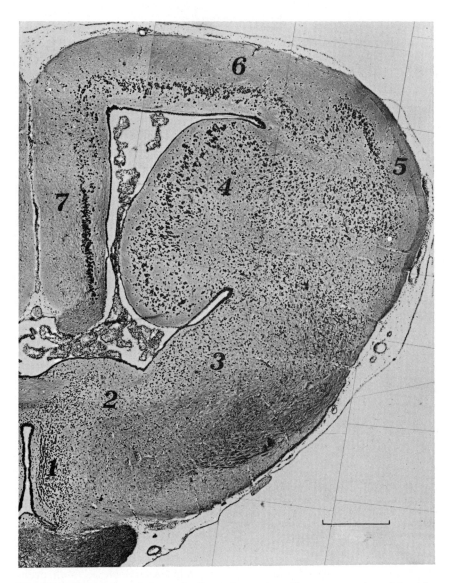

FIG. 58. Telencephalon of the turtle *Sternotherus minor*. Transverse section, right side; bar scale indicates 500 μm. 1, Nucleus praeopticus (diencephalon); 2, area cellularis reuniens; 3, striatum; 4, dorsal ventricular ridge; 5, lateral cortex; 6, dorsal cortex; 7, medial cortex.

F. Telencephalon

Ontogenesis of the reptilian telencephalon has been discussed by Herrick (1892), Johnston (1916), Faul (1926), Warner (1946), Källén (1951), Kirsche (1972), Hetzel (1974), and Rudin (1975); however, these authors emphasized different aspects of development. Källén focused primarily on the

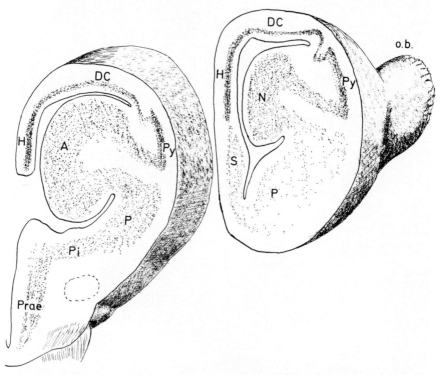

Fig. 59. Reptilian telencephalic hemispheres—turtles and *Sphenodon*. Caudolaterodorsal view of transverse section through right hemisphere. A, Caudal dorsal ventricular ridge; DC, dorsal cortex; H, medial cortex; N, anterior dorsal ventricular ridge; o.b., olfactory bulb; P, striatum; Pi, area cellularis reuniens; Prae, nucleus praeopticus; Py, lateral cortex (pyriform cortex); S, septum.

longitudinal zones (basal and alar plates), Kirsche and Hetzel both dealt with matrix growth and cell migration, Johnston emphasized the relationship between dorsal ventricular ridge and the basal telencephalic area, and Rudin focused on simultaneous development of the olfactory nuclei and olfactory and Jacobson's epithelia.

The earliest ontogenic stages of the telencephalon are described by von Kupffer (1906). The prosencephalic vesicle gives rise to diencephalic and telencephalic vesicles. The telencephalon then evaginates paired vesicles which constitute the hemispheres. The matrix of the preoptic area, a transitional region between the diencephalon and telencephalon, reveals extreme proliferation coinciding with hemispheric evagination. During hemispheric evagination, the matrix of the rostral preoptic hypothalamus shifts dorsolaterally and rostrally. Later, the cellular matrix surrounding the hemispheric ventricle differentiates into distinct regions. The various striatal and pallial regions differentiate (Hetzel, 1974) by additional cell proliferation and migration.

In adult reptiles (Figs 58, 59), the base of the hemisphere is connected to the hypothalamus by a continuous cell lamina. This area cellularis reuniens (pars inferior massae cellularis reunientis, Kuhlenbeck, 1931) embryonically forms a continuous matrix lamina from the preoptic hypothalamus to the base of the hemisphere. However, Källén (1951) and Kirsche (1972) also reported thalamic masses continuous with the hemispheres, and both claimed that the major telencephalic subdivision was a continuation of alar and basal plates. Källén distinguished four longitudinal telencephalic zones in embryonic *Alligator*, *Chrysemys*, *Chamaeleo*, *Lacerta*, and *Natrix*. Ventrally, zones a, b, and c represent the floor: a differentiates into the septum and nucleus of the diagonal band; b forms the olfactory tubercle, nucleus accumbens and nucleus lateralis septi; c gives rise to the striatum. The roof, a longitudinal zone d, develops into the pallial cortex and hypopallium (dorsal ventricular ridge). The dorsal ventricular ridge may differentiate as a laminated structure—e.g. in turtles, *Sphenodon* (Figs 58, 59A), and some lizards (Fig. 59B)—or as a nuclear mass, as in crocodilians (Fig. 59C) and some lizards (iguanids, agamids, teiids and varanids).

V. Division and Continuity of the Central Nervous System

Ontogenetic patterns within the central nervous system have been used to classify CNS structures into major groups. These classifications apply particularly to reptiles. His (1893) recognized longitudinal zones in the central nervous system. The neural tube is divided into dorsal and ventral zones, their boundary indicated by a sulcus limitans. Sensory nuclei tend to be located in the dorsal zone, and motor nuclei tend to be located in the ventral zone. Herrick (1899, 1914) completed this classification by pointing out that each zone is subdivided into visceral and somatic components. Visceral components are related to non-segmented, coelomic mesoderm or to the branchial region of the head, whereas somatic components are related to exteroceptors and the derivatives of embryonic somites (Starck, 1963a, b, 1965). These zones or columns extend through the spinal cord and medulla, but their rostral extent is not clearly established. Haller (1929) was unable to trace the four columns through the diencephalon. Källén (1951) and Bergquist (1954) assert that the rostral pole of the somatosensory column is in the isthmus, while the somatomotor column reaches the boundary of the diencephalon and the mesencephalic tegmentum. This suggests that the pattern of longitudinal zones does not apply unambiguously to the roof of the midbrain, the diencephalon, and the telencephalon.

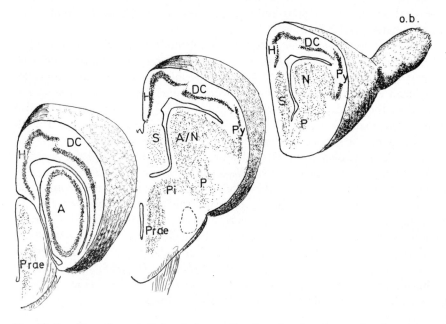

Fig. 60. Reptilian telencephalic hemispheres—lizards and snakes. Perspective the same as in Fig. 59.

A second divisional scheme recognizes rostrocaudal components in the neuraxis. Von Kupffer (1906) recognizes a series of brain vesicles in the rostral neural tube. Initially three vesicles are present, but the prosencephalon and rhombencephalon later subdivide, resulting in a total of five vesicles. However, Haller (1929) and Kuhlenbeck (1931) point out that major cell masses often do not originate from single vesicles, but instead stem from regions between vesicles. Thus, the embryonic vesicles do not entirely reflect the subsequent development of cell masses in the adult brain.

A third method of division emphasizes the laminar arrangement of the neural tube (Senn, 1968, 1970). The entire neural tube develops according to a pattern of matrix layer and stratum zonale formation. These layers ultimately form neuronal laminae, such as those present in cortical areas, or nuclear masses. They develop differently in different parts of the brain, giving each region its characteristic structure (Figs 60, 61); however, their continuity throughout the neuraxis can be used to compare the organization of different brain regions. The optic tectum is a convenient standard for these comparisons, as all major layers are present and can be traced rostrally and caudally. The tectal layers can be grouped into periventricular, central,

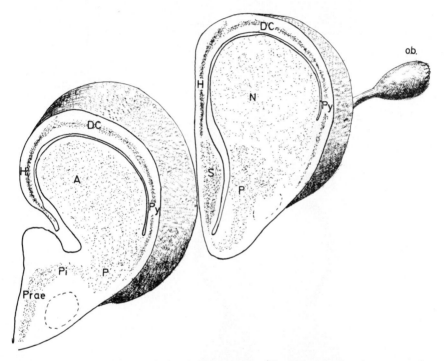

Fig. 61. Reptilian telencephalic hemispheres—crocodilians. Perspective the same as in Fig. 60.

and superficial groups. Figures 62 and 63 show diagrammatic horizontal and transverse sections through the neural tube. The periventricular, central, and superficial layers are indicated.

In the adult spinal cord, the ependyma represents the periventricular layers and the gray and white matter represent the central layers. The superficial layers are poorly developed. Similarly, the ependyma represents the periventricular layers in the rhombencephalon, while the cranial nerve nuclei, tegmental structures, and cerebellum represent the central layers. However, the ontogenesis of the mesencephalic tectum is very different; the periventricular layers include zones 6 and 7, and the superficial layers

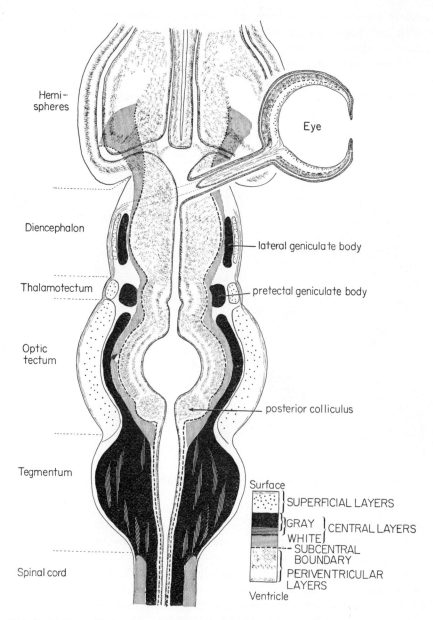

FIG. 62. Horizontal schematic of layers through the brain. The spinal cord and medulla oblongata comprise central layers; periventricular, central and superficial layers are present in the midbrain roof and diencephalon; the telencephalic hemispheres consist mainly of periventricular layers.

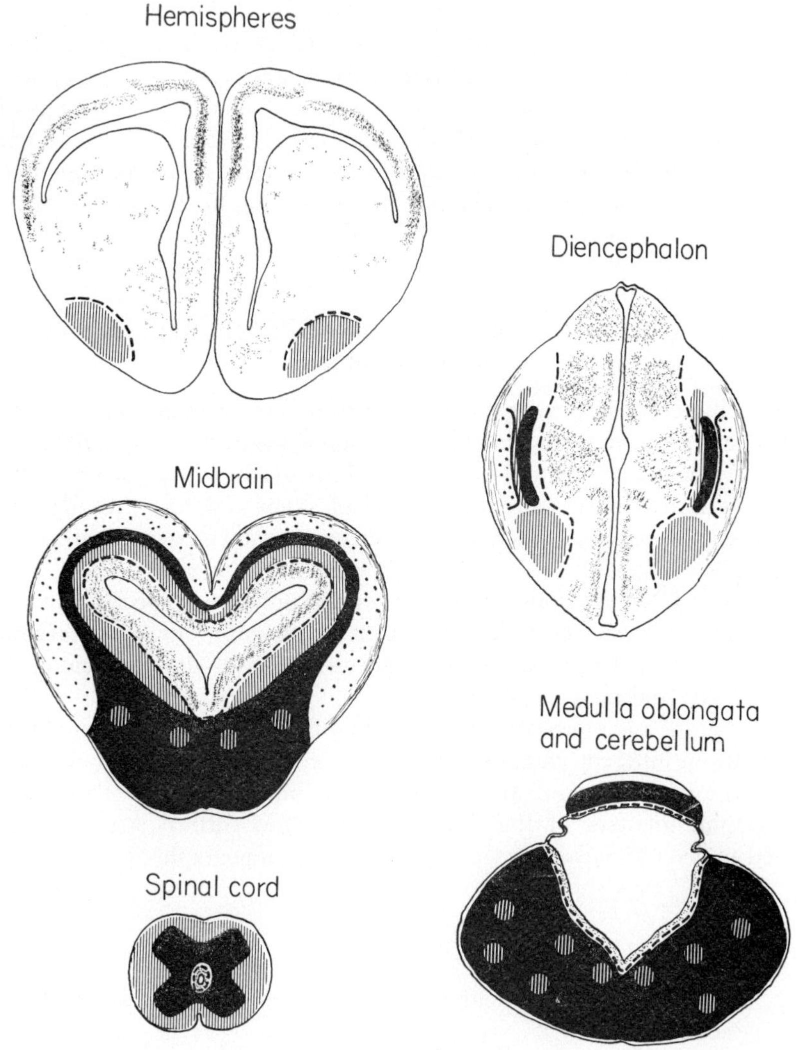

FIG. 63. A series of transverse schematics showing distribution of layers. See Fig. 62 for coding and shading.

include zones 9 through 14. The pretectum is basically similar. The periventricular layers include the ependyma, the pars plicata of nucleus lentiformis (= zones 3 and 5), and periventricular fiber system (= zones 2 and 4). The central layers include tangential fibers (= zone 6), the pars extensa of nucleus lentiformis thalami, and the medial cell plate of the pretectal

geniculate nucleus (= zone 7). The lateral neuropil of the pretectal geniculate and the optic tract represent the superficial layers. Diencephalic structures primarily represent the periventricular layers, with some exceptions.
The medial cell plate of the lateral geniculate, and fiber systems such as the
fornix and forebrain bundles, represent central layers, and the lateral
neuropil of the lateral geniculate and the optic tract represent superficial
layers. Most of the telencephalic cell masses belong to the periventricular
layers formed by migration within the matrix layer.

VI. Comparisons of Development in Different Reptiles and Persistent Problems

Few differences in development of reptilian nervous systems are known,
as few species have been examined. Embryonic series are unavailable for
Sphenodon, and a complete series of crocodilian stages is badly needed. The
brains of lizards vary more than those of other reptiles; thus data on
Lacerta are probably insufficient to characterize brain development among
lizards.

Details of CNS development are known for only a few species, but it is
clear that *Chelydra* and *Lacerta* possess remarkably similar embryonic
patterns and that *Natrix* exhibits some specializations in development of the
diencephalon and mesencephalic roof.

Cell migration is a major phenomenon in differentiation of the neural tube
and varies in different parts of the tube. Several types of migrations occur
within the telencephalon, diencephalon, and mesencephalon. Thus autoradiographic analyses of the different nuclei and cortical structures are
needed to determine the exact time of origin and topography.

VII. Summary

1. The early embryonic neural tube forms regions known as von Kupffer's vesicles.

2. The His–Herrick longitudinal zones constitute the major divisions of
the spinal cord and rhombencephalon.

3. The differentiating wall of the neural tube consists primarily of a
cellular matrix. A peripheral stratum zonale is populated by migrating
matrix cells which form the mantle layer.

4. The mantle layer in the spinal cord and rhombencephalon differentiates into nuclei.

5. The mantle layer of the metencephalic lamina forms the cerebellar
cortex.

6. The cortex of the optic tectum comprises up to 14 layers grouped into three primary zones: superficial, central, and periventricular zones. Early in development, cells migrate from the matrix layer forming the superficial and central zones, while the periventricular zone is formed by unmigrated matrix cells that differentiate *in situ*.

7. The tectal development of *Natrix* differs from that of turtles and lizards in that subdivision of the periventricular tectal layers is only transitory, and the superficial layers possess a unique subdivision.

8. The torus semicircularis of turtles and lizards originates in the matrix layer, but in snakes the mantle layer forms a new structure, the paratorus.

9. Cells of the lateral dorsal thalamus and geniculate nuclei migrate early from the matrix.

10. The epithalamic, thalamic, pretectal, and hypothalamic nuclei form by expansion of the matrix.

11. Pallial and striatal telencephalic areas differentiate *in situ* after the hemispheres evaginate mainly from the preoptic area.

Acknowledgements

Thanks are due to M. Durand-Wenger and D. Keller for their excellent technical assistance. I am grateful to Dr C. Gans (Ann Arbor), Dr R. G. Northcutt (Ann Arbor), Dr C. L. Yntema (Syracuse), Dr H. Wackernagel (Basel) and Dr P. Studer (Basel) for having contributed to my collection of reptilian brains. I would like to express my gratitude to Dr W. Stingelin (Basel), Dr G. Haas (Jerusalem), Dr R. G. Northcutt and Dr C. Gans for discussions on various questions regarding reptilian neuroanatomy and systematics. S. Bousani-Baur and O. Rieppel assisted me in completing the figures for this chapter, and I am grateful to Dr R. G. Northcutt and M. S. Northcutt for much aid and hospitality during the preparation of the final manuscript. Finally, I am indebted to Dr A. Sigg (Hergiswil), who graciously supported my neuroanatomical research on reptiles.

References

Ariëns Kappers, C. U. (1947). "Anatomie Comparée du System Nerveux." De Erven F. Bohn, Haarlem.

Ariëns Kappers, J. (1967). The sensory innervation of the pineal organ in the lizard, *Lacerta viridis*, with remarks on its position in the trend of pineal phylogenetic structural and functional evolution. *Z. Zellforsch. mikrosk. Anat.* 81, 581–618.

Ariëns Kappers, J., Huber, C. G. and Crosby, E. C. (1936). "The Comparative Anatomy of the Nervous System of Vertebrates, including Man." Macmillan, New York, 2 vol.

Armstrong, J. A. (1950). An experimental study of the visual pathways in a reptile (*Lacerta vivipara*). *J. Anat.* 84, 146–167.

Armstrong, J. A. (1951). An experimental study of the visual pathways in a snake (*Natrix natrix*). *J. Anat.* 85, 275–288.

Beccari, N. (1923). Il centro tegmentale o insterstiziale ed altre formazion poco note nel mesencefalo e nel diencefalo di un rettile. *Archo ital. Anat. Embriol.* 20, 560–619.

Beccari, N. (1943). "Neurologia Comparata Anatomo-funzionale dei Vertebrati Compreso l'Uomo." Sansoni, Firenze.

Bergquist, H. (1953). On the development of the diencephalic nuclei and certain mesencephalic relations in *Lepidochelys olivacea* and other reptiles. *Acta Zool., Stockh.* 34, 155–190.

Bergquist, H. (1954). Ontogenesis of diencephalic nuclei in vertebrates. *Lunds Univ. Arskrift.* 50, 1–33.

Burckhardt, R. (1894a). Über den Bauplan des Gehirns. *Anat. Anz.* 9, 159–162.

Burckhardt, R. (1894b). Die Homologien des Zwischenhirndaches bei Reptilien und Vögeln. *Anat. Anz.* 9, 320–324.

de Lange, S. J. (1913). Das Zwischenhirn und das Mittelhirn der Reptilien. *Folia neurobiol.* 7, 67–138.

Edinger, L. (1899). Untersuchungen über die vergleichende Anatomie des Gehirnes. 4. Studien über das Zwischenhirn der Reptilien. *Abh. senckenb. naturforsch. Ges.* 20, 161–197.

Faul, J. (1926). The comparative ontogenetic development of the corpus striatum in reptiles. *Proc. Acad. Sci. Amsterdam, Sect. Sci.* 29, 150–162.

Haller, G. (1929). Die Gliederung des Zwischen- und Mittelhirnes der Wirbeltiere. *Morph. Jb.* 63, 359–407.

Herrick, C. L. (1892). Embryological notes on the brain of the snake. *J. comp. Neurol.* 2, 160–172.

Herrick, C. J. (1899). The cranial and first spinal nerves of *Menidia*: a contribution upon the nerve components of the bony fishes. *J. comp. Neurol.* 9, 153–455.

Herrick, C. J. (1914). The medulla oblongata of larval *Amblystoma*. *J. comp. Neurol.* 24, 343–427.

Herrick, C. J. (1948). "The Brain of the Tiger Salamander." Univ. Chicago Press, Chicago.

Hetzel, W. (1974). Die Ontogenese des Telencephalons bei *Lacerta sicula* (Rafinesque), mit besonderer Berücksichtigung der pallialen Entwicklung. *Zool. Beitr. Neue Folge* 20, 361–458.

His, W. (1893). Vorschläge zur Einteilung des Gehirnes. *Arch. Anat. Physiol.* 17, 172–179.

Huber, G. C. and Crosby, E. C. (1926). On the thalamic and tectal nuclei and fiber paths in the brain of the American alligator. *J. comp. Neurol.* 40, 97–227.

Huber, G. C. and Crosby, E. C. (1933). The reptilian optic tectum. *J. comp. Neurol.* 57, 57–163.

Johnston, J. B. (1916). The development of the dorsal ventricular ridge in turtles. *J. comp. Neurol.* 26, 481–506.

Källén, B. (1951). On the ontogeny of the reptilian forebrain. Nuclear structures and ventricular sulci. *J. comp. Neurol.* 95, 307–347.

Kirsche, W. (1972). Die Entwicklung des Telencephalons der Reptilien und deren Beziehung zur Hirnbauplanlehre. *Nova Acta Acad. Caesar. Leop.* 37, 1–78.

Kuhlenbeck, H. (1927). "Vorlesungen über das Zentralnervensystem der Wirbeltiere." Fischer, Jena.

Kuhlenbeck, H. (1931). Über die Grundbestandteile des Zwischenhirnbauplans bei Reptilien. *Morph. Jb.* 66, 244–317.

Kupffer, K. V. von (1906). Die Morphogenie des Zentralnervensystems. *In* "Handbuch der vergleichenden und experimentellen Entwicklungslehre der Wirbeltiere". (O. Hertwig, ed.). Gustav Fischer, Jena, **2**, 1–272.

Landmann, L. (1971). Bau und Ontogenese des vestibulären Systems bei *Lacerta sicula*. Birkhäuser, Basel.

Larsell, O. (1926). The cerebellum of reptiles: lizard and snake. *J. comp. Neurol.* **41**, 59–94.

Larsell, O. (1932). The cerebellum of reptiles: chelonians and alligator. *J. comp. Neurol.* **56**, 299–345.

Nelsen, O. E. (1953). "Comparative Embryology of the Vertebrates." Blakiston, New York.

Nieuwenhtuys, R. and Bodenheimer, T. S. (1966). The diencephalon of the primitive bony fish *Polypterus* in the light of the problem of homology. *J. Morph.* **118**, 415–450.

Northcut, R. G. (1977). Retinofugal projections in the lepidosirenid lungfishes. *J. comp. Neurol.* **174**, 553–574.

Peter, K. (1904). Normentafel zur Entwicklungsgeschichte der Zauneidechse (*Lacerta agilis*). *In* "Normantafeln zur Entwicklungsgeschichte der Wirbeltiere". (F. Keibel, ed.). Fischer, Jena, 1–165.

Ramón, P. (1896). Estructura del encefalo del camaleon. *Revta trimest. Micrograf.* **1**, 46–82.

Rudin, W. (1975). Bau und Ontogenese der telencephalen olfaktorischen Zentren bei *Lacerta sicula* (Rafinesque). *Verh. naturf. Ges. Basel* **85**, 101–134.

Schwab, M. E. and Durand, M. (1974). An autoradiographic study of neuroblast proliferation in the rhombencephalon of a reptile, *Lacerta sicula. Z. Anat. EntwGesch.* **145**, 29–40,

Senn, D. G. (1966). Über das optische System im Gehirn squamater Reptilien. *Acta anat. Suppl.* **65**, 1–87.

Senn, D. G. (1968a). Bau und Ontogenese von Zwischen- und Mittelhirn bei *Lacerta sicula* (Rafinesque). *Acta anat., Suppl.* **71**, 1–150.

Senn, D. G. (1968a). Über den Bau von Zwischen- und Mittelhirn von *Anniella pulchra* Gray. *Acta anat.* **69**, 239–261.

Senn, D. G. (1968c). Der Bau des Reptiliengehirnes im Licht neuer Ergebnisse. *Verh. naturf. Ges. Basel* **79**, 25–43.

Senn, D. G. (1969). The saurian and ophidian colliculi posteriores of the midbrain. *Acta anat.* **74**, 114–120.

Senn, D. G. (1970a). The stratification in the reptilian central nervous system. *Acta anat.* **75**, 521–552.

Senn, D. G. (1970b). Zur Ontogenese des Tectum opticum von *Natrix natrix* (L.). *Acta anat.* **76**, 545–563.

Senn, D. G. (1971). Structure and development of the optic tectum of the snapping turtle (*Chelydra serpentina* L.). *Acta anat.* **80**, 46–57.

Senn, D. G. (1972). Development of tegmental and rhombencephalic structures in a frog (*Rana temporaria* L.). *Acta anat.* **82**, 525–548.

Shanklin, W. M. (1930). The central nervous system of *Chamaeleon vulgaris. Acta zool., Stckh.* **11**, 425–490.

Shanklin, W. M. (1933). The comparative neurology of the nucleus opticus tegmenti with special references to *Chamaeleon vulgaris. Acta zool., Stockh.* **14**, 163–184.

Starck, D. (1963a). Diskussionsbeitrag zu Herrn Remane. *Zool. Anz.* **170**, 508–510.

Starck, D. (1963b). Die Metamerie des Kopfes der Wirbeltiere. *Zool. Anz.* **170**, 393–428.

Starck, D. (1965). "Embryologie." Thieme, Stuttgart.

Stefanelli, A. (1941). I centri motori dell occhio e le loro connesioni nel *Chamaeleon vulgaris*, con riferimenti comparativi in altri rettili. *Archo ital. Anat. Embriol.* **45**, 360–412.

Warner, F. J. (1946). The development of the forebrain of the American watersnake *Natrix sipedon. J. comp. Neurol.* **84**, 385–418.

Weston, J. K. (1936). The reptilian vestibular and cerebellar gray with fiber connections. *J. comp. Neurol.* **65**, 93–199.

Will, L. (1892–95). Beiträge zur Entwicklungsgeschichte der Reptilien. *Zool. Jb.* (*Anat.*) **6**, 1–160, 529–615; **9**, 1–91.

Yntema, C. L. (1968). A series of stages in the embryonic development of *Chelydra serpentina. J. Morph.* **125**, 219–252.

Zehr, D. R. (1962). Stages in the normal development of the common garter snake, *Thamnophis sirtalis sirtalis. Copeia 1962*, 322–329.

CHAPTER 5

The Parietal Eye—Pineal Complex

W. B. QUAY

Department of Anatomy, University of Texas Medical Branch,
Galveston, Texas, U.S.A.

I. Introduction

The parietal eye-pineal complex of reptiles is a morphologically, and probably functionally, interrelated set of structures developed in the roof of the diencephalon (Table I). This complex is dominated by two organs, the pineal organ or gland (or epiphysis cerebri) and the parietal eye (Table II). One might also reasonably include within this complex, at least on the basis of developmental and anatomical proximity, the dorsal sac and paraphysis, structures that resemble the choroid plexuses that extend into the ventricles of the brain. However, several fragments of evidence suggest that it may be premature to relegate these two structures to the status of additional and unspecialized units in the set of choroid plexuses. The dorsal sac is more closely associated with the pineal gland than is the paraphysis, not only in terms of anatomical proximity, but also on the basis of developmental and functional relations. Unfortunately these have received relatively little attention to date.

↪Several brain structures border on the base of the pineal complex and are noted here primarily as anatomical reference points or landmarks. However, some of these have either demonstrated or suspected functional relations with the pineal complex. Most prominent among these landmarks are, from anterior to posterior, the posterior pallial commissure (commissura pallii posterior or commissura aberrans of the older literature; Elliot Smith 1903; Ariëns Kappers *et al.*, 1936), the habenular commissure (commissura habenularum or commissura superior of the older literature), and the posterior commissure (commissura posterior). The latter two are of interest both as developmental landmarks and as pathways associated with the courses taken by the nerve fibers of the pineal and parietal eyes. The posterior commissure bounds the pineal complex as well as the roof of the diencephalon posteriorly. Along its medial ventricular surface lies the sub-

W. B. QUAY

commissural organ, an ependymally derived secretory organ which produces Reissner's fiber and may have other secretory functions as well
(Olsson, 1958; Oksche, 1969; Palkovits, 1965). Although in some vertebrates
the secretory cells of the subcommissural organ are contiguous or sometimes intermixed (Quay, 1956) with pineal cells, this has not yet been reported

TABLE I

*Anatomical relations of structures in and about the reptilian parietal
eye–pineal complex*[a]

Putative Left-sided origin	Median or transmedian	Putative right-sided origin
	Lamina terminalis	
	Paraphysis	
	Posterior pallial commissure	
	Velum transversum	
	Dorsal sac Habenular commissure	
Parietal Eye Parietal Eye Nerve		
	Pineal recess	
		Pineal gland
		Pineal nerve
	Subcommissural organ	
	Posterior commissure	

(Left margin, top to bottom: ANTERIOR ↑ ... POSTERIOR ↓)

[a] Derived and modified in part from Burckhardt (1890, 1893, 1894), Minot (1901), Studnička
(1905), Schmidt (1909), and Tilney and Warren (1919).

in reptiles. The subcommissural organ appears to have different functional
relations too, but these are obscure and will not be reviewed here. It might be
treated most appropriately as a member of the circumventricular complex of
organs (Campos-Ortega, 1965; Vigh, 1971).

The pineal complex is bordered distally and dorsally by the mostly
mesodermal tissues of outer meninges, periosteum, skeletal elements of the
skull roof, and subcutaneous fascia or connective tissue. When the parietal

TABLE II

Synonyms of structures in and related to the reptilian parietal eye–pineal complex[a]

Relative position	Current designation—Synonyms
↑ A N T E R I O R	Lamina terminalis
	Paraphysis—paraphyseal arch, anterior epiphysis (Burckhardt 1890), pre-paraphysis (His, 1868), posterior choroid plexus (Sorenson, 1894)
	Posterior pallial commissure—commissura pallii posterior, commissura aberrans
	Velum transversum
	Dorsal sac—(of Goronowitsch, 1888) post-velar arch, parencephalon (von Kupffer, 1887), Zirbelpolster (Burckhardt, 1890), post-paraphysis (Sorenson, 1894)
	Habenular commissure—commissura habenularum, superior commissure, commissura tenuissima
	Parietal eye—frontal organ or stirnorgan (Leydig, 1872), Leydig's organ, anterior epiphysis (Hill, 1891), parapineal organ (Studnička, 1895–96), parapineal eye, parietal organ
P O S T E R I O R ↓	Parietal eye nerve—parietal nerve
	Pineal recess—recessus pinealis
	Pineal gland—epiphysis cerebri, posterior epiphysis (Hill, 1891), corpus pineale, Zirbel, Zirbeldrüse, glandula superior, pineal body, pineal organ
	Pineal nerve—nervus pinealis, pineal tract
	Subcommissural organ
	Posterior commissure

[a] Derived and modified in part from Burckhardt (1890, 1893, 1894), Minot (1901), Studnička (1905), Schmidt (1909), and Tilney and Warren (1919).

eye is extracranial (that is, when it lies dorsal to the skull roof), then integumentary tissues border this part of the complex and are often adaptively modified as transparent and cornea-like members of the parietal eye apparatus. The present review of the parietal eye-pineal complex will include considerations of two features in these dorsal tissues, the so-called parietal or pineal foramen and integumentary, cornea-like, structural modifications. The parietal foramen (which is not always in the parietal bones) variably contains the parietal eye and transmits the parietal eye nerve. Its size and structure in fossil reptiles are of especial interest, as only by such indirect evidence can we estimate the degree of development (or regression) of their parietal eye systems. Integumentary adaptations over the parietal eye of some living lizards will be seen to support and charac-terize the photoreceptive adaptations of this part of the complex.

Retrospectively, knowledge concerning the reptilian parietal eye–pineal complex appears to have advanced in a mostly fitful and disconnected manner. Also, the field has been burdened by the premature and faulty conclusion that the essential evolutionary trend of the pineal complex in tetrapods is one of regression to a vestigial, functionless organ. Evolutionary reduction and loss can be supported, at least in regard to the parietal eye. However, the glandular part of the complex has been remodeled extensively, distinctively and independently along separate evolutionary lines, especially within the classes Chondrichthyes, Osteichthyes, Reptilia, Aves and Mammalia. Within the living Reptilia separate lines of evolutionary remodeling of the glandular (pineal or epiphyseal) part of the complex are seen in the Testudines, Sauria, Serpentes and Rhynchocephalia (*Sphenodon*). The Crocodilia are the only living reptiles with neither the glandular nor the photoreceptive parts of the pineal complex. Although evolutionary reduction and loss are one pattern of advanced evolutionary status in reptilian parietal eyes and organs, it is not the only pattern that is properly considered advanced when the glandular pineal is considered. Moreover, evolutionary patterns of remodeling with distinctive structural and bio-chemical characteristics are seen in the pineal glands within advanced orders of both birds and mammals, including Passeriformes (Quay, 1965a; Quay and Renzoni, 1963, 1967) of the former, and Primates (Krabbe, 1920; Quay, 1970a) of the latter.

Research on the reptilian pineal complex can be viewed historically as having passed through three phases and as now being well into a fourth. The part of the complex which is now considered to be chiefly secretory, the reptilian pineal organ or epiphysis cerebri, was known anatomically by the beginning of the nineteenth century through the works of Cuvier (1805), Tiedemann (1823), and others. About a century ago a second phase arose having primarily morphogenetic, histological and cytological points of emphasis, and being based upon light microscopy. Early and notable contributors during this phase were Leydig (1872, 1887, 1889, 1890a, b, 1897), Strahl (1884), Spencer (1886a, b), de Graaf (1886), Hoffmann (1886,

1890), Francotte (1887, 1888, 1892, 1894, 1896), Béraneck (1887, 1892, 1893), Strahl and Martin (1888), McKay (1888), Hanitsch (1888), Owsjannikow (1888, 1890), Duval and Kalt (1889), Carriére (1890), Ritter (1890, 1894), Klinckowström (1893, 1894), Prenant (1893, 1894, 1895), Sorenson (1893, 1894), Locy (1894), Gaupp (1897) and Dendy (1899, 1909, 1910, 1911). The parietal eye was the focal point of much of the research during this second phase. Studnička's (1905) and Schmidt's (1909) reviews of the findings gathered during this phase remain classic and still useful. The subsequent fifty years, comprising the third phase, saw comparatively little research on the reptilian pineal complex; most work provided either additional details to earlier findings or morphological information on species not previously examined. The relatively rare and pioneering experimental investigations of this time, such as those of Clausen and Poris (1937), and Clausen and Mofshin (1939), apparently gained little recognition. Works reviewing the reptilian pineal complex during this third phase were mostly misleading and discouraging. This was at least largely due to their emphasis upon the regressive aspects of the morphology and presumed functional significance of the eyelike components and their adnexa (Camp, 1923; Gladstone and Wakeley, 1940).

A fourth major phase in parietal eye–pineal research commenced in the mid-1950s and continues still. Quantitative resurgence or rebirth and marked diversification into about eleven research approaches occurred during the ensuing decade. 1. Behavior: Stebbins and Eakin (1958); Glaser (1958); Stebbins (1960, 1963); Palenschat (1964). 2. Biochemistry: Quay and Wilhoft (1964); Quay (1965b, 1971); Vivien-Roels et al. (1971). 3. Histochemistry: Eakin et al. (1961); Grignon and Grignon (1963a); Quay et al. (1967); Collin (1968b); Quay et al. (1968); Wartenberg and Baumgarten (1969a, b); Quay (1969a); Vivien-Roels (1969); McDevitt (1970, 1972); Meiniel and Collin (1970); Petit (1971b). 4. Histophysiology and physiology: Hutton and Ortman (1957); Eakin et al. (1959); Stebbins (1960, 1963, 1970); Aron et al. (1960); Combescot and Demaret (1962, 1963). 5. Neurology: J. A. Kappers (1964, 1965, 1966, 1967); Quay et al. (1968); Vivien-Roels (1968); Collin and J. A. Kappers (1968). 6. Neurophysiology: Miller and Wolbarsht (1962); Dodt and Scherer (1967, 1968a, b); Hamasaki (1968, 1969a, b); Gruberg et al. (1968); Hamasaki and Dodt (1969). 7. Nutrition: Eakin (1964b). 8. Optics and ophthalmology: Gasson (1947); Sivak (1973). 9. Paleontology: Edinger (1955, 1956, 1964). 10. Pharmacology: Steyn (1958); Quay et al. (1967); Quay et al. (1968); Quay (1969a); Wartenberg and Baumgarten (1969a, b; Meiniel and Collin (1970); Petit (1971b); Petit et al. (1971). 11. Ultrastructure (electron microscopy): Eakin and Westfall (1959, 1960, 1962); Steyn (1959a, 1960a, b); Steyn and Steyn (1962, 1965); Eakin (1960, 1963, 1964a, b, 1968, 1970, 1973); Vivien

(1964b); Lierse (1965a, b); Oksche and Kirschstein (1966a, b, 1968); Collin (1967a, b, 1968a, b, 1969, 1971); Lutz and Collin (1967); Vivien and Roels (1967, 1968); Wartenberg and Baumgarten (1968, 1969a, b); and Petit (1968, 1969, 1971a).

Results obtained in at least several of these research lines have independently revealed the parietal eye–pineal complex to have probable functional significance at least in several of the major reptilian taxa. Perhaps we are at the point now where integration and broader correlations can be made concerning this complex, using the results from disparate lines of biological research. Surely this will most likely be easier in the future, but current timeliness of such a comprehensive review and integration is supportable by the argument that future research will be aided thereby.

Although in recent decades reviews have been written about the parietal eye–pineal complex the emphasis, if not overall coverage, has been on the mammalian pineal gland. Furthermore, most of these reviews are neither comprehensive in references to diverse aspects of the pineal gland nor do they present different points of view or schools of thought concerning pineal function. They remain useful, nevertheless, for students of the reptilian pineal complex. Therefore they are worthy of chronological citation here, as representative source materials and points of view in the fourth and current phase of pineal research: Kitay and Altschule (1954); Thiéblot and LeBars (1955); Oksche (1956); Steyn (1957, 1959b, 1961); Kelly (1962); Eakin (1963); Kamer (1965); Quay (1965a); Steyn (1966); Eakin (1968); Wurtman et al. (1968); Collin (1969); J. A. Kappers (1969); Quay (1969a, b); Eakin (1970); Hoffman (1970); Quay (1970b); Dodt et al. (1971); J. A. Kappers (1971b); Miline (1971); Oksche (1971a, b); Reiter (1972); Dodt (1973); Eakin (1973); Reiter (1973); Axelrod (1974); Quay (1974); Reiter (1974).

II. Developmental and Topographic Anatomy

A. General Features and Nomenclature

The reptilian parietal eye–pineal complex is most closely related to the primitive central nervous system in developmental origins and histogenetic relationships. Major features and the developmental morphology of the reptilian central nervous system have been described and illustrated by Senn in Chapter 4 of this volume. Our review, therefore, will be limited chiefly to the parietal eye and pineal organ themselves.

The development of these two small and closely associated structures in reptiles has been studied for over a century and by many investigators (Table III). With the clear exception of Dendy's classic and detailed work

TABLE III

Descriptions of developmental stages of the parietal eye–pineal complex or region in reptiles

Order Suborder Family	Species (References)

TESTUDINES
  Chelydridae — *Chelydra serpentina* (Humphrey, 1894; Krabbe, 1935; Studnička, 1905)
  Emydidae — *Chrysemys picta* (Krabbe, 1935; Warren, 1911). *Emys orbicularis* (Nowikoff, 1910)
  Testudinidae — *Testudo graeca* and *T. hermanni* (Vivien-Roels and Petit, 1973)
  Cheloniidae — *Eretmochelys imbricata* (Studnička, 1905; Voeltzkow, 1903)
  Trionychidae — *Trionyx muticus* (Gage, 1895)

SQUAMATA
  Sauria
    Iguanidae — *Iguana iguana* (de Klinckowström, 1893, 1894; Studnička, 1905). *Phrynosoma coronatum* (Sorenson, 1894). *Sceloporus occidentalis* (Eakin, 1964a). *Sceloporus* sp. (Sorenson, 1894)
    Agamidae — *Amphibolurus muricatus* (McKay, 1888). *Calotes cristatellus* (Schmidt, 1909). *Calotes versicolor* (Preisler, 1942). *Phrynocephalus vlangalii* (Owsjannikow, 1888; Studnička, 1905)
    Chamaeleonidae — *Chamaeleo bitaeniatus* (Krabbe, 1934)
    Gekkonidae — *Gehyra oceanica* (Stemmler, 1900; Studnička, 1905). *Hemidactylus mabouia* (Stemmler, 1900; Studnička, 1905). *Tarentola mauritanica* (Leydig, 1897; Melchers, 1900; Studnička, 1905)
    Teiidae — *Tupinambis teguixin* (de Klinckowström, 1894; Studnička, 1905)
    Scincidae — *Chalcides ocellatus* (Legge, 1897; Oksche, 1965; Schmidt, 1909; Studnička, 1905; Trost, 1952, 1953a, b). *Chalcides chalcides* (Schmidt, 1909; Boveri, 1925). *Lygosoma taeniolatum* (McKay, 1888). *Mabuya sulcata* (Steyn, 1957, 1959a, b). *Tiliqua gigas* (Schmidt, 1909).
    Lacertidae — *Lacerta agilis* (Francotte, 1894; de Graaf, 1886; C. K. Hoffmann, 1886; Leydig, 1872; 1890b; Nowikoff, 1910; Petit, 1967; Schmidt, 1909; Studnička, 1905; Warren, 1911). *Lacerta muralis* (Francotte, 1894; Leydig, 1872; Nowikoff, 1910; Warren, 1911). *Lacerta viridis* (Francotte, 1894; Petit, 1967; Warren, 1911). *Lacerta vivipara* (Francotte, 1894, 1896; von Haffner, 1953, 1955; Leydig,

(*Table III continued page 252*)

TABLE III—contd.

Order
  Suborder
    Family
	Species (References)

	1872; Meiniel, 1974a, b, 1975a, b; Meinel and Collin, 1970; Meiniel *et al.*, 1970, 1972, 1973, 1975; Nowikoff, 1910; Schmidt, 1909; Strahl and Martin, 1888)
Cordylidae	*Cordylus polyzonus* (Steyn, 1957, 1959)
Anguidae	*Anguis fragilis* (Béraneck, 1887, 1892, 1893; Francotte, 1888, 1894; de Graaf, 1886; Hanitsch, 1888; Leydig, 1872; Petit, 1967; Preisler, 1942; Strahl and Martin, 1888; Studnička, 1905; Trost, 1952, 1953a, b)
Serpentes	
Colubridae	*Coluber constrictor* (Sorenson, 1894; Studnička, 1905). *Coronella austriaca* (Leydig, 1883, 1897; Studnička, 1905). *Natrix natrix* (Francotte, 1894; C. K. Hoffmann, 1886; Leydig, 1883, 1897; Petit, 1969; Preisler, 1942; Ssobolew, 1907; Studnička, 1893, 1905; Trost, 1952, 1953a, b)
Viperidae	*Vipera berus* (Hanitsch, 1888; Ssobolew, 1907; Studnička, 1905). *Vipera ursinii* (Leydig, 1897; Studnička, 1905)
RHYNCHOCEPHALIA	
Sphenodontidae	*Sphenodon punctatus* (Dendy, 1899, 1910, 1911; Studnička, 1905; Wyeth, 1925)
CROCODILIA	
Crocodylidae	*Alligator mississippiensis* (Sorenson, 1894; Studnička, 1905). *Crocodylus niloticus madagascariensis* (Voeltzkow, 1903). *Melanosuchus niger* (Studnička, 1905; Voeltzkow, 1903)

on *Sphenodon* (1899, 1910, 1911), much of the embryological work on the reptilian parietal eye–pineal complex was rather fragmentary and superficial until the 1950s. At that time interest was renewed and more critical examinations appeared, authored by Trost (1952, 1953a, b), Haffner (1953, 1955), Steyn (1957, 1959b), Eakin (1964a), Petit (1967, 1969) and Vivien-Roels and Petit (1973).

Review of the development of the reptilian parietal eye and pineal necessarily focuses on the four separate major groups in which either the pineal alone (Testudines, some Sauria and Serpentes) or both pineal and parietal eye (many Sauria and *Sphenodon*) are found. Development of the components of the parietal eye–pineal complex will be considered first within each of these groups separately and then compared, primarily among the reptilian groups. Table III lists the forms for which data are available.

B. TESTUDINES

Useful descriptions of the entire course of early pineal development in turtles are found only in the detailed and important work of Vivien-Roels and Petit (1973). Their findings, based upon embryos of *Testudo graeca* and *T. hermanni* are outlined in the following paragraphs. Nine developmental stages (A to I, Table IV) have been designated and are characterized both

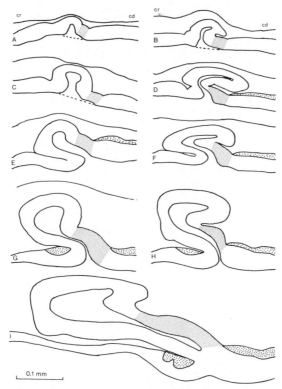

FIG. 1. Developmental morphology of the pineal complex in *Testudo graeca* and *T. hermanni*. The posterior pineal primordium is lightly stippled; the anterior and parietal primordium, to its left, is clear. The habenular (left) and posterior (right) commissures are coarsely stippled. Cranial (cr) and caudal (cd) orientations are the same in these sagittal sections of the diencephalic roof. (Courtesy of Vivien-Roels and Petit, 1973.)

by major morphological features and by correspondence with Yntema's (1968) table of development for *Chelydra serpentina*.

STAGE A: The posterior part of the diencephalic roof shows two median, dorsal evaginations (Fig. 1A), comparable to those of the pineal complex in

TABLE IV

Morphological correlates of pineal development in Testudo graeca and T. hermanni. (Data of Vivien-Roels and Petit, 1973)

Stage	Head length (mm)	Number of somites	Length of carapace (mm)	Testudo graeca and T. hermanni Pineal complex	Remarks	Chelydra serpentina comparable stage (of Yntema, 1968)
A	0·8-0·9	24-26 (T. graeca) 26-28 (T. hermanni)	—	Median anterior (parietal) and posterior (pineal) evaginations present	Limb primordia low swellings; branchial clefts 1 and 2 open	—
B	1·1-1·2	about 30	—	Growth mainly in anterior (parietal) primordium	Eyes not pigmented; limb buds grow	10
C	1·7	35-40	—	Growth mainly in anterior (parietal) primordium	Eyes pigmented; four pairs of branchial clefts	11
D	1·9	40-45	—	Leftward orientation taken by parietal primordium	Primordial limb paddles with apical crest	12
E	3·3	—	5-6 (first appears)	Ventricular connection of original pineal lumen lost	Anterior digit primordia and eyelids formed	16
F	4·9	—	11	Beginning of rapid growth of posterior (pineal) primordium with fusion of both primordia	Chondrification of cranial vault begins	—
G	6·5	—	16-16·5	Lengthening of pineal primordium with occasional loss of original diencephalic attachment	Secretory activity in subcommissural organ	—
H	8·5	—	23-25	Formation of folds and diverticula, with secondary attachments to diencephalic roof	Neurohypophysis forms; secreting chromophils in pars distalis	—
I	9·5	—	27-28	Pineal composed of epithelial vesicles or follicles; ganglion cells appear within pineal epithelium	Hatching occurs	—

lizard embryos. The more anterior of these is believed to correspond to the parietal component and the more posterior to the pineal (epiphyseal) component of the complex. The presumptive parietal component is better developed and closely approaches the overlying epidermis, from which it is separated by no more than a thin sheet of mesenchyme. The relatively smaller and posterior pineal (epiphyseal) primordium is scarcely raised from the level of the ependymal cells forming the diencephalic roof. A shallow transverse furrow separates the two primordia. From the standpoint of their comparative histogenesis it is interesting that two cell types are encountered within the primordia at this time. The first cell type has an elongate oval nucleus, dense chromatin and a very distinct nucleolus. Due to their resemblance to ependymal cells, the cells of this first type are considered precursors of supporting cells. The second cell type, which is more prevalent in the parietal primordium, has paler, smaller and more spheroidal nuclei. The cells of this second type are believed to be the precursors for sensory cells. The density of cytoplasmic staining is similar in these two cell types. The luminal or ventricular surface of the evaginations is bordered by filamentous or vesiculated cytoplasmic processes. Significant and rapid growth of the primordia at this stage is indicated by observed autophagic bodies and apical mitotic figures. Just posterior to the parietal and pineal primordia, cells of the developing subcommissural organ are starting their organization and distinctive structural differentiation. Even at this time they are well differentiated from cells of the pineal primordium. The posterior commissure, however, is not yet distinct.

STAGE B: The parietal primordium is raised further above the third ventricle and takes on a generally dorsocaudal direction of growth (Fig. 1B). Because of this, it often appears partially to overlie the more posterior pineal primordium. However, this primordium becomes somewhat difficult to delimit with precision at this stage. The dorsal part of the parietal primordium is still closely applied against the epiblast in such a manner that it is externally visible as a slightly projecting button. The pineal primordium has changed little since the preceding stage and does not show any consistent pattern of dorsocaudal growth. Sections cut in transverse and frontal planes demonstrate that the two primordia are always median. The two cell types described in the previous stage are seen again here, but the cells considered to be precursors to a sensory type of cell are more numerous in the distal region of the parietal primordium than in other regions of the developing parietal–pineal complex. An interior crease separates the parietal primordium from the diencephalic roof. At this level the orientation and general aspect of the cell nuclei suggest the occurrence of an invagination of ependymal material within the parietal primordium. Mitotic figures and so-called autophagic bodies are frequently observed within cells of both parietal and pineal primordia as well as in cells of the neighbouring subcommissural organ.

STAGE C: The parietal primordium takes a cranial or slightly dorsocranial direction of growth (Fig. 1D, E, F), forming an important anterior fold with the diencephalic roof, which is thereby partially covered. The lumen, which is often bent posteriorly, still communicates broadly with the third ventricle. Tissue sections in transverse or parasagittal planes show that the parietal primordium has a tendency to form an anterior vesicle. Form and position of the vesicle are variable due to differential growth of the primordia and adjacent tissue. This active growth of the parietal primordium, still characterized by abundant mitoses, draws out as well the posterior pineal primordium. The latter thus becomes somewhat raised above the third ventricle, although in other respects it shows little change since stage A (Fig. 2A and B).

At this point Vivien-Roels and Petit (1973) call attention to a phenomenon similar to that in stage E of the development of the saurian pineal complex (Petit, 1967): the development of the pineal primordium seems to undergo an inhibition that might be imposed by the ocular or terminal vesicle in the complex.

Cellular differentiation within the two primordia of the tortoise pineal complex proceeds, but still with a distinct retardation of the pineal primordium. The orientation and shape of the cell nuclei of the anterior fold show that periparietal ependymal cells continue to be incorporated into the primordium. The presumptive sensory cells are still the most numerous within the parietal primordium. The nucleus occupies the basal cytoplasm in these cells and the apical cytoplasm is denser and longitudinally striated. Nuclei of ependymal cells are more elongate, more or less triangular, and have dense chromatin distributed in irregular masses. Ependymal cytoplasm is clear and lacks any particular affinity for staining.

It may be noted in passing that at this stage (C) the first primordium of the paraphysis appears, consisting of two or three cellular thickenings in the anterior median region of the diencephalic roof. Also, the first evident fibers of the posterior commissure appear above the caudal part of the subcommissural organ.

STAGE D: The parietal primordium takes on again a more dorsal or vertical orientation (Fig. 1G and H; Fig. 2C). Reconstructions from tracings of serial sections (in the sagittal, transverse and frontal planes) show that the parietal primordium has a true anterior vesicle at this time. The vesicle has a lumen connected to the third ventricle by only a narrow canal and is orientated slightly to the left in relation to the sagittal plane. Although the tortoise parietal vesicle morphologically resembles that of lizards (Petit, 1967), this vesicle in *Testudo* lacks retinal or lens-like differentiations. The dorsal

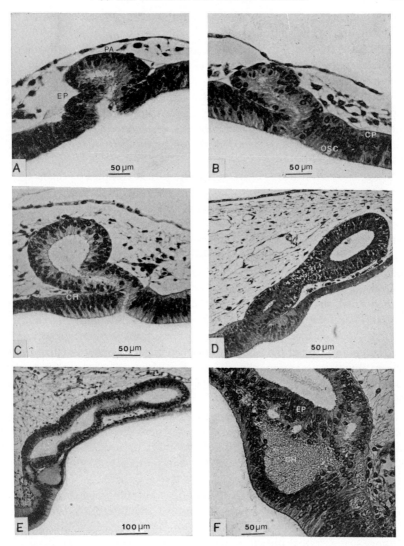

FIG. 2. Sagittal sections of the developing pineal complex in *Testudo hermanni* (A, B, C) and *T. graeca* (D, E, F), and representing stages C (A, B), D (C), E (D) and F (E, F). CH, habenular commissure; CP, posterior commissure; EP, posterior pineal (epiphyseal) primordium; OSC, subcommissural organ; PA, anterior or parietal primordium. (Courtesy of Vivien-Roels and Petit, 1973.)

furrow that separates the parietal vesicle from the pineal primordium extends laterally, attaining thereby the ventral wall (Fig. 1H).

A part of the periparietal ependymal material incorporated within the primordium in the course of the preceding stages probably participates in the formation of the ventral and lateral walls of the pineal primordium. The latter begins at this stage an active growth phase, noted on the basis of increased numbers of mitotic figures (Fig. 2c). Interestingly, postepiphyseal subcommissural material also seems to be incorporated within the pineal primordium at this stage. The supportive ependymal cells and the primitive, supposedly sensory cells, that appeared in earlier stages, now occur within both primordia and project filamentous or vesicular cytoplasmic extensions within the lumen. Their exact nature remains uncertain in the absence of electron micrographs.

STAGE E: Two features characterize the pineal complex at this stage, the obliteration of the original, or primary, pineal canal that no longer connects with the third ventricle, and the greater difficulty in defining the boundary between parietal and pineal tissue regions. In effect one sees continuity between the still slightly leftward directed anterior vesicle and the posterior pineal or epiphyseal primordium. Frequently at this time only a slight constriction marks the junction of the two primordia, which now start to form ventral or lateral accessory vesicles (Fig. 2D). Together, these participate in the formation of the definitive or adult pineal gland or organ in subsequent stages. Therefore, no parietal eye forms. Cellular differentiation continues; the supposed sensory cells terminate with an inner segment projecting into the lumen and tipped by a filamentous structure of probably ciliary nature. Ciliary formations are equally abundant at the level of the closure of the epiphyseal lumen, as at the level of the pineal recess, which is clearly evident at this time (Fig. 2D, lower left corner).

Vascularization of the diencephalic roof becomes notably richer and extends anteriorly, forming a kind of canopy between the paraphysis and the parietal and pineal primordia. The latter takes on a dorsocranial direction of growth, and the superior sagittal sinus appears and caps the distal extremity of the parietal vesicle.

STAGE F: The pineal, now flattened dorsoventrally, regains what appears to be a sagittal position, perhaps because of the adjacent bilateral growth and pressures of the cerebral hemispheres and optic lobes. Pineal growth continues in a cranial direction, with support gained from the diencephalic roof and elongation from the base at the cranial end of the subcommissural organ. The pineal remains attached by a stout stalk, which extends dorso-cranially, drawing along with it subjacent subcommissural cells (Fig. 2E, lower left corner).

Following upon the flexure at the level of the posterior commissure and the subcommissural organ, the proximal and ventral part of the pineal wall comes to lie close to the habenular commissure, and secondary contacts are established between these structures (Fig. 2F, center). There is a basal blending or continuity of pineal and habenular tissues at the level of the contact zone, and a similar relationship is established with cells in the adjacent diencephalic roof. From this stage onward, the relations of the pineal with the diencephalon show a series of individual variations which are accentuated in the course of the last stages, but which need not concern us further here.

STAGE G: Three changes are seen in the pineal primordium: (1) the pineal, which continues its growth in a dorsocranial direction, remains attached basally by a stout and clearly defined stalk at the level of which occur basal cytoplasmic processes from the tanycytes in the cranial end of the subcommissural organ. The two adjacent commissures, habenular and posterior, are thus narrowly separated, one from the other by the pineal stalk and the pineal recess (Fig. 1I; Fig. 3B). (2) Although the anterior and posterior basal portions of the pineal are entirely fused with the habenular commissure and subcommissural organ respectively, a completely separated anterior vesicle appears at the distal end. This is separated from the more posteriorly lying pineal by one or more folds of choroid plexus (Fig. 3C). The figures (Fig. 3C and E) suggest, however, that these epithelial folds possibly may represent the dorsal sac. (3) In some instances the epiphysis, during the course of its growth, is so stretched out from the cranial end of the subcommissural organ that it appears to lose completely its connection with this region of the diencephalic roof (Fig. 3D). Only an isolated strand of cells stretching out from the cranial end of the subcommissural organ may remain as a vestige of the original zone of pineal attachment.

Cells within the anterior part of the pineal continue their structural differentiation. The internal segments of the supposed sensory cells are well developed and numerous within the anterior part of the pineal. They take the form of large vesicles projecting into the lumen. However, within the more proximal or basal part of the pineal one observes such inner segments but rarely. Sensory and supportive types of cells are arranged in an alternating fashion, and their basal or external cytoplasmic extensions tend to form a basal plexiform layer along the external margin. The pineal at this stage does not show neurons, at least when treated with the usual staining techniques. Only in the region of the habenular commissure are there cells having the characteristics of neurons (Fig. 3B, arrow). These cells have a large spherical nucleus and cytoplasmic granulation that stains strongly with Gomori's chrome alum hematoxylin and with aldehyde fuchsin.

STAGE H: Pineal growth continues, with the formation of folds and lateral and ventral diverticula, all of which generally still maintain their continuity with each other and with the central lumen of the organ. However, there is great individual variation in the structural relations between the pineal and the region ("*épidiencephalique*") of its origin and former basal attachment,

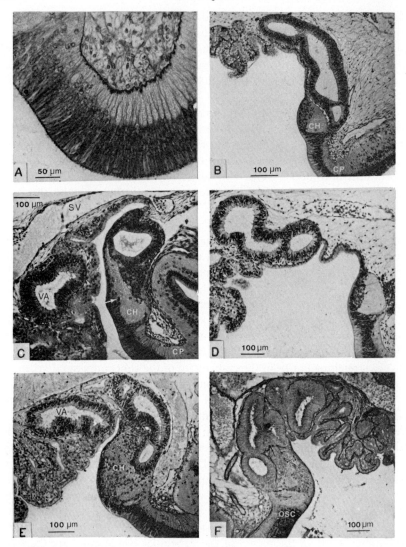

FIG. 3. Sagittal sections of the developing subcommissural organ (A) and pineal complex (B to F) in *Testudo graeca*, and representing stages F (A), G (B, C, D) and H (E, F). A. Tanycytes with PAS-positive basal cytoplasm and characteristic structure are shown. B. Pineal stalk and recess separate the habenular (CH) and posterior (CP) commissures. C. An anterior (parietal) vesicle (VA) appears to be completely separated from the rest of the pineal; the proximal (posterior) part of the pineal is attached to the habenular commissure in which a nerve cell body (arrow) is strongly stained with Gomori chrome alum hematoxylin; SV, superior sagittal venous sinus. D. The pineal has lost continuity with the diencephalic roof. E. The anterior (parietal) vesicle (VA) is separate from the posterior pineal, which is closely attached to the neurone-containing habenular commissure (CH). F. The posterior pineal's extensions or diverticula are secondarily joined to the diencephalic roof at several points (arrows); the subcommissural organ (OSC) is strongly stained with aldehyde fuchsin. (Courtesy of Vivien-Roels and Petit, 1973.)

and also with more anterior (cranial) structures in the diencephalic roof. Secondary attachments are formed not only in the proximal or basal region of the pineal but also between the ventral wall of the intermediate pineal region and parts of the diencephalic roof anterior to as well as including the habenular commissure. Sometimes, direct continuity occurs between pineal tissue and the choroidal roof, with the pineal lumen then opening directly into the third ventricle in this region anterior to the habenular commissure (Fig. 4A). Finally, some embryos have a pineal which is either completely disconnected from the diencephalic roof structures or contains an anterior pineal vesicle which is entirely separated from the remainder of the organ.

A large number of cell bodies having the characteristics of neurons are revealed in the vicinity of the habenular commissure, the cranial end of the subcommissural organ and at the base of the proximal part of the pineal organ. Nevertheless, these cells do not appear to colonize the pineal epithelium (Fig. 3E). They are seen in slides stained with aldehyde fuchsin, Gomori's chrome alum hematoxylin or alcian blue. With silver impregnations a nerve tract within the pineal stalk is not yet demonstrable. However, one specimen showed a slender nerve fascicle directed towards the posterior commissure, and in *Chrysemys* (Vivien-Roels, 1970) a nerve tract is commonly observed running caudally between the posterior commissure and the subcommissural organ. At this stage no nerve fiber is seen running from the pineal towards the habenular commissure.

In contrast, at this stage three or four large nerve cell bodies are seen dorsal to the pineal and between it and the superior sagittal sinus (Fig. 4B). Their cytoplasm stains with Gomori hematoxylin, alcian blue and aldehyde fuchsin, as well as with silver impregnation. These cells, which are in direct contact with the epiphysis, send processes dorsally along the ventral wall of the superior sagittal sinus. But they rapidly fade out and disappear when they are traced by light microscopy. It is not ascertainable as yet whether these cells differentiate from cells within the pineal organ or whether they come from elsewhere.

Within the pineal epithelium, and equally well proximally and distally, two cell types are present (Fig. 4D). One of these, the supposed sensory line, shows above the pale nucleus a rather voluminous inner segment protruding into the lumen and tipped by an elongate, club-shaped structure probably representing a primordial outer (external) segment. The ependymal supportive cells alternate with the preceding type and have elongate or somewhat triangular and hyperchromatic nuclei. Both cell types have basally or externally directed cytoplasmic extensions that make up a basal plexiform layer underlying the pineal epithelium.

STAGE I: The pineal appears to be composed of many vesicles or follicle-like structures which have variable relations with each other. When connected

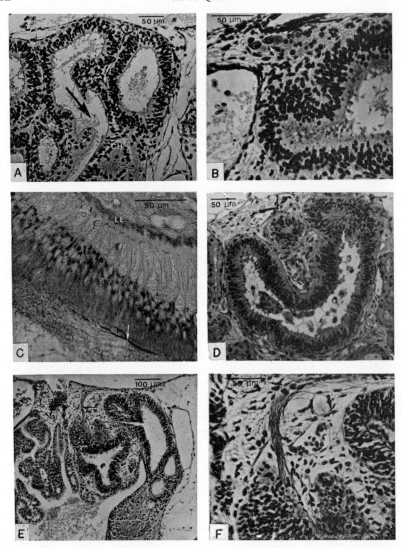

FIG. 4. Sagittal (A, B, C, E, F) and transverse (D) sections of the developing subcommissural organ (C) and pineal complex (A, B, D, E, F) in *Testudo graeca*, and representing stages H (A, B, C, D) and I (E. F). A. Secondary attachments of vesicles, or of diverticula, of the posterior or proximal part of the pineal are shown with the roof of the third ventricle (confluence of lumens at arrow) and the habenular commissure (CH). Bodian-Fitzgerald technique. B. Neuron cell bodies (arrow) forming a ganglionic mass dorsal to a pineal vesicle. Bodian-Fitzgerald technique. C. Secretion of the subcommissural organ cells, stained here with aldehyde fuchsin, extends basally towards the external boundary (LE) and apically to form Reissner's fiber (arrow) within the ventricle. D. Distal part of pineal. Gomori's chrome alum hematoxylin technique. E. The pineal is reattached to the cranial part of the habenular commissure; the arrow points to the dorsal nerve tract which comes to branch out at the level of the dorsal wall of the pineal. Bodian-Fitzgerald technique. F. Enlargement of the nerve tract shown in E. Bodian-Fitzgerald technique. (Courtesy of Vivien-Roels and Petit, 1973.)

to the diencephalon they are seen to be reattached generally to the cranial (anterior) extremity of the habenular commissure (Fig. 4E). Here, one or more short but stolid pineal stalks make the connection. Within these are some ependymal cells, rare neuron cell bodies, and, more rarely, isolated nerve fibers directed either towards the base of the habenular commissure or towards the posterior commissure. Anterior to the habenular commissure, the diencephalic roof forms an important fold, directed at first upward and backward and forming the dorsal sac above which lie the anterior pineal vesicles. This posterior fold of the roof, or dorsal sac, frequently separates the vesicles of the anterior part of the pineal from the posterior part of the pineal. It also shows continuity with one or another of the pineal vesicles, which consequently open directly into the ventricular cavity of the diencephalon.

What seem to be ganglion cell bodies appear within the pineal epithelium at this stage. In addition, silver impregnation demonstrates a nerve with apparently afferent pineal relations. It runs along the ventral surface of the superior sagittal venous sinus in a cranial direction (Fig. 4E and F) and distributes nerve fibers to the periphery of the pineal vesicles. Both origin and nature of this nerve remain obscure. It has no relation either to the existing pineal stalk or to the habenular and posterior commissures. A group of three or four large nerve cells now form a veritable ganglion above the cranial (anterior) part of the pineal. Nerve fibers extend from this ganglion, which appears to relay innervation to the pineal.

The pineal lumen contains a coagulum that stains more or less intensely with either PAS (periodic acid–Schiff) or aldehyde fuchsin. Associated with this are cells, some pyknotic and in groups, others isolated and probably representing macrophages.

Comparisons: The above outlined work of Vivien-Roels and Petit (1973) is the first to present evidence of a parietal eye primordium in any testudinian embryo. Earlier studies failed to find indications of such distal eye-like structures in either embryos (references in Table III) or adults. These very old embryological studies depended upon relatively few specimens and stages. A study in progress (Vivien-Roels and Petit) on an aquatic turtle (*Emys orbicularis*) suggests that a parietal primordium within the developing pineal complex may occur more generally and that it is not restricted to *Testudo*.

The recent and detailed studies on the development of the parietal eye–pineal complex in *Testudo* demonstrate also the complicated nature of the development of this system. It should become obvious, therefore, that it is impossible to compare developmental morphology or mechanisms between two or more taxa on the basis of data from isolated and arbitrary stages. For this reason, it is difficult if not impossible to interpret or compare many of the isolated embryological descriptions in the early literature (Table III). Continuous series of carefully staged embryos and later stages are needed.

C. Sauria

Developmental stages in the morphogenesis of the pineal region have been described in many more lizards than in members of any other major group of reptiles (Table III). However, only in a very few of these has the entire developmental sequence been followed. One of the best studied is the slow-worm, blindworm, or orvet, *Anguis fragilis*. It was frequently studied in the past and described in the greatest detail recently by Petit (1967), using 253 embryos. The development of the pineal complex in this species, outlined in Table V, can serve both as a representative model of the developmental events in the saurian pineal complex and as a standard with which variations in other species may be compared. Recent studies suggest few differences in major and functionally important features among the developmental patterns of the pineal complex within lizards. This tends to be obscured by controversies promulgated very early in the literature from study of very few and dissimilar developmental stages, and from the use of inadequate techniques for resolving particular cytological and micromorphological questions. The early developmental changes are well illustrated by the diagrams (Fig. 5) from Petit's (1967) work with *Anguis fragilis*. Overlapping and later stages taken from Steyn's (1957) descriptions based on *Mabuya sulcata* illustrate the later developmental morphology of the lizard pineal complex (Fig. 6).

Recent studies on pineal embryology in lizards have employed techniques of incubation and care described by Panigel (1956) and Raynaud (1959a, b) and modified by Dufaure (1966) and Meiniel (1974a). These and related methods will increase in importance in further comparative and experimental investigations on the development of the pineal complex.

Beyond the basic developmental patterns (Table V and Figs 5 and 6) we shall select three important subtopics for brief review concerning the state of understanding of the formation of the saurian pineal complex.

a. *Symmetry*. A long-continued controversy has kept open the question of whether the major components of the pineal complex, the parietal eye (parapineal) and the epiphysis (pineal) represent primitively paired, and left *vis-à-vis* right-sided structures, respectively. Some of the best evidence for such primitively bilateral relations comes from studies of the developmental morphology of the pineal complex in lizards. An early leftward orientation of the parietal eye bud is seen in at least some specimens of a number of species, as noted in stage G (Table V) of *Anguis fragilis* (Petit,

1967) and in a later stage (Fig. 7) of *Sceloporus occidentalis* (Eakin, 1964a, 1973). The precise relations are clear only in transverse sections. In the presumptive parietal eye the epithelial cells destined to become the lens can be distinguished by their higher columnar shape (Fig. 7c).

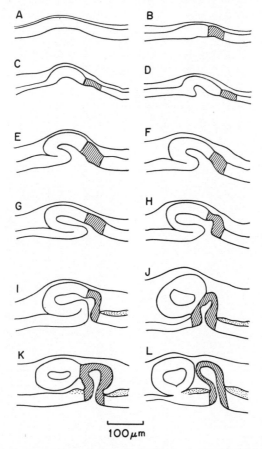

100 μm

FIG. 5. A–L. Diagrammatic parasagittal sections of stages in the normal development of the pineal complex in *Anguis fragilis*. The pineal primordium is cross-hatched, while the parietal eye primordium to its left in the figures is blank. Correspondence of figures with designated stages and morphological correlates is noted in Table V. (Adapted from Petit, 1967.)

The epithelial cells of the epiphyseal part of the diverticulum are distinguished from those of the presumptive parietal eye by their greater density and tinctorial darkness (Fig. 7D). The constriction which will separate the presumptive parietal eye from the epiphysis passes obliquely at the level shown in Fig. 7D. Asymmetry is most apparent at this level and

TABLE V

Development of the pineal complex in Anguis fragilis. (Data of Petit, 1967)

Stage	Head length (mm)	Pineal complex	Correlates
A	0·8	A single, shallow and median evagination appears in the presumptive pineal region (Fig. 5A)	Secondary vesicle of lateral eyes well developed and not closed; otic cups generally open; dorsal wall of hypophyseal diverticulum joins the floor of the IIIrd ventricle; branchial slits 1 and 2 begin to open
B	1·0	The evagination has two thickenings: the anterior one will form the lens and the greater part of the retina of the parietal eye, the posterior (= epiphyseal) one is relatively slight (Fig. 5B)	Lateral eye lens a closed vesicle having a bistratified epithelium; otic cups horseshoe-shaped; Rathke's pocket deeper; branchial slits 1 and 2 open
C	1·2	Anterior (parietal) primordium grows in cranial or dorsocranial direction, forming a fold which defines internally a presumptive parietal lumen; posterior (epiphyseal) primordium little changed from stage B (Fig. 5C)	Lateral eye lens still attached to the epiblast by a cellular cord; otic vesicles appear completely closed: Rathke's pocket still touches the notochord
D	1·3	A stage characterized by active growth of the parietal primordium, whose dorsal region contacts the epiblast; epiphyseal primordium lies exactly within the plane of bilateral symmetry of the ocular primordia; posterior to the epiphyseal primordium the subcommissural organ budding appears as two paired thickenings (Fig. 5D)	Lateral eye lens' connection with epiblast is lost; lens lumen reduced; three pairs of open branchial slits; Rathke's pocket, deeper, loses contact with notochord
E	1·5	Parietal vesicle opens broadly into the IIIrd ventricle and has a generally cranial direction of growth; epiphyseal primordium little changed—appearing to be the only dorsal diencephalic region in static condition (Fig. 5E, F)	Fibers appear within the lateral eye lens; four pairs of branchial slits present; evagination begins in the paraphyseal thickenings in the cranial brain wall; pars tuberalis begins budding as two little lateral cell masses

F	1·7	Parietal vesicle shows two distinct regions: a lens dorsally and a retina lateroventrally; posterior (epiphyseal) primordium begins to evaginate; paraphysis becomes digitiform; caudal part of the subcommissural organ shows its secretory character (Fig. 5G and H)	Lateral eyes pigmented; anterior limb buds well developed; a cerebellar plate appears; behind Rathke's pocket a depression is shown in the floor of the diencephalon
G	2·1	Parietal eye separated from the posterior (epiphyseal) primordium through a process of constriction; canal connecting the lumen of the parietal eye with that of the epiphysis progressively obliterated; a slightly leftward orientation of the parietal eye occurs as the epiphysis remains median (Fig. 5I, J and K)	Only the aboral region of Rathke's pocket adheres to the floor of the diencephalon
H	2·7	Parietal eye separated from the epiphysis although still in contact; one or two layers of cells lie between the parietal eye lens and the epidermis; the epiphyseal digitation opens into the IIIrd ventricle, is slightly inclined in a cranial direction and presents two regions—an anterior (cranial, distal) and a posterior (caudal, proximal) forming between themselves an angle of 110–130°; parietal nerve and habenular commissure formed simultaneously (Fig. 5K and L)	Hypophyseal anterior lobe buds off Rathke's pocket; diencephalic roof, formerly smooth, shows sinuosity leading to formation of tela chorioidea; subcommissural organ and posterior commissure abut against the posterior wall of the epiphysis; aldehyde fuchsin+ and Gomori+ cytoplasmic granules appear in the subcommissural organ
I	3·0	Parietal eye, elevated above the habenular commissure, accomplishes a dorsocranial shift; parietal nerve composed of a large number of nerve fibers joins the brain roof just anterior to the habenular commissure, which is well developed; connective tissue cells completely enclose the parietal eye and nerve, forming "sclerotic" and perineural-like layers respectively; epiphysis, further separated from the parietal eye, still has a narrow luminal connection with the IIIrd ventricle; vascularity becomes greater in the epiphyseal vicinity as compared with that of the parietal eye; accessory vesicles are formed by budding, apparently from the distal or ventral walls of the epiphysis; parietal eye and epiphysis are displaced towards the left in relation to the median sagittal plane of the embryo; basal zone of the parietal eye contains bipolar and multipolar ganglion cells	Hypophyseal anterior lobe well developed; distal end of the paraphysis approaches the parietal eye; velum transversum establishes a telencephalo–diencephalic boundary, with its anterior wall formed by the paraphysis and its posterior wall in continuity with the diencephalic roof

(*Table V continued on page 268*)

J	3·8	Parietal eye flattens dorsoventrally and its retina loses its central depression; epiphysis arched in shape with apex touching the parietal eye, its base tapering towards the IIIrd ventricle and the epiphyseal canal very reduced but still connecting the epiphyseal lumen with the IIIrd ventricle; parietal nerve is applied to the ventral wall of the epiphysis and enters the habenular commissure slightly to the left of the midsagittal plane passing through the pineal recess; within the commissure the nerve divides into a larger left branch to the left habenular nucleus and a small right branch to the right habenular nucleus; nerve observed was either a parietal nerve directed unilaterally to one nucleus or fibers entering the posterior commissure; a peripheral nerve plexus forms within the epiphysis, analogous to that of the parietal eye but looser; a thicker layer is formed thereby in the ventral as compared with the dorsal epiphyseal walls; epiphyseal histogenesis at this stage appears to be comparable to that of the parietal eye at stage H; accessory vesicles, having both parietal eye and epiphyseal origins, are strongly pigmented	Hypophyseal pars intermedia tends to encircle the neurohypophysis; hypophyseal canal disappears; vertebrae and cranial base are in process of chondrification; caudal end of the paraphysis reaches the epiphysis; tela chorioidea compressed between epiphysis and paraphysis as a consequence of the expansion of cerebral hemispheres and optic lobes; velum transversum gains a vertical position and its ventral end shows the first fibers of the posterior pallial commissure (Table II); paraphyseal cells lose their ciliation and contain various vacuoles with PAS+ contents
K	5·0	Parietal eye reaches the level of the posterior edge of the cerebral hemispheres; epiphyseal growth dorsally is limited by the formation of cranial cartilages, and thus bends and passes dorsal to the tela chorioidea (of ventricle III and dorsal sac) and paraphysis (Fig. 6D); two epiphyseal regions can be distinguished: a distal or anterior one of horizontal orientation, and a proximal or posterior one of vertical orientation (Fig. 6D); the epiphyseal lumen loses its communications with the IIIrd ventricle; between posterior and habenular commissures the epiphysis is reduced to a thin cellular cord; in addition to the non-myelinated	Cranial vault chondrified; epidermis plicated and scaled; neurohypophysis connected to the infundibulum by a short stalk

parietal nerve fibers noted above, fascicles of myelinated fibers appear now within the epiphysis; these fascicles, few in number and preferentially in the lateral walls, suggest a bilateral innervation of the organ; a nerve tract at the base of the epiphyseal stalk runs caudally between the subcommissural organ and the posterior commissure; retinal sensory cells of the parietal eye show very well developed, flame-shaped outer or external segments; one to three accessory vesicles are frequently found between the epiphysis and parietal eye; no nerve connections or relations are found for these accessory vesicles—neither with the parietal nerve nor with the epiphysis

L   6·0   Very dorsoventrally flattened parietal eye fits into the parietal foramen; the epiphysis is able to be described as showing three regions: (1) an epiphyseal tube (or vesicle) or anterior epiphysis, (2) a slightly folded sac or middle epiphysis, and (3) a stalk or posterior epiphysis; within the epiphyseal stalk, especially its basal part, ganglion cells are found; the pineal complex at this (hatching) stage possesses all of the morphological features of the adult animal

Hatching occurs

just anterior to it. The lumen of the diverticulum and the bulk of the parietal eye vesicle lie to the left of the midline and the anterior part of the pineal or epiphyseal component lies on the right side of the midline. The leftward budding of the presumptive parietal eye is a relatively fleeting sign of the asymmetry of this part of the lizard pineal complex. A more durable

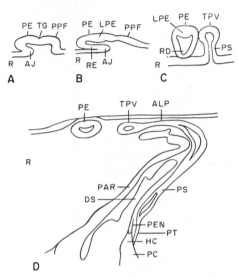

FIG. 6. Pineal primordia and complex in embryos of *Mabuya sulcata*. A. Sagittal section of the primordia in an embryo with head length of 0·71 mm, × 150. B. Median sagittal plane of the complex, embryo head length 0·9 mm, × 150. C. Parasagittal section of the complex, embryo head length 1·12 mm, × 120. D. Parasagittal section slightly left of the median sagittal plane, showing all components of the pineal complex, embryo head length 4·7 mm, × 45. (Adapted from Steyn, 1924.)

Abbreviations: AJ, anterior (rostral) junction of the parietal organ evagination with the diencephalic roof; ALP, anteriorly directed limb of the pineal body; DS, dorsal sac; HC, habenular commissure; LPE, lens of the parietal eye; PAR, paraphysis; PC, posterior commissure; PE, parietal eye; PEN, parietal eye nerve; PPF, posterior pineal (epiphyseal) fold; PS, pineal (epiphyseal) stalk; PT, pineal tract (nerve); R, rostral side; RD, retinal depression in parietal eye; RE, retina of parietal eye; TG, transverse groove; TPV, terminal pineal vesicle.

sign is the path of the parietal eye nerve noted in stages H, I and J, Table V. The parietal nerve is considered in more detail in a later section.

However, Petit (1967) has argued that the relative positions of parietal eye and epiphysis do not constitute proof of a primitively sinestral origin of the eye. He has suggested that: (1) the innervation of the parietal eye, and probably also that of the epiphysis, is bilateral; and (2) in some specimens both parietal eye and epiphysis seem to have individually bilateral origins.

    b. *Cell types.* Many of the more detailed descriptions of the development

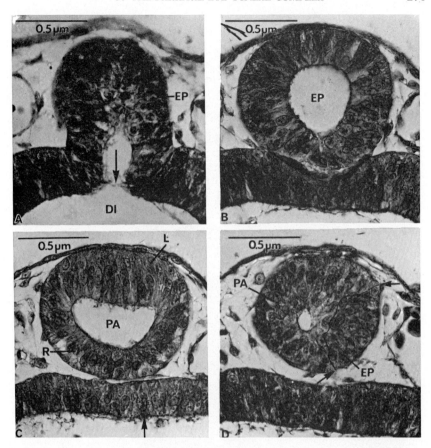

FIG. 7. Transverse sections through different anteroposterior levels of the pineal Complex in an embryonic *Sceloporus occidentalis*. The sequence of sections is from posterior (A) to anterior (D). Compare with Fig. 5I, a diagrammatic parasagittal section of a comparable stage. DI, Third ventricle of diencephalon; the arrow indicates the continuity of the lumen of the pineal diverticulum with the third ventricle; EP, epiphyseal component of the pineal diverticulum; L, presumptive lens of the parietal eye; PA, parietal eye component of the pineal diverticulum; R, presumptive retina of the parietal eye. Arrow in C marks the midline (median sagittal plane) of the embryo. Arrows and line in D demark the parietal (left) and epiphyseal (right) components of the pineal diverticulum. Overlying superficial ectodermal epithelium of the embryo is shown at the top in all four sections. (Courtesy of Eakin, 1964a, 1973, and University of California Press.)

of the pineal complex in lizards include comments on cytological differentiations within the diverticulum and neighboring parts of the diencephalic neuroectoderm (Petit, 1967; Preisler, 1942; Steyn, 1957, 1959a; Trost, 1952, 1953a, b). These are based on light microscopy only and cannot be accepted uncritically. Thus it is not at all clear without electron microscopic

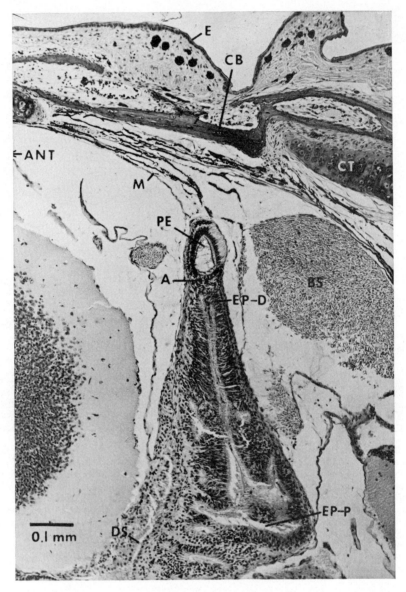

FIG. 8. Sagittal section of the pineal complex in a subadult male *Sceloporus occidentalis*, with an anomalous or ectopic parietal eye (PE) attached to the tip of the epiphysis (EP). (Adapted from Eakin, 1964a, 1973.) A, Zone of attachment of parietal eye and epiphysis ANT, anterior direction and direction to normal position of the adult parietal eye; BS, blood in venous sinus; CB, cranial bone; CT, cartilage; DS, dorsal sac; E, epidermis; EP-D and EP-P, distal and proximal portions of the epiphysis; M, meninges (artifactually pulled away from the brain).

studies which of the embryonic cells can be designated as presumptive photoreceptors or as in some way related to photoreceptors. Furthermore, it is unclear to what extent particular luminal cells represent natural occurrences and which may have been distorted or modified through artifact or imperfect or delayed fixation. Nevertheless, here in the lizard pineal complex the descriptive cytology shows an early structural differentiation of cell types, whatever their functional significance may eventually be. Also, it is frequently observed that the cellular differentiation, as well as the growth of the epithelium, is earlier in the parietal eye component than in the epiphyseal component of the diverticulum. The difference in timing of growth of the two components can be appreciated by noting their developmental changes in Figs 5 and 6.

c. *Developmental variations and anomalies.* Several kinds of morphological variations and anomalies have been reported, as a consequence of recent studies employing large series of microscopically examined lizard specimens. Some of these variations may be instructive in our gaining an understanding of the normal developmental processes and relations. Others are more difficult either to understand morphogenetically or to relate to particular postulated functional activities or relations.

Variation in the developmental directions of growth and separation of parietal eye and epiphyseal primordia have been noted in early stages of several species by Petit (1967), Steyn (1957) and Trost (1952) among others. Less commonly observed are incomplete separations of parietal and pineal divisions of the complex in adult lizards. Eakin (1964a, 1973) has described two examples in *Sceloporus occidentalis* (Figs 8 and 9) and noted a third in a specimen of *Gerrhonotus multicarinatus*. The specimen figured here (Figs 8 and 9) showed no parietal eye, corneal elevation or transparent region externally, though the animal appeared to be otherwise normal. Histological examination later revealed that in this specimen the parietal eye had failed to advance anteriorly to its normal position and remained attached to the apex of the epiphysis. Beyond the zone of junction with the epiphysis, the structure and cellular composition of this ectopic eye appeared to be essentially normal (Fig. 9). In a second case, the parietal eye was normal in position, but an abnormally elongate epiphysis was connected to it.

Another kind of variation observed both in early developing stages and in adults pertains to so-called accessory vesicles (stages I, J and K, Table V). These epithelial vesicles derive from and resemble, at least superficially, the parietal and epiphyseal vesicles. Generally, however, they have neither sensory nor neural elements, and they often become heavily pigmented. It is assumed that these are functionless, epithelial derivatives of the primary components of the pineal complex. However, there is no information on their biochemical and metabolic characteristics.

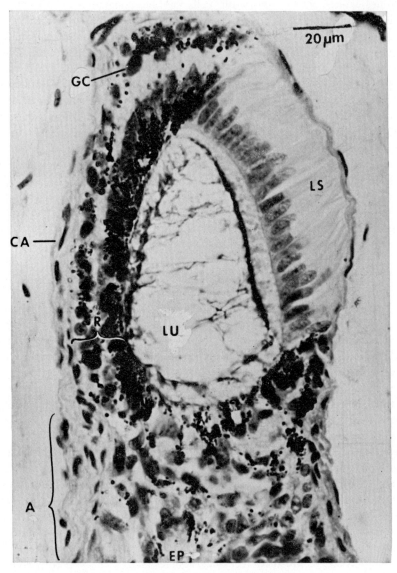

FIG. 9. Ectopic parietal eye of Fig. 8 shown in higher magnification. (Adapted from Eakin, 1964a, 1973.) A, Zone of attachment of parietal eye and epiphysis; CA, connective tissue capsule of the parietal eye; EP, distal end of epiphysis; GC, ganglion cell in parietal eye retina; LS, lens of parietal eye; LV, lumen of parietal eye; R, retina of parietal eye.

D. SERPENTES

Pineal development has been studied in detail in only one species of snake, the European ring-necked snake or common grass snake, *Natrix natrix*. The culmination of this work is Petit's (1969) excellent account, which is outlined in Table VI and summarized in Figs 10–15. Data on developmental stages in other snakes are scant and fragmentary (Table III).

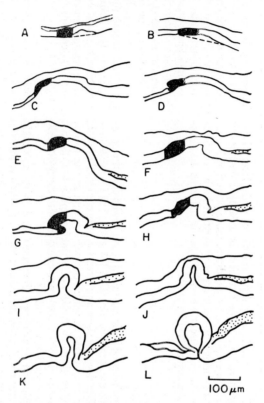

FIG. 10. A–L. Diagrammatic parasagittal sections of stages in the normal development of the pineal complex in *Natrix natrix*. The parietal primordium is black; the epiphyseal primordium behind it (right in each figure) is unshaded; the area occupied by the posterior commissure is stippled. Correspondence of figures (A–L) with designated developmental stages and morphological correlates is noted in Table VI. (Adapted from Petit, 1969.)

One of the most interesting, as well as most generally agreed upon, features in the early morphogenesis of the pineal complex of snakes is that two distinct but contiguous buds or primordia occur. This was noted early and confirmed in embryos of *Natrix natrix* by Ssobolew (1907), Trost (1952) and Petit (1969). However, as noted by Petit (1969), the figured embryonic

TABLE VI

Development of the pineal complex in Natrix natrix. *(Data primarily of Petit, 1969)*

Stage	Head length (mm)	Pineal complex	Correlates
A	1·5	Parietal and epiphyseal buds distinguishable, as in lacertilians; parietal primordium, more anterior, is a simple ependymal thickening; the epiphyseal primordium, more posterior, is very slightly evaginating; two cell types present in both primordia and claimed to represent primitive ependymal cells and presumptive sensory cells (Fig. 10A)	Embryonic brain cavity divided into five segments; hypophyseal primordium consists of primitive pharyngeal evagination with dorsal wall applied against the infundibular region; paired subcommissural organ primordia distinguishable; posterior commissure not yet formed; lateral eye lens composed of an epithelium of more or less radiating cells surrounding a reduced central cavity
B	2·3	Parietal and epiphyseal buds are raised above the level of the ependyma in the diencephalic roof (Fig. 10B and C); this very shallow outpocketing does not show any direction of preferential growth, except for one variant in which the parietal bud in the rostral end of the evagination consists of a thicker and more distinct small mass of cells (Fig. 10D); presumed primitive sensory cells in both buds are few in number	Only the aboral tip of Rathke's pocket contacts the infundibulum; above the subcommissural organ the first fibers of the posterior commissure appear; lateral eye lens contains primary lens fibers
C	2·8	Parietal–epiphyseal evagination increased and with a weakly marked transverse furrow (Fig. 10E); the evagination appears to grow dorsally and sometimes dorsocaudally affecting principally the epiphyseal rather than the presumed parietal portion of the evagination—a directionally opposite trend as compared with the lacertilian pineal complex (Fig. 5C, D, E; Table V stages C–D and E); cells of the presumed sensory and primitive ependymal types become separated from the base and occupy a more internal position; initial pinealocytes or pinealoblasts differentiate from ependymal cells	Posterior commissure well developed; subcommissural organ well developed and organized, with possibly some of its more cranial cells becoming incorporated with the epiphyseal primordium

D	3·2	Parietal-epiphyseal outgrowth rises dorsally or slightly dorso-caudally with the opening onto the IIIrd ventricle becoming reduced (Fig. 10G); it becomes difficult to clearly delimit the presumed parietal bud where it impinges on the presumed epiphyseal bud (Fig. 10G and H); the parietal bud appears to become annexed to the epiphysis, contributing thereby to epiphyseal tissue, and with the same patterns of cellular differentiation occurring in both; differentiation of pinealoblasts from ependymal cells continues; pinealoblasts, situated on the side of the external limiting membrane, consist of masses of three to five cells; cells bordering on the lumen of the parietal-epiphyseal evagination are either of the presumed sensory type or, for the greater part, of the ependymal category	Diencephalic roof notably extended; paraphysis appears as two or three cellular masses at first seen as evaginations
E	3·5	Epiphysis takes the shape of a little pocket with a central lumen higher than broad and still communicating with the IIIrd ventricle (Fig. 10I, J, and K); in the formation of this epiphyseal pocket the parietal and epiphyseal buds have been fused; through folding of the epiphyseal pockets' walls, vesicles and a contorted epithelial structure are formed; pinealoblasts are more abundant than previously in the more external epithelial regions; primitive pinealocytes with faintly granular cytoplasm are more evident	This constitutes the time of laying; the second hypophyseal invagination (that forms the pars distalis) appears; the paraphysis is a large evagination in the anterior diencephalic roof; ependymal tissue differentiates between the cranial end of the subcommissural organ's epithelium and the posterior commissure
F	4·1	Epiphyseal pocket closes (Fig. 10L); the obliteration of the epiphyseal canal to the IIIrd ventricle coincides with the appearance of the habenular commissure; the longitudinal venous sinus is constituted; islets of pinealoblasts are most notable dorsally in the epiphyseal pocket while some of the cells of the presumed sensory category are eliminated into the epiphyseal lumen	
G	5·0	Epiphysis undergoes important growth phase, and can be noted as composed of two regions—a dorsal, saccular portion, elongated vertically or slightly dorsocaudally, and a ventral stalk interposed between posterior and habenular commissures (Fig. 11); epithelium of the saccular part of the epiphysis consists of one to three layers of cells among which can be distinguished: (1)	Subcommissural organ complex in structure and with secretory tanycytes having apical (toward the IIIrd ventricle) granulations that are stained by various techniques (e.g. Gomori, aldehyde fuchsin, PAS, alcian blue, etc.) Within the hypophysis a constriction appears, separating intermediate and anterior lobes; paraphysis a broad tube with a slightly plicated posterior wall

(Table VI continued page 278)

		ependymal cells—either undifferentiated or on the way to becoming pinealoblasts, (2) pinealoblasts (Fig. 11) and (3) presumed sensory cells that seem to show an apical (lumenward) secretory activity; epiphyseal stalk composed of undifferentiated ependymal cells; marked epithelial growth of the epiphysis at this stage is due to the mitotic activity of the ependymal cells; during early prophase these cells individually increase greatly in volume (Fig. 11)	
H	5·5	Intense cellular proliferation in the distal (dorsal) part of the epiphysis leads to reduction in size of the epiphyseal lumen and an increasing thickness of the epiphyseal wall dorsally; epiphyseal tissue at this time consists of: (1) vesicles with small central lumen either connecting with the principal epiphyseal lumen or separated from it, (2) groups of 6 to 20 pinealoblasts, (3) cords of pinealoblasts between the vesicles and cellular masses, (4) connective tissue fibers which penetrate between the above epithelial formations, and (5) small lacunae	Hypophyseal canal disappears and an epithelial stalk connects the hypophyseal anterior lobe to pharyngeal epithelium; the diencephalic choroid plexus forms a dome between paraphysis and epiphysis
I	5·7	Epiphysis elongates from the cranial end of the subcommissural organ, to which it remains attached by a stalk (Fig. 12); pinealocytes differentiate from pinealoblasts, take on an irregular shape and have cytoplasmic expansions applied to capillaries	Between intermediate and anterior hypophyseal lobes a curvature is produced; the anterior lobe is well vascularized and cartilages surround the hypophysis-infundibular plate sends deep indentations towards the pars intermedia
J	6·5	Epiphysis covered by the cranial end of the superior sagittal sinus, which has ramifications receiving pineal capillary drainage; other epiphyseal capillaries come from the choroid plexus; no epiphyseal arterial vascularization is seen; within the subcommissural organ neuron cell bodies are always present, and sometimes lie near to the pineal stalk (Fig. 13)	Compression of the diencephalic roof brought about by growth of telencephalon and tectum leads to paraphysis and epiphysis being closer together and the choroid plexus extending deeper within the IIIrd ventricle

K	7·2	Ovoid epiphysis with major axis dorsoventral and with reduction of the central lumen to some small lacunar spaces; epiphysis maintained in position by numerous connective tissue fibers, which in part radiate ventrally to anchor within the external limiting membrane of the habenular and posterior commissures, and which in part expand dorsally to attach to the dura mater; secretory-appearing pinealocytes constitute the major cell type in the epiphysis; within many of these the juxtanuclear, and probably Golgi, zone stains strongly with chrome hematoxylin; interlobular and perivascular connective tissue fibers and cells (including histiocytes and mast cells) occur within the epiphysis; silver impregnations and other techniques do not show any nerve fibers within the epiphyseal stalk, but on the other hand nerve fibers originating from hypendymal cell bodies extend to the vascular and connective tissue covering of the epiphysis; sometimes these fibers form a tract extending from the cranial ependyma to the posterior part of the epiphysis; this "epiphyseal" (properly, hypendymo-epiphyseal) nerve tract can be traced to neurone cell bodies such as those shown in Fig. 14	Hypophyseal pars distalis in active growth; subcommissural organ in active secretion with Reissner's fiber visible within the ventricle
L	8·0	The short epiphyseal stalk has a small central lumen and is connected to the cranial end of the subcommissural organ by a slender cord (Fig. 15) which is composed of tanycytes, nonsecretory glia, histiocytes and mast cells; pigmented cells, a new cell-type, appear within the epiphysis and apparently differ from pinealocytes only by their cytoplasmic content of yellow-brown granules which are discharged into the epiphyseal lumen; neurone cell bodies are dispersed within the cranial ependyma of the subcommissural organ and some occur at the base of the cellular cord attaching epiphysis to subcommissural organ; this dispersion of nerve cell bodies appears to be related to the expansion of the posterior commissure in this region	Hatching occurs; hypophyseal pars distalis undergoes a 90° retroflexion; paraphysis forms a vertical tube which does not regain the dorsal sac; number of nerve fibers in posterior commissure increased especially at its cranial end; some of these fibers are alleged to ascend toward the epiphyseal stalk without attaining or redescending to the opposite side of the commissure, in a manner like that of similar fibers described in *Lacerta* by Ariëns Kappers (1967)

snake pineal complex of earlier authors, as well as that of more recently
studied specimens shows a wide range of variation in relative size and
distinctness of the two primordia. Especially variable is the alleged or
presumed parietal eye homologue, lying anteriorly to the more actively
expanding epiphyseal bud or primordium. In any case, the fate of the

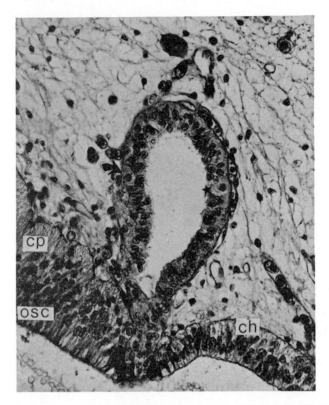

FIG. 11. Sagittal section through the epiphysis of *Natrix natrix* at stage G (Table VI).
Gomori's chrome alum hematoxylin and phloxine, × 320. The arrow points to a pinealo-
blast; the star is adjacent to an ependymal cell in early prophase. ch, Habenular commissure; cp, posterior commissure; osc, subcommissural organ. (Courtesy of Petit, 1969.)

primordia appears to be fusion, with the anterior or presumed parietal eye
component becoming incorporated within and contributing to the cellular
content of the posterior or epiphyseal component. The single, median epiphysis or glandular pineal thus formed becomes the only structure remaining
in the adult pineal complex in snakes, so far as is known at this time.

     A theme of great interest both in the ontogeny and the phylogeny of the
pineal gland is the derivation of the pineal endocrine secretory cells—the

so-called pinealocytes. In Petit's (1969) account such cells are described as arising from pinealoblasts which are most notable in the outer portions of the epiphyseal primordium. Cells which are alleged to represent the sensory cell line are encountered mostly within the inner layers of the epiphysis

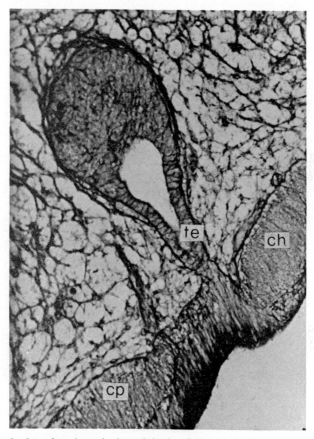

FIG. 12. Sagittal section through the epiphysis of *Natrix natrix* at stage I (Table VI). Aldehyde fuchsin, × 272. The arrow points to epiphyseal material stained with aldehyde fuchsin. ch, Habenular commissure; cp, posterior commissure; te, epiphyseal stalk. (Courtesy of Petit, 1969.)

and bordering on the cell lumen. The extent to which these resemble sensory cells ultrastructurally and their possible relation to cells giving rise to pinealoblasts will have to await clarification by means of electron microscopic study. The present and suggestive observations have nevertheless encouraged the view (Petit, 1969) that ancestors of snakes had photoreceptor and secretory components in the pineal complex, much as can be observed in some living lizards. Nevertheless, an early developmental dominance of the epiphyseal rather than the parietal primordium is seen in the pineal complex of developing *Natrix* in contrast with that of developing lizards. This may be taken to suggest tentatively that the shift in snake ancestors from a primarily photosensory to an exclusively endocrine secretory pineal function occurred relatively early.

Some of the other characteristics of the developing *Natrix* pineal gland, especially those involving the vasculature, innervation and relations with

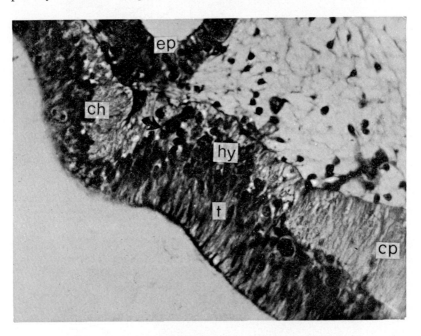

FIG. 13. Parasagittal section of the cranial end of the subcommissural organ and the adjacent basal portion of the epiphysis (ep) in *Natrix natrix* at stage J (Table VI). Gomori's chrome hematoxylin and phloxine, × 360. The arrow points to a neuron cell body within the subcommissural organ and near the base of the epiphysis. ch, Habenular commissure; cp, posterior commissure; hy, hypendymal cells of the subcommissural organ; t, columnar epithelial cells of the subcommissural organ. (Courtesy of Petit, 1969.)

the subcommissural organ (Table VI), may be more strictly snake-like and may be presumed to depart more from, or not be as comparable to, what is seen in the developing pineal complex in other groups of reptiles. Some of these features suggest a morphological convergence with respect to pineal patterns in birds and mammals. This springs from the solid, parenchymatous nature of the organ in adult snakes in contrast to the looser and circumventricular pineal epithelial structure seen in other adult reptiles.

E. RHYNCHOCEPHALIA

Most of what we know about the pineal complex in *Sphenodon* we owe to the detailed and pioneering descriptions by Dendy (1899, 1910, 1911). However, there remain sources of possible uncertainty and confusion in this early work. The most important of these is the relative incompleteness and arbitrary nature of Dendy's series of designated embryonic stages, especially

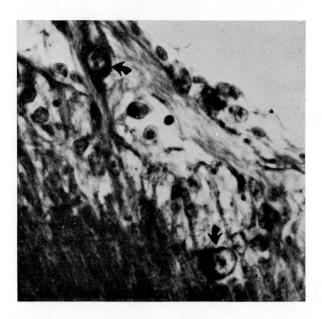

FIG. 14. Sagittal section through the "epiphyseal" (hypendymo-epiphyseal) nerve tract in *Natrix natrix* at stage K (Table VI). Gomori's chrome hematoxylin and phloxine, ×720. The arrows point to two bipolar neuron cell bodies. (Courtesy of Petit, 1969.)

the earlier ones. For this reason, the precise early interrelations of parietal eye and epiphyseal primordia are uncertain. Dendy (1899) thought that the second (epiphyseal) primordium appeared sometime between stages L–M and N, probably as an independent evagination of the brain roof. However, in his monograph of 1911 he figured a stage, designated as "about stage O" with continuous or joined primordia (Fig. 16B). In the earliest stage shown (stage L) a single diverticulum is seen and was termed the "primary parietal vesicle" (Table VII, Fig. 16A). While he apparently believed that this gave rise to only the parietal eye and not the epiphysis, there is no apparent proof for such a contention. It appears more likely, from the figures published in the 1911 monograph, that both primordia arise from the same "primary parietal vesicle". A stage L "primary parietal vesicle" figured at this date (1911, Fig. 29) shows a distinct and abrupt thinning in the dorsal epithelium, which might be expected to give rise to the constriction seen here at the later stage we show in Fig. 16B (taken from Dendy, 1911, Fig. 30). The

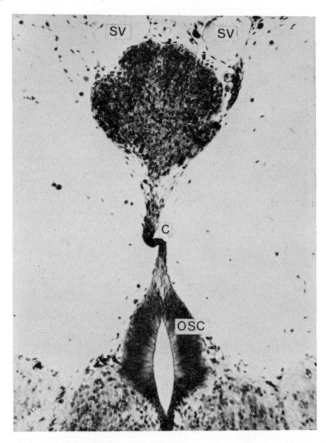

FIG. 15. Transverse section through the epiphysis (above) and its connection (c) with the subcommissural organ (OSC) in *Natrix natrix* at stage L (Table VI). Venous sinuses (SV) overlying the now solid epiphysis bilaterally. Klüver-Barrera Luxol blue technique, ×114. (Courtesy of Petit, 1969.)

joined primordia in the latter figure (designated at "about stage O") would seem to represent an earlier stage than those showing completely separated primordia (Fig 16c and D) but designated as "stage N" and "about stage N–O". From these considerations it seems possible that the two primordia may be parts of the same diverticulum in early development, although comprising different regions of the epithelium of this diverticulum.

Other possible sources of confusion derive from differences in orientation, interpretation and terminology in the early descriptions of the pineal region and its components. The second outgrowth of the pineal complex in *Sphenodon* Dendy first designated as "parietal stalk" (1899), but he later

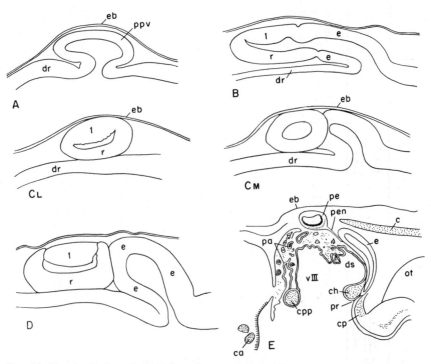

Fig. 16. Longitudinal vertical sections (not to same scale) through the pineal region of embryos of *Sphenodon punctatus* (adapted from Dendy, 1899, 1911). Anterior is to left in all figures. A. "Stage L". B. "About stage O". C. Slightly left (cl) and rear midline (cm) sections of the same specimen—"stage N". D. Stage "about N–O". E. "Stage R (late)". c, cartilage; ca, anterior commissure; ch. habenular commissure; cp, posterior commissure; cpp, posterior pallial commissure; dr, diencephalic roof; ds, dorsal sac; e, epiphysis (= "parietal stalk" and "pineal sac" of Dendy, 1899 and 1911 respectively); eb, epiblast; ot, optic lobes (tectum); pa, paraphysis; pe, parietal eye; pen, pariental eye nerve; ppv, "primary parietal vesicle"; pr, pineal recess; r, parietal eye retina; VIII, third ventricle.

called it "pineal sac". This structure is clearly comparable in all essential morphological features and relations with the pineal, posterior pineal or epiphyseal primordium as described in embryos of lizards (compare Figs 5l, 6c and 16c and d). Another such difference is the designation of the dorsal sac as "paraphysis" in the 1899 description, with its correction by the time of the monograph of 1911.

TABLE VII

Development of the pineal complex in Sphenodon punctatus. (*Data of Dendy,* 1899, 1911)

Stage	Pineal complex	Correlates
K	A parietal vesicle or "primary parietal vesicle" appears as a bud on the forebrain roof slightly, but consistently, to the left of the midline	Forebrain already bent ventrally and posteriorly; optic vesicles have begun invagination to form optic cups, while the lens appears as a thickening of the superficial epiblast
L	"Primary parietal vesicle" still communicates by a wide cavity with the IIIrd ventricle, but is somewhat dorsoventrally flattened and extends farther anteriorly than posteriorly (Fig. 16A)	
M	"Primary parietal vesicle" still a simple outgrowth slightly left of the midline	Beginning of limb buds
N	Two small diverticula present: the "primary parietal vesicle" closes off from the brain ventricle and lies on the forebrain roof slightly anterior and to the left of a fingerlike and cranially curving diverticulum with a lumen continuous with the IIIrd ventricle; this second diverticulum was called by Dendy at first the "parietal stalk" (1899) although the parietal eye at this stage appeared to be nearly if not entirely separated from the "stalk" (Fig. 16B, C); he later called it "pineal sac" (1911), and it is comparable to the epiphysis or glandular pineal of other authors	Paraphysis appears
O	Parietal eye lens thickens and is composed of elongated columnar cells; coagulum present in central lumen of both parietal eye and epiphysis; epiphyseal anterior wall flattened against posterior wall of parietal eye and its lumen still opens into the brain ventricle (Fig. 16D)	Cerebral hemispheres begin to bud off from the prosencephalon; habenular commissure begins to develop; beginning of paraphysis as median evagination; infundibulum a wide diverticulum with pituitary attached to its floor.

R — Parietal eye now median in position and with its retina marginally pigmented; epiphysis now much elongated, but remaining attached to the brain at a point now lying between the habenular and posterior commissures; and the lumen of its basal portion here being obliterated (Fig. 16E); an increasing space develops between the anterior end of the epiphysis and the parietal eye, due to the anterior shifting of the latter. Towards the end of this stage a pigmented patch appears in the antero-ventral wall of the distal extremity of the epiphysis and the parietal eye nerve appears as a posteriorly directed outgrowth of the parietal eye retina and can be traced along the distal and anteroventral surface of the epiphysis without being actually connected with it

Limbs and digits well formed; integument pigmented with pattern of "transverse bands and longitudinal stripes"; cerebral hemispheres and optic lobes much enlarged and compressing the area of the diencephalic roof medially; habenular ganglia and commissure very feebly developed

S — Parietal eye shows externally as a dark spot through the translucent "corneal" skin over the parietal foramen; all components of the parietal eye and epiphysis essentially adult

Last stage before hatching; dorsal sac becomes infolded with the formation of a choroid plexus; subcommissural organ present

In the early embryology of the pineal complex Dendy showed well that when both components were formed as separate vesicles or primordia, the parietal eye vesicle generally was found to the left of the midline or midsagittal plane, and the epiphyseal primordium behind and to its right was at about the midline. However, he also claimed, both in an early (1899) and in a later study (1911), that the primary parietal vesicle lay "a little to the left of the middle line" (1911, p. 309). Certainly this must have been generally true for its anterior and early more actively growing end. Dendy (1911) drew further evidence for a fundamentally bilateral nature for the pineal complex from the courses of the parietal eye and pineal (epiphyseal) nerve fibers, which were said to be also left-sided and more or less median respectively. Emphasized, too, was the fact that at least during early and middle phases of development, the histological structure of the pineal sac (= epiphysis) was "essentially identical with the very characteristic structure of the retina of the pineal [parietal] eye".

Some of the major features in *Sphenodon's* embryology of the pineal complex are outlined in Table VII. Additional features pertaining more to late development morphology will be reviewed in the section on adult pineal structure and composition.

F. Comparative Conclusions

In early development, the pineal complex of all suitably examined reptiles consists of two neuroectodermal buds, swellings or evaginations in the posterior roof of the diencephalon. The more anterior or anterosinestral of these is either the primordium of the adult parietal eye (lizards and rhynchocephalians) or shows transient evidence of being probably homologous with the parietal eye primordium (turtles and snakes). In later stages of turtles and snakes the presumed homologue of the parietal eye primordium contributes to tissue of the more posterior primordium in the formation of the adult epiphysis or pineal gland and does not form an eyelike structure. The epiphyseal primordium in turn, while apparently homologous among reptilian groups in very early stages of development, is variously modified and added to by adjacent structures in later developmental stages. Thus anteriorly, ventrally and laterally there may be epiphyseal accretions from the parietal primordium (turtles and snakes) and accessory vesicles (especially in turtles) which originate apparently as products of both parietal and epiphyseal primordia.

The possibility that the dorsal sac contributes epithelial vesicles to reptilian epiphyseal tissue has received little attention, but deserves study in the light of later developmental contributions of this sort in some birds (Quay and Renzoni, 1967). Basally or proximally the reptilian epiphysis, particularly in turtles and snakes, receives variable amounts of cellular or tissue accretions from the subcommissural organ and the habenular and posterior commissures.

The result of these different patterns and tissue sources of later epiphyseal growth is that the adult reptilian epiphysis or pineal gland may be only partially homologous from one group to another. Whereas the epiphyses of lizards and *Sphenodon* on developmental grounds. Various structural developmental and histological evidence, the epiphyses of turtles and snakes are only partially homologous with each other and with the epiphyses in lizards and *Spenodon* on developmental grounds. Various structural similarities in epiphyses of adult turtles and snakes, such as the more compact and parenchymatous nature, represent developmental convergence by means of differences in later epiphyseal morphogenetic changes. Therefore, epiphyseal similarities between turtles and snakes are not to be taken as evidence of closer ancestral similarity and relations as compared with the corresponding features and relations of lizards and snakes for example.

Within reptiles the two primordia forming the early pineal complex vary greatly in their spatial relations to each other and to the midsagittal plane of the diencephalic roof. One does generally see a more anterior position of the parietal primordium in relation to the epiphyseal position. The parietal primordium generally lies on the left side in early stages of lizards and *Sphenodon*, while the epiphyseal primordium remains more median. Although particular spatial interrelations of the developing pineal components characterize particular reptilian taxa in a statistical sense, there is much intra- as well as intergroup variability. This variability precludes use of such information to support phylogenetic interpretations.

One of the most often considered, and still academic, speculations is that the parietal and epiphyseal primordia necessarily represent the left- and right-sided members of primitively paired and matching organs. Perhaps, primitively, there was such a relationship, most likely in a very early ancestor such as suggested by certain Devonian fishes (Edinger, 1955, 1956). The very early, transient, imperfect and variable nature of the signs of bilaterality in the developing reptilian complex suggests that the reptilian type of pineal complex is considerably modified and removed from a theoretical, simple, bilateral ancestral model.

Patterns of pineal histogenesis within reptiles show three major lines or types, which progressively differ from each other. The theoretically most primitive pattern is that seen in *Sphenodon* and in some lizards. Here there is evidence of sensory cell precursors, as well as similar patterns of cellular organization, in both primordia. More highly modified are the histogenetic patterns seen in the pineal complexes of the two lines comprised of turtles and snakes. Many remaining questions about pineal histogenesis can only be resolved on the basis of careful electron microscopic studies of developmental stages.

III. Evolutionary Patterns and Relations

A. INTRODUCTION

Direct evidence concerning the evolutionary history of the parietal eye–pineal complex can come only from the paleontological or fossil record. As the tissue components of the complex are not preserved as fossils, one has to utilize the size, shape and position of those cranial spaces that may once have housed one or more components of the parietal–pineal organs. There are only two possible choices—to disregard such fossil evidence on the grounds that it is indirect and possibly misleading or to utilize it as wisely as we can and with appropriate reservations. The second decision is made here, and has been most ably defended by Edinger (1955).

Osteological evidence concerning the possible size and anatomical relations of the parietal eye–pineal complex is of two kinds. The first comprises the parietal or pineal foramen in the skull roof, and can be studied in the greatest number of fossil reptiles. The second kind of osteological evidence is based upon characteristics of endocranial casts, or the impressions found on the ventral surfaces of cranial vaults. Useful and informative endocranial casts from fossil reptiles are relatively rare, especially in terms of their being able to provide evidence of anatomical details in the parietal eye–pineal organ complex. The parietal foramina are believed to have diagnostic value as evolutionary indicators chiefly or solely for the photoreceptive or eyelike portion of the complex. However, only the endocranial impressions and casts can tell us anything about the state of the nonphotoreceptive and presumably secretory parts of the complex (Edinger, 1955; also see Chapter 2).

B. PARIETAL OR PINEAL FORAMINA

Parietal or pineal foramina are restricted to particular lizards and to *Sphenodon* among the living reptiles, but they are found in many extinct reptilian groups as well (Fig. 17). When such a foramen occurs in either living or fossil reptiles, it is single and median, but varies in its size, shape and anteroposterior position. The fact that paired pineal foramina are demonstrable in some representatives of several orders of Devonian fish (Arthrodira, Crossopterygii, and Stegoselachii) has been interpreted by Edinger (1956, 1964) as supporting the theory of paired pineal, or parapineal-pineal organs in the most ancient vertebrates. In reptiles the single remaining foramen can occur between the two parietal bones or between the frontals, or in the region of the frontoparietal suture or fontanelle (Fig. 18). An extensive tabulation of the relative anteroposterior positions of the foramen in recent reptiles has been published by Trost (1956), with earlier summaries provided by Cope (1892) and Camp (1923). The foramina have shifted anteroposteriorly at different times and in different reptilian lines. Trost

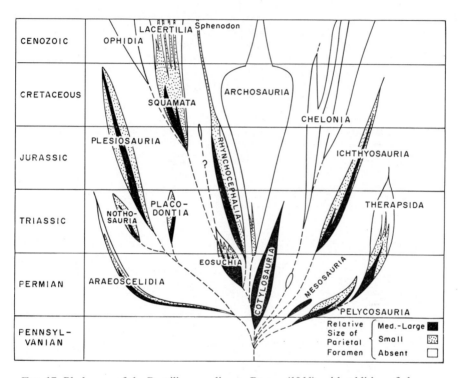

FIG. 17. Phylogeny of the Reptilia according to Romer (1966), with addition of chronological and phylogenetic distribution of parietal (pineal) foramina of different relative size classes.

(1956) believes that among modern reptiles a forward shifting of the parietal eye and its foramen depends principally upon increasing elevation of the forebrain, at least in part reflecting an increase in the size of the orbit. Such relations are illustrated in Fig. 19.

Several caveats attend these considerations on the recognition and importance of the parietal foramen. It has been shown that within both living and extinct groups of reptiles one cannot homologize particular cranial bones solely on the basis of the position of this foramen, in spite of earlier practices and claims to the contrary (Westoll, 1938; Parrington, 1967; Romer, 1941, 1968). Furthermore, not all median openings in the cranial roof are necessarily foramina for the transmittal or housing of the parietal eye or its nerve. Various median gaps between the bones, especially the fontanelles, occurring chiefly during cranial development, may have no

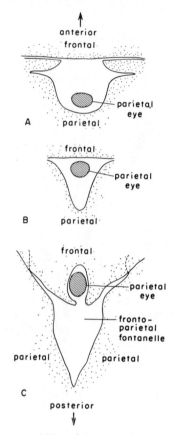

FIG. 18. Examples of different positions of the parietal or pineal foramen in living lizards. The enclosing frontal and parietal bones are stippled. The parietal eye is cross-hatched. (Adapted from Trost, 1956.) A. *Eremias velox* (Lacertidae). B. *Phrynocephalus scutellatus* (Agamidae). C. *Agama ruderata* (Agamidae).

relation or proximity to a parietal eye or organ. Moreover, in some dinosaurs a foramen in advance of the parietals and that was once called a "pineal foramen" is seen to have communication with cavities in the postfrontals and to have no relation or connection with the pineal region (Hatcher *et al.* 1907; Janensch, 1935). However, in adult and heavily ossified reptilian

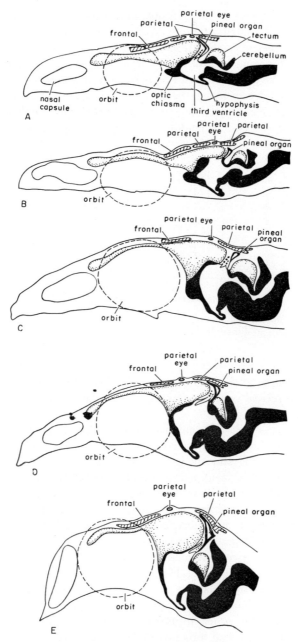

FIG. 19. Diagrammatic median sections through heads of Recent saurians to illustrate the anatomical correlates of a relatively more anterior position of parietal eye and foramen in particular species. Increasingly more anterior position and separation from the glandular pineal organ are shown in the series from A to E. (Adapted from Trost, 1956.) A. *Tiliqua omolepida* (Scincidae). B. *Lacerta saxicola defilippi* (Lacertidae). C. *Eremias velox* (Lacertidae). D. *Liolaemus pictus* (Iguanidae). E. *Phrynocephalus scutellatus* (Agamidae).

skulls a median foramen in the frontoparietal region generally represents the parietal or pineal foramen, a foramen transmitting or housing a photo-receptive and either presumed (fossil) or observed (recent) parietal eye organ.

A rationale for using size of the parietal foramen as an indicator of the relative size of the parietal eye can be derived from comparisons of foramen and parietal eye size in living species. Such comparisons have been made by Edinger (1955), although they are largely based upon published illustrations rather than measurements taken directly from specimens (Fig. 20). In

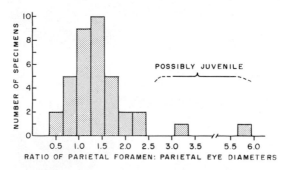

FIG. 20. Histogram of distribution of ratio of diameter of parietal foramen to diameter of the parietal organ in published illustrations of lizards (based upon data of Edinger, 1955).

general, a near 1·0 ratio of eye to foramen exists in adult reptiles. There is no reason to suppose that the diameter of the parietal foramen of fossil reptiles is correlated with something other than a presumably present parietal eye.

Superficial surveys have been made of the general evolutionary trends suggested by the sizes of parietal foramina in fossil reptiles (von Huene, 1933; Gregory, 1951) and the generality or validity of certain of these proposed trends and correlations has been questioned (Edinger, 1955). Thus the idea that the foramen followed a consistent pattern of reduction through reptilian evolution (as, for example, suggested by Gregory, 1951, Figs 12, 53b) is an oversimplification, because, as we shall see, the foramen shows different evolutionary patterns in various groups of fossil reptiles, and the timing of parietal foramen reduction or loss in the geologic scale differs according to reptile group (Fig. 17). Moreover, among gnathostomes most if not all of the relatively largest parietal foramina occur in the Reptilia; nearly all of the exceptions are members of the Seymouriamorpha, a group variously placed with either amphibians or stem reptiles (Romer, 1956, 1966). Examples of parietal foramina of the largest size may be seen in the seymouriamorph genera *Nycteroleter*, *Diadectes* and *Chilonyx* (as illustrated by Romer, 1956).

In animals of vastly different sizes and cranial morphologies, comparisons and statements concerning the sizes of parietal foramina can only be relative and imprecise at best. In the smaller and more delicately built of the fossil forms the parietal foramen generally appears misleadingly larger than in larger forms with massive development or extension of jaws or other bony cranial structures. Perhaps the best guide available for judging in fossil reptiles the relative size of the parietal foramen and its presumed contents, the parietal eye apparatus, is the size of the foramen relative to that of the brain or that of the foramen magnum (Edinger, 1955). The area of the foramen magnum is not much greater than the cross-sectional area of the junction of medulla oblongata and spinal cord. However, measurements either of the volume of the brain (endocranial cast) or of the area of the foramen magnum are available from very few fossil reptiles (Table VIII).

TABLE VIII

Comparative measurements of parietal (pineal) foramen and foramen magnum in selected fossil and living forms. (Data of Edinger, 1955)

Order Suborder Genus species (N)	Dimensions (mm)		
	Parietal foramen	Foramen magnum	Area ratio
	Fossil:		
Anthracosauria			
Seymouriamorpha			
Diadectes (2)	16 × 20	17 × 19	1:1·0
	28 × 15	?	—
Therapsida			
Anomodontia			
Delphinognathus			
conocephalus (1)	2 × 2	2·7 ×	1:0·9
Lystrosaurus (2)	9 × 7	13 × 18	1:3·7
	10 × 7	17 × 23	1:5·6
	Living:		
Rynchocephalia			
Sphenodon punctatus (2)	3 × 1	5 × 4·5	1:7
Squamata			
Sauria			
Iguana sp. (8)	<1 × <1 to 1 × 1	4 × 5 to 7 × 7	1:21
Ctenosaura pectinata (6)	<1 × <1 to 1 × 1	5 × 5 to 6 × 6	1:36
Varanus komodoensis (1)	2 × 3	12 × 14	1:28

Meaningful review of evolutionary patterns shown by reptilian parietal foramina must focus on the characteristics and changes seen within natural phylogenetic assemblages or lines. This is possible now, at least provisionally, for such major groups as are outlined below and the relationships of which are summarized in Fig. 17. The following outline follows the classification and sequence of reptilian groups used by Romer (1966) and is based on published illustrations and descriptions.

Cotylosauria. Parietal foramina are medium to large in size in nearly all representatives of this, the stem or basal, reptile group. This is true for *Hylonomus*, *Protorothyris*, *Romeria*, *Captorhinus* and *Labidosaurus* in the suborder Captorhinomorpha, and for *Procolophon*, *Bradysaurus*, *Pareiasaurus*, *Scutosaurus*, *Milleretta*, *Millerina* and *Millerettops* in the suborder Procolophonia (Romer, 1956, 1966).

Mesosauria. These constitute the earliest of the groups of aquatic reptiles and inhabited bodies of fresh water (Romer, 1966). *Mesosaurus* had a medium-sized parietal foramen (von Huene, 1941).

Testudines. Throughout the known history of this group, parietal or pineal foramina were lacking (Romer, 1956).

Eosuchia. These small reptiles, giving rise to the Squamata, and possibly the Archosauria (Romer, 1966), had parietal foramina that varied both in presence and relative size. The foramen was usually medium to large in size in Permian and lowermost Triassic (*Mesenosaurus*, *Palaeagama*, *Paliguana*, *Youngina*, *Youngoides*), absent in at least some later genera such as *Prolacerta* and *Champsosaurus*, while remaining medium-sized in others such as *Askeptosaurus* and *Thalattosaurus* (Broom, 1925, 1926; Romer, 1956, 1966; Williston, 1925). *Prolacerta* is structurally an advanced eosuchian and *Champsosaurus* is considered by Romer (1966) to be a late survivor of the group. The parietal eye apparently followed different tendencies in two aquatic sidelines of the eosuchians, remaining sizeable in marine, fish-eating thalattosaurians (*Askeptosaurus* and *Thalattosaurus*) and disappearing in *Choristoderan*, a freshwater, fish-eating choristoderan.

Squamata. A parietal foramen is lacking in snakes and almost all amphisbaenians and is variably present or absent in genera or species of other squamate subgroups. Where present among lizards, it is generally small in size (Camp, 1923; Cope, 1892; Edinger, 1955; McDowell and Bogert, 1954; Gilmore, 1928; Zangerl, 1944). Examples of small to medium-sized parietal foramina are found in upper Cretaceous marine lizards, the mosasaurs (*Platecarpus* and *Tylosaurus*) (Baur, 1892; Romer, 1966; Williston, 1925).

Rhynchocephalia. The parietal foramen is usually either small (*Spheno-*

don, Mesosuchus, and *Sapheosaurus,* for example) or absent (*Hyper-odapedon, Stenometopon, Scaphonyx, Sauranodon*) (von Huene, 1952; Osawa, 1898; Romer, 1956, 1966; Williston, 1925).

Archosauria. A parietal foramen is lacking in nearly all members of this large subclass (Hatcher *et al.,* 1907; Kälin, 1933; Lull and Wright, 1942; Newton, 1889; Romer, 1956, 1966). A couple of exceptions can be noted among early representatives, such as *Erythrosuchus* and *Mesorhinus* of the Triassic (Romer, 1956; Williston, 1925). *Pleurosaurus,* an aquatic reptile of uncertain relations but included here (Romer, 1966), has a medium-sized foramen (von Huene, 1952; Watson, 1914; Williston, 1925).

Euryapsida. Each of the major orders or suborders of this subclass shows great differences both in terms of presence and of size of the parietal foramen. This pertains to the Araeoscelidia, Nothosauria, Plesiosauria and Placodontia and is diagrammed for them in the left side of Fig. 17. In the Araeoscelidia the parietal foramen may be absent (*Trilophosaurus*), small or medium-sized (*Araeoscelis*). Among nothosaurs it is generally present but variable in size (*Nothosaurus, Pachypleurosaurus, Simosaurus*). Among plesiosaurs, the foramen ranges from absent (*Hydrotherosaurus, Styxosaurus*) (Welles, 1952), to small (*Muraenosaurus, Pistosaurus*) (Williston, 1925) and to medium or large (*Peloneustes, Pliosaurus, Brachauchenius*) (Edinger, 1955; Linder, 1913; Williston, 1925). The Placodontia in turn include an example of a large parietal foramen (*Placodus*), as well as a form lacking it (*Henodus*) (Edinger, 1955). Some of these groups of semiaquatic to aquatic reptiles have a very large parietal foramen (Table IX).

Ichthyopterygia. Ichthyosaurs are considered to be the reptiles that were the most highly adapted for aquatic life. These generally have a parietal foramen, and it reaches medium size in some (*Ichthyosaurus, Ophthalmosaurus*) (Romer, 1956; Williston, 1925).

Pelycosauria. The pelycosaurs, primitive synapsida, provide more information about evolutionary changes in the parietal foramen than do most other fossil groups of reptiles. Not only is there an abundance of specimens and known forms, but we also have a wealth of careful observations compiled by Romer and Price (1940). Members of this group generally have parietal foramina (Fig. 21). Some different trends in the relative size of foramen may be suggested in the three major pelycosaurian subdivisions. The Sphenacodontia, carnivores leading to the therapsids, show a tendency for reduction in foramen size in such late forms as *Dimetrodon* as compared with *Varanops* and *Sphenacodon* (Romer and Price, 1940; Williston, 1925) (Figs 21 and 22). The other two pelycosaur groups suggest an opposite trend, with larger parietal

foramina occurring in some of the later and more specialized genera
(Romer, 1966). This is shown in the Edaphosauria, with very large
foramina in the caseids (*Casea*, *Cotylorhynchus*) and medium-sized ones
in nitosaurids (*Mycterosaurus*) and edaphosaurids (*Edaphosaurus*,
Naosaurus) (Romer and Price, 1940; Williston, 1925) (Figs 20 and 21).
In the Ophiacodontia, the relative size of the foramen is larger in

TABLE IX

Measurements of large parietal foramina among selected euryapsids. (*Data of Edinger, 1955*)

Order Suborder Genus	Skull length (mm)	Parietal foramen	
		Length (mm)	Breadth (mm)
Sauropterygia			
Nothosauria			
Nothosaurus	125–800	4–23	2·5–23
Plesiosauria			
Brachauchenius	800	40	
Pliosaurus	1160	40	15
Placodontia			
Placodus	158–200	10–19	10–14

Eothyris than in either *Ophiacodon* or *Varanosaurus*, although the
foramen of this smaller animal has a smaller absolute size (Fig. 22).

The pelycosaur data permit one to point out that evaluation of
relative size of the parietal foramen depends upon the anatomical
standard or scale used for comparison, whether the median basal
skull length or width of foramen magnum (Fig. 22). With median
basal skull length as a standard (top of Fig. 22), the relative size of the
parietal foramen is clearly greatest in *Casea* and *Cotylorhynchus*. If
width of the foramen magnum is taken as the standard (middle of Fig.
22), then the relative size of the parietal foramen is clearly greater in
the two more basal or primitive pelycosaur representatives, *Varanops*
and *Varanosaurus*. Another anatomical base for comparisons of the size
of the parietal foramen is the relative size of the orbit, as an indicator
of possible order of size of the lateral eyes. In this instance *Dimetrodon*
and the caseids (*Cotylorhynchus* and *Casea*) have the relatively largest
parietal foramina (Fig. 22, bottom).

Pelycosaurs also are of interest for the different structural characteristics of their parietal foramina. In *Ophiacodon* the margins of the foramen are not raised above the general surface contours of the parietal bone, but are sunken, forming a cup of bone around the base of the presumed pineal eyeball, as suggested by Romer and Price (1940, p. 201; Fig. 21B). Illustrations of skulls of *Dimetrodon limbatus*, on the other hand, show the parietal foramen in the center of a medial swelling or boss of the parietal bones (Fig. 21C). A similar structural feature occurs in other and only distantly related reptilian genera, such as *Gorgonops* and *Prorubidgea* among the gorgonopsian therapsids (Manten, 1958).

Therapsida. These advanced synapsid and mammal-like reptiles show different patterns of evolutionary change in the parietal foramen and pineal region. In the Theriodontia, therapsid lines leading to mammals, the parietal foramen is reduced and eventually lost. Here the foramen is: (i) nearly always present but small in infraorders Gorgonopsia (*Prorubidgea, Gorgonops, Scymnognathus, Leontocephalus, Scylacops, Arctognathus* and *Lycaenops*) (Kemp, 1969; Manten, 1958; Williston, 1925) and Cynodontia (*Leavachia, Prosynosuchus, Scalopocynodon, Cynosuchoides, Glochinodontoides, Platycraniellus, Thrinaxodon* (Fig. 23), *Cynognathus, Cynidiognathus, Lycaenognathus, Diademodon, Gomphognathus* and *Trirachodon* (Fig. 23) (Brink, 1955a, b, c, 1960a; Broom, 1911; Kemp, 1972; Parrington, 1946; Watson, 1942; Williston, 1925); (ii) usually small or lacking in infraorders Therocephalia (present: *Scylacosaurus, Lycosuchus, Trochosaurus, Hofmeyria, Moschorhinus, Notaelurops, Notosollasia*; absent: *Aneugomphius*) (Brink, 1958; Broom, 1936; Kemp, 1972) and Bauriamorpha (present: *Ictidosuchoides, Ictidosuchops, Ictidostoma*; absent: *Tetracynodon, Bauria*) (Brink, 1960b; Broom, 1911; Kemp, 1972; Williston, 1925); and (iii) lacking in infraorder Tritylodontoidea (*Bienotherium, Oligokyphus*) (Romer, 1956; Watson, 1942). In the Anomodontia, specialized, often herbivorous, sidelines of therapsid evolution, the parietal foramen is not only generally present throughout, but is often medium to large in size. This is demonstrable for the two infraorders with the largest numbers of known genera, the Dinocephalia and the Dicynodontia, but in the latter group the range of variation is greater. Thus, in illustrated dinocephalians the parietal foramen is generally medium to large in size (*Jonkeria, Delphinognathus* (Table VIII), *Mormosaurus, Moschops, Strutiocephalus, Ulemosaurus*) (Brink, 1957; Edinger, 1955; Romer, 1956; Williston, 1925). In dicynodontians it may be absent (*Dinanomodon*) or its size small (*Synostocephalus*), medium-sized (*Emydops, Aulacocephalodon, Dicynodon, Cistecephalus, Pelanomodon, Proaulacocephalodon, Pro-*

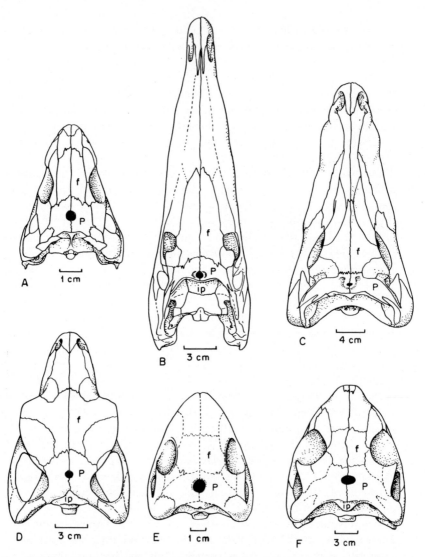

FIG. 21. Dorsal views of pelycosaur skulls, illustrating variation in size and relative uniformity in position of the parietal foramen in genera of widely different habits and cranial morphology (adapted from Romer and Price, 1940). A. *Eothyris parkeyi*. B. *Ophiacodon uniformis*. C. *Dimetrodon limbatus*. D. *Edaphosaurus pogonias*. E. *Casea broilii*. F. *Cotylorhynchus romeri*. f, Frontal; ip, interparietal; P, parietal.

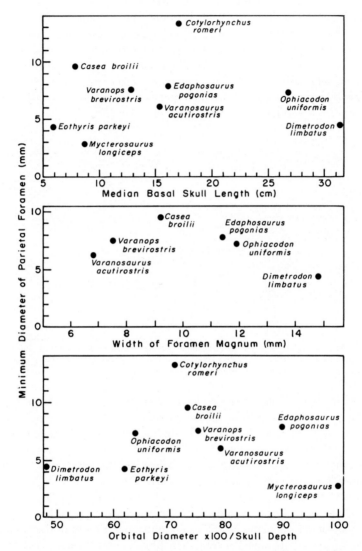

FIG. 22. Plots of minimum parietal foramen diameter against three standards for size comparisons. Some measurements were taken as listed by Romer and Price (1940); others, including those of the parietal foramen, were calculated from skull illustrations in Romer and Price (1940). The validity or estimated accuracy of the latter technique was tested by comparing measurements from both sources. Measurements calculated from skull illustrations were within 4·5% of those made from specimens directly and listed by Romer and Price (1940).

pelanomodon) or large (*Lystrosaurus* (Table VIII) (Agnew, 1958; Edinger, 1955; Romer, 1956; Toerien, 1955; Williston, 1925).

Among these therapsids, a cynodont line presumably near mammal ancestry consisted for the most part of rather lightly built and active carnivores (Romer, 1966). Although the temporal region in many of these is broadly expanded, with increased mass and cranial attachment of jaw muscles, the parietal foramen persists and rises to the dorsal surface via a high and narrow sagittal crest or ridge (Fig. 23). The persistence

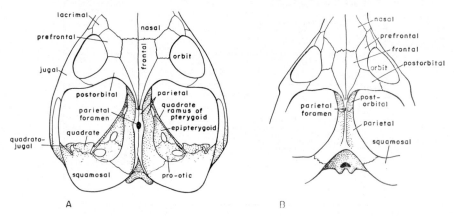

FIG. 23. Anatomical relations of the reduced parietal foramen in cynodont, mammal-like reptiles, in dorsal views. A. *Thrinaxodon liorhinus* (adapted from Parrington, 1946). B. *Trirachodon kannemeyeri* (adapted from Broom, 1911).

of the parietal foramen in such circumstances in so many genera suggests that its presumed content, the parietal eye, remained functionally significant. Beyond this, the sagital crest may have functioned not only for bilateral muscle attachment, but also for protection of the medial parietal eye. In three more advanced therapsid lines, generally a little later than the cynodonts, the parietal foramen is lost. In these, the Tritylodontoidea, Bauriamorpha and Ictidosauria, we are witnessing the demise of the parietal foramen in or very near the immediate ancestors of the mammals. This circumstance viewed in the perspective of suggested therapsid-mammalian phylogenies (Olson, 1944; Romer, 1966) can form the basis for an estimated loss of the ancestral mammalian parietal foramen and eye in upper Permian to lower Triassic time, or approximately 230 million years ago. This might be about the same length of time since the loss of the parietal foramen in the archosaurian line leading to birds (Fig. 17). In all fossil and living birds and in all but a few early to mid-Triassic archosaurians the parietal foramen is lacking.

C. ENDOCRANIAL CASTS

Endocranial brain casts and the internal morphology of fossil braincases strongly suggest that the parietal-pineal organ complex was larger in some extinct reptiles than in any living representatives (Case, 1921; Nopsca, 1926; Edinger, 1929; and others; Fig. 24). However, difficulties remain, preventing full utilization of information from this source for interpretation of the evolution of the parietal eye–pineal complex in reptiles. There are

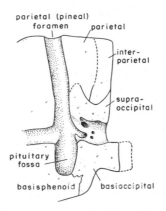

FIG. 24. Median sagittal section through the posterior region of a skull of a tapinocephaloid therapsid to show the great length and size of the parietal–pineal canal (adapted from Nopsca, 1926).

still comparatively few reptiles for which we have detailed studies of intra-cranial morphology (see Hopson, Chapter 2 of this volume). Anatomical identifications of particular intracranial features are often difficult or debatable. Furthermore, the vault of the braincase may not have been applied closely enough to the contained soft structures to render a good impression of them. Nevertheless, several general observations can be made. (1) Among therapsids the endocranial space presumably occupied by the parietal–pineal complex was frequently relatively very large compared both to the foramen magnum and the space occupied by the brain (Figs 24 and 25; Table X). However, the size of this space was, at least sometimes, poorly correlated with the size of the parietal foramen, as pointed out by Edinger (1955) in comparisons of *Delphinognathus* and *Lystrosaurus*. (2) The divergence of size or presence of the parietal foramen and the size of the endocranial outlines of the parietal–pineal complex is even greater among the archosaurs. Here parietal foramina are usually absent (see above), but the endocranial casts sometimes suggest parietal–pineal organs of large size (Table X). One extreme example, *Belodon buceros*, lacks a parietal foramen,

TABLE X

Status of size of parietal and pineal organs, in examples from selected fossil reptiles judged from endocranial casts. (Data and figures of Hatcher et al., 1907; Case, 1921; Nopsca, 1926; Edinger, 1929, 1955; Kemp, 1969)

Subclass Order Suborder Genus	Suggested size of parietal–pineal organ complex
Archosauria	
Thecodontia	
Aetosauria	
Desmatosuchus spurensis	Small
Phytosauria	
Belodon buceros	Large
Crocodilia	
Mesosuchia	
Macrorhynchus	Absent
Eusuchia	
Gavialis	Absent
Pterosauria	
Pterodactyloidea	
Pteranodon	Absent
Saurischia	
Theropoda	
Ceratosaurus	Absent
Tyrannosaurus rex	Small
Ornithischia	
Ornithopoda	
Claosaurus	Absent
Edmontosaurus	Absent
Ceratopsia	
Triceratops serratus	Small
Euryapsida	
Sauropterygia	
Nothosauria	
Nothosaurus mirabilis	Large
Placadontia	
Placodus gigas	Large
Synapsida	
Therapsida	
Theriodontia	
Arctognathus	Medium-large (Fig. 25)
Anomodontia	
Tapinocephalian sp.	Large (Fig. 24)
Delphinognathus conocephalus	Large
Lystrosaurus	Large

but shows an endocranial morphology suggesting the presence of a complex and large structure in the epiphyseal–parietal organ region (Case, 1921). (3) Some of the endocranial casts have led investigators to believe that there are two component structures in the pineal region or complex. One example that has been proposed from such an interpretation is shown in Fig. 25.

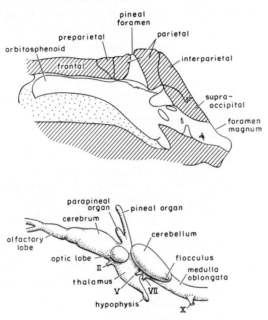

FIG. 25. A. Composite reconstruction of the gorgonopsid braincase—internal view of a sagittally sectioned skull. B. Lateral view of restored brain and pineal complex based upon reconstruction of the above braincase. (Adapted from Kemp, 1969.)

There are others in the paleontological literature, but they are difficult to evaluate without study of the original specimens and specimens of other and related reptilian taxa.

IV. Morphology and Composition in Living Reptiles

A. TESTUDINES

1. *Anatomy and Histology*

The pineal region of the few adult turtles that have been examined shows only a single member of the complex—a parenchymatous and saccular pineal organ or epiphysis. Although an eyelike component is not known in the pineal complex of any adult turtle, we have noted above (Section IIB the transient occurrence developmentally of an epithelial vesicle possibly of this nature or homology. Furthermore, cells having structural characteristics reminiscent of photoreceptors do survive in the adult pineal organ and are described below.

Detailed information on testudinian pineal structure and composition is available only from one or two families out of the dozen often recognized (Table XI). Only some of the grosser features have been described in the pineals of sea and soft-shelled turtles, and this was done near the end of the last century (Table XI). The pineal has not been examined critically in

TABLE XI

Descriptions of structure and composition of the pineal organ in adult Testudines

Family	Species (References)
Chelydridae	*Chelydra serpentina* (Humphrey, 1894; Studnička, 1905)
Emydidae	*Pseudemys callirostris* (Oksche and Kirchenstein, 1966a, b)
	Chrysemys picta (Vivien and Roels, 1968)
	Chrysemys scripta (Vivien, 1964; Vivien and Roels, 1967, 1968; Vivien-Roels, 1969, 1970)
	Emys orbicularis [*Cistudo europaea, Testudo iberica*] (Bojanus 1819–21; Faivre, 1857; Herrick, 1893; Scatizzi, 1933; Sorenson, 1893; Studnicka, 1905; Vivien-Roels, 1970)
	Mauremys caspica (Combescot and Demaret, 1963; Vivien-Roels, 1970)
Testudinidae	*Testudo hermanni* (Collin and Meiniel, 1971; Lutz and Collin, 1967; Mehring, 1972)
	Geochelone gigantea (Collin and Meiniel, 1971; Grignon and Grignon, 1963a, b, c; Vivien and Roels, 1967, 1968)
	Testudo sp. (Oksche, 1965)
Cheloniidae	*Eretmochelys imbricata* (Studničks, 1905; Voeltzkow, 1903)
	Chelonia mydas (Rabl-Rückhard, 1886; Studnička, 1905)
Trionychidae	*Trionyx muticus* (Gage, 1895; Studnička, 1905)

any member of the Pleurodira, although this is considered as the more primitive one of the two living suborders.

Recent studies suggest that there may be some major morphological differences or variations in the pineal glands of turtles. There are two major structural patterns described: (1) The pineal is composed of a series of thick-walled epithelial vesicles the central cavities of which interconnect with each other and with the third ventricle of the brain. This is the pineal morphology described by Grignon and Grignon (1963a) in presumably adult *Testudo graeca* and found as well in late developmental stages of *Testudo graeca* and

T. hermanni by Vivien-Roels and Petit (1973, Section IIB above, Figs 3F and 4E). (2) The pineal is a thick-walled epithelial sac, closed off from the third ventricle in both juveniles and adults, and with a distinct and solid stalk containing nerve fibers and attached near the posterior commissure

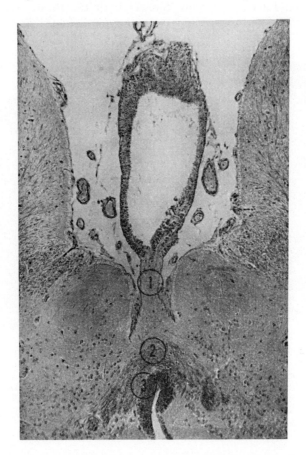

FIG. 26. Transverse section through the posterior part of the epiphysis of a young *Chrysemys scripta* (courtesy of Vivien-Roels, 1969). (1), Pineal or epiphyseal stalk; (2), posterior commissure; (3), cranial end of the subcommissural organ. Hematoxylin and eosin stains. × 100.

(Fig. 26). This is the pineal morphology described in *Chrysemys scripta* (Vivien, 1964a, b; Vivien and Roels, 1968; Vivien-Roels, 1969). Any sort of consistent association, however, of one of these kinds of pineal morphology with tortoises (*Testudo* sp.) on the one hand or aquatic emydids on the other may be premature. There remain contradictory descriptions in both old and recent publications. For example, Mehring (1972) has suggested that *Testudo hermanni* lacks a continuous pineal lumen.

The cellular composition of the testudinian pineal appears to be essentially the same whether or not the organ is saccular or vesicular, and whether or not its central lumen or lumina connect with the third ventricle. The epithelial wall of the pineal appears to be more folded and complexly

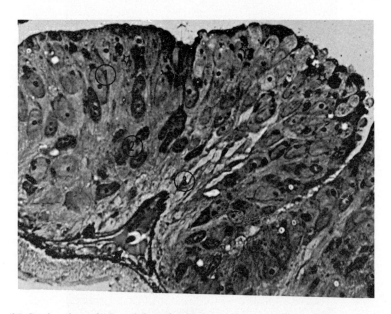

FIG. 27. Section through the epiphyseal epithelium of a young *Chrysemys scripta* (courtesy of Vivien-Roels, 1969). The epiphyseal lumen is at the top right, and a small area of the capsule of the organ with penetrating capillary (arrow) is at the lower left. Two more or less regularly alternating cell types are seen: (1), "pseudosensory cells", having ovoid and relatively clear nuclei and a supranuclear mass of glycogen (*); (2), ependymal or supportive cells, having more granular and darkly stained nuclei. (3), Basal plexiform layer of the epithelium. Periodic acid–Schiff technique.

expanded in older animals, but its basic cellular composition remains the same from juvenile through adult ages. The thickest and innermost layer of the pineal epithelial wall resembles a pseudostratified epithelium (Figs 27 and 28). It is composed of two, nearly alternating kinds of columnar epithelial cells: (i) a so-called "pseudosensory" pinealocyte, having the structure of a rudimentary or regressing photosensory cell, but showing also evidence of secretory activity (Figs 29 to 32); (ii) ependymal, supportive or interstitial cells. Besides these two primary cell types there are present cells of intermediate structure and staining characteristics (Grignon and

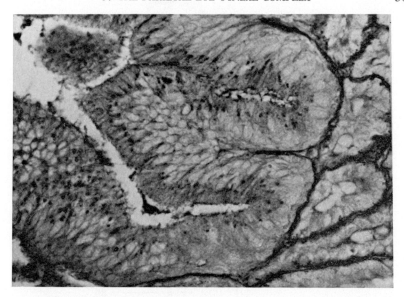

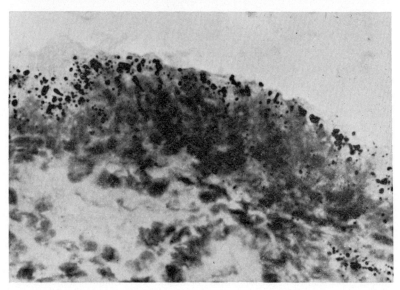

FIG. 28. Sections through the epiphyseal epithelium of a young *Chrysemys scripta* (courtesy of Vivien-Roels, 1969). Top. Aldehyde fuchsin (of Gabe) is shown here to stain strongly: granular material in the zone of "pseudosensory cells", coagulum within the lumen, and the basal membrane or lamina. × 480. Bottom. Lipid droplets in the apical cytoplasm are colored with Sudan black B (Mayer's Carmalum counterstain shows cell nuclei). × 750.

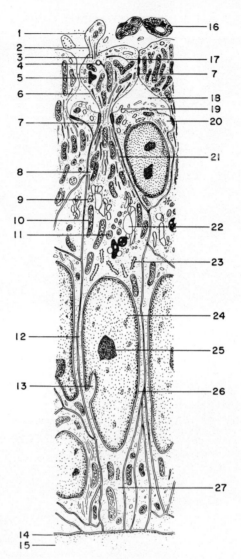

FIG. 29. Diagrammatic vertical section through cells of the pineal epithelium at an intermediate level, from *Testudo hermanni*. 1, Outer (or external) segment; 2, neck or connecting piece; 3, axial centriole; 4, oblique centriole; 5, lipoidal bodies; 6, apical extension or bulblike process of the ("pseudosensory") pinealocyte; 7, zonule of adhesion between ependymoid or supporting cell and pinealocyte (left) and between two pinealocytes (right); 8, inner segment; 9, multivesicular body in pinealocyte cytoplasm; 10, mitochondrion; 11, lysosome-like bodies; 12, cell body of pinealocyte; 13, nuclear crease or invagination; 14, basal lamina; 15, perivascular space; 16, concentric membrane systems in lumen; 17, rootlet; 18, lumen; 19, microvilli of ependymoid cell; 20, apical cytoplasm of ependymoid cell; 21, microtubules in inner segment; 22, dilated Golgi cisterns; 23, rough endoplasmic reticulum (ER) or ergastoplasm; 24, nucleus of pinealocyte; 25, nucleolus; 26, nuclear membrane; 27, basal cytoplasmic process of pinealocyte; × approx. 1200. Adapted from Lutz and Collin (1967).

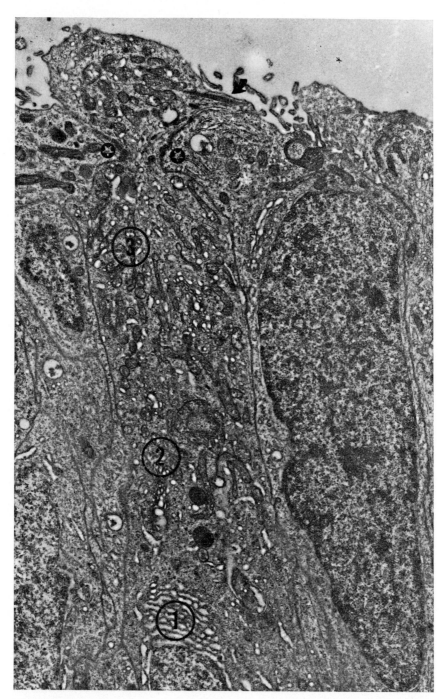

FIG. 30. Apical ends of epiphyseal epithelial cells of a young *Chrysemys scripta* showing the contents and relations of the apical and supranuclear cytoplasm of a "pseudosensory" pinealocyte *in situ* (courtesy of Vivien-Roels, 1969). (1), Paraboloid, just above the nucleus; (2), Golgi zone; (3), zone of numerous mitochondria; ←, ciliary rootlet; *, desmosomal junctions (maculae adhaerentes) between "pseudosensory" pinealocyte at isthmus region and adjacent ependymal supportive cells. ×11 000.

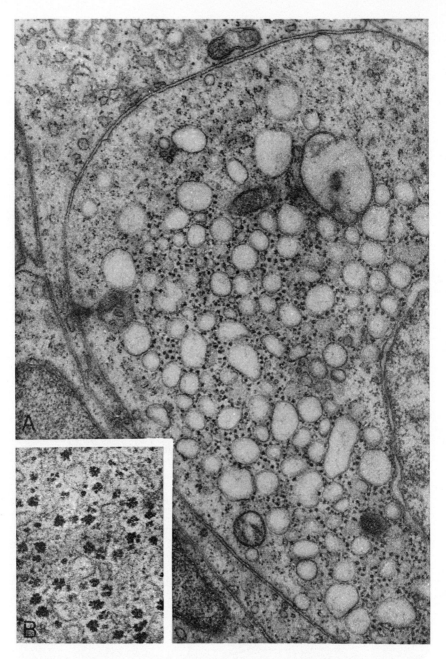

FIG. 31. A. Paraboloid region of the juxtanuclear cytoplasm of a "pseudosensory" pine-alocyte from the epiphysis of a young *Chrysemys scripta*. Numerous cisternae and glycogen granules are shown. × 27 000. (Courtesy of Vivien-Roels, 1969.) B. Small area enlarged to show structure of glycogen granules. × 54 000.

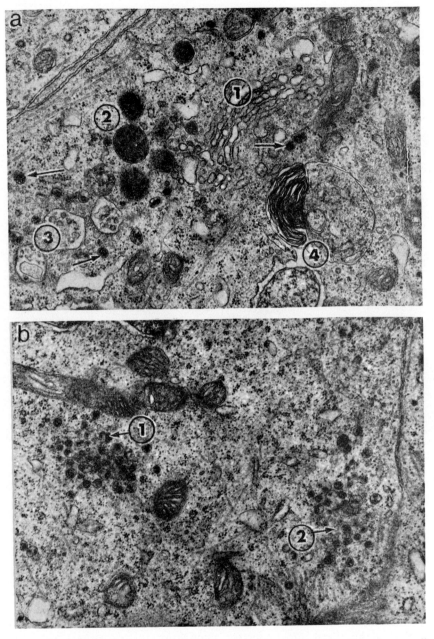

FIG. 32. Cytoplasmic contents and evidence of secretory activity in "pseudosensory" pinealocytes of an adult *Chrysemys scripta* (courtesy of Vivien-Roels, 1970). a. Golgi region: (1) Golgi saccules; (2), lysosomes; (3), multivesicular body; (4), pseudomyelin figure; ↑, formation of dense-cored vesicles of type I. ×24 000. b. Cytoplasm in basal process: (1), vesicles of type I; (2), vesicles of type II. ×20 000.

Grignon, 1963a) and also nerve or ganglion cells, that are discussed below under the heading of pineal innervation.

The luminal ends of the epithelial cell types of the pineal and of their interrelations are relatively simple to examine (Fig. 27). But their slender, peripherally directed, processes enter a fibrous zone that is difficult to sort out and understand. It is composed also of nerve and neuroglial fibers and

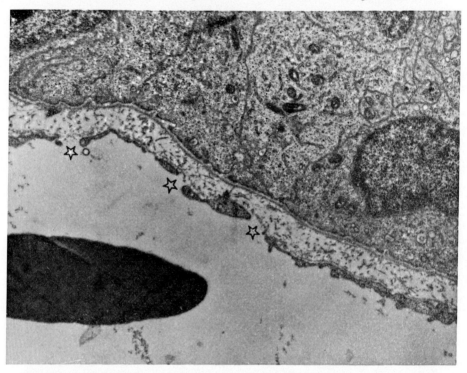

Fig. 33. Relations of basal or peripheral portion of a pineal epithelial cell (right) to a capillary wall (erythrocyte in capillary lumen at lower left). Two basal laminae and a narrow connective tissue space separate the pineal epithelium and endothelium. Pores in the capillary endothelium are seen at the starred sites. ×9000 (courtesy of Vivien-Roels, 1969).

will be discussed under innervation. More peripherally yet, the pineal is bounded by a basal lamina and thin connective tissue layers and creases through which a rich blood supply reaches the pineal epithelium (Fig. 33).

Within the pineal lumen electron microscopy reveals various materials, often lumped together with a "coagulum" by earlier light microscopic investigations, and often of uncertain origin and significance. Some of the cellular debris and products in the lumen are believed to be derived from the "pseudosensory" pinealocytes, and are certainly partly degenerative (Fig. 36). Macrophages are commonly associated with this material (Fig. 37). Although a pineal secretory activity may in part be luminally oriented, the specific identification of such a luminal secretory product remains unclear.

2. Pseudosensory Pinealocytes

"Pseudosensory" pinealocytes stand out especially well on the basis of their paler and more ovoid nuclei and their relatively dense cytoplasm, rich in mitochondria and free ribosomes (Fig. 27). As tall, columnar, epithelial cells they each can be descriptively divided into three regions (Fig. 29): (i) a complex supranuclear region, toward the pineal lumen; (ii) a cell body or nuclear region; and (iii) a basal process. The supranuclear region supports apically a ciliary formation (Fig. 29, 1), often termed an outer or external segment, but only in the most rudimentary way resembling such a structure in photoreceptor cells of either the lateral eyes or of lower vertebrate parietal eyes. The outer (external) segment is attached to a bulblike process of the cell by a neck or connecting piece at the base of which an axial centriole may be seen. The bulblike apical process also contains the oblique centriole, lipoidal bodies, microtubules, dense granules, dense-cored vesicles and mitochondria (Figs 29, 30 and 34). At its basal constriction the bulblike process shows desmosomal connections with adjacent ependymal or support-ive cells (Figs 29, 30 and 34). Through this constricted region extend many, mostly parallel, microtubules (Figs 29 and 34). Below this is encountered the region sometimes termed the "inner segment" (Fig. 29, 8) with abundant mitochondria and microtubules. This apical region with numerous mito-chondria is sometimes considered closely analogous to the "ellipsoid" of lateral eye cones, which also is often associated with a lipid droplet or globule. As one descends still farther in the supranuclear cytoplasm one encounters a greater variety of organelles and inclusions, such as multi-vesicular bodies, lysosomes, Golgi cisterns and rough endoplasmic reticulum or ergastoplasm. Just above the nucleus a paraboloid region occurs, con-taining Golgi cisterns and glycogen granules (Figs 30 and 31). On the basis of composition and structure this region appears to be comparable to the paraboloid described within the cones of the lateral eye retinas of amphibians, reptiles and birds (Vivien-Roels, 1969). In the cell body or circumnuclear cytoplasm of pseudosensory pinealocytes one sees sparse mitochondria, and some free ribosomes and parts of endoplasmic reticula. In the basal process of these cells there are mitochondria, microtubules, dense granules, vesicles and sometimes synaptic structures (Fig. 32). The granules and vesicles in the basal process are assumed to include secretory products of these cells which will be released in the vicinity of the blood vessels in the outer circum-ference of the organ (Fig. 33). However, the opposite, or apical, end of the

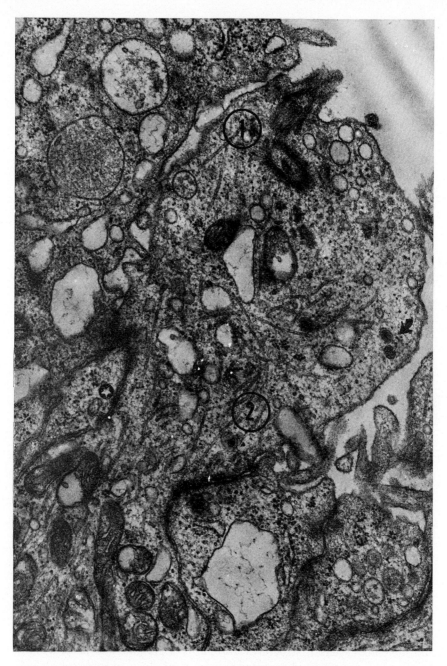

FIG. 34. Apical extension or bulblike process of "pseudosensory" pinealocyte (compare with item 6, Fig. 29) from *Chrysemys scripta* (courtesy of Vivien-Roels, 1969). (1), Two centrioles at right, the distal one is giving rise to a cilium; (2), microtubules; ↓, dense-cored vesicles; *, desmosomal junctions with neighboring ependymal cells.

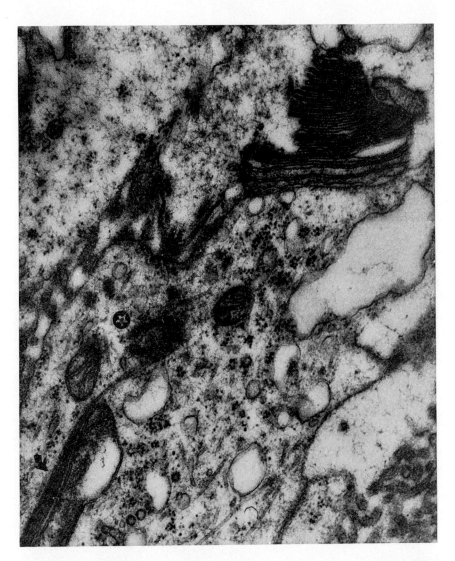

FIG. 35. Formation of the outer (or external) segment (compare with item 1, Fig. 29) at the luminal apex of a "pseudosensory" pinealocyte in a young *Chrysemys scripta* (courtesy of Vivien-Roels, 1969). The outer segment (upper right corner) is composed of flat disks stacked in a more or less regular pattern. Two centrioles (*) and a ciliary rootlet (↑) are shown in the apical extension or bulblike process extending from the lower left corner. × 25 000.

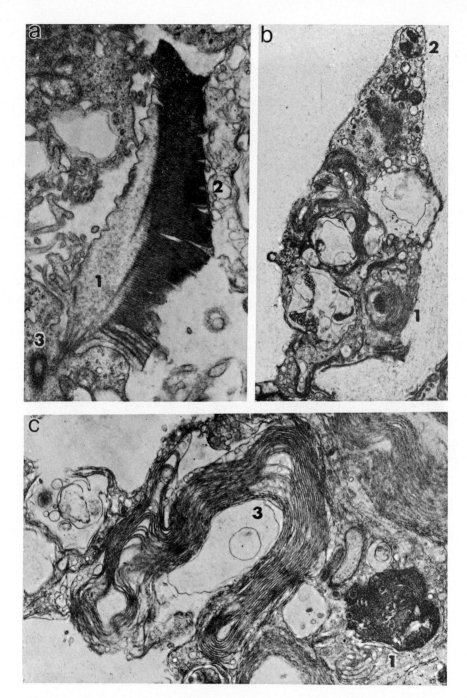

FIG. 36. Typical (a) and degenerating (b and c) outer (external) segments of adult turtle "pseudosensory" pinealocytes (courtesy of Vivien-Roels, 1960). a. *Chrysemys scripta*, ×15 000: 1, ciliary axis (compare with item 1, Fig. 29); 2, saccules; 3, proximal centriole. b. *Chrysemys scripta*, ×6000: 1, tubules; 2, vacuoles containing heterogeneous material. c. *Mauremys caspica*, ×12 000: 1, tubules and dense material; 3, lamellar complexes free within the lumen.

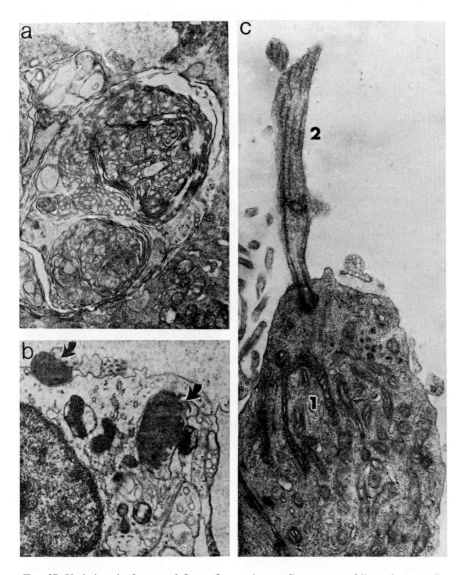

FIG. 37. Variations in forms and fates of outer (external) segments of "pseudosensory" pinealocytes of adult turtles (courtesy of Vivian-Roels, 1970). a. Degeneration of the outer segment through tubule formation; *Mauremys caspica*, ×10 500. b. Macrophage containing pieces from outer segments (at arrows); *Chrysemys scripta*, ×11 300. c. Apical extension (1), containing elongate mitochondria and supporting a rudimentary outer segment (2); anterior epiphyseal region of *C. scripta*, ×18 000.

cell is also sometimes credited with secretory activity. In this case the secretion would pass into the pineal lumen. In addition to possible granular and vesicular products that might possibly pass in this direction there are also the products of fragmented and degenerated outer segments (Figs 34 to 37). It remains debatable, nevertheless, whether such heterogeneous luminal materials truly function as secretions on the basis of a meaningful use of the

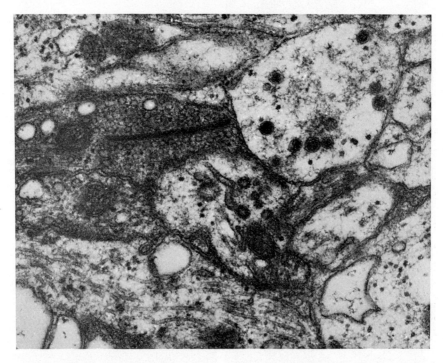

FIG. 38. Basal termination of a "pseudosensory" pinealocyte in *Chrysemys scripta* (courtesy of Vivien-Roels, 1969). The pinealocyte terminal (at left) contains vesicles and a typical synaptic ribbon. It lies in the vicinity of a nerve fiber (upper right) containing a few dense-cored vesicles. × 37 500.

term. Although variations in quality of fixation may have sometimes added to the uncertainty about proposed luminal secretory products and processes, it does seem clear that luminal release and breakdown of outer segment materials occurs naturally—whatever significance be attributed to these events.

3. *Ependymal or Supportive Cells*

Ependymal cells have many synonyms in the descriptions of the pineal–parietal complex of lower vertebrates. They include "interstitial cells"

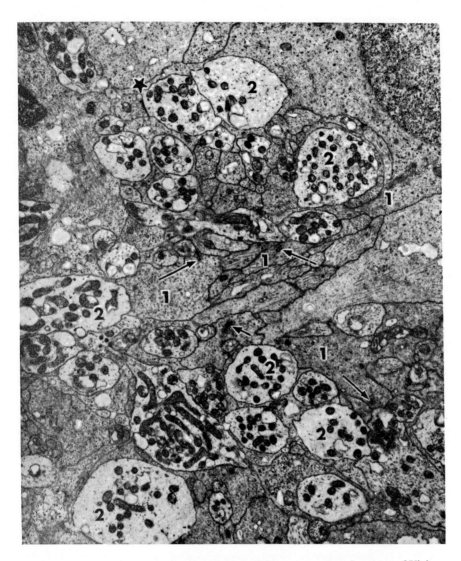

FIG. 39. Synaptic relations in the pineal gland of *Chrysemys scripta* (courtesy of Vivien-Roels, 1970). Neurosensory synapses are seen between basal processes (1) of "photo-receptorial" or "pseudosensory" pinealocytes containing synaptic ribbons (at ↑) surrounded by vesicles, and postsynaptic nerve terminals (2). Interneuronal synapses are seen also, as at *. ×20 000.

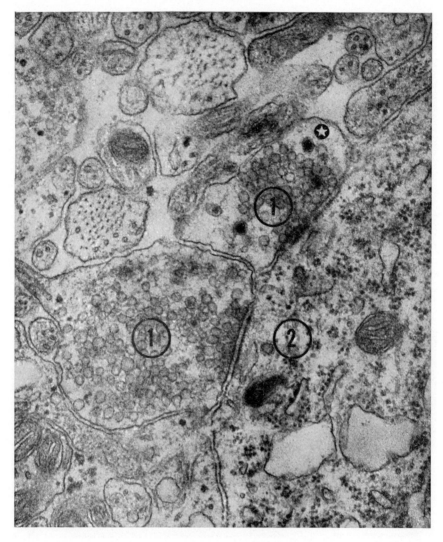

FIG. 40. Two nerve terminals (1) making synaptic contact with a neuron cell body (2) in the pineal of *Chrysemys scripta* (courtesy of Vivien-Roels, 1969). The presynaptic terminals are characterized by an abundance of vesicles, 150–450 Å in diameter, and a few of which are dense-cored (as at star). Within the postsynaptic neurone cytoplasm Nissl substance is shown. × 24 000.

(Petit, 1967), "nutritive cells" (Scatizzi, 1933) and "epithelial cells of type II" (Grignon and Grignon, 1963a), as well as the more frequently and generally applied categories, "ependymal" and "supportive cells". Additionally, a more conservative approach would entail considering them ependymal-like ("ependymoid") rather than comparable to the fully differentiated ependymal cells of the brain's ventricular system. More remotely yet, these cells may be in some degree analogous to the pigment cells in the retina of the parietal eye of lizards and to the cells of Müller in the retina of its lateral eye. In the pineal gland of *Chrysemys* the luminal ends of the ependymoid or supportive cells are characterized by microvilli

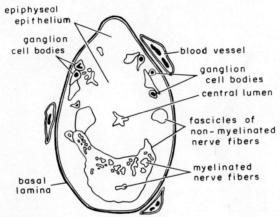

FIG. 41. Diagrammatic transverse section through a posterior or basal region of the pineal (epiphysis) of *Chrysemys* sp., showing the organization of the nerve (ganglion) cells and fibers (adapted from Vivien and Roels, 1968).

and cilia (Figs 29 and 30). Their cytoplasm contains microfilaments (microfibrillae).

4. *Neurons and Innervation*

The nervous tissue within the pineal organ of turtles provides the strongest evidence for pineal sensory function in these animals (Vivien-Roels, 1969). The pineal of turtles is in this regard intermediate between the clearly sensory parietal eye structure of some lizards and the essentially non-sensory pineal structure of snakes. This structural, and presumably functional intermediacy, of the testudinian pineal does not imply an evolutionarly intermediate position. Rather, the evolutionary transformation from a presumably mostly sensory structure to a glandular one has not progressed as far in turtles as in living snakes, mammals and many birds in separate evolutionary lines of descent.

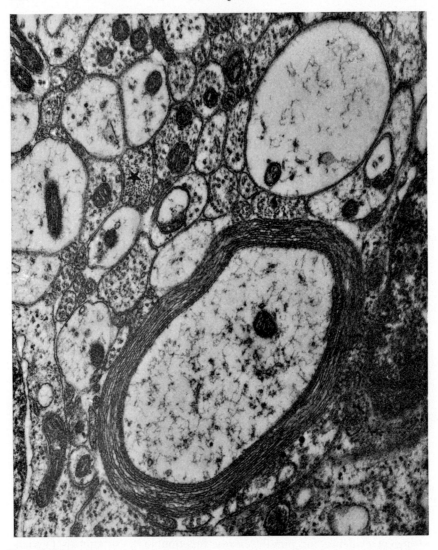

FIG. 42. Ultrastructure of the plexiform or nerve fiber zone in the posterior pineal of *Chrysemys scripta* (courtesy of Vivien-Roels, 1969). A large myelinated nerve fiber, non-myelinated nerve fibers, fibers and processes containing microtubules, and a process containing microfilaments (*) are shown. × 30 000.

The functionally most suggestive component or linkage in the neural tissue of the testudinian pineal is the synaptic contact made by the basal cytoplasmic processes of the "pseudosensory" pinealocytes, especially in the nerve fiber or plexiform layer of the posterior wall of the organ (Vivien

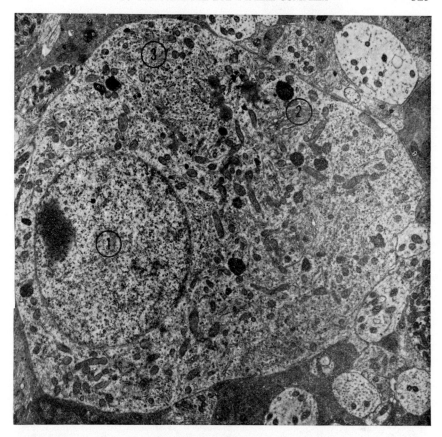

FIG. 43. Neuron cell body within the basal plexiform or nerve fiber zone of the postero-dorsal pineal of *Chrysemys scripta* (courtesy of Vivien-Roels, 1969). (1), Nucleus; (2), Golgi vesicles; (3), Nissl substance. ×7200.

and Roels, 1968; Vivien-Roels, 1969, 1970). Typical neurosensory junctions are seen (Fig. 38), while other kinds of synaptic contacts also occur (Figs. 39 and 40) in this outer fibrous or plexiform layer. Some of these junctions involve typical ganglion or nerve cell bodies, which are found both in this outer zone (Figs 41, 42 and 43) and in the stalk region (Figs 44, 45 and 46). A "pineal nerve" is formed (Figs 44 to 47). It consists of two lateral bundles of myelinated fibers along with many non-myelinated fibers, some of which contain granulated vesicles (Fig. 48). Some pineal nerve fibers course rostrally to the habenular commissure, but most of them run caudally between the posterior commissure and the subcommissural organ (Figs 45, 46 and 47). The ultimate destinations of any of these pineal nerve fibers remain to be demonstrated. This information would be of the greatest

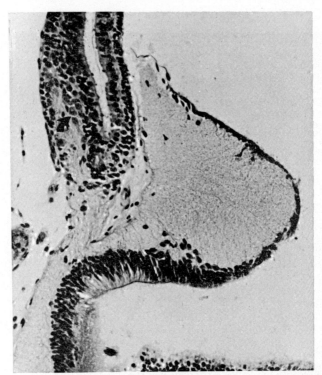

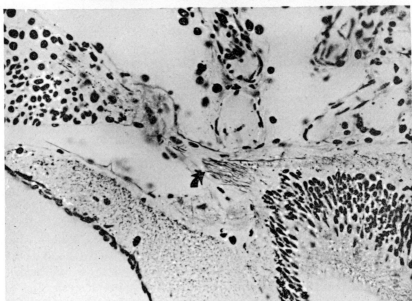

FIG. 44. Nervous tissue in the epiphyseal stalk of *Chrysemys scripta* (courtesy of Vivien-Roels, 1969). Top. Near sagittal section of posterior epiphysis and stalk (upper left), containing nerve fibers along the length of the dorsal wall and nerve cell bodies (at arrow) in this stalk region. Hematoxylin and eosin. ×224. Bottom. Fascicles of nerve fibers (at arrow) in the region of the stalk. Impregnation according to the Bodian–Ziesmer technique. ×320.

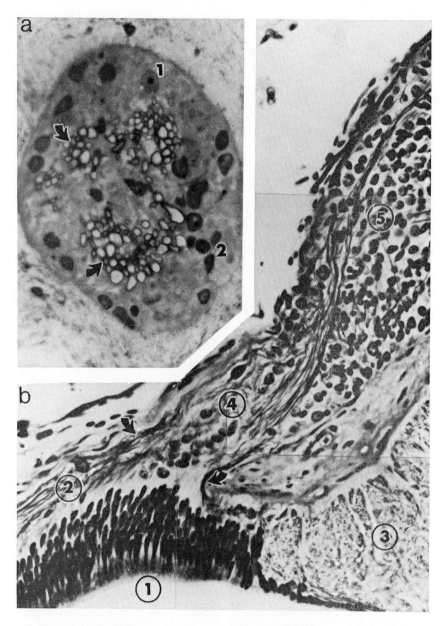

FIG. 45. Nervous tissue of the epiphyseal stalk region in *Chrysemys scripta* (courtesy of Vivien-Roels, 1970). a. Transverse section of epiphyseal stalk. Mallory (azure II) stain. Evident at this intermediate magnification ($\times 720$) are fascicles of myelinated nerve fibers (as at arrows), neurone cell body (1), and "supportive" cells (2). b. Parasagittal section of the epiphyseal stalk region, showing the subcommissural organ (1), posterior commissure (2), habenular commissure (3), epiphyseal stalk tissue (4), epiphyseal or pineal tissue (5), and fascicles of nerve fibers (as at arrows). Fitzgerald impregnation technique. $\times 480$.

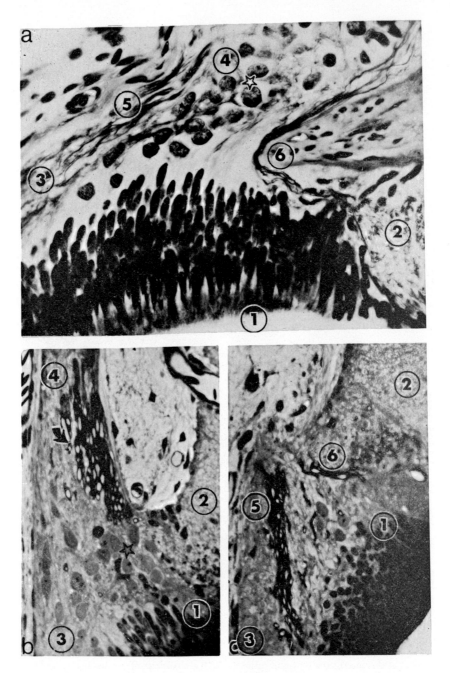

FIG. 46. Parasagittal sections of basal portions and nerve fiber relations of the epiphyseal stalk in *Chrysemys scripta* (courtesy of Vivien-Roels, 1970). a. Histological section, Fitzgerald technique, ×640. b and c. Thin section, Mallory technique, ×400.

Key: (1), subcommissural organ; (2), habenular commissure; (3), posterior commissure; (4), epiphyseal stalk; (5), dorsoposterior branch or division of the epiphyseal nerve tract; (6), anteroventral branch or division of the epiphyseal nerve tract directed towards the habenular commissure; →, point of division or separation of the two branches of the epiphyseal nerve tract; *, neuron cell bodies in epiphyseal stalk.

importance in ascertaining the neurological and possible functional relations of the presumably sensory pineal input.

5. *Vasculature*

The vascular contents and relations of the testudinian pineal organ are comparatively poorly known. Electron micrographs of the organ in *Testudo hermanni* show a very wide perivascular space containing fibrocytes and collagen fibers (Mehring, 1972). Communications between the perivascular

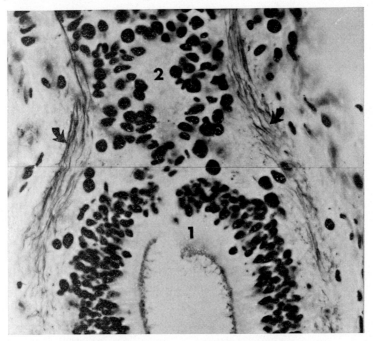

FIG. 47. Vertical (horizontal) section through the subcommissural organ (1) and epiphyseal stalk (2) of *Chrysemys scripta* (courtesy of Vivien-Roels, 1970). Bilateral fascicles of the epiphyseal nerve tract are shown at arrows. Bodian–Ziesmer impregnation. × 480.

space and the intercellular spaces within the parenchyma of the organ could not be demonstrated. Furthermore, an osmiophilic material of unknown nature often fills the intercellular spaces, but not the perivascular ones.

B. SAURIA

1. *Anatomy and Histology*

The parietal eye–pineal complex has been studied microscopically in more genera and species of lizards than in those of any other group of reptiles (Table XII). Relatively little has been published about the complex in the

TABLE XII

Descriptions of fundamental and adult structures of the parietal eye–pineal complex in saurians

Family	Species (References)
Iguanidae	*Anolis carolinensis* (Lierse, 1965a, b; McDevitt, 1972; Ortman, 1960)
	Anolis cristatellus (Schmidt, 1909)
	Anolis extremus (Lierse, 1965a, b)
	Anolis pulchellus (Saurez, 1969)
	Anolis sp. (Schmidt, 1909; Spencer, 1886c)
	Crotaphytus collaris (Trost, 1956)
	Iguana iguana (Oksche and Kirschstein, 1966a, b; Sivak, 1973
	Iguana iguana (de Klinckowström, 1893, 1894; Leydig, 1896; Oksche and Kirschstein, 1966a, b; Schmidt, 1909; Sivak, 1973; Spencer, 1886c)
	Iguana sp. (Spencer, 1886a, c)
	Liolaemus chiliensis (Trost, 1954, 1956)
	Liolaemus nitidus (Schmidt, 1909; Spencer, 1886a, c)
	Liolaemus pictus (Trost, 1956)
	Liolaemus tenuis (Schmidt, 1909; Spencer, 1886c)
	Oplurus sebae (Schmidt, 1909)
	Phrynosoma coronatum (Ritter, 1890, 1894; Schmidt, 1909; Sorenson, 1893)
	Phrynosoma douglassii (Ritter, 1890; Schmidt, 1909)
	Phrynosoma orbiculare (Studnička, 1905)
	Phymaturus palluma (Schmidt, 1909)
	Plica umbra (Schmidt, 1909; Spencer, 1886a, c)
	Sceloporus occidentalis (Eakin, 1960, 1963, 1964a, 1968, 1970, 1973; Eakin et al., 1961; Eakin and Stebbins, 1959; Eakin and Westfall, 1959, 1960, 1962; Stebbins and Eakin, 1958; Stebbins and Tong, 1973)
	Sceloporus striatus (Schmidt, 1909; Sorenson, 1894)
	Sceloporus undulatus (Herrick, 1893; Schmidt, 1909; Trost, 1956)
	Uta stansburiana (Ritter, 1890; Schmidt, 1909)
Agamidae	*Agama agilis* (Trost, 1956)
	Agama agilis sanguinolenta (Schmidt, 1909)
	Agama atra (Steyn, 1958)
	Agama impalearis (Schmidt, 1909)
	Agama caucasica (Owsjannikow, 1888; Ritter, 1894; Schmidt, 1909; Trost, 1954, 1956)
	Agama agama (Stigler, 1950)
	Agama hispida (Schmidt, 1909; Spencer, 1886c)
	Agama microlepis (Trost, 1954, 1956)
	Agama mutabilis (Schmidt, 1909; Trost, 1956)
	Agama ruderata (Trost, 1954, 1956)
	Agama stellio (Spencer, 1886c; Trost, 1950, 1954)

TABLE XII—contd.

Family	Species (References)
	Amphibolurus barbatus (Schmidt, 1909)
	Amphibolurus barbatus (McKay, 1888; Spencer, 1886a, c)
	Amphibolurus muricatus (Schmidt, 1909)
	Calotes calotes (Schmidt, 1909; Spencer, 1886c)
	Calotes cristatellus (Schmidt, 1909)
	Calotes versicolor (Schmidt, 1909; Spencer, 1886c)
	Calotes sp. (Spencer, 1886c)
	Ceratophora aspera (Schmidt, 1909; Spencer, 1886b)
	Ceratophora stoddartii (Trost, 1956)
	Draco volans (Schmidt, 1909; Spencer, 1886c)
	Draco sp. (Trost, 1956)
	Lyriocephalus scutatus (Schmidt, 1909; Spencer, 1886c)
	Moloch horridus (Schmidt, 1909; Spencer, 1886c; Trost, 1956)
	Phrynocephalus helioscopus (Trost, 1956)
	Phrynocephalus maculatus (Trost, 1956)
	Phrynocephalus scutellatus (Trost, 1956)
	Phrynocephalus vlangalii (Owsjannikow, 1888; Schmidt, 1909)
	Agama stellio (Spencer, 1886a, c)
	Uromastyx acanthinurus (Schmidt, 1909)
Chameleonidae	*Brookesia stumpffi* (Schmidt, 1909)
	Chamaeleo bifidus (Spencer, 1886c)
	Chamaeleo chamaeleon (Owsjannikow, 1888; Schmidt, 1909; Spencer, 1886a, c; Studnička, 1905)
	Chamaeleo gracilis (Schmidt, 1909)
	Chamaeleo lateralis (Grignon and Grignon, 1963b)
	Chamaeleo pardalis (Schmidt, 1909)
	Chamaeleo sp. (Schauinsland, 1903)
Gekkonidae	*Cosymbotus platyurus* (Yeager and Chang, 1972)
	Gehyra oceanica (Schmidt, 1909; Stemmler, 1900)
	Gekko gecko (Schmidt, 1909; Spencer, 1886c)
	Hemidactylus mabouia (Schmidt, 1909; Stemmler, 1900)
	Hemidactylus turcicus (Leydig, 1890a, b, 1897; Schmidt, 1909)
	Phelsuma madagascariensis (Schmidt, 1909)
	Tarentola annularis (Schmidt, 1909)
	Tarentola delalandii (Schmidt, 1909)
	Tarentola mauritanica (Collin, 1968b; Collin and Kappers, 1968; Leydig, 1897; Schmidt, 1909; Spencer, 1886c)
	Tarentola (Leydig, 1890b; Melchers, 1900; Spencer, 1886c; Studnička, 1905)
	Tarentola neglecta (Schmidt, 1909)
Teiidae	*Ameiva corvina* (Schmidt, 1909; Spencer, 1886c)

TABLE XII—contd.

Family	Species (References)
Scincidae	*Tupinambis teguixin* (Schmidt, 1909)
	Ablepharus kitaibelii (Trost, 1956)
	Acontias percivali (Gundy and Ralph, 1971)
	Chalcides chalcides (Boveri, 1925; Gundy and Ralph, 1971; Leydig, 1890b; Schmidt, 1909; Spencer, 1886a, b, c; Trost, 1956)
	Chalcides monodactylus (Trost, 1956)
	Chalcides ocellatus (Oksche, 1965; Schmidt, 1909; Trost, 1952, 1953b, 1956)
	Eumeces fasciatus (Gundy and Ralph, 1971)
	Eumeces obsoletus (Gundy and Ralph, 1971)
	Eumeces schneiderii (Schmidt, 1909)
	Feylinia currori (Gundy and Ralph, 1971)
	Lygosoma smaragdinum (Schmidt, 1909)
	Lygosoma sp. (McKay, 1888; Sorensen, 1894)
	Lygosoma taeniolatum (Schmidt, 1909)
	Mabuya elegans (Schmidt, 1909)
	Mabuya multicarinata (Schmidt, 1909)
	Mabuya quinquetaeniata (Schmidt, 1909)
	Mabuya sulcata (Steyn, 1957, 1958, 1959a)
	Mabuya vittata (Trost, 1956)
	Riopa sundevalli (Gundy and Ralph, 1971)
	Scincella lateralis (Gundy and Ralph, 1971)
	Scincus scincus (Prenant, 1895; Schmidt, 1909)
	Scincus scincus (Trost, 1956)
	Tiliqua casuarinae (Trost, 1956)
	Tiliqua gigas (Schmidt, 1909)
	Voeltzkowia mira (Schmidt, 1909)
Lacertidae	*Acanthodactylus boskianus* (Schmidt, 1909)
	Acanthodactylus erythrurus (Schmidt, 1909)
	Acanthodactylus pardalis (Trost, 1956)
	Acanthodactylus scutellatus (Schmidt, 1909; Trost, 1956)
	Eremias argutas (Schmidt, 1909)
	Eremias guttulata (Schmidt, 1909; Trost, 1956)
	Eremias velox (Schmidt, 1909; Trost, 1956)
	Lacerta agilis (de Graaf, 1886; Grignon and Grignon, 1963b; von Haffner, 1953; Leydig, 1872, 1889, 1890a, b; 1896; Nowikoff, 1907, 1910; Oksche, 1965; Owsjannikow, 1888; Preisler, 1942; Schmidt, 1909; Studnička, 1905; Trost, 1956)
	Lacerta cauasica (Stammer, 1967)
	Lacerta dugesi (Schmidt, 1909)
	Lacerta galloti (Schmidt, 1909)
	Lacerta laevis (Trost, 1956)

TABLE XII—contd.

Family	Species (Family)
	Lacerta lepida (Leydig, 1889, 1890a, b; Schmidt, 1909; Spencer, 1886a, c)
	Lacerta muralis (Collin, 1968a, b, 1971; Collin and Kappers, 1968; Leydig, 1872, 1889, 1890a, b; Nowikoff, 1910; Preisler, 1942; Schmidt, 1909; Studnička, 1893; Swain, 1968; Wartenberg, 1969; Wartenberg and Baumgarten, 1968, 1969a, b)
	Lacerta saxicola (Trost, 1956)
	Lacerta sicula (Preisler, 1942)
	Lacerta viridis (Collin, 1967a, b, c, 1968a, 1971; Collin and Kappers, 1968; Grignon and Grignon, 1963b; Kappers, 1966, 1967; Leydig, 1890a, b; Lierse, 1965a, b; Schmidt, 1909; Spencer, 1886c; Wartenberg, 1969; Wartenberg and Baumgarten, 1968, 1969a)
	Lacerta vivipara (Collin and Kappers, 1971; Collin and Meiniel, 1972, 1973; Grignon and Grignon, 1963b; von Haffner, 1953, 1955; Leydig, 1872; Meiniel and Collin, 1970; Meiniel *et al.*, 1972; Meiniel *et al.*, 1973; Nowikoff, 1910; Schmidt, 1909; Spencer, 1886a, c; Studnička, 1905)
	Lacerta sp. (Leydig, 1887)
	Ophisops elegans (Trost, 1956)
	Ophisops occidentalis (Schmidt, 1909)
	Psammodromus algirus (Schmidt, 1909; Trost, 1956)
Cordylidae	*Cordylus polyzonus* (Steyn, 1957, 1958, 1959a, 1960a, b; Steyn and Steyn, 1962, 1965)
Gerrhosauridae	*Gerrhosaurus nigrolineatus* (Schmidt, 1909)
	Zonosaurus madagascariensis (Schmidt, 1909)
Anguidae	*Anguis fragilis* (Béraneck, 1892; Carriére, 1890; Collin, 1968a, b; Duval and Kalt, 1889; Francotte, 1896; de Graaf, 1886; Hanitsch, 1888; Leydig, 1872, 1887, 1889, 1896; Nowikoff, 1907; Owsjannikow, 1888; Petit, 1968, 1969; Prenant, 1894; Schmidt, 1909; Spencer, 1886a, b, c; Strahl and Martin, 1888; Studnička, 1893; Trost, 1952, 1953b)
	Ophisaurus apodus (Hoffmann, 1890; Owsjannikow, 1888; Schmidt, 1909, Studnička, 1905)
Anniellidae	*Anniella pulchra* (Coe and Kunkel, 1906)
Varanidae	*Varanus bengalensis* (Schmidt, 1909; Spencer, 1886a, c)
	Varanus bengalensis nebulosus (Leydig, 1890a, b; Schmidt, 1909)
	Varanus giganteus (Schmidt, 1909; Spencer, 1886a, c; Studnička, 1905)
	Varanus griseus (Schmidt, 1909)
	Varanus niloticus (Leydig, 1889)

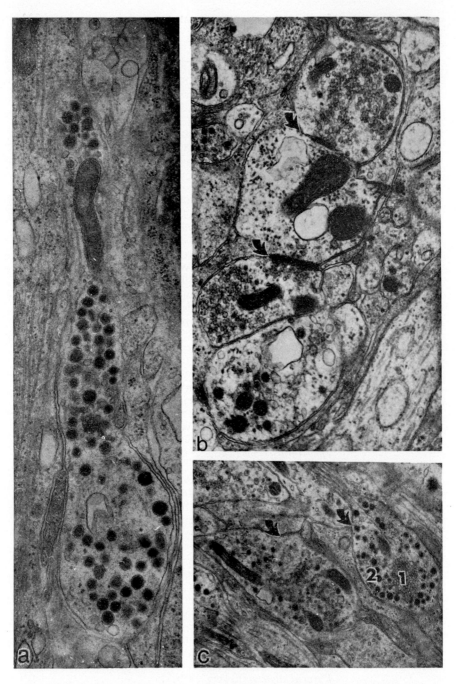

Fig. 48. Sagittal sections within (a) and at the base (b and c) of the epiphyseal stalk, of *Chrysemys scripta* (courtesy of Vivien-Roels, 1970). a. Non-myelinated nerve fiber containing granulated vesicles, ×24 000. b. Interneuronal synapses (at arrows), ×22 500. c. Terminal boutons (at arrows) of non-myelinated fibers containing both small synaptic vesicles (as at 1) and dense granules or granulated vesicles (as at 2), ×16 000.

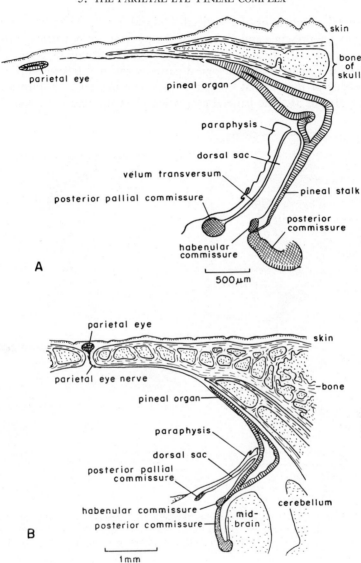

FIG. 49. Diagrammatic sagittal sections through the parietal eye–pineal complex of: (A) an iguanid, *Oplurus sebae*; and (B) a chameleonid, *Chamaeleo pardalis*. Anterior is to the left. (Adapted from Schmidt, 1909.)

families Pygopodidae, Dibamidae, Xantusiidae, Anelytropsidae, Xenosauridae, Helodermatidae and Lanthanotidae. There are many statements scattered in the literature on these and other groups that only indicate the presence or absence of some superficially visible component, usually either the parietal foramen or the parietal ("pineal") eye. More concentrated listings of the presence and absence of the parietal eye in particular lizards have been given by McKay (1888), Camp (1923) and Gundy *et al.* (1975).

The wide variety of morphological patterns and interrelationships of the components of the parietal eye–pineal complex in lizards is illustrated in Figs 49, 50 and 51. The parietal eye, when present, often lies considerably

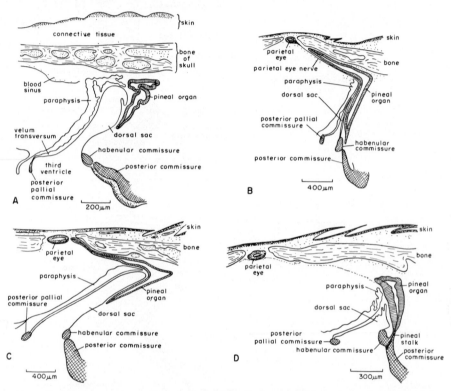

FIG. 50. Diagrammatic sagittal sections through the parietal eye–pineal complex of: (A) a gekkonid, *Phelsuma madagascariensis*; and three scincids—(B) *Mabuya elegans*, (C) *Eumeces schneiderii*, (D) *Chalcides chalcides*. Anterior is to the left. (Adapted from Schmidt, 1909.)

anterior to and from the pineal organ. But in some instances adults show it closer to the distal tip of the pineal organ, in part due to an anterior extension of the latter (Fig. 50B, C). Phylogenetic losses of the parietal eye and foramen usually but not always occur in parallel, as demonstrated by the survival of the eye under the imperforate parietal bones of *Gerrhosaurus* (Fig. 51D) and *Anniella* (Coe and Kunkel, 1906; Schmidt, 1909).

For over sixty years there have been attempts to correlate presence versus absence of the parietal eye with differences in habits or environments of lizards. Families that have lost the parietal eye in living genera examined thus far (Table XIII) range from mostly arboreal representatives (geckos) to terrestrial and burrowing types (pygopodids, dibamids and others). Other

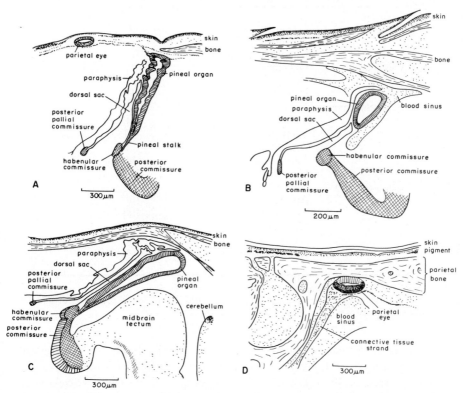

FIG. 51. Diagrammatic sagittal sections through the parietal eye–pineal complex (A, B, C) or the parietal eye alone of (A) a lacertid, *Lacerta galloti*; (B) a scincid, *Voeltzkowia mira*; and two gerrhosaurids—(C) *Zonosaurus madagascariensis*, (D) *Gerrhosaurus nigrolineatus*. Anterior is to the left. (Adapted from Schmidt, 1909.)

groups that have burrowing or snake-like members often retain the parietal eye (Anguidae, Anniellidae). Thus at best only an incomplete correlation is the basis of belief "that a subterreanean habit may result in regression of the pineal complex", as was suggested by Gundy and Ralph (1971) as well as by some earlier investigators.

Correlation of loss of the parietal eye with nocturnality in lizards has numerous exceptions (such as diurnal species of teiids and some geckos). However, most of the saurian species that lack parietal eyes are believed to

TABLE XIII

Occurrence of the parietal eye in families of lizards
(Adapted from Gundy et al., 1975)

Infraorder	Family	Genera in which parietal eye visible (%)
Iguania	Iguanidae (53/53)[a]	96–98
	Agamidae (29/33)[a]	83
	Chamaeleonidae	100
Gekkota	Gekkonidae	0[b]
	Pygopodidae	0
	Dibamidae	0
Scincomorpha	Xantusiidae	100
	Teiidae	0[b]
	Scincidae	91–95
	Anelytropsidae	0
	Lacertidae	90
	Cordylidae	100
Anguimorpha	Anguidae	100
	Anniellidae	100
	Xenosauridae	100
	Helodermatidae	0
	Varanidae	100
	Lanthanotidae	0

[a] Number of genera examined/number of genera known for family.
[b] Absence of the parietal eye could not be confirmed definitely in one of the genera because of insufficient specimens (G. C. Gundy, pers. commun.).

be either nocturnal or crepuscular. At the family level, the correlation appears to be true for six of the seven families that lack parietal eyes (G. C. Gundy, pers. commun.). Such relatively simple, single factor correlations remain chancy due to the seasonal or other variables that may lead to shifts in timing of daily activity (as in *Xantusia, Heloderma* among others). Most recently, Gundy *et al.* (1974, 1975) have suggested that lack of parietal eyes is primarily restricted to species that are geographically restricted to relatively low (tropical) latitudes (Table XIV) and that possession of a parietal eye might in some way facilitate survival at higher latitudes, perhaps in relation to timing of reproductive activity and thermoregulation. If the parietal eye is physiologically important for such adaptations at higher latitudes, it would seem of interest to evaluate and compare the possible clines in presence or size of parietal eyes in relation to altitude in equatorial and low temperate zones. It might be hypothesized that if the parietal eye is functionally advantageous in monitoring changing photoperiod in order

TABLE XIV

Occurrences and absences of the parietal eye in genera in relation to latitude.
(Adapted primarily from Gundy et al., 1975)

Family	Parietal eye occurrence	Centers of abundance by latitude			Latitudinal range
		°S Latitude	Equator 0°	°N Latitude	
Iguanidae	with (52)[a]		21°[9]	32°[10]	55°S 48°N
	without (1)[1]		1°		12°S 10°N
Agamidae	with (24)	30°[7]	24°[8]; 0°[7]; 10°[7]; 12°[8]; 24°[8]		44°S 50°N
	without (5)[2]		0°		8°S 24°N
Teiidae	with (0)				
	without (31)		0°[18]		40°S 43°N
Scincidae	with (61)				46°S 48°N
	without (3)[3]	6°			25°S 13°N
Lacertidae	with (18)				66½°N
	without (2)[4]		9·5°		4°S 10°N
Gekkonidae	with (0)				
	without (67)	25°[10]; 22°[9]	0°[9]; 5°[9]; 9°[10]		45°S 46°N

[a] ( ) = Number of general in which parietal eye is known to be present (with) or absent (without).
[ ] = number of general that geographically overlap at that particular latitude (center of abundance)
[1] = *Uracentron.*
[2] = *Cophotis, Harpesaura, Leiolepis, Lophocalotes* and *Phoxophrys.*
[3] = *Corucia, Ristella* and *Voeltzkowia.*
[4] = *Holaspis* and *Philochortus.*

to optimize seasonal timing of reproductive and other activities, it would be maintained more at higher altitudes especially as one passes away from the equatorial zone. On the other hand, if parietal eye function includes a significant physiological relation to shorter term thermoregulation and behavior, then one might expect it to be maintained more frequently at higher elevations whether or not in equatorial or temperate zones. Beyond such relatively gross and speculative hypotheses there remains a need for tracing evolutionary changes of the parietal eye–pineal complex within particular taxa of lizards. As yet, the phylogenetic and ecological histories of lines showing loss of parietal eyes have not been studied in this way.

The integument over a parietal eye is often modified to form a cornea, with at least some modification of pigmentation and physical characteristics. Most superficially or externally this is usually visible as a raised and less pigmented spot within the interparietal scale. The ranges in relative size

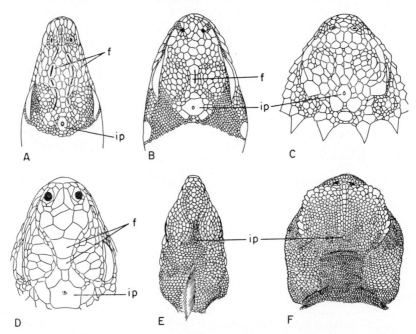

FIG. 52. Head shield scales in the region of the parietal eye (under the interparietal scale) of iguanid (A–D) and agamid (E, F) lizards. Magnification varies. (Adapted from M. A. Smith, 1935, and H. M. Smith, 1946.) A. *Anolis carolinensis*; B. *Callisaurus draconoides*; C. *Phrynosoma platyrhinos*; D. *Sceloporus cyanogenys*; E. *Calotes emma*; F. *Phrynocephalus maculatus*. f, Frontal scale(s); ip, interparietal scale.

and position of this scale and its part of the parietal eye cornea are illustrated in Figs 52 and 53.

While approximately 41% of all examined living lizard genera lack parietal eyes (Gundy *et al.*, 1975), apparently all still have a pineal organ or epiphysis. However, the pineal organ has been studied in fewer genera than has the parietal eye; the pineal is usually invisible externally and requires serial histological sections of the region between brain roof and skull for a reliable evaluation of either its presence or its structure. Where the parietal eye is lacking the pineal organ may be either somewhat smaller than usual (gekkonids, Fig. 50A) or retain its normal size. When the parietal eye is missing the pineal organ is often more club-shaped, clavate or saccular, in contrast to the often more complex, bent and folded patterns common in taxa possessing a parietal eye.

In general, the distal or dorsal part of the pineal organ extends dorsally to, and sometimes along, the connective tissue underlying or bounding the inner lamina of the medial bones of the skull (Figs 49, 50 and 51). Proximally or basally the pineal organ of adult lizards varies greatly differing in

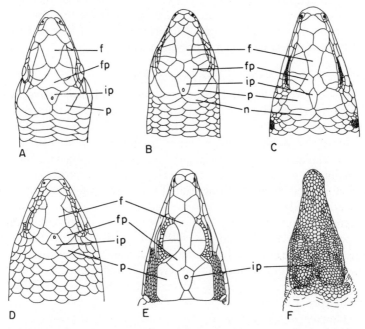

FIG. 53. Head shield scales in the region of the parietal eye (under the interparietal scale) of scincid (A–D), lacertid (E) and varanid (F) lizards. Magnification varies. (Adapted from M. A. Smith, 1935; and H. M. Smith, 1946.) A. *Ablepharus pannonicus*. B. *Eumeces septentrionalis*. C. *Mabuya rudis*. D. *Ateuchosaurus chinensis*. E. *Eremias guttulata*. F. *Varanus bengalensis nebulosus*. f, Frontal scale(s); fp, frontoparietal scale(s); ip, interparietal scale; n, nuchal scale(s); p, parietal scale(s).

the retention of the embryonic attachment of parenchyma to the brain in the form of a stalk, as contrasted to a parenchyma more or less distant from the roof of the brain (Figs 49, 50 and 51). In either case the pineal lumen is nearly always closed off in the stalk region (Schmidt, 1909), resulting in its isolation from the brain's ventricular system and suggesting the unlikelihood that a luminal pineal secretion would have direct access to cerebrospinal fluid in the ventricular system. In this regard the lizard pineal organ differs from that of amphibians and most closely resembles that of many birds.

The medial roof of the lizard forebrain has two thin-walled and ependy-mally lined diverticula or sacculations anterior, and often closely applied, to the pineal organ. These are the dorsal sac and the paraphysis (Figs 49, 50 and 51). Although they have received only scant attention in the literature on the reptilian pineal organ, it has been suggested recently that in some mammals the dorsal sac is part of a theoretically possible indirect route whereby secretions may reach the cerebrospinal fluid circulation in the third ventricle (Quay, 1973; Reiter *et al.*, 1975). The actual functioning of such a humoral transport route in reptiles or mammals presupposes more detailed anatomical and physiological information about this structure and its pineal vascular relations than is presently available.

2. *Structure and Composition of the Parietal Eye*

The parietal eye of lizards is usually a single epithelial vesicle, with its dorsal wall transformed into a lens and its more ventral portions represent-ing a retina (Fig. 54). However, the parietal eye vesicle in some individuals may atypically be double or may contain, or be associated with, accessory vesicles of similar or sometimes simpler composition (von Haffner, 1955). Occasionally the parietal eye may be developmentally anomalous or ectopic in position, and be incompletely separated from the epithelium of the pineal organ (Eakin, 1964a, 1973).

The lens, as typified by that of *Sceloporus occidentalis*, is composed of a closely packed palisade of elongate cells with nuclei toward their luminal end (Fig. 54). At the other and more superficial end the lens is fused with the cornea. This consists of an inner fibrous layer, a middle less dense connective tissue layer continuous with the dermis of adjacent skin, and an outer epidermal layer (Fig. 54).

The elements of the retina are the structurally and functionally most important components of the parietal eye. Three kinds of retinal cells are generally prominent: sensory (photoreceptoral), supportive and ganglionic (neuronal) cells. The sensory cells are columnar, devoid of dark pigment, and have, one per cell, a photoreceptoral process projecting into the lumen of the eye. The forward projection of these parietal eye photoreceptoral processes is opposite to that of the rods and cones of vertebrate lateral eyes. The fine structure of the parietal eye photoreceptor cells and of their photoreceptor processes (Figs 55, 56) share many features with analogous receptor cells and cell processes in the retina of the lateral eye. The support-ive cells, interspersed among the retinal sensory cells, are also columnar, but contain melanin pigment granules. At least in some lizard species these pigment granules are subject to photomechanical responses, moving toward the cell apex (lumenward) during light adaptation, and toward the cell base in darkness (Nowikoff, 1910; Eakin *et al.*, 1961; Eakin, 1973). Retinal

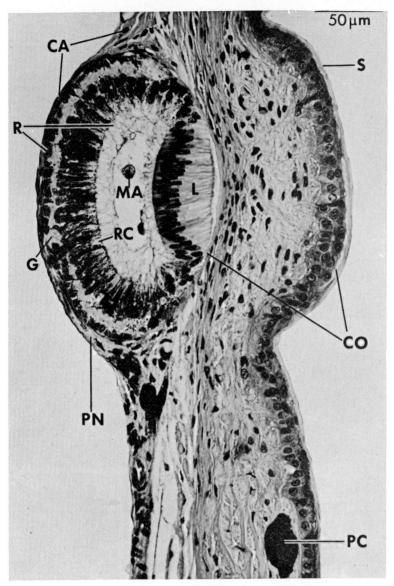

FIG. 54. Structure and composition of the parietal eye and its adnexa in the western fence lizard (*Sceloporus occidentalis*) as seen in a median longitudinal (sagittal) section. (Courtesy of Eakin, 1973.) CA, Connective tissue capsule of the eye; CO, cornea (= essentially slightly modified integument overlying the eye); G, ganglion (nerve) cell; L, lens of the parietal eye; MA, macrophage (variably present and positioned) within the lumen of the parietal eye; PC, pigment cell in adjacent dermal connective tissue; PN, parietal (eye) nerve; R, retina of the parietal eye; RC, location of a receptor cell in the inner, columnar epithelium of the retina.

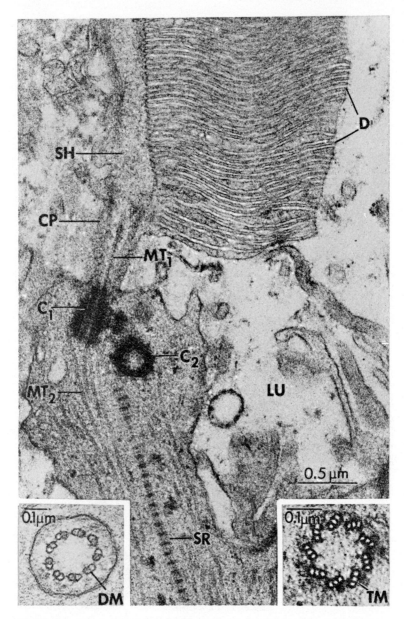

FIG. 55. Ultrastructure of the basal attachment, in longitudinal section, of a photoreceptor process (= modified cilium) of a western fence lizard (*Sceloporus occidentalis*). The inserts at lower left and right show cross sections respectively of the connecting piece and distal centriole. (Courtesy of Eakin, 1968, 1973.) C_1, distal centriole (kinetosome); C_2, accessory or proximal centriole; CP, connecting piece; D, disks in the outer segment of the photo-receptor process; DM, doublet of microtubules within the connecting piece; LU, lumen of the parietal eye; MT_1, a microtubule within the connecting piece; MT_2, a microtubule within the inner segment of the photoreceptor process; SH, shaft of the photoreceptor process (or modified cilium); SR, striated rootlet; TM, triplet of microtubules within the distal centriole.

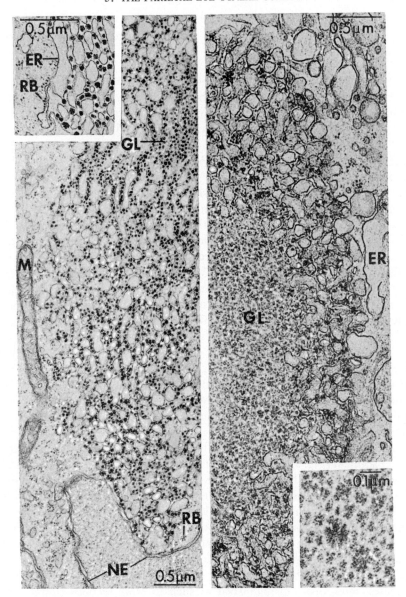

FIG. 56. Ultrastructure of the supranuclear masses of cisternae and glycogen (= so-called paraboloid) in sensory (receptor) cells in the western fence lizard's (*Sceloporus occidentalis*) parietal eye. (Courtesy of Eakin, 1964b, 1973.) ER, Cisternae of endoplasmic reticulum; GL, glycogen granules (beta particles in left and upper left insert, alpha particles in right and lower right insert); M, mitochondrion; NE, nuclear envelope (membrane); RB, ribosomes.

ganglion cells are relatively less numerous, but they stand out due to their large size, large nucleus and position within the outer and less pigmented tissue zone of the retina (Fig. 54).

3. *Ultrastructure and Identity of Parietal Eye Photoreceptors*

The distal or outer segment of the saurian parietal eye is a modified cilium, consisting of a series of superimposed disks or flattened sacs which are open to the cavity of the parietal eye (Fig. 55). Outer segments in the parietal eyes of *Sceloporus* and *Anguis* range from 10 to 17 μm in length and contain from 250 to 450 disks (Petit, 1968; Eakin, 1973). Each disk is about 2·5 μm in diameter and is 25–30 nm in thickness. The upper and lower membranes forming each disk are essentially comparable to cell membranes, each being about 7·5 nm thick. The space between the membranes of a disk is 10–15 nm in width. The disks are held together at the shaft, where their membranes are reflected (Fig. 55). The cytoplasm of this shaft of the outer segment (cilium) contains a bundle (axoneme) of microtubules. These (such as MT_2 in Fig. 55) extend distally from the base of the outer segment for much, perhaps about half, of the total length of the shaft. The outer segment below its first or most basal disk is constricted, forming the connecting piece (CP, Fig. 55), which joins it with the apical swelling of the cell proper, the region termed inner segment. Within and through the connecting piece the microtubules of the outer segment can be seen to run basally into the inner segment as far as the distal centriole (C_1, Fig. 55), also sometimes known as axial centriole, basal body or kinetosome. In cross section, the connecting piece shows the microtubules arranged in a ring of nine doublets (lower left insert, Fig. 55); central microtubules are missing.

As one progresses basally or away from the lumen one next encounters the inner segment (Fig. 55). This is essentially the apical cytoplasmic bulge of the photoreceptor cell beyond the level of close intercellular attachments bordering the lumen of the parietal eye. These cellular attachments, involving receptor and adjacent supportive cells, consist of junctional complexes, the most notable component of which is the desmosome. A centriolar apparatus is prominent within the inner segment and consists of a distal centriole (noted above) and a proximal (or accessory) centriole oriented at right angles to it (Fig. 55). Both are composed of bundles of nine triplets of microtubules, most easily distinguished as such in cross sections (lower right insert, Fig. 55). Extending basally from the centrioles and through the inner segment is the striated rootlet. Its cross banding consists of alternating light (about 55 nm wide) and dark (about 35 nm wide) bands or zones (SR, Fig. 55). It probably functions to anchor the centrioles and axoneme, while the distal centriole serves developmentally as the organizer of the sensory (outer segment) process. The function of the proximal centriole in this type of relationship remains enigmatic (Eakin, 1973).

The cytoplasmic region below the bulblike part of the inner segment has been called at times the ellipsoid, in analogy with a region having the corresponding position in cone cells of the frog's lateral eye retina. This ellipsoid region is notable primarily for its numerous mitochondria, especially at or near the basal end of the inner segment.

A still deeper or more basal cytoplasmic region in the parietal eye photoreceptor cell, but lying above the nucleus (supranuclear), has been called a paraboloid. Again this terminology begs analogy with a corresponding region in lateral eye photoreceptors of lower vertebrates. However, unlike the latter the paraboloid region of parietal eye receptor cells does not display a regularity or suggest optical function in its shape. On this basis and because of its distinctive ultrastructure, Eakin (1973) has suggested the wisdom of discarding this term from descriptions of this cytoplasmic region in parietal eye receptor cells. This supranuclear region is distinctive for its wealth of cisternae and interspersed cytoplasmic granules, including both ribosomes and glycogen granules (Fig. 56). The cisternae are parts of the fluid-filled channels of the endoplasmic reticulum, which ramifies and extends widely within each cell. In the supranuclear, so-called "paraboloid" region the cisternae vary in appearance from irregular interconnected spaces to more organized piles of more or less parallel cisternae (Petit, 1968). Within the center of this region glycogen granules are most densely concentrated, often to the near exclusion of cisternae, as at right in Fig. 56. The granular subunits of the clusters of glycogen granules are sometimes termed "beta particles", while the clusters themselves, often astral in appearance (lower right insert, Fig. 56), are called "alpha particles". The glycogen composition of the particles was determined by cytochemical studies showing that they stain by the periodic acid–Schiff (PAS) procedure and are selectively removed by prior treatment with α-amylase (Eakin et al., 1961; Petit, 1968). It appears likely that this region and its glycogen content are important during changing metabolic conditions, but data are insufficient for defining such a relationship. Variability in the glycogen deposits have been attributed tentatively to seasonal differences (Eakin, 1964a, 1973). Seemingly contradictory effects on the glycogen deposits have been observed following light or dark treatment. Several days of illumination have been reported to increase the glycogen granules in this region in *Anguis fragilis* (Petit, 1968); while dark-adapted rather than light-adapted *Sceloporus occidentalis* show glycogen granules more abundantly (Eakin et al., 1961).

The basal end of each of the parietal eye receptor cells is most notable for tapering to form a neurite or axon that makes synaptic contact with a ganglion cell (Fig. 54) towards the outer zone of the retina of the parietal eye.

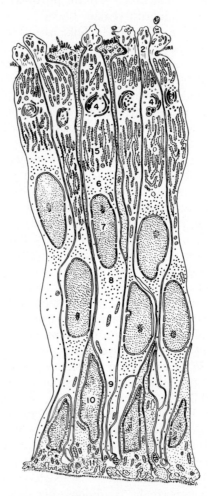

FIG. 57. Diagrammatic vertical section through a group of cells forming the wall of the pineal organ in *Lacerta viridis*. The luminal ends of the cells are at the top and their basal attachments are at the bottom of the figure. 1 to 9, Pinealocyte structures: 1, clublike portion of the inner segment; 2, neck or connecting piece; 3, ellipsoid, with a collection of mitochondria in its outer portion; 4, Golgi field with cytosome (type C); 5, zone containing rough endoplasmic reticulum (ER) in parallel arrays, and cytosome of type B; 6, cytoplasmic granules (type A) in supranuclear cytoplasm of pinealocyte; 7, nucleus; 8, cytoplasmic granules (type A) in subnuclear cytoplasm; 9, basal cytoplasmic process of pinealocyte. 10 and 11, Supporting cell (Stützzelle): 10, nucleus; 11, labyrinthine dilation of the supporting cell's basal and boundary region. ×1200. Adapted from Wartenberg and Baumgarten (1968).

Although it remains possible that some receptor axons or their collaterals, if there be such, bypass the ganglion cells and enter the parietal nerve directly, no such situation has yet been described (Eakin, 1973).

4. *Structure and Composition of the Pineal Organ*

The fine structure and intercellular relations of the saurian pineal have been described in *Lacerta viridis* and *L. muralis,* and have clarified and corrected many of the impressions gained during previous decades of dependence on light microscopy.

The most notable features of the cellular composition of the epithelial wall of the pineal organ are, firstly, the basic similarity to cell types in the retina of the parietal eye and, secondly, the partial transformation for secretory activity and for the probable control of such activity of certain of these cell types and of adjacent nerve and cell processes. These two themes have been described and discussed in detail by Collin (1967a, b, c, 1968a, b, 1969, 1971), Collin and Kappers (1968, 1971), Collin and Meiniel (1972b) and Meiniel (1974a, 1975a), Oksche (1971a, b), Oksche and Kirschstein (1966a, 1968), and Petit (1969). Although there is some general agreement about functional and evolutionary trends in the pineal organ of lizards, there remain many uncertainties and contradictions about important details and their proper interpretation. Electrophysiological recording (Hamasaki and Dodt, 1969) and electron microscopy (Hamasaki and Dodt, 1969) prove functional photoreceptive capacity in the saurian pineal organ. However, the pineal differs physiologically from the parietal eye (Hamasaki and Dodt, 1969) and the idea that photoreception occurs is not in accord with the absence of synaptic junctions between presumed sensory-type pinealocytes and the ganglion cells (Petit, 1969).

The structural and cytoplasmic zonation of the pinealocytes (Fig. 57) has many similarities to that of the parietal eye photo-receptor cells. The luminal tips of the pinealocytes develop through a similar sequence outer (external) segments or photoreceptor-type processes from a ciliary precursor (Fig. 58). However, their fates, secondary relations and functions may diverge from what might be expected of the outer segments of typical photoreceptors. These outer segments sometimes undergo cyclic degenerative changes and are associated with other luminal cell processes and cell products (Fig. 59). This includes axonal or cellular processes having the characteristics of noradrenergic fibers and endings (Fig. 60). The presumably efferent nature of these processes, and their association with the transformed receptor pinealocytes containing diverse granules and vesicles, has been viewed as supporting the acquisition of secretory function by the pinealocytes. However, the interrelations and complexity, as well as the diversity, of the luminal fibers, processes and endings within the saurian

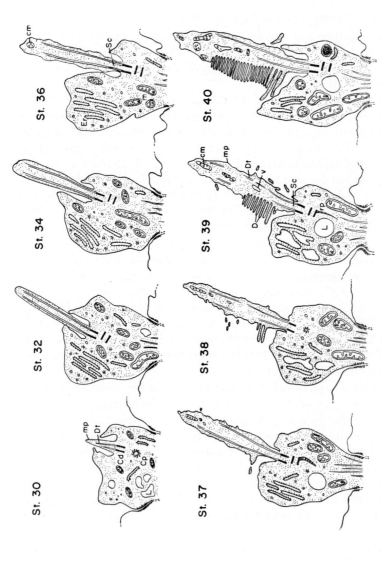

FIG. 58. Morphogenesis of the outer segment of pineal (epiphyseal) cells of the sensory type from embryonic stages of *Lacerta vivipara*. (Adapted from Meiniel, 1974a.) Compare with the same regions of parietal eye sensory cells (Fig. 55). cd, Distal centriole; cm, multi-vesicular body; Cp, proximal centriole; D, disks in the outer (external) segment; Dt, microtubule doublets in the shaft of the outer segment; Er, ergastoplasm; L, (lipid?) vacuole; m, mitochondria in basal portion of inner segment; mp, plasma membrane; rp, striated rootlet; Sc, connecting piece; v, vesicles.

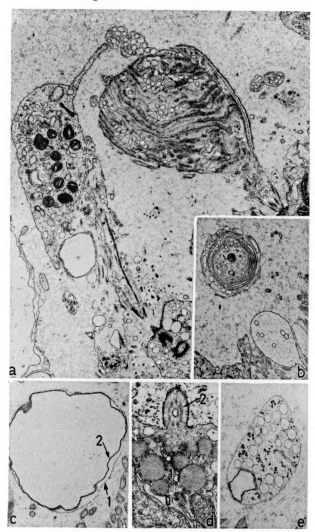

Fig. 59. Luminal structures in the pineal organ of *Lacerta viridis*. (Courtesy of Wartenberg and Baumgarten, 1968.) a. Rudimentary outer segment extending from a pinealocyte into the lumen. × 11 600. b. Structure resembling an outer segment. ×9 600. c. Large luminal vesicle in section bounded by an outer "contrast-poor" (less dense) membrane (1), and an inner "contrast-rich" (electron-dense) membrane (2). ×17 600. d. Section through the apical part of an inner segment, showing dense, homogenous granules (1) and an obliquely cut cilium (2). ×17 600. e. Section through a membrane-bounded body containing numerous small vesicles and glycogen granules. ×17 600.

352   W. B. QUAY

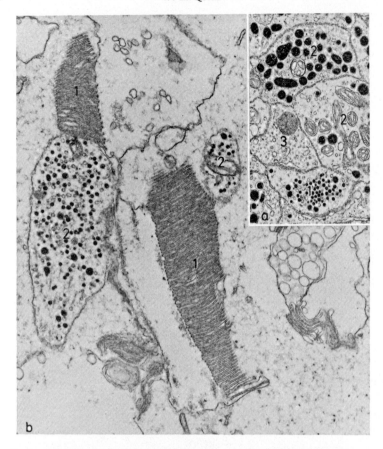

FIG. 60. Sections from the epithelial zone (a) and lumen (b) of the pineal organ of a
Lacerta muralis that had been injected with 200 mg/kg body weight of 5-hydroxydopa
24 and 2 hours prior to death and fixation. (Courtesy of Wartenberg and Baumgarten,
1969.) a. Small area of epithelial cells: 1, axon containing granulated vesicles as a result of
the treatment with 5-hydroxydopa; 2, pinealocyte processes containing larger granulated
vesicles the contents of which were not notably influenced by the prior treatment; 3, cell
process of unknown origin. × 16 800. b. Luminal structures: 1, outer segments of sensory-
type pinealocytes; 2, apparent axonal endings, which are recognized by their numerous
granulated vesicles. × 20 000.

pineal organ (Fig. 61) are still insufficiently understood to enable either a
facile or wholly convincing functional interpretation. Intercellular relations
are easier to ascertain within the epithelium of the pineal organ, and the
characteristics of cytoplasmic differentiation are more readily defined here
than in the photoreceptor cells of the parietal eye (Figs 62–65). The pinealocytes contain both apically (Figs 60, 62) and basally (Fig. 66) granular and/or

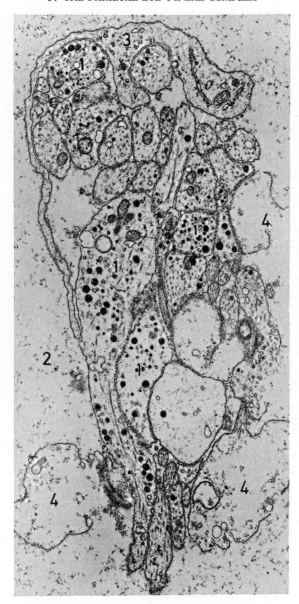

FIG. 61. Bundle of adrenergic nerve fibers or processes in the lumen of the pineal organ of a *Lacerta muralis*. This animal had been injected with 200 mg/kg body weight of 5-hydroxydopa 24 and 2 hours prior to death and fixation. × 11 200. (Courtesy of Wartenberg and Baumgarten, 1969b.) 1, Nerve fibers or processes in lumen of pineal organ; 2, lumen; 3, processes of glial cells partially covering the bundle; 4, axons or glial processes probably artifactually modified.

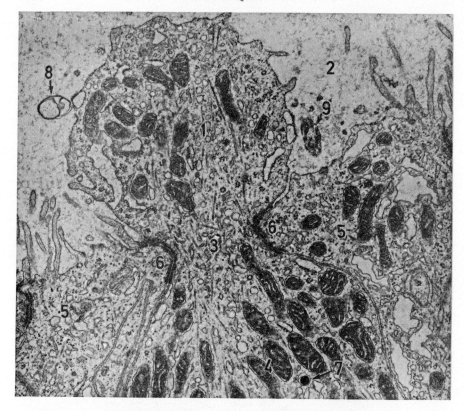

FIG. 62. Apical end of a pinealocyte in *Lacerta viridis*. (Courtesy of Wartenberg and Baumgarten, 1968. × 14 400. 1, Bulblike portion of the inner segment; 2, lumen of the pineal organ; 3, axis of the neck piece; 4, ellipsoid region (note numerous mitochondria); 5, apical cytoplasm of adjacent supporting cells; 6, intermediate junctions; 7, cytoplasmic granule of "type A"; 8, putative secretion vesicle; 9, obliquely cut cilium.

vesicular products that may represent presecretory materials. The electron-dense bodies and granules of the pinealocyte cytoplasm have been variously subdivided and classified into at least three categories (Wartenberg and Baumgarten, 1968; Petit, 1969).

1. Type A: Very dense, homogeneous and round bodies 60–200 nm in diameter and enveloped by a single membrane; the granule within the body generally does not fill the space enclosed by the membrane and often is eccentric in position (Figs 62, 64, 65, 66). Granules of type A are concentrated in cytoplasmic zones both above (toward the lumen) and below the nucleus, and in both the distal (luminal) and the basal processes of the pinealocytes. Various kinds of comparisons of these in

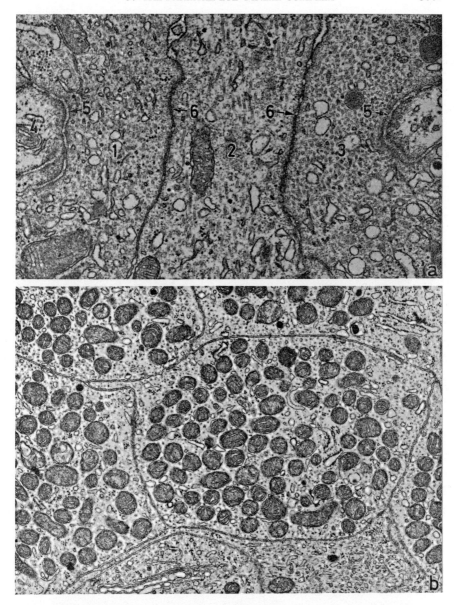

FIG. 63. Supranuclear cytoplasmic zones in pinealocytes of *Lacerta viridis*. (Courtesy of Wartenberg and Baumgarten, 1968.) a. Diagonal section through the neck piece of three adjacent pinealocytes (1, 2, 3). 4, Supporting cell; 5, "intermediate junctions"; 6, "tight junctions". × 30 000. b. Cross section through an inner zone with ellipsoid mitochondria. × 18 000.

356 W. B. QUAY

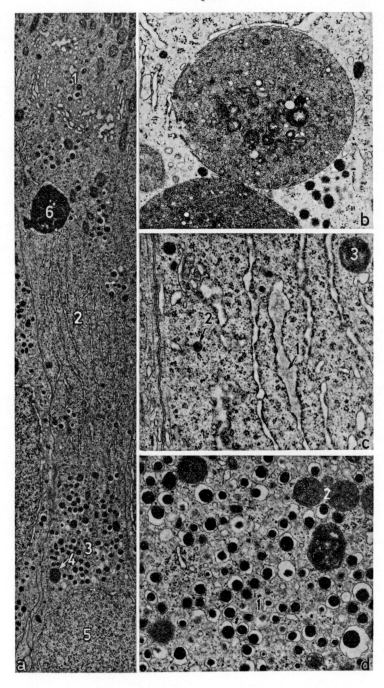

adults with patterns observed in cytochemical preparations (Falck-Hillarp method) suggest that they represent, at least in part, granules containing 5-hydroxytryptamine (serotonin) and related compounds (W. B. Quay, unpublished). Recent studies on such correlations have been extended to embryonic stages as well (Meiniel, 1975b).

2. Type B: Bodies of significantly greater diameter (400 nm) when fully developed, and with a usually less electron-dense granular content than those of type A. This granule content or interior consists of a finely granulated mass in which are embedded vesicles of varying size (Fig. 64b, c, d). Type B bodies (or granules) are only rarely found elsewhere than in the supranuclear zone of the inner segment.

3. Type C: Bodies of irregular shape and of very large (1–3 μm) diameter. Like the preceding two types of granules this one is also within a membrane, but its contents consist of subdivisions having diverse densities (Figs 64a and 65a, b). Type C are similar to type B bodies in appearing only in the supranuclear region of the pinealocyte cytoplasm.

The basal ends of the pinealocytes taper and split into very thin cell processes (Fig. 66) that are recognizable as pinealocyte processes by their content of type A bodies. The processes are partly concentrated in fascicles that generally follow a horizontal course through the outer or reticular zone of the epithelial wall of the pineal organ (Fig. 67). They frequently terminate in dilations of the extracellular space and in many respects resemble processes seen at the apical end of the pinealocytes and within the lumen of the organ.

In addition to the above described, and typical, kind of pinealocyte, there is a much less common second type ("type II", Fig. 65). These differ from the chief type ("type I") pinealocytes in two characteristics: (i) their mito-chondria are larger and less dense, as can be observed especially well within

---

FIG. 64. Structure of the supranuclear cytoplasmic regions of pinealocytes of *Lacerta*. (Courtesy of Wartenberg and Baumgarten, 1968.) a. Longitudinal (vertical) section through the supranuclear regions of *Lacerta viridis*. 1, Zone containing a Golgi field beneath the ellipsoid (at top edge of figure); 2, zone containing rough endoplasmic reticulum (ER) in a parallel (longitudinal) orientation; 3, cytoplasmic region capping the nucleus and containing dense granules of "type A" and "B" (4); 5, nucleus of the pinealocyte; 6, cytoplasmic body of "type C". ×7 600. b. Cytoplasmic body of "type B" (cytosome) from *Lacerta muralis*. ×20 000. c. Enlarged sector from the zone containing parallel ER (*Lacerta viridis*). 1, Widened ER cistern containing a flocculent material; 2, granule of "type A", 3, granule of "type B". ×20 000. d. Enlarged sector from the region capping the nucleus (*Lacerta viridis*). Compare with the paraboloid region of parietal eye receptor cells (Fig. 56). 1, Granule of "type A"; 2, granule of "type B". × 20 000.

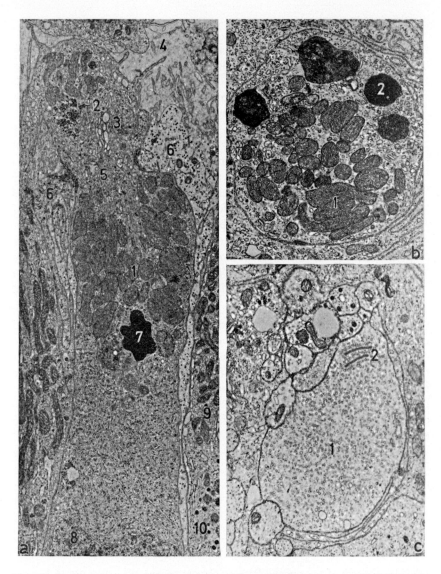

FIG. 65. Supranuclear zones of pinealocytes of "type II" from *Lacerta viridis* (a and b) and the plexiform zone of the pineal organ of *Lacerta muralis* (c). (Courtesy of Wartenberg and Baumgarten, 1968.) a. Supranuclear zones of "type II" (center) and other (on each side) pinealocytes. The "type II" pinealocytes differ from the others (type I) in having larger mitochondria in the ellipsoid region (1), in lacking dense granules of "type A" and in having an aggregation of glycogen granules (2) in the inner segment (3). 4, Lumen of the pineal organ; 5, axis of neck piece; 6, adjacent supporting cells; 7, cytoplasmic body ("cytosome") of "type C"; 8, nucleus of "type II" pinealocyte; 9, neighboring pinealocytes ("type I") with dense granules (10) and mitochondria of specific form. × 7 600. b. Cross section through the ellipsoid region of a pinealocyte of "type II". 1, Mitochondria; 2, cytoplasmic bodies of "type C". × 12 800. c. Section from plexiform zone. 1, Club-shaped process containing numerous (synaptic?) vesicles and two "synaptic ribbons" (2). × 11 200.

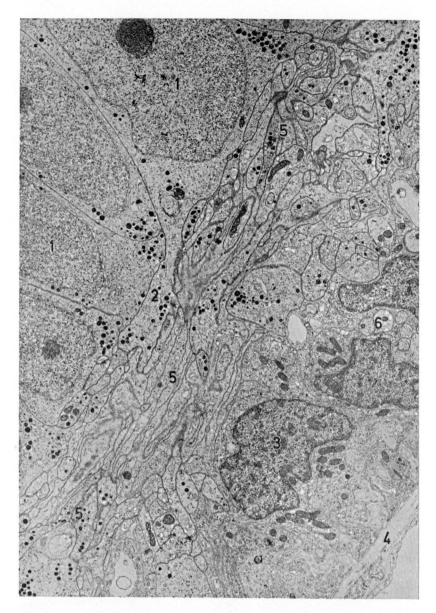

FIG. 66. Section through the outer zones of the pineal organ of *Lacerta viridis*, extending from pinealocyte nuclei (1) and basal cytoplasmic processes (2) at upper left, to outer supportive cells (3) bordering the perivascular space (4) at the lower right. 5, The plexiform or reticular zone, consisting largely of basal cytoplasmic processes from pinealocytes and most easily recognized by their content of dense granules of "type A"; 6, a group of non-myelinated axons between supporting cells. × 800. (Courtesy of Wartenberg and Baumgarten, 1968.)

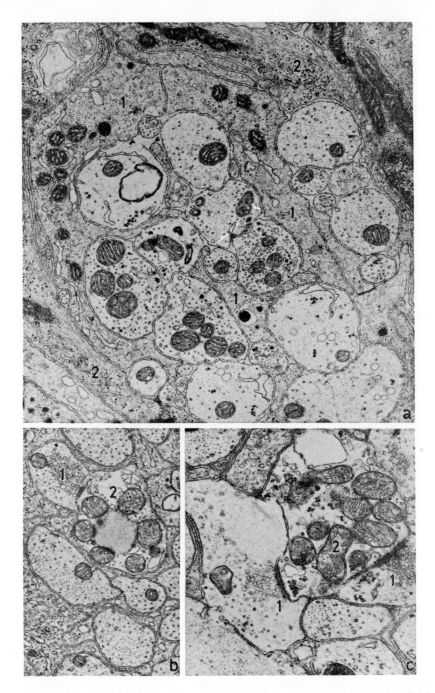

FIG. 67. Ultrastructural relations of non–myelinated axons and cell processes in the pineal organ of *Lacerta viridis*. (Courtesy of Wartenberg and Baumgarten, 1968.) a. Fascicle of non-myelinated axons penetrated and enclosed by cytoplasmic processes of pinealocytes (1) and supporting cells (2). ×17 600. b. and c. 1, Non-myelinated processes or axons with synaptic formations; 2, post-synaptic portion of cellular process of unknown origin. × 17 600 and 20 000 respectively.

the so-called ellipsoid region (Figs 65a, b); (ii) they contain no granules or bodies of "type A".

In addition to pinealocytes, two other cell types have been designated as typical constituents of the pineal epithelial wall in lizards. The supporting or interstitial cells ("Stützzellen") are not notably different from those observed in the retina of the saurian parietal eye, nor indeed from retinal cells in the parietal eye–pineal complex of other reptiles. They can be distinguished from pinealocytes (in the pineal organ of *Lacerta*) by the irregular form and density of their nucleus and the lighter or less compact appearance of their cytoplasm with its content of glial filaments.

The third cell type of the saurian pineal organ is relatively very rare. It is a round, light (less electron-dense) cell, basal in position and often with a broad cytoplasmic process. These "light cells", probably analogous to the ganglion cells of the parietal eye retina, and corresponding to the sensory nerve cells of J. A. Kappers (1967), apparently show no synaptic relations with pinealocytes in *Lacerta* (Wartenberg and Baumgarten, 1968).

5. *Neurons and Innervation*

As noted above, the photoreceptor cells of the saurian parietal eye often make synaptic contact with the retinal ganglion cells. The photoreceptor terminals on the ganglion cells contain synaptic vesicles of similar diameter, about 30 nm in *Sceloporus occidentalis* (Eakin, 1973) and 44–55 nm in *Anguis fragilis* (Petit, 1968). The synapse between photoreceptor terminal and ganglion cell process or dendrite is characterized also by the presence of a dense bar, the "synaptic ribbon", that is usually oriented perpendicularly to the membrane of the photoreceptor cell terminal. Axons of the ganglion cells from the parietal eye collect into fascicles which enter the parietal eye nerve at the posteroventral side of the retina (*Sceloporus occidentalis*, Eakin, 1973) or more nearly midventrally (*Anguis fragilis*, Nowikoff, 1910; Petit, 1968). Within the parietal nerve of *Sceloporus*, Eakin (1973) has counted 273 nerve fibers. This number is similar to the number of ganglion cells presumed to occur in the parietal eye. This suggests a relationship of approximately 1:1 between fibers and ganglion cells of origin. The retina of the parietal eye has approximately 2500 photoreceptor cells in this species. It is inferred that, on the average, about ten of these sensory cells synapse with each ganglion cell (Eakin, 1973).

The nerve of the parietal eye, the "parietal nerve" of many authors, has long been known in lizards (Strahl and Martin, 1888). Its relatively small size, and content mostly of non-myelinated nerve fibers, may explain statements that it degenerates in the adult (Steyn, 1957; Roth and Braun, 1958). However, degeneration has never been conclusively demonstrated, nor has it been supported with electron microscopic observations. On the

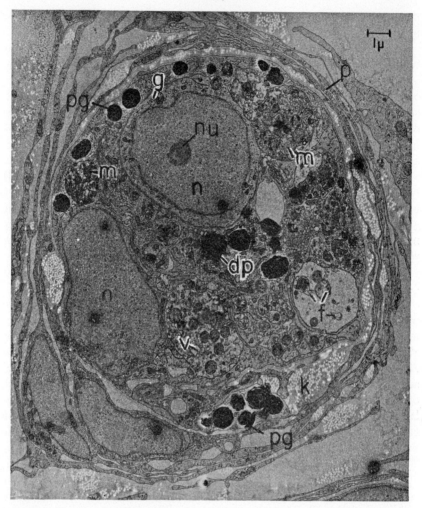

FIG. 68. Cross-sectional view of entire parietal nerve of an adult *Sceloporus occidentalis* caudal to a surgical transection performed four days earlier. This is the same nerve as that shown in Fig. 69, but at this level, between the transection and the brain, there is marked degeneration. (Courtesy of Eakin, 1964a.) dp, Osmiophilic (lipid?) droplet; f, fragments of organelles; g, small granules; k, collagenous fibers; m, swollen and aggregated mitochondria; n, nuclei of sheath cells; nu, nucleolus; p, perineurium; pg, pigment granules; v, vesicles.

contrary, the most recent evidence, of both light and electron microscopic origin, supports the structural and functional maintenance of the parietal nerve in adult lizards (Eakin and Stebbins, 1959; Eakin and Westfall, 1960; Ortman, 1960). The controversy concerning the origin of the nerve fibers within the nerve appears also to have been resolved, at least in terms of the quantitatively dominant component. The belief of most of the early investigators, including Nowikoff (1910) among others, was that the fibers originate from ganglion cells of the parietal eye retina. This contrasted with the beliefs of other investigators (Béraneck, 1887, 1892; Steyn, 1959c), but has been confirmed experimentally by Eakin (1964a). Surgical transection of the parietal nerve produced degeneration of nerve fibers in the part caudal to the section (Fig. 68), while nerve fibers rostral to the section, that is between the section and the parietal eye, remained essentially normal (Fig. 69). Consequently, the nerve cell bodies giving rise to the fibers in the parietal nerve are believed to be in the retina of the parietal eye rather than in the brain (Eakin, 1964a). Although this relationship seems true for the majority of the fibers of this nerve, it is possible that a small number of fibers may originate elsewhere. This might be true, for example, for the rare myelinated fibers. Such myelinated fibers are found infrequently in the parietal nerve of *Sceloporus occidentalis* (Eakin, 1973). However, Oksche and Kirschstein (1968) found 50 myelinated fibers out of a total of 638 fibers in the parietal nerve of *Lacerta sicula*.

The parietal nerve in its caudal, and then more ventrally directed course, passes along the anterior surface of the pineal organ. In this passage, the nerve is oriented progressively towards the left side. This asymmetry is confirmed by noting its entrance to the brain in the vicinity of the left habenular nuclei (Eakin, 1973). This relationship has been observed in various species of lizards (von Haffner, 1953; J. A. Kappers, 1965, 1967; Ortman, 1960), as well as the tuatara, *Sphenodon punctatus* (Dendy, 1899, 1911). Recent work on the parietal nerve of *Lacerta* indicates that the nerve may actually consist of two branches, with the left one thicker, and with the two branches apparently crossing below the tip of the pineal organ (Wartenberg and Baumgarten, 1968). The ultimate destination(s) of the sensory fibers coursing down the parietal nerve within the brain remain unknown.

The innervation of the saurian pineal organ differs from that of its parietal eye in its reduction in sensory or pinealofugal fibers and its greater number of efferent, noradrenergic or pinealopetal fibers (J. A. Kappers, 1966, 1967, 1969, 1971a, b; Collin and Kappers, 1968, 1971). The sensory fibers of the pineal nerve run in small bundles towards the pineal stalk where they assemble to form the "pineal nerve". As described in *Lacerta viridis* (J. A. Kappers, 1967), many of these fibers are myelinated, and run ventralward in the sagittal plane just caudal to the habenular commissure. After reaching the dorsal border of the subcommissural organ these fibers turn into the periventricular brain tissue both ventrally and caudally. They apparently do not contribute to habenular or posterior commissural systems,

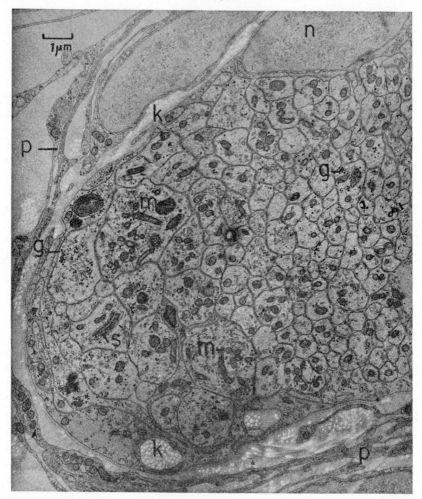

FIG. 69. Cross-sectional view of about half of the nerve fibers in the parietal nerve of an adult *Sceloporus occidentalis* rostral to a surgical transection performed four days earlier. Nerve fibers shown here are normal in appearance, except possibly for the scattered dense granules (g) in the axoplasm of many. (Courtesy of Eakin, 1964a.) g, Granules; k, bundle of collagenous fibers; m, mitochondria; n, nucleus of sheath cell; p. perineurium; s, stack of cisternae with granules.

nor to innervation of the subcommissural organ (J. Ariëns Kappers, 1967). The ultimate destination within the brain of the sensory fibers of the pineal nerve has not been ascertained.

The efferent fibers of the lizard pineal organ consist of an augmented autonomic system, that is mostly sympathetic and secretomotor. Nora-drenergic or sympathetic fibers have been identified by means of electron

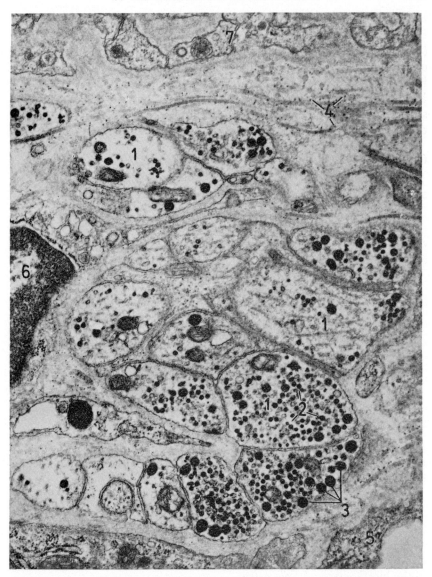

FIG. 70. Ultrastructure of perivascular "space" and its content of monoaminergic nerve fibers, in the pineal organ of *Lacerta muralis*. This animal had been injected with 400 mg/kg body weight of 5-hydroxydopamine 11 and 2 hours prior to death and fixation. × 20 000. (Courtesy of Wartenberg and Baumgarten, 1969.) 1, Monoaminergic nerve fibers distinguishable on the basis of their granulated vesicles; 2, smaller dense-cored vesicles (or granules) measuring 300–500 Å in diameter; 3, larger dense-cored vesicles measuring 700–1200 Å in diameter; 4, very fine dense granules lying between collagen fibrillae; 5, capillary endothelium; 6, nucleus of connective tissue cell; 7, basal (outer) part of the pineal epithelial layer, consisting here of a basal membrane (lamina) and basal cytoplasmic extensions (processes) of supporting cells.

microscopy in three pineal tissue regions of *Lacerta muralis*: (i) adjacent to blood vessels in the perivascular connective tissue compartment (Fig. 70); (ii) between cells and their processes within the epithelial layer of the organ (Figs 66, 67), and (iii) partially free and glia-covered within the lumen of the organ (Figs 59, 60, 61) (Wartenberg and Baumgarten, 1969). It is still uncertain which, if any, of the observed terminations and synaptic structures within the pineal organ are in fact secretomotor, and which control synthetic or secretory activities of the pinealocytes.

6. *Vasculature*

The vasculature of the parietal eye–pineal region in lizards has been studied in *Agama atra*, *Cordylus polyzonus* and *Mabuya sulcata* (Steyn,

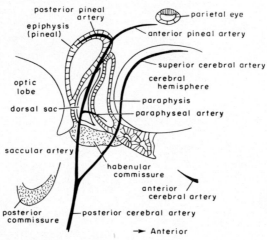

FIG. 71. Arterial supply of the pineal complex in *Lacerta muralis*, in diagrammatic sagittal reconstruction. (Modified from Swain, 1968.)

1958); in *Anolis carolinensis*, *A. extremus* and *Lacerta viridis* (Lierse, 1965a); and in *Lacerta muralis*, *L. viridis*, *Chalcides chalcides*, *Agama cyanogaster* and *Varanus niloticus* (Swain, 1968). The terminology employed in descriptions generally follows Dendy's (1909, 1910) earlier detailed descriptions of the blood vessels of *Sphenodon*.

The vascular patterns in the pineal of lizards show relatively less variation on the arterial than on the venous side (Swain, 1966, 1968). The vascular anatomy in *Lacerta muralis* (Figs 71 and 72) may be taken as a standard. The arterial supply of the pineal is bilaterally supplied via the internal carotid arteries and the posterior cerebral arteries. Each posterior cerebral artery bifurcates as it passes medially between the optic lobe and cerebral hemisphere. The anterior branch or superior cerebral artery extends over the posterior surface of the cerebral hemisphere. The posterior branch or saccular artery continues dorsad, supplies blood to paraphysis and dorsal sac, and then gives off posterior and anterior branches supplying the pineal organ and parietal eye respectively (Fig. 71). Only on the left side is there an anterior pineal artery, the branch extending anteriorly to the parietal eye.

The veins of the pineal complex of *Lacerta muralis* all drain into the median longitudinal sinus, which extends between the roof of the brain and

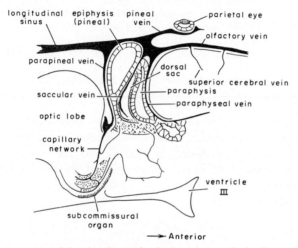

Fig. 72. Venous system of the pineal complex in *Lacerta muralis*, in diagrammatic sagittal reconstruction. (Modified from Swain, 1968.)

the meningeal connective tissue that lies above it. The dorsal sac and the anterior wall of the pineal organ are drained by bilateral saccular veins. A median pineal vein forms a circle around and beneath the parietal eye and drains into the longitudinal sinus above the distal tip of the pineal organ (Fig. 72). Just behind the pineal, the median parapineal vein joins the longitudinal sinus. The vein originates by fusion of veins, superficial to the optic lobes, and not only receives blood from the pineal organ but also from the habenular, posterior and subcommissural regions (Swain, 1968). Major differences in patterns of pineal venous drainage among lizard species center on variations in the saccular vein(s).

C. Serpentes

Although a glandular pineal organ has been found in all snakes that have been examined, amazingly few species have been studied (Table XV). In

TABLE XV

Descriptions of the pineal complex in adult serpentes

Family	Species (References)
Boidae	*Python molurus* (Rabl-Rückhard, 1894; Studnička, 1905)
Colubridae	*Coronella austriaca* (Leydig, 1897)
	Elaphe longissima (Studnička, 1893, 1905)
	Natrix natrix (Milcou *et al.*, 1968; Milcou and Dancâsiu, 1967; Oksche and Kirschstein, 1966a, b; Petit, 1971a, b; Quay *et al.*, 1967, 1968; Ssobolew, 1907; Studnička, 1893, 1905; Trost, 1953b; Vivien, 1964a, b; 1965)
	Natrix tessellata (Milcou *et al.*, 1968)
	Thamnophis sirtalis (Herrick, 1893; Sorenson, 1894; Studnička, 1905)
Viperidae	*Vipera berus* (Ssobolew, 1907; Studnička, 1905)

fact, detailed studies by modern methods have been made on the pineal gland of only a single species, *Natrix natrix*. Neither parietal eye nor its equivalent has ever been found in snakes, and the integumentary area overlying the pineal gland is always unmodified. In some smaller species, however, the venous vascular pattern around the pineal gland is discernible through the skin (Fig. 73).

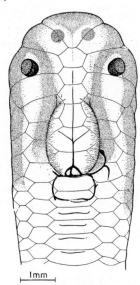

1mm

FIG. 73. Dorsal surface of the head of a *Leptotyphlops humilis* fixed in Bouins fluid and cleared in cedarwood oil. The median venous vascular pattern around the pineal gland is seen through the skin, which is unmodified in this region.

The pineal gland of Serpentes is a single, compact and median structure that is attached basally in the region between habenular and posterior commissures and encapsulated dorsally by connective tissue continuous with that of the dura mater (Fig. 74). The interior of the gland is composed of lobules containing closely spaced small parenchymal cells (pinealocytes) and intervening strands of stromal tissue containing sinusoidal capillaries

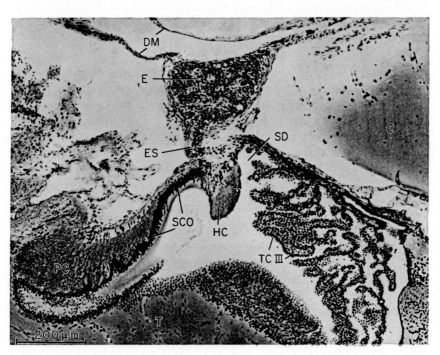

FIG. 74. Pineal gland of an adult female *Natrix natrix* in sagittal section. (From Quay *et al.*, 1968.) C, Cerebrum; DM, dorsal meninges; E, epiphysis (pineal gland); ES, epiphyseal stalk; HC, habenular commissure; PC, posterior commissure; SCO, subcommissural organ; SD, dorsal sac; T, thalamus; TC-III, tela chorioidea (choroid plexus) of roof of third ventricle. Bodian–Ziesmer protargol method.

(Vivien, 1964a, b, 1965; Quay *et al.*, 1968). In general, the microanatomy of the pineal gland of snakes is remarkably similar to that of mammals.

The pinealocytes of *Natrix natrix* consist of a cell body or perikaryon and of cytoplasmic processes that show a secretory polarity. Although the cytoplasmic density of the pinealocytes varies considerably, it has not yet been possible to distinguish distinct subtypes of these cells. Pinealocyte secretory granules appear first in Golgi vesicles, pass into cytoplasmic processes and accumulate in their perivascular terminations (Vivien, 1964a, b,

1965; Petit, 1971a). Cytochemical and autoradiographic methods show 5-hydroxytryptamine (serotonin, 5-HT) to be present within the pinealocytes, but apparently in a diffuse form rather than bound within granules or vesicles (Quay et al., 1967, 1968; Petit, 1971b).

Neither neurons nor ganglion cell bodies have ever been found within the pineal gland of a snake and neither sensory or nerve fiber connections have been demonstrated in the stalk region between the gland and the brain. Sympathetic fibers extend to the pineal gland of *Natrix*, at least in part by way of a median, dorsal, meningeal bundle (Quay et al., 1968). Sympathetic fibers are numerous within the gland, both in perivascular spaces and in parenchymal lobules. Some of these fibers are seen to terminate in direct contact with pinealocytes, but without showing typical synaptic junctions (Petit, 1971a). Nevertheless, they do contain large dense-cored vesicles and other small granular and non-granular ones. The occurrence of synaptic ribbons surrounded by synaptic vesicles is one of the few features of snake pinealocytes that is shared with the pinealocytes or transformed photoreceptors of lizards.

D. Rhynchocephalia

Detailed and excellently illustrated descriptions of the parietal eye–pineal complex in *Sphenodon* have been provided by Dendy (1899, 1909, 1910, 1911). Additional materials, discussions and interpretations of the complex in this sole surviving rhynchocephalian have been published by Gabe and Saint Girons (1964), Gasson (1947), Osawa (1898), Schauinsland (1903), Spencer (1886a, b, c), Studnička (1905), and Wyeth (1925). However, no electron microscopic, cytochemical and other recent techniques have yet been applied. For this reason it is still impossible to make a critical comparison of the cellular relations and composition of the complex in *Sphenodon* and that in other reptiles. However, on the basis of the anatomy and general histology of the complex, it is most similar to that of lizards.

The structure of the adult parietal eye (= "pineal eye" of some authors) of *Sphenodon* varies only slightly. It lies in the lower portion of the parietal foramen, under a mass of gelatinous and more or less transparent connective tissue that Dendy termed the "parietal plug". This plug nearly fills the parietal foramen and has an outer convex and an inner concave surface, the parietal eye being embedded in the latter. The parietal eye itself is covered by internal and external connective tissue capsules, which Dendy considered to be parts of, or continuations of, the dura mater. The *Sphenodon* parietal eye, like that of lizards (Fig. 54), is a simple vesicle without cupping by invagination and consists of an outer epithelial lens and an inner retinal formation. Similarly the retina contains sensory (photoreceptor), supporting

(= "radial fibers" of Dendy) and ganglion cells. The relative positions of the nuclei of these cell types within the parietal eye retina give the impression of three layers: inner (sensory), middle (ganglion) and outer (supportive).

The pineal gland, or "pineal sac" of Dendy, in *Sphenodon* has an essentially similar histological structure to that of the parietal eye retina, in so far as seen with light microscopy. The anatomical relations of the pineal gland to adjacent structures, its arterial supply and venous drainage are diagrammed in Fig. 75. A highly vascular connective tissue covers the outside of the pineal gland and contains as well bundles of nerve fibers. Sensory cells with

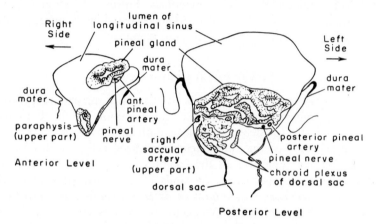

FIG. 75. Transverse sections of the pineal gland and adjacent structures in *Sphenodon*, at relatively anterior (left) and posterior (right) levels. (Modified from Dendy, 1909.)

photoreceptor-like outer segments are numerous in the wall of the pineal gland and have tapering basal processes extending into a layer or zone of nerve fibers and cell processes. The lumen of the pineal gland contains a considerable number of free cells, probably leucocytic or macrophagic in nature.

E. COMPARATIVE CONCLUSIONS

The adult morphology and cellular composition of the parietal eye–pineal complex in reptiles is known in detail for relatively few and distantly related taxa. The most serious gaps in knowledge relate to the Amphisbaenia, primitive groups of turtles and most groups of snakes. Within the groups in which the structure of the complex is somewhat known, four conditions are observed: (i) apparent absence of both parietal eye and pineal gland (Crocodilia); (ii) parietal eye and pineal gland both usually present, with the former probably remaining primarily photoreceptive in function and the latter showing various degrees of transformation from photoreceptor to secretory cellular activity (lizards and Rhynchocephalia); (iii) only a parenchymatous and presumably mostly non-sensory and actively secretory pineal gland remains, but this is possibly composite in origin and complex in composition (Testudines); (iv) only a compact, homogeneous and glandular pineal organ remains, much like that of mammals (by evolutionary convergence) (Serpentes). From an evolutionary point of view the cellular transformations in the saurian pineal gland are pivotal to our gaining understanding about how the jump can be made from photoreceptor to secretory (presumably endocrine) cellular functions. Presumably similar but not necessarily identical pineal transformations occurred in the separate phylogenies leading to turtles, snakes, birds and mammals.

V. Chemical Characteristics

Chemical characteristics of the cells and tissues of the parietal eye–pineal complex are important not only for the definition of the biosynthetic capacities, but also for determination of both the phylogenetic origin and functional relations of the component specialized cells. At this time our knowledge of the chemistry of the complex in reptiles is derived nearly entirely from three approaches or kinds of concerns: (i) general histochemical and cytochemical methods of diverse sorts that are broadly descriptive; (ii) pharmacological, cytochemical and biochemical methods for biogenic monamines and the enzymes involved in their synthesis and metabolism; and (iii) methods relating to demonstration of visual pigments and related aspects of receptor or photobiology. Some of the findings concerning the first two of these have been presented correlatively in the sections above, concerning developmental and adult structure and composition, and will not be repeated. I will limit myself here to brief and selective review of some of the findings of the second and third groups, particularly those that appear to be most interesting functionally.

A. BIOGENIC AMINES

Biogenic amines are small molecular derivatives of amino acids, found and synthesized in diverse cells and tissues, often as chemical mediators. Two chemical categories of these have been demonstrated in the reptilian pineal complex: (i) the catecholamines, typified by norepinephrine (noradrenaline), the primary neurotransmitter of sympathetic nerve endings within parts of the parietal eye–pineal complex as well as elsewhere in the body, and (ii) the indoleamines, including pineal melatonin and its more widely distributed precursor, 5-hydroxytryptamine (= serotonin, 5-HT).

TABLE XVI

Hydroxyindole O-methyltransferase activities of lateral eye retina, parietal eye and pineal gland in selected reptiles.[a] (*Data of Quay, 1965b*)

Group Species	Retina	Parietal eye	Pineal gland
Testudines			
Chrysemys scripta	$29\cdot0 \pm 22\cdot6(3)$	—	$432\cdot0 \pm 32\cdot0(3)$
Sauria			
Cnemidophorus lemniscatus	$5\cdot4 \pm 1\cdot9(4)$	—	$6651\cdot0(1)$
Iguana iguana	$6\cdot3 \pm 1\cdot4(5)$	$3562\cdot0 \pm 1279\cdot0(4)$	$1237\cdot0 \pm 309\cdot0(5)$
Serpentes			
Nerodia valida	$0\cdot0 \quad (4)$	—	$2903\cdot0 \pm 1526.0(3)$

[a] Results are expressed as nmoles of melatonin formed hourly/g tissue; means $\pm$ standard errors (number of samples).

High levels of activity of melatonin-forming enzyme, hydroxyindole *O*-methyltransferase (HIOMT, also known as acetylserotonin methyltransferase, ASMT), are found in both parietal eye and pineal gland (Table XVI), but the cellular localization is not known, although generally assumed to be pinealocytes and possibly, but even more tenuously, their parietal eye

TABLE XVII

Comparison of concentrations of 5-hydroxytryptamine in pineal glands and brain regions of different reptiles[a]. (*Data of Quay and Wilhoft, 1964*)

Group Species	(N)	Range in brain regions	Pineal gland[a]
Testudines			
Terrapene carolina	(3–4)	0·42–4·76	$6\cdot98 \pm 0\cdot74$
Gopherus berlandieri	(3)	0·57–6·19	$9\cdot84 \pm 1\cdot55$
Sauria			
Sauromalus varius	(1)	0·73–2·59	0·87
Gerrhonotus multi-carinatus	(1)	2·30–5·50	41·00
Serpentes			
Nerodia sipedon	(1–3)	0·24–3·08	10·00
Pituophis melanoleucus	(1)	0·69–3·20	3·80

[a] Results are expressed as mean ($\pm$ standard error for pineal glands) μg 5-HT base/g tissue wet weight.

relatives, the photoreceptor cells. Levels of HIOMT activity have been determined in individual pineal glands from a field population of *Sceloporus occidentalis* sampled in April and May (California) (Quay, 1971; Quay *et al.*, 1971). Enzyme activity was lowest during the coldest day, when all animals

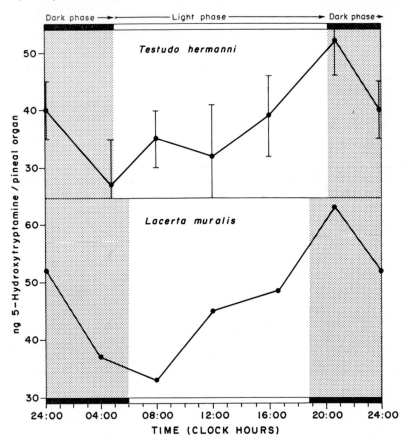

FIG. 76. Twenty-four-hour rhythms in pineal content of 5-hydroxytryptamine in *Testudo hermanni* and *Lacerta muralis*. (Adapted from Vivien-Roels *et al.*, 1971.)

were inactive, and was yet lower at that time in animals from which the parietal eye had been removed surgically during the previous autumn.

Reptilian pineal glands, like those of birds and mammals, have relatively high concentrations of serotonin (Table XVII; also, Petit *et al.*, 1971). As noted in Section IV above, cytochemical and radioautographic studies demonstrate pinealocyte cytoplasm to be the primary locus of pineal serotonin in turtles, lizards and snakes (Collin, 1967c, 1968b; Collin and

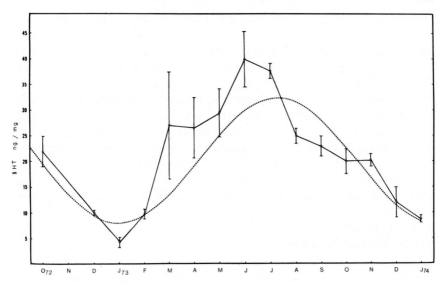

FIG. 77. Seasonal changes in pineal content of 5-hydroxytryptamine (5-HT) in *Testudo hermanni* (October 1972 to January 1974). At near monthly intervals animals were sampled every 4 hours within a 24-hour period; in one graph means (ng 5-HT/mg pineal tissue) $\pm$ standard errors are plotted; in the other the periodic function calculated by the method of least squares is shown. (Courtesy of Vivien-Roels and Petit, 1975.)

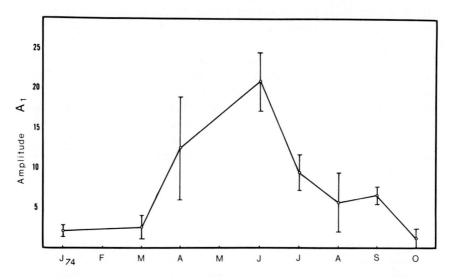

FIG. 78. Seasonal changes in the amplitude (A_1) of the 24-hour rhythm in pineal content of 5-hydroxytryptamine (5-HT) in *Testudo hermanni* (January to October 1974). (Courtesy of Vivien-Roels and Petit, 1975.)

Meiniel, 1971, 1972a, 1973; Meiniel, 1974a, b, 1975a, b; Meiniel and Collin, 1970; Meiniel *et al.*, 1975; Quay *et al.*, 1968; Wartenberg and Baumgarten, 1969a, b). Results from both cytochemical and biochemical studies on pineal serotonin content in *Lacerta muralis* show a circadian rhythm or day–night difference (Quay, 1969a); Quay *et al.*, 1967; Vivien-Roels *et al.*, 1971) of the type demonstrated earlier in mammals and birds. Fluorometry of pineal serotonin in tortoises and lizards, sampled at different times through a standard day–night, light–dark cycle, shows a similar 24-hour pattern in the two species (Fig. 76). Longer term and detailed studies on pineal serotonin content in *Testudo hermanni* by Vivien-Roels and Petit (1975) have revealed a summer acrophase and winter nadir in the mean content of serotonin (Fig. 77) and a similar seasonal (circannual) rhythm in the amplitude of the 24-hour (circadian) rhythm (Fig. 78). Further work is needed in order to tie these results to possible pineal contributions to either 24-hour or seasonal cyclic physiological mechanisms.

B. Photobiological Constituents

Two recent studies indicate that particular chemical constituents of functional importance in visual photophysiology are shared by the parietal and lateral eyes of lizards. Immunofluorescence techniques have shown that crystallins, specific lens proteins, occur in the lenses of both parietal and lateral eyes in *Anolis carolinensis* (McDevitt, 1972). Although direct demonstration of one of the known photopigments in the retina or photoreceptor cells of the parietal eye has so far been unsuccessful (R. M. Eakin and Crescitelli, unpublished), indirect evidence for the possibility of such occurrence has been obtained (Eakin, 1964b). This is based on the fact that vitamin A provides the prosthetic group for cone photopigments as well as that for rhodopsin and porphyropsin, and that vitamin A deficiency leads to vesicular degeneration of the disks in lateral eye retinal rods (Dowling and Wald, 1960). A similar event occurs in the photoreceptor processes of sensory cells in the parietal eye of lizards made deficient in vitamin A (Fig. 79; Eakin, 1964b).

VI. Physiology

The functional importance and physiological relations of either the reptilian parietal eye–pineal complex as a whole or of its component parts are still unsettled. Nevertheless, there are two well-consolidated beachheads resulting from diverse and repeated attacks on the problem of parietal eye–pineal function. One of these concerns optical and photoreceptoral properties

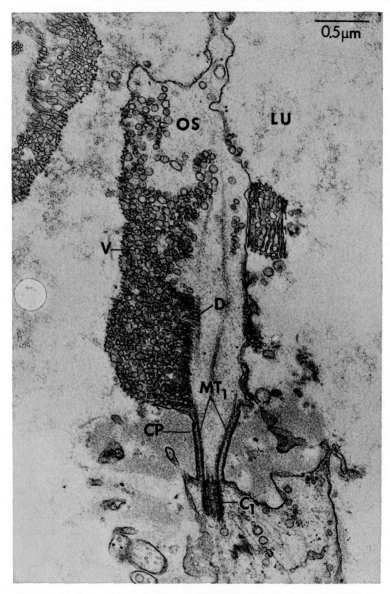

FIG. 79. Longitudinal section through a photoreceptor process in the parietal eye of a lizard (*Sceloporus occidentalis*) deficient in vitamin A. Vesicles (V) are being formed as the photoreceptor disks (D) degenerate (compare with Fig. 55). (Courtesy of Eakin, 1964b, 1973.) C_1, Distal centriole (kinetosome); CP, connecting piece; D, remnants of disks; LU, lumen of parietal eye; MT_1, microtubules (axoneme) of photoreceptor cilium; OS, outer segment; V, vesicles resulting from breakdown of the disks. $\times 27\,000$.

of the parietal and pineal components of the complex and the other concerns the peripheral, organic, metabolic and behavioral effects of removal or other manipulations of these components or their presumed secretory products. In both of these subjects the available information, diverse and sometimes conflicting, is extensive and depends upon presentation of detailed background data and interpretational analysis for adequate understanding and review. For this reason, and because of limitations of space, our coverage here will be brief and selective, with emphasis on positive and well-supported findings, and omitting consideration of most of those that are equivocal, incomplete or less easily interpreted.

A. OPTICAL AND PHOTORECEPTORAL CHARACTERISTICS

The interparietal scale overlying the parietal eye is generally nearly transparent and is externally convex; therefore, it resembles a cornea, as

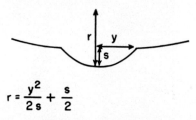

$$r = \frac{y^2}{2s} + \frac{s}{2}$$

FIG. 80. Diagrammatic representation of the bisected edge of the interparietal scale from a green iguana (*Iguana iguana*), showing a central portion of short radius of curvature (*r*). Formula and measurements used to calculate *r* are noted. (Modified from Sivak, 1973.)

noted by early as well as recent investigators (Gasson, 1947; Stebbins and Eakin, 1958). The rigidity and measurements (radius of curvature, Fig. 80) of this part of the scale are consistent with corneal function (Sivak, 1973). Likewise of interest is the spectral transmittance (Fig. 81). Although these characteristics may suggest the possibility of optical imagery on the part of the parietal eye (Sivak, 1973), other kinds of information are essential before such a complex visual capacity can be proven. It has generally been assumed that the small parietal eye seen in recent animals is more likely to serve as a radiation dosimeter without true visual function (Eakin, 1973; Glaser, 1958; Stebbins and Eakin, 1958).

Responses to illumination have been demonstrated in both parietal eye and pineal gland (epiphysis cerebri) of adult lizards by means of electrical recording (neurophysiological) techniques (Dodt, 1973; Dodt and Scherer, 1968a, b; Engbretson and Lent, 1974; Gruberg *et al.*, 1968; Hamasaki, 1968, 1969a, b; Hamasaki and Dodt, 1969; Miller and Wolbarsht, 1962). The parietal eye of lizards (*Lacerta sicula*) shows a much slower electrical response on exposure to light than does its lateral eye retina (Dodt and Scherer, 1968a). Stimulation with different wavelengths of light reveals consistent differences between the electroretinogram obtained from the lateral eye and the slow (graded) response of the parietal eye. While the polarity of the electrical response of the parietal eye changes with the color (wavelength) of the stimulus, that of the lateral eye does not. Potentials obtained from the parietal eye are positive in response to blue and negative in response to green light. Photic effects carried onward to the level of the ganglion cells of the parietal

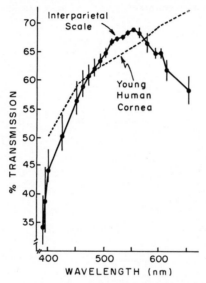

FIG. 81. Mean percentage transmittance of light by the interparietal scales of three green iguanas (*Iguana iguana*) as a function of wavelength. For comparative purposes the percentage transmittance by the young human cornea is plotted by a dashed line. (Modified from Sivak, 1973.)

eye are excitatory or inhibitory, depending on both wavelength and intensity of the stimulus. With cessation of the stimulus off-discharges, one sees transient (post-excitatory) depression to sustained inhbition of nerve impulses.

Electrical responses (electroretinogram) obtained from the parietal eye of the green iguana (*Iguana iguana*) under achromatic light stimulation are complex, rather than in the form of a simple negative wave; they show deflections at both lights-on and lights-off (Fig. 82). The shape of recordings from fully dark-adapted parietal eyes differ little from those obtained from light-adapted parietal eyes, but the threshold is about 1·5 log units lower (Fig. 82). In the iguana dark-adaptation range of the parietal eye is markedly greater than that of its own lateral eye, but it resembles that of lateral eyes of two distantly related nocturnal reptiles (Fig. 83). The flicker fusion frequency in relation to intensity determined for parietal and lateral eyes of the green iguana and for the lateral eyes of the Tokay gecko shows a relatively constant slope for the lateral eyes, but a marked curvature for the parietal eye (Fig. 84). The responses of the parietal eye of the iguana to paired flashes of light (Fig. 85) resemble those of the lateral eye of *Gekko gecko*. Thus in a number of properties the parietal eye of the green iguana

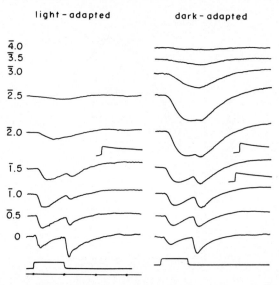

FIG. 82. Electrical responses recorded from light-adapted (left) and dark-adapted (right) parietal eyes of the green iguana (*Iguana iguana*). Stimulus intensities are denoted by the numbers at the left. Calibration: 100 μV for the light-adapted ERGs (electroretinograms) and from $1 = \bar{4}\cdot0$ to $\bar{2}\cdot0$ for the dark-adapted ERGs; 250 μV for the dark-adapted ERGs from $1 = \bar{1}\cdot5$ to 0. Time: 1 second. (Adapted from Hamasaki, 1968.)

resembles more the lateral eyes of nocturnal reptiles, than its own (Hamasaki, 1968).

Light sensitivity has been demonstrated by electrophysiological techniques also in the pineal gland of several lizards (*Lacerta sicula, Acanthodactylus erythrurus* and *Iguana iguana*) (Hamasaki and Dodt, 1969). In this work the parietal eye was removed before stimulation of, and recording from, the pineal gland. In general, the pineal photic responses differ from those of the parietal eye by being purely inhibitory in response to all light stimuli, and by demonstrating an absolute intensity threshold within the photopic range (4 lm/m^2) and maximal sensitivity near 600 nm.

When the vascular filtering effect of blood over the pineal gland is corrected

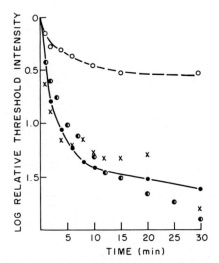

FIG. 83. Curves showing the courses of dark-adaptation in lateral (open circles and broken line) and parietal (dots and solid line) eyes of the green iguana (*Iguana iguana*). For comparative purposes dark-adaptation data for the lateral eyes of Tokay geckos (Xs) and spectacled caimans (*Caiman crocodylus*) (half-filled circles) are shown also. Ordinate units = log of relative light intensity required to elicit criterion response (= 30 μV for the parietal eye). (Adapted from Hamasaki, 1968.)

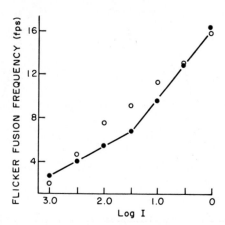

FIG. 84. Flicker fusion frequency curve for the parietal eye of the green iguana (*Iguana iguana*) (dots and solid line) and lateral eye of the Tokay gecko (open circles). (Adapted from Hamasaki, 1968.)

for, one observes a shift of maximal sensitivity to shorter wavelengths (Fig. 86). These results have been taken to suggest that the pineal gland contains a photopigment similar to that found in lateral eyes ($\lambda_{max} = 570$ nm) (Hamasaki and Dodt, 1969).

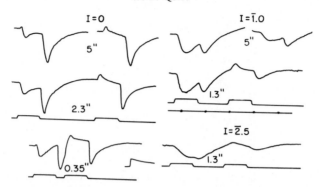

FIG. 85. Responses of the parietal eye of the green iguana (*Iguana iguana*) to paired flashes of light. The interflash intervals (in seconds) are denoted between the two responses in each record and the stimulus intensities (*I*) above each series of records. Calibrations: 100 μV; 1 second.

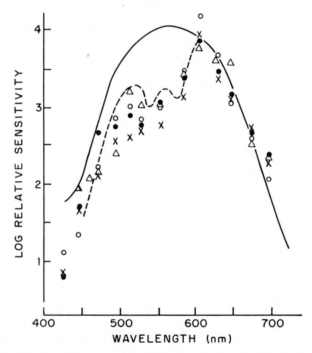

FIG. 86. Determination of the spectral sensitivity (symbols) of single cells ("neurons") of *Lacerta sicula*, determined by measurement of the relative number of quanta necessary for a just detectable inhibitory action of light between 428 and 693 nm. Different sites ("neurons") of recording are indicated by different symbols. The continuous line shows the spectral sensitivity of the lateral eye of the same species, and the dotted line corrects for the absorption by blood within vessels overlying the epiphysis (pineal gland). (Adapted from Hamasaki and Dodt, 1969.)

B. Peripheral and Behavioral Effects

Even though photoreceptor activity has been clearly demonstrated for the parietal eye–pineal complex of lizards and photic information is relayed from complex to brain, consistent peripheral and behavior effects of ablation or manipulation of the complex are not always obtained. Much of the difficulty may stem from the need for recognizing permissive factors, such as season or phase of the circannual cycle, or from the need for conditioning the animals by photic, thermal or other environmental factors. For example, it has been shown in diverse groups, from teleost fishes to placental mammals, that pinealectomy may only have an effect on the reproductive organs at one season, or only under particular environmental conditions (Fenwick, 1970; Quay, 1969b; Reiter, 1972, 1974; Vodicnik, 1974).

Other probable sources of obscurity and inconsistency, in studies on peripheral effects of the reptilian complex, include the likelihood of indirect mediation or modulation of some of the effects and problems with experimental design as well as the quantitative evaluation and interpretation of results. Removal of the parietal eye may have widespread secondary repercussions, for instance on aspects of metabolism and thermoregulation. An early study by Clausen and Mofshin (1939) suggests that the parietal eye of *Anolis carolinensis* can contribute to reception of photic information and that the animal utilizes this in regulation of oxygen consumption. However, the effect is quantitatively small and has been ignored by many experimentors.

Investigations by Stebbins and associates on the effects of parietalectomy (removal of the parietal eye) in lizards have provided evidence for behaviorally increased environmental or surface exposure and increased thyroid activity in the absence or covering of the parietal eye (Eakin *et al.*, 1959; Glaser, 1958; Quay *et al.*, 1970; Stebbins, 1960, 1963, 1970; Stebbins and Cohen, 1973; Stebbins and Eakin, 1958; Stebbins *et al.*, 1967; Stebbins and Tong, 1973; Stebbins and Wilhoft, 1966). Other researchers have carried out related studies on parietal eye function (Packard and Packard, 1972; Palenschat, 1964; Roth and Braun, 1958). Therefore, Francis and Brooks (1970), hypothesized that parietalectomy should lead to an increase in metabolic rate and concomitantly in heat and ventilatory rates. Although the results of their experiments do not support this, their data for ventilatory rate suggest that the slope of ventilatory rate increased with increased temperature may have been greater in the parietalectomized animals (Fig. 87).

In extensive studies on Australian lizards, Firth (1974) demonstrates a seasonally dependent influence of the parietal eye on panting behavior, in terms of quantitative aspects of the "panting threshold". This relationship is stated to be presumably secondary to the effects of the parietal eye on

activity cycles and exposure to sunlight. It may also be consistent with
theories (Stebbins and Eakin, 1958; Stebbins and Wilhoft, 1966) relating
parietal eye activity to such functions (Firth, 1974). Studies on oxygen
consumption in the blue granite lizard (*Sceloporus cyanogenys*) suggest that

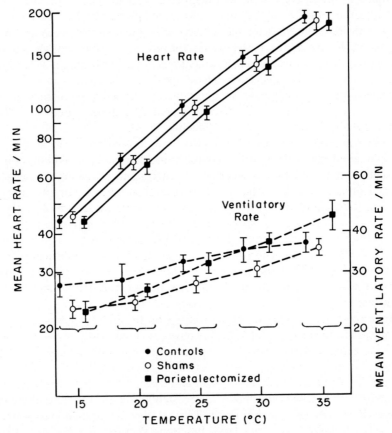

FIG. 87. Relations of heart-beat rate and body ventilatory movement rate to body temperature on day 30 in control, sham-operated and parietalectomized lizards (*Sceloporus
occidentalis*). (Adapted from Francis and Brooks, 1970.)

removal of the parietal eye does not significantly affect the mean rate of
metabolism, nor its rhythms of oxygen consumption (Songdahl and Hutchinson, 1972). However, at least those animals acclimated to higher temperature
(25°C) and a short photoperiod need either the lateral or the parietal eyes
to increase oxygen consumption under the conditions of the experiment
(Fig. 88). Studies on the thermal relations of parietalectomized lizards
(*Anolis carolinensis*) show that parietalectomized animals have a significantly

lower thermal tolerance (Fig. 89), but select significantly higher temperatures when placed in a thermal gradient, than do controls, except for a brief time in the first half of the daily light phase (Kosh and Hutchinson, 1972; Hutchinson and Kosh, 1974).

These results reinforce the suspected importance of preexisting or conditioning circumstances and the time of day at which comparisons are made between parietalectomized and control animals. We also lack simplistic interpretation of parietal eye–pineal gland function, in terms of providing a "biological clock" for the circadian activity rhythm. Removal

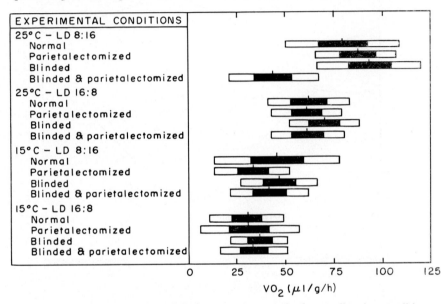

FIG. 88. Oxygen consumption of *Sceloporus cyanogenys* in four acclimation conditions. Vertical (midscale) lines are the means; one white and black rectangle on each side of a mean = 1 standard deviation; one black rectangle on either side of a mean = 2 standard errors. (Modified from Songdahl and Hutchinson, 1972.)

of parietal eye and pineal organ, even in blinded lizards, does not prevent reentrainment of the circadian activity cycle to a new environmental photoperiod (Underwood, 1973, 1975; Underwood and Menaker, 1970). Therefore, experimental designs for testing photic mediation by either parietal eye or pineal organ in lizards must take into appreciation not only lateral eye reception but also a so-called "extraretinal" photoreception lying outside of the lateral eyes and the parietal eye–pineal complex.

In comparison to the extensive work on pineal–gonadal relations in mammals, there are many fewer experiments testing for such a physiological relationship in reptiles. Nevertheless, the available data not only

suggest that the reptilian parietal eye–pineal complex may have physiological effects extending to the gonads, but also that seasonal timing and
ambient conditions are similarly critical for such effects to be demonstrable.
This was early suggested by the results of Clausen and Poris (1937) using
the testis of *Anolis carolinensis* (Fig. 90). However, negative or inconclusive

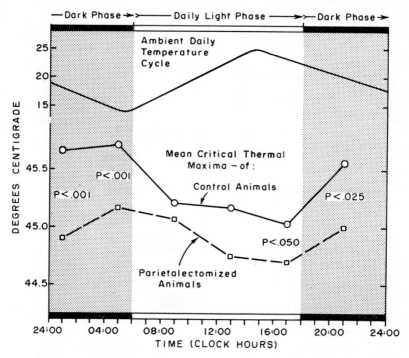

FIG. 89. Twenty-four-hour variations of critical thermal maxima of control (normal) and
parietalectomized *Anolis carolinensis* acclimated to a 15–25°C daily temperature cycle and
an LD 12:12 light cycle. Significant differences between the group means are shown by
probability (*P*) values between the graphs. Each mean is based upon 20 (controls) or
18 (parietalectomized) determinations. (Data of Kosh and Hutchinson, 1972.)

results from similar experiments by some subsequent investigators led to
various interpretations to explain the results (Fox and Dessauer, 1958;
Hutton and Ortman, 1957; Licht and Pearson, 1970; Underwood, 1975).
More recently, further studies with *Anolis carolinensis* show that parietalectomy plus blinding is more effective than either operation alone (Ridgway,
1972; Ridgway and Kent, 1971). However, parietalectomy between March
and mid-June has inhibitory effects on the testes, while it is without effect
when performed from December to March.

Removal of the pineal gland of *Anolis carolinensis* and evaluation of ovarian effects has provided clearer evidence of a pineal-gonadal physiological relationship (Levey, 1972, 1973). Pinealectomy in November or January leads to significant follicular development within 14 days, while this is reversed by daily injections of melatonin (Fig. 91). Ovarian sensitivity to the effects of pinealectomy appears to decrease with the onset of seasonal reproductive activity and is absent at the end of the usual breeding season (September). These and related observations support the interpretations that under conditions of short photoperiod and high ambient temperature

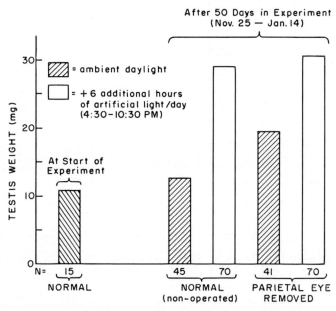

FIG. 90. Replotted data of Clausen and Poris (1937) suggesting increased testis weight following removal of the parietal eye in winter and under conditions of short (ambient) photoperiod.

(1) the pineal gland can modify ovarian activity in *Anolis*, (2) the ovary shows a seasonal dependency of sensitivity or responsiveness to effects of pinealectomy, and (3) melatonin can reverse the ovarian effect of pinealectomy suggesting that it could be part of the mediation mechanism whereby the pineal can influence the ovaries.

Other lines or targets of investigation of parietal eye–pineal function either have not been carried to meaningful depth or have provided only negative or fragmentary results, that are often difficult, if not impossible, to interpret confidently at this time. Among such negative findings are those concerning color changes in *Anolis carolinensis* following either removal or covering of the parietal eye (Meyer and Brooks, 1968; Wilson, 1939).

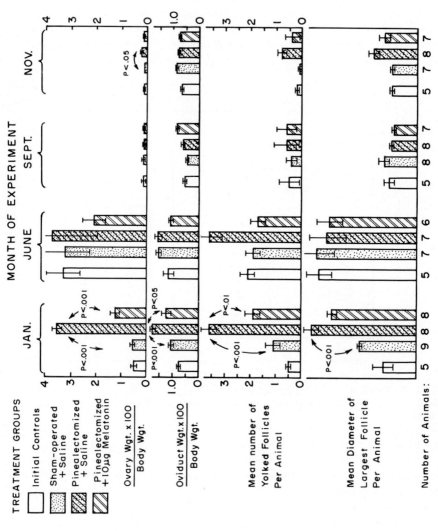

FIG. 91. Effects of pinealectomy (removal of the pineal gland) and melatonin administration on ovarian activity in *Anolis carolinensis* at different seasons of the year. (Data of Levey (1973) replotted and *P* values recalculated using Student–Fisher *t*.)

VII. Conclusions

This review of the structure, development, composition, evolution and function of the reptilian parietal eye–pineal complex should not only serve to indicate the major gaps in available information and fundamental understanding, but also to show that this organ complex is of great interest, both evolutionarily and functionally. The paleontological record has been reviewed on the basis of parietal foramina and endocranial casts. The probable size of the parietal eye, and possibly of the epiphysis or pineal organ in fossils, suggests that the complex may have been more elaborate and had a relatively greater significance than in living reptiles. Nevertheless, physiological evidence from living reptiles, albeit nearly exclusively from lizards, demonstrates distinctive photoreceptoral activities in both parietal eye and pineal components, along with probable endocrine secretory activity in the latter.

Recent developmental and ultrastructural studies have provided evidence of important differences, similarities and probable cellular derivations of components of the complex in Testudines, Sauria and Serpentes. Especially interesting for both developmental and evolutionary studies is the finding, within the pineal organ of living lizards, of a cellular transformation, in which rudimentary photoreceptor cells are changed into presumptively endocrine secretory cells of a new kind, namely pinealocytes. The latter comprise the functionally and cytologically distinct parenchymal cells of the mammalian pineal gland or organ. The photoreceptor-to-pinealocyte transformation process in reptiles, and the photic, adrenergic and inductive mechanisms associated with it, offer an exceedingly interesting and responsive cellular system for the study of intercellular, molecular and neuro-endocrine control mechanisms.

Correlations among structures and functions within the pineal complex of reptiles have advanced further in regard to incoming (sensory) rather than outgoing (neural and endocrine) functional relations. Associated with this situation and related deficiencies in our understanding, is the still obscure question of functional and evolutionary divergence of the two major components of the complex, the parietal eye and the pineal organ (gland). Review of the evidence, particularly from those lizards that retain both organs, and in part from mammals, in which more is known concerning neural and pineal physiology, leads to the following general hypothesis.

The structural and functional changes that have taken place in the evolution of the reptilian pineal complex appear to be most readily interpreted when one considers the parietal eye and pineal organ separately. Although these two organs may have been, and may be still, functionally interrelated in some vertebrates, including lizards, they have clearly changed differently to attain different fates within Reptilia.

Let us consider first the probable functional relations of the evolution of the parietal eye. Where the parietal eye occurs within reptilian groups, it is either seen (living species) or suspected (fossil forms) to have its primary function as a photoreceptor. The photic information received and selected by the parietal eye is probably relayed primarily to anterior levels of the brainstem, i.e. those anterior to the level of the habenular nuclei. The photosensory activity of the parietal eye, and the information provided by it, may be interpreted as accessory or ancillary with respect to activities and connections of the lateral eyes. It seems possible that functional overlap and replacement have occurred in those aspects of lateral eye function which do not involve imagery of visual field, and which relate more to characteristics of ambient illumination. Such projections of photic information from the lateral eyes of mammals to the brain include that of the retino-hypothalamic fibers and the accessory optic system. Both of these transmit photic information having regulatory significance in mammalian neuro-vegetative and neuroendocrine functions. It appears likely that these mammalian lateral eye projection systems have replaced to some extent the parietal eye projection systems of lower tetrapods and ancestral reptiles. Although much less is known, as yet, about the evolution of comparable non-visual retinal projections in non-mammalian vertebrates, it seems desirable to investigate this relationship in future work. The foregoing thus leads to the suggestion that the photoreceptive parietal eye was reduced and disappeared in most groups of reptiles, possibly in parallel with the advent of specialized subdivision of the accessory or non-visual inputs and projections from the lateral eyes.

Let us consider next the probable functional relations of the evolution of the pineal or epiphyseal component of the complex. Where this component in some vertebrates retains photosensory capacity and projects photic information to the brain, evidence suggests that the pineal sensory nerves terminate in, or course towards, more posterior and periventricular regions of the brainstem. These same regions of the brainstem contain, among other things, relatively primitive ascending tracts, many of which are mono-aminergic. These monoaminergic pathways, employing such neurotrans-mitters as norepinephrine and serotonin, contribute to the regulation of arousal and sleep phase by higher centers in the brain. In mammals the same behaviors are affected both by removal of the pineal gland and by admini-stration of melatonin, which is one of the presumptive hormones of the pineal. It is suggested here that the physiological evolution of the pineal component in reptiles, and possibly in tetrapods generally, has involved the replacement of neural pineal projections affecting monoaminergic control mechanisms, with essentially secretory and endocrine pineal activities affecting still primarily monoaminergic control mechanisms. This evolutionary replacement of neurosensory by neuroendocrine function in the pineal organ is most sharply defined within reptiles. It is suggested that both the transformation of pineal photoreceptors to endocrine pinealocytes within the reptilian pineal organ, and functional target relationships that involve monoaminergic neurotransmitter and molecular control mechanisms, were maintained throughout this evolutionary progression.

Acknowledgements

The author is especially grateful to Drs Richard Eakin and Robert Stebbins, who as colleagues were most important in stimulating and furthering productive interest in the subject of this review. Gratitude is extended also to Cheryle Hughes and John Dallman for aid with the illustrations.

References

Agnew, J. D. (1958). Cranio-osteological studies in *Dicynodon grimbeeki* with special reference to the sphenethmoid region and cranial kinesis. *Palaeont. Afr.* **6**, 77–107.

Aron, E., Combescot, C. and Deméret, J. (1960). Exophtalmie de la Tortue d'eau *Emys leprosa* Schw. produite par la destruction de la région épiphysaire. *C. r. hebd. Acad. Sci., Paris* **250**, 3386–3387.

Ariëns Kappers, C. U., Huber, G. C. and Crosby, E. (1936). "The Comparative Anatomy of the Nervous System of Vertebrates, Including Man." Macmillan, New York.

Axelrod, J. (1974). The pineal gland: A neurochemical transducer. *Science, N.Y.* **184**(4144) 1341–1348.

Baur, G. (1892). On the morphology of the skull in the Mosasauridae. *J. Morph.* **7**, 1–22.

Boveri, V. (1925). Untersuchungen über das Parietalauge der Reptilien. *Acta zool. Stockh.* **6**, 1–57.

Béraneck, E. (1887). Über das Parietalauge der Reptilien. *Jena. Z. Naturwiss* **21**, 374–411.

Béraneck, E. (1892). Sur le nerf pariétal et la morphologie du troisième oeil des vertébrés. *Anat. Anz.* **7**, 674–689.

Béraneck, E. (1893). L'individualité de l'oeil pariétal. Réponse á Mr Klinckowstroem. *Anat. Anz.* **8**, 669.

Bojanus, L. H. (1819–21). "Anatome Testudinis Europaeae." Vilnae (also 1970 reprint Soc. Stud. Amph. Rept.).

Brink, A. S. (1955a). A study on the skeleton of *Diademodon*. *Palaeont. Afri.* **3**, 3–39.

Brink, A. S. (1955b). On the Cynognathidae. *Palaeont. Afr.* **3**, 47–55.

Brink, A. S. (1955c). Note on a very tiny specimen of *Thrinaxodon liorhinus*. *Palaeont. Afr.* **3**, 73–76.

Brink, A. S. (1957). *Struthiocephalus kitchingi* sp. nov. *Palaeont. Afr.* **5**, 39–56.

Brink, A. S. (1958). Notes on some whaitsiids and moschorhinids. *Palaeont. Afr.* **6**, 23–49.

Brink, A. S. (1960a). A new type of primitive cynodont. *Palaeont. Afr.* **7**, 119–154.

Brink, A. S. (1960b). On some small therocephalians. *Paleont. Afr.* **7**, 155–182.

Broom, R. (1911). On the structure of the skull in cynodont reptiles. *Proc. zool. Soc. Lond.* **1911**(2), 893–925.

Broom, R. (1925). On the origin of lizards. *Proc. zool. Soc. Lond.* **1925**(1), 1–16.

Broom, R. (1926). On a nearly complete skeleton of a new eosuchian reptile (*Palaeagama vielhaueri*, gen. et sp. nov.). *Proc. zool. Soc. Lond.* **1926**(1), 487–491.

Broom, R. (1936). On the structure of the skull in the mammal-like reptiles of the sub-order Therocephalia. *Phil. Trans. R. Soc. Ser. B*, **226**, 1–42.

Burckhardt, R. (1890). Die Zirbel von *Ichthyophis glutinosus* und *Protopterus annectens*. *Anat. Anz.* **6**, 348–349.

Burckhardt, R. (1893). Die Homologien des Zwischenhirndaches und ihre Bedeutung für die Morphologie des Hirns bei niederen Vertebraten. *Anat. Anz.* **9**, 152–155.

Burckhardt, R. (1894). Die Homologien des Zwischenhirndaches bei Reptilien und Vögeln. *Anat. Anz.* **9**, 320–324.

Camp, C. L. (1923). Classification of the lizards. *Bull. Am. Mus. nat. Hist.* **48**, 289–481.

Campos-Ortega, J. A. (1965). Aportaciones a la organización de las cubiertas ventriculares del encéfalo de los reptiles, referidas a los llamados "órganos circunventriculares". *Anal. Anat.* **14**, 171–216.

Carrière, J. (1890). Neuere Untersuchungen über das Parietalorgan. *Biol. Zbl.* **9**, 136.

Case, E. C. (1921). On an endocranial cast from a reptile, *Desmatosuchus spurensis*, from the Upper Triassic of western Texas. *J. comp. Neurol.* **33**, 133–147.

Clausen, H. J. and Mofshin, B. (1939). The pineal eye of the lizard (*Anolis carolinensis*), a photoreceptor as revealed by oxygen consumption studies. *J. cell. comp. Physiol.* **14**, 29–41.

Clausen, H. J. and Poris, E. G. (1937). The effect of light upon sexual activity in the lizard, *Anolis carolinensis*, with especial reference to the pineal body. *Anat. Rec.* **69**, 39–53.

Coe, W. R. and Kunkel, B. W. (1906). Studies of the Californian limbless lizard, *Anniella*. *Trans. Conn. Acad. Sci.* **12**, 349–403.

Collin, J.-P. (1967a). Structure, nature sécretoire, degenerescence partielle des photo-recepteurs rudimentaires epiphysaires chez *Lacerta viridis* (Laurenti). *C. r. hebd. Acad. Sci., Paris* **264**, 647–650.

Collin, J.-P. (1967b). Nouvelles remarques sur l'épiphyse de quelques Lacertiliens et Oiseaux. *C. r. hebd. Acad. Sci., Paris* **265**, 1725–1728.

Collin, J.-P. (1967c). Recherches préliminaires sur les propriétes histochimiques de l'épiphyse de quelques lacertiliens. *C. r. hebd. Acad. Sci., Paris* **265**, 1827–1830.

Collin, J.-P. (1968a). Pluralité des photorecepteurs dans l'épiphyse de *Lacerta C. r. hebd. Acad. Sci., Paris* **267**, 1047–1050.

Collin, J.-P. (1968b). L'épiphyse des Lacertiliens: Relations entre les données micro-electroniques et celles de l'histochimie (en fluorescence ultraviolette) pour la détection des indole- et catécholamines. *C. r. hebd. Acad Sci., Paris* **162**, 1785–1789.

Collin, J.-P. (1969). Contribution à l'étude de l'organe pineal. De l'épiphyse sensorielle à la glande pinéale: Modalités de transformation et implications fonctionelles. *Annls Stn. Biol. Besse-en-Chandesse, Suppl.* **1**, 1–359.

Collin, J.-P. (1971). Differentiation and regression of the cells of the sensory line in the epiphysis cerebri. *In* "The Pineal Gland." CIBA Foundation Symposium. Churchill Livingstone, Edinburgh, 79–125.

Collin, J.-.P. and Ariëns Kappers, J. (1968). Electron microscopic study of pineal innervation in lacertilians. *Brain Res.* **11**, 85–106.

Collin, J.-P. and Ariëns Kappers, J. (1971). Synapses of the ribbon type in the pineal organ of *Lacerta vivipara*. *Experientia* **27**, 1456–1457.

Collin, J.-P. and Meiniel, A. (1971). L'organe pineal: Études combinées ultrastructurales, cytochimiques (monoamines) et experimentales, chez *Testudo mauritanica*;

grains denses des cellules de la lignée "sensoriette" chez les vertébres. *Arch. Anat. microsc. Morph. exp.* **60**, 269–304.

Collin, J.-P. and Meiniel, A. (1972a). Amines biogènes de l'organe pinéal des reptiles. *Gen. comp. Endocr.* **18**, 583–584.

Collin, J.-P. and Meiniel, A. (1972b). L'organe pinéal du genre *Lacerta* (reptile, lacertilien): Action d'enzymes proteolytiques sur les grains denses (500–3400 Å) des photorécepteurs rudimentaires. *C. r. Séanc. Soc. Biol.* **166**, 370–374.

Collin, J.-P. and Meiniel, A. (1973). Metabolisme des indolamines dans l'organe pinéal de *Lacerta* (reptiles, lacertiliens). II. L'activité MAO et l'incorporation de 5-HTP-^{3}H et de 5-HT-^{3}H, dans les conditions normales et expérimentales. *Z. Zellforsch. mikrosk. Anat.* **145**, 331–361.

Combescot, C. and Demaret, J. (1962). The histophysiology of the epiphysis in the water turtle, *Emys leprosa*. *Gen. comp. Endocr.* **2**, 605.

Combescot, C. and Demaret, J. (1963). Histophysiologie de l'épiphyse chez la tortue d'eau *Emys leprosa* (Schw.). *Ann. Endocr.* **24**, 204–212.

Cope, E. D. (1892). The osteology of the Lacertilia. *Proc. Am. Phil. Soc.* **30**, 185–221.

Cuvier, G. (1805). "Leçons d'Anatomie Comparée." 5 Volumes. Crochard et Cie Libraires, Paris.

de Graaf, H. W. (1886). Zur Anatomie und Entwicklung der Epiphyse bei Amphibien und Reptilien. *Anat. Anz.* **9**, 191–194.

Dendy, A. (1899). On the development of the parietal eye and adjacent organs in *Sphenodon* (*Hatteria*). *Q. J. microsc. Sci.* **42**, 111–153.

Dendy, A. (1909). The intracranial vascular system of *Sphenodon*. *Phil. Trans. R. Soc. Ser. B*, **200**, 403–426.

Dendy, A. (1910). On the structure, development and morphological interpretation of pineal organs and adjacent parts of the brain in the tuatara (*Sphenodon punctatus*). *Anat. Anz.* **37**, 453–462.

Dendy, A. (1911). On the structure, development and morphological interpretation of the pineal organs and adjacent parts of the brain in the tuatara (*Sphenodon punctatus*). *Phil. Trans. R. Soc. Lond. Ser. B* **201**, 227–331.

Dodt, E. (1973). The parietal eye (pineal and parietal organs) of lower vertebrates. *In* "Handbook of Sensory Physiology". (R. Jung, ed.). Springer Verlag, New York, 7(3B), 113–140.

Dodt, E. and Scherer, E. (1967). The electroretinogram of the third eye. II. *Symp. int. Soc. Clin. Electroretinography* **29**, 10.

Dodt, E. and Scherer, E. (1968a). Photic responses from the parietal eye of the lizard *Lacerta sicula campestris* (De Betta). *Vision res.* **8**, 61–72.

Dodt, E. and Scherer, E. (1968b). The electroretinogram of the third eye. *Adv. Electrophysiol. Path. Visual System* **6**, 231–237.

Dodt, E., Scherer, E., Ueck, M. and Oksche, A. (1971). Relations of structure and function: The pineal organ of lower vertebrates. *In* "J. E. Purkyně Centenary Symposium". (V. Kruta, ed.). Universita Jana Evangelisty Purkyně, Brno, 253–278.

Dowling, J. E. and Wald, G. (1960). The biological function of vitamin A acid. *Proc. natn. Acad. Sci., U.S.A.* **46**, 587–608.

Dufaure, J. P. (1966). Recherches descriptives et expérimentales sur les modalités et facteurs du dévelopment de l'appareil génital chez le lézard vivipare (*Lacerta vivipara* Jacquin). *Arch. Anat. microsc. Morph. exp.* **55**, 437–537.

Duval, M. and Kalt. (1889). Des yeux pinéaux multiples chez l'orvet. *C. r. Séanc. Soc. Biol.* **41**, 85–86.

Eakin, R. M. (1960). Number of photoreceptors and melanocytes in the third eye of the lizard, *Sceloporus occidentalis*. *Anat. Rec.* 138, 345.

Eakin, R. M. (1963). Lines of evolution of photoreceptors. *In* "General Physiology of Cell Speciation". (D. Mazia and A. Tyler, eds). McGraw-Hill, New York, 393–425.

Eakin, R. M. (1964a). Development of the third eye in the lizard *Sceloporus occidentalis*. *Rev. suisse Zool.* 71, 267–285.

Eakin, R. M. (1964b). The effect of vitamin A deficiency on photoreceptors in the lizard *Sceloporus occidentalis*. *Vision Res.* 4, 17–22.

Eakin, R. M. (1968). Evolution of photoreceptors. *In* "Evolutionary Biology". (T. Dobzhansky, M. K. Hecht and W. C. Steere, eds). Appleton-Century-Crofts, New York 2, 194–242.

Eakin, R. M. (1970). A third eye. *Am. Scient.* 58, 73–79.

Eakin, R. M. (1973). "The Third Eye." Univ. California Press, Berkeley.

Eakin, R. M. and Stebbins, R. C. (1959). Parietal eye nerve in the fence lizard. *Science, N.Y.* 130, 1573–1574.

Eakin, R. M. and Westfall, J. A. (1959). Fine structure of the retina in the reptilian third eye. *J. biophys. biochem. Cytol.* 6, 133–134.

Eakin, R. M. and Westfall, J. A. (1960). Further observations of the fine structure of the parietal eye of lizards. *J. biophys. biochem. Cytol.* 8, 483–499.

Eakin, R. M. and Westfall, J. A. (1962). Effects of vitamin A deficiency on photoreceptors in the lateral and median eyes of the lizard, *Sceloporus occidentalis*. *Am. Zool.* 2, 520.

Eakin, R. M., Stebbins, R. C. and Wilhoft, D. C. (1959). Effects of parietalectomy and sustained temperature on thyroid of lizard, *Sceloporus occidentalis*. *Proc. Soc. exp. Biol. Med.* 101, 162–164.

Eakin, R. M., Quay, W. B. and Westfall, J. A. (1961). Cytochemical and cytological studies of the parietal eye of the lizard, *Sceloporus occidentalis*. *Z. Zellforsch. Mikrosk. Anat.* 53, 449–470.

Edinger, T. (1929). Die fossilen Gehirne. *Ergebn. Anat. EntwGesch.* 28, 1–249.

Edinger, T. (1955). The size of parietal foramen and organ in reptiles. A rectification. *Bull. Mus. comp. Zool. Harv.* 114, 1–34.

Edinger, T. (1956). Paired pineal organs. *In* "Progress in Neurobiology". (J. Ariëns Kappers, ed.). Elsevier, Amsterdam, 121–129.

Edinger, T. (1964). Recent advances in paleoneurology. *Prog. Brain Res.* 6, 147–160.

Elliot Smith, G. (1903). On the morphology of the cerebral commissures in the Vertebrata with special reference to an aberrant commissure found in the forebrain of certain reptiles. *Trans. Linn. Soc. Lond. Ser.* 2, 8, 455–500.

Engbretson, G. A. and C. M. Lent (1974). Sensory information and feedback in the parietal eye–pineal gland complex of a lizard. *Am. Zool.* 14, 1280.

Faivre, E. (1857). Étude sur le conarium et les plexus choroides chez l'homme et les animaux. *Annls. Sci. nat. (Zool.) ser.* 4, 7, 52–90.

Fenwick, J. C. (1970). The pineal organ: photoperiod and reproduction cycles in the goldfish, *Carassius auratus* L. *J. Endocr.* 46, 101–111.

Firth, B. T. (1974). "Functional Aspects of the Pineal Complex in Lacertilia." Ph.D. Thesis, University of New England, Armidale, N.S.W., Australia.

Fox, W. and Dessauer, H. C. (1958). Response of the male reproductive system of lizards (*Anolis carolinensis*) to unnatural day-lengths in different seasons. *Biol. Bull. mar. biol. Lab., Woods Hole* 115, 421–439.

Francis, C. and Brooks, G. R. (1970). Oxygen consumption, rate of heart beat and ventilatory rate in parietalectomized lizards, *Sceloporus occidentalis*. *Comp. Biochem. Physiol.* 35, 463–469.

Francotte, P. (1887). Contribution à l'étude du développement de l'épiphyse et du troisième oeil chez les reptiles. *Bull. Acad. r. Belg.* **14**, 699–702.

Francotte, P. (1888). Recherches sur le développement de l'épiphyse. *Arch. Biol.*, *Liege* **8**, 757–821.

Francotte, P. (1892). "Contribution à l'Étude de l'Épiphyse et de la Paraphyse chez les Lacertiliens." Brussels.

Francotte, P. (1894). Note sur l'oeil pariétal, l'épiphyse, la paraphyse et les plexus choroides du troisième ventricule. *Bull. Acad. r. Belg.* **27**, 84–109.

Francotte, P. (1896). Contribution à l'étude de l'oeil pariétal, de l'épiphyse et de la paraphyse chez les Lacertilia. *Acad. r. Belg. Mem. Cour.*, **55**, 1–45.

Gabe, M. and St. Girons, H. (1964). "Contribution à l'Histologie de *Sphenodon punctatus* Gray." Editions du C.N.R.S., Paris.

Gage, S. P. (1895). Comparative morphology of the brain of the soft-shelled turtle (*Amyda mutica*) and the English sparrow (*Passer domestica*). *Proc. Am. Micr. Soc.* **17**, 185–238.

Gasson, W. (1947). The normal and parietal eyes of the tuatara. *Optician* **37**, 261–265.

Gaupp, E. (1897). Zirbel, Parietalorgan und Paraphysis. *Ergebn. Anat. Entw. Mech.* **7**, 208–285.

Gilmore, C. W. (1928). Fossil lizards of North America. *Mem. Nat. Acad. Sci.* **22**, 1–201.

Gladstone, R. J. and Wakeley, C. P. (1940). "The Pineal Organ." Baillière, Tindall and Cox, London.

Glaser, R. (1958). Increase in locomotor activity following shielding of the parietal eye in night lizards. *Science, N.Y.* **128**, 1577–1578.

Goronowitsch, N. (1888). Das Gehirn und die Cranialnerven von *Acipenser ruthenus*. *Morph. Jb.* **13**, 515.

Gregory, W. K. (1951). "Evolution Emerging." Macmillan, New York, 2 vols.

Grignon, M. and Grignon, G. (1963a). Étude histologique et histophysiologique de l'épiphyse chez la tortue terrestre (*Testudo mauritanica* Dumér.). *Annls Endocr.* **24**(2), 356–364.

Grignon, M. and Grignon, G. (1963b). Étude de la structure de l'épiphyse chez quelques reptiles. *Gen. comp. Endocr.* **3**, 704.

Grignon, G. and Grignon, M. (1963c). Sur la structure de l'épiphyse de la tortue terrestre (*Testudo mauritanica* Dumér.). *C. r. Assoc. Anat.*, *Bull. Assoc. Anat.* **118**, 685–696.

Gruberg, E. R., Heath, J. E. and Northcutt, R. G. (1968). Photosensitivity of the parietal eye of the lizard, *Phrynosoma cornutum*. *Proc. Int. Union Physiol. Sci.* **7**, 171.

Gundy, G. C. and Ralph, C. L. (1971). A histological study of the third eye and related structures in scincid lizards. *Herpetol. Rev.* **3**, 65.

Gundy, G. C., Ralph, C. L. and McCoy, C. J. (1974). The significance of third eyes in lizards: a zoogeographical approach. *Am. Zool.* **14**(4), 1271.

Gundy, G. C., Ralph, C. L. and Wurst, G. Z. (1975). Parietal eyes in lizards: Zoogeographical correlates. *Science, N.Y.* **190**, 671–673.

Haffner, K. von (1953). Untersuchungen über die Entwicklung des Parietalorgans und des Parietalnerven von *Lacerta vivipara* und das Problem der Organe der Parietalregion. *Z. wiss. Zool.* **157**, 1–34.

Haffner, K. von (1955). Über "accessorische Parietalorgane" und "Nebenparietalaugen" als degenerative Bildungen am Parietalauge von *Lacerta vivipara*. *Mitt. Zool. Mus. Inst. Hamb.* **53**, 25–32.

Hamasaki, D. I. (1968). Properties of the parietal eye of the green iguana. *Vision Res.* **8**, 591–599.

Hamasaki, D. I. (1969a). Spectral sensitivity of the parietal eye of the green iguana. *Vision Res.* **9**, 512–523.

Hamasaki, D. I. (1969b). Interaction of the slow responses of the parietal eye. *Vision Res.* **9**, 1453–1459.

Hamasaki, D. I. and Dodt, E. (1969). Light sensitivity of the lizard's epiphysis cerebri. *Pflügers Arch. ges. Physiol.* **313**, 19–29.

Hanitsch, R. (1888). On the pineal eye of the young and adult of *Anguis fragilis. Proc. Liverpool biol. Soc.* **3**, 87–95.

Hatcher, J. B., Marsh, O. C. and Lull, R. S. (1907). The Ceratopsia. *Monogr. U.S. Geol. Survey* **49**, 1–157.

Herrick, C. L. (1893). Contributions to the comparative morphology of the central nervous system. II. Topography and histology of the brain of certain reptiles. *J. comp. Neurol.* **3**, 92–94.

Hill, C. (1891). Development of the epiphysis in *Coregonus albus. J. Morph.* **3**, 503.

His, W. (1868). "Untersuchungen über die ersten Anlage Wirbeltierleibes." W. Engelmann, Leipzig, 1–237.

Hoffman, R. A. (1970). The epiphyseal complex in fish and reptiles. *Am. Zool.* **10**, 191–199.

Hoffmann, C. K. (1886). Weitere Untersuchungen zur Entwicklung der Reptilien. *Morph. Jb.* **11**, 176–219.

Hoffmann, C. K. (1890). Epiphyse und Parietalauge. *In* "Klassen und Ordnungen des Thier-reichs". (H. G. Bronn, ed.). C. F. Winter'sche Verlagshandlung, Leipzig, 6(3), Reptilien, 1981–1993.

Huene, F. von (1933). Zur Lebensweise und Verwandtschaft von *Placodus. Abh. senckenb. naturf. Ges.* **38**, 365–382.

Huene, F. von (1941). Osteologie und systematische Stellung von *Mesosaurus. Palaeontographica* **92**, 45–58.

Huene, F. von (1952). Revision der Gattung *Pleurosaurus* auf Grund neuer und alter Funde. *Paleontographica* **101**, 167–200.

Humphrey, O. D. (1894). On the brain of the snapping turtle (*Chelydra serpentina*). *J. comp, Neurol.* **4**, 73–116.

Hutchinson, V. H. and Kosh, R. J. (1974). Thermoregulatory function of the parietal eye in the lizard *Anolis carolinensis. Oecologia* **16**, 173–177.

Hutton, K. E. and Ortman, R. (1957). Blood chemistry and parietal eye of *Anolis carolinensis. Proc. Soc. exp. Biol. Med.* **96**, 842–844.

Janensch, W. (1935). Die Schädel der Sauropoden *Brachiosaurus, Barosaurus* und *Dicraeosaurus* aus den Tendaguru-schichten Deutsch-ostafrikas. *Palaeontographica Suppl.* 7(2), 147–298.

Kälin, K. A. (1933). Beiträge zur vergleichenden Osteologie des Crocodilidenschädels. *Zool. Jb. (Anat.)* **57**, 535–714.

Kamer, J. C. van de (1965). Histological structure and cytology of the pineal complex in fishes, amphibians and reptiles. *Prog. Brain Res.* **10**, 30–48.

Kappers, J. A. (1964). Survey of the innervation of the pineal organ in vertebrates. *Am. Zool.* **4**, 47–51.

Kappers, J. A. (1965). Survey of the innervation of the epiphysis cerebri and the accessory pineal organs of vertebrates. *Prog. Brain Res.* **10**, 87–153.

Kappers, J. A. (1966). Note préliminaire sur l'innervation de l'épiphyse du lézard *Lacerta viridis. Bull. Ass. Anat., Nancy* **134**, 111–116.

Kappers, J. A. (1967). The sensory innervation of the pineal organ in the lizard, *Lacerta viridis*, with remarks on its position in the trend of pineal phylogenetic structure and functional evolution. *Z. Zellforsch. mikrosk. Anat.* **81**, 581–618.

Kappers, J. A. (1969). The morphological and functional evolution of the pineal organ during its phylogenetic development. *In* "Progress in Endocrinology" (C. Gual, ed.). Excerpta Med. Fdn, Amsterdam, 619–626.

Kappers, J. A. (1971a). Innervation of the pineal organ. Phylogenetic aspects and comparison of the neural control of the mammalian pineal with that of other endocrine systems. *Mem. Soc. Endocrinol.* **19**, 27–48.

Kappers, J. A. (1971b). The pineal organ: An introduction. *In* "The Pineal Gland." (G. E. W. Wolstenholme and J. Knight, eds). CIBA Foundation Symposium. Churchill Livingstone, Edinburgh, 3–34.

Kelly, D. E. (1962). Pineal organs: Photoreception, secretion and development. *Am. Scient.* **50**, 597–625.

Kemp, T. S. (1969). On the functional morphology of the gorgonopsid skull. *Phil. Trans. R. Soc. Ser. B.* **256**, 1–83.

Kemp, T. S. (1972). Whaitsiid Therocephalia and the origin of cynodonts. *Phil. Trans. R. Soc. Ser. B* **264**, 1–54.

Kitay, J. I. and Altschule, M. D. (1954). "The Pineal Gland. A Review of the Physiologic Literature." Harvard University Press, Cambridge, Mass.

de Klinckowström, A. (1893). Le premier développement de l'oeil pinéal, l'épiphyse et le nerf pariétal chez *Iguana tuberculata*. *Anat. Anz.* **8**, 289–298.

de Klinckowström, A. (1894). Beiträge zur Kenntnis des Parietalorgans. *Zool. Jb. (Anat.)* **7**, 249.

Kosh, R. J. and Hutchinson, V. H. (1972). Thermal tolerance of parietalectomized *Anolis carolinensis* acclimated at different temperatures and photoperiods. *Herpetologica* **28**, 183–191.

Krabbe, K. H. (1920). Histologie, développement et functions de la glande pinéale chez les mammiferes. *Biol. Meddedr. Dansk. Vidensk. Selskab.* **2**, 1–126.

Krabbe, K. H. (1934). Embryonal development of parietal organs in *Chamaelo bitaeniatus* Fischer. *Psychiat. Neurol. Amsterdam* **38**, 750–760.

Krabbe, K. H. (1935). Recherches embryologiques sur les organes parietaux chez certains reptiles. *Biol. Meddedr. Danske Vidensk. Selskabs.* **12**, 1–111.

Kupffer, D. von (1887). Über die Zirbeldrüse des Gehirns. *Münch. Med. Wochenschrift* **34**, 205.

Legge, F. (1897). Sul sviluppo dell'occhio pineale nel *Gongylus ocellatus. Bull. R. Acc. Med., Roma.* **23**,

Levey, I. L. (1972). Reproductive function of the pineal complex in female lizards. *J. Colo.-Wyo. Acad. Sci.* **7**, 74.

Levey, I. L. (1973). Effects of pinealectomy and melatonin injections at different seasons on ovarian activity in the lizard *Anolis carolinensis. J. exp. Zool.* **185**, 169–174.

Leydig, F. (1872). "Die in Deutschland lebenden Arten der Saurier." H. Laupp'sche Buchhandlung, Tübingen.

Leydig, F. (1887). Das Parietalorgan der Wirbeltiere. *Zool. Anz.* **10**, 534–539.

Leydig, F. (1889). Das Parietalorgan der Reptilien und Amphibien, kein Sinneswerkzeug. *Biol. Zbl.* **8**, 707–718.

Leydig, F. (1890a). Das Parietalorgan. *Biol. Zbl.* **10**, 278–285.

Leydig, F. (1890b). Das Parietalorgan der Amphibien und Reptilien. *Abh. senckenb. Naturforsch. Ges.* **16**, 441–550.

Leydig, F. (1896). Zur Kenntnis der Zirbel und Parietalorgane. *Abh. senckenb. naturforsch. Ges.* **19**, 217–278.

Leydig, F. (1897). Zirbel und jacobsonsche Organe einiger Reptilien. *Arch. Mikrosk. Anat. EntwMech.* **50**, 385–418.

Leydig, J. (1883). Über die einheimischen Schlangen. *Abh. senckenb. naturforsch. Ges.* 8, 167–221.

Licht, P. and Pearson, A. K. (1970). Failure of parietalectomy to affect the testes in the lizard *Anolis carolinensis. Copeia* 1970(1), 172–173.

Lierse, W. (1965a). Die Gefässversorgung der Epiphyse und Paraphyse bei Reptilien. *Prog. Brain Res.* 10, 183–192.

Lierse, W. (1965b). Electronenmikroskopische Untersuchungen zur Cytologie und Angiologie des Epiphysensteils von *Anolis carolinensis. Z. Zellforsch. mikrosk. Anat.* 65, 397–408.

Linder, H. (1913). Beiträge zur Kenntnis der Plesiosaurier-gattungen *Peloneustes* und *Pliosaurus. Geol. Paläont. Abh.* 15, 337–409.

Locy, W. A. (1894). The derivation of the pineal eye. *Anat. Anz.* 9, 169–180.

Lull, R. S. and Wright, N. E. (1942). Hadrosaurian dinosaurs of North America. *Geol. Soc. Am., Spec. Pap.* 40, 1–242.

Lutz, H. and Collin, J. P. (1967). Sur la regression des cellules photoreceptrices épiphysaires chez la tortue terrestre: *Testudo hermanni* (Gmelin) et la phylogénie des photorécepteurs épiphysaires chez les vertébrés. *Bull. Soc. zool. Fr.* 92, 797–801.

Manten, A. A. (1958). Two new gorgonopsian skulls. *Palaeont. Afr.* 6, 51–76.

McDevitt, D. S. (1970). Presence of lens-specific proteins (crystallins) in the pineal eye of the American chameleon, *Anolis carolinensis. Am. Zool.* 10, 532.

McDevitt, D. S. (1972). Presence of lateral eye lens crystallins in the median eye of the American chameleon. *Science, N.Y.* 175, 763–764.

McDowell, S. B., Jr. and Bogert, C. M. (1954). The systematic position of *Lanthanotus* and the affinities of the anguinomorphan lizards. *Bull. Am. Mus. nat. Hist.* 105, 1–142.

McKay, W. J. (1888). The development and structure of the pineal eye in *Hinulia* and *Grammatophora. Proc. Linn. Soc. N.S.W.* (series 2) 3, 876–889.

Mehring, G. (1972). Licht- und elektronenmikrosckopische Untersuchung des Pinealorgans von *Testudo hermanni. Anat. Anz.* 131, 184–203.

Meiniel, A. (1974a), L'épiphyse et l'oeil pariétal de l'embryon de *Lacerta vivipara* J.-Recherche qualitative des monoamines en fluorescence ultraviolette et incorporation de 5-hydroxytryptophane-^{3}H (=5-HTP-^{3}H) au niveau des photorécepteurs rudimentaires sécrétoires. *Arch. Anat. Histol. Embryol.* 56, 111–130.

Meiniel, A. (1974b). Biosynthèse d'amines biogènes dans l'organe pinéal embryonnaire de *Lacerta vivipara* J. *J. Physiol., Paris* 68, 5B.

Meiniel, A. (1975a). The ultrastructure of the secretory rudimentary photoreceptor cells in the embryonic pineal organ of *Lacerta vivipara. C. r. hebd. Acad. Sci., Paris* 281, 1163.

Meiniel, A. (1975b). Mise en évidence d'une relation entre les sites de stockage des indolamines et les zones de concentration des grains denses dans les photorécepteurs rudimentaires sécrétoires de l'epiphyse embryonnaire de *Lacerta vivipara* J. *J. Physiol., Paris* 70, 4B–5B.

Meiniel, A. and Collin, J.-P. (1970). Monoamines de l'organe pineal au cours des stades de développement intra-utérins d'un amniote. Recherches chez *Lacerta vivipara* (Jacquin), reptile, lacertilien. *C. r. hebd. Acad. Sci., Paris* 271, 2373–2376.

einiel, A., Collin, J.-P. and Calas, A. (1972). Incorporation du 5-hydroxytryptophane M(5-HTP) dans l'organe pinéal du lacertilien *Lacerta vivipara* (J.): étude par radioautographie à haute résolution. *C. r. hebd. Acad. Sci., Paris* 274, 2897–2900.

Meiniel, A., Collin, J.-P. and Hartwig, H. G. (1973). Pinéale et troisième oeil de *Lacerta vivipara* (J.), au cours de la vie embryonnaire et postnatale. Étude cytophysiologique des monoamines en microscopie de fluorescence et en microspectrofluorimetrie. *Z. Zell-forsch. mikrosk. Anat.* 144, 89–115.

Meiniel, A., Collin, J.-P. and Moskowska, A. (1975). Pinéale et 3éme oeil de l'embryon de *Lacerta vivipara*: étude qualitative et quantitative, en microscopie photonique, de l'incorporation de 5-hydroxytryptophanne-^{3}H, au cours de l'ontogenèse. *J. neur. Transm.* 36, 249–279.

Melchers, F. (1900). Über rudimentäre Hirnanhangsgebilde beim Gecko (Epi-, Para- und Hypophyse). *Z. wiss. Zool.* 67, 139–166.

Meyer, J. and Brooks, G. R. (1968). Effect of blinding and parietalectomy on color change in *Anolis carolinensis* (Reptilia: Ignanidae). *Virginia J. Sci.* 19, 122–125.

Milcou, S. M., Dancâsiu, M., Cîmpeanu, L., Petrovici, A. and Ionescu, M. D. (1968). Ultrastructure de la glande pinéale chez les ophidiens. *Rev. roumaine Endocrinol.* 5, 303–307.

Milcou, S. M. and Dancâsiu, M. (1967). The ultrastructure of pineal gland in reptiles (ophidians). *Proc. Nat. Congr. Endocrinol., Bucharest*, 30 May–2 June, p. 211.

Miline, R. (1971). Role of the pineal in cold adaptation. *In* "The Pineal Gland." (G. E. W. Wolstenholme and J. Knight, eds). CIBA Foundation Symposium. Churchill Livingstone, Edinburgh, 372–373.

Miller, W. H. and Wolbarsht, M. L. (1962). Neural activity in the parietal eye of a lizard *Science, N.Y.* 135, 316–317.

Minot, C. S. (1901). On the morphology of the pineal region, based upon its development in *Acanthias. Am. J. Anat.* 1, 81–98.

Newton, E. T. (1889). On the skull, brain and auditory organ of a new species of ptero-saurian (*Scaphognathus purdoni*), from the Upper Lias near Yorkshire. *Phil. Trans. R. Soc. Ser. B* 179, 503–537.

Nopsca, F. (1926). Heredity and evolution. *Proc. zool. Soc. Lond.* 1926(1), 633–666.

Nowikoff, M. (1907). Über das Parietalauge von *Lacerta agilis* und *Anguis fragilis. Biol. Zbl.* 27, 364–370, 405–414.

Nowikoff, M. (1910). Untersuchungen über den Bau, die Entwicklung und die Bedeutung des Parietalauges von Sauriern. *Z. wiss. Zool.* 96, 118–207.

Oksche, A. (1956). Funktionelle histologische Untersuchungen über die Organe des Zwischenhirndaches der Chordaten. *Anat. Anz.* 102, 404–419.

Oksche, A. (1965). Survey of the development and comparative morphology of the pinea. organ. *Prog. Brain Res.* 10, 3–28.

Oksche, A. (1969). The subcommissural organ. *J. neuro-visceral Relations* Suppl. 9, 111–139.

Oksche, A. (1971a). Pineal organ. *In* "Subcellular Organization and Function in Endocrine Tissues". (H. Heller and K. Lederis, eds). Cambridge Univ. Press, 5–76.

Oksche, A. (1971b). Sensory and glandular elements of the parietal organ. *In* "The Pinea Gland". (G. E. W. Wolstenholme and J. Knight, eds). CIBA Foundation Symposium Churchill Livingstone, Edinburgh, 127–146.

Oksche, A. and Kirschstein, H. (1966a). Zur Frage der Sinneszellen im Pinealorgan der Reptilien. *Naturwissenschaften* 53, 46.

Oksche, A. and Kirschstein, H. (1966b). Elektronenmikroskopische Feinstruktur der Sinneszellen im Pinealorgan von *Phoxinus laevis* L. (Pisces, Teleostei, Cyprinidae) (mit vergleichenden Bemerkungen). *Naturwissenschaften* 53, 591.

Oksche, A. and Kirschstein, H. (1968). Unterschiedlicher elektronenmikroskopischer Feinbau der Sinneszellen im Parietalauge und im Pinealorgan (Epiphysis cerebri) der

Lacertilia. Ein Beitrag zum Epiphysenproblem. *Z. Zellforsch. mikrosk. Anat.* **87**, 159–192.

Olson, E. C. (1944). Origin of mammals based upon cranial morphology of the therapsid suborders. *Geol. Soc. Am., Spec. Pap.* **55**, 1–136.

Olsson, R. (1958). Studies on the subcommissural organ. *Acta zool., Stockh.* **39**, 71–102.

Ortman, R. (1960). Parietal eye and nerve in *Anolis carolinensis. Anat. Rec.* **137**, 386.

Osawa, G. (1898). Beiträge zur Anatomie der *Hatteria punctata. Arch. Mikrosk. Anat. EntwMech.* **51**, 481–690.

Owsjannikow, P. (1888). Über das dritte Auge bei *Petromyzon fluviatilis*, nebst einigen Bemerkungen über dasselbe Organ bei anderen Tieren. *Mém. Acad. Imper. St. Pétersbourg* (ser. 7), **36**, 1–27.

Owsjannikow, P. (1890). Übersicht der Untersuchungen über das Parietalauge bei Amphibien, Reptilien and Fischen. *Revue Sci. Nat. Soc. Nat. St. Pétersbourg* **2**, pt. 2.

Packard, G. C. and Packard, M. J. (1972). Photic exposure of the lizard *Callisaurus draconoides* following shielding of the parietal eye. *Copeia* **1972**(4), 695–701.

Palenschat, D. (1964). "Beiträge zur locomotorischen Aktivität der Blindschleiche (*Anguis fragilis* L.) unter besonderer Berücksichtigung des Parietalorgans." Dokt. Diss., Georg-August Universität, Göttingen.

Palkovits, M. (1965). Morphology and function of the subcommissural organ. *Studia Biol. Hungarica* **4**, 1–105.

Panigel, M. (1956). Contribution à l'étude de l'ovoviviparité chez les reptiles: gestation et parturition chez le lézard vivipare *Zootoca vivipara. Annls. Sci. nat. (Zool.)* **18**, 569–668.

Parrington, F. R. (1946). On the cranial anatomy of cynodonts. *Proc. zool. Soc. Lond.* **116**, 181–197.

Parrington, F. R. (1967). The identification of the dermal bones of the head. *J. Linn. Soc. (Zool.)* **47**, 231–239.

Petit, A. (1967). Nouvelles observations sur la morphogénèse et l'histogénèse du complexe épiphysaire des lacertiliens. *Arch. Anat. Histol. Embryol.* **50**, 227–257.

Petit, A. (1968). Ultrastructure de la rétine de l'oeil pariétal d'un lacertilien, *Anguis fragilis. Z. Zellforsch. mikrosk. Anat.* **92**, 70–93.

Petit, A. (1969). Ultrastructure, innervation et fonction de l'épiphyse de l'orvet (*Anguis fragilis* L.). *Z. Zellforsch. mikrosk. Anat.* **96**, 437–465.

Petit, A. (1971a). L'épiphyse d'un serpent: *Tropidonotus natrix* L. I. Étude structurale et ultrastructurale. *Z. Zellforsch. mikrosk. Anat.* **120**, 94–119.

Petit, A. (1971b). L'épiphyse d'un serpent: *Tropidonotus natrix* L. II. Études cytochimique, autoradiographique et pharmacologique. *Z. Zellforsch. mikrosk. Anat.* **120**, 246–260.

Petit, A., Vivien-Roels, B. and Lichte, C. (1971). Dosage spectrofluorimétrique de la 5-hydroxytryptamine (5-HT = sérotonine) épiphysaire chez les reptiles. Étude des variations du taux de 5-HT en fonction de quelques drogues. *C. r. hebd. Acad. Sci., Paris* **272**, 1283–1285.

Preisler, O. (1942). Zur Kenntnis der Entwicklung des Parietalauges und des Feinbaues der Epiphyze der Reptilien. *Z. Zellforsch. mikrosk. Anat.* **32**, 209–216.

Prenant, A. (1893). Sur l'oeil pariétal accessoire. *Anat. Anz.* **9**, 103–112.

Prenant, A. (1894). Les yeux pariétaux accessoires d'*Anguis fragilis*. Sous le rapport de leur situation, de leur nombre et de leur fréquence. *Bibliogr. anat.* **2**, 223–229.

Prenant, A. (1895). L'appareil pinéal de *Scincus officinalis* et d'*Agama bibronii* (Duméril). *Bull. Soc. Sci. Nancy* **14**, 52.

Quay, W. B. (1956). Volumetric and cytologic variation in the pineal body of *Peromyscus leucopus* (Rodentia) with respect to sex, captivity and day-length. *J. Morph.* **98**, 471–495.

Quay, W. B. (1965a). Histological structure and cytology of the pineal organ in birds and mammals. *Prog. Brain Res.* **10**, 49–86.

Quay, W. B. (1965b). Retinal and pineal hydroxyindole-*O*-methyl transferase activity in vertebrates. *Life Sci.* **4**, 983–991.

Quay, W. B. (1969a). Catecholamines and tryptamines. *J. neuro-visceral Relations* Suppl. **9**, 212–235.

Quay, W. B. (1969b). Evidence for a pineal contribution in the regulation of vertebrate reproductive systems. *Gen. comp. Endocrinol.* Suppl. **2**, 101–110.

Quay, W. B. (1970a). Pineal structure and composition in the orangutan (*Pongo pygmaeus*). *Anat. Rec.* **168**, 93–104.

Quay, W. B. (1970b). The significance of the pineal. *Mem. Soc. Endocr.* **18**, 423–444.

Quay, W. B. (1971). Factors in the measurement of pineal acetylserotonin methyltransferase activity in the lizard *Sceloporus occidentalis*. *Gen. comp. Endocr.* **17**, 220–226.

Quay, W. B. (1973). Retrograde perfusions of the pineal region and the question of pineal vascular routes to brain and choroid plexuses. *Am. J. Anat.* **137**, 387–401.

Quay, W. B. (1974). "Pineal Chemistry In Cellular and Physiological Mechanisms." Charles C Thomas, Springfield, Ill.

Quay, W. B. and Renzoni, A. (1963). Comparative and experimental studies of pineal structure and cytology in passeriform birds. *Rivista Biol.* **56**, 363–407.

Quay, W. B. and Renzoni, A. (1967). The diencephalic relations and variably bipartite structure of the avian pineal complex. *Rivista. Biol.* **60**, 9–75.

Quay, W. B., Stebbins, R. C., Kelley, T. D. and Cohen, N. W. (1971). Effects of environmental and physiological factors on pineal acetylserotonin methyltransferase activity in the lizard *Sceloporous occidentalis*. *Physiol. Zoöl.* **44**, 241–248.

Quay, W. B. and Wilhoft, D. C. (1964). Comparative and regional differences in serotonin content of reptilian brains. *J. Neurochem.* **11**, 805–811.

Quay, W. B., Jongkind, J. F. and Kappers, J. A. (1967). Localizations and experimental changes in monoamines of the reptilian pineal complex studied by fluorescence histochemistry. *Anat. Rec.* **157**, 304–305.

Quay, W. B., Kappers, J. A. and Jongkind, J. F. (1968). Innervation and fluorescence histochemistry of monoamines in the pineal organ of a snake (*Natrix natrix*). *J. neuro-visceral Relations* **31**, 11–25.

Quay, W. B., Kelley, T. D., Stebbins, R. C. and Cohen, N. W. (1970). Experimental studies on brain 5-hydroxytryptamine and monoamine oxidase in a field population of the lizard *Sceloporus occidentalis*. *Physiol. Zoöl.* **45**, 90–97.

Rabl-Rückhard, H. (1886). Zur Deutung der Zirbeldrüse (Epiphysis). *Zool. Anz.* **9**, 405–407.

Rabl-Rückhard, H. (1894). Einiges über das Gehirn der Riesenschlange. *Z. wiss. Zool.* **54**, 694.

Raynaud, A. (1959a). Une technique permettant d'obtenir le développement des oeufs d'orvet (*Anguis fragilis*) hors de l'organisme maternel. *C. r. hebd. Acad. Sci., Paris* **249**, 1715–1717.

Raynaud, A. (1959b). Développement et croissance des embryons d'orvet (*Anguis fragilis*) dans l'oeuf incubé in vitro. *C. r. hebd. Acad. Sci., Paris* **249**, 1813–1815.

Reiter, R. J. (1972). The role of the pineal in reproduction. *In* "Reproductive Biology." (H. Balin and S. Glasser, eds). Excerpta Medica, Amsterdam, 71–114.

Reiter, R. J. (1973). Comparative physiology—pineal gland. *Am. Rev. Physiol.* **35**, 305–328.

Reiter, R. J. (1974). Pineal-anterior pituitary gland relationships. *In* "MTP Int. Review of Science, Physiology. Series I, Vol. 5, Endocrine Physiology" (S. M. McCann, ed.). Butterworths, London, 277–308.

Reiter, R. J., Vaughan, M. K. and Blask, D. E. (1975). Possible role of the cerebrospinal fluid in the transport of pineal hormones in mammals. *In* "Brain–Endocrine Interaction II." (K. M. Knigge and D. E. Scott, eds). S. Karger AG, Basel, 337–354.

Ridgeway, P. M. (1972). "Effects of Blinding and Parietalectomy on the Testes of Male Lizards (*Anolis carolinensis*)." Ph.D. Thesis, Memphis State University.

Ridgeway, P. M. and Kent, G. C. (1971). Effects of parietalectomy and blinding on the testes of the lizard *Anolis carolinensis*. *Am. Zool.* **11,** 651.

Ritter, W. E. (1890). The parietal eye in some lizards from the western United States. *Bull. Mus. comp. Zool. Harv.* **20,** 209–228.

Ritter, W. E. (1894). On the presence of a parapineal organ in *Phrynosoma coronata*. *Anat. Anz.* **9,** 766–772.

Romer, A. S. (1941). Notes on the crossopterygian hyomandibular and braincase. *J. Morph.* **69,** 141–160.

Romer, A. S. (1956). "Osteology of the Reptiles." Univ. Chicago Press, Chicago.

Romer, A. S. (1966). "Vertebrate Palaeontology." 3rd edn. Univ. Chicago Press, Chicago.

Romer, A. S. (1968). "Notes and Comments on Vertebrate Paleontology." Univ. Chicago Press, Chicago.

Romer, A. S. and Price, L. I. (1940). Review of the Pelycosauria. *Geol. Soc. Am., Spec. Pap.* **28,** 1–538.

Roth, C. and Braun, R. (1958). Zur Funktion des Parietalauges der Blindsch-leiche *Anguis fragilis* (Reptilia; Lacertilia, Anguidae). *Naturwissenschaften* **45,** 218–219.

Saurez, V. T. (1969). "El Ojo Parietal de *Anolis pulchellus* y Algunos aspectos de su Relacion con la Luz." Unpublished M.S. Thesis, University of Puerto Rico.

Scatizzi, J. (1933). Ricerche sulla fine costituzione dell'epfisi dei cheloni. *Arch. Zool. Ital.* 407–420.

Schauinsland, H. (1903). Beiträge zur Entwickelungsgeschichte und Anatomie der Wirbeltiere. I. *Sphenodon, Callorhynchus, Chamaeleo. Zoologica* **16,** 1–98.

Schmidt, W. J. (1909). Beiträge zur Kenntnis der Parietalorgane der Saurier. *Z. wiss. Zool.* **92,** 359–426.

Sivak, J. G. (1973). Optical properties of the interparietal scale of the green iguana (*Iguana iguana*). *Herpetologica* **29,** 254–255.

Smith, H. M. (1946). "Handbook of Lizards. Lizards of the United States and Canada." Comstock, New York.

Smith, M. A. (1935). "The Fauna of British India. Reptilia and Amphibia. II. Sauria." Taylor and Francis, London.

Songdahl, J. H. and Hutchinson, V. H. (1972). The effect of photoperiod, parietalectomy and eye enucleation on oxygen consumption in the blue granite lizard, *Sceloporus cyanogenys. Herpetologica* **28,** 148–156.

Sorensen, A. D. (1893). The pineal and parietal organ in *Phrynosoma coronata. J. comp. Neurol.* **3,** 48–50.

Sorensen, A. D. (1894). Comparative study of the epiphysis and roof of the diencephalon. *J. comp. Neurol.* **4,** 12–72, 153–171.

Spencer, W. B. (1886a). The parietal eye of *Hatteria. Nature, Lond.* **34,** 33–35.

Spencer, W. B. (1886b). Preliminary communication on the structure and presence in *Sphenodon* and other lizards of the median eye described by von Graaf in *Anguis fragilis. Proc. R. Soc.* **40,** 559–565.

Spencer, W. B. (1886c). On the presence and structure of the pineal eye in Lacertilia. *Qut. Jl. Microsc. Sci.* **17,** 165–238.

Ssobolew, L. W. (1907). Zur Lehre Über die Entwicklung von Paraphysis und Epiphysis bei den Schlangen. *Arch. mikrosk. Anat. EntwMech.* **70**, 318–329.

Stammer, A. (1967). The structure of the pineal gland in the sand lizard. *Gen. comp. Endocr.* **9**, 521.

Stebbins, R. C. (1960). Effects of pinealectomy in the western fence lizard *Sceloporus occidentalis. Copeia* **1960**(4), 276–283.

Stebbins, R. C. (1963). Activity changes in the striped plateau lizard with evidence on influence of the parietal eye. *Copeia* **1963**(4), 681–691.

Stebbins, R. C. (1970). The effect of parietalectomy on testicular activity and exposure to light in the desert night lizard (*Xantusia vigilis*). *Copeia* **1970**(2), 261–270.

Stebbins, R. C. and Cohen, N. W. (1973). The effect of parietalectomy on the thyroid and gonads in free-living western fence lizards, *Sceloporus occidentalis. Copeia* **1973**(4), 662–668.

Stebbins, R. C. and Eakin, R. M. (1958). The role of the "third eye" in reptilian behavior. *Am. Mus. Novit.* **1870**, 1–40.

Stebbins, R. C. and Tong, W. (1973). Epithelial cell height as a measure of thyroid activity in free-living western fence lizards, *Sceloporus occidentalis. Copeia* **1973**(4), 668–672.

Stebbins, R. C. and Wilhoft, D. C. (1966). Influence of the parietal eye on activity in lizards. *In* "The Galapagos" (R. I. Bowman, ed.). Proc. Galapagos Int. Science Proj. Univ. California Press, 258–268.

Stebbins, R. C., Lowenstein, J. M. and Cohen, N. W. (1967). A field study of the lava lizard (*Tropidurus albemarlensis*) in the Galapagos Islands. *Ecology* **48**, 839–851.

Stemmler, J. (1900). "Die Entwicklung der Anhänge am Zwischenhirndach beim Gecko (*Gehyra oceanica* und *Hemidactylus mabouia*). Ein Beitrag zur Kenntnis der Epiphysis, des Parietalorganes und der Paraphyse." Leipziger Dissertation, Limburg.

Steyn, W. J. (1957). The morphogenesis and some functional aspects of the epiphyseal complex in lizards. *J. comp. Neurol.* **107**, 227–251.

Steyn, W. J. (1958). The pineal circulation in some lizards. *S. Afr. J. Sci.* **54**, 143–147.

Steyn, W. J. (1959a). Ultrastructure of pineal eye sensory cells. *Nature, Lond.* **183**, 764–765.

Steyn, W. J. (1959b). Some problems of the diencephalic roof in lower vertebrates. *S. Afr. J. Sci.* **55**, 93–95.

Steyn, W. J. (1959c). Epithelial organization and histogenesis of the epiphyseal complex in lizards. *Acta Anat.* **4**, 310–335.

Steyn, W. J. (1960a). Observations on the ultrastructure of the pineal eye. *J. R. microsc. Soc.* **3**, 47–58.

Steyn, W. J. (1960b). Electron microscopic observations on the epiphyseal sensory cells in lizards and the pineal sensory cell problem. *Zellforsch. mikrosk. Anat.* **51**, 735–747.

Steyn, W. J. (1961). Some epithalamic organs, the subcommissural organ, and their possible relation to vertebrate emergence on dry land. *S. Afr. J. Sci.* **57**, 283–287.

Steyn, W. J. (1966). Three eyes: wider implications of a narrow specialty. *S. Afr. J. Sci.* **62**, 13–20.

Steyn, W. and Steyn, S. (1962). Verdere lig- en electronemikroskopie van die derde oog met aanmerkings oor sy termoregulatiewe funksie. *Cimbebasia* **4**, 7–16.

Steyn, W. and Steyn, S. (1965). Further light and electron microscopy of the pineal eye, with a note on thermoregulatory aspects. *Prog. Brain Res.* **10**, 288–295.

Stigler, R. (1950). Versuche über das Parietalauge von *Agama colonorum. Zool. Anz.* **145**, 316–318.

Strahl, H. (1884). Das Leydigsche Organ bei Eidechsen. *Sitzungsber. Gesell. Beford. Ges. Naturwiss. Marburg* (1884), 81–83.

Strahl, H. and Martin, E. (1888). Die Entwickelung des Parietalauges bei *Anguis fragilis* und *Lacerta vivipara. Arch. Anat. Physiol.* (1888), Anat. Abt., 146–164.

Studnička, F. K. (1893). Sur les organes parietaux de *Petromyzon planeri. Sber. k. Ges. Wiss. Prague* 1, 1–50.

Studnička, F. K. (1895–96). Beiträge zur Anatomie und Entwicklungsgeschichte des Vorderhirns der Kranioten. *Sber. k. Ges. Wiss. Prague* Abt. 1 (1895), Abt. 2 (1896).

Studnička, F. K. (1905). Die Parietalorgane. *In* "Lehrbuch der vergleichenden mikroskopischen Anatomie der Wirbeltiere." (A. Oppel, ed.). Gustav Fischer, Jena, pt. 5.

Swain, R. (1966). "Studies on the structure and function of the parietal complex in Lacertilia." Ph.D. Thesis, University of Birmingham, England.

Swain, R. (1968). The pineal vascular system in *Lacerta muralis*, with notes on the venous system of other lizards. *J. Zool., Lond.* 154, 487–493.

Thiéblot, L. and LeBars, H. (1955). "La Glande Pinéale ou Épiphyse." Libraire Maloine, Paris.

Tiedemann, F. (1823). "Anatomie du Cerveau." Trad. par A. Jourdan, Paris.

Tilney, F. and Warren, L. F. (1919). The morphology and evolutional significance of the pineal body. *Am. Anat. Mem.* 9, 1–257.

Toerien, M. J. (1955). Important new Anomodontia. *Paleont. Afr.* 3, 65–72.

Trost, E. (1952). Untersuchungen über die frühe Entwicklung des Parietalauges und der Epiphyse von *Anguis fragilis, Chalcides ocellatus* und *Tropidonotus natrix. Zool. Anz.* 148, 58–71.

Trost, E. (1953a). Die Histogenese und Histologie des Parietalauges von *Anguis fragilis* und *Chalcides ocellatus. Z. Zellforsch. mikrosk. Anat.* 38, 185–217.

Trost, E. (1953b). Die Entwicklung, Histogenese und Histologie der Epiphyse, der Paraphyse, des Velum transversum, des Dorsalsackes und des subcommissuralen Organs bei *Anguis fragilis, Chalcides ocellatus* und *Natrix natrix. Acta anat.* 18, 326–342.

Trost, E. (1954). Zur Morphologie der Parietalorgane der Eidechsen. *Anat. Anz.* 100, 368–374.

Trost, E. (1956). Über die Lage des Foramen parietale bei rezenten Reptilien und Labyrinthodontia. *Acta anat.* 26, 318–339.

Underwood, H. (1973). Retinal and extraretinal photoreceptors mediate entrainment of the circadian locomotor rhythm in lizards. *J. comp. Physiol.* 83, 187–222.

Underwood, H. (1975). Extraretinal light receptors can mediate photoperiodic photoreception in the male lizard *Anolis carolinensis. J. comp. Physiol.* 99, 71–78.

Underwood, H. and Menaker, M. (1970). Extraretinal light perception: entrainment of the biological clock controlling lizard locomotor activity. *Science, N.Y.* 170, 190–193.

Vigh, B. (1971). Das Paraventrikularorgan und das Zirkumventrikulare System des Gehirns. *Stud. Biol. hung.* 10, 1–149.

Vivien, J. H. (1964a). Organisation et structure de l'organe pinéal d'un ophidien, *Tropidonotus natrix* L. *J. Microscopie* 3, 57.

Vivien, J. H. (1964b). Ultrastructure des constituants de l'épiphyse de *Tropidonotus natrix* L. *C. r. hebd. Acad. Sci., Paris* 258, 3370–3372.

Vivien, J. H. (1965). Signes de stimulation des activités sécrétoires des pinéalocytes chez couleuvre *Tropidonotus natrix* L. traitée par des principes gonadotropes. *C. r. hebd. Acad. Sci., Paris* 260, 5370–5372.

Vivien, J. H. and Roels, B. (1967). Ultrastructure de l'épiphyse des chéloniens. Présence d'un "paraboloide" et de structure de type photorecepteur dans l'épithelium sécrétoire de *Pseudemys scripta elegans. C. r. hebd. Acad. Sci., Paris* 264, 1743–1746.

Vivien, J. H. and Roels, B. (1968). Ultrastructure synaptiques dans l'épiphyse des chéloniens. Présence de rubans synaptiques au niveau des articulations entre cellules pseudosensorielles et terminaisons nerveuses dans l'épiphyse de *Pseudemys scripta elegans* et *Pseudemys picta*. *C. r. hebd. Acad. Sci., Paris* **266**, 600–603.

Vivien-Roels, B. (1969). Etude structurale et ultrastructurale de l'épiphyse d'un reptile: *Pseudemys scripta elegans*. *Z. Zellforsch. mikrosk. Anat.* **94**, 352–390.

Vivien-Roels, B. (1970). Ultrastructure, innervation et function de l'épiphyse chez les chéloniens. *Z. Zellforsch. mikrosk. Anat.* **104**, 429–448.

Vivien-Roels, B. and Petit, A. (1973). Embryogenèse du complexe épiphysaire chez la tortue mauresque (*Testudo graeca* L.). *Annls Embryol. Morph.* **6**, 151–168.

Vivien-Roels, B. and Petit, A. (1975). Dosage spectrofluorimetrique de la sérotonine (5-hydroxytryptamine = 5-HT) épiphysaire chez les reptiles. Étude des variations du taux de 5-HT en fonction du cycle saisonnier chez *Testudo hermanni*. *C. r. hebd. Acad. Sci., Paris* **D280**. 463.

Vivien-Roels, B., Petit, A and Lichté, C. (1971). Dosage spectrofluorimétrique de la sérotonine épiphysaire chez les reptiles. Étude des variations du taux de sérotonine en fonction de la période d'éclairement. *C. R. Hebd. Acad. Sci., Paris* **272**, 459–461.

Vodicnik, M. J. (1974). The effects of pinealectomy on gonadal development, pituitary cytology and ultrastructure in the teleost, *Notemigonus chrysoleucas*. *Am. Zool.* **14**, 1271.

Voeltzkow, A. (1903). Beiträge zur Entwicklungsgeschichte der Reptilien, Epiphyse und Paraphyse bei Krokodilen und Schildkröten. *Abh. Senckenb. naturforsch. Ges.* **27**, 165–177.

Warren, J. (1911). The development of the paraphysis and pineal region in Reptilia. *Am. J. Anat.* **11**, 313–392.

Wartenberg, H. (1969). Vergleichende Untersuchungen über die Feinstruktur des Pinealorgans der Säuger und anderer Wirbeltiere. *Anat. Anz.* **125**, Suppl., 439–445.

Wartenberg, H. and Baumgarten, H. G. (1968). Elektronenmikroskopische Untersuchungen zur Frage der photosensorischen und sekretorischen Funktion des Pinealorgans von *Lacerta viridis* und *Lacerta muralis*. *Z. Anat. EntwGesch.* **127**, 99–120.

Wartenberg, H. and Baumgarten, H. G. (1969a). Untersuchungen zur fluorescenz- und elektronenmikroskopischen Darstellung von 5-Hydroxytryptamine (5-HT) im Pineal Organ von *Lacerta viridis* und *Lacerta muralis*. *Z. Anat. EntwGesch.* **128**, 185–210.

Wartenberg, H. and Baumgarten, H. G. (1969b). Über die elektronenmikroskopische Identifizierung von noradrenergen Nervenfasern durch 5-Hydroxydopamin und 5-Hydroxydopa im Pinealorgan der Eidechse (*Lacerta muralis*). *Z. Zellforsch. mikrosk.* **94**, 252–260.

Watson, D. M. S. (1914). *Pleurosaurus* and the homologies of the bones of the temporal region of the lizard's skull. *Ann. Mag. nat. Hist.* **14**, 84–95.

Watson, D. M. S. (1942). On Permian and Triassic tetrapods. *Geol. Mag.* **79**, 81–116.

Welles, S. P. (1952). A review of the North American Cretaceous elasmosaurs. *Univ. Calif. Publ. Geol. Sci.* **29**, 47–144.

Westoll, T. S. (1938). Ancestry of the tetrapods. *Nature, Lond.* **141**, 127–128.

Williston, S. W. (1925). "The Osteology of the Reptiles." Harvard Univ. Press, Cambridge, Mass.

Wilson, F. H. (1939). Preliminary experiments on the color changes of *Anolis carolinensis* (Cuvier). *Am. Nat.* **73**, 190–192.

Wurtman, R. J., Axelrod, J. and Kelly, D. E. (1968). "The Pineal." Academic Press, New York and London.

Wyeth, F. J. (1925). The development and neuromery of the midbrain and the hindbrain in *Sphenodon punctatus*. *Proc. zool. Soc. Lond.* Part I, 507–558.

Yeager, V. L. and Chang, P.-L. (1972). Microscopic anatomy of the pineal gland of the
    lizard *Platyurus platyurus*. *Anat. Rec.* **172**, 430–431.
Yntema, C. L. (1968). A series of stages in the embryonic development of *Chelydra
    serpentina*. *J. Morph.* **125**, 219–252.
Zangerl, R. (1944). Contributions to the osteology of the skull of the Amphisbaenidae.
    Am. Midl. Nat. **31**, 417–454.

CHAPTER 6

Sensory Nerve Endings of the Skin and Deeper Structures

MONICA VON DÜRING

Department of Anatomy II, Ruhr-University, 4630 Bochum
Federal Republic of Germany

and

MALCOLM R. MILLER

Department of Anatomy, University of California, San Francisco, California,
U.S.A.

I. Introduction

This chapter deals with the sensory nerve endings found in the skin (epidermis and dermis) and the deeper lying tissues (joint capsules, perichondrium, periosteum, tendons and muscles) of reptiles. It does not deal with such innervations as that of the heart and vessels (cf. Ábrahám, 1964). The organs of special sense, such as the olfactory, optic, auditory and vestibular, and taste, are considered elsewhere. The pit organ of snakes has already been treated in the second volume of the "Biology of the Reptilia." Further studies report on the radiant heat receptors in the head scales of *Boa constrictor*, which are homologous with some pit organs (von Düring, 1974a).

The first detailed reports of sensory receptors in reptiles are those of Leydig (1871, 1873) and Merkel (1880). Other major earlier studies are those of Retzius (1892) and Maurer (1895). Early in the twentieth century appeared the detailed and excellent studies of Hulanicka (1913, 1914) and Schmidt (1910, 1913, 1917, 1920). In 1924, L. Plate synthesized what was then known about sensory innervation and sense organs. Particularly important, both as an original report and for its extensive discussion of earlier work, is Jaburek's analysis (1927). In 1934, Boeke summarized the basic literature on vertebrate nerve endings and sensory organs.

More recently, Miller and Kasahara (1967) reported on the innervation of lizard skin, Proske (1969b) on that of the snake, *Pseudechis porphyriacus*, and Påc (1968a, 1968b, 1972) on the innervation of joint capsules in turtles and lizards. Landmann (1975) presented a very detailed light microscopical study of the integumentary sense organs of Squamata and gave a good synopsis of the different papillae before and during moulting. Of particular importance are the recent ultrastructural studies of the sensory endings in the skin of some snakes, lizards, and crocodilians (von Düring, 1973a, b, 1974a, b). These studies (1) enabled the resolution of past disputes, (2) established a less artificial scheme for the classification of nerve endings, (3) provided a firm basis for phylogenetic comparison, and (4) made possible more accurate correlations of structure and function.

II. The Skin

Before describing the nerve endings in the skin, it is necessary to present a brief overview of reptilian skin.

The morphology of the epidermis shows extensive variation among reptiles, whereas the lamina propria and corium remain relatively unaltered both in structure and in differentiation. The collagen fibers of the lamina propria are somewhat smaller and interwoven in a loose network instead of aggregating in large bundles, as is typical for the corium. A restricted amount of ground substance lies among the formed connective tissue elements. The dermal chromatophore units, responsible both for reptilian color and color change, lie in the lamina propria. The units are composed of xanthophores, containing pterinosomes and carotenoid granules, iridophores, which contain rows of reflecting platelets, and melanophores, which contain melanosomes (Alexander, 1968). The position and distribution of the mela-nosomes in the dendritic branchings are hormone dependent and result in a particularly fast color change in some reptiles (Alexander and Fahrenbach, 1969; Taylor and Hadley, 1970), while the iridophores induce color changes in the skin of *Anolis carolinensis* (Rohrlich and Porter, 1972).

The epidermis of Testudines and that of Crocodilia is shed in the form of small flakes. In the shell region, there is a stiff β-keratin layer over the stratified epithelium, whereas in the neck and leg regions the cornified layer is composed of the pliable α-keratin.

The structure of the crocodilian epidermis closely resembles that of birds and mammals. The stratified epithelium has a layer of cornified cells, which varies in thickness and shape across the scale depending on the function. The middle of each scale is covered by a stiff keratin, while the cornified layer of the hinge region has some morphological characteristics of both α- and β-keratin; the β-keratinlike layer is thinner here (Alexander, 1968).

Histological observations of the epidermis of *Sphenodon punctatus* (Maderson, 1968) indicate that it is similar to that of squamates and is shed periodically; distinct epidermal generations are then formed and lost. The cornified epidermis is composed of a β- and α-keratin layer, but the meso-layer is apparently absent (Maderson, 1968).

The very complex epidermis of squamates is shed periodically. Apart from the different stages of epidermal regeneration before and after moulting (Roth and Jones, 1970; Maderson *et al.*, 1972; Landmann, 1975), the epithelium is composed of layers of α-keratin, meso-, and β-keratin, and of the Oberhäutchen (Maderson, 1965, 1966, 1967, 1970). The stiff β-keratin layer is very much thinner along the free edge of each scale and is almost completely lacking in the scale folds itself. The keratinous covering in the region of the tactile papillae and tactile hairs differs considerably from that of adjacent regions. Particularly noticeable in all reptiles is the reduction of the stiff β-keratin in such areas. The pliable α-keratin and meso- layers in the tactile papillae and tactile hair regions are variably reduced in squamates Landmann, 1975; Hiller, 1976a). In gekkos, for example, the α-keratin layer is reduced from 13 μm to 0·8 μm, whereas that of iguanas remains unaltered (Fig. 10A).

A peculiarity of the keratinous covering is seen in the tactile papillae of the monitors and crocodilians. Flat cell processes with fine granules lie interpolated between the stiff β-keratin lamellae. These processes might help to make the β-keratin layer of the tactile papillae more pliable (Figs 11A, B, 12D). Experiments on living monitors, such as *Varanus orientalis*, show that the papillary dome, but not the neighboring scale region, may be relatively easily indented with a brush (M. von Düring, unpublished).

III. Classification of Nerve Endings

A. GENERAL

The advent of recent ultrastructural studies of the sensory nerve endings in a variety of vertebrates provides the basis for a realistic, rather than an arbitrary or artificial, classification of sensory nerve endings. The peripheral receptors of vertebrates have recently been reviewed (Andres, 1969; Munger, 1971; Andres and von Düring, 1973; Andres, 1974; Halata, 1975). These reviews are concerned largely with nerve terminations in mammals and birds; little ultrastructural work has yet been completed in fishes, amphibians or reptiles.

During the past century, a considerable amount of work was done on the light microscopy of vertebrate nerve endings. The criteria for classifying endings used then are still in use today. Formerly, nerve endings were mainly classified by criteria such as the separation of the nerve terminal from modified neural, epithelial or connective tissue cells, or its incorporation into these. Plate's (1924) scheme classifies "sense organs", that is, nerve terminals together with the modified tissues to which they relate. Boeke's (1934) classification is relatively more simple in that it classifies nerve endings on the basis of the primary nature of the nerve terminal. In studies of mammalian (Miller et al., 1958; Miller and Kasahara, 1959) and reptilian skin (Miller and Kasahara, 1967), nerve endings are classified as (1) free, (2) complex unencapsulated, and (3) encapsulated. At the time this scheme was established, it was indicated that the divisions are arbitrary and that a firm basis for classification depends on information about the exact relationships of the tissues involved in any nerve terminal (Miller and Kasahara, 1967).

Vertebrate tissue receptors are here characterized using the following morphological criteria: (i) diameter and quality of the axon, (ii) receptive field and the involved tissue, and (iii) matrix of the receptor (Andres and von Düring, 1973).

Most vertebrate cutaneous and visceral receptors are neurons with either myelinated or unmyelinated axons. The receptive field is defined as the receptive area of the skin within which lies the telodendron, namely the axonal arborization of a single neurone. Ultrastructural studies (Andres and von Düring, 1973; Andres, 1974) have documented differences within the receptor axon, namely between the conductive part of the telodendron and its receptive part (Fig. 1). Therefore, it is necessary to differentiate between the ultrastructural organization of these two regions of the receptor axon. In contrast to the conductive part of the telodendrons of all vertebrate mechano- and thermoreceptors, the receptive area has a receptor matrix (Figs 2A, B, 3), which is a particularly differentiated axoplasm, made up of a fine filamentous net in which lie varying numbers and sizes of clear and granulated vesicles, as well as mitochondria and sometimes multivesicular bodies. The excitable and strongly contrasting axon membrane lies below the receptor matrix. In some terminal regions of the receptive area, the mitochondria in the receptor matrix demarcate the receptor matrix itself, as well as the central axoplasm typical of the conductive part. Neurofilaments, microtubules and smooth endoplasmic reticulum are characteristic of the axoplasm of the conductive part of the receptor axon (Figs 1B, C, E, F, G, 2C).

Comparative observations on tissue receptors in amphibians (K. H. Andres and M. VON Düring, pers. commun.), reptiles (von Düring, 1974a), birds (M. von Düring et al., pers. comm.) and mammals (Andres, 1966, 1974) have shown that mechanoreceptors possess specific morphological structures. These structures, which are apparently necessary for the transfer of mechanical stimuli to the receptor, are lacking in thermoreceptors (von Düring, 1974a; Hensel et al., 1974).

Fingerlike processes occur in the mechanoreceptors of the connective tissue. The processes contain desmosomes at their bases but not at their

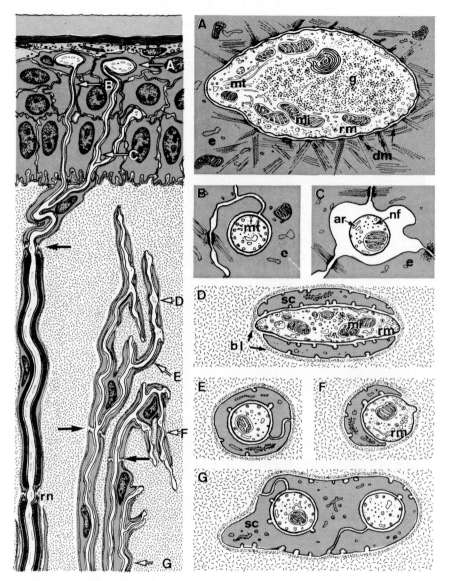

FIG. 1. Schematic representation of one myelinated and two non-myelinated afferent nerve fibers. The dark arrows indicate the beginning of the receptor axons with their conductive and receptive segments. Inserts A–G represent cross sections at higher magnification of different segments of the receptor axons. A–C. Discoid receptor with (A) terminal, (B) intraepidermal and (C) interepidermal segments of the receptor axons. D–G. Branched lanceolate terminals in the dermis with their receptive (D, F) and their conductive (E, F) segments. The receptive part of the receptor axon is characterized by the receptor matrix (rm), an accumulation of mitochondria (mi), lamellated bodies and often glycogen granules (g). The conductive part of the receptor axon contains microtubules (mt), neurofilaments (nf) and axoplasmic reticulum (ar). In A note the tonofibrillar basket of the epidermal cell (e) which is connected by desmosome-like plaques (dm) to the discoid receptor terminal. bl, Basement lamella; rn, node of Ranvier; sc, Schwann cell.

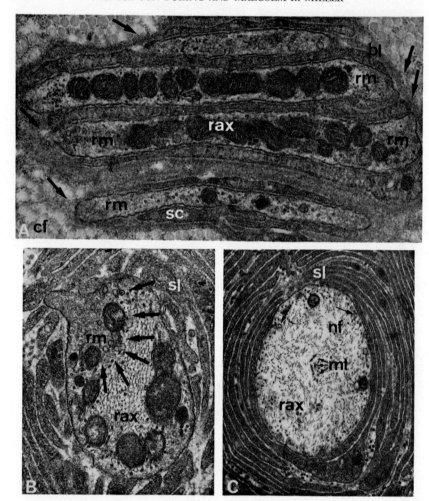

FIG. 2. A. Branched lanceolate terminal of the corium of supralabial scale of *Boa constrictor*. × 29,750. The receptor matrix (rm) is clearly seen where the receptor axon (rax) contacts the surrounding tissue (arrows) in its receptive part. bl, Basement lamella; cf, collagen fiber; sc, Schwann cell. B. *Caiman crocodilus*. Receptor axon (rax) with its Schwann cell lamellation (inner core) emanating from an encapsulated receptor with capsular space. × 29,750. Note the receptor matrix (rm) in and at the base of the finger-like protrusion. Arrows indicate the delineation of receptor matrix from the conductive part (von Düring, 1973b). C. *Caiman crocodilus*. Receptor axon (rax) with its Schwann cell lamellation (sl; inner core) emanating from an encapsulated receptor with capsular space. × 15,300. The conductive part of the receptor axon (rax) contains neurofilaments (nf), microtubuli (mt) and cisterns of the endoplasmic reticulum.

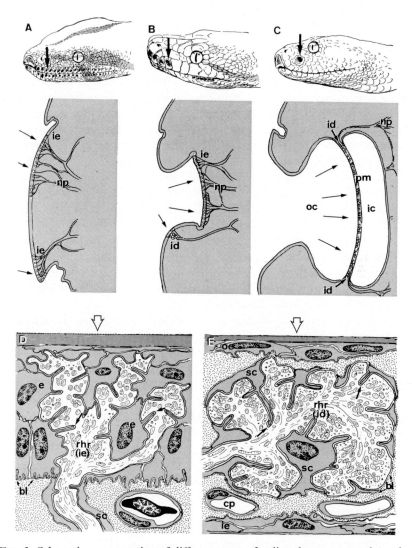

Fig. 3. Schematic representation of different types of radiant heat receptors in snakes. A. Distribution of the radiant heat receptor in the supra- and infralabials of *Boa constrictor*. The intraepidermal radiant heat receptors have been marked in black. No specialization of the scale surface is seen. B. Radiant heat receptors in *Python reticulatus*. The receptor terminals lie in different grooves of the supra- and infralabials. The grooves are marked in black. C. Radiant heat receptors in the pit organ of *Crotalus durissus*. Only one pit is present on each side. Large black arrows indicate the scale region, which is shown in schematic representations below. These cross sections show the intraepidermal (ie) and intradermal (id) location of the radiant heat receptors. The nerve fibers form a plexus-like structure (np) within the dermis. In cross section the pit organ shows the pit membrane (pm) dividing the pit into an outer (oc) and inner (ic) cavity. The channel connecting the inner cavity of the scale surface is not shown in the diagram. D. Schematic representation of the intraepidermal radiant heat receptor (rhr; ie) of *Boa constrictor* and *Python reticulatus*. Notice the invaginated crests (arrows) of the epidermal cells (e). E. Schematic drawing of the intradermal radiant heat receptor (rhr; id) in the pit membrane of *Crotalus*. The invaginated crests (arrow) are formed by the Schwann cell covering (sc). bl, Basement lamella; cp, capillary; ie. inner epidermis of the pit membrane; oe, outer epidermis of the pit membrane.

tips. Depending on the structure of the receptor, these finger- or ribbon-like processes may project freely into surrounding connective tissue, thus having a functional contact without anchorage to either collagen or elastic fibres. The processes may also project between the lamellae of the Schwann cells. The processes can have varying lengths and contain a receptor matrix (Fig. 2B). Additional criteria for the differentiation of different mechanoreceptors are the occurrence of (i) specialized lamellar formations of the Schwann cell, (ii) particularly well-developed endoneural connective tissue and (iii) a perineural sheath, which forms a capsule around the receptor terminal. A second group of mechanoreceptors is made up of the Merkel cell and its axon terminal, which forms the Merkel cell neurite complex (Andres, 1966; Iggo and Muir, 1969; Winkelmann and Breathnach, 1973).

These established morphological criteria permit the following classification of reptilian mechanoreceptors: (1) intraepidermal mechanoreceptors, (2) mechanoreceptors of the connective tissue, that lack Schwann cell specialization, (3) mechanoreceptors covered by lamellated Schwann cells, and (4) Merkel cell neurite complexes.

A morphological and physiological identification of reptilian thermo- and nociceptors, has been unsuccessful as yet. The specialized temperature receptors of the Boidae and Crotalinae represent an exception (Bullock and Cowles, 1952; Bullock and Diecke, 1956; Bullock and Fox, 1957; Bleichmar and De Robertis, 1962; Terashima et al., 1968, 1970; Warren and Proske, 1968; Meszler, 1970; Barrett, 1970; von Düring, 1974a; Hensel, 1975). Their structural organization is compared in Fig. 5, but the lack of specific structural criteria make it difficult for the morphologist to identify these receptors. A further difficulty in the morphological and physiological analysis of thermo- and nociceptors is that their axons belong, for the most part, to the unmyelinated group of C fibers. Advances are only likely to be achieved by close morphological and physiological collaboration. Physiological identification and classification of a receptor and the labeling of its receptive field must be followed by systematic morphological examination, using alternating series of semi- and ultrathin sections (Hensel et al., 1974).

B. Intraepidermal Mechanoreceptors

1. Introductory

The reptilian epidermis is generally innervated in a distinct fashion and differs from that of all other vertebrates; the distinction resides essentially in the nature of the terminals of the free nerve endings. All vertebrates, except for reptiles, have small, tapered free nerve terminals that end between the epithelial cells (Hulanicka, 1909; Munger, 1965, 1971; Whitear, 1971, 1974; Andres and von Düring, 1973). In contrast, most of the intraepithelial nerves of reptiles terminate not as tapered tips but as relatively large, terminal expansions (Retzius, 1892; Hulanicka, 1913, 1914; Jaburek, 1927; Miller and Kasahara, 1967; von Düring, 1973a, b, 1974a, b; Landmann and Villiger, 1975).

In light microscopic studies, such as those using silver impregnation or methylene blue staining, the intraepidermal endings appear to be relatively constant in structure (Fig. 17A). However, in electron microscopical studies, there are differences in the structural relationships of the terminals to the epithelium which vary with the state of differentiation of the epithelium itself. These relationships seem to be responsible for the stimulus specificity of the receptor, i.e. they may indicate whether the receptor is particularly sensitive to pressure, tension or stretch.

2. *Discoid Terminals*

Comparative electron microscopic studies suggest that the fine structure and presence of the ubiquitous discoid receptors in the receptor field of the scale epithelium are the same in all groups of reptiles (von Düring, 1973a, 1974a, b). The large, free intraepidermal terminals arise from myelinated axons of about 2–4 μm in diameter. The unmyelinated branches of the axons (0·2–0·6 μm in diameter) pass in deep grooves within the epithelium up to the outermost layer of living cells. The terminal expansion, which is termed "bubble receptor" (von Düring, 1974a), has a discoid shape and measures up to 10 μm in diameter and 4 μm in height. These terminals generally lie parallel to the surface. The term "bubble receptors" is unfortunate, though the receptor terminals are swollen. To avoid future confusion, the less ambiguous term "discoid" (Landmann and Villiger, 1975) is here adopted.

The receptor terminal is filled with glycogen granules, identified histo-chemically, and has a narrow border of fine, filamentous receptor matrix, containing granulated and clear vesicles (Fig. 4B). Mitochondria are unevenly distributed and may be more common in the receptor matrix than in the glycogen pool. The terminals may also contain lamellated dense bodies or large vacuoles.

An important characteristic of all the discoid terminals is a typical inti-mate association with the epithelial tonofibrillar system (Fig. 1A). A receptor terminal is always invaginated within an epithelial cell and surrounded by condensed bundles of tonofibrils, which are arranged in a basket-like manner (Figs 1, 4A, B). The intercellular space between the membrane of the discoid nerve terminal and the covering epithelial cell membrane is narrowed wherever tonofibrils contact the terminal membrane. The tonofibrillar bundles, on the other hand, form desmosomal connections with neighboring epithelial cells. The specialized association of the discoid receptor and the tonofibrillar system suggests that vertical or tangential dislocation of the

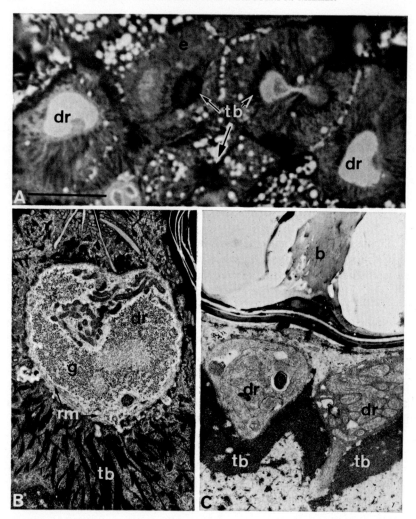

FIG. 4. A. Horizontal section through the epithelium of the scale region of *Natrix natrix*. Semithin section, × 2125. The tonofibrils of the epithelial cell (e) form a tonofibrillar basket (tb) around the discoid receptor (dr). Scale = 10 μm. (After von Düring, 1973a.) B. Large discoid receptor (dr) from a neck scale of *Natrix natrix*. × 11,050. The discoid receptor is invaginated into an epithelial cell and contains large numbers of glycogen granules (g), numerous mitochondria and a peripheral layer of receptor matrix (rm). tb, Bundles of tonofibrils. (From von Düring, 1973a.) C. An area with two discoid receptors seen in a tangential section of the tactile sense organ in the jaw region of *Pachydactylus bibronii*. × 11,050. A dense tonofibrillar basket (tb) system comparable to that of Figs 4A, B, is seen around the discoid receptor (dr). Note the bristle (b) and the reduced cornified layer.

surface of the skin produces a mechanical deformation of the tonofibrillar "basket" and thus activates the receptor membrane (von Düring, 1973a, 1974a, b).

The high percentage of glycogen, which is typically observed in the cutaneous receptors of all ectotherms, could be explained in one of two ways. Either it represents an energy reservoir or it maintains a high internal turgor in the terminal. This turgor might tense the terminal membrane, facilitating its stimulation.

The distribution of the discoid receptors varies among reptiles. In turtles, crocodillians, and lizards, the discoid receptor terminals are more or less scattered in the superficial living cell layer and are covered by cornified layers, which are variously differentiated according to the order.

It is important to note the varying distribution of receptor terminals, such as the intraepidermal terminals in the tactile sense organs of crocodilians and lizards (Figs 4C, 10, 11, 12B, D). The modified cornified layers and surrounding tissue modifications of such organs suggest that they represent mechanoreceptors for distinct stimuli. However, these tactile organs also show association of tonofibril and basket. Consequently, they can be classified with the intraepithelial discoid receptors.

3. Hinge Region Receptor

A branched intraepithelial receptor is located in the hinge region, which is the epidermal folds between scales. The stiff β-keratin layer is almost completely lacking in this hinge region, and the overall depth of the epithelium is reduced. The epidermis directly overlies the thick collagen bundles of the corium, which run continuously under the whole epithelium. The axon terminals are branched and run parallel to the surface. Along the intraepithelial part of the axon itself, small localized swellings are observed (Fig. 15; von Düring, 1974a). These receptors could possibly act as stretch receptors, because the epithelium of the hinge region moves as the scales shift relative to each other.

The intrapithelial receptors have been classified here according to those morphological criteria thus far available. There is an obvious need for complementary investigations of these receptors.

C. Those Mechanoreceptors of the Connective Tissue Lacking Schwann Cell Specialization

1. General

Complex unencapsulated nerve endings occur in lizards (Miller and Kasahara, 1967), freely ending fibers with tapered tips have been noted in *Alligator mississippiensis* and *Testudo graeca* (Hulanicka, 1913, 1914) and complex coiled endings have been described in the dermis of turtles (Hin-Ching and Maneely, 1962), all with the aid of silver impregnation techniques and by staining with methylene blue. These techniques show the path of the axon and of its telodendral arborization. However, axon and sheath cannot be visualized in terms of their structural relationships to the surrounding tissues. Complementation of such morphological data with electron microscopic studies allowed von Düring (1973a, b, 1974a, b) to identify different mechanoreceptors in the dermis of *Caiman crocodilus*, *Boa constrictor*, *Natrix natrix* and *Varanus bengalensis*.

The unsheathed receptors represent a less complex and perhaps a phylogenetically old kind of receptor. They appear in fishes (Lowenstein, 1957), while the lamellated receptors apparently first appeared in amphibians (Bolgarskij, 1964; von Düring and Seiler, 1974). Their main characteristic is that the unmyelinated receptor axon has an incomplete Schwann cell covering. Where the sheath is lacking, the receptor axon is in contact with the surrounding connective tissue, from which it is separated only by a basement lamella. This group of endings can be further divided into three subgroups, depending on variations in the location of the structures as well as on differences concerned with the formation of the receptor.

2. *Free Nerve Terminals of the Dermis*

Free nerve terminals can be identified as they enter the collagen fiber bundles, run parallel with the fibers and possess all the main characteristics mentioned above (Figs 5A, 9A, 10B, 11A). The incorporation of the receptor into collagen fiber bundles suggests that it may be a type of stretch receptor that registers displacements of these fiber bundles.

3. *Branched Lanceolate Terminals in the Dermis*

Branched lanceolate terminals have been described in the dermis of *Boa constrictor*. They show relatively more axonal organization and polarization than the preceding group and enter those collagen fiber bundles lying in parallel to the scale surface. In cross section, the terminals have a lanceolate appearance. Also, these receptor types lack a covering of Schwann cells at their tips.

4. *Branched Coiled Terminals of the Dermis*

Branched coiled terminals of the dermis are more compactly organized and have been described only in the soft-shelled turtle *Trionyx sinensis*, where they show a complex coiled ending (Hin-Ching and Maneely, 1962); their structure was verified during our electron microscopical studies. These receptors are not incorporated into the collagen fiber bundles, as are the others, but lie between the bundles; the coiled nature of their receptor axons make these receptors corpuscle-like (Fig. 5c). Different mechanical parameters are suggested for this receptor type. Its distinct position and construction suggest that this receptor has different mechanical parameters from the precedings ones. Its appearance resembles the Krause corpuscles of mammals (Chouchkov, 1972, 1973; Andres and von Düring, 1973).

D. MECHANORECEPTORS COVERED BY LAMELLATED SCHWANN CELLS

The lamellated receptors are more complex than unsheathed receptors and are characterized by flat, lamellated Schwann cell processes (Figs 6A,

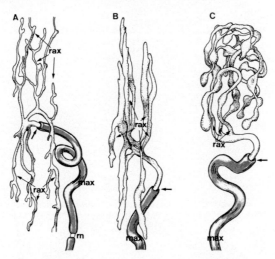

FIG. 5. Schematic representation of different types of mechanoreceptors of the connective tissue without Schwann cell specialization. The different course of the receptor axons indicates the different correlations to the surrounding connective tissue structures involved. A. Free nerve terminal. B. Branched lanceolate terminal. C. Branched coiled terminal. Arrows indicate the beginning of the myelination. max, Myelinated afferent axon; rax, branches of the receptor axons; rn, node of Ranvier.

B, C, 17C, D, E, F). They occur in all orders of reptiles. The receptive portions of the axon terminals have fingerlike protrusions that extend distally between the lamellae (Figs 2B, 7). It is phylogenetically interesting that reptiles show two forms of lamellation in these receptors, similar in turn to the inner core lamellations of receptors found respectively in birds and mammals. For example, lizards have very compact lamellations of the Schwann cell with no interposition of connective tissue elements (Figs 6A, B, 7B). The lamellations are comparable in structure to the inner core lamellations of the Herbst corpuscle of birds (Schwartzkopff, 1973). However, caimans show a looser lamellation, while endoneural tissue lies among the lamellae (Figs

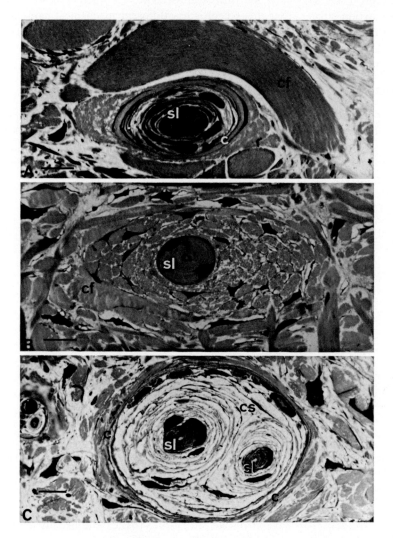

FIG. 6. A. Encapsulated lamellated receptor from the foot pad of *Varanus bengalensis*. Scale = 10 μm. × 900. c, Capsule; cf, collagen fibers of the surrounding connective tissue. B. Lamellated receptor from jaw region of *Boa constrictor*. × 900. Note the absence of a capsule and the densely packed collagen fibers (cf) around the lamellated receptor. Scale = 10 μm. C. *Caiman crocodilus*. Lamellated encapsulated receptor with capsular space (cs). Scale = 10 μm. × 750. sl, Schwann cell lamellation. (From von Düring, 1973b.)

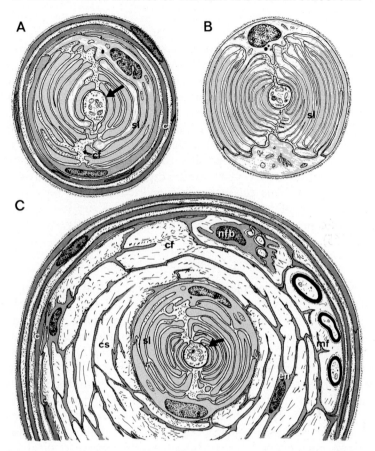

FIG. 7. A–C. Semischematic representation of a cross section of lamellated integumentary receptors. A. Encapsulated lamellated receptor (*Caiman crocodilus*). B. Unencapsulated lamellated receptor (*Boa constrictor*). C. Encapsulated lamellated receptor with capsular space (*Caiman crocodilus*). The arrow points to a receptor axon. c, Capsule; cf, collagenous fibrillae of the endoneural connective tissue; cs, capsular space; en, endoneural cells in the capsular space; mf, myelinated nerve fibers; nfb, transmigrating bundles of non-myelinated nerve fibers; sl, lamellae of the inner core. (After von Düring, 1973b.)

6B, 7C). This is comparable to the inner core lamellation of the Vater-Pacini corpuscle in the skin of mammals (Andres, 1969).

The lamellated receptors, which may be 0·5 mm long, can be further subdivided into two groups: those with and those without a capsule. The lamellated receptor without a capsule occurs in the skin of lizards and snakes, as well as in the tip of the dermal part of the touch papilla of *Caiman crocodilus* (von Düring, 1973a, b, 1974a; Fig. 11A).

Encapsulated lamellated receptors occur in *Testudo graeca*, and *Caiman crocodilus*, as well as in *Varanus orientalis* and *Varanus bengalensis* (M. von Düring, unpublished observations). The capsule is derived from the perineural sheath of the myelinated nerve fiber (diameter 8–10 μm), which enters the corpuscle. A capsular space lies between the inner core and the capsule of the encapsulated receptor of *Caiman crocodilus* (Fig. 6c). It contains dispersed collagen fibers and lamellated endoneural cell processes. Neurophysiological investigators (Siminoff and Kruger, 1968; Proske, 1969a) describe rapidly adapting mechanoreceptors in the alligator, as well as in the skin of snakes. It is possible that both lamellated receptors and lamellated encapsulated receptors within a capsular space are rapidly adapting mechanoreceptors. This suggestion is supported by the strong similarity between this type of receptor and the mammalian Vater-Pacini corpuscle, which is, of course, a rapidly adapting mechanoreceptor (Loewenstein and Skalak, 1965).

E. MERKEL CELL NEURITE COMPLEXES

Merkel cell neurite complexes are exceptional in that the receptor axon is closely associated with a specialized cell, termed the Merkel cell. The Merkel cell neurite complex appears to be a secondary, slowly adapting type I mechanoreceptor as is that reported in physiological studies in mammals (Iggo and Muir, 1969; Burgess and Perl, 1973).

Morphological criteria for identifying the Merkel cells are the straight, finger-like processes with their content of glycogen granules, the networks of tonofibrils and the typical dense core vesicles (Munger, 1965; Andres, 1966), which often appear to be concentrated towards the nerve ending. The finger-like processes contain straight filaments of about 8 nm diameter. Synaptic membrane complexes are associated with the nerve terminal. Desmosomes connect the tonofibrillar system of the Merkel cell either to the tonofibrillar system of the epidermis or to the Schwann cell envelope. The desmosomes only occur at the base of fingerlike processes (Andres, 1969; von Düring, 1974b; Figs 8A, B), so that the latter do not appear to function as mechanical anchors.

The positions of the integumentary Merkel cells differ among the classes and orders of vertebrates. Those found in the dermis of some reptiles (von Düring, 1974b) and birds (Andres, 1969) are indistinguishable morphologically from those in the epidermis of mammals (Munger, 1965; Andres, 1966; Halata, 1970). It is best to be cautious about possible homologies, as no physiological work has been done on these receptors. They are here referred to as epidermal and dermal Merkel cells. Epidermal Merkel cells occur in fishes (Lane and Whitear, 1977), amphibians (Nafstad and Baker, 1973; von Düring and Andres, 1976), reptiles (*Testudo graeca, Trionyx sinensis*, *Caiman crocodilus*, *Gekko gecko*; M. von Düring and K. H. Andres, unpublished) and mammals (Munger, 1965; Andres, 1966; Halata, 1970).

Dermal Merkel cells occur throughout the corium of the upper and lower jaw region of *Testudo graeca* and *Trionyx sinensis* (M. von Düring and K. H. Andres, unpublished). They are enveloped by a covering Schwann cell,

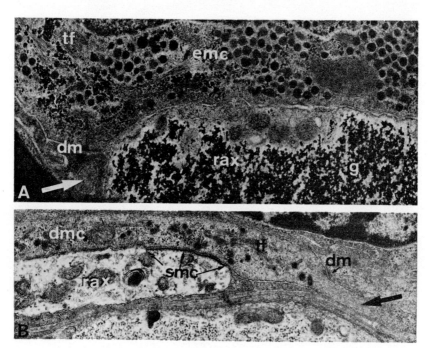

Fig. 8. A. Merkel cell neurite complex with epidermal Merkel cell (emc) and receptor axon (rax) from the snout epidermis of *Trionyx sinensis*. × 21,250. The dense core vesicles of the Merkel cell are prominent. Note the bundles of tonofibrils (tf) and glycogen (g), as well as a desmosome (dm) at the base of the finger-like process (arrow), seen in cross section. B. Dermal Merkel cell (dmc) of the touch papillar region of *Caiman crocodilus*. × 17,000. As in A, the desmosome (dm) is present at the base of the finger-like process (arrow). Note the receptor axon (rax) having a synaptic membrane complex (smc), the bundles of tonofilaments (tf) and the dense core vesicles.

while the finger-like processes penetrate either into the Schwann cell envelope or extend into the connective tissue, where they are covered only by the basement lamella. Several axon terminals with their receptor matrices are directly associated with the Merkel cell membrane (Fig. 8B). Electron microscopy indicates that the dermal Merkel cell of *Caiman crocodilus* is limited to the region of the touch papilla (von Düring, 1974b). Such Merkel cells occur in a regular pattern, and several Merkel cells may lie

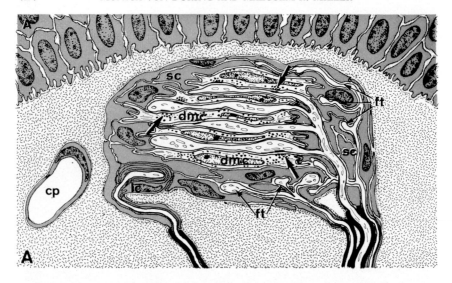

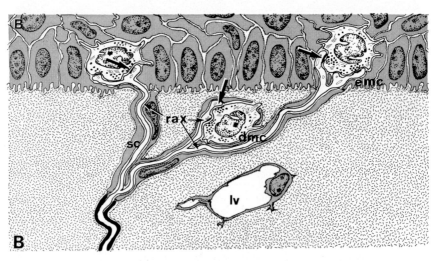

FIG. 9. Schematic representation of epidermal and dermal Merkel cell neurite complexes. A. Dermal Merkel cell column in the tactile sense organ (touch papilla) of crocodilians. Note the flattened Merkel cells (dmc) and intercalated receptor axon terminals. The column is covered by Schwann cells (sc); synaptic membrane complexes (arrows) lie between the dermal Merkel cells and the intercalated receptor axons. Other receptors, such as small unencapsulated lamellated receptors (lc) and intradermal free receptors (ft) with terminal swelling, are associated with the Merkel cell column. cp, Capillary. B. Single epidermal (emc) and dermal (dmc) Merkel cell neurite complexes as they are seen in tortoises; note synaptic membrane complexes (arrows). lv, Lymphatic vessel; sc, Schwann cell.

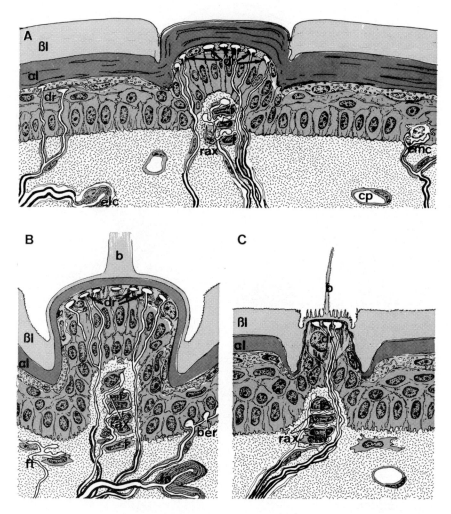

FIG. 10. Schematic representation of different tactile sense organs of lizards. Note the structural differentiation of the β-keratin layer (βl) as well as the reduction of the α- and β-keratin layer. A. Tactile sense organ of *Iguana iguana*. B. Tactile sense organ of *Agama stellio*. C. Tactile sense organ of *Pachydactylus bibronii*. The discoid receptors (dr) lie just deep to the modified keratinous covering. The connective tissue papillae contain columns of connective tissue cells (f) that contact nerve fiber endings (rax) of another receptor type. Other receptors occur in the vicinity of the tactile sense organ. al, α-Keratin layer; b, bristle; ber, basal epithelial receptor; cp, capillary; dr, freely distributed discoid receptor; elc, encapsulated lamellated receptor; emc, epidermal Merkel cell neurite complex; ft, free nerve terminals in the connective tissue; lc, unencapsulated lamellated receptor.

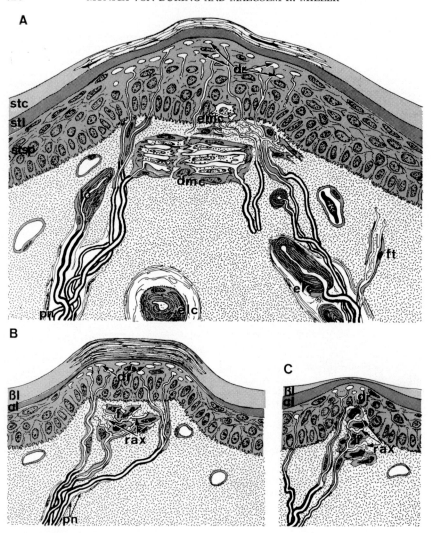

FIG. 11. Schematic representation of tactile sense organs. A. *Caiman crocodilus*. B. *Varanus bengalensis*. C. *Python reticulatus*. Note the modification in the stratum corneum (stc) of *Caiman* and in the β-keratin layer of *Varanus*. These indicate the more pliable tip region of the tactile sense organ. The most complex arrangement of different receptor types is seen in *Caiman*, whereas *Varanus* and *Python* show mainly discoid receptors and branched receptors in the connective tissue papillae. αl, α-Keratin layer; βl, β-keratin layer; dmc, dermal Merkel cell column; dr, discoid receptor; elc, encapsulated lamellated receptor; emc, epidermal Merkel cell neurite complex; f, papilla with fibrocytes; ft, free branched receptor in the connective tissue; lc, unencapsulated lamellated receptor; pn, perineural sheath; rax, branched receptor axons in the connective tissue papilla; stl, stratum lucidum; stsp, stratum spinosum.

deep to each other, forming a Merkel cell column (Fig. 9A). The nerve terminals are sandwiched among the Merkel cells. Two such columns are found separated from one another by connective tissue in the touch papilla region. Siminoff and Kruger (1968) and Kenton et al. (1971) described two classes of slowly adapting receptors in alligator skin; one of these may be the dermal Merkel cell neurite complex.

F. Tactile Sense Organs

While Merkel cell neurite complexes are rarely found in reptiles, another type of sensory structure, the tactile sense organ or touch papilla, is well developed and occurs in the skin of all orders. Tactile sense organs consist of an epidermal and a dermal component.

Landmann (1975) summarizes the tactile sense organs in the skin of the head region in squamates. He describes the different light microscopic appearance of the touch papilla of representative squamates. Except for papillae of the Teiidae, Xantusiidae, Lacertidae, Boidae, Anguidae, and Elapidae, each touch papilla contains discoid termina. However, electron microscopy of *Natrix natrix* also demonstrates discoid terminals (von Düring, 1973a). Consequently, further electron microscopic studies and better fixation techniques might demonstrate discoid terminals in other families as well.

The differentiation of the touch papilla in the different orders of reptiles is shown in Figs 10, 11. in *Varanus orientalis*, *V. bengalensis* (Figs 11B, 12D) and *Caiman crocodilus* (Fig. 11A) differentiation in the β-keratin layer may help make the cornified layer more pliable for the reception of mechanical stimuli.

In *Agama stellio* and *Gekko gecko* the touch papilla possesses a bristle differentiated from the β-keratin layer (Figs 10B, C, 14B). Functionally, the bristle may be compared to a lever arm. The degree, direction and displacement of the bristle may be transferred as a mechanical stimulus to the discoid receptor membrane by the attachment plaques and desmosomes of the meso- and α-keratin layers via the tonofibrillar system (Figs 4C, 10, 12B).

The cornified layer of *Iguana iguana* (Figs 10A, 12A), *Boa constrictor*, *Python reticulatus* and *Natrix natrix* is reduced in the region of the touch papilla, but otherwise shows no individual differentiation (Fig. 11C). Epithelial cells, which contain the discoid terminals, have been described as sensory cells (Landmann, 1975). Other ultrastructural observations give no morphological indication that these cells are sensory (unpublished observations), although they can be easily distinguished from the surrounding cells.

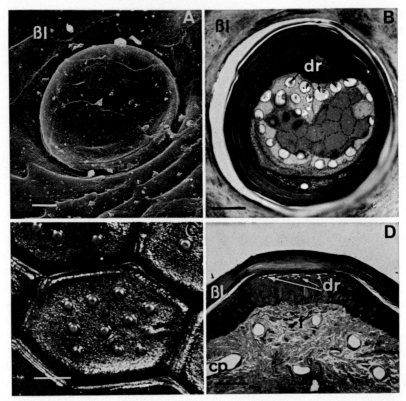

FIG. 12. A. Tactile sense organ of *Iguana iguana*. Scanning micrograph. × 680. A groove separates the tactile area from the surrounding scale area, but the smooth surface of the tactile sense organ otherwise lies at the same level as the scale surface. Scale = 10 μm. αl, α-Keratin layer. B. Horizontal section of tactile sense organ of *Iguana iguana*. Semithin section, × 680. Scale = 10 μm. Note the numerous discoid receptors (dr) lying below the α-keratin layer, indicating a highly receptive area. The space between the α- and β-keratin layers is an artifact. C. *Varanus bengalensis*. × 20. Scale = 0·5 mm. Scale surface with ten touch papillae of a supralabial scale as seen by the interference reflecting light method (Andres and von Düring, 1978). D. Semithin section of a touch papilla on the supralabial scale of *Varanus bengalensis*. × 213. Scale = 100 μm. The discoid receptors are concentrated deep to the differentiated β-keratin layer, which is more pliable. The papillar layered fibrocytes (f) can be seen in the dermis. cp, Capillary.

The number of discoid terminals per touch papilla varies by size and species (Figs 12A, B, C, D).

Species	Number of discoid terminals
Caiman crocodilus	60–100
Iguana iguana	30–40
Gekko gecko	8–12
Boa constrictor	6–8

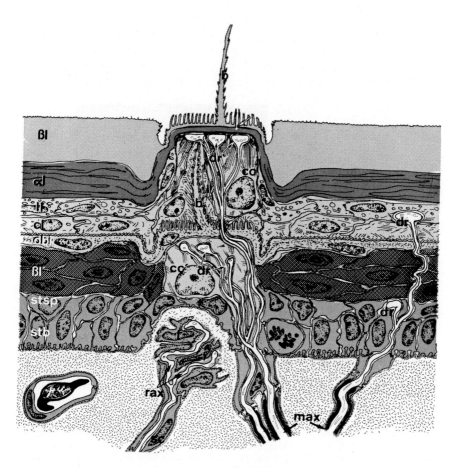

FIG. 13. Schematic representation of a tactile sense organ of *Gekko gecko* in stage 4 of the shedding cycle according to Maderson's classification. In this stage the inner generations of the epidermal layers are developed. The border between the clear cells (cl) and the Oberhäutchen cell (obi) already indicates the surface structure of the Oberhäutchen. The presumptive β-keratin cells (βl′) are rich in keratohyaline granules. The presumptive central cell (cc′) takes up new proliferation branches of the discoid receptors (dr′). During the last phase of sloughing the discoid receptors of the outer generation (dr) will become detached together with their central cell (cc). The little channel through which the receptor axons pass the Oberhäutchen cell (obi) during development, persists (arrows) αl, Outer generation of α-keratin layer; βl, outer generation of β-keratin layer; b, bristle; b′, presumptive bristle; f, fibrocyte column; ll, lacunar cell layer; max, myelinated afferent axon; rax, branched receptor axons in the connective tissue papilla; sc, Schwann cell; stb, basal cell layer; stsp, spinus cell layer which will produce the presumptive cells of the α-keratin layer.

The discoid receptors of the touch papilla of *Tarentola mauritanica* regenerate each time the skin is shed (Hiller, 1976a). Recent studies (in *Gekko gecko* and *Pachydactylus bibronii*; M. von Düring and K. H. Andres, unpublished) show that the central cell as well as its discoid terminals are lost during sloughing. Consequently, the bristle must regenerate from cells

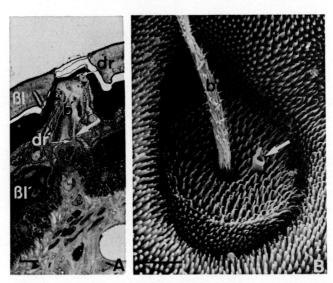

Fig. 14. A. *Gekko gecko*. Semithin section through a tactile sense organ in stage 4 (Maderson) of the sloughing cycle, in the supralabial region. × 510. The β-keratin layer (βl) as well as the α-keratin layer are significantly reduced in the region of the tactile sense organ. A complete, but as yet immature, outer epidermal generation appears. The inner generation is represented by an Oberhäutchen and layers of presumptive β-cells (βl'). The thick arrow indicates the hole where the receptor axons penetrate the Oberhäutchen. The developing bristle (b') derives from the Oberhäutchen of the inner epidermal generation. The section does not pass through the bristle of the outer epidermal generation. Scale = 10 μm. dr, Discoid receptor of the outer epidermal generation; dr', discoid receptors of the inner epidermal generation. B. *Gekko gecko*. Tactile sense organ in the eye rim. Scanning micrograph. × 2040. The scale surface, as well as the tactile sense organ surface, exhibits several spinules and a bristle (b). A grove separates the sunken tactile sense organ from the surrounding scale surface. The arrow indicates the hole in the Oberhäutchen through which the receptor axons pass. Scale = 5 μm.

of the Oberhäutchen (Landmann, 1975). During stage 4 of Maderson's classification of the sloughing process, the outer epidermal generation is reflected in the appearance of the inner epidermal generation (Figs 13, 14A). During this stage, each axon of the discoid receptors develops a lateral swelling, just below the Oberhäutchen of the inner epidermal generation. After sloughing, these axons become the new discoid terminals of the new epithelium. The place where the axons penetrate the Oberhäutchen remains as a small hole, visible under the scanning microscope (Figs 13, 14B; Hiller, 1976b).

The dermal component of the touch papilla contains layered cells, shown by electron microscopy to be fibrocytes. However, in *Caiman crocodilus*, the layered cells have been described as dermal Merkel cells. The diameter of the connective tissue papilla is specific and reflects the number of layered fibrocytes. The connective tissue of the touch papilla consists of a filamentous, ground substance with loosely dispersed collagen fibers. Nerve terminals with expanded tips, containing glycogen and a receptor matrix, lie interspersed among these. They may exhibit a thin Schwann cell covering or be in contact with the fibrocytes (Figs 10, 11B, c), but their function is still unknown.

G. Complex Sensory Structures

Both the bristled and bristleless touch papillae of lizards appear to indicate very sensitive integumentary areas with such different receptor terminals as discoid terminals and branched free endings between the layered fibrocytes in the dermal part of the papilla, as well as lamellated receptors.

This situation may be compared with the combination of receptor types forming complex sensory structures in the bill-tip organ of geese (Gottschaldt *et al.*, 1976), Eimer organs of moles (Andres and von Düring, 1973) and the sinus hair of cats (Andres, 1966). A particularly complex sensory structure is seen in the touch papilla of caimans (von Düring, 1974b), which show practically all of these forms of mechanoreceptors concentrated in a small area (Fig. 11). Thus a detailed picture of the environment may be transmitted to the brain via a wide variety of stimuli.

Physiological studies of the sensory receptors in the skin of the green lizard (*Lacerta viridis*) show that discharges from integumentary mechanoreceptors cover the complete range between brief, high frequency bursts and slowly adapting, low frequency discharges (Bailey, 1969). Both unimodal "cold units" and bimodal units (responding also to pressure) occur and respond to rapid cooling of more than 3 to 5°C.

It becomes ever more necessary to appreciate the importance of the topographical distribution of receptors (Figs 15, 16), as this provides the morphological basis for further physiological examination.

IV. Joint Capsules

The joint capsules of *Agama stellio*, *Physignathus lesueurii* and *Lacerta viridis* contain free nerve endings, non-encapsulated clews (skeins), non-

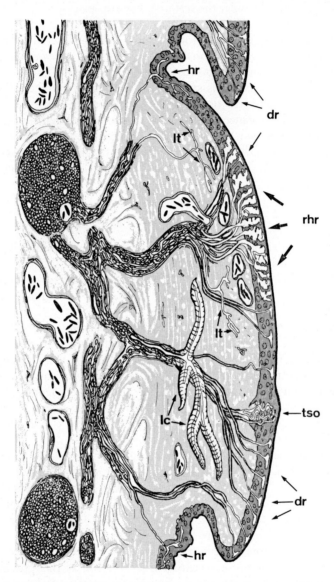

FIG. 15. Schematic representation of the tissue receptors in the scales of *Boa constrictor*. dr, Discoid receptor; hr, epithelial terminals in the hinge region between the scales; lc, unencapsulated lamellated receptor; lt, lanceolate terminal; rhr, radiant heat receptor; tso, tactile sense organ. (After von Düring, 1974a.)

encapsulated spraylike endings, and simple encapsulated corpuscles with an inner core (Păc, 1968a, b, 1972). In all probability, these structures correspond to a variety of free and lamellated types and, when examined with the electron microscope, will probably prove to be structurally similar to the nerve endings in the dermis.

The joint capsule of the tortoise *Testudo graeca* contains only free fibers and a peculiar type of spraylike encapsulated corpuscles (Păc, 1968a),

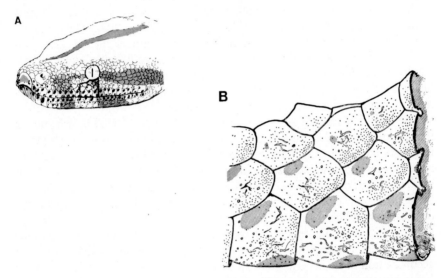

Fig. 16. A. Head of *Boa constrictor* with the location of the supralabials. B. Reconstruction of the supralabials with their sensory innervation pattern. Stipled area, radiant heat receptor; open circle, tactile sense organ; single dot, discoid receptor; lengthy profile, unencapsulated lamellated receptor. (After von Düring, 1974a.)

while the joint capsules of *Caiman crocodilus* (Palmieri and Panu, 1972) contains both free and encapsulated nerve endings. The encapsulated corpuscles are similar to corpuscles of the Pacinian and Golgi–Mazzoni types.

The joint capsules of amphibians show only arborized free fiber endings, but lack endings with auxiliary cells and encapsulated corpuscles (Păc, 1970).

V. Perichondrium and Periosteum

The only description of nerve endings in the reptilian perichondrium and periosteum is that by Stefanelli (1934); he stated that *Tarentolo mauritanica* and *Elaphe quatuorlineata* have numerous multibranched endings with varicose terminals.

VI. Tendon and Muscle

Barker (1974), on whose work this section is based, notes that the tendons of reptiles are innervated by large afferent fibers that branch to terminate in a number of plaques. In lizards, these are 60–100 μm long and 40–50 μm wide (Regaud, 1907). They consist of irregular, leaflike blobs of axoplasm distributed among the tendon fascicles, which are smaller and more densely nucleated in the area of termination than in the surrounding tendon (Fig. 17A). In *Emys*, some of the receptors are invested with a thin capsule and form rudimentary tendon organs (Huber and De Wit, 1900). These organs generally have more elaborate endings and are confined to the musculo-tendinous junction, while simple and non-encapsulated plaques occur wholly within tendons. The muscle of pythons contains thin non-myelinated fibers that branch extensively to terminate as free endings in the intra-muscular connective tissue (Kulchitsky, 1924).

The reptilian muscle spindle is discussed by Barker (1974), who notes that reptilian muscles are like amphibian muscles in containing both plate-innervated and grape-innervated muscle fibers. However, the latter are relatively less common and sometimes absent altogether. Spindles have been studied in four orders. Those of snakes and lizards are remarkable. Wherever found, they consist of one muscle fiber only, rarely of two. Of the two types of muscle spindles thus far recognized, one has a short, wide, and obvious capsule. The capsule encloses a muscle fiber that loses its cross-striations over a short length, increases in diameter, and becomes filled with an accumulation of nuclei and granular sarcoplasm. The second type of spindle has a long, narrow, indistinct capsule, which encloses a muscle fiber that remains cross-striated throughout and shows equatorial nucleation in the form of a chain.

In tortoises, the spindles are composed of both plate- and grape-innervated muscle fibers, while the spindles consist of two to 17 muscle fibers. The sensory endings consist of varicose threads, among which lie forked, tri-angular, and leaflike terminals. A sensory fiber may branch to supply two or three capsular regions of adjacent spindles.

The spindles of alligators are composed of two to five muscle fibers. The sensory ending is occasionally varicose but "generally compact" (Barker, 1974).

VII. Summary

1. Reptilian peripheral receptors are characterized by differences in the diameter and quality of the axon, receptive field and the involved tissue, and the matrix of the receptor. Using these morphological criteria, reptilian receptors can be grouped as follows: intraepidermal mechanoreceptors,

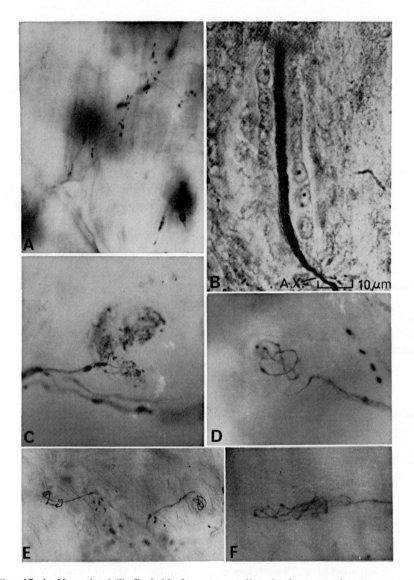

FIG. 17. A. *Xantusia vigilis*. Probable free nerve endings in the connective tissue sheath or fascia overlying skeletal muscle fibers. Methylene blue. × 300. (After Miller and Kasahara, 1967.) B. *Pseudechis porphyriacus*. An enlarged view of a "club corpuscle." The axon enters an indistinct capsule and then expands to several times its original diameter. Within the capsule it is surrounded by a collar of tightly packed cells. Ranson pyridine silver. (After Proske, 1969.) C. *Varanus griseus*. Probable lamellated (encapsulated) type of receptor in the deep dermal connective tissue of the ventral snout. Light micrographs of this type of nerve ending show no distinct connective tissue elements. Methylene blue. × 280. (After Miller and Kasahara, 1967.) D. *Varanus griseus*. Lamellated (encapsulated) nerve ending in the dermal connective tissue of the ventral snout. Methylene blue. × 280. (After Miller and Kasahara, 1967.) E. *Varanus griseus*. Lamellated (encapsulated) nerve ending in the dermal connective tissue of the eyelid. Methylene blue. × 100. (After Miller and Kasahara, 1967). F. *Varanus griseus*. Lamellated (encapsulated) nerve ending in the conjunctival connective tissue. Methylene blue. × 119. (After Miller and Kasahara, 1967.)

connective tissue mechanoreceptors lacking Schwann cell specializations, mechanoreceptors covered by lamellated Schwann cells, Merkel complexes, tactile sense organs, complex sensory organs, joint capsule endings, and sensory endings associated with the perichondrium, periosteum, tendons and muscles.

2. Reptiles differ from other vertebrates in possessing relatively large terminal expansions of the free nerve ending the epithelial cells of the epidermis termed intraepidermal mechanoreceptors. These terminal receptors are discoid in shape, filled with glycogen granules and surrounded by a tonofibrillar basket that responds to mechanical deformation. A similar but branched receptor occurs in the hinge region between scales and possibly acts as a stretch receptor.

3. Complex unencapsulated nerve endings occur in reptiles as in anamniotes, and they are characterized by an unmyelinated receptor axon in contact with the surrounding connective tissue. Three groups can be recognized in the dermis: free nerve terminals, branched lanceolate terminals, and branched coiled terminals.

4. Lamellated receptors possess flat, lamellated Schwann cell processes with the axon terminal branching between the lamellae. These receptors are similar to the inner core lamellated receptors of birds and mammals, and may be rapidly adapting mechanoreceptors.

5. Merkel cell neurite complexes occur in the skin of fish, reptiles, birds and mammals. These receptors, while rare in reptiles, consist of a receptor axon closely associated with a specialized cell (Merkel cell) with finger-like processes filled with glycogen granules, networks of tonofibrils and dense core vesicles. The Merkel complex appears to be a secondary, slowly adapting mechanoreceptor.

6. Tactile sense organs or touch papillae are common in reptiles and consist of an epidermal and dermal component. The epidermis associated with the discoid terminal may be reduced in the region of the touch papillae, or a differentiated bristle may develop from the β-keratin layer. The dermal component consists of layered fibrocytes with nerve terminals having expanded tips interspersed among the fibrocytes.

7. The bristled and bristleless touch papillae of reptiles contain a wide variety of nerve terminals similar to complex sensory structures in birds and mammals, and these integumentary mechanoreceptors may cover the complete range of integumentary stimuli: brief, high frequency bursts; slowly adapting, low frequency discharges; cold units; and bimodal cold and pressure units.

8. Reptilian joint capsules contain free nerve endings, non-encapsulated clews and spray-like endings, as well as simple encapsulated corpuscles with an inner core.

9. Little information exists on the nerve endings of reptilian perichondrium and periosteum. Multibranched endings with varicose terminals are known.

10. Reptilian tendons contain free nerve endings and simple non-encapsulated plaques distributed among the tendon fascicles, as well as receptors invested with a thin capsule forming rudimentary tendon organs.

11. Reptilian muscle spindles are highly variable. Snakes and lizards possess spindles consisting of a single muscle fiber; whereas turtles possess spindles with 2–17 muscle fibers. The sensory endings consist of varicose threads with leaflike terminals. A single sensory fiber may innervate adjacent spindles.

Acknowledgements

We should like to thank Mrs Christine Parker for her assistance in the preparation of this chapter. The research was supported by the German Research Council, SP "Receptor Physiology" and SFB 114 grants.

References

Ábrahám, A. (1964). "Die mikroskopische Innervation des Herzens und der Blutgefässe von Vertebraten." Akademia Kiado, Budapest.

Alexander, N. J. (1968). The chromatophores of anolis lizard skin. *J. Cell Biol.* 39, 5a.

Alexander, N. J. and Fahrenbach, W. H. (1969). The dermal chromatophores of *Anolis carolinensis* (Reptilia, Iguanidae). *Am. J. Anat.* 126, 41–56.

Andres, K. H. (1966). Über die Feinstruktur der Rezeptoren an Sinushaaren. *Z. Zellforsch. mikrosk. Anat.* 75, 339–365.

Andres, K. H. (1969). Zur Ultrastruktur verschiedener Mechanorezeptoren von höheren Wirbeltieren. *Anat. Anz.* 124, 551–565.

Andres, K. H. (1974). Morphological criteria for the differentiation of mechanoreceptors in vertebrates. *Rhein-Westf. Akad. Wiss.* 53, 135–152.

Andres, K. H. and Düring, M. von (1973). The morphology of cutaneous receptors. *In* "Handbook of Sensory Physiology." (A. Iggo, ed.). Springer Verlag, Berlin, Heidelberg, New York 2(1), 1–28.

Andres, K. H. and Düring, M. von (1978). Interference phenomenon on osmium tetroxide-fixed specimens for systematic electron microscopic study. *In* "Principles and Techniques of Electron Microscopy." (M. A. Hayat, ed.). Van Nostrand Reinhold, New York 8, 241–261.

Bailey, S. E. R. (1969). The responses of sensory receptors in the skin of the green lizard *Lacerta viridis* to mechanical and thermal stimulation. *Comp. Biochem. Physiol.* 29, 161–172.

Barker, D. (1974). The morphology of muscle receptors. *In* "Handbook of Sensory Physiology." (C. C. Hunt, ed.). Springer Verlag, Berlin, Heidelberg, New York 3-2(1), 2–174.

Barrett, R. (1970). The pit organs of snakes. *In* "Biology of the Reptilia." (C. Gans and T. S. Parsons, eds). Academic Press, London and New York 2(4), 277–300.

Bleichmar, H. and De Robertis, E. (1962). Submicroscopic morphology of the infrared receptor of pit vipers. *Z. Zellforsch. mikrosk. Anat.* **56,** 748–761.

Boeke, J. (1934). Niedere Sinnesorgane. Freie Nervenendigungen und Endorgane sensibler Nerven. *In* "Handbuch der vergleichenden Anatomie der Wirbeltiere." (L. Bolk, E. Göppert, E. Kallius and W. Lubosch, eds). Urban und Schwartzenberg, Berlin and Vienna, 2(2), 841–1283.

Bolgarskij, J. A. (1964). Zur Frage über die besonderer Formen der rezeptorischen Nervenapparate der Haut der Amphibien. *Anat. Anz.* **114,** 38–47.

Bullock, T. H. and Cowles, R. B. (1952). Physiology of an infrared receptor: The facial pit of pit vipers. *Science, N.Y.* **115,** 541–543.

Bullock, T. H. and Diecke, F. P. J. (1956). Properties of an infrared receptor. *J. Physiol., Lond.* **134,** 47–87.

Bullock, T. H. and Fox, W. (1957). The anatomy of the infrared sense organ in the facial pit of pit vipers. *Q. Jl. microsc. Sci.* **98,** 219–234.

Burgess, P. R. and Perl, E. R. (1973). Cutaneous mechanoreceptors and nociceptors. *In* "Handbook of Sensory Physiology." (A. Iggo, ed.). Springer Verlag, Berlin, Heidelberg, New York 2(2), 30–78.

Chouchkov, C. N. (1972). On the fine structure of free nerve endings in human digital skin, oral cavity and rectum. *Z. Zellforsch. mikrosk. Anat.* **86,** 273–288.

Chouchkov, C. N. (1973). On the fine structure of Krause's bulbs in human skin, oral cavity and rectum. *Arch. hist. jap.* **35(5),** 365–375.

Düring, M. von (1973a). Zur Feinstruktur der intraepidermal Nervenfasern von Nattern (*Natrix*). *Z. Anat. EntwGesch.* **141,** 339–350.

Düring, M. von (1973b). The ultrastructure of lamellated mechanoreceptors in the skin of reptiles. *Z. Anat. EntwGesch.* **143,** 81–94.

Düring, M. von (1974a). The radiant receptor and other tissue receptors in the scales of the upper jaw of *Boa constrictor*. *Z. Anat. EntwGesch.* **145,** 299–319.

Düring, M. von (1974b). The ultrastructure of cutaneous receptors in the skin of *Caiman crocodilus*. Symposium: "Mechanoreception", Bochum 1973. *Abhdlg. Rhein. Westf. Akad. Wiss.* **53,** 123–134.

Düring, M. von and Andres, K. H. (1976). The ultrastructure of taste and touch receptors of the frog's taste organ. *Z. Zellforsch. mikrosk. Anat.* **165,** 185–198.

Düring, M. von and Seiler, W. (1974). The fine structure of lamellated receptors in the skin of *Rana esculenta*. *Z. Anat. EntwGesch.* **144,** 165–172.

Gottschaldt, K. M., Andres, K. H. and Düring, M. von (1976). Fine structure and function of the bill tip organ in geese. *Neuroscience Abstracts* **2,** 912–913.

Halata, Z. (1970). Zu den Nervenendigungen (Merkel'sche Endigungen) in der haarlosen Nasenhaut der Katze. *Z. Zellforsch. mikrosk. Anat.* **106,** 51–60.

Hensel, H. (1975). Static and dynamic activity of warm receptors in *Boa constrictor*. *Pflügers Arch. ges. Physiol.* **353,** 191–199.

Hensel, H., Andres, K. H. and Düring, M. von (1974). Structure and function of cold receptors. *Pflügers Arch. ges. Physiol.* **352,** 1–10.

Hiller, U. (1976a). Ultrastruktur und Regeneration mechanorezeptiver Hautsinnesorgane bei Gekkoniden. *Naturwissenschaften* **63,** 200–201.

Hiller, U. (1976b). Elektronenmikroskopische Untersuchungen zur funktionellen Morphologie der borstenführenden Hautsinnesorgane bei *Tarentola mauritanica* L. (Reptilia, Gekkonidae). *Zoomorphologie* **84,** 211–221.

Hin-Ching, L. and Maneely, R. B. (1962). Some cutaneous nerve endings in the soft-shelled turtle of South China. *J. comp. Neurol.* **10,** 159–208.

Huber, G. C. and De Wit, L. M. A. (1900). A contribution on the nerve terminations in neuro-tendinous end organs. *J. comp. Neurol.* 10, 159–208.

Hulanicka, R. (1909). Recherches sur les terminaisons nerveuses dans la peau du *Rana esculenta*. *Bull. int. Acad. Crac.*, *Ser. B*, *Ann.*, 687–703.

Hulanicka, R. (1913). Recherches sur les terminaisons nerveuses dans la langue, le palais et la peau du crocodile. *Arch. Zool. exp. gén.* 53, 1–14.

Hulanicka, R. (1914). Über die Nervenendigungen bei der Schildkröte. *Anat. Anz.* 46, 485–490.

Iggo, A. and Muir, A. R. (1969). The structure and function of a slowly adapting touch corpuscle in hairy skin. *J. Physiol.*, *Lond.* 200, 763–796.

Jaburek, L. (1927). Über Nervenendigungen in der Epidermis der Reptilien. *Z. Zellforsch. mikrosk. Anat.* 10, 1–49.

Kenton, B., Kruger, L. and Woo, M. (1971). Two classes of slowly adapting mechano-receptor fibres in reptile cutaneous nerve. *J. Physiol.*, *Lond.* 212, 21–44.

Kulchitsky, N. (1924). Nerve endings in muscles. *J. Anat.* 58, 152–168.

Landmann, L. (1975). The sense organs in the skin of the head of Squamata (Reptilia). *Israel J. Zool.* 24, 99–135.

Landmann, L. and Villiger, W. W. (1975). Glycogen in epidermal nerve terminals of *Lacerta sicula* (Squamata: Reptilia). *Experientia* 31, 967–968.

Lane, E. B. and Whitear, M. (1977). On the occurrence of Merkel cells in the epidermis of teleost fishes. *Cell Tiss. Res.* 182, 235–246.

Leydig, F. (1871). Zur Kenntniss der Sinnesorgane der Schlangen. *Arch. Mikrosk. Anat. EntwGesch.* 8, 317–357.

Leydig, F. (1873). Über die äusseren Bedeckungen der Reptilien und Amphibien. *Arch. Mikrosk. Anat. EntwGesch.* 9, 753–794.

Loewenstein, W. R. and Skalak, R. (1965). Mechanical transmission in a Pacinian corpuscle. *J. Physiol.*, *Lond.* 177, 377–397.

Lowenstein, O. (1957). Pressure receptors in the fins of the dogfish *Scylliorhinus canicula*. *Exp. Biol.* 33(2), 417–421.

Maderson, P. F. A. (1965). The structure and development of the squamate epidermis. *In* "Biology of the Skin and Hair Growth." (A. G. Lyne and B. F. Short, eds). Angus and Robertson, Sydney, pp. 129–153.

Maderson, P. F. A. (1966). Histological changes in the epidermis of the tokay (*Gekko gecko*) during the sloughing cycle. *J. Morph* 119, 39–50.

Maderson, P. F. A. (1967). Epidermal morphology and sloughing frequency in normal and prolactin treated *Anolis carolinensis* (Iguanidae, Lacertilia). *J. Morph.* 123, 157–172.

Maderson, P. F. A. (1968). Observations on the epidermis of the tuatara (*Sphenodon punctatus*). *J. Anat.* 103, 311–320.

Maderson, P. F. A. (1970). Endocrine-epidermal relationships in squamate reptiles. *Mem. Soc. Endocr.* 18, 259–284.

Maderson, P. F. A., Flaxman, B. A., Roth, S. J. and Szabo, G. (1972). Ultrastructural contribution to the identification of cell types in the lizard epidermal generation. *J. Morph.* 136, 191–210.

Maurer, F. (1895). "Die Epidermis und ihre Abkömmlinge." Wilhelm Engelmann, Leipzig.

Merkel, F. (1880). "Über die Endigungen der sensiblen Nerven in der Haut der Wirbeltiere." Rostock.

Meszler, R. M. (1970). Correlation of ultrastructure and function. *In* "Biology of the Reptilia". (C. Gans and T. S. Parsons, eds). Academic Press, London and New York 2(4), 305–314.

Miller, M. R. and Kasahara, M. (1959). The pattern of cutaneous innervation of the human foot. *Am. J. Anat.* **105**, 233–256.

Miller, M. R. and Kasahara, M. (1967). Studies on the cutaneous innervation of lizards. *Proc. Calif. Acad. Sci.* **34**, 549–568.

Miller, M. R., Ralston, H. J., III and Kasahara, M. (1958). The pattern of cutaneous innervation of the human hand. *Am. J. Anat.* **102**, 183–218.

Munger, B. L. (1965). The intraepidermal innervation of the snout skin of the opossum. *J. Cell. Biol.* **26**, 79–97.

Munger, B. L. (1971). Patterns of organization of peripheral sensory receptors. *In* "Handbook of Sensory Physiology." (W. R. Loewenstein, ed.). Springer Verlag, Berlin, Heidelberg, New York 1(17), 523–556.

Nafstad, P. H. and Baker, R. E. (1973). Comparative ultrastructural study of normal and grafted skin in the frog *Rana pipiens*, with special reference to neuroepithelia connections. *Z. Zellforsch. mikrosk. Anat.* **139**, 451–462.

Păc, L. (1968a). Sensory nerve endings in joint capsule of some Lacertilia (*Agama stellio*, *Physignathus lesueurii*). *Scripta med.* **41**, 155–161.

Păc, L. (1968b). Sensory nerve endings in the joint capsules of the tortoise (*Testudo graeca*). *Folia morph., Praha* **18**, 43–47.

Păc, L. (1970). A contribution to the study of the joint receptors of the frog (*Rana temporaria* L.). *Folia morph., Praha* **18**, 46–51.

Păc, L. (1972). Sensory nerve endings in the joint capsules of the green lizard (*Lacerta viridis*). *Scripta med.* **45**, 115–120.

Palmieri, G. and Panu, R. (1972). Innervazione sensitive nelle articolazioni di *Caiman sclerops*. *Boll. Soc. ital. Biol. sper.* **48**, 507–511.

Plate, L. (1924). Die Sinnesorgane der Tiere. *In* "Allgemeine Zoologie und Abstammungslehre." Gustav Fischer, Jena, Part 2.

Proske, U. (1969a). Vibration-sensitive mechanoreceptors in snake skin. *Expl. Neurol.* **23**, 187–194.

Proske, U. (1969b). Nerve endings in skin of the Australian black snake. *Anat. Rec.* **164**, 259–266.

Regaud, C. (1907). Les terminaisons nerveuses et les organes nerveus sensitifs de l'appareil locomoteur. II. Les terminaisons nerveuses et les organes nerveux sensitifs des tendons, de leurs gaines, des enveloppes conjonctives musculo-tendineuses du périoste et des tissus articulaires. *Rev. gen. Histol.* **1**, 578–689.

Retzius, G. (1892). Über die sensiblen Nervenendigungen in den Epithelien bei Wirbeltieren. *In* "Biologische Untersuchungen." G. Fischer, Jena, N.F. 4.

Rohrlich, S. T. and Porter, K. R. (1972). Fine structural observations relating to the production of color by the iridophores of a lizard, *Anolis carolinensis*. *J. Cell Biol.* **53**, 38–52.

Roth, S. J. and Jones, W. A. (1970). The ultrastructure of epidermal maturation in the skin of the Boa constrictor (*Constrictor constrictor*). *J. Ultrastruct. Res.* **32**, 69–93.

Schmidt, W. J. (1910). Das Integument von *Voeltzkowia mira* Bttgr. Ein Beitrag zur Morphologie und Histologie der Eidechsenhaut. *Z. wiss. Zool.* **94**, 605–720.

Schmidt, W. J. (1913). Studien am Integument der Reptilien. IV. *Uroplatus fimbriatus* und die Geckoniden. *Zool. Jb.* (*Anat.*) **36**, 377–464.

Schmidt, W. J. (1917). Studien am Integument der Reptilien. VIII. Über die Haut der Acrochordinen. *Zool. Jb.* (*Anat.*) **40**, 155–202.

Schmidt, W. J. (1920). Einiges über die Hautsinnesorgane der Agamiden, insbesondere von *Calotes*, nebst Bemerkungen über diese Organe bei Geckoniden und Iguaniden. *Anat. Anz.* **53**, 113–139.

Schwartzkopff, J. (1973). Mechanoreception. *In* "Avian Biology." (D. S. Farner, J. R. King, and K. C. Parker, eds). Academic Press, New York and London 2(7), 417–477.

Siminoff, R. and Kruger, L. (1968). Properties of reptilian cutaneous mechanoreceptors. *Expl. Neurol.* **20**, 403–414.

Stefanelli, A. (1934). Su di alcune espansioni nervose nel periostio e nel pericondrio dei Rettile. *Monit. Zool. ital.* **45**, 115–120.

Taylor, J. D. and Hadley, Mac. E. (1970). Chromatophores and color change in the lizard, *Anolis carolinensis. Z. Zellforsch. mikrosk. Anat.* **104**, 282–294.

Terashima, S. J., Goris, R. C. and Katsuki, Y. (1968). Generator potential of crotaline snake infrared receptor. *J, Neurophysiol.* **31**, 682–688.

Terashima, S. J., Goris, R. C. and Katsuki, Y. (1970). Structure of warm fiber terminals in the pit membrane of vipers. *J. Ultrastruct. Res.* **31**, 494–506.

Warren, J. W. and Proske, U. (1968). Infrared receptors in the facial pits of the Australian python, *Morelia spilotes. Science, N.Y.* **159**, 439–441.

Whitear, M. (1971). The free nerve endings in fish epidermis. *J. Zool. Lond* **163**, 231–236.

Whitear, M. (1974). The nerves in frog skin. *J. Zool. Lond.* **172**, 503–529.

Winkelmann, R. K. and Breathnach, A. S. (1973). The Merkel cell. *J. invest. Derm.* **60**, 2–15.

Author Index

A

Ábrahám, A., 407, *437*
Agnew, J. D., 302, *391*
Albrecht, P. W., *35*
Alexander, N. J., 408, *437*
Altschule, M. D., 250, *397*
Andres, K. H., 409, 410, 414, 419, 421, 422, 423, 428, 431, *437, 438*
Andrews, C. W., 65, 101, *140*
Anthony, R., 147, *169*
Ariëns Kappers, C. U., 193, *241*, 245, 397
Ariëns Kappers, J., 183, 222, *241*, 249, 250, 331, 333, 349, 361, 363, 364, 368, 369, 370, 376, *392, 396, 397, 401*
Armstrong, J. A., 225, *242*
Aron, E., 249, *391*
Aronson, L. R., 53, *140*
Arranz, S. B., *391*
Axelrod, J., 250, *391, 405*

B

Bailey, S. E. R., 431, *437*
Baird, I. L., 15, 16, *35*
Baker, R. E., *440*
Bakker, R. T., 63, 93, *140*
Barghusen, H. R., 127, *140*
Barker, D., 434, *437*
Barrett, R., 414, *437*
Barry, T. H., 3, *35*
Barsbold, R., 92, *140*
Bauchot, R., 147, 148, 149, 150, 154, 156, 160, 164, 166, 168, *169, 171*
Baumgarten, H. G., 249, 250, 333, 348, 351, 352, 353, 354, 355, 357, 358, 359, 360, 361, 363, 365, 366, 376, *405*
Baur, G., 296, *391*
Beccari, N., 193, 222, *242*
Bellairs, A. d' A., 24, 33, *35*, 166, *169*
Béraneck, E., 249, 252, 333, 363, *391*
Bergquist, H., 173, 177, 222, 236, *242*

Blanc, C. P., 149, *169*
Blask, D. E., 342, *402*
Bleichmar, H., 414, *438*
Bodenheimer, T. S., 222, *243*
Boeke, J., 407, 410, *438*
Bogert, C. M., 296, *398*
Bojanus, L. H., 22, *35*, 306, *391*
Bolgarskij, J. A., 418, *438*
Bonaparte, J.-F., 133, *140*
Bonin, G., von., 147, 158, *169*
Boonstra, L. D., 42, 71, 127, 128, 129, 130, *140*
Boveri, V., 251, 332, *391*
Brandt, A., 149, 160, *169, 171*
Braun, R., 361, 383, *402*
Breathnach, A. S., 414, *441*
Brink, A. S., 129, *140*, 299, *391*
Brooks, G. R., 383, 384, 387, *394, 399*
Broom, R., 296, 299, 302, *391, 392*
Brown, B., 101, 105, 107, 108, 114, 117, 118, *140*
Brummelkamp, R., 149, *169*
Bullock, T. H., 414, *438*
Burckhardt, R., 173, 222, *242*, 246, 247, *392*
Burgess, P. R., 422, *438*
Butler, A. B., 161, *170*

C

Calas, A., 252, *398*
Camp, C. L., 59, 75, 77, 79, 81, *140*, 249, 291, 296, 336, *392*
Campos-Ortega, J. A., 246, *392*
Carriére, J., 249, 333, *392*
Carroll, R. L., 65, 124, *140, 141*
Case, E. C., 79, 81, 118, 125, 126, *141*, 303, 304, 305, *392*
Chang, P.-L., 331, *406*
Chouchkov, C. N., 419, *438*
Cimpeanu, L., 368, *399*
Clausen, H. J., 249, 383, 386, 387, *392*
Cluver, M. A., 130, 131, *141*

443

Subject Index

A

Ablepharus, 332, 340
Acanthodactylus, 20, 332, 380
Accessory optic system, 390, *also see* Nucleus, basal optic
Acontias, 8, 332
Acrochordal plate, 2
Aetosauria, 66, 79, 81, 304
Afferent fiber, 410
Agama, 26, 28, 29, 151, 157, 292, 331, 363, 366, 425, 427, 431
Agamidae, 28, 161, 163, 235, 251, 330, 338, 339
Agkistrodon, 158
Alar plate, 179, 234
Alligator, 43, 154, 164, 182, 186, 196, 199, 214, 226, 235, 252, 417
Allometry, 53, 61, 106, 132, 136, 137, 151, 157, 160, 166, *also see* Coefficient, allometric
Allosaurus, 157, 332
Amphibia, 11, 17, 156, 341, 409, 433, *also see* Anura, and Urodeles
Amphibolurus, 28, 251 331,
Amphisbaenia, 8, 10, 16, 19, 26–27, 31, 34, 43, 57, 66, 75, 78, 157, 158, 163, 166, 296, 371
Ampulla, 13
Anapsida, 65
Anatosaurus, 61, 101, 102
Anchiceratops, 114–118
Anelytropsidae, 335, 338
Aneugomphius, 299
Anguidae, 8, 161, 163, 252, 337, 338, 427
Anguimorpha, 338
Anguis, 151–154, 157, 161, 166, 252, 264–269, 332, 346, 361
Ankylosauria, 55, 67, 111, 138
Anniella, 22, 333, 336
Anniellidae, 332, 337, 338
Anolis, 20, 27, 28, 157, 330, 340, 363, 376, 383, 386, 387, 388, 408

Anomodontia, 68, 127, 295, 299, 304
Antarctosaurus, 98
Anthracosauria, 57, 295
Anura, 166, 167, 347
Arachnoid, 23
Archaeopteryx, 167
Archencephalon, 174, 177
Archosauria, 19, 43, 52, 56, 58, 59, 66, 78, 79, 109, 135, 137, 138, 139, 296, 297, 304
Arctognathus, 299, 304
Area cellularis reuniens, 233, 234, 235
Areoscelidia, 67, 297
Areoscelis, 297
Artery, basilar, 50, 76, 77, 103, 121
    internal carotid, 5, 8, 18, 44, 47, 48, 56, 76, 77, 80, 81, 82, 84, 95, 99, 103, 104, 107, 108, 113, 114, 117, 366
    median palatine, 103, 114
    pineal, 366, 371
    posterior cerebral, 46, 366
    saccular, 367
Askeptosaurus, 296
Ateuchosaurus, 341
Aulacephalodon, 299
Auricle, 50

B

Bactrosaurus, 101, 104
Barosaurus, 57, 98
Basal plate, 179, 234
Basal telencephalic area, 234
Basipterygoid process, 2
Bat, 85, *also see* Chiroptera
Bauria, 299
Bauriamorpha, 132, 299, 302
Belodon, 79, 303, 304
Bienotherium, 133
Bill-tip organ, 431
Biogenic amine, 372, *also see* Norepinephrine, 5-Hydroxydopa and 5-Hydroxytryptamine

450

O

Q

R